AMERICA at odds

AN INTRODUCTION TO AMERICAN GOVERNMENT

SECOND EDITION

AMERICA at odds

AN INTRODUCTION TO AMERICAN GOVERNMENT

SECOND EDITION

EDWARD SIDLOW
College of Arts and Sciences
Eastern Michigan University

BETH HENSCHEN
Department of Political Science
Eastern Michigan University

 **Wadsworth**
Thomson Learning™

An International Thomson Publishing Company

Australia · Canada · Mexico · Singapore · Spain · United Kingdom · United States

POLITICAL SCIENCE PUBLISHER:	Clark Baxter
SENIOR DEVELOPMENT EDITOR:	Sharon Adams Poore
ASSISTANT EDITOR:	Cherie Hackelberg
EDITORIAL ASSISTANTS:	Peggy Marshall and Melissa Gleason
MARKETING MANAGER:	Pamela Shaffer
MARKETING ASSISTANT:	Cara Dur
PRODUCTION, ART, AND DESIGN:	Doug Abbott and Ann Borman
PRODUCTION ASSISTANCE:	Megan Ryan
COVER DESIGN AND PHOTOGRAPHIC ILLUSTRATION:	Doug Abbott
PROJECT EDITOR:	Hal Humphrey
PRINT BUYER:	Barbara Britton
PERMISSIONS EDITOR:	Joohee Lee
COPY EDITOR:	Suzie Franklin DeFazio
PROOFREADING:	Pat Lewis
INDEXER:	Bob Marsh, HTP Services
COVER PHOTOGRAPHS:	Columbine High School Students, © Rodolfo Gonzalez/Denver Rocky Mountain News/Corbis Sygma; Voters Rally, © Bob Daemmrich, Corbis Sygma;
COMPOSITOR:	Parkwood Composition Service
PRINTER:	The West Group

This book is printed on acid-free recycled paper

Photo Credits appear on the page following the index.

Printed in the United States of America
1 2 3 4 5 6 7 8 9 10
For more information, contact Wadsworth Publishing Company, 10 Davis Drive, Belmont, CA 94002, or electronically at http://www.wadsworth.com

Library of Congress Cataloging-in-Publication Data

Sidlow, Edward, 1952–
    America at odds: an introduction to American government / Edward Sidlow, Beth Henschen.—2nd. ed.
        p.   cm
    Includes bibliographical references and index.
    ISBN:0–534-56988-9
    1. United States—Politics and government. I. Henschen, Beth, 1953–   .   II. Title.
JK274.S5415   1999
320.473—dc21   99-049174

 *For Sarah*

CONTENTS IN BRIEF

Institutions

CONTENTS

Features of Special Interest xxxi

To the Instructor xxxiii

The Foundations of Our American System

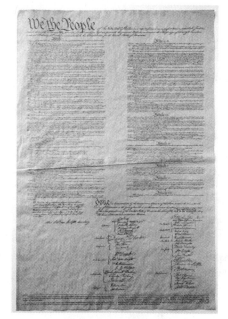

Chapter 2
The Constitution   21

Chapter 3
Federalism   53

Our Liberties and Rights

Comparative Politics • Church and State under Islamic Law 86

Perception versus Reality • The Effect of Supreme Court Decisions 88

Politics on the Far Side • Accommodating Snake Bites 90

Politics on the Far Side • Online Obscenity and the Starr Report 94

The American Political Spectrum • To Regulate or Not to Regulate the Internet—That is the Question 95

A Question of Ethics • Should Gang Members Be Deprived of Their Right to Assemble? 98

The
Politics of
Democracy

Chapter 6
Political Culture and Ideology 139

Chapter 7
Interest Groups 159

Chapter 8
Political Parties   185

Chapter 9
Public Opinion and Voting   211

Chapter 10
Campaigns and Elections 237

The American Political Spectrum °
Comparing Republican and
Democratic Convention
Delegates 242

A Question of Ethics ° Should PACs
Be Allowed to Influence Judicial
Elections? 250

Perception versus Reality ° Are
Americans Really All that Concerned
about the Democrats' Fund-Raising
Tactics? 251

A Question of Ethics ° Why Was All
That Foreign Money Donated? 254

Politics on the Far Side ° Outlaw Soft
Money—Are You Kidding? 260

Institutions

Chapter 13
Congress   309

Chapter 14
The Presidency 337

Chapter 15
The Bureaucracy   363

Chapter 16
The Judiciary   389

Public Policy

Chapter 17
Domestic Policy   415

Chapter 18
The Politics of Regulation   439

Chapter 19
Foreign Policy   463

State and
Local Government

Chapter 20
State and Local Politics   489

Features of Special Interest

Perception versus Reality

The American Political Spectrum

Politics on the Far Side

To the Instructor

It does not take long for a student of American government to get the message: Americans are at odds over numerous political issues. Political conflict is certainly not new to this country. Indeed, there have been times when many Americans doubted whether our democracy could endure. Nonetheless, it has endured, and the U.S. Constitution has been the model for most of the world's new democracies in the 1990s.

We believe that it is important for students to realize how political conflict and divergence of opinion have always helped to forge our political traditions and way of governing. *America at Odds: An Introduction to American Government,* Second Edition, looks at government and politics in this country as a series of conflicts that have led to compromises. Along the way, your students will sometimes encounter a bit of irreverence—none of us should take ourselves so seriously all of the time!

This text was written with today's generation of students in mind. As such, it does the following:

- Forthrightly presents different perspectives on key issues.
- Helps your students test their beliefs and assumptions.
- Assists your students in forming enlightened political values and opinions.
- Uses a thematic as well as an analytical approach, with emphasis on the various challenges that face our enduring democracy.
- Fully explains the major problems facing the American political system today.
- Integrates the global connections that exist between American politics and those of the rest of the world.
- Captures the excitement of cyberspace with respect to its effect on American politics, and makes available numerous Web resources, ranging from a book-specific site to the online library of InfoTrac College Edition.
- Offers links to an issues-driven, fully interactive CD-ROM.

Today's Reality—The World Is Wired

It is always in the news magazines. It is always in the newspaper. And it is always talked about on radio and television. "It" is cyberspace—the Internet and the World Wide Web (and who knows what else is around the corner). Cyberspace affects not only our home lives and the way we do business but also American politics. *America at Odds,* Second Edition, fully integrates the world of cyberspace into the study of American politics.

Throughout this text, your students are exposed to the numerous political issues that have come about because of the rapid changes in communications technology. For example, Chapter 2 opens with an issue that widespread use of the Internet has propelled into the foreground: Should privacy rights outweigh community interests? A section in Chapter 4 explores the problem of online obscenity, including a special feature presenting views across the political spectrum on whether the government should regulate the Internet. Who should be accountable for inaccurate news stories on the Web, particularly when those stories harm the interests of certain individuals or groups? How are special interest groups in the United States—and indeed throughout the world—using the Web to further their causes? These questions and many others are discussed in Chapter 12, entitled "Politics in Cyberspace."

POLITICS ON THE WEB

The amount of information available to students of American government on the Web is almost without limits. Where do they start? And where do they go? We solve this thorny problem by providing, at the end of each chapter, an entire section entitled *Politics on the Web*. There your students can discover the best Web sites for each chapter's subject matter. Many of those Web sites offer additional hot links.

USING WEB RESOURCES

New to the Second Edition of *America at Odds* is an Internet exercise, entitled *Using Web Resources,* which appears in each chapter just following the *Politics on the Web* feature. This exercise directs the student to a specific Web site that contains information on one of the topics covered in the chapter. The student is asked to find certain materials on the site, read or analyze them, and then answer specific questions about those materials.

THE *AMERICA AT ODDS,* SECOND EDITION, WEB SITE

In addition to the *Politics on the Web* and the *Using Web Resources* sections just described, there is a fully functioning Web page for *America at Odds,* Second Edition. Through the Political Science Resource Center at

http://politicalscience.wadsworth.com

you and your students can access the *America at Odds,* Second Edition, companion site. There you will find a wealth of information developed especially for *America at Odds*. This Web site offers numerous helpful resources, including the following:

- Chapter-by-chapter tutorial quizzes that allow students to test their knowledge.
- Hyperlinks to relevant Web sites for each chapter—including URLs that update materials in the text and the CD-ROM.
- A discussion forum designed to encourage dialogue among students from around the country.
- Internet and InfoTrac activities that relate to each chapter.

And as the World Wide Web develops, so, too, will this Web site. We will always be interested in your suggestions on how we can improve it.

INFOTRAC FOR REAL RESEARCH ON THE INTERNET

Many professors require their students to undertake research projects. Users of this text are fortunate to have at their disposal the finest existing search system on the Internet for questions relating to American government and politics. Wadsworth Publishing Company has an exclusive agreement with InfoTrac, the premiere research service on the Web, developed by Information Access Corporation. InfoTrac lets your students ask specific questions. Through exclusive search agreements with many important politi-

cal science journals and other related sources, the system takes the student to exactly where he or she needs to go to find the relevant information, including full-text articles. When full text is available, the student prints it directly. Otherwise, the full text can be sent to the student's e-mail address.

When appropriate, a special icon appears in the margin of the text page, indicating to your students that InfoTrac will provide especially helpful information, or links to related materials, on the subject being discussed.

Professors who use this book can order a one-month free subscription to this service. If the professor requests that the service be bundled with each student copy of the text (for a nominal fee), then he or she will receive a four-month free subscription. Ask your sales representative for your free password to log on at **www.infotrac-college.com/wadsworth** on the Web.

INFOTRAC RESOURCE GUIDE

This online guide to InfoTrac, your twenty-four-hour-a-day reference resource, contains approximately fifteen articles tied to each of the twenty major topics in the text. Activities that include exercises in obtaining research materials are also included. The guide is updated quarterly to keep you up to date with the latest news.

WESTLAW

There is one name that stands out in online legal research, and that name is WESTLAW. Adopters of *America at Odds,* Second Edition, can obtain free hours on WESTLAW and thus have ready access to a variety of legal materials. For example, professors who wish to read the entire text of a particular court case mentioned in the book can access WESTLAW online and download or print out the full text of that case. Federal and state statutes are also available through this legal-research service, as are the world's leading newspapers and magazines. For more information on how to obtain free hours on WESTLAW, just ask your sales representative.

INTERNET ACTIVITIES

To make sure that your students can not only master the Web but at the same time improve their understanding of American politics, we have a specially designed booklet that you can order for them. It is called *American Government Internet Activities,* Second Edition. Each exercise relates to topics that are covered in the text. The exercise takes your students on a navigation path and then asks them to complete various exercises related to the data that they discover.

A Fully Interactive CD-ROM

Available with *America at Odds,* Second Edition, is a fully interactive CD-ROM. We are especially proud of this student supplement because of the creativity that went into its planning, organization, and execution. Your students can view video clips, listen to speeches, and learn more about the chapter-opening features in this text. A Web component provides an online forum for students to discuss and debate the issues. Links specific to these issues offer additional information and point students to important resources. There is also a link to the *America at Odds,* Second Edition, home page. In addition, there is an interactive study guide that further tests the students' knowledge and understanding of the various issues over which Americans are at odds. Free access to ATT World Net for one month is included on the CD-ROM.

The Modern Text—
Features That Teach

Any American government text must present the basics of the American political process and its institutions. Any *modern* American government text, however, must go further; it must excite and draw the student into the subject materials. That is exactly what we do in *America at Odds,* Second Edition. Among other things, we present many of today's controversial political issues in special features. Each of these features is referred to within the text itself so that the student understands the connection between the feature and the topic being discussed. We describe below the various types of features that we have included in *America at Odds,* Second Edition.

- *America at Odds*—This chapter-opening feature examines a major controversy over which the public is divided and has strong views. Each of these features concludes with a section entitled *Where Do You Stand?* These concluding sections, which consist of two or three questions, invite the student to form or express his or her own opinions on the arguments presented in the features. Most of these features are expanded on in the accompanying CD-ROM. A final concluding section entitled *On the Web* directs the student to one or more Web sites for more information on the topic discussed in the feature. The chapter-opening *America at Odds* features include the following:

  - Do Americans Care about Politics and Government? (Chapter 1).
  - Should Privacy Rights Outweigh Community Interests? (Chapter 2).
  - Should the Death Penalty Be Banned? (Chapter 4).
  - Should the United States be the World's Police Officer? (Chapter 19).

- *The American Political Spectrum*—On many issues, there is a relatively well established position that has been laid out by political conservatives and another, usually contrasting position claimed by political liberals. Not only are your students presented with these two views, but they are guided in understanding the reasons why conservatives and liberals have taken such stands. At the end of each of these features there is a critical-thinking exercise. Some of the titles to these features are as follows:

  - The Politics of Impeachment (Chapter 2).
  - To Regulate or Not to Regulate the Internet—That Is the Question (Chapter 4).
  - Should Same-Sex Couples Have the Legal Right to Marry? (Chapter 5).
  - Homelessness (Chapter 17).

- *Perception versus Reality*—Perhaps nowhere in our media-generated view of the world are there more misconceptions than in the area of American government and politics. This feature tries to help your students understand the difference between the public's general perception of a particular political event or issue and the reality of the situation. The perception is often gleaned from responses to public opinion surveys. The reality usually is presented in the form of objective data that show that the world is not quite what the public often thinks it is. At the end of each of these features is a section entitled *You Be the Judge,* in which the student is encouraged to think about why there is such a disparity between the perception and the reality. Some of the titles of these features are as follows:

  - Devolution? (Chapter 3).
  - What Do the Parties Really Stand For? (Chapter 8).
  - Does Online Information Really Mean the Death of Traditional News? (Chapter 12).
  - How Accurate Is the U.S. Census? (Chapter 13).

■ *A Question of Ethics*—Ethical behavior in government has become a serious issue. Questions of ethics arise frequently both within and without government and are commented on daily by the media. Most of the chapters in this text have one or more features dealing with ethical issues that should be of concern to every student of American politics. Each feature ends with a critical-thinking question. A few of these features are the following:

- Can Personal Ethics Be Separated from Politics? (Chapter 1).
- Do National Security Interests Justify Secret Courts? (Chapter 16).
- Has the War on Drugs Made Matters Worse? (Chapter 17).
- Is "Environmental Justice" Fair to Minority Communities? (Chapter 18).

■ *Comparative Politics*—One of the best ways to understand the American political system is by examining how it compares to other political systems. Students need to know that in much of the world, the political process is different. That is how they can better understand and appreciate what goes on in this country, both in Washington, D.C., and in state capitals. Nearly every chapter has at least one of these features. At the end of each of these features, the student is asked to further examine some part of the argument in a question "For Critical Analysis." Some examples of the *Comparative Politics* features are as follows:

- Is Having a Written Constitution All That Important? (Chapter 2).
- Church and State under Islamic Law (Chapter 4).
- Patriotism: A Cross-National Comparison (Chapter 6).
- Legal Systems of the World (Chapter 16).

■ *Politics on the Far Side*—Sometimes you just cannot believe what goes on in politics. That is why we created this feature. It is meant to grab your students' attention. For the Second Edition, we have added a question for critical analysis at the end of each of these features. Here are some examples of the *Politics on the Far Side* features:

- The Information Explosion (Chapter 1).
- How to Tackle Your Opponents (Chapter 2).
- Outlaw Soft Money—Are You Kidding? (Chapter 10).
- Elections 1998—Where Were the Media? (Chapter 11).

Chapter-Ending Issues and Pedagogy

Every chapter ends with the following sections:

- **Americans at Odds over [chapter topic].** This concluding portion of each chapter discusses selected political issues over which Americans are currently at odds—and will continue to be at odds until some consensus of opinion is reached.
- **Key Terms.** This is a list of the terms that were boldfaced and defined within the chapter. Each term in the list is followed by the page number on which it first appeared and was defined.
- **Chapter Summary.** This point-by-point feature gives a full summary of every important point within the chapter.
- **For Critical Analysis.** This section presents seven thought-provoking questions designed to stimulate critical thinking and discussion of various topics covered in the chapter.
- **Suggested Readings.** Several suggested readings, along with annotations describing each book, are given at the end of each chapter. Except for classic references, they are all from the late 1990s.
- **Politics on the Web.** As explained earlier, this section gives selected Web sites that students can access for more information.
- **Using Web Resources.** This section, as explained earlier, consists of an Internet exercise that students can perform to learn more about a particular issue discussed within the chapter's text.

■ **Notes.** We have included numerous footnotes to provide documentation for information provided in the text. These footnotes appear at the end of each chapter.

The Supplements

Both instructors and students today expect, and indeed require, a variety of accompanying supplements to teach and learn about American government. *America at Odds,* Second Edition, takes the lead in providing the most comprehensive and user-friendly supplements package on the market today. These supplements include those listed below.

PRINTED MATERIALS FOR INSTRUCTORS

■ Instructor's Manual with Test Bank, written by Beth Henschen. This supplement now includes a Multimedia Guide, prepared by Larry Elowitz.

MULTIMEDIA SUPPLEMENTS FOR INSTRUCTORS

■ An online Resource Center for political science at

> http://politicalscience.wadsworth.com

■ A special, book-specific Web site for *America at Odds,* Second Edition, which can be accessed through the Resource Center.
■ CNN Today: American Government videos, Volumes 1 and 2.
■ A video library, including new selections.
■ Online Instructor's Manual, Test Bank, and Multimedia Guide.
■ Thomson Learning Testing Tools.
■ Transparency Acetates.
■ PowerPoint Presentation on multi-platform CD-ROM.
■ InfoTrac College Edition.
■ InfoTrac Resource Guide.

PRINTED MATERIALS FOR STUDENTS

■ Study Guide, written by Beth Henschen.
■ Readings in American Government.
■ An Introduction to Critical Thinking and Writing in American Politics.
■ American Government Internet Activities, Second Edition.
■ Handbook of Selected Legislation and Other Documents.
■ Handbook of Selected Court Cases.
■ College Survival Guide.
■ Thinking Globally, Acting Locally.

MULTIMEDIA SUPPLEMENTS FOR STUDENTS

■ *America at Odds* Interactive CD-ROM.
■ A special online Resource Center for political science at

> http://politicalscience.wadsworth.com

■ A special, book-specific Web site for *America at Odds,* Second Edition, which can be accessed through the Resource Center.
■ InfoTrac College Edition, offering a fully searchable online library of readings.
■ InfoTrac Resource Guide.
■ Your Research: Data Analysis for American Government and Politics.
■ *American Government: An Introduction Using MicroCase ExplorIt,* Sixth Edition—The Sixth Edition of this popular ancillary for American government courses includes computer-based assignments, a student version of MicroCase's ExplorIt software, and current real data sets. Each

assignment is packed with dozens of issues that are guaranteed to grab student interest.

What's New in the Second Edition?

We thought that those of you who have used the First Edition of *America at Odds* would like to know what changes have been made for the Second Edition. Generally, all of the text, tables, figures, and features in this book have been rewritten or updated as necessary to reflect the most recent developments in American government and politics. The Second Edition incorporates the results of the 1998 elections throughout the text as they relate to chapter topics, as well as coverage of the impeachment and trial of President Bill Clinton. Other key changes and additions made for the Second Edition include those described below.

SPECIAL NEW FEATURES AND PEDAGOGY

If you look at the list of "Features of Special Interest" at the end of the Table of Contents, you will note that the Second Edition of *America at Odds* includes a large number of newly written features. In addition, the following special new features and pedagogy have been added:

- *Politics on the Far Side* (similar to the *Politics in the Extreme* of the First Edition), each of which now concludes with a *For Critical Analysis* section posing a critical-thinking question about the feature topic.
- *On the Web* sections at the end of each chapter-opening *America at Odds* feature.
- *For Critical Analysis* questions at the end of each chapter.
- *Using Web Resources.*

SIGNIFICANT CHANGES TO THE CHAPTERS

As already indicated, each chapter in *America at Odds,* Second Edition, has been updated and revised in order to reflect the most current developments in American politics and government. When appropriate, new features have been added, and references to new laws and court decisions have been included. Here we list some other significant changes made to selected chapters.

- Chapter 1 (America Enters the Twenty-first Century)—This chapter now includes a new section that looks at the "big picture" of American democracy and shows the student how the topics covered in the text interrelate. Other new sections include one titled "Rating the Nation's Performance" and "Is Our Democracy Facing a Crisis?" Elements of the First Edition section titled "The Challenges of a Multiracial Society" have been incorporated into Chapter 6 in order to streamline the coverage of this topic. Also, pluralism, formerly treated in this chapter, is now discussed in Chapter 7, in the context of interest groups.
- Chapter 2 (The Constitution)—A new section comparing the Constitution to the Articles of Confederation has been added. We have also added a section titled "The Constitution—A Document for the Ages."
- Chapter 3 (Federalism)—This chapter now includes a text discussion of categorical and block grants, a new section on "Whatever Happened to Devolution?" and a section titled "Do State and Local Selective Purchasing Laws Violate the Constitution?"
- Chapter 4 (Civil Liberties)—Now includes a subsection discussing the erosion of the *Miranda* ruling and a new section discussing the issue of student fees and the right to free speech.

- Chapter 5 (Civil Rights)—The discussion of bilingualism was moved to Chapter 6 for the Second Edition. Additionally, the discussion of laws protecting gay rights has been largely rewritten, as has the final subsection in the affirmative action section. A discussion of sexual harassment versus free speech has been added to the end-of-chapter "Americans at Odds" section.
- Chapter 6 (Political Culture and Ideology)—Now includes a substantial section discussing political values in a multicultural society.
- Chapter 10 (Campaigns and Elections)—Includes newly written subsections on front-loading the primaries and on soft money contributions in recent elections.
- Chapter 11 (Politics and the Media)—Now includes coverage of TV news magazines, a discussion (and a table) on the erosion of media values, and a new section titled "Are Americans Really Less Interested in Political News?"
- Chapter 12 (Politics in Cyberspace)—Because the world of cyberspace changes so rapidly, much of this chapter had to be totally rewritten—or extensively revised—in order to include the latest developments in how Internet use is affecting American politics. The chapter now includes discussions of online fund raising, the rise of the Internet campaign strategist, the question of whether the Internet will change political campaigning as we know it, how online interest groups are using the Internet, and a number of other topics.
- Chapter 17 (Domestic Policy)—The chapter now includes a discussion of the relationship between age and crime, plus a new figure illustrating this relationship.
- Chapter 20 (State and Local Politics)—A new section titled "Voter Initiatives and American Democracy" was added to the chapter-ending "Americans at Odds" topics.

Acknowledgments

A number of political scientists reviewed the manuscript of the First Edition of *America at Odds*. We remain indebted to the following scholars for their thoughtful suggestions on how to create a text that best suits the needs of today's students and faculty:

Weston H. Agor
University of Texas, El Paso

Ross Baker
Highland Park, New Jersey

Glenn Beamer
University of Virginia

Lynn Brink
Northlake College, Texas

John Francis Burke
University of Houston

Richard Christofferson
University of Wisconsin,
Stevens Point

Lane Crothers
Illinois State University

Larry Elowitz
Georgia College and State University

Craig Emmert
Texas Tech University

Terri Fine
University of Central Florida

Scott R. Furlong
University of Wisconsin, Green Bay

Jim Graves
Kentucky State University

Joanne Green
Texas Christian University

William E. Kelly
Auburn University, Alabama

Matt Kerbel
Villanova University, Pennsylvania

James D. King
University of Wyoming

James J. Lopach
University of Montana

William McLauchlan
Purdue University, Indiana

Gabriel Ume
Palo Alto College, Texas

J. David Woodard
Clemson University, South Carolina

In preparing the Second Edition of *America at Odds*, we benefited from the criticism and comments of a number of users and reviewers of the First Edition. We thank the following reviewers for their conscientious work:

Wendy E. Scattergood
University of Wisconsin, Green Bay

Sam W. Mckinstry
East Tennessee State University

Michele Zebich-Knos
Kennesaw State University, Georgia

Christian Goergen
College of DuPage, Illinois

Ruth Ann Strickland
Appalachian State University,
North Carolina

Paul Savoie
Long Beach City College, California

Larry Elowitz
Georgia College and State
University

Brian Cherry
Northern Michigan University

We received our professional training at The Ohio State University in the late 1970s, benefiting from the guidance of several political scientists who shaped our styles of teaching and working with students. In particular, we thank Lawrence Baum, Herbert Asher, Elliot Slotnick, and Randall Ripley for lessons well taught. As faculty members, we have had the good fortune of learning from—and being rewarded by—generations of thoughtful students at Miami University (Ohio), Purdue University, Northwestern University, Loyola University Chicago, and Eastern Michigan University. We trust that some of what appears on these pages reflects their insights, and we hope that what we have written will capture the interest of current and future students. We have also worked with a number of dedicated colleagues from whom we have learned a great deal. Of course, we owe an immeasurable debt to our families, whose divergent views on political issues reflect an America at odds.

We thank Susan Badger, president of Wadsworth Publishing Company, for all of her encouragement and support throughout our work on this project. We were also fortunate to have the editorial advice of Clark Baxter, publisher, and the assistance of Sharon Adams Poore, senior developmental editor, who supervised all aspects of the supplements and the text. Additionally, we have benefited from the valuable advice and guidance offered by Cheri Hackelberg, our assistant editor. We also thank Lavina Leed Miller for her tremendous help in coordinating the project and for her research, copyediting, and proofreading assistance. We received additional copyediting and proofreading assistance from Suzie DeFazio and Pat Lewis. We are also grateful to Sue Jasin of K&M Consulting and Roxie Lee. With their help, we were able to meet our ambitious publishing schedule. We appreciate the enthusiasm of Pamela Shaffer, our hard-working marketing manager at Wadsworth Publishing Company. We would also like to acknowledge Doug Abbott, our wonderful designer, and Ann Borman, our production manager. We believe that they have produced the most attractive and user-friendly American government text on the market today.

Finally, we are indebted to all of those who worked on various supplements for *America at Odds*. For their tireless and expert work on the CD-ROM that accompanies this text, we would like to give special thanks to Maureen Rosener (project director), Stephen E. Frantzich of the U.S. Naval Academy (author of the CD-ROM), Kit Eastman (instructional designer),

Eric Iverson (programmer), and Tracy Claude (graphic artist). We also thank Becky Stovall, creator of the CNN videos, as well as Abbie Baxter, who undertook the CNN video correlation and supervised the production of some of the supplements. We further wish to thank Larry Elowitz for his work on the Multimedia Guide that is now a part of the Instructor's Manual and Jeffrey Bernstein for providing the InfoTrac citations in the text.

If you or your students have ideas or suggestions, you can write us directly or send us information through Wadsworth Publishing Company.

E.I.S.
B.M.H.

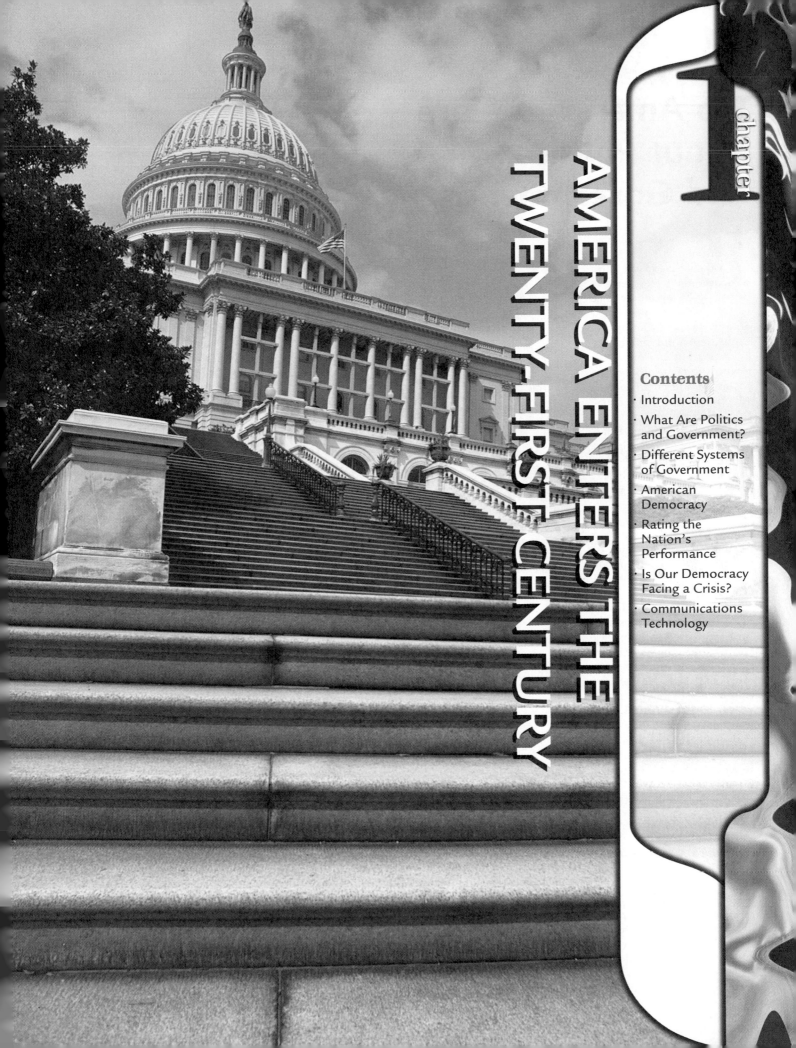

chapter 1

AMERICA ENTERS THE TWENTY-FIRST CENTURY

Contents

Do Americans Care about Politics and Government?

In recent years, a number of political scholars and others have voiced alarm over what they perceive to be a growing indifference to politics and government among the American public. In their view, this indifference is causing our system of government to come apart at the seams, or will do so shortly. After all, if our democratic form of government is to endure, the people must participate in government. Americans must keep informed about political events, issues, and candidates.

Above all, they must go to the polls to vote for those who will represent them.

Others say such doom-and-gloom conclusions and predictions are nonsense. They claim that the American democracy is in many ways more vital than ever before. And even if citizen participation in civic life is declining, that could mean that people are simply satisfied with their government and see no need to "get involved" to change the status quo.

Political Indifference Will Destroy Our Democracy, Say Some

Those who claim that Americans are increasingly detached from the political process support their argument by pointing to, among other things, the low voter turnout in recent elections. In the presidential elections of 1996, only 49 percent of the voting-age population turned out to cast their votes. A turnout below 50 percent had not occurred since 1924, when voting was still new to women.

Other studies supporting the idea that Americans are in the process of political disengagement include a 1998 survey of college students conducted by the American Council on Education. The survey compared its results to those obtained in surveys conducted in the late 1960s by the same organization and containing the same questions. Answers given in the 1998 survey showed a significant change in students' attitudes. The percentage of students who felt that keeping up to date with political affairs was an important "life goal" dropped from about 50 percent in 1966 to about 25 percent in 1998. Responses to the 1998 survey also indicated that just 14 percent of the respondents frequently discussed politics, down from 30 percent in 1968. Generally, the comparison showed that students were more politically detached in 1998 than they had ever been in the history of the survey.[1]

Those who fear that our democracy may be in serious trouble also argue that the American public has become increasingly cynical about politics and the political process. President Clinton has commented on numerous occasions about the cynicism prevailing in America. According to Vice President Al Gore,

cynicism is becoming a "malignant habit in democracy." Some political commentators have remarked that cynicism is widespread, if not "rampant," in our political culture. Indeed, some writers have labeled the 1990s a "cynical age." They say this cynicism about politics reflects an indifference to our political process that is threatening our democracy.

Don't Jump to Conclusions, Say Others

Others feel that such alarmist conclusions are not merited. To be sure, turnouts in recent elections have been lower than in the past, but this does not necessarily mean that Americans are politically apathetic. On the contrary, low voter turnouts can be interpreted to mean that things are going all right. To this group, the low voter turnout in the 1996 presidential elections might simply reflect a well-running economy, little threat from abroad, and few major social issues at home.

The same can be said with respect to the political attitudes of today's college students compared to students during the 1960s. The so-called disengagement from politics noted among today's college students could simply reflect contentment—there are no bad things to get upset about and to get people involved in politics. During the 1960s, in contrast, there were a number of pressing social issues. African Americans were organizing protests to achieve civil rights. Ralph Nader was spearheading the movement to obtain rights for consumers. The public was increasingly becoming aware of the need to protect our

environmental resources. Americans were being killed in an undeclared war in Vietnam.

This more optimistic group of Americans also feels that the idea that cynicism is rampant in America is a misperception. According to Robert Eisinger, a political science professor at Lewis and Clark College, those who infer that the American citizenry has become cynical are "misunderstanding the public's message." For one thing, there is no real way to measure cynicism. Often, distrust in government is equated with cynicism toward politics, yet there is no justification for making this connection. According to Eisinger, "When reporters and pollsters conflate mistrust with cynicism, without reflecting on what cynicism is or how it can be measured, they may conclude that Americans are cynical, when they actually have identified some (arguably healthy) manifestations of distrust."[2]

Where Do You Stand?

1. To what extent, if any, do low unemployment rates, low crime rates, and the lack of pressing social issues affect political participation?

2. If you were asked for suggestions on how to increase political interest and participation, what would you suggest?

On the Web

For more information on how Americans feel about government—and other topics—go to the Web sites for the Gallup Organization (at http://www.gallup.com), the Harris Poll (at http://www.louisharris.com), and the Pew Research Center (at http://www.people-press.org).

Go to CD-ROM

Introduction

Regardless of how Americans feel about government, one thing is certain: they can't live without it. James Madison (1751–1836) once said, "If men were angels, no government would be necessary." Today, we can expand his statement to include women, and it still holds true. People are not perfect. People need an organized form of government and a set of rules to live by.

Note, though, that even if people were perfect, they would still need to establish rules to guide their behavior. They would somehow have to agree on how to divide up a society's resources, such as its land, among themselves and how to balance individual needs and wants against those of society generally. These perfect people would also need to decide whether they should permit people from other lands to enter their society, just as Americans today are trying to reach agreement on the issue of immigration. They would also have to establish some form of government to enforce the rules they make. It is thus not difficult to understand why government is one of humanity's oldest and most universal institutions. No true society has existed without some form of government. The need for authority and organization will never disappear.

As you will read in this chapter, a number of different systems of government exist in the world today. In the United States, we have a democracy, in which decisions about pressing issues ultimately are made by the people, through their representatives in government. Not surprisingly, Americans are at odds about many issues facing the nation, just as they are over whether perceived political apathy or detachment on the part of the citizenry is threatening our political system. Later in this chapter, we will look at some of the issues facing Americans as we enter the twenty-first century—you will read about other issues in later chapters of this book. First, though, we examine more closely the nature of politics and government, including the purposes and origins of government, and different government systems.

I N F O T R A C *

Hotbeds of activisms

What Are Politics and Government?

Politics means many things to many people. To some, politics is an expensive and extravagant game played in Washington, D.C., in state capitols, and in city halls, particularly during election time. To others, politics involves all of the tactics and maneuvers carried out by the president and Congress.

Most formal definitions of politics, however, begin with the assumption that **social conflict**—disagreements among people in a society over what the society's priorities should be—is inevitable. Conflicts will naturally arise over how the society should use its scarce resources and who should receive various benefits, such as wealth, status, health care, and higher education. Resolving such conflicts is the essence of **politics.** Political scientist Harold Lasswell perhaps said it best when he defined politics as the process of determining "who gets what, when, and how" in a society.[3] Another political scientist, David Easton, defined politics as "the authoritative allocation of values."[4] According to Easton's model of politics, the question concerns how values (scarce resources) are allocated (apportioned among various groups) in a society. Both definitions imply that a set of procedures is needed to resolve the questions of who is to receive which benefits in a society.

There are also many different notions about the meaning of government. A citizen who has broken the law might view government as an interference, while another citizen might view government as a "rescuer" that provides such services as transportation, health care, and protection from crime in her neighborhood. From the perspective of political science, though, **government** can best be defined as the individuals and institutions that make society's rules and that also possess the *power* and *authority* to enforce those rules.

SOCIAL CONFLICT ● Disagreements among people in a society over what the society's priorities should be with respect to the use of scarce resources.

POLITICS ● The process of resolving conflicts over how society should use its scarce resources and who should receive various benefits, such as wealth, status, health care, and higher education. According to Harold Lasswell, politics is the process of determining "who gets what, when, and how" in a society. According to David Easton, politics is "the authoritative allocation of values" in a society.

GOVERNMENT ● The individuals and institutions that make society's rules and that also possess the power and authority to enforce those rules.

Some conflict occurs when people disagree over what society's priorities should be. As such, it is inevitable. One way to resolve such conflicts is through physical force. Another way is through politics, which can be defined as who gets what, when, and how. Here, two Texas legislators argue their respective views on an issue.

A key question here, of course, is this: How do specific individuals obtain the power and authority to govern? As you will read shortly, the answer to this question varies from one type of political system to another.

THE ORIGINS OF GOVERNMENT

There are numerous theories about why and how governments emerged. The most widely studied theories focus on evolution, force, and social contracts.

Evolution

The **evolutionary theory** holds that government developed gradually, step by step. The first state of human political development was the primitive family, usually headed by the father. Over a period of many years, families joined together into clans and worked cooperatively for protection. Clans gradually combined into larger units, called tribes. Usually, one of the older males (or a group of males) led the tribe and was expected to make decisions and resolve conflicts between members of the tribe. As the years went by, the number of families and clans in the tribe grew, and the "government" became larger and more formalized. These tribal groups eventually gave up the nomadic life and settled down to an agricultural existence.

Force

According to the **force theory**, governments first originated when strong persons or groups conquered territories and then forced everyone living in those territories to submit to their will. Then, **institutions**—police, courts, and tax collectors—were created to make people work and to collect all or part of what they produced for the conquerors. Certainly, force has been an element in many governments around the world, and, as you will read shortly, dictatorships are usually created or maintained by force.

EVOLUTIONARY THEORY ● A theory that holds that government evolved gradually over time as families first joined together into clans, then into tribes, and then into a larger, more formal unit.

FORCE THEORY ● A theory that holds that government originated when strong persons or groups conquered territories and forced everyone living in those territories to submit to their will.

INSTITUTIONS ● Organizations and establishments in a society that are devoted to the promotion of a particular cause. Some of the institutions in our government are the legal system, Congress, and the social welfare system.

SOCIAL CONTRACT ● A voluntary agreement among individuals to create a government and to give that government adequate power to secure the mutual protection and welfare of all individuals.

NATURAL RIGHTS ● Rights that are not bestowed by governments but are inherent within every single man, woman, and child by virtue of the fact that he or she is a human being.

POWER ● The ability to influence the behavior of others, usually through the use of force, persuasion, or rewards.

AUTHORITY ● The ability to exercise power, such as the power to make and enforce laws, legitimately.

Social Contracts

The *social contract theory* was developed in the seventeenth and eighteenth centuries by philosophers such as John Locke (1632–1704) and Thomas Hobbes (1588–1679) in England, and Jean-Jacques Rousseau (1712–1778) in France. According to this theory, individuals voluntarily agree with one another, in a social contract, to create a government and to give that government adequate power to secure the mutual protection and welfare of all individuals.

John Locke argued that people are born with natural rights to life, liberty, and property. He theorized that the purpose of government was to protect those rights; if it did not, it would lose its legitimacy and need not be obeyed. The creation of government stemmed from an agreement (social contract) among society's members to voluntarily give up some of their freedoms to obtain the benefits of orderly government. Locke's assumption that people, by nature, are rational and are endowed with certain rights is an essential component of his theory that people can govern themselves.

Hobbes and Rousseau also posited social contracts as the bases of governments, but their approach was markedly different from that of Locke. For example, Hobbes contended that there was no such thing as a natural right. Whereas Locke's vision of the state of nature—a hypothetical state that existed before any government was created—was benign, Hobbes's was violent. To Hobbes, human beings were like monkeys fighting over the bananas on a banana tree, and life in the state of nature was "nasty, brutish, and short." Only if the people agreed, through a social contract, to establish a sovereign whose power was absolute—for better or worse—could there be rights, including the right to personal security. Rousseau had yet another theory. For him, the social contract meant an agreement among society's members to submit their individual wills to a "majority will." Majority rule would determine the outcome of social conflicts.

THE PURPOSES OF GOVERNMENT

The first step in understanding how government works is to understand what it actually does for people and society. Government serves at least four major purposes: (1) it resolves conflicts; (2) it provides public services; (3) it sets goals for public policies; and (4) it preserves culture.

Resolving Conflicts

Even though people have lived together in groups since the beginning of time, none of these groups has been free of social conflict. As mentioned, disputes over how to distribute the society's valued resources inevitably arise because valued resources, such as property, are limited, while people's wants are unlimited. To resolve such disputes, people need ways to determine who wins and who loses, and how to get the losers to accept that decision. Who has the legitimate power and authority to make such decisions? This is where government steps in.

Governments decide how conflicts will be resolved so that public order can be maintained. Governments have power—the ability to influence the behavior of others. Power is getting someone to do something he or she would not do otherwise. Power may involve the use of force (often called coercion), persuasion, or rewards. Governments also have authority, which they can exercise only if their power is legitimate. As used here, the term *legitimate power* means power that is collectively recognized and accepted by society as legally and morally correct. Power and authority are central to a government's ability to resolve conflicts by making and enforcing laws, placing limits on what people can do, and developing court systems to make final decisions.

John Locke (1632–1704), an English philosopher. Locke argued that human beings were equal and endowed by nature with certain rights, such as the right to life, liberty, and property. The purpose of government, according to Locke, was to protect those rights. Locke's theory of natural rights and his contention that government stemmed from a social contract among society's members were an important part of the political heritage brought to this country by the English colonists.

One of the primary purposes of government is, of course, to resolve conflicts in society. Governments also serve other purposes, however, one of which is to provide public services that individuals cannot provide for themselves. The creation and preservation of national and state parks are examples of public services undertaken by the government. Pictured here is a park ranger at the Grand Canyon National Park.

Providing Public Services

Another purpose of government is to provide **public services**—essential services that individuals cannot provide for themselves. Governments undertake projects that individuals usually would not or could not do on their own, such as building and maintaining roads, providing welfare programs, operating public schools, and preserving national parks. Governments also provide such services as law enforcement, fire protection, and public health and safety programs. As Abraham Lincoln once said:

> The legitimate object of government is to do for a community of people whatever they need to have done but cannot do at all, or cannot so well do for themselves in their separate and individual capacities. But in all that people can individually do for themselves, government ought not to interfere.

An important public service provided by government is national security and defense against attacks from other nations. Historically, defense matters have been given high priority by governments and have demanded considerable time, effort, and expense. In the twentieth century, however, national defense became an especially expensive and complex activity for almost every government in the world.

The U.S. government provides for the common defense and national security with its Army, Navy, Air Force, Marines, and Coast Guard. The State Department, Defense Department, Central Intelligence Agency, National Security Agency, and other agencies also contribute to this defense network. As part of an ongoing policy of national security, many departments and agencies in the federal government are constantly dealing with other nations. The Constitution gives our national government exclusive power over relations with foreign nations. No individual state can negotiate a treaty with a foreign nation.

Setting Goals for Public Policies

Governments set goals designed to improve the lives of their citizens. These goals may affect the people on a local, state, or national scale. On setting these goals, governments design plans of action, known as **public policies**, to support or achieve the goals. Public-policy goals may be short term, such as improving a city's educational system by adding new classes, or long term, such as discovering new energy sources. Examples of politi-

PUBLIC SERVICES ● Essential services that individuals cannot provide for themselves, such as building and maintaining roads, providing welfare programs, operating public schools, and preserving national parks.

PUBLIC POLICIES ● Plans of action to support or achieve government goals that are designed to improve the lives of citizens.

cal and social goals for the United States might be the decision to launch an orbiting space station by the year 2005 or to clean up the environment in the twenty-first century.

As you will read in Chapters 17 and 19, public policymaking is a difficult and complex undertaking. In part, this is because policy decisions ultimately involve ethical choices. Because resources are limited, establishing one policy goal may mean sacrificing another.

Preserving Culture

A nation's culture includes the customs, language, beliefs, and values of its people. Governments have worked to preserve their nations' cultures in ways that citizens cannot. For example, the observance of Independence Day on July 4 in the United States helps carry on a tradition that celebrates our history. In France, Bastille Day is celebrated every year on July 14. In the People's Republic of China, National Day is celebrated on October 10.

Of course, a government also helps to preserve a nation's culture, as well as its integrity as an independent unit, by defending the nation against attacks by other nations. Failure to defend successfully against foreign attacks may have significant results for a nation's culture. For example, consider what happened in Tibet. When the former government of that country was unable to defend itself against China, the conquering Chinese set out on a systematic program to destroy Tibet's culture.

Different Systems of Government

Through the centuries, the functions of government just discussed have been performed by many different types of government structures. A government's structure is influenced by a number of factors, such as history, customs, values, geography, climate, resources, and human experiences and needs. No two nations have exactly the same form of government. Over time, however, political analysts have developed various ways of classifying different systems of government. One of the most meaningful ways of classifying governments is according to *who* governs. Who has the power to make the rules and laws that all must obey?

One of the ways that we preserve our unique American political culture is through celebrating important historical events, such as the date we declared independence from Britain. Fourth of July parades, such as the one shown here, remind Americans of their history and contribute to feelings of patriotism.

AUTOCRACY ● A form of government in which the power and authority of the government are in the hands of a single person.

MONARCHY ● A form of autocracy in which a king, queen, emperor, empress, tsar, or tsarina is the highest authority in the government; monarchs usually obtain their power through inheritance.

ABSOLUTE MONARCHY ● A form of monarchy in which the monarch has complete and unlimited power as a matter of divine right.

DIVINE RIGHT THEORY ● A theory that the right to rule by a king or queen was derived directly from God rather than from the consent of the people.

CONSTITUTIONAL MONARCHY ● A form of monarchy in which the monarch shares governmental power with elected lawmakers; the monarch's power is limited, or checked, by other government leaders and perhaps by a constitution or a bill of rights.

DICTATORSHIP ● A form of government in which absolute power is exercised by a single person who has usually obtained his or her power by the use of force.

TOTALITARIAN ● A term describing a dictatorship in which a political leader (or group of leaders) seeks to control almost all aspects of social and economic life. Totalitarian dictatorships are rooted in the assumption that the needs of the nation come before the needs of individuals.

DEMOCRACY ● A system of government in which the people have ultimate political authority. The word is derived from the Greek *demos* (people) and *kratia* (rule).

DIRECT DEMOCRACY ● A system of government in which political decisions are made by the people themselves rather than by elected representatives. This form of government was widely practiced in ancient Greece.

RULE BY ONE: AUTOCRACY

In an **autocracy**, the power and authority of the government are in the hands of a single person. At one time, autocracy was a common form of government, and it still exists in some parts of the world. Autocrats usually obtain their power either by inheriting it (as the heir to a divine right monarchy, for example) or by force.

Monarchy

One form of autocracy, known as a **monarchy**, is government by a king, queen, emperor, empress, tsar, or tsarina. In a monarchy, the monarch, who usually acquires power through inheritance, is the highest authority in the government.

Historically, many monarchies were **absolute monarchies**, in which the ruler held complete and unlimited power as a matter of divine right. Prior to the eighteenth century, the theory of divine right was widely accepted in Europe. The **divine right theory**, variations of which had existed since ancient times, held that God gave those of royal birth the unlimited right to govern other men and women. In other words, those of royal birth had a "divine right" to rule. According to this theory, only God could judge those of royal birth. Thus, all citizens were bound to obey their monarchs, no matter how unfair or unjust they seemed to be. Challenging this power was regarded not only as treason against the government but also as a sin against God.

Most modern monarchies, however, are **constitutional monarchies**, in which the monarch shares governmental power with elected lawmakers. The monarch's power is limited, or checked, by other government leaders and perhaps by a constitution or a bill of rights. These constitutional monarchs serve mainly as *ceremonial* leaders of their governments, as in Great Britain, Denmark, and Sweden.

Dictatorship

Another form of autocracy is a **dictatorship**, in which a single leader rules, although not through inheritance. Dictators often gain supreme power by using force, either through a military victory or by overthrowing another dictator or leader. Dictators hold absolute power and are not accountable to anyone else.

A dictatorship can also be **totalitarian**, which means that the leader (or group of leaders) seeks to control almost all aspects of social and economic life. The needs of the nation come before the needs of individuals, and all citizens must work for the common goals established by the government. Examples of this form of government include Adolf Hitler's government in Nazi Germany from 1933 to 1945, Benito Mussolini's rule in Italy from 1923 to 1943, and Josef Stalin's rule in the Soviet Union from 1929 to 1953. More contemporary examples of totalitarian dictators include Saddam Hussein in Iraq, Fidel Castro in Cuba, and Kim Jong Il in North Korea.

RULE BY MANY: DEMOCRACY

The most familiar form of government to Americans is **democracy**, in which the supreme political authority rests with the people. The word *democracy* comes from the Greek *demos*, meaning "the people," and *kratia*, meaning "rule." The main idea of democracy is that government exists only by the consent of the people and reflects the will of the majority.

The Athenian Model of Direct Democracy

Democracy as a form of government began long ago. **Direct democracy** exists when the people participate directly in government decision making.

This New Hampshire town meeting is an example of direct democracy.

In its purest form, direct democracy was practiced in Athens and other ancient Greek city-states about 2,500 years ago. Every Athenian citizen participated in the governing assembly and voted on all major issues. Although some consider the Athenian form of direct democracy ideal because it demanded a high degree of citizen participation, others point out that most residents in the Athenian city-state (women, foreigners, and slaves) were not deemed to be citizens and thus were not allowed to participate in government.

Clearly, direct democracy is possible only in small communities in which citizens can meet in a chosen place and decide key issues and policies. Nowhere in the world does pure direct democracy exist today. Some New England town meetings, though, and a few of the smaller political subunits, or cantons, of Switzerland still use a modified form of direct democracy. (See the feature entitled *Comparative Politics: Direct Democracy in Switzerland.*)

Representative Democracy

Although the founders of the United States were aware of the Athenian model and agreed that government should be based on the consent of the governed, many feared that a pure, direct democracy would deteriorate into mob rule. They believed that large groups of people meeting together

comparative politics

Direct Democracy in Switzerland

In a modern democracy, there is a belief that every qualified adult is entitled to an equal say in the conduct of public affairs. Nowhere in the modern world has this idea been taken further than in Switzerland, a country in which direct democracy reigns. In that country, only 50,000 signatures—about 1 percent of the qualified voters—are needed on a petition to bring a new countrywide law passed by the parliament before the vote of the whole people in a referendum for possible recall. If 150,000 signatures can be gathered, a proposal that the parliament has not even considered can be brought before the whole people for possible enactment into law.

Since the current system was instituted in Switzerland 130 years ago, 450 questions have been the subjects of nationwide referenda. Three or four times a year, all Swiss citizens are invited to read detailed documents sent to them in the mail, presented on TV, or available on the Internet that present arguments for and against as many as a dozen different issues. One issue involved an attempt to stop the Swiss Air Force from buying any new fighter aircraft until after the year 2000. The measure almost passed. Another issue concerned the legalization of drugs. The electorate was asked to vote on a constitutional amendment that would make legal "the consumption, cultivation or possession of drugs, and their acquisition for personal use." Nearly three-fourths of the voters who turned out for the election voted against the amendment.

Swiss voters have accepted about half of the laws that were questioned in referenda. But the voters have turned down nine-tenths of the proposed new legislation.

For Critical Analysis
Is direct democracy compatible with a strong legislature?

REPRESENTATIVE DEMOCRACY ● A form of democracy in which the will of the majority is expressed through smaller groups of individuals elected by the people to act as their representatives.

REPUBLIC ● Essentially, a term referring to a representative democracy—in which the will of the majority is expressed through smaller groups of individuals elected by the people to act as their representatives.

PRESIDENTIAL DEMOCRACY ● A form of democracy in which the lawmaking and law-enforcing branches of government are separate but equal, as in the United States.

PARLIAMENTARY DEMOCRACY ● A form of democracy in which the lawmaking and law-enforcing branches of government overlap. In Great Britain, for example, the prime minister and the cabinet are members of the legislature, meaning that they both enact and enforce the laws.

would ignore the rights and opinions of people in the minority and would make decisions without careful thought. They concluded that a representative democracy would be the better choice, because it would enable public decisions to be made in a calmer and fairer manner.

In a **representative democracy,** the will of the majority is expressed through a smaller group of individuals elected by the people to act as their representatives. These representatives are responsible to the people for their conduct and can be voted out of office. Our founders preferred to use the term **republic,** which means essentially a representative democracy. As our population grew, this republic became increasingly removed from the Athenian model.

In the modern world, there are two forms of representative democracy: presidential and parliamentary. In a **presidential democracy,** the lawmaking and law-enforcing branches of government are separate but equal. For example, in the United States, Congress is charged with the power to make laws, and the president is charged with the power to carry them out. In a **parliamentary democracy,** the lawmaking and law-enforcing branches of government overlap. In Great Britain, for example, the prime minister and the cabinet are members of the legislature and enact the laws as well as carry them out.

American Democracy

> This country, with all its institutions, belongs to the people who inhabit it. Whenever they shall grow weary of the existing government, they can exercise their constitutional right to amend it, or their revolutionary right to dismember or overthrow it.

With these words, Abraham Lincoln underscored the most fundamental concept of American government: that the people, not the government, are ultimately in control.

PRINCIPLES OF AMERICAN DEMOCRACY

American democracy is based on five fundamental principles:

■ *Equality in voting.* Citizens need equal opportunities to express their preferences about policies or leaders.

■ *Individual freedom.* All individuals must have the greatest amount of freedom possible without interfering with the rights of others.

■ *Equal protection of the law.* The law must entitle all persons to equal protection of the law.

■ *Majority rule and minority rights.* The majority should rule, while guaranteeing the rights of minorities so that the latter may sometimes become majorities through fair and lawful means.

■ *Voluntary consent to be governed.* The people who make up a democracy must agree voluntarily to be governed by the rules laid down by their representatives.

These principles, which lie at the heart of American political culture (see Chapter 6), frame many of the political issues that you will read about in this book. In the next chapter, for example, you will read about the debate among the framers of the Constitution over what type of government structure could best protect certain principles, including individual freedom and minority rights. Later chapters deal with such questions as whether the principle of minority rights means that minorities should be given preferential treatment in hiring and firing decisions, or whether the principle of individual freedom means that individuals suffering from a terminal illness have the right to commit physician-assisted suicide. How these issues are resolved in the future may have a significant impact on our political system and, ultimately, on our individual freedoms and rights.

I N F O T R A C ®

Direct democracy delivers

The U.S. Constitution. In this document, the founders established a form of democratic government that has endured for more than two hundred years. The Constitution is the supreme law of the land and, as such, provides a focal point for any study of American law, history, or politics.

These issues—and others that you will read about in this text—are resolved through the political process. How does this process work? Who are the key players? These questions will be answered in the remaining chapters of this book. In the meantime, though, it is helpful to have some kind of a "road map" to guide you through these chapters so that you can see how each topic covered in the text relates to the big picture.

AMERICAN DEMOCRACY AT WORK—THE BIG PICTURE

Our democracy did not come out of nowhere. Rather, it resulted from what can be viewed as a type of "social contract" among early Americans to create and abide by a set of governing rules. These rules are set forth in the U.S. Constitution. It is appropriate, then, that we begin this text, following this introductory chapter, with a discussion of how and why the Constitution was created, the type of governing structure it established, and the rights and liberties it guarantees for all Americans. These topics, covered in Chapters 2 through 5, are necessarily the point of departure for any discussion of our system of government. As you will see, some of the most significant political controversies today have to do with how various provisions in this founding document should be applied, over two hundred years later, to modern-day events and issues.

We then explore various aspects of the key question mentioned earlier: Who acquires the power and authority to govern, and how do they obtain that power and authority? Generally, of course, the "winners" in our political system are the successful candidates in elections. But the electoral process is influenced by more than just the issue positions taken by the candidates. As you read Chapters 6 through 12, keep the following questions in mind: How do interest groups influence elections? How essential are political parties to the electoral process? To what extent do public opinion and voting behavior play a role in determining who the winners and losers will be? Why are political campaigns so expensive, and what are the implications of high campaign costs for our democracy? Finally, what role do the media and the Internet play in fashioning the outcomes of campaigns?

Once a winning candidate assumes a political office, that candidate becomes a part of one of the institutions of government discussed in Chapters 13 through 16 of this text. He or she also becomes one of the decision makers in the policymaking process (discussed in Chapters 17, 18, and 19), the process of deciding "who gets what, when, and how" in our society. When formulating and implementing federal policies, as well as state and local policies (see Chapter 20), the wishes of interest groups cannot be ignored, particularly those of wealthier groups that can help to fund policymakers' reelections. Public opinion and the media, of course, not only affect election outcomes but also influence which issues will be included on the policymaking agenda.

The political system established by the founders of this nation has endured for over two hundred years. The question facing Americans, as we enter the twenty-first century, is whether it will continue to endure.

America at the Turn of the Twenty-first Century

Chronologically, the United States, as well as the rest of the world, is now entering into the twenty-first century. From a historical perspective, however, the twentieth century really ended with the collapse of the Soviet Union in 1991. As you will read in Chapter 19, that development brought to a close a century of strife, including two world wars and a "Cold War" between the United States and the Soviet Union that lasted for over forty years. As a new century dawns, there is hope that somehow a new world order can be achieved.

In the United States, new issues are emerging, and Americans have conflicting opinions as to how today's problems should be solved. In the remaining pages of this chapter, we examine some of the issues currently facing Americans. Numerous other issues will be explored in later chapters of this text.

Rating the Nation's Performance

According to a Pew Research Center report issued in 1997, the United States seemed to be a nation overwhelmed by political, social, and moral problems. According to the center's report, only once in four decades of polling (in 1974, in the midst of the Watergate scandal) did the public rate the current state of the nation and its future prospects lower than they did in 1996. Of the four national problems thought by over 60 percent of respondents to be increasing in severity, three related to moral and social issues.[5] Subsequent surveys have shown a similar concern over morals. In a Gallup poll conducted in early 1999, for example, respondents included moral decline as one of the top three problems facing the nation.

MORALITY AND POLITICAL LEADERSHIP

Certainly, the morality of some of our political leaders, particularly President Clinton, came under question in 1998, as the scandal over Clinton's relationship with White House intern Monica Lewinsky unfolded. Clinton was not the only politician under fire. Some members of Congress, fearing exposure by the press, felt compelled to either confess their "sins" (previous extramarital affairs) or resign from office. (An interesting question emerging out of these events is whether personal ethics can be separated from politics—see this chapter's *A Question of Ethics: Can Personal Ethics Be Separated from Politics?* for a discussion of this topic.) These moral low points in political leadership—as well as school shootings, hate crimes committed against ethnic and other minority groups, and the supposedly increasing political detachment of the citizenry—seemed to confirm the prediction that our nation was on the verge of an ethical and social collapse.

Monica Lewinsky became the focus of widespread media attention in 1998 after the press learned about her relationship with President Clinton. Here, she is shown being whisked away from reporters.

ARE THINGS REALLY ALL THAT BAD?

Interestingly, in spite of the morality drama being played out in Washington, D.C., the president was able to maintain relatively high job approval ratings. Although the majority of Americans gave Clinton low marks for his moral behavior, at the same time they appeared to approve of the job he was doing as president. In fact, it was Congress, not the president, that saw its approval ratings drop during the impeachment proceedings. Some observers believe that the public's response to the Clinton-Lewinsky scandal confirms the importance of economic factors in shaping public opinion. According to political scientist Everett Carll Ladd, a president's job approval ratings are directly related to economic conditions.[6] Certainly, the fact that the country was experiencing one of the healthiest economies in history worked to Clinton's advantage in 1998 and 1999.

In addition to a healthy economy, the nation was experiencing remarkable progress in other areas. The crime rate had fallen by one-third since the mid-1980s. Cocaine and marijuana use had also fallen—by nearly one-half since 1980. Welfare caseloads had dropped dramatically, by nearly 40 percent since 1993. Racial and gender discrimination, while still a significant concern, was less of a problem than it had been in earlier decades. Stephen Moore, an economist at the Cato Institute, contends that "the daily dose of sleaze" in Washington, D.C., has overshadowed these and other developments in American society. Outside the nation's capital, contends Moore, there have been signs that America is in the early stages of "remarkable cultural renaissance." To be sure, today's social problems are

a question of ethics

Can Personal Ethics Be Separated from Politics?

Clearly, there is a distinction between a political *office,* such as the office of the presidency, and the *person* who holds that office, just as there is a distinction between *official* conduct and *private* conduct. Yet can the personal and official elements of any political office ever be totally separated? This question came to the forefront in 1998 with respect to the presidency.

Certainly, many Americans—including President Clinton—tried to draw a line between the president's personal conduct with Monica Lewinsky and his official conduct as chief executive and head of state. After all, claimed this group, several American presidents in the past had also engaged in extramarital affairs. Yet never before had the media gone into such a frenzy over a president's private conduct. Although the extramarital sexual activities of such presidents as Franklin D. Roosevelt and John F. Kennedy later became publicized in biogra-

phies, the media generally pursued a "hands-off" policy until those presidents left office. Should the media have similarly "looked the other way" with respect to Clinton's private activities?

The issue here is whether the private behavior of a president is really anyone's business. Is there any relationship between private ethical standards and official conduct? Some claim that personal ethics and official conduct can be compartmentalized. In other words, a president's private morality and activities should matter little to the public, as long as they do not affect official decisions. Indeed, during 1998, polls showed that many Americans were not really very concerned about the president's behavior with respect to Monica Lewinsky.

According to at least one scholar, however, people should be concerned about the private ethical standards and conduct of their presidents. University of Texas professor Marvin Olasky claims

that "a study of presidential history shows a link between lying about adultery and lying about other matters." He cites several examples of past presidents who, following sexual affairs and their cover-ups, found it easier to break faith with others, including the American people, in their official conduct.

Olasky concludes that journalists and voters should scrutinize closely the sexual allegations made about presidential candidates. To do otherwise would be negligent, because faithlessness to a wife "is generally a leading indicator of trouble. Small betrayals in marriage generally lead to larger betrayals, and leaders who break a large vow to one person find it easy to break relatively small vows to millions."[7]

For Critical Analysis

Is character likely to be more of an issue in future elections than it has been in the past?

worse than those experienced during the 1950s, but, at least for Moore, the underlying trends are reassuring.[8]

Is Our Democracy Facing a Crisis?

i INFOTRAC®
Americans distrust their government

In this chapter's opening feature—on whether Americans care about government—we discussed the fears of some Americans that political detachment and cynicism were threatening our democracy. These fears are bolstered by data that show a decline in Americans' trust in government in the last several decades. In the mid-1960s, around three-fourths of the American public said they trusted the federal government to do the right thing most of the time. In recent years, depending on the poll, only about one-fourth to one-third of Americans do so. Harris polls show that public confidence in the nation's major institutions reached the lowest point ever in the 1990s. Table 1–1 shows the confidence ratings given to the three branches of the federal government since 1997. As you can see, although the scores for these institutions are increasing, they remain very low, especially for Congress and the executive branch.

Some scholars have concluded that our democracy is facing a crisis. American citizens are losing faith in their government and becoming alienated from the political system. Others are not so worried. For one thing, they point to the increasing levels of confidence in government during the past few years. Also, polling data can be acquired and used differently.

Table 1-1

Confidence in the Leadership of the Nation's Major Institutions

This table shows the percentage of respondents in recent Harris polls who expressed "a great deal of confidence" in the leaders of the three branches of the national government.

	YEAR		
	1997	**1998**	**1999**
Congress	11%	12%	12%
Executive branch	12	17	17
Judicial branch	28	37	42

Source: Harris Poll, February 3, 1999.

For example, it may be true that only a small percentage of Americans have a "great deal of confidence" in their leaders and institutions. But what if you add to those figures the number of Americans who express "a fair amount" of confidence or trust in government? In a recent Gallup poll, for example, respondents expressing a "great deal" and a "fair amount" of trust in government were combined. Not surprisingly, a much rosier picture emerged. The results revealed that 63 percent of Americans expressed a "high degree of trust" in the executive branch, 61 percent expressed a similarly high degree of trust in the legislative branch, and 78 percent gave a high rating to the judicial branch. The pollsters concluded that, overall, "public trust in the federal government remains high."[9]

Political scientist Joseph Nye suggests that while trust in government may be at lower levels than some would like, the problem may be that American expectations of government became too high after World War II (1941–1945). Nye also notes that at the underlying constitutional level, public opinion is still positive. The vast majority of Americans (over 80 percent) say that the United States is the best place in the world to live, and 90 percent approve of the democratic system of government. Similarly, in other democratic countries experiencing a decline in confidence in government, the majority of citizens approve of the political system itself. Nye believes, however, that cynicism and lack of trust in government should not be taken lightly. He notes that in the past three decades, the media and films have tended to portray politics and government with a negative slant. In the long run, this "devaluation of government and politics" could affect the strength of democratic institutions.[10]

Communications Technology

One of the great promises of the twenty-first century is that it will truly become the age of information. Indeed, the digital age is already upon us, as you will read throughout the remainder of the text. (For a discussion of the rate at which information is expanding, if not "exploding," see this chapter's *Politics and the Far Side: The Information Explosion*.) How will developments in communications technology affect politics and government?

POLITICS IN CYBERSPACE

One thing is certain: political leaders who have understood each new wave in communications technology have been able to use it to their advantage. George Washington and Thomas Jefferson were great writers of letters and cheap pamphlets. Lincoln was an excellent orator, and his publicly spoken words were carried through the telegraph. Theodore Roosevelt used political publicity stunts to get front-page coverage in metropolitan tabloids. Franklin Roosevelt learned how to use the radio. Kennedy and Reagan conquered TV. What is left in the digital world of today and tomorrow? Perhaps the next generation of politicians will master superservers capable of conducting simultaneous real-time discrete conversations with tens of thousands of voters at once.

politics on the far side

The Information Explosion

Are we really experiencing an information explosion? Professional forecaster Graham Molitor, after researching this question for five years, compiled his results in an "Encyclopedia of the Future." Molitor concluded that the world's fund of information is doubling every two to two and a half years. Scientific information doubles every five years, and the number of scientific articles doubles in four to five years. Literature doubles every ten to fifteen years. He states that by the time a child born today reaches the age of fifty, there will have been a thirty-two-fold increase in knowledge. According to Molitor, as much as 97 percent of the world's knowledge will be accumulated over one person's lifetime.[11]

For Critical Analysis: What effects might this rapid expansion of information have on traditional educational concepts and structures?

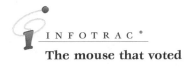

I N F O T R A C °

The mouse that voted

MEDIATING INSTITUTIONS ●
Institutions that assume a mediating role between Americans and their government. Mediating institutions include political party conventions (which decide who will be candidates for political office) and network news organizations (which determine what political events should be reported to the public).

The Web has become the bulletin board and the walkie-talkie of interest groups throughout the land. Access to political information has been amazingly democratized. Voters can find the record of any candidate on any issue at any time. Citizens can go online to contact their representatives in Congress, their state legislators, or virtually any public official. They can form or join political interest groups, learn who contributed to a particular politician's campaign, and find information on virtually any political issue or policy.

In the future, politicians may become completely connected to all voters. Some people envision a truly electronic democracy, in which the entire population, via online voting forums, will vote on important policy issues as they arise. The specter of even more electronic interactions between citizens and their governments suggests a future that is characterized by very different patterns of political behavior than those to which we are now accustomed.

Cyberspace has also created new issues and forced them onto the agenda of the establishment in Washington, D.C. Free speech on the Internet (see Chapters 4 and 12) and free Web access are two such issues.

NO MEDIATING INSTITUTIONS

The future of digital democracy may be messy, however. The digital future may eliminate **mediating institutions,** such as political party conventions (to decide who will be candidates for political office) and network news (to inform the public of political issues and events). In the past, mediating institutions have decided what is or is not important and, in effect, have assumed a mediating role between Americans and their government. In today's digital age, however, everybody with an obsession can be linked to everybody else with the same obsession—disregarding the facts. This may lead to the fragmentation of politics. Of course, radical groups have already learned how to use the Web to propel their propaganda to all corners of the globe. Neo-Nazis and skinheads, who could never get mainstream press, can now reach millions of people virtually for free on the Internet. Indeed, rebel groups as diverse as Mexico's Zapatista guerrillas and Colombia's Revolutionary Armed Forces have their own Web pages to spread their "truths."

Another issue is perhaps even more disturbing for some Americans: the Internet's lack of a common starting point or context for discussion and analysis. If every view has the same value and can be presented almost free of charge on the Internet, then how can one have any perspective? Without a known perspective, it is difficult to judge anything.

COMMUNICATIONS TECHNOLOGY AND THE GLOBAL SOCIETY

The Internet has built new communities and fractured old ones around the world. The global telecommunications network has linked the youth of the world to common events, ranging from the "ethnic cleansing" in Bosnia and Kosovo to the launching of the latest line of lingerie from Victoria's Secret. Financial markets now operate twenty-four hours a day. They link and discipline the world's greatest economies.

As the world gets richer, particularly in Asia, the rising middle class everywhere will seek the same autonomy that individuals have in the United States. The free flow of information will also be a liberating force, as the intransigent leaders of the People's Republic of China, Iran, Iraq, North Korea, and other countries will sooner or later discover.

key terms

absolute monarchy 8
authority 5
autocracy 8
constitutional monarchy 8
democracy 8
dictatorship 8
direct democracy 8
divine right theory 8
evolutionary theory 4
force theory 4
government 3
institutions 4
mediating institutions 15

monarchy 8
natural rights 5
parliamentary democracy 10
politics 3
power 5
presidential democracy 10
public policies 6
public services 6
representative democracy 10
republic 10
social conflict 3
social contract 5
totalitarian 8

chapter summary

1. Politics can be formally defined as the process of resolving social conflict—disagreements over how the society should use its scarce resources and who should receive various benefits, such as wealth, status, health care, and higher education.

2. There are numerous theories as to the origin of governments. The most widely studied theories are the evolutionary theory, the force theory, and the social contract theory.

3. Government can be defined as the individuals and institutions that make society's rules and that also possess the power and authority to enforce those rules. Government serves four major purposes: (1) it resolves conflicts; (2) it provides public services; (3) it sets goals for public policies; and (4) it preserves culture.

4. In an autocracy, the power and authority of the government are in the hands of a single person. Monarchies and dictatorships, including totalitarian dictatorships, are all forms of autocracy. In a constitutional monarchy, however, the monarch shares power with elected lawmakers.

5. Democracy is a form of government in which the government exists only by the consent of the people and reflects the will of the majority. In a direct democracy, the people participate directly in government decision making. In a representative democracy, or republic, people elect representatives to government office to make decisions for them. Forms of representative democracy include presidential democracy and parliamentary democracy.

6. The five principles of American democracy are (1) equality in voting, (2) individual freedom, (3) equal protection of the law, (4) majority rule and minority rights, and (5) voluntary consent to be governed.

7. The collapse of the Soviet Union in 1991 and developments in communications technology promise to alter the national (and international) political landscape in the coming century in ways that cannot yet be fully understood. How the world will be refashioned in view of these developments will depend on the world's governments and the people who participate in those governments.

8. Challenges facing the United States today include a perceived decline in the ethical standards of political leaders, the low level of confidence in government leaders and institutions (as reported by some pollsters), and, perhaps most significantly, the impact of communications technology on American life, including American politics and government.

for critical analysis

1. Ask at least three of your classmates, friends, family members, or others whether they care about politics and government. Also ask them why they do or do not care. What were their responses? How would *you* answer these questions?

2. Is voter turnout necessarily a good indicator of political interest or disinterest? Explain.

3. Does democracy have a better chance of succeeding in countries that are highly developed economically than in countries that are less developed? Why or why not?

4. In your opinion, should morality be an important factor in political leadership?

5. Ironically, in an age when more political information is available than ever before, Americans seem to have less time to take advantage of that information to become knowledgeable about political issues. Will the dual pressures of more information and less time eventually have a negative effect on our democratic system?

6. Suppose that electronic voting were possible and that policymakers, before making decisions on any important question, called for a vote on the issue. What would be the advantages and disadvantages of such a "direct democracy"?

7. Is the global communications system made possible by the Internet necessarily a boon to democracy?

suggested readings

Bouza, Anthony V. *The Decline and Fall of the American Empire: Corruption, Decadence, and the American Dream.* New York: Plenum Press, 1996. Bouza sounds a wake-up call to Americans. He claims that Americans, like the ancient Romans, have become corrupt and hedonistic and that, unless we do something soon, we will meet the same fate as the Roman Empire. Bouza offers inventive and practical solutions to the current problems facing the United States and argues that we need to work hard to make sure that common decency and wisdom will triumph over intolerance and ignorance.

Eberly, Don E. *America's Promise: Civil Society and the Renewal of American Culture.* New York: Rowman and Littlefield, 1999. The author explains why civil society is crucial to the preservation of democratic values and institutions and why the concern over America's moral decay must be a top priority. The author believes that American society cannot thrive without strong social institutions, moral order, and participation in the political process by all sectors of society.

Skocpol, Theda, and Morris Fiorina, eds. *Civic Engagement in American Democracy.* Washington, D.C.: Brookings Institution Press, 1999. This collection of essays looks at various aspects of citizen participation in America in an attempt to find some reasons to explain why Americans are withdrawing from involvement with community affairs and politics.

Weisberg, Jacob. *In Defense of Government: The Fall and Rise of Public Trust.* New York: Scribner, 1996. The author, a political columnist for *New York* magazine and a contributing editor of the *New Republic,* examines the public's loss of confidence in national government institutions. He challenges government to undertake actions in those areas in which government action has traditionally yielded benefits—such as in righting racial wrongs and protecting against personal and national economic disasters—and to abandon involvement in other areas.

politics on the web

Each chapter of *America at Odds,* Second Edition ends with a list of Internet resources and addresses. Once you are on the Internet, you can use the addresses, or uniform resource locators (URLs), listed in the *Politics on the Web* sections in this book to access the ever-growing number of resources available on the Internet relating to American politics and government.

Internet sites tend to come and go, and there is no guarantee that a site included in some of the *Politics on the Web* features will be there by the time this book is in print. We have tried, though, to include sites that have so far proved to be fairly stable. If you do have difficulty reaching a site, do not immediately assume that the site does not exist. First, recheck the URL shown in your browser. Remember, you have to type the URL exactly as written: upper case and lower case are important. If the URL appears to be keyed in correctly, then try the following technique: delete all of the information to the right of the forward slash mark that is farthest to the right in the address, and press enter. Sometimes, this will allow you to reach a home page from which you can link to the topic at issue.

A good point of departure for your online search for information is, of course, the home page for InfoTrac. As described in the Preface to this book, Wadsworth Publishing Company, the publisher of this text, has an exclusive agreement with InfoTrac, developed by Information Access Corporation. InfoTrac, which has become the premiere research service on the Web, can help you find a virtually endless number of resources relating to American politics and government. To access this site, go to

http://www.infotrac-college.com/wadsworth

There are now a seemingly infinite number of sites on the Web that offer information on American government and politics. A list of even the best sites would fill pages. For reasons of space, in this chapter and in those that follow, the *Politics on the Web* sections will include references to only a few selected sites. Following the links provided by these sites will take you to a host of others.

One good site to explore is that of the Cyberspace Law Institute (CLI). By using the CLI site, you can find articles and information on various topics that raise constitutional questions. Go to

http://www.cli.org

Another site that offers information on the effect of new computer and communications technologies on the constitutional rights and liberties of Americans is the Center for Democracy and Technology, which can be accessed at

http://www.cdt.org

The Pew Research Center for the People and the Press offers survey data online on a number of topics relating to American politics and government. The URL for the center's site is

http://www.people-press.org

Yale University Library, one of the great research institutions, has an excellent collection of sources relating to American politics and government. Go to

http://www.library.yale.edu/socsci

using web resources

Rock the Vote (RTV) is a nonprofit organization dedicated to protecting freedom of expression and to helping young people realize and utilize their power to effect change in the civic and political lives of their communities. RTV conducts Rock the Nation forums in cities across the country to provide young people with the opportunity to meet and discuss issues of mutual interest. Access RTV's Web site at

http://www.rockthevote.org

1. Select "Inside Rock the Vote" and then click on "Artists Who Rock the Vote." What do you believe these artists have in common? Is it just politics, or is there an artistic connection? Are your favorite artists listed?

2. Return to the main page and select "Artist Spotlight." Which artists are featured? Why were they selected?

3. In your opinion, does RTV provide an effective message? Why or why not?

notes

1. "A Long Way from Flower Power," *The Economist,* January 17, 1998, p. 26.

2. Robert M. Eisinger, "Cynical America? Misunderstanding the Public's Message," *The Public Perspective,* April/May 1999, pp. 45–48.

3. Harold Lasswell, *Politics: Who Gets What, When and How* (New York: McGraw-Hill, 1936).

4. David Easton, *The Political System* (New York: Knopf, 1953).

5. Based on 1996 data collected in a survey conducted in conjunction with *State of the Union,* a PBS series.

6. Everett Carll Ladd. "Nixon, Clinton and the Polls," *The Wall Street Journal,* April 1, 1998, p. A18.

7. Marvin Olasky, "Sex and the Presidency," *The Wall Street Journal–Europe,* January 27, 1998.

8. Stephen Moore, "Civil Society Is Making a Comeback in America," *Los Angeles Times,* February 19, 1999, p. B7.

9. David W. Moore, "Public Trust in Federal Government Remains High," Gallup Poll Release, January 8, 1999.

10. Joseph S. Nye, Jr., "Dissatisfaction with Government Is an Early Warning," *International Herald Tribune,* January 12, 1999, p. 6.

11. Graham T. T. Molitor, "Trends and Forecasts for the New Millennium," *The Futurist,* August/September 1998, p. 53.

2 chapter

THE CONSTITUTION

Contents

Should Privacy Rights Outweigh Community Interests?

Nowhere in the U.S. Constitution is there any mention of a right to privacy. Yet for some time the courts have inferred such a right from other rights and liberties specifically spelled out in the Constitution. State laws also typically provide for some protection of individual privacy. Most Americans consider the right to privacy to be one of their most precious rights.

One of the issues facing Americans and their political leaders today is how to protect privacy rights in an infotech age. In this feature, we focus on a particular aspect of the current debate over privacy rights. Specifically, should privacy rights be given the fullest protection possible, or are there times when individual privacy rights should give way to community needs? Many privacy advocates believe that privacy rights should be protected, no matter what. Others contend that the right to privacy, as with any other right, should be balanced against the interests of the larger community.

Go to CD-ROM

Protect Privacy Rights, No Matter What, Say Some

In the past several years, privacy advocates have consistently rejected any attempt to infringe on the right to privacy. For example, some type of a national identification system using biometric data—such as fingerprints or "eyeprints"—would be useful for tracking criminals and protecting against fraud and identity theft. Yet this group regards such a system as too intrusive on our individual privacy. Similarly, proposals to give the government expanded authority to wiretap electronic communications in order to detect criminal actions and conspiracies, including terrorist plots, have been rejected as invasive of privacy rights.

The fear is that sacrificing a portion of our privacy rights, even for a good cause, would be the first step on the "slippery slope" toward no privacy rights at all. According to Marc Rotenberg, the head of the Electronic Privacy Information Center, "we have invariably found that when the rights of the individual are balanced against the claims of the community, the individual loses out."[1]

Some believe that if the government does take action, it should be to further protect, rather than infringe on, individuals' privacy rights. For example, Rod Dixon, an attorney at the U.S. Department of Education, argues that the government should enact a "bold privacy law" to ensure that the right of privacy does not become a "scapegoat of technology." If the government fails to pass such a law, the protection of our personal privacy will be left in the hands of technological innovation. If that happens, claims Dixon, Americans may be left with no more than "a remnant of our privacy."[2]

Balance Privacy Rights and the Common Good, Say Others

Another group of Americans believes that the intense focus on individual privacy rights causes us to lose sight of the common good—the needs of the community. Why should the government stand aside when the means exist to monitor the activities of criminals and terrorists? Why shouldn't Americans allow their government more control over civilian electronic communications networks, such as the Internet, to keep our nation from becoming vulnerable to the efforts of enemy hackers? What is wrong with having sobriety checkpoints on the streets and highways, if such efforts help to reduce the number of injuries and fatalities caused by drunk driving?

Sociologist Amitai Etzioni of George Washington University acknowledges that "without privacy, no society can long remain free." Yet he also suggests that there is another side to the privacy equation: there are times when serving the common good entails violating privacy. Etzioni claims that we need a new conception of privacy. We need to forge a new privacy doctrine that protects individuals from irresponsible government and snooping corporations but that cedes individual privacy rights when public health and safety are at stake.

According to Etzioni, government intrusion is not the real problem anyway. Rather, it is a small group of corporations that have more information about private citizens than the police force of any dictatorship.[3] Indeed, a recent Federal Trade Commission survey of 1,400 commercial Internet sites found that more than 85 percent of those surveyed collected personal information on visitors, yet only 14 percent provided any notice to site users regarding such information-collection practices.[4]

Etzioni and others argue that we should look at the right to privacy as we do other rights. For example, the First Amendment to the U.S. Constitution guarantees freedom of speech, but the courts have routinely held that certain forms of speech (such as false speech that is detrimental to another's reputation) are not permissible because they are harmful to society's interests. Why shouldn't we place similar constraints on individual privacy rights, which are not even specifically mentioned in the Constitution?

Where Do You Stand?

1. Do you think that some of our privacy rights should be sacrificed for the sake of more effective crime prevention efforts?

2. In your opinion, which should take first priority, constitutional rights or national security?

On the Web

For an example of how corporations gather and sell personal data obtained from their Web sites, see the Federal Trade Commission's description of the deceptive practices of GeoCities at http://www.ftc.gov/os/1998/9808/geo-cmpl.htm. For more information on privacy rights generally, visit the Web site of the American Civil Liberties Union at http://www.aclu.org.

Introduction

MAGNA CARTA ● The great charter that King John of England was forced to sign in 1215 as protection against the absolute powers of the monarchy. It included such fundamental rights as trial by jury and due process of law.

LIMITED GOVERNMENT ● A form of government based on the principle that the powers of government should be clearly limited either through a written document or through wide public understanding; characterized by institutional checks to ensure that government serves public rather than private interests.

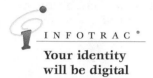

INFOTRAC®

Your identity will be digital

Whether some of our privacy rights should be sacrificed for the common good is just one of many debates concerning our constitutional rights. Although the Constitution was written over two hundred years ago, it continues to be the supreme law of the land. Time and again, its provisions have been adapted to the changing needs and conditions of society. The challenge before today's citizens and political leaders is to find a way to apply those provisions to an information age that could not possibly have been anticipated by the founders. Will the Constitution survive this challenge? Most Americans assume that it will—and with good reason: no other written constitution in the world today is as old as the U.S. Constitution.

Since the collapse of Communist governments in the former Soviet Union and elsewhere, a number of new governments have been formed. Many of these governments have asked constitutional scholars from the United States to lend a hand in developing their constitutions. Why? For much of the rest of the world, our Constitution serves as a model—a model that has withstood the test of time. To understand why, you have to go back to the beginnings of our nation's history.

The Beginnings of American Government

The ideas embedded in our Constitution did not appear out of nowhere. When the framers of the Constitution met in Philadelphia in 1787, they brought with them some valuable political assets. One asset was their English political heritage. Another was the hands-on political experience they had acquired during the colonial era. Their political knowledge and experience enabled them to establish a constitution that could meet not only the needs of their own time but also the needs of generations to come.

THE BRITISH LEGACY

In writing the Constitution, the framers incorporated two basic principles of government that had evolved in England: *limited government* and *representative government*. In a sense, then, the beginnings of our constitutional form of government are linked to events that occurred centuries earlier in England. They are also linked to the writings of European philosophers, particularly the English political philosopher John Locke; from these writings, the founders of our nation derived ideas to justify their rebellion against England and the establishment of a "government by the people."

Limited Government

The Magna Carta (1215) is the most famous document in British constitutional history.

At one time, the English monarch had virtually unrestricted powers. This changed in 1215, when King John was forced by his nobles to sign the **Magna Carta,** or Great Charter. This monumental document provided for a trial by a jury of one's peers (equals). It prohibited the taking of a person's life, liberty, or property except by the lawful judgment of that person's peers. The Magna Carta also forced the king to obtain the nobles' approval of any taxes he imposed on his subjects. Government thus became a contract between the king and his subjects.

The Magna Carta's importance to England cannot be overemphasized, for it clearly established the principle of **limited government**—a government on which strict limits are placed, usually by a constitution. Hence, the Magna Carta signaled the end of the monarch's absolute power. Although the rights provided under the Magna Carta originally applied only to the nobility, it formed the basis of the future constitutional government for all individuals in England and eventually in the United States.

REPRESENTATIVE GOVERNMENT ●
A form of government in which
representatives elected by the people
make and enforce laws and policies.

PARLIAMENT ● The name of the
national legislative body in countries
governed by a parliamentary system, as
in England and France.

BICAMERAL LEGISLATURE ● A
legislature made up of two chambers,
or parts. The United States has a
bicameral legislature, composed of the
House of Representatives and the
Senate.

The principle of limited government was expanded four hundred years later, in 1628, when Charles I signed the Petition of Rights. Among other things, this petition prohibited the monarch from imprisoning political critics without a jury trial. Perhaps more important, the petition declared that even the king or queen had to obey the law of the land.

In 1689, the English Parliament (described shortly) passed the English Bill of Rights, which further extended the concept of limited government. This document included several important ideas:

- The king or queen could not interfere with parliamentary elections.
- The king or queen had to have Parliament's approval to levy (collect) taxes or to maintain an army.
- The king or queen had to rule with the consent of the people's representatives in Parliament.
- The people could not be subjected to cruel or unusual punishment or to excessive fines.

The British colonists in North America were also British citizens, and thus the English Bill of Rights of 1689 applied to them as well. As a result, virtually all of the major concepts in the English Bill of Rights became part of the American system of government.

Representative Government

In a **representative government**, the people, by whatever means, elect individuals to make governmental decisions for all of the citizens. Usually, these representatives of the people are elected to their offices for specific periods of time. In England, this group of representatives is referred to as **Parliament**, which is a **bicameral** (two-house) **legislature** consisting of an upper chamber (the House of Lords) and a lower chamber (the House of Commons). The English form of representative government provided a model for Americans to follow. Many of the American colonies had bicameral legislatures—as did, eventually, the U.S. Congress that was established by the Constitution.

Political Philosophy—John Locke's Influence

Locke expounded his political theories in *Two Treatises on Government*, published in 1690. Locke argued that neither custom nor tradition nor the fact of being born in a certain society was sufficient reason to obey rulers. He further argued that all persons were born free, equal, and independent, and that all possessed certain natural rights, including the rights to life, liberty, and property. Government did not give these rights to the people, for the rights already existed in a hypothetical "state of nature" before governments were even created. According to Locke, the primary purpose of government was to protect these natural rights. Essentially, government resulted from a social contract—an agreement by the people to establish a government and abide by its rules.

John Locke's treatises clearly set forth an alternative to divine right monarchy, the prevailing political system of his day. As you will see, when the American colonists rebelled against English rule, such concepts as "natural rights" and a government based on a "social contract" became important theoretical tools in justifying the rebellion.

POLITICS AND PRACTICES IN THE AMERICAN COLONIES

The American colonies were settled by individuals from many nations, including England, France, Spain, Holland, Sweden, and Norway. The majority of the colonists, though, came from England. The British colonies in North America were established by private individuals and private trading companies and were under the rule of the British Crown. The

MAYFLOWER COMPACT ● A document drawn up by Pilgrim leaders in 1620 on the ship *Mayflower*. The document stated that laws were to be made for the general good of the people.

FUNDAMENTAL ORDERS OF CONNECTICUT ● America's first written constitution, developed by some of the Pilgrims who left the Massachusetts Bay Colony and settled in what is now Connecticut. The document provided for an assembly of elected representatives from each town and for the popular election of a governor and judges.

BILL OF RIGHTS ● The first ten amendments to the U.S. Constitution. They list the freedoms—such as the freedoms of speech, press, and religion—that a person enjoys and that cannot be infringed on by the government.

Figure 2–1
The Thirteen Colonies
Georgia, the last of the thirteen colonies, was established in 1732. By this time, each of the thirteen colonies had developed its own political system, complete with necessary political documents and a constitution.

New Hampshire

Massachusetts*

New York

Rhode Island

Connecticut

New Jersey

Pennsylvania

Delaware

Maryland

Virginia

North Carolina

South Carolina

Georgia

ATLANTIC OCEAN

*Maine was under the governance of Massachusetts until 1832.

British colonies, which were located primarily along the Atlantic seaboard of today's United States, eventually numbered thirteen.

Although American politics owes much to the English political tradition, the colonists actually derived most of their understanding of social compacts, the rights of the people, limited government, and representative government from their own experiences. Years before Parliament adopted the English Bill of Rights or John Locke wrote his *Two Treatises on Government,* the American colonists were putting the ideas expressed in those documents into practice.

The First British Settlements

In the 1580s, Sir Walter Raleigh convinced England's queen, Elizabeth I, to allow him to establish the first English outpost in North America on Roanoke Island, off the coast of what was to become North Carolina. The attempted settlement was unsuccessful, however. The first permanent English settlement in North America was Jamestown, in what is now Virginia. Jamestown was established in 1607 as a trading post of the Virginia Company of London.[5]

The Plymouth Company founded the first New England colony in 1620 in what is now Plymouth, Massachusetts. The settlers at Plymouth, who called themselves Pilgrims, were a group of English Protestants who came to the New World on the ship *Mayflower.* Even before the Pilgrims went ashore, they drew up the **Mayflower Compact,** in which they set up a government and promised to obey its laws. The reason for the compact was that the group was outside the jurisdiction of the Virginia Company, which had arranged for them to settle in Virginia, not Massachusetts. The leaders on board the *Mayflower* feared that some of the passengers might decide that they were no longer subject to any rules of civil order and that some form of governmental authority was thus necessary. The Mayflower Compact, which was essentially a social contract, has historical significance because it was the first of a series of similar contracts among the colonists to establish fundamental rules of government.[6]

The Massachusetts Bay Company established another trading outpost in New England in 1630. In 1639, some of the Pilgrims at Plymouth, who felt that they were being persecuted by the Massachusetts Bay Colony, left Plymouth and settled in what is now Connecticut. They developed America's first written constitution, which was called the **Fundamental Orders of Connecticut.** This document called for the laws to be made by an assembly of elected representatives from each town. The document also provided for the popular election of a governor and judges. Other colonies, in turn, established fundamental governing rules. The Massachusetts Body of Liberties protected individual rights. The Pennsylvania Frame of Government, passed in 1682, and the Pennsylvania Charter of Privileges of 1701 established principles that were later expressed in the U.S. Constitution and **Bill of Rights** (the first ten amendments to the Constitution).

By 1732, all thirteen colonies had been established, each with its own political documents and a constitution (see Figure 2–1).

Colonial Legislatures

As mentioned, the British colonies in America were all under the rule of the British monarchy. Britain, however, was thousands of miles away (it took two months to sail across the Atlantic). Thus, to a significant extent, colonial legislatures carried on the "nuts and bolts" of colonial government. These legislatures, or *representative assemblies,* consisted of representatives elected by the colonists. The earliest colonial legislature was the Virginia House of Burgesses, established in 1619. By the time of the American Revolution, all of the colonies had representative assemblies, many of which had been in existence for more than a hundred years.

Through their participation in colonial governments, the colonists gained crucial political experience. Colonial leaders became familiar with the practical problems of governing. They learned how to build coalitions among groups with diverse interests and how to make compromises. Because of their political experiences, the colonists were able to quickly set up their own constitutions and state systems of government—and eventually a new national government—after they declared their independence from Great Britain in 1776.

The Rebellion of the Colonists

Scholars of the American Revolution point out that, by and large, the American colonists did not want to become independent of Great Britain. For the majority of the colonists, Britain was the homeland, and ties of loyalty to the British monarch were strong. Why, then, did the colonists revolt against Britain and declare their independence? What happened to sever the political, economic, and emotional bonds that tied the colonists to Britain? The answers to these questions lie in a series of events in the mid-1700s that culminated in a change in British policy with respect to the colonies. Table 2–1 shows the chronology of the major political events in early U.S. political history.

One of these events was the Seven Years' War (1756–1763) between Britain and France, which Americans often refer to as the French and Indian War. The Seven Years' War and its aftermath permanently changed the relationship between Britain and the American colonists. To pay its war debts and to finance the defense of its expanded empire, Britain needed revenues. The British government decided to obtain some of these revenues by imposing taxes on the American colonists and exercising more direct control over colonial trade. At the same time, Americans were beginning to distrust the British. Having fought alongside British forces, Americans thought they deserved some credit for the victory. The British, however, attributed the victory solely to the British war effort.

Additionally, Americans began to develop a sense of identity separate from the British. Americans were shocked at the behavior of some of the British soldiers and the cruel punishments meted out to enforce discipline among the British troops. The British, in turn, had little good to say about the colonists with whom they had fought, considering them brutish, uncivilized, and undisciplined. It was during this time that the colonists began to use the word *American* to describe themselves.

"TAXATION WITHOUT REPRESENTATION"

In 1764, in an effort to obtain needed revenues, the British Parliament passed the Sugar Act, which imposed a tax on all sugar imported into the American colonies. Some colonists, particularly in Massachusetts, vigorously opposed this tax and proposed a boycott of certain British imports. This boycott launched a "nonimportation" movement that soon spread to other colonies.

The Stamp Act of 1765

The following year, Parliament passed the Stamp Act, which imposed the first direct tax on the colonists. Under the act, all legal documents, newspapers, and other items, including playing cards and dice, had to use specially embossed (stamped) paper that was purchased from the government.

The Stamp Act generated even stronger resentment among the colonists. James Otis, Jr., a Massachusetts attorney, declared that there could be "no taxation without representation." The American colonists could not vote in British elections and therefore were not represented in the British Parliament. They viewed Parliament's attempts to tax them as contrary to

Table 2–1

Significant Events in Early U.S. Political History

1585	British outpost set up in Roanoke.
1607	Jamestown established; Virginia Company lands settlers.
1620	Mayflower Compact signed.
1630	Massachusetts Bay Colony set up.
1639	Fundamental Orders of Connecticut adopted.
1641	Massachusetts Body of Liberties adopted.
1682	Pennsylvania Frame of Government passed.
1701	Pennsylvania Charter of Privileges written.
1732	Last of thirteen colonies established.
1756	French and Indian War declared.
1765	Stamp Act; Stamp Act Congress meets.
1770	Boston Massacre.
1774	First Continental Congress.
1775	Second Continental Congress; Revolutionary War begins.
1776	Declaration of Independence signed.
1777	Articles of Confederation drafted.
1781	Last state signs Articles of Confederation.
1783–1789	"Critical period" in U.S. history; weak national government.
1786	Shays' Rebellion.
1787	Constitutional Convention.
1788	Ratification of Constitution.
1791	Ratification of Bill of Rights.

FIRST CONTINENTAL CONGRESS ●
The first gathering of delegates from twelve of the thirteen colonies, held in 1774.

SECOND CONTINENTAL CONGRESS ● The congress of the colonies that met in 1775 to assume the powers of a central government and establish an army.

the principle of representative government. The British saw the matter differently. From the British perspective, it was only fair that the colonists pay taxes to help support the costs incurred by the British government in defending its American territories and maintaining the troops that were permanently stationed in the colonies following the Seven Years' War.

In October 1765, nine of the thirteen colonies sent delegates to the Stamp Act Congress in New York City. The delegates prepared a declaration of rights and grievances, which they sent to King George III. This action marked the first time that a majority of the colonies had joined together to oppose British rule. The British Parliament repealed the Stamp Act.

Further Taxes and the Coercive Acts

Soon, however, Parliament passed new laws designed to bind the colonies more tightly to the central government in London. Laws that imposed taxes on glass, paint, lead, and many other items were passed in 1767. The colonists protested by boycotting all British goods. In 1773, anger over taxation reached a powerful climax at the Boston Tea Party, in which colonists dressed as Mohawk Indians dumped almost 350 chests of British tea into Boston Harbor as a gesture of tax protest.

The British Parliament was quick to respond to the Tea Party. In 1774, it passed the Coercive Acts (sometimes called the "Intolerable Acts"), which closed the harbor and placed the government of Boston under direct British control.

THE CONTINENTAL CONGRESSES

In response to the "Intolerable Acts," Rhode Island, Pennsylvania, and New York proposed a colonial congress. The Massachusetts House of Representatives requested that all colonies select delegates to send to Philadelphia for such a congress.

The First Continental Congress

On September 5, 1774, the **First Continental Congress** met at Carpenter's Hall in Philadelphia. Of the thirteen colonies, Georgia was the only one that did not participate. The First Continental Congress decided that the colonies should send a petition to King George III to explain their grievances, which they did. The congress also passed other resolutions continuing the boycott of British goods and requiring each colony to establish an army. (During this period, neighbors spied on neighbors. See the feature *Politics on the Far Side: Let Freedom Ring?*)

politics on the far side

Let Freedom Ring?

To enforce the boycott and other trading sanctions against Britain, the delegates to the First Continental Congress urged that "a committee be chosen in every county, city and town, by those who are qualified to vote for representatives in the legislature, whose business it shall be attentively to observe the conduct of all persons." Over the next several months, all colonial legislators supported this action. The committees of "safety" or "observation," as they were called, organized militias, held special courts, and suppressed the opinion of those who remained loyal to the British Crown. Committee members spied on neighbors' activities and reported to the press the names of those who violated the trading sanctions against Britain. The names were then printed in the local papers, and the transgressors were harassed and ridiculed in their communities.

For Critical Analysis: Does today's government ever permit actions that cause people to feel "harassed and ridiculed in their communities"?

The Second Continental Congress

Almost immediately after receiving the petition, the British government condemned the actions of the First Continental Congress as open acts of rebellion. Britain responded with even stricter and more repressive measures. On April 19, 1775, British soldiers (Redcoats) fought with colonial citizen soldiers (Minutemen) in the towns of Lexington and Concord in Massachusetts, the first battles of the American Revolution. The battle at Concord was memorialized by the poet Ralph Waldo Emerson as the "shot heard round the world." Less than a month later, delegates from all thirteen colonies gathered in Pennsylvania for the **Second Continental Congress**, which immediately assumed the powers of a central government. It declared that the militiamen who had gathered around Boston were now a full army. It also named George Washington—a delegate to the Second Continental Congress who had some military experience—as its commander in chief.

JULY 4, 1776 – KING GEORGE'S THRONE

INDEPENDENCE·HALL

©97 SCRIPPS HOWARD. E-MAIL: hpayne@cais.com (www.unitedmedia.com/inkwell/payne)

HENRY PAYNE reprinted by permission of United Feature Syndicate, Inc.

The delegates to the Second Continental Congress still intended to reach a peaceful settlement with the British Parliament. One declaration stated specifically that "we [the congress] have not raised armies with ambitious designs of separating from Great Britain, and establishing independent States." The continued attempts to effect a reconciliation with Britain, even after the outbreak of fighting, underscore the colonists' reluctance to sever their relationship with the home country. As one scholar put it, "Of all the world's colonial peoples, none became rebels more reluctantly than did Anglo-Americans in 1776."[7]

Breaking the Ties: Independence

Public debate about the problems with Great Britain continued to rage, but the stage had been set for declaring independence. One of the most rousing arguments in favor of independence was presented by Thomas Paine, a former English schoolmaster and corset maker,[8] who wrote a pamphlet called *Common Sense*. In that pamphlet, which was published in Philadelphia in January 1776, Paine addressed the crisis using "simple fact, plain argument, and common sense." He mocked King George III and attacked every argument that favored loyalty to the king. He called the king a "royal brute" and a "hardened, sullen-tempered Pharaoh."[9]

Paine's writing went beyond a personal attack on the king. He contended that America could survive economically on its own and no longer needed its British connection. He wanted the developing colonies to become a model nation for democracy in a world in which other nations were oppressed by strong central governments.

None of Paine's arguments was new; in fact, most of them were commonly heard in tavern debates throughout the land. Instead, it was the pungency and eloquence of Paine's words that made *Common Sense* so effective:

> A government of our own is our natural right: and when a man seriously reflects on the precariousness of human affairs, he will become convinced, that it is infinitely wiser and safer, to form a constitution of our own in a cool and deliberate manner, while we have it in our power, than to trust such an interesting event to time and chance.[10]

Thomas Paine (1737–1809). In addition to his successful pamphlet *Common Sense,* Paine also wrote a series of sixteen pamphlets, under the title *The Crisis,* during the American Revolution. He returned to England and, in 1791 and 1792, wrote *The Rights of Man,* in which he defended the French Revolution. To escape prosecution by the British government for treason, he fled to Paris, where he was imprisoned in 1793 and 1794 during the Reign of Terror. Paine returned to the United States in 1802.

Many historians regard Paine's *Common Sense* as the single most important publication of the American Revolution. The pamphlet became a bestseller; more than 100,000 copies were sold within a few months after its publication.[11] It put independence squarely on the agenda. Above all, *Common Sense* severed the remaining ties of loyalty to the British monarch, thus removing the final psychological barrier to independence. Indeed, later John Adams would ask,

> What do we mean by the Revolution? The War? That was no part of the Revolution. It was only an effect and consequence of it. The Revolution was in the minds of the people, and this was effected, from 1760 to 1775, in the course of fifteen years before a drop of blood was drawn at Lexington.[12]

THE RESOLUTION OF INDEPENDENCE

In June 1776, Richard Henry Lee of Virginia introduced the Resolution of Independence into the Second Continental Congress. By this time, the congress had already voted for free trade at all American ports for all countries except Britain. The congress had also suggested that all colonies establish state governments separate from Britain. On July 2, 1776, the congress adopted the Resolution of Independence:

> RESOLVED, That these United Colonies are, and of right ought to be free and independent States, that they are absolved from allegiance to the British Crown, and that all political connection between them and the state of Great Britain is, and ought to be, totally dissolved.

Although it was not legally binding, the Resolution of Independence was one of the first necessary steps to establish the legitimacy of the new nation in the eyes of foreign governments. The new nation required supplies for its armies and commitments of foreign military aid. Unless officials of foreign nations believed that this new land was truly independent from Britain, they would not support its new leaders.

THE DECLARATION OF INDEPENDENCE

Immediately after adopting the Resolution of Independence, the congress was ready to pass a full declaration. On July 4, 1776, the Declaration of Independence finally became law in the new nation. On that day, King George III, unaware of the events taking place three thousand miles away, wrote in his diary, "Nothing of importance happened today."

Minor changes to the Declaration of Independence were made during the next two weeks. On July 19, the modified draft became the "Unanimous Declaration of the Thirteen United States of America."[13] On August 2, the members of the Second Continental Congress signed the document. The first official printed version carried only the signatures of the congress's president, John Hancock, and of its secretary, Charles Thompson.

THE SIGNIFICANCE OF THE DECLARATION OF INDEPENDENCE

The Declaration of Independence is one of the world's most famous documents. Like Paine, Thomas Jefferson, who wrote most of the document, elevated the dispute between Britain and the American colonies to a universal level. Jefferson opened the second paragraph of the declaration with the following words, which have since been memorized by countless American schoolchildren and admired the world over:

> We hold these Truths to be self-evident, that all Men are created equal, that they are endowed by their Creator with certain unalienable Rights, that among these are Life, Liberty, and the Pursuit of Happiness—That to secure these Rights, Governments are instituted among Men, deriving their just Powers from the Consent of the Governed, that whenever any Form of Government becomes destructive of these Ends, it is the Right of the People to alter or to abolish it, and to institute new Government. . . .

UNICAMERAL LEGISLATURE ● A legislature with only one chamber.

CONFEDERATION ● A league of independent states that are united only for the purpose of achieving common goals.

ARTICLES OF CONFEDERATION ● The nation's first national constitution, which established a national form of government following the American Revolution. The articles provided for a confederal form of government in which the central government had few powers.

The concepts expressed in the Declaration of Independence clearly reflect Jefferson's familiarity with European political philosophy, particularly the works of John Locke.[14] Locke's philosophy, though it did not cause the American Revolution, provided the philosophical underpinnings by which it could be justified.

For Americans, the political concepts—particularly that of equality—set forth in the Declaration of Independence became standards by which future political developments were to be measured. For example, as you will see, the Constitution did not allow for equal treatment for many Americans, including African Americans and women. The disparity between the declaration's promise of equality and the Constitution's unequal treatment of Americans set the stage for future conflicts over the issue of equality.

FROM COLONIES TO STATES

Even prior to the Declaration of Independence, some of the colonies had transformed themselves into sovereign states with their own permanent governments. In May 1776, the Second Continental Congress had directed each of the colonies to form "such government as shall . . . best be conducive to the happiness and safety of their constituents [voters]." Before long, all thirteen colonies had created constitutions. Eleven of the colonies had completely new constitutions; the other two colonies, Rhode Island and Connecticut, made minor modifications to old royal charters. Seven of the new constitutions contained bills of rights that defined the personal liberties of all state citizens. All constitutions called for limited governments.

Many citizens were fearful of a strong central government because of their recent experiences under the British Crown. They opposed any form of government that resembled monarchy in any way. Consequently, wherever such antiroyalist sentiment was strong, the legislature—composed of elected representatives—itself became all-powerful. In Pennsylvania and Georgia, for example, unicameral (one-house) legislatures were unchecked by any executive authority. Indeed, antiroyalist sentiment was so strong that the executive branch was extremely weak in all thirteen states. This situation would continue until the ratification of the U.S. Constitution.

The Confederation of States

Antiroyalist sentiments also influenced the thinking of the delegates to the Second Continental Congress, who formed a committee to draft a plan of confederation. A **confederation** is a voluntary association of *independent* states (see Chapter 3). The member states agree to let the central government undertake a limited number of activities, such as forming an army, but the states do not allow the central government to place many restrictions on the states' own actions. The member states typically can still govern most state affairs as they see fit.

On November 15, 1777, the Second Continental Congress agreed on a draft of the plan, which was finally signed by all thirteen colonies on March 1, 1781. The **Articles of Confederation,** the result of this plan, served as this nation's first national constitution and represented an important step in the creation of our governmental system.[15]

THE GOVERNMENT OF THE CONFEDERATION

The Articles of Confederation established the Congress of the Confederation as the central governing body. This congress was a unicameral assembly of ambassadors, as they were called, from the various states. Although each state could send anywhere from two to seven ambassadors, or representatives, to the congress, each state, no matter what its size, had only one vote. The issue of sovereignty was an important part of the Articles of Confederation:

NORTHWEST ORDINANCE ● A 1787 congressional act that established a basic pattern for how states should govern new territories north of the Ohio River.

Each State retains its sovereignty, freedom and independence, and every power, jurisdiction, and right, which is not by this Confederation expressly delegated to the United States in Congress assembled.

The structure of government under the Articles of Confederation is shown in Figure 2–2.

Strengths of the Government of the Confederation

Congress had several powers under the Articles of Confederation, including the powers to do the following:

- Enter into treaties and alliances.
- Establish and control armed forces.
- Declare war and make peace.
- Regulate coinage (but not paper money).
- Borrow money from the people.
- Create a postal system.
- Regulate Indian affairs.
- Set standards for weights and measures.
- Create courts for problems related to ships at sea.
- Settle disputes between the states under certain circumstances.
- Guarantee that citizens visiting other states would have the same rights and privileges as the states' residents.

The new nation achieved a number of accomplishments under the Articles of Confederation. Certain states' claims to western lands were settled with the **Northwest Ordinance,** which established a basic pattern for how states should govern new territories north of the Ohio River. Additionally, and perhaps most significantly, the United States under the Articles of Confederation won the Revolutionary War. Congress was then able to negotiate a peace treaty with Great Britain. Under the 1783 treaty, Britain not only recognized American independence but also granted to the United States all of the territory from the Atlantic Ocean to the Mississippi River and from the Great Lakes and Canada to what is now northern Florida.

Figure 2–2
American Government under the Articles of Confederation

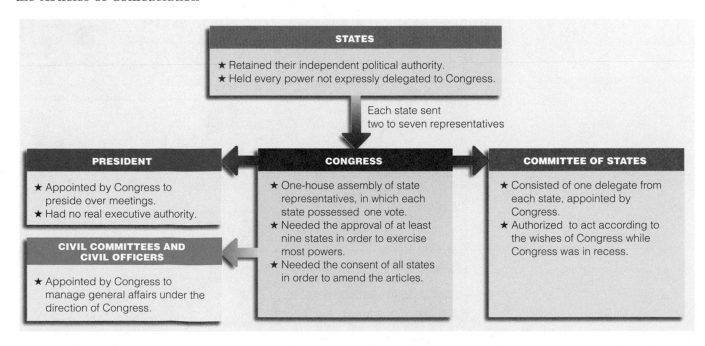

STATES
★ Retained their independent political authority.
★ Held every power not expressly delegated to Congress.

Each state sent two to seven representatives

PRESIDENT
★ Appointed by Congress to preside over meetings.
★ Had no real executive authority.

CIVIL COMMITTEES AND CIVIL OFFICERS
★ Appointed by Congress to manage general affairs under the direction of Congress.

CONGRESS
★ One-house assembly of state representatives, in which each state possessed one vote.
★ Needed the approval of at least nine states in order to exercise most powers.
★ Needed the consent of all states in order to amend the articles.

COMMITTEE OF STATES
★ Consisted of one delegate from each state, appointed by Congress.
★ Authorized to act according to the wishes of Congress while Congress was in recess.

The Articles of Confederation proved to be a good "first draft" for the Constitution, and at least half of the text of the articles would later appear in the Constitution. The articles were an unplanned experiment that tested some of the principles of government that had been set forth earlier in the Declaration of Independence. Some argue that without the experience of government under the Articles of Confederation, it would have been difficult, if not impossible, to arrive at the compromises that were necessary to create the Constitution several years later. The articles, though, had some important weaknesses.

Weaknesses of the Government of the Confederation

In spite of its accomplishments, the central government created by the Articles of Confederation was, in fact, quite weak. The articles also had other major weaknesses, which are listed in Figure 2–3. These weaknesses stemmed from the fact that the Confederation was made up of independent states that had no intention of giving up their sovereignty.

As you can see from Figure 2–3, much of the functioning of the government under the Articles of Confederation basically depended on the good-will of the states. Article 3, for example, simply established a "league of friendship" among the states, with no central government intended.

**Figure 2–3
Weaknesses in the
Articles of Confederation**

WEAKNESS	RESULT
Congress could not force the states to meet military quotas.	The central government could not draft soldiers to form a standing army.
Congress could not regulate commerce between the states or with other nations.	Each state was free to set up its own system of taxes on goods imported from other states. Economic quarrels among the states broke out. There was difficulty in trading with other nations.
Congress could enter into treaties, but could not enforce its power or control foreign relations.	The states were not forced to respect treaties. Many states entered into treaties independent of Congress.
Congress could not directly tax the people.	It had to rely on the states to collect and forward taxes, which the states were reluctant to do. The central government was always short of money.
Congress had no power to enforce its laws.	The central government depended on the states to enforce its laws, which they rarely did.
Nine states had to approve any law before it was enacted.	Most laws were difficult, if not impossible, to enact.
Any amendment to the articles required all 13 states to consent.	The powers of the central government could not be changed in practice.
There was no national judicial system.	Most disputes among the states could not be settled by the central government.
There was no executive branch.	Coordinating the work of the central government was almost impossible.

A TIME OF CRISIS—THE 1780S

The Revolutionary War ended on October 18, 1781. The Treaty of Paris, which confirmed the colonies' independence from Britain, was signed in 1783. Peace with the British may have been won, but peace within the new nation was hard to find. The states bickered among themselves and refused to support the new central government in almost every way. As George Washington stated, "We are one nation today and thirteen tomorrow. Who will treat us on such terms?"

The states also increasingly taxed each other's imports and at times even prevented trade altogether. By 1784, the new nation was suffering from a serious economic depression. States started printing their own money at dizzying rates, which led to inflation. Banks were calling in old loans and refusing to issue new ones. Individuals who could not pay their debts were often thrown into prison.

Shays' Rebellion

The tempers of angry farmers in western Massachusetts reached the boiling point in August 1786. Former Revolutionary War captain Daniel Shays, along with approximately two thousand armed farmers, seized county courthouses and disrupted the debtors' trials. Shays and his men then launched an attack on the national government arsenal in Springfield. **Shays' Rebellion** continued to grow in intensity and lasted into the winter, when it was finally stopped by the Massachusetts volunteer army, paid by private funds.

Similar disorders occurred throughout most of the New England states and in some other areas as well. The upheavals, and particularly Shays' Rebellion, were an important catalyst for change. The revolts scared American political and business leaders and caused more and more Americans to realize that a *true* national government had to be created.

The Annapolis Meeting

The Virginia legislature called for a meeting of representatives from all of the states at Annapolis, Maryland, on September 11, 1786, to address the problems facing the nation. Five of the thirteen states sent delegates, two of whom were Alexander Hamilton of New York and James Madison of Virginia. Both of these men favored a strong central government.[16] They persuaded the other delegates to issue a report calling on the states to hold a convention in Philadelphia in May of the following year.

The Congress of the Confederation at first was reluctant to give its approval to the Philadelphia convention. By mid-February 1787, however, seven of the states had named delegates to the Philadelphia meeting. Finally, on February 21, the congress called on the states to send delegates to Philadelphia "for the sole and express purpose of revising the Articles of Confederation." That Philadelphia meeting became the **Constitutional Convention.**

Drafting the Constitution

Although the convention was supposed to start on May 14, 1787, few of the delegates had actually arrived in Philadelphia on that date. The convention formally opened in the East Room of the Pennsylvania State House on May 25, after fifty-five of the seventy-four delegates had arrived.[17] Only Rhode Island, where feelings were strong against creating a more powerful central government, did not send any delegates.

WHO WERE THE DELEGATES?

Among the delegates to the Constitutional Convention were some of the nation's best-known leaders. George Washington was present, as were

James Madison (1751–1836). Madison's contributions at the Constitutional Convention in 1787 earned him the title "Master Builder of the Constitution." As a member of Congress from Virginia, he advocated the Bill of Rights. He was secretary of state under Thomas Jefferson (1801–1809) and became our fourth president in 1809.

Alexander Hamilton, James Madison, George Mason, Robert Morris, and Benjamin Franklin (then eighty-one years old), who had to be carried to the convention on a portable chair. Some notable leaders were absent, including Thomas Jefferson and John Adams, who were serving as ambassadors in Europe, and Patrick Henry, who did not attend because he "smelt a rat." (Henry favored local government and was wary that the convention might favor a stronger central government.)

For the most part, the delegates were from the best-educated and wealthiest classes. Thirty-three delegates were lawyers, nearly half of the delegates were college graduates, three were physicians, seven were former chief executives of their respective states, six owned large plantations, at least nineteen owned slaves, eight were important business owners, and twenty-one had fought in the Revolutionary War. In other words, the delegates to the convention constituted an elite assembly. No ordinary farmers, workers, women, African Americans, or Native Americans were present.

Indeed, in his classic work on the Constitution, Charles Beard maintained that the Constitution was produced primarily by wealthy property owners who wanted a stronger government that could protect their property rights.[18] (Whether the Constitution was favored by a majority of Americans is the topic of the *Perception versus Reality* feature later in this chapter.)

THE VIRGINIA PLAN

James Madison had spent months reviewing European political theory before he went to the Philadelphia convention. When his Virginia delegation arrived before anybody else, he immediately put its members to work. On the first day of the convention, Governor Edmund Randolph of Virginia was able to present fifteen resolutions outlining what was to become known as the Virginia Plan. This was a masterful political stroke on the part of the Virginia delegation. Its proposals immediately set the agenda for the remainder of the convention.

The fifteen resolutions contained in the Virginia Plan proposed an entirely new national government under a constitution. The plan, which favored large states such as Virginia, called for the following:

- A bicameral legislature. The lower house was to be chosen by the people. The smaller upper house was to be chosen by the elected members of the lower house. The number of representatives would be in proportion to each state's population (the larger states would have more representatives). The legislature could void any state laws.
- A national executive branch, elected by the legislature.
- A national court system, created by the legislature.

The smaller states immediately complained because they would have fewer representatives in the legislature. After two weeks of debate, they offered their own plan—the New Jersey Plan.

THE NEW JERSEY PLAN

William Paterson of New Jersey presented an alternate plan favorable to the smaller states. He argued that because each state had an equal vote under the Articles of Confederation, the convention had no power to change this arrangement. The New Jersey Plan proposed the following:

- Congress would be able to regulate trade and impose taxes.
- Each state would have only one vote.
- Acts of Congress would be the supreme law of the land.
- An executive office of more than one person would be elected by Congress.
- The executive office would appoint a national supreme court.

GREAT COMPROMISE ● A plan for a bicameral legislature in which one chamber would be based on population and the other chamber would represent each state equally. The plan, also known as the Connecticut Compromise, resolved the small-state/large-state controversy.

THREE-FIFTHS COMPROMISE ● A compromise reached during the Constitutional Convention by which it was agreed that three-fifths of all slaves were to be counted both for tax purposes and for representation in the House of Representatives.

THE COMPROMISES

Most delegates were unwilling to consider the New Jersey Plan. When the Virginia Plan was brought up again, delegates from the smaller states threatened to leave, and the convention was in danger of dissolving. On July 16, Roger Sherman of Connecticut broke the deadlock by proposing a compromise plan. Compromises on other disputed issues followed.

The Connecticut Plan: The Great Compromise

Sherman's plan, which has become known as the Great Compromise (or the Connecticut Compromise), called for a legislature with two houses:

■ A lower house (the House of Representatives), in which the number of representatives from each state would be determined by the number of people in that state.

■ An upper house (the Senate), which would have two members from each state; the members would be elected by the state legislatures.

The Great Compromise gave something to both sides: the large states would have more representatives in the House of Representatives than the small states, yet each state would be granted equality in the Senate—because each state, regardless of size, would have two senators. The Great Compromise thus resolved the small-state/large-state controversy.

The Three-Fifths Compromise

A second compromise settled a disagreement over how to count slaves for the purposes of determining how many representatives each state would have in the House and how to count slaves for tax purposes. Although slavery was legal everywhere except in Massachusetts, most slaves and slave owners lived in the South. The southern states wanted slaves to be counted equally in determining representation in Congress but not for tax purposes.

Because they did not have many slaves, the northern states took the opposite position. They wanted slaves to be counted for tax purposes but not for representation. The three-fifths compromise settled this

This woodcut of slaves prior to the Civil War shows the slave overseer with a whip in his hand. The terrible history of slavery dates back at least to the ancient Greeks and to the Roman Empire. Slavery had been accepted by early Christians, as well as by Muslims. During the fifteenth and sixteenth centuries, the British, French, Dutch, Spanish, and Portuguese engaged in a brutal slave trade along the African coast. Slaves were first brought to Virginia in 1619. Britain outlawed the slave trade in 1807 and abolished slavery in the entire British empire in 1833.

deadlock. Three-fifths of the slaves were to be counted for both tax purposes and representation. (The three-fifths compromise was eventually overturned in 1868 by the Fourteenth Amendment, Section 2.)

The Slavery Question

The three-fifths compromise did not satisfy everyone at the Constitutional Convention. Many delegates wanted slavery to be banned completely in the United States. The delegates compromised on this question by agreeing that Congress could limit the number of slaves imported into the country after 1808. The issue of slavery itself, however, was never really addressed by the delegates to the Constitutional Convention. As a result, the South won twenty years of unrestricted slave trade and a requirement that escaped slaves in free states be returned to their owners in slave states. Domestic slave trading was untouched. (How ethical this was is addressed in the feature entitled *A Question of Ethics: Should the Framers Have Banned Slavery?*)

Banning Export Taxes

The South's economic health depended in large part on its exports of agricultural products. The South feared that the northern majority in Congress might pass taxes on these exports. This fear led to yet another compromise: the South agreed to let Congress have the power to regulate **interstate commerce** as well as commerce with other nations; in exchange, the Constitution guaranteed that no export taxes would ever be imposed on products exported by the states. Today, the United States is one of the few countries that does not tax its exports.

THE FINAL DRAFT IS APPROVED

The Great Compromise was reached by mid-July. Still to be determined was the makeup of the executive branch and the judiciary. A five-man Committee of Detail undertook the remainder of this work and on August 6 presented a rough draft to the convention. On September 8, a committee was named to "revise the stile [style] of, and arrange the Articles which had been agreed to" by the convention. The Committee of Stile was headed by Gouverneur Morris of Pennsylvania.[19] On September 17, 1787, the final draft of the Constitution was approved by thirty-nine of the remaining forty-two delegates.

The Debate over Ratification

The ratification of the Constitution set off a national debate of unprecedented proportions. The battle was fought chiefly by two opposing groups—the **Federalists** (those who favored a strong central government and the new Constitution) and the **Anti-Federalists** (those who opposed a strong central government and the new Constitution).

THE FEDERALISTS ARGUE FOR RATIFICATION

In the debate over ratification, the Federalists had several advantages. They assumed a positive name, leaving their opposition with a negative label. The Federalists also had attended the Constitutional Convention and thus were familiar with the arguments both in favor of and against various constitutional provisions. The Anti-Federalists, in contrast, had no actual knowledge of those discussions because they had not attended the convention. The Federalists also had time, money, and prestige on their side. Their impressive list of political thinkers and writers included Alexander Hamilton, John Jay, and James Madison. The Federalists could communicate with each other more readily, because they were mostly bankers, lawyers, and merchants who lived in urban areas, where communication

INTERSTATE COMMERCE ● Trade that involves more than one state.

FEDERALISTS ● A political group, led by Alexander Hamilton and John Adams, that supported the adoption of the Constitution and the creation of a federal form of government.

ANTI-FEDERALISTS ● A political group that opposed the adoption of the Constitution because of the document's centralist tendencies and because it did not include a bill of rights.

Should the Framers Have Banned Slavery?

The delegates to the Constitutional Convention were not ordinary citizens. Indeed, they included some of America's best-educated people and greatest luminaries. How could these supposedly enlightened men have created a Constitution that permitted the continued existence of slavery?

Certainly, many of the delegates thought that slavery was morally wrong and that the Constitution should ban it entirely. This group, as well as many other Americans, regarded the framers' failure to deal with the slavery issue as a betrayal of the Declaration of Independence, which proclaimed that "all Men are created equal." Others pointed out how

contradictory it was that the framers of the Constitution complained about being "enslaved" by the British yet ignored the problem of slavery in this country.

Perhaps the most compelling argument supporting the framers' action (or lack of it) with respect to slavery is that they had no alternative but to ignore the issue. If they had taken a stand on slavery, the Constitution certainly would not have been ratified. Indeed, if the antislavery delegates had insisted on banning slavery, the delegates from the southern states might have walked out of the convention—and there would have been no Constitution to ratify.

Thus, the Constitution that was presented to the states for ratifica-

tion neither banned slavery nor explicitly permitted it. It did not mention the words *slave* and *slavery*. Nevertheless, everyone understood that the "all other Persons" in the phrase "three-fifths of all other Persons" referred to slaves and that the Constitution implicitly acknowledged the institution of slavery. Essentially, the framers simply tabled the issue and left it for future generations to solve.

For Critical Analysis

If you had had to choose between getting the Constitution ratified and banning slavery, what position would you have taken?

was easier. The Federalists organized a quick and effective ratification campaign to elect themselves as delegates to each state's ratifying convention.

The Federalist Papers

Alexander Hamilton, a leading Federalist, started answering the Constitution's critics in New York by writing newspaper columns under the pseudonym "Caesar." The Caesar letters appeared to have little effect, so Hamilton switched his pseudonym to "Publius" and enlisted John Jay and James Madison to help him write the papers. In a period of less than a year, these three men wrote a series of eighty-five essays in defense of the Constitution. These essays, which were printed not only in New York newspapers but also in other papers throughout the states, are collectively known as *The Federalist Papers.*

Allaying the Fears of the Constitution's Critics

Generally, the papers attempted to allay the fears expressed by the Constitution's critics. One fear was that the rights of minority groups would not be protected. Another was that a minority might block the passage of measures that the majority felt were in the national interest. Many critics also feared that a republican form of government would not work in a nation the size of the United States. Various groups, or **factions,** would struggle for power, and chaos would result. Madison responded to the latter argument in *Federalist Paper* No. 10 (see Appendix F), which is considered a classic in political theory. Among other things, Madison argued that the nation's size was actually an advantage in controlling factions: in a large nation, there would be so many diverse interests and factions that no one faction would be able to gain control of the government.[20]

THE ANTI-FEDERALISTS' RESPONSE

FACTION ● A group or clique within a larger group.

Perhaps the greatest advantage of the Anti-Federalists was that they stood for the status quo. Usually, it is more difficult to institute changes than it is

TYRANNY ● The arbitrary or unrestrained exercise of power by an oppressive individual or government.

to stay with what is already known, experienced, and understood. Among the Anti-Federalists were such patriots as Patrick Henry and Samuel Adams. Patrick Henry said of the proposed Constitution: "I look upon that paper as the most fatal plan that could possibly be conceived to enslave a free people."

In response to the *Federalist Papers,* the Anti-Federalists published their own essays, using such pseudonyms as "Montezuma" and "Philadelphiensis."

politics on the far side

How to Tackle Your Opponents

Political chicanery in American politics has a long history. Certainly, some of the Federalists were not above using questionable tactics during the debate over ratification. In one case, for example, Pennsylvania Federalists could not get a quorum (the number of representatives required before a resolution can be passed) for the Pennsylvania legislature so that the Federalist majority could approve a measure that would establish a ratifying convention. The Federalists surmounted this problem by forcibly dragging some Anti-Federalists from a tavern to the statehouse and locking the statehouse doors until the vote was taken. In another case, to prevent the details of the ratification debate occurring in the Pennsylvania legislature from being published (which the Federalists felt might harm their cause in other states), the Federalists simply bought the local paper, the *Pennsylvania Herald.* The *Herald* published no further reports on the constitutional debate until after the Constitution was ratified.[22]

For Critical Analysis: Does ownership of the media affect politics today?

They also wrote brilliantly, attacking nearly every clause of the new document. Many Anti-Federalists contended that the Constitution had been written by aristocrats and would lead the nation to aristocratic **tyranny** (the exercise of absolute, unlimited power). Other Anti-Federalists feared that the Constitution would lead to an overly powerful central government that would limit personal freedom.[21]

The Anti-Federalists strongly argued that the Constitution needed a bill of rights. They warned that without a bill of rights, a strong national government might take away the political rights won during the American Revolution. They demanded that the new Constitution clearly guarantee personal freedoms. The Federalists generally did not think that a bill of rights was all that important. Nevertheless, to gain the necessary support, the Federalists finally promised to add a bill of rights to the Constitution as the first order of business under the new government. This promise turned the tide in favor of the Constitution. (Some of the Federalists' attempts to gain votes for ratification went beyond persuasive arguments and compromises—see, for example, the tactics described in the *Politics on the Far Side* feature.)

RATIFICATION

The contest for ratification was close in several states, but the Federalists finally won in all of them. After unanimous ratifications in Delaware, New Jersey, and Georgia, Pennsylvania voted in favor of the Constitution by a margin of two to one, and Connecticut by a margin of three to one. Even though the Anti-Federalists were perhaps the majority in Massachusetts, a successful political campaign by the Federalists led to ratification by that state on February 6, 1788.

New Hampshire became the ninth state to ratify the Constitution on June 21, 1788, by a fifty-seven to forty-six margin, thus formally putting the Constitution into effect. New York and Virginia had not yet ratified, however, and without them the Constitution would have no true power. Those worries were dispelled in the summer of 1788, when both Virginia and New York ratified the new Constitution. North Carolina waited until November 21 of the following year to ratify the Constitution, and Rhode Island did not ratify until May 29, 1790. (For ideas on how democratic ratification really was, see the feature, *Perception versus Reality: Was the Constitution Favored by a Majority?*)

The Constitution's Major Principles of Government

The framers of the Constitution were fearful of the powerful British monarchy, against which they had so recently rebelled. At the same time, they wanted a central government strong enough to prevent the kinds of crises that had occurred under the weak central authority of the Articles of

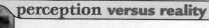

perception versus reality

Was the Constitution Favored by a Majority?

We think of our government as being formed by the will of the people. But who were the "people" who ratified the U.S. Constitution? Was the Constitution really favored by a majority of Americans?

The Perception

Many Americans never question the idea that the U.S. Constitution resulted from a democratic process and was favored by a majority of Americans. After all, the state conventions that ratified the Constitution consisted of representatives of the people. Thus, the process of adopting the Constitution was essentially democratic. If the majority had not favored the Constitution, the state conventions would not have adopted it.

The Reality

In reality, the evidence points to the contrary. There was never any popular vote on whether to hold a constitutional convention in the first place. Furthermore, only male property owners were eligible to vote. This means that most people in the country (white males without property, women, African Americans, and Native Americans) had no say in the matter. Additionally, of the white males who were eligible to vote, only about one-sixth of them actually voted for ratification. In all, the delegates at the various state ratifying conventions had been selected by only about 150,000 of the approximately four million citizens of that time. Even Federalist John Marshall, who

became chief justice of the Supreme Court after serving as John Adams's secretary of state, believed that in some of the adopting states a majority of the people opposed the Constitution.[23] If a Gallup poll could have been taken at that time, those supporting the Anti-Federalists' position would probably have widely outnumbered those supporting the Federalists' arguments.[24]

You Be the Judge

Does it really matter whether a majority of Americans supported the Constitution when it was adopted?

Confederation. The principles of government expressed in the Constitution reflect both of these concerns.

LIMITED GOVERNMENT AND POPULAR SOVEREIGNTY

The Constitution incorporated the principle of limited government, which means that government can only do what the people allow it to do through exercise of a duly developed system of laws. This principle can be found in many parts of the Constitution. For example, while Articles I, II, and III indicate exactly what the national government *can* do, the first nine amendments to the Constitution list the ways in which the government *cannot* limit certain individual freedoms.

Implicitly, the principle of limited government rests on the concept of popular sovereignty. Remember the phrases that frame the Preamble to the Constitution: "We the People of the United States . . . do ordain and establish this Constitution for the United States of America." In other words, it is the people who form the government and decide on the powers that the government can exercise. If the government exercises powers beyond those granted to it by the Constitution, it is acting illegally. The idea that no one is above the law, including government officers, is often called the **rule of law.**

THE PRINCIPLE OF FEDERALISM

The Constitution also incorporated the principle of federalism. In a **federal system** of government, the central (national) government shares sovereign powers with the various state governments. Federalism was the solution to the debate over whether the national government or the states should have ultimate sovereignty.

The Constitution gave to the national government significant powers—powers that it had not had under the Articles of Confederation. For example, the Constitution expressly states that the president is the nation's

RULE OF LAW ● A basic principle of government that requires both those who govern and those who are governed to act in accordance with established law.

FEDERAL SYSTEM ● A form of government in which a written constitution provides for a division of powers between a central government and several regional governments. In the United States, the division of powers between the national government and the fifty states is established by the Constitution.

MADISONIAN MODEL ● The model of government devised by James Madison in which the powers of the government are separated into three branches: executive, legislative, and judicial.

SEPARATION OF POWERS ● The principle of dividing governmental powers among the executive, the legislative, and the judicial branches of government.

CHECKS AND BALANCES ● A major principle of American government in which each of the three branches is given the means to check (to restrain or balance) the actions of the others.

VETO POWER ● A constitutional power that enables the chief executive (president or governor) to reject legislation and return it to the legislature with reasons for the rejection. This prevents or delays the bill from becoming law.

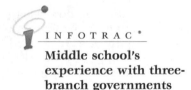

INFOTRAC®

Middle school's experience with three-branch governments

chief executive as well as the commander in chief of the armed forces. The Constitution also declares that the Constitution and the laws created by the national government are supreme—that is, they take precedence over conflicting state laws. Other powers given to the national government include the power to regulate interstate commerce, to coin money, and to levy and collect taxes. Finally, the national government was authorized to undertake all laws that are "necessary and proper" to carrying out its expressly delegated powers.

Because the states feared too much centralized control, the Constitution also allowed for numerous states' rights. These rights include the power to regulate commerce within state borders and generally the authority to exercise any powers that are not delegated by the Constitution to the central government. (See Chapter 3 for a detailed discussion of federalism.)

CHECKS AND BALANCES

As James Madison (1751–1836) once said, after you have given the government the ability to control its citizens, you have to "oblige it to control itself." To force the government to "control itself" and to prevent the rise of tyranny, Madison devised a scheme, the **Madisonian Model,** in which the powers of the national government were separated into different branches: the legislative, executive, and judicial.[25] The legislative branch (Congress) passes laws; the executive branch (the president) administers and enforces the laws; and the judicial branch (the courts) interprets the laws. By separating the powers of government, no one branch would have enough power to dominate the others. This principle of **separation of powers** is laid out in Articles I, II, and III.

The separation of powers is part of a system of **checks and balances** that was devised to ensure that no one group or branch of government can exercise exclusive control. Even though each branch of government is independent of the others, it can also check the actions of the others. Look at Figure 2–4, and you can see how this is done. As the figure shows, the president checks Congress by holding **veto power,** which is the ability to return bills to Congress for reconsideration. Congress, in turn, controls taxes and spending, and the Senate must approve presidential appointments. The judicial branch of government can also act as a check on the other branches of government through its power of *judicial review*—the power to rule congressional or presidential actions unconstitutional.[26] In turn, the president (and the Senate) exercise some control over the judiciary through the president's power to appoint federal judges and the Senate's role in confirming presidential appointments.

Among the other checks and balances built into the American system of government are staggered terms of office. Members of the House of Representatives serve for two years, members of the Senate for six, and the president for four. Federal court judges are appointed for life but may be impeached and removed from office by Congress for misconduct. Staggered terms and changing government personnel make it difficult for individuals within the government to form controlling factions, majorities, or minorities. The American system of government also includes numerous other checks and balances, many of which you will read about in later chapters of this book. We look next at another obvious check on the powers of government: the Bill of Rights.

THE BILL OF RIGHTS

To secure the ratification of the Constitution in several important states, the Federalists had to provide assurances that amendments would be passed to protect individual liberties against violations by the national government. At the state ratifying conventions, delegates set forth specific rights that should be protected. James Madison considered these recommendations as he labored to draft what became the Bill of Rights.

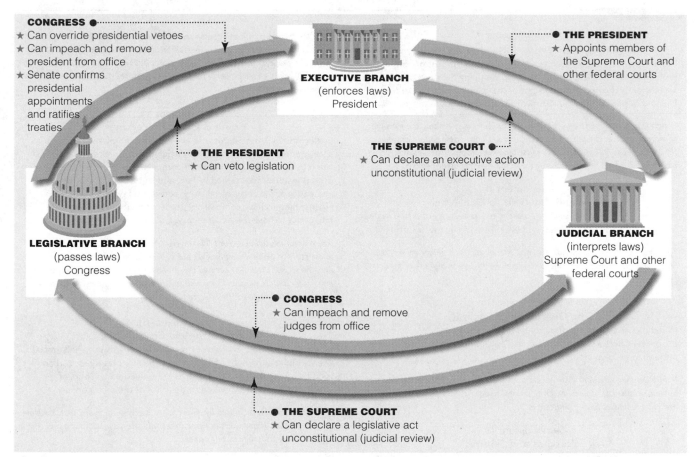

CONGRESS ●
★ Can override presidential vetoes
★ Can impeach and remove president from office
★ Senate confirms presidential appointments and ratifies treaties

EXECUTIVE BRANCH
(enforces laws)
President

● THE PRESIDENT
★ Appoints members of the Supreme Court and other federal courts

● THE PRESIDENT
★ Can veto legislation

THE SUPREME COURT ●
★ Can declare an executive action unconstitutional (judicial review)

LEGISLATIVE BRANCH
(passes laws)
Congress

JUDICIAL BRANCH
(interprets laws)
Supreme Court and other federal courts

● CONGRESS
★ Can impeach and remove judges from office

● THE SUPREME COURT
★ Can declare a legislative act unconstitutional (judicial review)

Figure 2–4
Checks and Balances among the Branches of Government

After sorting through more than two hundred state recommendations, Madison came up with sixteen amendments. Congress tightened the language somewhat and eliminated four of the amendments. Of the remaining twelve, two—one dealing with the apportionment of representatives and the other with the compensation of the members of Congress—were rejected by the states during the ratification process.[27] By 1791, all of the states had ratified the ten amendments that now constitute our Bill of Rights. Table 2–2 on the next page presents the text of the first ten amendments to the Constitution, along with explanatory comments. (Note that the Bill of Rights, in itself, is no guarantee that those rights will be enforced. See this chapter's *Comparative Politics* on page 43 for a discussion of this topic.)

The Constitution Compared to the Articles of Confederation

As mentioned earlier, the experiences under the government of the Confederation, particularly the weakness of the central government, strongly influenced the writing of the Constitution. The Constitution shifted many powers from the states to the central government—the Constitution's division of powers between the states and the national government is discussed at length in Chapter 3.

One of the weaknesses of the Confederation had been the lack of an independent executive authority. The Constitution remedied this problem by creating an independent executive—the president—and by making the

I N F O T R A C °

The pop-up Bill of Rights

Table 2–2

Amendment I.
Religion, Speech, Press, Assembly, and Petition

Congress shall make no law respecting an establishment of religion, or prohibiting the free exercise thereof; or abridging the freedom of speech, or of the press; or the right of the people peaceably to assemble, and to petition the Government for a redress of grievances.

Congress may not create an official church or enact laws limiting the freedom of religion, speech, the press, assembly, and petition. These guarantees, like the others in the Bill of Rights (the first ten amendments), are not absolute—each may be exercised only with regard to the rights of other persons.

Amendment II.
Militia and the Right to Bear Arms

A well regulated Militia, being necessary to the security of a free State, the right of the people to keep and bear Arms, shall not be infringed.

To protect itself, each state has the right to maintain a volunteer armed force. States and the federal government regulate the possession and use of firearms by individuals.

Amendment III.
The Quartering of Soldiers

No Soldier shall, in time of peace be quartered in any house, without the consent of the Owner, nor in time of war, but in a manner to be prescribed by law.

Before the Revolutionary War, it had been common British practice to quarter soldiers in colonists' homes. Military troops do not have the power to take over private houses during peacetime.

Amendment IV.
Searches and Seizures

The right of the people to be secure in their persons, houses, papers, and effects, against unreasonable searches and seizures, shall not be violated, and no Warrants shall issue, but upon probable cause, supported by Oath or affirmation, and particularly describing the place to be searched, and the persons or things to be seized.

Here the word warrant means "justification" and refers to a document issued by a magistrate or judge indicating the name, address, and possible offense committed. Anyone asking for the warrant, such as a police officer, must be able to convince the magistrate or judge that an offense probably has been committed.

Amendment V.
Grand Juries, Self-Incrimination, Double Jeopardy, Due Process, and Eminent Domain

No person shall be held to answer for a capital, or otherwise infamous crime, unless on a presentment or indictment of a Grand Jury, except in cases arising in the land or naval forces, or in the Militia, when in actual service in time of War or public danger; nor shall any person be subject for the same offense to be twice put in jeopardy of life or limb; nor shall be compelled in any criminal case to be a witness against himself, nor be deprived of life, liberty, or property, without due process of law; nor shall private property be taken for public use, without just compensation.

There are two types of juries. A grand jury considers physical evidence and the testimony of witnesses, and decides whether there is sufficient reason to bring a case to trial. A petit jury hears the case at trial and decides it. "For the same offense to be twice put in jeopardy of life or limb" means to be tried

twice for the same crime. A person may not be tried for the same crime twice or forced to give evidence against herself or himself. No person's right to life, liberty, or property may be taken away except by lawful means, called the due process of law. Private property taken for use in public purposes must be paid for by the government.

Amendment VI.
Criminal Court Procedures

In all criminal prosecutions, the accused shall enjoy the right to a speedy and public trial, by an impartial jury of the State and district wherein the crime shall have been committed, which district shall have been previously ascertained by law, and to be informed of the nature and cause of the accusation; to be confronted with the witnesses against him; to have compulsory process for obtaining witnesses in his favor, and to have the Assistance of Counsel for his defence.

Any person accused of a crime has the right to a fair and public trial by a jury in the state in which the crime took place. The charges against that person must be so indicated. Any accused person has the right to a lawyer to defend him or her and to question those who testify against him or her, as well as the right to call people to speak in his or her favor at trial.

Amendment VII.
Trial by Jury in Civil Cases

In Suits at common law, where the value in controversy shall exceed twenty dollars, the right of trial by jury shall be preserved, and no fact tried by a jury, shall be otherwise re-examined in any Court of the United States, than according to the rules of the common law.

A jury trial may be requested by either party in a dispute in any case involving more than $20. If both parties agree to a trial by a judge without a jury, the right to a jury trial may be put aside.

Amendment VIII.
Bail, Cruel and Unusual Punishment

Excessive bail shall not be required, nor excessive fines imposed, nor cruel and unusual punishments inflicted.

Bail is that amount of money that a person accused of a crime may be required to deposit with the court as a guarantee that she or he will appear in court when requested. The amount of bail required or the fine imposed as punishment for a crime must be reasonable compared with the seriousness of the crime involved. Any punishment judged to be too harsh or too severe for a crime shall be prohibited.

Amendment IX.
The Rights Retained by the People

The enumeration in the Constitution, of certain rights, shall not be construed to deny or disparage others retained by the people.

Many civil rights that are not explicitly enumerated in the Constitution are still held by the people.

Amendment X.
Reserved Powers of the States

The powers not delegated to the United States by the Constitution, nor prohibited by it to the States, are reserved to the States respectively, or to the people.

Those powers not delegated by the Constitution to the federal government or expressly denied to the states belong to the states and to the people. This clause in essence allows the states to pass laws under its "police powers."

comparative politics

Is Having a Written Constitution All That Important?

Throughout our nation's history, the courts have zealously guarded the rights and protections for Americans that are set forth in the Bill of Rights. Indeed, America is known the world over for the extensive rights and liberties enjoyed by its citizens. Yet it is important to realize that it takes more than a written constitution and a bill of rights to create and maintain these rights and liberties.

The truth is, political traditions play an important role in determining whether citizens of a given nation will enjoy civil rights and liberties. Consider that Great Britain, to whom we owe our constitutional and legal heritage, has no single document that serves as its constitution. Ironically, that country, which invented the concept of a bill of rights, has no written bill of rights specifically protecting the rights and liberties of British citizens. Yet for centuries, Britain has been regarded by the rest of the world as a "beacon of liberty."

In contrast, China does have a written constitution. Among other things, China's constitution provides that the citizens of that nation "have the right to criticize and make suggestions to any state organ or functionary." Yet after the massacre of students who launched a pro-democracy demonstration in Beijing's Tiananmen Square in 1989, it was clear that freedom of expression would not be tolerated.

Iraq also has a written constitution that guarantees a number of rights for its citizens. Its constitution guarantees equality of citizens before the law, freedom of religion, and "freedom of opinion, publication, meeting, demonstrations, and the formation of political parties, syndicates, and societies." Yet pity the Iraqi who dares to voice an opinion that is contrary to the views of Iraq's dictatorial ruler.

These are just a few examples of how citizens' rights are not dependent on a written constitution or bill of rights. Ultimately, it may be that, as American federal court judge Learned Hand once said, "Liberty lies in the hearts of men and women; when it dies there, no constitution, no law, no court can ever do much to help it."

For Critical Analysis

Which is more important for Americans' civil rights and liberties, the written Bill of Rights or the American political tradition?

president commander in chief of the army and navy and of the state militias when called into national service. The president was also given extensive appointment powers, although the president was required to obtain Senate approval for certain appointments.

Another problem under the Confederation was the lack of a judiciary that was independent of the state courts. The Constitution established the United States Supreme Court and authorized Congress to establish other "inferior" federal courts.

To protect against possible wrongdoing, the Constitution also provided for a way to remove federal officials from office—through the impeachment process. The Constitution provides that a federal official who commits "Treason, Bribery, or other high Crimes and Misdemeanors" may be impeached (accused, or charged with wrongdoing) by the House of Representatives and tried by the Senate. If found guilty of the charges by a two-thirds vote in the Senate, the official can be removed from office and prevented from ever assuming another federal government post. The official may also face judicial proceedings for the alleged wrongdoing after removal from office. (For a discussion of the politics of impeachment, see this chapter's *The American Political Spectrum.*)

The Constitution—A Document for the Ages

The Constitution that was drafted by the framers and ratified by the states has proved to be a lasting foundation for American government. At the time the Constitution was created, however, there was a great deal of doubt about whether the arrangement would actually work. James Madison, among others, hoped that the framers had created a government "for the ages." Indeed, Madison's vision has been realized, in large part because of the checks and balances that were incorporated in the Constitution and that have safeguarded the nation from tyranny—one of the greatest fears of the founders.

Another reason for the Constitution's long life is the brevity of its wording. Rather than set forth the details of government, the founders established broad principles that could—and have been—applied to changing conditions over time. Moreover, for all the stress on private property in the founding era, the framers did not require any property qualification for holding political office. The Constitution also provides that compensation be given for elective posts, meaning that, at least in theory, anyone—no matter how poor—could hold a federal office.

The Constitution also provided for an easier amendment process than that provided under the Articles of Confederation. Under the Articles of Confederation, amendments to the articles required the unanimous consent of the states. As a result, it was virtually impossible to amend the articles. The framers of the Constitution provided for an amendment process that required the approval of only three-fourths of the states. While the process is still extraordinarily cumbersome, it does facilitate amendments to a much greater extent than was possible under the Articles of Confederation.

Amending the Constitution

Since the Constitution was written, more than 11,000 amendments have been introduced in Congress. Of that number, only twenty-seven have been added to our Constitution. One of the reasons there are so few amendments is that the framers, in Article V, made the formal amendment process extremely difficult—although it was much easier than it was under the Articles of Confederation, as just discussed.

There are two ways to propose an amendment and two ways to ratify one. As a result, there are only four possible ways for an amendment to be added to the Constitution.

METHODS OF PROPOSING AN AMENDMENT

The two methods of proposing an amendment are as follows:

1. A two-thirds vote in the Senate and in the House of Representatives is required. All of the twenty-seven existing amendments have been proposed in this way.

The Politics of Impeachment

As mentioned elsewhere, the U.S. Constitution provides that the president and other federal officers can be removed from office through the impeachment process. The impeachment process has rarely been used, however, and only seven federal officials (all federal judges) have ever been both impeached *and* convicted. Prior to President Clinton's impeachment in 1998, only one other U.S. president—Andrew Johnson, in 1868—had been impeached, but he was acquitted by the Senate. In 1974, President Richard Nixon opted to resign from office rather than face almost certain impeachment and probable conviction for his role in covering up the Watergate break-in.[28]

The impeachment and trial of President Clinton caused the nation to focus once again on this constitutional process. The major issue before Congress was whether Clinton's actions constituted "high Crimes and Misdemeanors," as required by the Constitution. Many Republicans in the Republican-controlled Congress thought that they did; most Democrats disagreed. Indeed, one of the most notable aspects of Clinton's impeachment was the partisan character of the proceedings.

The Republicans Vote for Impeachment

When the House of Representatives voted to launch an impeachment inquiry against Clinton in October 1998, the House Judiciary Committee began its investigation into the matter. The committee reviewed Independent Counsel Kenneth Starr's lengthy report and supporting documents—the results of Starr's investigation into Clinton's

affair with White House intern Monica Lewinsky.

Starr had concluded his report with a section stating that there was "substantial and credible information" supporting impeachment on the basis of perjury (both in testimony given in relation to Paula Jones's lawsuit against Clinton, in which Clinton denied having had a sexual relationship with Monica Lewinsky, and in testimony given before Starr's grand jury), obstruction of justice (by the attempt to thwart the investigation in various ways), and abuse of presidential authority (by Clinton's lying to the public, among other things). To be sure, perjury and obstruction of justice were crimes, but were they high crimes and misdemeanors? And was Clinton's abuse of presidential authority sufficiently serious to constitute a ground for impeachment?

Certainly, the Republicans on the Judiciary Committee thought so. In a strikingly partisan series of votes, the committee approved four articles of impeachment against Clinton. (There were twenty-one Republicans and sixteen Democrats on the committee; the votes for approval were twenty-one to sixteen on three of the articles, and twenty to seventeen on the remaining article.) The chairman of the committee, Illinois Republican Henry Hyde, declared that the question before the House was "rather simple": "It's not about sex . . . . The matter before the House is lying under oath. This is called perjury." Hyde stated that perjury and obstruction of justice "cannot be reconciled with the office of the president of the United States. . . . The people's trust has been betrayed."

The articles were then put up for a vote by the full House of Representatives, in which 206 seats were held by Democrats and 228 by Republicans. The House approved two of the four articles in a largely partisan vote, but enough Republicans broke ranks to defeat the other two articles.

The Democrats Disagree

No one was pleased with the president's moral conduct, but a majority of the Democrats (and over 60 percent of Americans, according to polls taken at that time) did not feel that Clinton should be impeached. The Democrats generally believed that the allegations against Clinton, which stemmed from his attempts to cover up an extramarital affair and avoid public embarrassment, did not rise to the level of impeachable offenses. Although a few Democrats in the House crossed party lines to vote for impeachment, by and large they rejected the idea. In the Senate trial, all forty-five Democrats and ten of the fifty-five Republicans in that chamber voted "not guilty" on the perjury charge. The vote on the obstruction-of-justice article was fifty-fifty.

For Critical Analysis

Federal judges are appointed for life, and thus impeachment provides a means of removing these officials from office when Congress deems it necessary. Why did the founders also provide that the president—who is elected every four years—could be impeached?

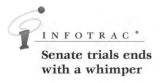

INFOTRAC®

Senate trials ends with a whimper

2. If two-thirds of the state legislatures request that Congress call a national amendment convention, then Congress could call one. The convention could propose amendments to the states for ratification. There has yet to be a successful amendment proposal using this method.

The notion of a national amendment convention is exciting to many people. Many national political and judicial leaders, however, are uneasy about the prospect of convening a body that conceivably could do what the Constitutional Convention did—create a new form of government.

In two separate instances, the call for a national amendment convention almost became reality. Between 1963 and 1969, thirty-three state legislatures (out of the necessary thirty-four) attempted to call a convention to amend the Constitution to eliminate the Supreme Court's "one person, one vote" decisions (see Chapter 13). Since 1975, thirty-two states have asked for a national convention to propose an amendment requiring that the federal government balance its budget. Because the federal government has managed to balance its budget in recent years, however, this issue—at least for the time being—has become moot. Generally, the major national convention campaigns have reflected dissatisfaction, on the part of certain conservative and rural groups, with the national government's social and economic policies.

METHODS OF RATIFYING AN AMENDMENT

There are two methods of ratifying a proposed amendment:

1. Three-fourths of the state legislatures can vote in favor of the proposed amendment. This method is considered the "traditional" ratification method and has been used twenty-six times.
2. The states can call special conventions to ratify the proposed amendment. If three-fourths of the states approve, the amendment is ratified. This method has been used only once—to ratify the Twenty-first Amendment.

You can see the four methods for proposing and ratifying amendments in Figure 2–5. As you can imagine, to meet the requirements for proposal *and* ratification, any amendment must have wide popular support in all regions of the country.

 # Americans at Odds over the Constitution

Our Constitution is a "living" document because of its relatively imprecise language. The broad language of the Constitution allows its principles to be adapted to different needs as American society and government institutions change over time. Because of this flexibility, the

Figure 2–5
The Process of
Amending the Constitution

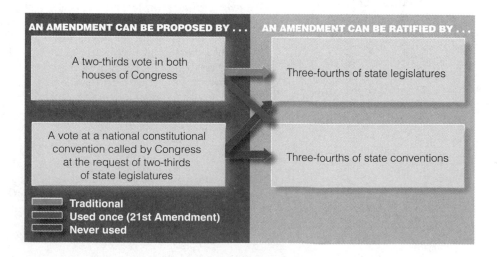

AN AMENDMENT CAN BE PROPOSED BY . . .	AN AMENDMENT CAN BE RATIFIED BY . . .
A two-thirds vote in both houses of Congress	Three-fourths of state legislatures
A vote at a national constitutional convention called by Congress at the request of two-thirds of state legislatures	Three-fourths of state conventions

- ☐ Traditional
- ☐ Used once (21st Amendment)
- ☐ Never used

Constitution still maintains its effectiveness more than two hundred years after its ratification. At the same time, the loose language of the Constitution leads to continuing disagreements among Americans over the meaning of its provisions.

Differing Interpretations of the Bill of Rights

The U.S. Constitution, primarily in the Bill of Rights (the first ten amendments to the Constitution), set forth the rights and liberties that are guaranteed for all Americans. Because these amendments are broadly worded, however, their exact nature has been disputed time and again. For example, one of today's significant controversies has to do with gun control. One aspect of the controversy involves the right to bear arms, which is guaranteed by the Second Amendment. Do only state militias have this right, as some scholars believe, or do all individuals have the right to bear arms?

Look again at the Bill of Rights in Table 2–2. Notice how various phrases are broadly crafted. For example, the First Amendment states that "Congress shall make no law . . . abridging the freedom of speech." Does this mean that *any* law restricting speech will be unconstitutional? According to the courts, no. Certain types of speech, such as speech that harms another's good reputation, are not protected. Where, however, do you draw the line between permissible and impermissible speech, including communications transmitted over the Internet? As we discuss in Chapter 4, how the courts have interpreted this amendment has generated substantial controversy among Americans.

Now look at the Second Amendment, which states that a "well regulated Militia, being necessary to the security of a free State, the right of the people to keep and bear Arms, shall not be infringed." Does this mean that *individuals* have a right to bear arms to protect themselves against the government (as citizens' militias believe)? Or does it mean that only the *states* are constitutionally authorized to maintain militias (as most constitutional scholars maintain)? We return to this issue in Chapter 7.

Consider still other examples. The Fourth Amendment protects the people against "unreasonable searches and seizures." Who decides when a search or seizure is unreasonable, however? Many Americans think that the courts, in interpreting this amendment, give too much weight to the rights of criminals and too little weight to the rights of society to be protected from crime. Regarding the Eighth Amendment, what exactly constitutes "cruel and unusual punishments"? Many Americans think that the death penalty qualifies as cruel and unusual punishment; others do not.

Finally, what about the Tenth Amendment? This amendment states that the "powers not delegated to the United States by the Constitution, nor prohibited by it to the States, are reserved to the States respectively, or to the people." Throughout the history of this nation, Americans have been at odds over the scope and nature of these "reserved powers" of the states. The debate over the division of powers in our federal system (see Chapter 3) often centers on just this issue.

The Power of the Federal Courts

As you will read in Chapter 4, the courts—and ultimately the Supreme Court—decide what the Constitution means, and thus the nature and scope of our constitutional rights and liberties. The views of the Supreme Court naturally change over time in response to changing circumstances. For example, in 1896 the Court ruled that "separate-but-equal" public facilities for African Americans were constitutional; but by 1954 the times had changed, and the Court reversed the decision.[29]

In fact, Americans are at odds not only about the meaning of various constitutional provisions but also about the fact that the Supreme Court, an unelected body, has, in some respects, the final say on such important issues. Many Americans feel that the courts need to be more accountable to the American people[30] and that more checks on this power of the courts are necessary. (See Chapter 16 for a further discussion of this issue.)

key terms

Anti-Federalists 36
Articles of Confederation 30
bicameral legislature 24
Bill of Rights 25
checks and balances 40
confederation 30
Constitutional Convention 33
faction 37
federal system 39
Federalists 36
First Continental Congress 27
Fundamental Orders of
    Connecticut 25
Great Compromise 35
interstate commerce 36
limited government 23

Madisonian Model 40
Magna Carta 23
Mayflower Compact 25
Northwest Ordinance 31
Parliament 24
representative government 24
rule of law 39
Second Continental
    Congress 27
separation of powers 40
Shays' Rebellion 33
three-fifths compromise 35
tyranny 38
unicameral legislature 30
veto power 40

chapter summary

1. The British legacy to the American form of government consisted of two principles of government: (1) limited government—a government whose powers are strictly limited, usually by a constitution; and (2) representative government—a system of government in which the people elect individuals to make governmental decisions for all citizens.

2. American colonists came from numerous countries, but the majority were English. The first successful English colonies were established at Jamestown (Virginia) in 1607 and at Plymouth (Massachusetts) in 1620. The Mayflower Compact created the first formal government in the colonies. By 1732, all thirteen colonies had been established.

3. For all their distance from Britain, the colonists had strong ties of loyalty to the home country and to the British monarch. A series of events during and following the Seven Years' War (1756–1763) served to loosen, and finally sever, these ties.

4. The colonies eventually transformed themselves into sovereign states, each having its own permanent government. Because antiroyalist sentiment was strong, the executive branch was extremely weak in all thirteen states. The government created by the Articles of Confederation was also weak. Shays' Rebellion focused the nation's attention on the need for a strong national government.

5. General dissatisfaction with the Articles of Confederation prompted the states to send delegates to a meeting in Philadelphia in 1787. Although the purpose of the Philadelphia convention (now known as the Constitutional Convention) was to revise the Articles of Confederation, discussions soon focused on creating a constitution for a new form of government.

6. The Federalists, who favored a strong central government, and the Anti-Federalists, who opposed ratification, intensely debated the ratification issue. By 1790, however, all of the states had ratified the Constitution. The final version of the Constitution provided for limited government and popular sovereignty; a federal system of government; and a system of checks and balances, including the separation of government powers among the three branches of government, to prevent any one group or branch of government from exercising too much control. Fears of a strong central government prompted the addition of the Bill of Rights (the first ten amendments) to the Constitution.

7. The Constitution addressed several problems that the Articles of Confederation had not resolved. Among other things, the Constitution shifted many of the powers from the states to the central government, and it created a strong executive authority, a judiciary independent of the states, and provisions for impeachment.

8. A constitutional amendment may be proposed either by a two-thirds vote in each house of Congress or by a national convention called by Congress at the request of two-thirds of the state legislatures. Ratification of an amendment can occur either by a

positive vote in three-fourths of the legislatures of the various states or by a positive vote in three-fourths of special conventions called in the states for the specific purpose of ratifying the proposed amendment.

9. The broad language of the Constitution means that it can be interpreted in different ways. As a result, Americans have been—and continue to be—at odds over the meaning of certain constitutional provisions.

for critical analysis

1. Read through the first ten amendments to the Constitution—the Bill of Rights—in Table 2–2. Which of these amendments would seem to imply a right to privacy?

2. How would you argue in support of the British government's position on the "taxation without representation" issue?

3. What are some factors, aside from those mentioned in this chapter, that might help to explain why the Constitution and the system of government it created have endured for over two centuries?

4. What might the United States be like today if the Bill of Rights had not been added to the Constitution?

5. Of the rights and freedoms set forth in the Bill of Rights, which one do you think is the most essential in a democracy? Why?

6. When the Constitution was created, the founders were very uncertain of whether the government that they had established would last. Today, Americans seem to think that the Constitution can withstand almost any challenge. Do you think that Americans tend to take their political system for granted? Should Americans work harder to protect their democracy?

7. Why did the founders make it so difficult to amend the Constitution? If they had made the process easier, what effect might this have had on our political system and procedures?

suggested readings

CASPER, Gerhard. *Separating Power: Essays on the Founding Period.* Cambridge, Mass.: Harvard University Press, 1997. Some constitutional scholars argue that we must use the founders' understanding of the Constitution as a guide for its interpretation today. This author contends that with respect to the separation of powers set forth in the Constitution, such an inquiry yields few results because the founders had not fully worked out many of their ideas.

DWORKIN, Ronald. *Freedom's Law: The Moral Reading of the Constitution.* Cambridge, Mass.: Harvard University Press, 1997. The author takes a stand against those who would interpret the Constitution literally. He argues that the judicial function is not mechanical, as politicians and judges alike maintain, but creative. Only when we openly recognize this fact can there be democratic accountability: the public can understand what is being done on its behalf and have the opportunity to influence constitutional law by comment and criticism.

HAMILTON, Alexander, James Madison, and John Jay. *The Federalist Papers.* Cambridge, Mass.: Harvard University Press, 1961. The book contains the complete set of columns from the *New York Packet* defending the new Constitution.

HOFFMAN, Daniel F. *Our Elusive Constitution.* Albany, N.Y.: State University of New York Press, 1997. This book draws attention to important questions in constitutional thought. Among the topics the author explores are the relationship between law and politics, the relationship between the citizen and the state, the jurisprudence of personal rights, and the need for expanded political and economic rights to restore balance to the constitutional system.

STORING, Herbert J. *The Complete Anti-Federalist.* 7 vols. Chicago: University of Chicago Press, 1981. An analysis of the views of those who argued against the adoption of the Constitution.

WHITTINGTON, Keith E. *Constitutional Construction: Divided Powers and Constitutional Meaning.* Cambridge, Mass.: Harvard University Press, 1999. This book argues that the American Constitution has a dual nature. The first is the degree to which the Constitution acts as a binding set of rules that can be neutrally interpreted and externally enforced by the courts against government actors. This is the process of constitutional interpretation. According to the author, however, the Constitution also permeates politics itself, to guide and constrain political actors in the very process of making public policy.

politics
on the web

The World Wide Web version of the Constitution provides hypertext links to amendments and other changes. Go to

http://www.law.cornell.edu/constitution/constitution.overview.html

The home page of Emory University School of Law offers access to a number of early American documents, including scanned originals of the Constitution and the Bill of Rights. This page is located at

http://www.law.emory.edu/FEDERAL

The National Constitution Center in Philadelphia has a Web page at

http://www.constitutioncenter.org

The site offers a Constitution quiz, information about the center, basic facts about the Constitution, exhibits and attractions, Constitution Week, and other information.

For information on the effect of new computer and communications technologies on the constitutional rights and liberties of Americans, go to the Center for Democracy and Technology at

http://www.cdt.org

The Cyberspace Law Institute (CLI) also focuses on law and communications technology. Go to

http://www.cli.org

The constitutions of almost all of the states are now online. You can find them at

http://www.findlaw.com/11stategov

To find historical documents relating to the founding period, including the charter to Sir Walter Raleigh in 1584, the Royal Proclamation of 1763, and writings by Thomas Paine, go to

http://www.yale.edu/lawweb/avalon/alfalist.htm

using
web resources

Thomas Jefferson, the third president of the United States, was one of the most important leaders in the patriot faction during the American Revolution and an important voice in shaping the new independent government. At the Second Continental Congress, Jefferson drafted the Declaration of Independence and, as the governor of Virginia, guided that state through the difficult years of the revolution. In 1785, he became minister to France. In 1787, from Paris, Jefferson wrote to James Madison explaining his beliefs on the new federal constitution. To view Jefferson's letter to Madison, go to

http://odur.let.rug.nl/~usa/P/tj3/writings/brf/jef176.htm

1. What are three things mentioned in the letter that Jefferson likes about the Constitution?

2. What are Jefferson's criticisms of the Constitution?

3. Near the end of the letter, Jefferson writes that he is "not a friend to a very energetic government." What does he mean by this statement?

4. Why, according to Jefferson, is education so vital to a democratic people?

notes

1. As quoted by John Schwartz in "A Middle Ground in the Privacy War," *The Washington Post,* March 29, 1999, p. F11.

2. Rod Dixon, "Needed: A Bold Privacy Law," *The National Law Journal,* April 19, 1999, p. A29.

3. Amitai Etzioni, *The Limits of Privacy* (New York: Basic Books, 1999).

4. Paul Terry, "FTC Protects Privacy of Web Site Visitors," *The Internet Newsletter,* March 1999, p. 3.

5. The first *European* settlement in North America was St. Augustine, Florida (a city that still exists), which was founded on September 8, 1565, by the Spaniard Pedro Menéndez de Ávilés.

6. John Camp, *Out of the Wilderness: The Emergence of an American Identity in Colonial New England* (Middleton, Conn.: Wesleyan University Press, 1990).

7. Paul S. Boyer *et al., The Enduring Vision: A History of the American People* (Lexington, Mass.: D. C. Heath, 1996).

8. Corsets are close-fitting undergarments that were worn at the time by both men and women to give the appearance of having a smaller waist. Whalebone was inserted in the corsets to make them stiff, and lacing was used to tighten them around the body.

9. Much of the colonists' fury over British policies was directed personally at King George III, who had ascended the British throne in 1760 at the age of twenty-two, rather than at Britain or British rule *per se.* If you look at the Declaration of Independence in Appendix B, you will note that much of that document focuses on what "He" (George III) has or has not done. George III's lack of political experience, his personality, and his temperament all combined to lend instability to the British government at this crucial point in history.

10. *The Political Writings of Thomas Paine,* Vol. 1 (Boston: J. P. Mendum Investigator Office, 1870), p. 46.

11. The equivalent in today's publishing world would be a book that sells between eight and ten million copies in its first year of publication.

12. As quoted in Winthrop D. Jordan *et al., The United States,* 6th ed. (Englewood Cliffs, N.J.: Prentice-Hall, 1987).

13. Many historians believe that the term *United States* was coined in a series of articles written in the 1770s by Thomas Paine. See, for example, A. J. Ayer, *Thomas Paine* (New York: Atheneum, 1988), p. 42.

14. Some scholars feel that Locke's influence on the colonists, including Thomas Jefferson, has been exaggerated. For example, Jay Fliegelman states that Jefferson's fascination with the ideas of Homer, Ossian, and Patrick Henry "is of greater significance than his indebtedness to Locke." Jay Fliegelman, *Declaring Independence: Jefferson, Natural Language, and the Culture of Performance* (Stanford, Calif.: Stanford University Press, 1993).

15. Well before the articles were ratified, many of them had, in fact, already been implemented. The Second Continental Congress and the thirteen states conducted American military, economic, and political affairs according to the standards and form specified later in the Articles of Confederation. See Robert W. Hoffert, *A Politics of Tensions: The Articles of Confederation and American Political Ideas* (Niwot, Colo.: University Press of Colorado, 1992).

16. Madison was much more "republican" in his views than Hamilton. See Lance Banning, *The Sacred Fire of Liberty: James Madison and the Founding of the Federal Republic* (Ithaca, N.Y.: Cornell University Press, 1995).

17. The State House was later named Independence Hall. This was the same room in which the Declaration of Independence had been signed eleven years earlier.

18. Charles A. Beard, *An Economic Interpretation of the Constitution of the United States* (New York: Macmillan, 1913; New York: Free Press, 1986).

19. Morris was partly of French descent, which is why his first name may seem strange. Note, though, that naming one's child *Gouverneur* was not common at the time in any language, even French.

20. Some scholarship suggests that the *Federalist Papers* did not play a significant role in bringing about the ratification of the Constitution. Nonetheless, the papers have lasting value as an authoritative explanation of the Constitution.

21. For an analysis of the views of the Anti-Federalists, see Herbert J. Storing, *What the Anti-Federalists Were For* (Chicago: University of Chicago Press, 1981). Storing also edited seven volumes of the Anti-Federalist writings, *The Complete Anti-Federalist* (Chicago: University of Chicago Press, 1981). See also Josephine F. Pacheco, *Antifederalism: The Legacy of George Mason* (Fairfax, Va.: George Mason University Press, 1992).

22. Richard Shenkman, *Legends, Lies, and Cherished Myths of American History* (New York: HarperCollins, 1988), p. 18.

23. Beard, *An Economic Interpretation of the Constitution,* p. 299.

24. Jim Powell, "James Madison—Checks and Balances to Limit Government Power," *Freeman,* March 1996, p. 178.

25. The concept of the separation of powers is generally credited to the French political philosopher Montesquieu (1689–1755), who included it in his monumental two-volume work entitled *The Spirit of Laws,* published in 1748.

26. The Constitution does not explicitly mention the power of judicial review, but the delegates at the Constitutional Convention probably assumed that the courts would have this power. Indeed, Alexander Hamilton, in *Federalist Paper* No. 78, explicitly outlined the concept of judicial review. In any event, whether the founders intended for the courts to exercise this power is a moot point, because in an 1803 decision, *Marbury v. Madison,* the Supreme Court claimed this power for the courts—see Chapter 16.

27. Eventually, Supreme Court decisions led to legislative reforms relating to apportionment. The amendment concerning compensation of members of Congress became the

Twenty-seventh Amendment to the Constitution when it was ratified 203 years later, in 1992.

28. In 1972, Republican operatives, with the approval of the head of Nixon's reelection committee (Nixon's attorney general), had broken into the Democratic headquarters at the Watergate apartment/office complex in Washington, D.C., to wiretap the phones. Nixon immediately took steps to cover up the affair, while publicly declaring that neither he nor anyone in his administration had anything to do with this "bizarre incident."

29. *Brown v. Board of Education of Topeka,* 347 U.S. 483 (1954). See Chapter 5 for a discussion of this case.

30. For an excellent discussion of this issue, see Ronald Dworkin, *Freedom's Law: The Moral Reading of the Constitution* (Cambridge, Mass.: Harvard University Press, 1997).

3 chapter

FEDERALISM

Contents

Should the States Take Orders from the National Government?

During the 1996 and 1998 elections, voters in several states approved laws that permit the use of marijuana for medical purposes. Such laws would allow physicians to prescribe marijuana for patients suffering from AIDS (acquired immune deficiency syndrome) or other terminal illnesses. Shortly after the passage of the California law in 1996, national government officials warned physicians practicing in that state that if they prescribed marijuana for their patients, they could have their licenses to prescribe all controlled drugs and narcotics revoked, be excluded from the Medicare and Medicaid programs, and even be subject to criminal prosecution. How can this be? Don't the voters in California (and elsewhere) have the right to regulate drug policy within their borders?

The answer to this question is yes—but only to the extent that state laws do not conflict with national drug policy. In all states, the possession of marijuana continues to be subject to a national law governing drugs: the Comprehensive Drug Abuse Prevention and Control Act of 1970, as amended. The national government's author-ity to control drugs is laid out very specifically in that law. The law gives a detailed schedule of specific substances that are to be controlled. It also delineates specific offenses and establishes a complex set of penalties for each offense. The fact is, drug strategy in the United States is fundamentally a policy of the national government, although each state has its own set of laws that operates concurrently with national law.

Let the States Control

Many members of the medical community support the prescription of marijuana for certain patients. Leading the medical community's counterattack on the federal policy, Dr. Jerome Kassirer stated in an article in the *New England Journal of Medicine* that the long-standing "federal policy that prohibits physicians from alleviating suffering by prescribing marijuana for seriously ill patients" is "misguided, heavy-handed, and inhumane."[1]

Those in favor of permitting the medical use of marijuana are only one part of a larger group who think that the national government should get out of the drug control business altogether. They argue that the national drug policy imposes costs on all Americans while accomplishing few of its goals. A single policy on drugs cannot work because there are simply too many conflicting preferences and circumstances to produce a valid national compromise.

This group argues that drug policy should be formed by the states, cities, and neighborhoods in which we live, rather than by the national government. State and local governments could then tailor drug policies to reflect local views and interests. Those who think that the national drug policy goes too far could relax their regulations, while people who think that the policy does not go far enough could impose stricter controls on drugs.

Let the National Government Control

Many Americans disagree with the proposal that state and local governments should have exclusive control over the illegal drug problem in the United States. They believe that it is in the best interests of the country, not just of each state, to have a national drug policy so that American citizens, regardless of which state they live in, will be protected uniformly from the consequences of drug possession and the crimes that result from drug use and distribution.

Supporters of a national drug policy emphasize that illegal drug use and drug trafficking are nationwide problems. In any given year, more than forty million Americans violate some drug law at least once, and the number of crimes associated with illegal drugs continues to increase.

Furthermore, certain states—notably, Texas, California, Florida, and New York—are more adversely affected than other states because they act as involuntary ports of entry for drugs for the whole country. If the task of controlling drugs were left to the states, these states would face far higher costs than others. Additionally, many state legislators and governors are reluctant to tackle the drug problem by themselves. Consequently, the resources of the national government must be used in the fight against illegal drug manufacturing, importation, shipment, and use.

Where Do You Stand?

1. What would result if the states were allowed to control drug policy? What might happen if the use of certain drugs was legal in some states but not in others?

2. If the states exercised ultimate control over drug policy, how could they arrange to handle the problem of interstate drug trafficking?

On the Web

The American Civil Liberties Union offers information on drugs and drug policies, including articles on the federal-state conflict over the medical use of marijuana, at **www.aclu.org.**

CALIFORNIA Rx PROHIBITED

Go to CD-ROM

Introduction

DEVOLUTION ● In the context of American politics, the transfer to the states of some of the responsibilities assumed by the national government since the 1930s.

INFOTRAC®
State-federal tug of war

Whether drug policy should be controlled by the national government or by state governments is just one example of how different levels of government in our federal system can be at odds with one another. Let's face it. Those who work for the national government based in Washington, D.C., probably would not like to see power taken away from Washington and given to the states. At the same time, those who work in state governments don't like to be told what to do by the national government. Finally, those who work in local governments would like to run their affairs with the least amount of interference from both their state governments and the national government.

The relationship between the national government and the governments at the state and local levels has never been free of conflict. Indeed, even before the Constitution was adopted, the Federalists and Anti-Federalists engaged in a heated debate over the issue of national versus state powers. As you learned in Chapter 2, the Federalists won the day, in terms of convincing Americans to adopt the Constitution. The Anti-Federalists' concern for states' rights, however, has surfaced again and again in the course of American history. Today, for example, we see the concern for states' rights reflected in arguments supporting **devolution**—the transfer to the states of some of the responsibilities assumed by the national government since the 1930s.

Such conflicts arise because our government is based on the principle of *federalism,* which means that government powers are shared by the national government and the states. When the founders of this nation opted for federalism, they created a practical and flexible form of government capable of enduring for centuries. At the same time, however, they planted the seeds for future conflict between the states and the national government over how government powers should be shared. As you will read in this chapter—and throughout this book—many of today's most pressing issues have to do with which level of government should exercise certain powers, such as the power to control drug policy.

Who shall control public policy—the national government or the states? This question is at the heart of the *devolution* movement in the United States. One example of an attempt by the states to "control their own destinies" involves the legalization of the medicinal use of marijuana. In 1996, citizens in both California and Arizona passed propositions legalizing marijuana for medical use. Immediately thereafter, the Clinton administration reacted negatively. The head of the Drug Enforcement Administration said, "We are going to take very serious action against [physicians who prescribe marijuana]." Attorney General Janet Reno urged local authorities to "make arrests and prosecute" those who violate federal drug laws. In 1998, voters in several other states approved ballot measures legalizing the medical use of marijuana.

Federalism and Its Alternatives

UNITARY SYSTEM ● A centralized governmental system in which local or subdivisional governments exercise only those powers given to them by the central government.

There are various ways of ordering relations between central governments and local units. Federalism is one of these ways. Learning about federalism and how it differs from other forms of government is important to understanding the American political system.

WHAT IS FEDERALISM?

Nowhere in the Constitution does the word *federalism* appear. Since the Federalists and the Anti-Federalists argued more than two hundred years ago about what form of government we should have, hundreds of definitions of federalism have been offered. Basically, though, as mentioned in Chapter 2, in a *federal system,* government powers are divided between a central government and regional, or subdivisional, governments.

Although this definition seems straightforward, its application certainly is not. After all, virtually all nations—even the most repressive totalitarian regimes—have some kind of subnational governmental units. Thus, the existence of national and subnational governmental units by itself does not make a system federal. *For a system to be truly federal, the powers of both the national units and the subnational units must be specified in a constitution.* Under true federalism, individuals are governed by two separate governmental authorities (national and state authorities) whose expressly designated constitutional powers cannot be altered without rewriting or altering (by amendment, for example) the constitution. The Central Intelligence Agency estimates that only eleven countries, constituting 32 percent of the world's population, have a truly federal system (see Table 3–1).[2]

Federalism in theory is one thing; federalism in practice is another. As you will read shortly, the Constitution sets forth specific powers that can be exercised by the national government and provides that the national government has the implied power to undertake actions necessary to carry out its expressly designated powers. All other powers are "reserved" to the states. The broad language of the Constitution, though, has left much room for debate over the specific nature and scope of certain powers, such as the national government's implied powers and the powers reserved to the states. Thus, the actual workings of our federal form of government have depended, to a great extent, on the historical application of the broad principles outlined in the Constitution.

To further complicate matters, the term *federal government,* as it is currently used, refers to the national, or central, government. When individuals talk of the federal government, they mean the national government; they are not referring to the federal *system* of government, which is made up of both the national government and the state governments.

ALTERNATIVES TO FEDERALISM

Most of the nations in the world today have a **unitary system** of government. In such a system, the constitution vests all powers in the national government. If the national government so chooses, it can delegate certain activities to subnational units. The reverse is also true: the national government can take away, at will, powers delegated to subnational governmental units. In a unitary system, any subnational government is a "creature of the national government." The governments of Britain, France, Israel, and the Philippines are examples of unitary systems. In the United States, because the Constitution does not mention local governments (cities and counties), we say that city and county governmental units are "creatures of state government." That means that state govern-

Table 3–1

Countries That Have a Federal System Today

COUNTRY	POPULATION (IN MILLIONS)
Argentina	36.2
Australia	18.6
Austria	8.1
Brazil	169.8
Canada	30.6
Germany	82.1
India	984.0
Malaysia	20.9
Mexico	98.6
Switzerland	7.3
United States	270.3

SOURCE: Central Intelligence Agency, *The World Fact Book, 1998* (Washington, D.C.: U.S. Government Printing Office, 1998).

Great Britain has a unitary system of government, in which governmental power is centralized at the national level. The key government institution in that country is Parliament, the origins of which go back to the medieval Great Council—a body of noble and church advisers to the monarch that eventually became the House of Lords (the upper chamber of Parliament). Today, only the House of Commons (the lower chamber of Parliament) exercises significant power. It consists of 651 democratically elected members.

ments can—and do—both give powers to and take powers from local governments.

The Articles of Confederation created a confederal system (see Chapter 2). In a **confederal system,** the national government exists and operates only at the direction of the subnational governments. Few true confederal systems are in existence today.

FEDERALISM—AN OPTIMAL CHOICE FOR THE UNITED STATES?

The Articles of Confederation failed because they did not allow for a sufficiently strong central government. The framers of the Constitution, however, were fearful of tyranny and a too-powerful central government. The natural outcome had to be a compromise—a federal system.

The appeal of federalism was that it retained state powers and local traditions while establishing a strong national government capable of handling common problems, such as national defense. A federal form of government also furthered the goal of creating a division of powers (to be discussed shortly). There are other reasons why the founders opted for a federal system, and a federal structure of government continues to offer many advantages (as well as some disadvantages) for U.S. citizens.

Advantages of Federalism

One of the reasons a federal form of government is well suited to the United States is its size relative to that of many other countries. Even in the days when the United States consisted of only thirteen colonies, its geographic area was larger than that of France or England. In those days, travel was slow, and communication was difficult, so people in outlying areas were isolated. The news of any particular political decision could take several weeks to reach everyone. Therefore, even if the framers of the Constitution had wanted a more centralized system (which most of them did not), such a system would have been unworkable.

Look at Figure 3–1 on the next page. As you can see, to a great extent the practical business of governing this country takes place not in Washington, D.C., but in state and local government units. Federalism, by providing a multitude of arenas for decision making, keeps government closer to the people and helps make democracy possible.

The existence of numerous government subunits in the United States also makes it possible to experiment with innovative policies and programs at the state or local level. Many observers, including Supreme Court

CONFEDERAL SYSTEM ● A league of independent sovereign states, joined together by a central government that has only limited powers over them.

Figure 3–1
Governmental Units in the United States Today

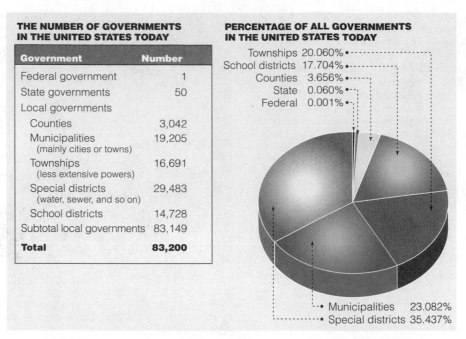

THE NUMBER OF GOVERNMENTS IN THE UNITED STATES TODAY	
Government	Number
Federal government	1
State governments	50
Local governments	
Counties	3,042
Municipalities (mainly cities or towns)	19,205
Townships (less extensive powers)	16,691
Special districts (water, sewer, and so on)	29,483
School districts	14,728
Subtotal local governments	83,149
Total	**83,200**

PERCENTAGE OF ALL GOVERNMENTS IN THE UNITED STATES TODAY

Townships 20.060%
School districts 17.704%
Counties 3.656%
State 0.060%
Federal 0.001%

Municipalities 23.082%
Special districts 35.437%

SOURCE: U.S. Department of Commerce, *Statistical Abstract of the United States, 1998* (Washington, D.C.: U.S. Government Printing Office, 1998).

Justice Louis Brandeis, have emphasized that in a federal system, state governments can act as "laboratories" for public policy experimentation. When a state adopts a program that fails, any negative effects are relatively limited. A program that succeeds can be copied by other states. For example, several states today are experimenting with new educational programs, including voucher systems (discussed in Chapter 20). Depending on the outcome of a specific experiment, other states may (or may not) implement similar programs. State innovations can also serve as models for federal programs. For example, California was a pioneer in air-pollution control. Many of that state's regulations were later adapted by the federal government to federal regulatory programs.

We have always been a nation of different political subcultures. The Pilgrims who founded New England were different from the settlers who established the agricultural society of the South. Both of these groups were different from those who populated the Middle Atlantic states. The groups who founded New England were religiously oriented, while those who populated the Middle Atlantic states were more business oriented. Those who settled in the South were more individualistic than the other groups; that is, they were less inclined to act as a group and more inclined to act independently of each other. A federal system of government allows the political and cultural interests of regional groups to be reflected in the laws governing those groups.

Some Drawbacks to Federalism

Federalism offers many advantages, but it also has some drawbacks. For example, although federalism in many ways promotes greater self-rule, or democracy, some scholars point out that local self-rule may not always be in society's best interests. These observers argue that the smaller the political unit, the higher the probability that it will be dominated by a single political group, which may or may not be concerned with the welfare of the majority of the local unit's citizens. Certainly, there have been dominant groups in states and cities that have exhibited corruption, encouraged racial segregation, and generally denied equal rights for citizens.

Federalism also poses the danger that national powers will be expanded at the expense of the states. President Ronald Reagan once said, "The Founding Fathers saw the federalist system as constructed something like a masonry wall. The States are the bricks, the national government is the mortar. . . . Unfortunately, over the years, many people have increasingly come to believe that Washington is the whole wall."[3]

At the same time, powerful state and local interests can block progress and impede national plans. State and local interests often diverge from those of the national government. As mentioned in this chapter's introduction, conflicts between the national government and state and local governments have characterized this nation from the outset. Finding acceptable solutions to these conflicts has not always been easy. Indeed, as you will read shortly, in the 1860s, war—not politics—decided the outcome of a struggle that was essentially a conflict over states' rights.

Federalism has other drawbacks as well. One of them is the lack of uniformity of state laws, which can complicate business transactions that cross state borders. Another problem is the difficulty of coordinating government policies at the national, state, and local levels. Regulation of business by all levels of government creates considerable red tape that imposes substantial costs on the business community.

The Constitutional Division of Powers

The founders created a federal form of government by dividing sovereign powers into powers that could be exercised by the national government and powers that were to be reserved to the states. Although there is no systematic explanation of this **division of powers** between the national and state governments, the original Constitution, along with its amendments, states what the national and state governments can (and cannot) do.

THE POWERS OF THE NATIONAL GOVERNMENT

The Constitution delegates certain powers to the national government. It also prohibits the national government from exercising certain powers.

Powers Delegated to the National Government

The Constitution delegates three types of powers to the national government: expressed powers, implied powers, and inherent powers. Article I, Section 8, of the Constitution expressly enumerates twenty-seven powers that Congress may exercise. Two of these **expressed powers** are the power to coin money and the power to regulate interstate commerce. Constitutional amendments have provided for other expressed powers. For example, the Sixteenth Amendment, added in 1913, gives Congress the power to impose a federal income tax. Article II, Section 2, of the Constitution expressly delegates certain powers to the president. These powers include making treaties and appointing certain federal officeholders.

The constitutional basis for the **implied powers** of the national government is found in Article I, Section 8, Clause 18, often called the **necessary and proper clause.** This clause states that Congress has the power to make "all Laws which shall be necessary and proper for carrying into Execution the foregoing [expressed] Powers, and all other Powers vested by this Constitution in the Government of the United States, or in any Department or Officer thereof." The necessary and proper clause is often referred to as the *elastic clause,* because it gives elasticity to our constitutional system.

The powers delegated to the national government also include **inherent powers**—powers that governments have simply to ensure the nation's integrity and survival as a political unit. For example, any national government must have the inherent ability to make treaties, regulate immigration, acquire territory, wage war, and make peace. Although the national government's inherent powers are few, they are important.

INFOTRAC®

Unnecessary and unintelligible

DIVISION OF POWERS ● A basic principle of federalism established by the U.S. Constitution. In a federal system, powers are divided between units of government (such as the federal and state governments).

EXPRESSED POWERS ● Constitutional or statutory powers that are expressly provided for by the Constitution or by congressional laws.

IMPLIED POWERS ● The powers of the federal government that are implied by the expressed powers in the Constitution, particularly in Article I, Section 8.

NECESSARY AND PROPER CLAUSE ● Article I, Section 8, Clause 18, of the Constitution, which gives Congress the power to make all laws "necessary and proper" for the federal government to carry out its responsibilities; also called the elastic clause.

INHERENT POWERS ● The powers of the national government that, although not expressly granted by the Constitution, are necessary to ensure the nation's integrity and survival as a political unit. Inherent powers include the power to make treaties and the power to wage war or make peace.

One of the expressed powers of Congress is the power to coin money. On April 2, 1792, Congress established the Mint of the United States in Philadelphia. Today, the U.S. Bureau of the Mint also maintains mints in Denver and San Francisco. The earliest mints were started in ancient Greece. The name "mint" comes from the Roman temple of Juno Moneta (*moneta* is Latin for *mint*), where silver coins were made as early as 269 B.C.E.

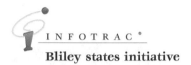
Bliley states initiative

POLICE POWERS ● The powers of a government body that enable it to create laws for the protection of the health, morals, safety, and welfare of the people. In the United States, most police powers are reserved to the states.

States have the power to protect the health, safety, morals, and welfare of their citizens.

Powers Prohibited to the National Government

The Constitution expressly prohibits the national government from undertaking certain actions, such as imposing taxes on exports, and from passing laws restraining certain liberties, such as the freedom of speech or religion. Most of these prohibited powers are listed in Article I, Section 9, and in the first eight amendments to the Constitution. Additionally, the national government is prohibited from exercising powers, such as the power to create a national public school system, that are not included among its expressed and implied powers.

THE POWERS OF THE STATES

The Tenth Amendment to the Constitution states that powers that are not delegated to the national government by the Constitution, nor prohibited to the states, "are reserved to the States respectively, or to the people."

Police Powers

The Tenth Amendment thus gives numerous powers to the states, including the power to regulate commerce within their borders and the power to maintain a state militia. In principle, each state has the ability to regulate its internal affairs and to enact whatever laws are necessary to protect the health, morals, safety, and welfare of its people. These powers of the states are called **police powers.** The establishment of public schools and the regulation of marriage and divorce are uniquely within the purview of state and local governments.

Because the Tenth Amendment does not specify what powers are reserved to the states, these powers have been defined differently at different times in our history. In periods of widespread support for increased regulation by the national government, the Tenth Amendment tends to recede into the background of political discourse. When the tide turns the other way, as it has in recent years (see the discussion of the new federalism later in this chapter), the Tenth Amendment is resurrected to justify arguments supporting increased states' rights. Because the Supreme Court

CONCURRENT POWERS ● Powers held by both the federal and state governments in a federal system.

is the ultimate arbiter of the Constitution, the outcome of disputes over the extent of state powers often rests with the Court.

Powers Prohibited to the States

Article I, Section 10, denies certain powers to state governments, such as the power to tax goods that are transported across state lines. States also are prohibited from entering into treaties with other countries. In addition, the Thirteenth, Fourteenth, Fifteenth, Nineteenth, Twenty-fourth, and Twenty-sixth Amendments also prohibit certain state actions.

CONCURRENT POWERS

Concurrent powers can be exercised by both state governments and the federal government. Generally, a state's concurrent powers apply only within the geographic area of the state and do not include functions that the Constitution delegates exclusively to the national government, such as the coinage of money and the negotiation of treaties. An example of a concurrent power is the power to tax. Both the states and the national government have the power to impose income taxes—and a variety of other types of taxes. States, however, are prohibited from imposing tariffs (taxes on imported goods), and the federal government may not tax real estate. Figure 3–2, below, which

Figure 3–2
The Constitutional Division of Powers

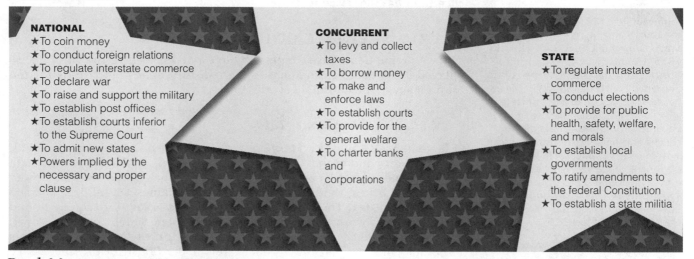

NATIONAL
★ To coin money
★ To conduct foreign relations
★ To regulate interstate commerce
★ To declare war
★ To raise and support the military
★ To establish post offices
★ To establish courts inferior to the Supreme Court
★ To admit new states
★ Powers implied by the necessary and proper clause

CONCURRENT
★ To levy and collect taxes
★ To borrow money
★ To make and enforce laws
★ To establish courts
★ To provide for the general welfare
★ To charter banks and corporations

STATE
★ To regulate intrastate commerce
★ To conduct elections
★ To provide for public health, safety, welfare, and morals
★ To establish local governments
★ To ratify amendments to the federal Constitution
★ To establish a state militia

Panel (a) Powers Granted by the Constitution

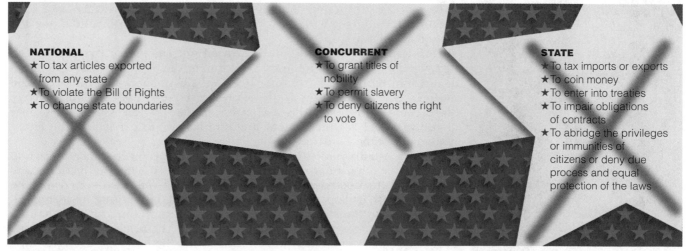

NATIONAL
★ To tax articles exported from any state
★ To violate the Bill of Rights
★ To change state boundaries

CONCURRENT
★ To grant titles of nobility
★ To permit slavery
★ To deny citizens the right to vote

STATE
★ To tax imports or exports
★ To coin money
★ To enter into treaties
★ To impair obligations of contracts
★ To abridge the privileges or immunities of citizens or deny due process and equal protection of the laws

Panel (b) Powers Denied by the Constitution

SUPREMACY CLAUSE ● Article VI, Clause 2, of the Constitution, which makes the Constitution and federal laws superior to all conflicting state and local laws.

summarizes the powers granted and denied by the Constitution, lists other concurrent powers.

THE SUPREMACY CLAUSE

The Constitution makes it clear that the federal government holds ultimate power. The **supremacy clause** in Article VI, Clause 2, states that the U.S. Constitution and the laws of the federal government "shall be the supreme Law of the Land." In other words, states cannot use their reserved or concurrent powers to counter national policies. Whenever state or local officers, such as judges or sheriffs, take office, they become bound by an oath to support the U.S. Constitution. National government power always takes precedence over any conflicting state action.[4]

The Struggle for Supremacy

Much of the political and legal history of the United States has involved conflicts between the supremacy of the national government and the desires of the states to remain independent. The most extreme example of this conflict was the Civil War in the 1860s. Through the years, because of the Civil War and several key Supreme Court decisions, the national government has increased its power.

EARLY SUPREME COURT DECISIONS

Two Supreme Court cases, both of which were decided in the early 1800s, played a key role in establishing the constitutional foundations for the supremacy of the national government.

McCulloch v. Maryland (1819)

John Marshall (1755–1835) served as the fourth chief justice of the United States Supreme Court from 1801 to 1835. He did much to establish the prestige and the independence of the Supreme Court. In *Marbury v. Madison,* he clearly enunciated the principle of judicial review, which has since become an important part of the checks and balances in the American system of government. He was an opponent of states' rights and established, in a series of cases, the superiority of federal authority under the Constitution. He has been called the "Great Chief Justice."

The issue in *McCulloch v. Maryland,*[5] a case decided in 1819, involved both the necessary and proper clause and the supremacy clause. When the state of Maryland imposed a tax on the Baltimore branch of the Second Bank of the United States, the branch's chief cashier, James McCulloch, decided not to pay the tax. The state court ruled that McCulloch had to pay it, and the national government appealed to the United States Supreme Court. The case involved much more than a question of taxes. At issue was whether Congress had the authority under the Constitution's necessary and proper clause to charter and contribute capital to the Second Bank of the United States. A second constitutional issue was also involved: If the bank was constitutional, could a state tax it? In other words, was a state action that conflicted with a national government action invalid under the supremacy clause?

Chief Justice John Marshall pointed out that no provision in the Constitution grants the national government the expressed power to form a national bank. Nevertheless, if establishing such a bank helps the national government exercise its expressed powers, then the authority to do so could be implied. Marshall also said that the necessary and proper clause included "all means that are appropriate" to carry out "the legitimate ends" of the Constitution.

Having established this doctrine of implied powers, Marshall then answered the other important constitutional question before the Court and established the doctrine of national supremacy. Marshall stated that no state could use its taxing power to tax an arm of the national government. If it could, the Constitution's declaration that the Constitution "shall be the supreme Law of the Land" would be empty rhetoric without meaning. From that day on, Marshall's decision became the basis for strengthening the national government's power.

Gibbons v. Ogden (1824)

Article I, Section 8, gives Congress the power to regulate commerce "among the several States," but the framers of the Constitution did not define the word *commerce*. At issue in *Gibbons v. Ogden*[6] was how the **commerce clause** should be defined and whether the national government had the exclusive power to regulate commerce involving more than one state. The New York legislature had given Robert Livingston and Robert Fulton the exclusive right to operate steamboats in New York waters, and they licensed Aaron Ogden to operate a ferry between New York and New Jersey. Thomas Gibbons, who had a license from the U.S. government to operate boats in interstate waters, decided to compete with Ogden, but he did so without New York's permission. Ogden sued Gibbons in the New York state courts and won. Gibbons appealed.

Chief Justice Marshall defined *commerce* as including all business dealings, including steamboat travel. Marshall also stated that the power to regulate interstate commerce was an *exclusive* national power and had no limitations other than those specifically found in the Constitution. Since this 1824 decision, the national government has used the commerce clause numerous times to justify its regulation of virtually all areas of economic activity.

THE ULTIMATE SUPREMACY BATTLE—THE CIVIL WAR

In part, the Civil War (1861–1865) was a fight to free the slaves. Although freedom for the slaves was an important aspect of the war, it was not the only one—or even necessarily the most important one, according to many scholars. At the heart of the controversy that led to the Civil War was the issue of states' rights versus national supremacy. The war brought to a bloody climax the ideological debate that had been outlined by the Federalist and Anti-Federalist factions even before the Constitution was ratified.

As just discussed, the Supreme Court headed by John Marshall interpreted the commerce clause in such a way as to increase the power of the national government at the expense of state powers. By the late 1820s, however, a shift

The Civil War is known in the South as the War between the States, but the official Union designation was the War of the Rebellion. Certainly, the question of slavery and its extension into new territories was an important cause of this conflict. Equally important, though, was the fundamental disagreement about the relative powers of the federal government and the state governments—or the issue of states' rights. Efforts toward a peaceful solution to the conflict failed, and ultimately the issue was decided by war. The first shot of the Civil War was fired on April 12, 1861, at Fort Sumter, South Carolina.

CONCURRENT MAJORITY ● A principle advanced by John C. Calhoun that states that democratic decisions should be made only with the agreement of all segments of society affected by the decisions. Without their agreement, a decision should not be binding on those whose interests it violates.

SECESSION ● The act of formally withdrawing from membership in an alliance; the withdrawal of a state from the federal Union.

DUAL FEDERALISM ● A system of government in which both the federal and state governments maintain diverse but sovereign powers.

COOPERATIVE FEDERALISM ● The theory that the states and the federal government should cooperate in solving problems.

NEW DEAL ● A program ushered in by the Roosevelt administration in 1933 to bring the United States out of the Great Depression. The New Deal included many government spending and public-assistance programs, in addition to thousands of regulations governing economic activity.

back to states' rights began, and the question of the regulation of commerce became one of the major issues in federal-state relations. When the national government, in 1823 and again in 1830, passed laws imposing tariffs (taxes) on goods imported into the United States, the southern states objected, believing that such taxes were against their best interests.

One southern state, South Carolina, attempted to *nullify* the tariffs, or to make them void. South Carolina claimed that in conflicts between state governments and the national government, the states should have the ultimate authority to determine the welfare of their citizens. Additionally, some southerners believed that democratic decisions could only be made when all the segments of society affected by those decisions were in agreement. In other words, a **concurrent majority** had to agree. Without such agreement, a decision should not be binding on those whose interests it violates. Supporters of this concurrent majority concept used it to justify the **secession**—withdrawal—of the southern states from the Union.

When the South was defeated in the war, the idea that a state has a right to secede from the Union was defeated also. Although the Civil War occurred because of the South's desire for increased states' rights, the result was just the opposite—an increase in the political power of the national government.

THE EVOLUTION OF FEDERALISM SINCE THE CIVIL WAR

Scholars have devised various models to describe the relationship between the states and the national government at different times in our history. These models are useful in describing the evolution of federalism from the end of the Civil War to the present.

Dual Federalism

The model of **dual federalism** assumes that the states and the national government are more or less equals, with each level of government having separate and distinct functions and responsibilities. The states exercise sovereign powers over certain matters, and the national government exercises sovereign powers over others.

For much of this nation's history, this model of federalism prevailed. Some scholars maintain that dual federalism characterized federal-state relations from 1789 to the early 1930s. Others date the beginning of dual federalism to the 1830s or 1840s. In any event, after the Civil War, the courts tended to support the states' rights to exercise their police powers and concurrent powers to regulate intrastate activities. In 1918, for example, the Supreme Court ruled unconstitutional a 1916 federal law excluding from interstate commerce the products created through the use of child labor. The law was held unconstitutional because it attempted to regulate a local problem.[7] The era of dual federalism came to an end in the 1930s, when the United States was in the depths of the greatest depression it had ever experienced.

Cooperative Federalism

The model of **cooperative federalism,** as the term implies, involves cooperation by all branches of governments. This model views the national and state governments as complementary parts of a single governmental mechanism, the purpose of which is to solve the problems facing the entire United States. For example, federal law enforcement agencies, such as the Federal Bureau of Investigation (FBI), lend technical expertise to solve local crimes, and local officials cooperate with federal agencies.

Cooperative federalism grew out of the need to solve the tremendous national problems caused by the Great Depression, which began in 1929. In 1933, to help bring the United States out of the depression, President Franklin D. Roosevelt launched his **New Deal,** which involved many government spending and public-assistance programs. Roosevelt's New Deal legislation not only ushered in an era of cooperative federalism, which has

President Johnson displays his signature on the War on Poverty bill after he signed it into law in a ceremony in the Rose Garden at the White House on August 20, 1964.

more or less continued until the present day, but also marked the real beginning of an era of national supremacy.

Some scholars argue that even if the Great Depression had not occurred, we probably would still have witnessed a growth in the powers of the national government. As the country became increasingly populated, industrialized, and interdependent with other nations, problems and situations that once were treated locally began to have a profound impact on Americans hundreds or even thousands of miles away. Environmental pollution does not respect state borders, nor do poverty, crime, and violence. National defense, space exploration, and an increasingly global economy also call for national—not state—action. Thus, the ascendancy of national supremacy in the twentieth century has had a very logical and very real set of causes.

Certainly, the 1960s and 1970s saw an even greater expansion of the national government's role in domestic policy. The Great Society legislation of Lyndon Johnson's administration (1963–1969) created Medicaid, Medicare, the Job Corps, Operation Head Start, and other programs. The Civil Rights Act of 1964 prohibited discrimination in public accommodations, employment, and other areas on the basis of race, color, national origin, religion, or gender. In the 1970s, national laws protecting consumers, employees, and the environment imposed further regulations on the economy. Today, few activities are beyond the reach of the regulatory arm of the national government.

The New Federalism—More Power to the States

During the 1970s and 1980s, several administrations attempted to revitalize the doctrine of dual federalism, which they renamed the "new federalism." The **new federalism** involves returning to the states certain powers that have been exercised by the national government since the 1930s. The term *devolution*—the transfer of powers to political subunits—is often used to describe the goals of the new federalism.

The new federalism was launched in the early 1970s by President Richard Nixon and, to varying degrees, has continued to the present. This form of federalism involves a shift from *nation-centered* federalism to *state-centered* federalism. An example of the new federalism is the welfare reform legislation of 1996 (discussed in Chapter 17), which gave the states more authority over welfare programs. For a further discussion of devolution, see the feature entitled *Perception versus Reality: Devolution?* on the next page.

SUPREME COURT DECISIONS SINCE THE 1930s

The two Supreme Court decisions discussed earlier became the constitutional cornerstone of the regulatory powers the national government enjoys today.

The Commerce Power

On numerous occasions during the twentieth century, the national government's constitutional authority to enact certain laws was challenged. The Supreme Court, though, until recently, consistently upheld Congress's power to regulate domestic policy under the commerce clause.

Even activities that occur entirely within a state are rarely considered outside the regulatory power of the national government. For example, in 1942 the Supreme Court held that wheat production by an individual farmer intended wholly for consumption on his own farm was subject to federal regulation, because the home consumption of wheat reduced the demand for wheat and thus could have a substantial effect on interstate commerce.[8] By 1980, the Supreme Court acknowledged that the commerce clause had "long been interpreted to extend beyond activities actually in interstate commerce to reach other activities, while wholly local in nature, which nevertheless substantially affect interstate commerce."[9] Today,

NEW FEDERALISM ● A plan to limit the federal government's role in regulating state governments and to give the states increased power to decide how they should spend government revenues.

perception **versus reality**

Devolution?

Since the Republicans took control of Congress in 1995, both the Clinton administration and the Republican-dominated Congress have promised a historic transfer of power from Washington, D.C., to the states. Spending by the national government would thus be reduced, numerous federal programs would no longer be necessary, and so on. Has this promise been realized? Has such a historic transfer of power to the states really occurred?

The Perception

Many Americans believe that it has. In the last few years, the states have gained control in a number of areas, most notably in the area of welfare. The federal welfare reform legislation of 1996 transferred significant powers to the states, which now have much more discretion over how welfare programs are administered. The states can determine who is eligible for welfare benefits and on what conditions. Although the national legislation put a lifetime limit on how long people could stay on welfare, the states can extend this period—as long as state funds are used to pay for the benefits. Since 1996, the states have also gained control over the

ability to expand children's health insurance and the option of enrolling Medicaid clients in managed-care programs.

The Reality

The perception that devolution is occurring apace is understandable, given the press releases by the White House and congressional leaders when any devolutionary legislation is passed. Yet a close look at what has actually happened in the last several years shows a different picture. Consider the first three budgets passed by the Republican-dominated Congress (the budgets for fiscal years 1996, 1997, and 1998). Far from decreasing national government spending, these budgets increased it by $183 billion. And only a few of the three hundred federal programs that were targeted for closure actually have been terminated. Furthermore, although the welfare reform legislation of 1996 did indeed mark a significant transfer of power to the states, since that time the flow of power to the states has slowed to a trickle.

If anything, the states today are busy fending off federal attempts to intrude into areas traditionally governed by the states. For example, education has traditionally

been under state control, yet President Clinton has pushed, unsuccessfully, for national educational standards. In 1998, Congress tried to regulate state drunk-driving standards in a measure attached to a transportation-funding bill. The measure failed to pass.

Gambling is another area of American life that the federal government has largely left alone in the past. Yet the national government is now contemplating legislation to make gambling laws more uniform. There has also been a trend to bring more types of crimes under federal jurisdiction. In his 1998 year-end report on the federal judiciary, Chief Justice of the United States William Rehnquist pointed out that during 1998, the number of federal court cases dealing with new types of federal crimes rose by 15 percent—the largest increase in nearly three decades. According to Rehnquist, "The trend to federalize crimes . . . threatens to change entirely the nature of our federal system."[10]

You Be the Judge

Why do the states resent national government intrusion into such areas as education, crime, and gambling?

I N F O T R A C *

Devolution part II

Congress can regulate almost any kind of economic activity, no matter where it occurs.

The commerce clause was also used to validate congressional legislation in what would seem to be social and moral matters—concerns traditionally regulated by the states. In 1964, for example, a small hotel in Georgia challenged the constitutionality of the Civil Rights Act of that year, claiming that Congress had exceeded its authority under the commerce clause by regulating local, intrastate affairs to prohibit discrimination in public accommodations. In holding that the 1964 act was constitutional, the Supreme Court stated, "If it is interstate commerce that feels the pinch, it does not matter how local the operation that applies the squeeze."[11]

The Supremacy Clause

John Marshall's validation of the supremacy clause of the Constitution has also had significant consequences for federalism in this century. One important effect of the supremacy clause today is that the clause allows for

PREEMPTION ● A doctrine rooted in the supremacy clause of the Constitution that provides that national laws or regulations governing a certain area take precedence over conflicting state laws or regulations governing that same area.

federal **preemption** of certain areas in which the national government and the states have concurrent powers. When Congress chooses to act exclusively in an area in which the states and the national government have concurrent powers, Congress is said to have *preempted* the area. When Congress preempts an area, such as aviation, the courts have held that a valid federal law or regulation takes precedence over a conflicting state or local law or regulation covering the same general activity. Starting in the 1960s, the use of federal preemption has become increasingly popular, as you can see in Figure 3–3.

The Supreme Court and the New Federalism

In the 1990s, a more conservative Supreme Court showed a willingness to rein in the constitutional powers of Congress, at least to a degree. In a landmark 1995 decision, *United States v. Lopez,*[12] the Supreme Court held that Congress had exceeded its constitutional authority under the commerce clause when it passed the Gun-Free School Zones Act in 1990. The Court found that the act, which banned the possession of guns within one thousand feet of any school, was unconstitutional because it attempted to regulate an area that had "nothing to do with commerce, or any sort of economic enterprise." This was the first time in sixty years that the Supreme Court had placed a limit on the national government's authority under the commerce clause.

Since then, the Court has issued a number of other decisions that indicate the Court's willingness to place some constitutional limits on the powers of Congress. In a 1997 case, the Court upheld state laws prohibiting assisted suicide, concluding that the constitutional right to privacy did not include the right to commit assisted suicide when one is terminally ill (see Chapter 4).[13] In the same year, the Court also struck down portions of the Brady Handgun Violence Prevention Act of 1993, which obligated state and local law enforcement officers to do background checks on prospective handgun buyers until a national instant check system could be implemented. The Court stated that Congress lacked the power to "dragoon" state employees into federal service through an unfunded mandate of this kind.[14]

A series of Supreme Court decisions issued in 1999 significantly enhanced the sovereign powers of the states within the federal system. For

Figure 3–3
Federal Preemption from 1900 to the Present
This graph shows the number of federal laws that preempt state authority. As you can see, the greatest growth in federal preemption is in laws regulating the environmental, health, or safety areas. Laws affecting commerce, energy, labor, and transportation run a close second.

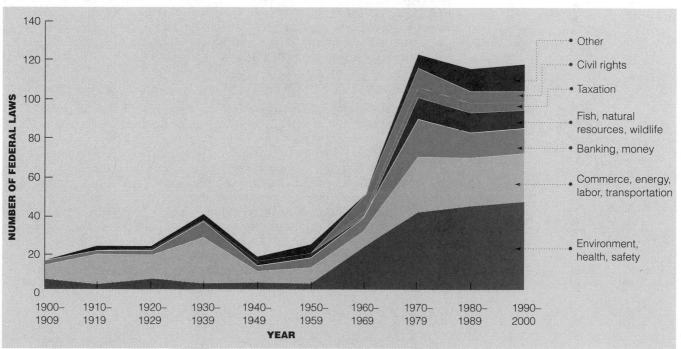

SOURCES: U.S. Advisory Commission on Intergovernmental Relations, plus authors' estimates.

FEDERAL MANDATE ● A requirement in federal legislation that forces states and municipalities to comply with certain rules.

example, in one case the issue had to do with whether Maine public employees could sue the state of Maine for violating the overtime pay provisions of a federal law. The Court held that the Constitution's structure and history shields states not only from being sued in federal courts but also makes them immune from private lawsuits brought in state court that seek to enforce a federal right. The Court emphasized that state immunity from such lawsuits "is a fundamental aspect of the sovereignty which [the states] enjoyed before the ratification of the Constitution, and which they retain today."[15]

Clearly, the border between federal and state authority is changing. Some commentators worry that the Supreme Court is going too far in reviving the authority of state governments. Others, however, believe that the Court's recent decisions emphasizing the authority of state governments merely "remind us of our constitutional framework of dual sovereignty."[16]

The Fiscal Side of Federalism

As everybody knows, big government is costly. But how can government spending be reduced without sacrificing government programs that some feel are essential? This question, which to a significant extent frames the debate over federalism today, requires an understanding of the fiscal side of federalism.

Since the advent of cooperative federalism in the 1930s, the national government and the states have worked hand in hand to implement programs mandated by the national government. Whenever Congress passes a law that preempts a certain area, the states are, of course, obligated to comply with the requirements of that law. A requirement that a state provide a service or undertake some activity in order to meet the national standards specified by the federal law is referred to as a **federal mandate.** Many federal mandates concern civil rights or environmental protection. Recent federal mandates require the states to provide persons with disabilities with access to public buildings, sidewalks, and other areas; to establish minimum water-purity and air-purity standards for specific localities; and to extend Medicaid coverage to all poor children.

To help the states pay for some of the costs associated with implementing national policies, the national government gives back some of the tax dollars it collects to the states—in the form of grants. As you will see, the states have come to depend on grants as an important source of revenue, yet grants are becoming harder and harder to get as the national government attempts to reduce its deficit.

FEDERAL GRANTS

Even before the Constitution was adopted, the national government granted lands to the states for the purpose of financing education. Using the proceeds from the sale of these lands, the states were able to establish numerous colleges, which came to be known as *land-grant colleges.* Cash grants started in 1808, when Congress gave money to the states to pay for the state militias. Federal grants were also made available for other purposes, such as building roads and railroads.

Only in the twentieth century, though, did federal grants become an important source of funds to the states. The major growth began in the 1960s, when the dollar amount of grants quadrupled to help pay for the Great Society programs of the Johnson administration. Grants became available for education, pollution control, conservation, recreation, highway construction and maintenance, and other purposes.

Bridging the Tenth Amendment—Fiscal Federalism

Grants of money to the states from the national government are one way that the Tenth Amendment to the U.S. Constitution can be bridged. Even

Many public services and projects carried out by the states are actually funded, at least in part, by federal grants. Our interstate highway system is a case in point.

when the power to regulate a particular activity is clearly reserved to the states (because the power is not one that was delegated to the national government), the national government can still influence that activity through its awarding (or withholding) of grants. The power of the national government to influence state policies through grants is often referred to as **fiscal federalism.**

There are two basic types of federal grants: categorical grants and block grants. A **categorical grant** is targeted for a specific purpose as defined by federal law—the federal government defines 578 categories of state and local spending. Categorical grants give the national government control over how states use the money by imposing certain conditions. For example, a categorical grant may require that the funds not be used for purposes that discriminate against any group or for construction projects that pay below the local union wage. Depending on the project, the government might require that an environmental impact statement be prepared.

In contrast, a **block grant** is given for a broad area, such as criminal justice or mental health programs. First started in 1966, block grants now constitute a growing percentage of all federal aid programs. The block grant is one of the tools of the new federalism because it gives the states more discretion over how the funds will be spent. Nonetheless, the federal government can exercise control over state decision making through these grants by using *cross-cutting requirements*. Title VI of the 1964 Civil Rights Act, for example, bars discrimination in the use of all federal funds, regardless of their sources.

The Intergovernmental Lobby

With so many different grants available for the states and cities, it is not surprising that those governments spend considerable resources trying to get their "fair share." The **intergovernmental lobby** is a powerful special interest lobby (see Chapter 7) made up of governors, mayors, highway commissioners, police chiefs, and superintendents of schools. All of them have learned to rely on the national government for some or all of their budgets. At least thirty states, perhaps one hundred cities, and about thirty

FISCAL FEDERALISM ● The power of the national government to influence state policies through grants.

CATEGORICAL GRANT ● A federal grant targeted for a specific purpose as defined by federal law.

BLOCK GRANT ● A federal grant given to a state for a broad area, such as criminal justice or mental health programs.

INTERGOVERNMENTAL LOBBY ● A special interest lobby formed by governors, mayors, highway commissioners, and others for the purpose of obtaining federal funds for state and local governments.

counties actually have offices in Washington, D.C. The state of Texas alone has twenty-five people there. Together, the five largest intergovernmental lobbying groups (listed below) spend more than $50 million a year trying to get more money from Washington.

- National Governors' Association
- National Conference of State Legislatures
- National League of Cities
- U.S. Conference of Mayors
- National Association of Counties

In spite of this impressive lobbying effort, the amount of funds going to the states is declining, particularly as a percentage of total state and local government spending. In addition, the national government has continued to centralize power in novel ways, such as by the use of federal mandates. The cost of these mandates for the states has generated controversy.

THE COST OF FEDERAL MANDATES

As mentioned, when the national government passes a law preempting an area in which the states and the national government have concurrent powers, the states must comply with that law in accordance with the supremacy clause of the Constitution. Thus, when such laws require the states to implement certain programs, the states must comply—but compliance with federal mandates can be costly.

For example, the estimated total cost of complying with federal mandates concerning water purity, over just a four-year period, is in the vicinity of $29 billion. In all, the cost of federal mandates to the states from 1994 through 1998 was almost $54 billion. Although Congress passed legislation in 1995 to curb the use of "unfunded" federal mandates (that is, mandates that are not funded by the federal government), the legislation was more rhetoric than reality.

The Revolt against Federal Mandates

Many states are at odds with the federal government over the issue of federal preemption—and particularly the use of federal mandates. Not only are mandates costly for the states, but they also prevent state and local governments from setting their own priorities.

The states have started to revolt. For example, California sued the national government over the National Voter Registration Act of 1993 (known as the Motor Voter Law). This law, which became effective in 1995, requires the states to provide all eligible citizens with the opportunity to register to vote when they apply for or renew their driver's licenses. The law also requires that states allow mail-in voter registration and that forms be provided at certain public agencies for this purpose. The underlying goal of the law, of course, was to increase voter turnout. (For a further discussion of this law, see Chapter 9.)

California refused to implement the law because, according to then Governor Pete Wilson, doing so would cost the state $18 million a year. Wilson claimed that the law was "flatly unconstitutional." He stated, "If the federal government thinks that it is important to have motor-voter registration, then let the federal agencies implement it."[17] California state agencies refused to implement the motor voter programs until ordered to do so by a federal judge in June 1995. The state appealed the judge's decision, but the higher court refused to overturn the lower court's ruling.[18] The state then appealed to the United States Supreme Court, but to no avail—the Supreme Court refused to hear the case, thus letting the decision stand.[19] Other states[20] have also tried to convince the courts to block the enforcement of the motor voter law, but also without success.

Those who oppose federal preemption argue that policy should be implemented by the level of government that establishes the policy. Addi-

A government worker samples water in a Texas reservoir for purity. Meeting environmental standards, including water purity standards, mandated by the federal government can be costly for state and local governments.

tionally, if the national government wants a particular policy result, it should pay for that result, rather than pass the costs on to other levels of government (or even the private sector, for that matter).

The Constitutional Question

As noted earlier, in 1997 the Supreme Court ruled that parts of the Brady Act were unconstitutional. In its decision, the Supreme Court stated that the federal government may "neither issue directives requiring the States to address particular problems, nor command the States' officers, or those of their political subdivisions, to administer or enforce a federal regulatory program." Such actions, the Court said, "are fundamentally incompatible with our constitutional system of dual sovereignty." In his dissent, Justice Stevens pointed out that several other laws, particularly in the environmental area, are constitutionally indistinguishable from the Brady Act in this respect. Should those laws be overturned also?

For example, consider the Emergency Planning and Community Right-to-Know Act (EPCRA) of 1986. This law was enacted to ensure that local communities are informed about potential environmental threats from hazardous materials. The act requires each governor to appoint a "state emergency response commission" to collect information from industrial facilities that use or store materials classified as "hazardous" by the federal Environmental Protection Agency. If the governor fails to appoint a commission, then the governor must personally fulfill the commission's duties. These duties include designating "emergency planning districts" for regulated industrial facilities and appointing a local "emergency planning commission" in each district. In other words, the act requires state officials, including the governor, to take specific actions and, in effect, to create new state agencies.

The implications of the Court decision ruling some provisions of the Brady Act unconstitutional are yet to be seen. But if the same reasoning is applied in cases challenging other acts of Congress involving unfunded federal mandates, the decision could have a broad impact on the federal regulatory scheme.

Federal Mandates—Another View

The controversy over the cost of unfunded federal mandates sometimes masks the importance of these mandates in creating a level playing field among the states. Consider an example. One of the most costly unfunded federal mandates for the states of Tennessee and Mississippi in the early 1990s was the requirement that states could no longer impose sales taxes on foods purchased with federally funded food stamps (see Chapter 17). These states had been imposing a 7 percent and 8 percent tax, respectively, on such foods. As a result, food stamps in those states did not purchase as much food as in other states, and poor families consequently found it more difficult to fulfill their nutritional requirements. Thus, in some instances, unfunded federal mandates force the states to pay their share of the costs involved in improving the welfare of the nation's citizens.

Consider another example—the problem of environmental pollution. What if the national government left environmental regulation entirely to the states? According to political scientist Thomas R. Dye's model of federalism, which he calls **competitive federalism,** state and local governments compete for businesses and citizens. Businesses and citizens in effect "vote with their feet" by moving to jurisdictions that offer a competitive advantage.

Thus, other things being equal, states with less stringent environmental regulations would attract more businesses because businesses in those states could avoid some of the costs associated with environmental regulations (such as the cost of installing pollution-control equipment). Yet

INFOTRAC®

Restoring watersheds, rebuilding communities

COMPETITIVE FEDERALISM ● A model of federalism devised by Thomas R. Dye in which state and local governments compete for businesses and citizens, who in effect "vote with their feet" by moving to jurisdictions that offer a competitive advantage.

pollution by those firms could affect the environmental health of other states. To illustrate: Suppose tire factories in Ohio emit substantial sulfur particles that are carried to Vermont and become acid rain. Ohio would refuse to require its factories to clean up their emissions because its politicians want to protect the state's employment. In the meantime, Vermonters bear the cost of the emissions in their tourism industry, their recreational fishing, and their own health costs associated with poor water quality.[21]

Americans at Odds over Federalism

The battle over unfunded federal mandates is only one part of the complicated landscape of American federalism today. Americans are also at odds over other issues relating to federalism, including those discussed next. (The United States is not the only nation in which citizens are at odds over issues involving federalism. See, for example, the discussion of such conflicts in Canada in this chapter's feature entitled *Comparative Politics: Ottawa versus the Provinces.*)

Whatever Happened to Devolution?

As discussed earlier in this chapter's *Perception versus Reality* feature, the devolutionary goals of congressional Republicans, which have also been espoused by the Clinton administration, have been far from realized. Why is this? Why is it so difficult for those in Washington, D.C., to let the states have more control over their affairs?

Some suggest that advances in technology may be responsible, at least to some extent. Consider, for example, the difficulties that states face when trying to control gambling within their borders. In most states, gambling is illegal, except when sanctioned by the state in the form of lotteries, off-track betting, and so on. Today, however, virtually any person, even a fourteen-year-old with a credit card, can play blackjack or other gambling games on the Internet. While a state government can exercise jurisdiction over the in-state resident, it cannot regulate gambling activities in other states. Texas, for example, has no constitutional authority to regulate gambling activities in New Jersey or Nevada. Only the federal government has the constitutional authority to regulate activities that extend beyond state borders (and even the federal government cannot regulate gambling companies located offshore).

Others emphasize that it is only natural for policymakers in the nation's capital to push for federal legislation rather than turn over funds to the states to accomplish the same ends. Federal legislators who want to be reelected will likely want to claim credit for passing laws or instituting programs in areas of public concern, such as crime and educational reform, so that they look good in the eyes of their constituents.[22]

Do State and Local Selective Purchasing Laws Violate the Constitution?

In our federal system, foreign policy is left in the hands of the national government in Washington, D.C. Recently, though, a number of state and local governments have enacted selective purchasing laws that seem to encroach on this exclusive domain of the federal government. These laws

comparative politics
Ottawa versus the Provinces

Canada, like the United States, has a federal system of government. And as in the United States, there have been a number of skirmishes in that country over issues of federalism. The most widely publicized conflict, of course, involved Quebec's nearly successful attempt in 1995 to secede from the federal union. Yet the clashes between Canada's central government and the provinces over federalism extend beyond Quebec.

A current divisive issue has to do with the federal government's imposing responsibilities on the provinces without adequate federal grants to pay for them. For example, in the 1960s the provincial governments agreed to administer federal health-care and social-assistance programs with matching funds from the federal government. Since the mid-1990s, however, the federal government has limited its contribution to a specified amount, and the provinces must cover the remainder of the costs. These costs have risen significantly in recent years, placing financial strains on the provinces. The provincial leaders want control over the programs to be taken out of federal hands so that the provinces can exercise more authority over the programs.

Western Canadians are at odds with the central government over another issue as well—gun control. In 1998, the Canadian government passed a sweeping gun-control law that requires all gun owners in Canada to be licensed, requires all rifles and handguns be registered, and bans sales or gifts of easily concealed handguns. Under the act, government officials are given broad discretion to deny licenses and to search homes for weapons. The legislation will have a significant impact on the western provinces, such as the Yukon Territory, where 70 percent of households own firearms. In contrast, in Ontario only about 15 percent of households own guns.[23]

Thousands of Canadians in the western provinces have announced their intention to break the law, and several provincial governments in the West resent what they see as Ottawa's meddling. The governments of the Yukon Territory, Alberta, Saskatchewan, Manitoba, and the Northwest Territories are all challenging the constitutionality of the legislation. These provincial governments argue that regulations governing property are the jurisdiction of the provinces, not the federal government.

For Critical Analysis

Are conflicts between the central government and regional (state or provincial) governments inevitable in a federal system?

place sanctions on nations to punish them for assorted human rights transgressions.

Consider a law recently enacted by the Massachusetts legislature. The law effectively prohibits state companies from forming contracts with any U.S. or foreign company doing business in Burma (now Myanmar), a country ruled by a brutal military regime. Some eighteen other governments in the United States impose similar sanctions on Burma. Dade County, Florida, has sanctions against Cuba, while the city of Oakland, California, places sanctions on Nigeria. Some business executives are worried that there may be a wave of state and city laws targeting China, a country in which many U.S. companies operate.

After Massachusetts passed its bill, Japan and a number of European countries objected to such sanctions and threatened to take their case to the World Trade Organization, which enforces international trade rules. The federal government, which would have to defend Massachusetts's actions before that international body, is not pleased. Neither are U.S. business groups involved in global business operations. Recently, one business group challenged the Massachusetts law on constitutional grounds in a federal court.

The question is, do selective purchasing laws, such as those against Burma, violate the Constitution? Some argue that state and local governments have no right to make such laws because they violate the Constitution. Among other things, claims this group, such laws are contrary to the commerce clause of the Constitution, which, as interpreted by the Supreme Court, gives the federal government the exclusive power to "regulate Commerce with foreign Nations." State and local sanctions against other nations, if they conflict with federal policy, may also violate the supremacy clause of the Constitution, under which federal law takes priority in such a situation. Finally, the Constitution gives the federal government broad authority in foreign affairs while restricting state actions to largely intrastate activities.

Others claim that states should be able to determine with whom companies within their borders will do business. Moreover, state and local governments should have the right to create laws that reflect their policy preferences with respect to human rights issues. If the state of New York doesn't want to do business with Swiss banks that held gold stolen by the Nazis during the Holocaust against the Jews in World War II (1941–1945), why can't New York create a law to that effect?

Federalism and States' Rights— The Debate Continues

Some conflicts concerning federal-state relations raise a question with important implications for democracy: If a majority of a state's citizens prefer to be (or not to be) governed by a certain policy favored by the national government, should those citizens be allowed to do so? The chapter-opening feature on drug policy raises this question. So do the recent decisions by California and Washington state voters to end affirmative action policies in those states (such policies are designed to remedy past discrimination based on such factors as race, national origin, and gender—see Chapter 5).

In 1996, 55 percent of California voters approved Proposition 209, which called for ending affirmative action policies in state employment, education, and contracting. Immediately after the election, however, a federal judge prevented the measure from being enforced until the issue of its constitutionality was decided—in effect, the court overruled the majority of California voters. A federal appellate court later declared that the law did not violate the Constitution.[24] The United States Supreme Court, without comment, decided not to hear the case, thereby leaving the lower court's ruling in place. Nevertheless, national government officials may support future challenges to the California law that will very likely be launched by civil rights groups.

In 1996, California voters also passed an initiative that in effect denied welfare payments to illegal aliens (60 percent of the voters approved the initiative). Again, a federal judge immediately stopped the state from enforcing the measure. (See the feature *A Question of Ethics: Should States Be Required to Treat All Welfare Recipients Equally?* for another example of a state policy that was overturned by a federal court decision.)

a question of ethics

Should States Be Required to Treat All Welfare Recipients Equally?

As mentioned earlier, in 1996 Congress passed welfare reform legislation that gave the states significant control over how welfare programs would be administered. One of the fears of the lawmakers was that under the new system states with more generous benefits might see an influx of newcomers who wanted to take advantage of those benefits. Another fear was that the states would engage in a "race to the bottom"—continuously cutting welfare benefits in order to keep poor people out of their states. In an attempt to avert these potential problems, the lawmakers added a provision to the 1996 legislation that allowed the states to pay newcomers lower benefits than long-time residents.

California and fourteen other states opted to do just that. During their first year in California, newcomers to the state received only as much as they would have received in their former states. For example, if a family of four from Mississippi moved to California, then for the first year on welfare in California it would receive $144 a month—the amount it would

have received in Mississippi. This is far less than the $673 a month allowed under the California program for families of four.

California's policy—and similar policies in other states—clearly raises questions of fairness. Should states be allowed to discriminate against newcomers in this fashion? According to the United States Supreme Court, the answer to this question is a firm "No." In a case challenging the constitutionality of California's policy, the Court held that the policy violated the Fourteenth Amendment. That amendment states, among other things, that "[a]ll persons born or naturalized in the United States . . . are citizens of the United States and of the State wherein they reside. No State shall make or enforce any law which shall abridge the privileges or immunities of citizens of the United States."

The state of California argued that by giving newcomers fewer benefits than residents, the state was able to save nearly $11 million. The policy also prevented the state from becoming a magnet to poor people in other states. More-

over, the 1996 welfare reform legislation specifically authorized California's actions. Attorneys in the U.S. Department of Justice also filed a "friend of the court" brief on California's behalf.

No matter, said the Supreme Court. "Citizens of the United States, whether rich or poor, have the right to choose to be citizens 'of the State wherein they reside.' The States, however, do not have any right to select their citizens." In the Court's eyes, California's interest in saving money provided no justification for discriminating among equally eligible citizens, and Congress had no right to allow the states to violate the Fourteenth Amendment.[25]

For Critical Analysis

If the decision were yours to make, how would you decide this issue?

Supposedly, a federal form of government promotes democracy because it brings government closer to the people, provides citizens with access to government at different levels, and so on. Yet Americans are currently at odds over whether federalism—particularly when the national government has the upper hand—truly promotes democracy. As you have seen, the question of whether the states should have the right to determine what policies will govern their citizens is not new in the American political landscape. Clearly, the struggle for supremacy continues.

key terms

block grant 69
categorical grant 69
commerce clause 63
competitive federalism 71
concurrent majority 64
concurrent powers 61
confederal system 57
cooperative federalism 64
devolution 55
division of powers 59
dual federalism 64
expressed powers 59
federal mandate 68

fiscal federalism 69
implied powers 59
inherent powers 59
intergovernmental lobby 69
necessary and proper clause 59
New Deal 64
new federalism 65
police powers 60
preemption 67
secession 64
supremacy clause 62
unitary system 56

chapter summary

1. The United States has a federal form of government, in which governmental powers are shared by the national government and the states. Alternatives to federalism include a unitary system and a confederal system.

2. Federalism has been viewed as well suited to the United States for the following reasons: (1) a federal form of government retained state traditions and local power while establishing a strong national government, thus effecting a compromise necessary for the Constitution's adoption; (2) federalism is a workable form of government in a country the size of the United States; (3) federalism allows state and local governments to experiment with innovative policies on a relatively small scale; and (4) federalism accommodates the political and cultural differences of different regional groups.

3. Federalism also has some drawbacks, including the following: (1) vested interests can control local governments at the expense of the welfare of the citizens; (2) the national government may expand its power at the expense of the states; (3) state interests may block progress and impede national plans; and (4) federalism leads to a lack of uniformity among state laws and to difficulty in coordinating government policies at the national, state, and local levels.

4. The powers delegated by the Constitution to the national government include expressed powers, such as the power to coin money and to regulate interstate commerce; implied powers, or powers that are "necessary and proper" to the carrying out

of the expressed powers; and inherent powers, which are necessary for any nation to survive and be a member of the community of nations.

5. All powers not delegated to the national government are "reserved" to the states, or to the people. State powers include police powers, which enable the states to enact whatever laws are necessary to protect the health, safety, morals, and welfare of their citizens. The Constitution prohibits both the national government and the states from exercising certain powers. Concurrent powers are powers, such as the power to tax, that can be exercised by both state governments and the national government. The supremacy clause provides that national laws are supreme—they take priority over any conflicting state laws.

6. Two Supreme Court cases that increased the powers of the national government are *McCulloch v. Maryland* (1819), in which the Court enhanced the implied powers of the national government and upheld the doctrine of national supremacy; and *Gibbons v. Ogden* (1824), in which the Court's broad interpretation of the commerce clause extended the regulatory powers of the national government. The power struggle between the states and the national government ultimately resulted in the secession of the southern states, but the effect of the South's desire for increased states' rights and the subsequent Civil War was an increase in the power of the national government.

7. Federalism has evolved through several stages since the Civil War. Under the doctrine of dual federalism, which prevailed until the 1930s, the states and

the national government were viewed as more or less equals, with each level of government having separate and distinct functions and responsibilities. During the Great Depression in the 1930s, dual federalism gave way to cooperative federalism, which involves cooperation by all branches of government. The new federalism, which involves returning to the states some of the powers assumed by the national government, dates to the Nixon administration during the 1970s and has continued, in varying degrees, to the present.

8. For much of the twentieth century, the Supreme Court by and large held that the national government had not overreached the powers given to it by the commerce clause and the supremacy clause of the Constitution. In the 1990s, however, a more conservative Supreme Court showed a willingness to support the new federalism by holding certain national government actions unconstitutional and emphasizing state sovereignty.

9. To help the states pay for the costs associated with implementing policies mandated by the national government, the national government awards grants to the states. Through the awarding of grants, the federal government can also influence activities that constitutionally are regulated by the states under their reserved powers.

10. A controversial issue today concerns federal preemption and particularly the use of unfunded federal mandates. Opponents of federal preemption argue that policy should be implemented by the level of government that decides that policy. Additionally, if the national government wants a particular policy result, it should pay the costs, rather than passing the costs on to other levels of government. Others acknowledge that federal mandates are one way to force the states to help pay for the costs of projects and programs that are in the national interest.

11. Federal issues over which Americans are at odds include state and local sanctions against foreign nations for various human rights violations and certain state initiatives passed by voters that are contrary to the policies of the federal government.

for critical analysis

1. The form of government created by the founders was a novel one—they invented the concept of federalism. If today's political leaders faced the task of creating a new constitution, do you think they would be as creative and farsighted as the founders were?

2. In your opinion, should the federal government be prohibited from passing laws that impose unfunded federal mandates on the states? Why or why not?

3. The French-speaking residents of Quebec have for years debated the question of whether they should withdraw from the Canadian union, in which English speakers predominate. Do you see a similar situation in the United States with the Latino population of the Southwest? Could Latinos become a political subculture with enough clout to cause fundamental changes in the relationship between the southwestern states and the national government?

4. Educational reform is of great importance to Americans. Yet some state legislators do not see the necessity of reforming the educational system. If a state fails to initiate effective educational reform, should the federal government be allowed to do so? Why or why not?

5. In recent years the federal government has been active in trying to clean up the environment. Why not leave it to the states? Isn't this an area that would be best left to the people closest to it—those at the state or local level?

6. One of the areas in which Americans are affected by federal law concerns traffic safety. Describe some of the ways in which the federal government could pressure state governments to pass laws that might be unpopular among state residents.

7. What are some important areas in which federal legislation affects the daily lives of Americans? Would we be better off if state governments regulated these areas?

suggested readings

BAUM, Dan. *Smoke and Mirrors: The War on Drugs and the Politics of Failure.* Boston: Little, Brown, 1996. In this attack on the national government's drug policy, Baum concludes that despite the government's massive (and costly) efforts, the use of illegal drugs continues to rise. Baum shows how the war on drugs began as a political campaign strategy and evolved into a multibillion-dollar fiasco. One of Baum's major concerns is with the civil liberties that have been sacrificed in the process.

BOK, Derek. *The State of the Nation.* Cambridge, Mass.: Harvard University Press, 1996. This book offers a counterargument to those who believe that downsizing the national government is essential to achieving America's goals. Bok agrees with Ronald Reagan that government is the problem, but he points out that government is also the most important part of the solution.

DONAHUE, John D. *Disunited States: What's at Stake as Washington Fades and the States Take the Lead.* Glenview, Ill.: Basic Books, 1997. The author candidly appraises the merits of devolution from a practical point of view. He argues that reality, not ideology, should shape policy.

LIGHT, Paul C. *The True Size of Government.* Washington, D.C.: The Brookings Institution, 1999. In this book, the author looks at the political incentives that make the idea of a small government so attractive and examines the tools used by bureaucrats to keep the official count of government employees low. In fact, claims Light, the real number is nearly nine times higher.

politics
on the web

There are numerous online resources that you can access to learn more about issues relating to federalism. Here are some sites that can serve as good points of departure for your search.

If you want to read *The Federalist Papers,* they are online at

http://www.mcs.net/~knautzr/fed/fedpaper.html

The Electronic Policy Network offers "timely information and leading ideas about federal policy and politics." It also has links to dozens of sites providing materials on federalism and public policy. Go to

http://epn.org

You can find a summary of some milestones in the growth of national power in the United States at

http://www.contrib.andrew.cmu.edu./

~heywood/literary/Federalism.In.The.US.html

The Brookings Institution, the nation's oldest think tank, is a good source for information on emerging policy challenges, including those relating to federal-state issues, and practical recommendations for dealing with those challenges. To access the institution's home page, go to

http://www.brook.edu

If you are interested in a more libertarian perspective on issues such as federalism, the Cato Institute has a Web page at

http://www.cato.org

using web resources

In our federal system, the relationship between the states and the national government is a dynamic, evolving story—one that has important effects on our daily lives. For an informative look at the history of federalism in the United States, go to

http://www.min.net/~kala/fed/history.htm

Once at the site, do the following:

1. Scroll down to the box labeled "1900s" and describe the "stream of commerce" doctrine.

2. Click on the link to "child labor laws." What do the photos at this Web site add to the discussion? Do they help you understand the issue of child labor and its relationship to federalism?

3. Return to the main page and scroll down to the "New Federalism" section. What are three examples of how the new federalism has been implemented since the 1970s?

notes

1. As cited in Harvey A. Silverglate, "States, Feds and Doctors Tangle in Drug War," *The National Law Journal*, April 14, 1997, p. A21.

2. According to another definition of a federal system, however, only one-fourth of the world's population lives under a federal form of government, with another one-third living in countries that have some element of federalism. See Daniel J. Elazar, "Opening a Third Century of American Federalism: Issues and Prospects," *Annals of the American Academy of Political and Social Sciences*, Vol. 509 (May 1990), p. 14.

3. Text of an address by the president to the National Conference of State Legislatures, Atlanta, Georgia (Washington, D.C.: The White House, Office of the Press Secretary, July 30, 1981).

4. An excellent illustration of this principle was President Dwight Eisenhower's disciplining of Arkansas governor Orval Faubus when he refused to allow a Little Rock high school to be desegregated in 1957. Eisenhower federalized the National Guard to enforce the court-ordered desegregation of the school.

5. 4 Wheaton 316 (1819).

6. 9 Wheaton 1 (1824).

7. *Hammer v. Dagenhart*, 247 U.S. 251 (1918). This decision was overruled in *United States v. Darby*, 312 U.S. 100 (1941).

8. *Wickard v. Filburn*, 317 U.S. 111 (1942).

9. *McLain v. Real Estate Board of New Orleans, Inc.*, 444 U.S. 232 (1980).

10. David G. Savage, "Rehnquist Urges Shorter List of Federal Crimes," *The Los Angeles Times*, January 1, 1999, p. A25.

11. *Heart of Atlanta Motel v. United States*, 379 U.S. 241 (1964).

12. 514 U.S. 549 (1995).

13. See *Washington v. Glucksberg*, 521 U.S. 702 (1997).

14. *Printz v. United States*, 521 U.S. 898 (1997).

15. *Alden v. Maine*, 119 S.Ct. 2240 (1999).

16. As cited in Marcia Coyle, "Is Rehnquist Tinkering with Revolution?" *The National Law Journal*, August 16, 1999, p. B7.

17. "Court Rejects 'Motor-Voter' Case, but the Battle Isn't Over," *Congressional Quarterly Weekly Reporter*, January 27, 1996, p. 6.

18. *Voting Rights Coalition v. Wilson*, 60 F.3d 1411 (9th Cir. 1995).

19. *Wilson v. Voting Rights Coalition*, 516 U.S. 1093 (1996).

20. These states include Illinois, Kansas, Michigan, Pennsylvania, and South Carolina.

21. This is an example of a *negative externality*, a cost not borne solely by those persons or entities involved in an activity but by others as well (see Chapter 18).

22. Richard Wolf, "States See Washington Trying to Grab Power," *USA Today*, July 24, 1998, p. 4A.

23. Anthony DePalma, "Western Canada Is Up in Arms over Gun Control," *The New York Times International*, March 28, 1999, p. 3.

24. *Coalition for Economic Equity v. Wilson*, 110 F.3d 1431 (9th Cir. 1997).

25. *Saenz v. Roe*, 119 S.Ct. 1518 (1999).

CIVIL LIBERTIES

Contents

Should the Death Penalty Be Banned?

Today, thirty-eight states and the federal government allow for the death penalty. The number of convicts on "death row" in America's prisons now stands at about three thousand and grows annually. During 1997 and 1998, 142 prisoners were executed. In all, there are more executions today than there have been in the past twenty-five years.

The United States is now the only Western democracy that continues to use the death penalty. All fifteen countries of the European Union have banned its use and are actively promoting its abolition elsewhere. The United Nations Commission on Human Rights recently passed a resolution calling for its restriction and eventual abolition on a global level. In contrast to the emerging international consensus that the death penalty should be banned, in the United States the opposite is occurring: polling data show that support for the death penalty has been rising in the past two decades. A Gallup poll taken in early 1999 showed that 71 percent of Americans approved of capital punishment.

Should the death penalty be banned in this country? Few questions stir such heated debate among Americans as this one. Many Americans think that the death penalty serves a useful function and should be maintained. Others claim that it is a barbaric, out-dated practice that is inconsistent with our society's morals and values.

Keep the Death Penalty—It Serves a Useful Function

Those who think that the death penalty should be maintained usually support their position with three basic arguments. First, the death penalty is useful as a deterrent to crime. It helps to prevent future violence and murder by showing would-be killers what the consequences of such actions may entail. This deterrent function was one of the reasons why executions were once public events in this nation. (The last public execution took place in 1936, in Kentucky.)

Those in favor of the death penalty also point out that it serves society's interests because it ensures that a convicted murderer will never be able to kill again.

Finally, supporters of the death penalty claim that someone who willfully takes another's life deserves to be put to death. The biblical concept of just retribution—"an eye for an eye"—is often cited by supporters of the death penalty: society should inflict on killers the punishment they deserve.

Ban the Death Penalty—It Is Ineffective, Outdated, and Wrong

Opponents of the death penalty argue that capital punishment violates the Eighth Amendment to the Constitution, which prohibits cruel and unusual punishments. They also point out that there is little evidence to support the argument that the death penalty deters crime. For one thing, the kinds of people who kill rarely are in a mental or emotional state to calculate the consequences of their actions. And even if they do make the calculation, what are the chances that a murderer will actually be executed? According to one study, the chances are only about one in one thousand.[1]

Furthermore, despite the use of the death penalty, America has the highest murder rates in the industrialized world, and those rates are highest in the southern states, where the most executions occur. In contrast, in the European countries that have abolished the death penalty, murder rates are far lower than those in the United States.

Clearly, the argument that putting a killer to death prevents that person from murdering again is true. Yet life imprisonment without parole would accomplish the same end. Interestingly, opinion polls indicate that support for capital punishment among Americans drops significantly (from 71 percent to 56 percent in a recent poll) when life imprisonment without parole is given as an alternative.

Opponents of the death penalty also point out that there can never really be a just retribution for the crime of murder. Some crimes are so heinous that death would seem insufficient as a penalty. A person who has tortured and killed many people and caused untold suffering, for example, can only be put to death once.

This group also argues that it is wrong to give any government the dangerous power to put citizens to death. Even with all of our legal guarantees and complex appeals systems, it has been difficult to apply the death penalty fairly and consistently—rich, well-educated murderers rarely get a capital sentence. Finally, and perhaps most significantly, the risk of executing innocent persons is very real. Since 1973, seventy-eight people have been released from death row after evidence of their innocence emerged.

Where Do You Stand?

1. Do you favor the death penalty? Why or why not?

2. The objectives of our criminal justice system include both punishment and rehabilitation. How can the concept of rehabilitation of wrongdoers be reconciled with the death penalty?

On the Web

There are a number of Web sites you can visit to obtain information on the death penalty. One is the U.S. Department of Justice, which compiles information on sentencing, at **http://www.ojp.usdoj.gov/bjs/welcome.html**. For views opposing the death penalty—and some fairly reliable statistics on the topic—go to Amnesty International's Web site at **http://www.amnesty.org**.

Introduction

The debate over the death penalty is but one of many controversies concerning our civil liberties. **Civil liberties** are legal and constitutional rights that protect citizens from government actions. The First Amendment freedoms of religion, speech, press, assembly (to gather together for a common purpose), and petition (to address the government about its policies) constitute important civil liberties. So do the freedoms and guarantees set forth in the remainder of the Bill of Rights. The government cannot infringe on these rights, nor can Congress pass laws abridging them.

The Constitutional Basis for Our Civil Liberties

The founders believed that the constitutions of the individual states contained ample provisions to protect their citizens' rights. Most references to individual civil liberties, therefore, were not included in the Constitution until the Bill of Rights was ratified in 1791. Nonetheless, the original Constitution did include some safeguards to protect citizens against an overly powerful government.

SAFEGUARDS IN THE ORIGINAL CONSTITUTION

Article I, Section 9, of the Constitution provides that the writ of *habeas corpus* (a Latin phrase that roughly means "you should hand over the body") will be available to all citizens except in times of rebellion or national invasion. A **writ of *habeas corpus*** is an order requiring that an official bring a specified prisoner into court and that the judge be shown why the prisoner is being kept in jail. If the court finds that the imprisonment is unlawful, it orders the prisoner to be released. If our country did not have such a constitutional provision, political leaders could jail their opponents without giving them the opportunity to plead their cases before a judge. Without this opportunity, many opponents might conveniently disappear or be left to rot away in prison.

The Constitution also prohibits Congress and the state legislatures from passing *bills of attainder*. A **bill of attainder** is a legislative act that directly punishes a specifically named individual (or a specifically named group or class of individuals) without a trial. For example, your state's legislature cannot pass a law that provides that students at your school who drive over the speed limit will automatically be sentenced to one night in jail.

The Constitution also prohibits Congress from passing *ex post facto* laws. The Latin term *ex post facto* roughly means "after the fact." An ***ex post facto* law** punishes individuals for committing an act that was legal when it was committed but that has since become a crime.

THE BILL OF RIGHTS

The Bill of Rights was ratified by the states and became part of the Constitution on December 15, 1791. Look at the text of the Bill of Rights in Appendix A. As you can see, the first eight amendments grant the people specific rights and liberties. The remaining two amendments reserve certain rights and powers to the people and to the states.

Basically, in a democracy, government policy tends to reflect the view of the majority. A key function of the Bill of Rights, therefore, is to protect the rights of minority groups against the will of the majority. When there is disagreement over how to interpret the Bill of Rights, the courts step in—particularly the Supreme Court, which has become known as the guardian of individual liberties. Ultimately, though, the responsibility for

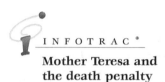

INFOTRAC®

Mother Teresa and the death penalty

CIVIL LIBERTIES ● Individual rights protected by the Constitution against the powers of the government.

WRIT OF *HABEAS CORPUS* ● An order that requires an official to bring a specified prisoner into court and explain to the judge why the person is being held in prison.

BILL OF ATTAINDER ● A legislative act that inflicts punishment on particular persons or groups without granting them the right to a trial.

***EX POST FACTO* LAW** ● A criminal law that punishes individuals for committing an act that was legal when the act was committed but that has since become a crime.

DUE PROCESS CLAUSE ● The constitutional guarantee, set out in the Fifth and Fourteenth Amendments, that the government will not illegally or arbitrarily deprive a person of life, liberty, or property.

DUE PROCESS OF LAW ● The requirement that the government use fair, reasonable, and standard procedures whenever it takes any legal action against an individual; required by the Fifth and Fourteenth Amendments.

ESTABLISHMENT CLAUSE ● The section of the First Amendment that prohibits Congress from passing laws "respecting an establishment of religion." Issues concerning the establishment clause often center on prayer in public schools, the teaching of fundamentalist theories of creation, and government aid to parochial schools.

FREE EXERCISE CLAUSE ● The provision of the First Amendment stating that the government cannot pass laws "prohibiting the free exercise" of religion. Free exercise issues often concern religious practices that conflict with established laws.

protecting minority rights lies with the American people. Each generation has to learn anew how it can uphold its rights by voting, expressing opinions to elected representatives, and bringing cases to the attention of the courts when constitutional rights are threatened.

THE INCORPORATION ISSUE

For many years the protections against government actions in the Bill of Rights were applied only to actions of the federal government, not those of state or local governments. The founders believed that the states, being closer to the people, would be less likely to violate their own citizens' liberties. Moreover, state constitutions, most of which contain bills of rights, protect citizens against state government actions.

The Right to Due Process

In 1868, three years after the end of the Civil War, the Fourteenth Amendment was added. The **due process clause** of this amendment ensures that state governments will protect their citizens' rights. The due process clause reads, in part, as follows:

> No State shall . . . deprive any person of life, liberty, or property, without due process of law.

The right to **due process of law** is simply the right to be treated fairly under the legal system. That system and its officers must follow "rules of fair play" in making decisions, in determining guilt or innocence, and in punishing those who have been found guilty. Generally, due process means that whenever the government takes a person's life, liberty, or property, the government must follow the correct procedures and give the person an equal opportunity to be heard.

Other Liberties Incorporated

The Fourteenth Amendment also states that no state "shall make or enforce any law which shall abridge the privileges or immunities of citizens of the United States." For some time, the Supreme Court considered the "privileges and immunities" referred to in the amendment to be those conferred by state laws or constitutions, not the federal Bill of Rights.

Starting in 1925, however, the Supreme Court gradually began using the due process clause to say that states could not abridge a right that the national government could not abridge. In other words, the Court *incorporated* the rights protected by the national Bill of Rights into the rights protected under the Fourteenth Amendment. As you can see in Table 4–1, the Supreme Court was particularly active during the 1960s in broadening its interpretation of the due process clause to limit state action in areas in which federal action is banned. Today, for all practical purposes, the Bill of Rights guarantees individual rights against infringement by both state and national governments. The main exceptions involve the right to bear arms, the right to refuse to quarter soldiers, and the right to a grand jury hearing.

Freedom of Religion

The First Amendment prohibits Congress from passing laws "respecting an establishment of religion, or prohibiting the free exercise thereof." The first part of this amendment is known as the **establishment clause.** The second part is called the **free exercise clause.**

That the Bill of Rights provides for the protection of religious liberty first is not a surprise—many of the colonists came here to escape religious persecution. Indeed, in 1802, President Thomas Jefferson referred to the

Table 4–1

Incorporating the Bill of Rights into the Fourteenth Amendment

YEAR	ISSUE	AMENDMENT INVOLVED	COURT CASE
1925	Freedom of speech	I	*Gitlow v. New York*, 268 U.S. 652.
1931	Freedom of the press	I	*Near v. Minnesota*, 283 U.S. 697.
1932	Right to a lawyer in capital punishment cases	VI	*Powell v. Alabama*, 287 U.S. 45.
1937	Freedom of assembly and right to petition	I	*De Jonge v. Oregon*, 299 U.S. 353.
1940	Freedom of religion	I	*Cantwell v. Connecticut*, 310 U.S. 296.
1947	Separation of state and church	I	*Everson v. Board of Education*, 330 U.S. 1.
1948	Right to a public trial	VI	*In re Oliver*, 333 U.S. 257.
1949	No unreasonable searches and seizures	IV	*Wolf v. Colorado*, 338 U.S. 25.
1961	Exclusionary rule	IV	*Mapp v. Ohio*, 367 U.S. 643.
1962	No cruel and unusual punishments	VIII	*Robinson v. California*, 370 U.S. 660.
1963	Right to a lawyer in all criminal felony cases	VI	*Gideon v. Wainwright*, 372 U.S. 335.
1964	No compulsory self-incrimination	V	*Malloy v. Hogan*, 378 U.S. 1.
1965	Right to privacy	Various	*Griswold v. Connecticut*, 381 U.S. 479.
1966	Right to an impartial jury	VI	*Parker v. Gladden*, 385 U.S. 363.
1967	Right to a speedy trial	VI	*Klopfer v. North Carolina*, 386 U.S. 213.
1969	No double jeopardy	V	*Benton v. Maryland*, 395 U.S. 784.

First Amendment's establishment clause as "a wall of separation between church and state."[2] This makes the United States different from countries that are ruled by religious governments, such as the Islamic government of Iran (see this chapter's feature, *Comparative Politics: Church and State under Islamic Law*, on the next page). It also makes us different from nations that have in the past strongly discouraged the practice of any religion at all, such as the People's Republic of China.

THE ESTABLISHMENT CLAUSE

The establishment clause forbids the government to establish an official religion. What does this separation of church and state mean in practice? For one thing, religion and government, though constitutionally separated

According to the Constitution as well as numerous Supreme Court decisions, there must be a separation of church and state in this country. Nonetheless, references to God are common in public life. Here you see a printed reference to God on our currency. It is also common for most public gatherings to open with prayer and references to God. Certainly, every recent presidential candidate has felt compelled to refer to God in public speeches.

comparative politics

Church and State under Islamic Law

Today, Muslims constitute over one-half of the population in thirty-five nations, a significant portion of the population in twenty-one other nations, and nearly one-fourth of the global population. The Muslim faith (Islam) is one of the great religions of the world. Increasingly, Americans deal with Muslims in the international marketplace. Yet Americans who would like to understand Islamic law often find it difficult to do so.

This is not really surprising, given the American legal tradition in which church and state are separate entities. Indeed, many Americans regard the idea of a state-sponsored religion as somehow inherently evil. Islamic law, in contrast, does not provide for the separation of church and state—law and religion are one and the same concept. The Islamic religion controls Islamic law and regulates all public and private matters. The governments of Islamic nations, such as Iran and Iraq, are to a large extent "theocracies" that govern in accordance with religious principles. This lack of any separation between church and state is perhaps the most difficult aspect of Islamic law for Americans to grasp.

For Critical Analysis

Is the union of religion and law incompatible with a democratic form of government?

in the United States, have never been enemies or strangers. The establishment clause does not prohibit government from supporting religion *in general;* it remains a part of public life. Most government officials take an oath of office in the name of God, and our coins and paper currency carry the motto "In God We Trust." Clergy of different religions serve with each branch of the armed forces. The Pledge of Allegiance contains a reference to God. Public meetings and even sessions of Congress open with prayers.

The "wall of separation" that Thomas Jefferson referred to, however, does exist and has been upheld by the Supreme Court on many occasions. An important ruling by the Supreme Court on the establishment clause came in 1947 in *Everson v. Board of Education.*[3] The case involved a New Jersey law that allowed the state to pay for bus transportation of students who attended parochial schools (schools run by churches or other religious groups). The Court stated as follows: "No tax in any amount, large or small, can be levied to support any religious activities or institutions." The Court upheld the New Jersey law, however, because it did not aid the church *directly* but provided for the safety and benefit of the students. The ruling both affirmed the importance of separating church and state and set the precedent that not *all* forms of state and federal aid to church-related schools are forbidden under the Constitution.

A full discussion of the various church-state issues that have arisen in American politics would fill volumes. Here we examine three of these issues: prayer in the schools, evolution versus creationism, and government aid to parochial schools.

Prayer in the Schools

On occasion, some schools have promoted a general sense of religion without proclaiming allegiance to any particular church or sect. Whether the states have a right to allow this was the main question presented in 1962 in

Is prayer permissible in school? This thorny issue continues to come to the fore in public debate and court cases. Public schools, according to the majority of Supreme Court decisions, cannot sponsor religious activities. Nonetheless, individuals can pray when and as they choose in any place.

INFOTRAC®

The ten commandments in Alabama

Engel v. Vitale,[4] also known as the "Regents' Prayer case." The State Board of Regents in New York had composed a nondenominational prayer (a prayer not associated with any particular religion) and urged school districts to use it in classrooms at the start of each day. The prayer read as follows:

> Almighty God, we acknowledge our dependence upon Thee, and we beg Thy blessings upon us, our parents, our teachers, and our Country.

Some parents objected to the prayer, contending that it violated the establishment clause. The Supreme Court agreed and ruled that the regents' prayer was unconstitutional. Speaking for the majority, Justice Hugo Black wrote that the First Amendment must at least mean "that in this country it is no part of the business of government to compose official prayers for any group of the American people to recite as a part of a religious program carried on by government."

In 1980, a Kentucky law requiring that the Ten Commandments be posted in all public schools was found unconstitutional in *Stone v. Graham.*[5] In 1985, the Supreme Court ruled that an Alabama law authorizing a daily one-minute period of silence for meditation and voluntary prayer also violated the establishment clause. The Court concluded that because the law specifically endorsed prayer, it appeared to support religion.[6]

In sum, the Supreme Court has ruled that the public schools, which are agencies of government, cannot sponsor religious activities. It has *not,* however, held that individuals cannot pray, when and as they choose, in schools or in any other place. Nor has it held that the Bible cannot be studied as a form of literature in the schools. (Furthermore, as indicated in the feature entitled *Perception versus Reality: The Effect of Supreme Court Decisions* on the following page, even when the Court does rule that a certain state law is unconstitutional, there is no guaranty that the opinion will actually be followed by all Americans.)

Evolution versus Creationism

Certain religious groups, particularly in the southern states, have long opposed the teaching of evolution in the schools. These groups contend that evolutionary theory, a scientific theory with overwhelming support, directly counters their religious belief that human beings did not evolve but were created fully formed, as described in the biblical story of the creation. The Supreme Court, however, has held unconstitutional state laws that forbid the teaching of evolution in the schools.

perception **versus reality**

The Effect of Supreme Court Decisions

Since the beginning of this nation, the Supreme Court has been the ultimate interpreter of our constitutional liberties, including the freedom of religion. Once the Supreme Court speaks on a constitutional issue, that ruling becomes the law on the matter.

The Perception

The general public widely perceives the Supreme Court to be the final arbiter of national laws. Through its power of judicial review (the power to decide whether a law is or is not constitutional—see Chapter 16), the Court can wield enormous powers. It can determine the nation's policy in regard to such matters as religion in the schools, abortion, the right to die, the rights of criminal defendants, and hundreds of other issues that affect our daily lives. Most Americans view the Court as the guardian of our civil rights and liberties. Many Americans also assume that if the Court decides that a particular law or practice is in violation of the

Constitution, the dispute over the matter is laid to rest.

The Reality

In reality, the Supreme Court has no tangible enforcement mechanisms. If a Supreme Court decision is noticeably at odds with public opinion, persons affected by the decision may simply ignore it. Suppose, for example, that a teacher continues to lead her or his students in prayer every day despite the Supreme Court ruling that such a practice violates the establishment clause. What can the courts do in this situation? Unless someone complains about the teacher's actions and initiates a lawsuit, the courts can do nothing. Similarly, what if a state passes a law that directly challenges a Supreme Court decision on the practice regulated by the law? What can the courts do? Again, the answer is nothing—unless the law is challenged in court.

Additionally, just as higher courts can reverse the decisions of lower courts, so can lower courts

act as a check on higher courts. Lower courts can ignore—and often have ignored—Supreme Court decisions. Usually, this is done indirectly. A lower court might conclude, for example, that the precedent set by the Supreme Court does not apply to the exact circumstances in the case before the lower court. Alternatively, the lower court may decide that the Supreme Court's decision was ambiguous with respect to the issue being decided by the lower court. In such cases, the lower court is free to fashion its own interpretation of what the Supreme Court meant by a particular ruling. The fact that the Supreme Court rarely makes broad, clear-cut statements on any issue allows the lower courts to interpret those statements differently.

You Be the Judge

Should the framers of the Constitution have given the Supreme Court enforcement powers?

For example, in *Epperson v. Arkansas,*[7] a case decided in 1968, the Supreme Court held that an Arkansas law prohibiting the teaching of evolution violated the establishment clause because it imposed religious beliefs on students. In 1987, the Supreme Court also held unconstitutional a Louisiana law requiring the biblical story of the creation to be taught along with evolution. The Court deemed the law unconstitutional, in part because it had as its primary purpose the promotion of a particular religious belief.[8] State and local groups in the so-called Bible Belt, however, continue their efforts against the teaching of evolution. Recently, for example, Alabama approved a disclaimer to be inserted in biology textbooks, indicating that evolution is "a controversial theory some scientists present as a scientific explanation for the origin of living things." A school district in Georgia adopted a policy that creationism could be taught along with evolution. The state board of education in Kansas garnered national media attention when it decided, in the fall of 1999, that statewide tests can no longer even mention the subject of evolution. No doubt, these laws and policies will eventually be challenged on constitutional grounds.

Aid to Parochial Schools

Under certain circumstances parochial schools can constitutionally obtain state aid. Many states have provided aid to church-related schools in the form of textbooks, transportation, and equipment. Other forms of aid,

LEMON TEST ● A three-part test enunciated by the Supreme Court in the 1971 case of *Lemon v. Kurtzman* to determine whether government aid to parochial schools is constitutional. To be constitutional, the aid must (1) be for a clearly secular purpose; (2) in its primary effect, neither advance nor inhibit religion; and (3) avoid an "excessive government entanglement with religion." The *Lemon* test has also been used in other types of cases involving the establishment clause.

such as funding teachers' salaries and paying for field trips, have been found unconstitutional.

Those who favor government financial aid to parochial schools argue that 12 percent of all American students attend private schools, 85 percent of which have some religious affiliation. These students would otherwise be attending public schools at public expense. Advocates of aid to parochial schools argue that parents should be relieved of some of the double financial burden of paying to send their children to private schools while also paying local property taxes to support public schools. Opponents argue that parents who send children to parochial schools know full well that such schools are not supported with tax dollars. The parents should accept the consequences and not expect society to pay for their choice.

Since 1971, the Supreme Court has held that, to be constitutional, a state's school aid must meet three requirements: (1) the purpose of the financial aid must be clearly secular (not religious); (2) its primary effect must neither advance nor inhibit religion; and (3) it must avoid an "excessive government entanglement with religion." The Court first used the test in *Lemon v. Kurtzman,*[9] and hence it is often referred to as the **Lemon test.** In the *Lemon* case, the Court denied public aid to private and parochial schools for the salaries of teachers of secular courses and for textbooks and instructional materials in certain secular subjects. The Court held that the establishment clause is designed to prevent three main evils: "sponsorship, financial support, and active involvement of the sovereign [the government] in religious activity."

The Supreme Court's Views on Excessive Entanglement

In a case decided in 1985, *Aguilar v. Felton,*[10] the Supreme Court addressed another issue: May federally funded special educational services for disadvantaged students be provided for parochial school students? More specifically, the issue was whether such services could be delivered to students on parochial school premises. The Court held that they could not, because that would constitute an excessive entanglement of church and state. After that decision, special educational services for disadvantaged, parochial school students had to be provided in public school classrooms, in mobile units parked near religious school property, or by computer.

In 1997, in *Agostini v. Felton,*[11] a case brought by a New York City school board and parents, the Supreme Court was asked to reconsider its decision in *Aguilar.* The school board and parents claimed that it would be much less costly to provide the special educational services on the religious schools' premises. The Court, declaring that *Aguilar* was "no longer good law," held that providing federally funded special educational services for disadvantaged students on the premises of sectarian schools does not violate the establishment clause.

THE FREE EXERCISE CLAUSE

As mentioned, the second part of the First Amendment consists of the free exercise clause, which forbids the passage of laws "prohibiting the free exercise of religion." This clause protects individuals' right to worship or believe as they wish without government interference. No law or act of government may violate this constitutional right.

Belief and Practice Are Distinct

The free exercise clause does not necessarily mean that individuals can act in any way they want on the basis of their religious beliefs. There is an important distinction between belief and practice. The Supreme Court has ruled consistently that the right to hold any *belief* is absolute. The government has no authority to compel you to accept or reject any particular religious belief. The right to *practice* one's beliefs, however, may have some limitations. As the Court itself once asked, "Suppose one believed that human sacrifice were a necessary part of religious worship?"

SYMBOLIC SPEECH ● The expression of beliefs, opinions, or ideas through forms other than speech or print; speech involving actions and other nonverbal expressions.

The Supreme Court first dealt with the issue of belief versus practice in 1878 in *Reynolds v. United States*.[12] Reynolds was a Mormon who had two wives. Polygamy, or the practice of having more than one spouse at a time, was encouraged by the practice and teachings of this religion. Polygamy was also prohibited by federal law. Reynolds was convicted and appealed the case, arguing that the law violated his constitutional right to freely exercise his religious beliefs. The Court did not agree. It said that to allow Reynolds to practice polygamy would be to make the doctrines of religious beliefs superior to the law.

Religious Practices and the Workplace

The free exercise of religion in the workplace was bolstered by Title VII of the Civil Rights Act of 1964, which requires employers to accommodate their employees' religious practices unless such accommodation causes an employer to suffer an "undue hardship." Thus, if an employee claims that his or her religious beliefs prevent him or her from working on a particular day of the week, such as Saturday or Sunday, the employer must attempt to accommodate the employee's needs. (For an extreme example of the application of this law, see this chapter's feature, *Politics on the Far Side: Accommodating Snake Bites*.)

Freedom of Expression

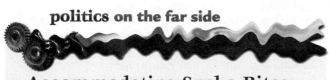

politics on the far side

Accommodating Snake Bites

Title VII of the 1964 Civil Rights Act requires employers to accommodate the religious needs of their workers. But to what extent must employers do so? There are no hard-and-fast answers to this question. For example, in one case a worker became ill after being bitten by a snake during a religious snake-handling service. The employee requested a leave of absence, but he refused to obtain the required physician's note because his religious beliefs precluded medical treatment. The employer granted the worker a leave of absence after the first snake bite but fired the worker after he took subsequent unexcused leaves for other snake bites.

The employer should have known better, at least according to the federal district court that heard the case brought by the employee for religious discrimination. The court held that the employer failed to accommodate the employee's religious beliefs and awarded the employee $20,500 in damages.[13]

For Critical Analysis: *Some critics of the court's decision in this case claimed that the court went overboard with respect to the religious rights of employees. Do you agree? Why or why not?*

No one in this country seems to have a problem protecting the free speech of those with whom they agree. The real challenge is protecting unpopular ideas. The protection needed is, in Justice Oliver Wendell Holmes's words, "not free thought for those who agree with us but freedom for the thought that we hate." The First Amendment is designed to protect the freedom to express *all* ideas, including those that may be unpopular or different.

The First Amendment has been interpreted to protect more than merely spoken words; it also protects **symbolic speech**—speech involving actions and other nonverbal expressions. Picketing in a labor dispute and wearing a black armband in protest of a government policy are fairly common examples. Even burning the American flag as a gesture of protest has been held to be protected by the First Amendment.

THE RIGHT TO FREE SPEECH IS NOT ABSOLUTE

Although Americans have the right to free speech, not *all* speech is protected under the First Amendment. Our constitutional rights and liberties are not absolute. Rather, they are what the Supreme Court—the ultimate interpreter of the Constitution—says they are. Although the Court has zealously safeguarded the right to free speech, at times it has imposed limits on speech in the interests of protecting other rights of Americans. These rights include security against harm to one's person or reputation, the need for public order, and the need to preserve the government.

Generally, throughout our history, the Supreme Court has attempted to balance our rights to free speech against these other needs of society. As Justice Holmes once said, even "the most stringent protection of free speech would not protect a man in falsely shouting fire

How far can we go in exercising our right to free speech? The First Amendment does not put any limits on our right to free speech. The courts have, though, in the interests of protecting other rights. Nonetheless, speech in the United States probably has more protection than anywhere else in the world.

in a theatre and causing a panic."[14] We look next at some of the ways that the Court has limited the right to free speech.

EARLY RESTRICTIONS ON EXPRESSION

At times in our nation's history, various individuals have not supported our form of democratic government. Our government, however, has drawn a fine line between legitimate criticism and the expression of ideas that may seriously harm society. Clearly, the government may pass laws against violence, espionage, sabotage, and treason. **Espionage** is the practice of spying for a foreign power. **Sabotage** involves actions normally intended to hinder or damage the nation's defense or war effort. **Treason** is specifically defined in the Constitution as levying war against the United States or adhering (remaining loyal) to its enemies (Article III, Section 3). But what about **seditious speech,** which urges resistance to lawful authority or advocates overthrowing the government?

As early as 1798, Congress took steps to curb seditious speech when it passed the Alien and Sedition Acts, which made it a crime to utter "any false, scandalous, and malicious" criticism against the government. The acts were considered unconstitutional by many but were never tested in the courts. Several dozen individuals were prosecuted under the acts, and some were actually convicted. In 1801, President Thomas Jefferson pardoned those sentenced under the acts, and Congress soon repealed them. During World War I, Congress passed the Espionage Act of 1917 and the Sedition Act of 1918. The 1917 act prohibited attempts to interfere with the operation of the military forces, the prosecution of the war, or the process of recruitment. The 1918 act made it a crime to "willfully utter, print, write, or publish any disloyal, profane, scurrilous [insulting], or abusive language" about the government. More than two thousand persons were tried and convicted under this act, which was repealed at the end of World War I.

In 1940, Congress passed the Smith Act, which forbade people from advocating the violent overthrow of the U.S. government. The Supreme Court first upheld the constitutionality of the Smith Act in *Dennis v. United States,*[15] which involved eleven top leaders of the Communist Party who had

ESPIONAGE ● The practice of spying, on behalf of a foreign power, to obtain information about government plans and activities.

SABOTAGE ● A destructive act intended to hinder a nation's defense efforts.

TREASON ● As enunciated in Article III, Section 3, of the Constitution, the act of levying war against the United States or adhering (remaining loyal) to its enemies.

SEDITIOUS SPEECH ● Speech that urges resistance to lawful authority or that advocates the overthrowing of a government.

COMMERCIAL SPEECH ● Advertising statements that describe products. Commercial speech receives less protection under the First Amendment than ordinary speech.

LIBEL ● A published report of a falsehood that tends to injure a person's reputation or character.

SLANDER ● The public utterance (speaking) of a statement that holds a person up for contempt, ridicule, or hatred.

"FIGHTING WORDS" ● Words that, when uttered by a public speaker, are so inflammatory that they could provoke the average listener to violence.

been convicted of violating the act. The Court found that their activities went beyond the permissible peaceful advocacy of change. According to the Smith Act, these activities threatened society's right to a certain national security. Subsequently, however, the Court modified its position. Since the 1960s, the Court has defined seditious speech to mean only the advocacy of immediate and concrete acts of violence against the government.[16]

LIMITED PROTECTION FOR COMMERCIAL SPEECH

Advertising, or **commercial speech,** is also protected by the First Amendment, but not as fully as regular speech. Generally, the Supreme Court has considered a restriction on commercial speech to be valid as long as the restriction "(1) seeks to implement a substantial government interest, (2) directly advances that interest, and (3) goes no further than necessary to accomplish its objective." Problems arise, though, when restrictions on commercial advertising achieve one substantial government interest yet are contrary to the interest in protecting free speech and the right of consumers to be informed. In such cases, the courts have to decide which interest takes priority.

Liquor advertising is a good example of this kind of conflict. For example, in one case, Rhode Island argued that its law banning the advertising of liquor prices served the state's goal of discouraging liquor consumption (because the ban discouraged bargain hunting and thus kept liquor prices high). The Supreme Court, however, held that the ban was an unconstitutional restraint on commercial speech. The Court stated that the First Amendment "directs us to be especially skeptical of regulations that seek to keep people in the dark for what the government perceives to be their own good."[17] Similarly, recent restrictions on tobacco advertising are the result of a policy choice that free speech can be restrained in the interests of protecting the health of society, particularly the health of young Americans.

UNPROTECTED SPEECH

Certain types of speech receive no protection under the First Amendment. These types of speech include libel and slander, "fighting words," and obscenity.

Libel and Slander

No person has the right to libel or slander another. **Libel** is a published report of a falsehood that tends to injure a person's reputation or character. **Slander** is the public utterance (speaking) of a statement that holds a person up for contempt, ridicule, or hatred. To prove libel and slander, however, certain criteria must be met. The statements made must be untrue, must stem from an intent to do harm, and must result in actual harm.

The Supreme Court has ruled that public figures (public officials and others in the public limelight) cannot collect damages for remarks made against them unless they can prove the remarks were made with "reckless" disregard for accuracy. Generally, it is felt that because public figures have greater access to the media than ordinary persons do, they are in a better position to defend themselves against libelous or slanderous statements.

"Fighting Words"

Another form of speech that is not protected by the First Amendment is what the Supreme Court has called **"fighting words."** This is speech that is so inflammatory that it will provoke the average listener to violence. The Court has ruled that fighting words must go beyond merely insulting or controversial language. The words must be a clear invitation to immediate violence or breach of the peace.

OBSCENITY ● Indecency or offensiveness in speech or expression, behavior, or appearance; what specific expressions or acts constitute obscenity normally are determined by community standards.

Obscenity

Obscene speech is another form of speech that is not protected under the First Amendment. Although the dictionary defines **obscenity** as that which is offensive and indecent, the courts have had difficulty defining the term with any precision. Supreme Court Justice Potter Stewart's famous statement, "I know it when I see it," certainly gave little guidance on the issue.

One problem in defining obscenity is that what is obscene to one person is not necessarily obscene to another; what one reader considers indecent, another reader might see as "colorful." Another problem is that society's views on obscenity change over time. Major literary works of such great writers as D. H. Lawrence, Mark Twain, and James Joyce were once considered obscene in most of the United States.

After many unsuccessful attempts to define obscenity, in 1973 the Supreme Court came up with a three-part test in *Miller v. California*.[18] The Court decided that a book, film, or other piece of material is legally obscene if it meets the following criteria:

1. The average person applying contemporary [present-day] standards finds that the work taken as a whole appeals to the prurient interest—that is, tends to excite unwholesome sexual desire.
2. The work depicts or describes, in a patently [obviously] offensive way, a form of sexual conduct specifically prohibited by an antiobscenity law.
3. The work taken as a whole lacks serious literary, artistic, political, or scientific value.

The very fact that the Supreme Court has had to set up such a complicated test shows how difficult defining obscenity is. The Court went on to state that, in effect, local communities should be allowed to set their own standards for what is obscene. What is obscene to many people in one area of the country might be perfectly acceptable to those in another area.

Obscenity in Cyberspace

One of the most controversial issues in regard to free speech in cyberspace concerns obscene and pornographic materials. Such materials can be easily accessed by anyone of any age anywhere in the world via numerous World Wide Web sites. Many strongly believe that the government should step in to prevent obscenity on the Internet. Others believe, just as strongly, that speech on the Internet should not be regulated. The issue came to a head in

Reprinted with special permission of King Features Syndicate.

politics on the far side

Online Obscenity and the Starr Report

In September 1998, the House of Representatives made an unprecedented decision: to publish online an independent counsel's report of an investigation of presidential conduct. The independent counsel was Kenneth Starr; the report contained numerous excerpts from testimony given during his investigation of the relationship between Monica Lewinsky and President Clinton.

Many disapproved of the decision to post the report on the Web. For one thing, the moment the report went online, it was available to every Internet user, holding the president up for ridicule throughout the world. For another, many found the sexually explicit descriptions of contacts between Clinton and Lewinsky to be offensive and obscene. Additionally, sites carrying the report often had links to pornographic sites. Even those who accessed the front page of the online *New York Times* on the day the report was published encountered nude photos of women, which had been placed there by hackers invading the site. There is some irony in the fact that Congress, which enacted the Communications Decency Act (CDA) of 1996 and the so-called CDA II of 1998, was responsible for publishing a report online that, in the opinion of at least one commentator, would have violated those acts.

For Critical Analysis: What did the House of Representatives hope to accomplish by publishing the Starr report online?

1996, when Congress passed the Communications Decency Act (CDA). The law made it a crime to transmit "indecent" or "patently offensive" speech or images to minors (those under the age of eighteen) or to make such speech or images available online to minors. Violators of the act could be fined up to $250,000 or imprisoned for up to two years.

Various groups supporting free speech rights immediately challenged the law as unconstitutional because of the restraints it placed on free speech. In 1997, the issue came before the Supreme Court, which held that the law's sections on indecent speech were unconstitutional. According to the Court, those sections of the CDA were too broad in their scope and significantly restrained the constitutionally protected free speech of adults.[19]

Congress made a further attempt to regulate Internet speech in 1998. Included in the federal budget bill passed in that year was the Child Online Protection Act, which became known as CDA II. The act imposed criminal penalties on those who distribute material that is "harmful to minors" without using some kind of age-verification system to separate adult and minor Web users. (Despite its concerns over online obscenity, Congress itself published materials on the Web that many Americans thought were offensive and obscene—see the *Politics on the Far Side: Online Obscenity and the Starr Report* for details.) Like the CDA of 1996, CDA II was immediately challenged in court by civil rights groups. In early 1999, a federal court in Philadelphia issued a preliminary injunction blocking the enforcement of the act until a full trial on the issue could be held.[20]

Notwithstanding these decisions, the debate continues, with strong arguments supporting both sides. (Some of the major arguments are set forth in the feature, *The American Political Spectrum: To Regulate or Not to Regulate the Internet—That Is the Question.*)

Freedom of the Press

The framers of the Constitution believed that the press should be free to publish a wide range of opinions and information, and generally the free speech rights just discussed also apply to the press. The courts have placed certain restrictions on the freedom of the press, however. Over the years, the Supreme Court has developed various guidelines and doctrines to use in deciding whether the freedom of speech and the press can be restrained.

CLEAR AND PRESENT DANGER

One guideline the Court has used resulted from a case in 1919, *Schenck v. United States*.[21] Charles T. Schenck was convicted of printing and distributing leaflets urging men to resist the draft during World War I. The government claimed that his actions violated the Espionage Act of 1917, which made it a crime to encourage disloyalty to the government or resistance to the draft. The Supreme Court upheld both the law and the convictions. Justice Holmes, speaking for the Court, stated as follows:

> The question in every case is whether the words used are used in such circumstances and are of such a nature as to create a *clear and present danger* that they will bring about the substantive evils that Congress has a right to prevent. It is a question of proximity [closeness] and degree. [Emphasis added.]

the american political spectrum

To Regulate or Not to Regulate the Internet—That Is the Question

Speech has always been subject to limitations, more so in the broadcast media than in the printed media. Now the telecommunications revolution that has given us a worldwide, interconnected speech vehicle—the Internet—has raised a new question: How much should government intervene to control speech transmitted via the Internet?

The Traditional American Liberal Argues for an Open Internet

Traditional American liberals—and liberal organizations such as the American Civil Liberties Union (ACLU)—routinely argue in favor of leaving the Internet alone. They point out that many of the materials on the Internet are useful and worthy. Additionally, any attempt to regulate the Internet will unconstitutionally restrain free speech for adults, who will have reduced access to such materials. According to liberals, government regulation isn't necessary because parents them-

selves can protect their children by using "filtering" software to block access to pornography on the Internet.

To be sure, the Internet has been used and will continue to be used to transmit pornography as well as hateful politics. Liberals point out, though, that most of these materials on the Internet are already available in other media, such as magazines, pamphlets, and books.

Finally, opponents of government controls point out that such controls wouldn't work anyway. Even if the U.S. government did impose restrictions on Internet speech, those restrictions wouldn't apply to people in other countries. Thus, a single national government has no means of controlling what is or is not posted on Internet bulletin boards. Furthermore, the definition of obscenity is based on community standards, yet what community standards can apply to the Internet, which has no geographical boundaries?

The Traditional American Conservative Supports Controls on the Internet

American social conservatives support government regulation of speech on the Internet, particularly because of children's potential exposure to pornography. Enough Is Enough, a typical group supporting government controls on the Internet, has shown that any nine-year-old child can access, without any problem, Web sites that show bestiality and the like. Other groups that support government censorship of the Internet include the Christian Coalition, the Family Research Council, and the National Coalition for the Protection of Children and Families.

Generally, proponents of controls on Internet speech want the government to ensure that children will not be able to access the hundreds of thousands of pornographic images available online. Perhaps more important, supporters of cyberspace controls argue that the federal government has routinely been able to control pornographic materials on the radio and television. Therefore, why shouldn't it be able to regulate similar speech on the Internet?

We should note here that not all of those who support government regulation of the Internet are traditional conservatives. Indeed, the main sponsor of the Communications Decency Act of 1996 was Senator Jim Exon, a Democrat from Nebraska.

For Critical Analysis

Should priority be given to the constitutional right of adults to exercise free speech, or should adults be compelled to curb their expression so that Web-surfing children will not be exposed to patently offensive content?

Using a popular Web browser and one simple search, a person can find scores of Internet sites dealing with pornographic materials.

Top:Business and Economy:Companies:Sex:Virtual Clubs:Online Picture Galleries

Search Options

⦿ Search all of Yahoo ○ Search only in **Online Picture Galleries**

- **Amateurs** *(74)*
- **Anal** *(11)*
- **Asian** *(57)*

- **BDSM@**
- **Lesbian, Gay and Bisexual@**
- **Nude Celebrities** *(28)*

- Ashley's World NEW! - featuring original photographs of beautiful amateur teenage girls.
- Daizee's Freaky Flashers NEW! - flashing photos.
- Darlings of the Web NEW! - amateur photos, links and adult site link list including cost and number of pictures for each link.
- Entrance To Heaven NEW!
- Erotic Warehouse NEW!
- Lovebyte NEW!
- NetSmut NEW!
- Sex-Palace NEW!
- Svetlana's Salon NEW!
- Teen Emporium NEW!

- "@"It Porn - instant access to XXX hardcore. Thumbnail images for easy browsing.
- "@"Sex - erotic, hardcore pics of women from all over the world.
- 1 Cheap Thrill - XXX hardcore photos, instant access, chat and free sex mpegs for members.

Thus, according to the *clear and present danger test,* government should be allowed to restrain speech only when that speech clearly presents an immediate threat to public order. It is often hard to say when speech crosses the line between being merely controversial and being a "clear and present danger," but the principle has been used in many cases since *Schenck.*

The clear and present danger principle seemed too permissive to some Supreme Court justices. Several years after the *Schenck* ruling, in the case of *Gitlow v. New York,*[22] the Court held that speech could be permissibly curtailed even if it had only a *tendency* to lead to illegal action. Since the 1920s, however, this guideline, known as the *bad-tendency test,* has generally not been supported by the Supreme Court.

THE PREFERRED-POSITION DOCTRINE

Another guideline, called the *preferred-position doctrine,* states that certain freedoms are so essential to a democracy that they hold a preferred position. According to this doctrine, any law that limits these freedoms should be presumed unconstitutional unless the government can show that the law is absolutely necessary. Thus, freedom of speech should rarely, if ever, be diminished, because printed and spoken words are the prime tools of the democratic process.

PRIOR RESTRAINT

Stopping an activity before it actually happens is known as *prior restraint.* With respect to freedom of the press, prior restraint involves *censorship,* which occurs when an official removes objectionable materials from an item before it is published or broadcast. An example of censorship and prior restraint would be a court's ruling that two paragraphs in an upcoming article in the local newspaper had to be removed before the article could be published. The Supreme Court has generally ruled against prior restraint, arguing that the government cannot curb ideas *before* they are expressed.

A widely publicized case involving prior restraint was *New York Times v. United States,*[23] also called the *Pentagon Papers* case. The *Times* was about to publish the *Pentagon Papers,* an elaborate secret history of the U.S. government's involvement in the Vietnam War (1964–1975), which had been obtained by a former Pentagon official. The government wanted a court order to bar publication of this series, arguing that national security was being threatened and that the documents had been stolen. The *New York Times* argued that the public had the right to know the information contained in the papers and that the press had the right to inform them. The Court rejected the government's plea to bar publication, holding that the government had not proved that printing the documents would in fact endanger national security.

On some occasions, however, the Court has allowed prior restraints. For example, in a 1988 case, *Hazelwood School District v. Kuhlmeier,*[24] a high school principal deleted two pages from the school newspaper just before it was printed. The pages contained stories on the students' experiences with pregnancy and discussed the impact of divorce on students at the school. The Supreme Court, noting that students in school do not have exactly the same rights as adults in other settings, ruled that high school administrators *can* censor school publications. The Court said that school newspapers are part of the school curriculum, not a public forum. Therefore, administrators have the right to censor speech that promotes conduct inconsistent with the "shared values of a civilized social order."

Freedom of Assembly

The First Amendment also protects the right of the people "peaceably to assemble" and communicate their ideas on public issues to government officials, as well as to other individuals. Parades, marches, protests, and

The Constitution guarantees freedom of assembly. Does that mean that any group should be allowed to stage a protest or hold a parade? Many Americans would like to prevent the Ku Klux Klan (KKK) from marching in downtown areas, such as in Austin, Texas, as seen here. Nonetheless, the Supreme Court has upheld the First Amendment rights of such marchers.

other demonstrations are daily events in this country and allow groups to express and publicize their ideas. The Supreme Court often has put this freedom of assembly, or association, on a par with freedom of speech and freedom of the press. In the interests of public order, however, the Court has allowed municipalities to require permits for parades, sound trucks, demonstrations, and the like.

Like unpopular speech, unpopular assemblies or protests often generate controversy. One controversial case arose in 1977, when the American Nazi Party decided to march through the largely Jewish suburb of Skokie, Illinois. The city of Skokie enacted three ordinances designed to prohibit the types of demonstrations that the Nazis planned to undertake. The American Civil Liberties Union (ACLU) sued the city on behalf of the Nazis, defending their right to march (in spite of the ACLU's opposition to the Nazi philosophy). A federal district court agreed with the ACLU and held that the city of Skokie had violated the Nazis' First Amendment guarantees by denying them a permit to march. The appellate court affirmed that decision. The Supreme Court refused to review the case, thus letting the lower court's decision stand.[25] (The California courts have shown less tolerance when it comes to whether gang members should be able to associate freely with one another. See the feature entitled *A Question of Ethics: Should Gang Members Be Deprived of Their Right to Assemble?* on the next page for a discussion of this issue.)

The Right to Privacy

Supreme Court Justice Louis Brandeis stated in 1928 that the right to privacy is "the most comprehensive of rights and the right most valued by civilized men."[26] The majority of the justices on the Supreme Court at that time did not agree. In the 1960s, though, the justices on the Supreme Court began to hold that a right to privacy is implied by other constitutional rights guaranteed in the First, Third, Fourth, Fifth, and Ninth Amendments. For example, consider the words of the Ninth Amendment: "The enumeration in the Constitution, of certain rights, shall not be construed to deny or disparage others retained by the people." In other words, just because the Constitution,

a question of ethics

Should Gang Members Be Deprived of Their Right to Assemble?

In the last decade or so, New York, Chicago, Los Angeles, and other major American cities have seen whole neighborhoods virtually overtaken by street gangs. City governments are beginning to strike back.

Chicago, for example, passed an "antiloitering" ordinance in 1992 that stated, "Whenever a police officer observes a person whom he reasonably believes to be a criminal street gang member loitering in any public place with one or more other persons, he shall order all such persons to disperse and remove themselves from the area. Any person who does not promptly obey such an order is in violation of [the ordinance]." Although antiloitering laws in some cities

have passed constitutional muster, Chicago's law did not. In 1999, the United States Supreme Court held that it was too vague to satisfy due process requirements. Among other things, the ordinance left far too much "lawmaking" power to the police, who were left to decide what actions constitute "loitering."[27]

Los Angeles has tried another approach—obtaining court injunctions prohibiting specified gang members in particular neighborhoods from being "public nuisances." For example, in early 1997 the city of Los Angeles brought a civil suit against Efrain "Woody" Moreno and seventeen other alleged members of the "Eighteenth Street" gang. The city convinced the court to grant an injunction permanently

barring the gang members from being "public nuisances." The injunction barred the gang members from engaging in any conduct that is "a precursor to criminal gang activities," such as using vulgar language, blocking sidewalks, carrying spray paint, or "riding a bicycle in any public place for the purpose of promoting or engaging in narcotics and other unlawful activity." Most significantly, the gang members were barred from appearing in public together.

The gang members claim that such injunctions are unconstitutional because they violate the right of assembly guaranteed by the First Amendment. The American Civil Liberties Union supports this position as well. The California Supreme Court, however, has a different perspective on the issue. Upholding a similar injunction against gang members in San Jose, California, the state's high court declared that society's rights to peace and quiet and to be free from harm outweighed the gang members' First Amendment associational rights.[28]

For Critical Analysis

Should the First Amendment associational rights of gang members be sacrificed in the interests of keeping others in society safe from harm?

Members of the Crips gang gather in San Fernando Valley, California.

including its amendments, does not specifically mention the right to privacy does not mean that this right is denied to the people.

As discussed in the opening *America at Odds* feature in Chapter 2, the courts have acknowledged a constitutional right to privacy. The nature and scope of this right are not always clear, however. For example, Americans continue to debate whether the right to privacy includes the right of terminally ill persons to commit physician-assisted suicide, an issue we explore later in this chapter. The extent to which our right to privacy applies in cyberspace is another disputed issue (see Chapter 12 for a fuller discussion of this topic).

An emotionally charged issue is whether the right to privacy means that women can choose to have abortions. In 1973, in the landmark case of *Roe v. Wade*,[29] the Supreme Court held that it did. According to the Court, the "right of privacy . . . is broad enough to encompass a woman's decision whether or not to terminate her pregnancy." The right is not absolute throughout preg-

The abortion controversy was certainly not put to rest by the *Roe v. Wade* decision in 1973. Americans continue to passionately express their differing views on this subject, as shown in the photo here. Abortion was long practiced as a form of birth control until pressure from the Roman Catholic Church and changing public opinion led to the passage of strict antiabortion laws in the nineteenth century. By the 1970s, though, abortion had been legalized not only in the United States but also in most European countries and in Japan. In recent years, abortion opponents in the United States have resorted to more militant tactics in attempts to disrupt abortion clinics; some have even resorted to bombings and murders.

nancy, however. The Court also said that any state could impose certain regulations to safeguard the health of the mother *after* the first three months of pregnancy and, in the final stages of pregnancy, could act to protect potential life.

Since the *Roe* decision, the Supreme Court has adopted a more conservative approach and has upheld restrictive state laws (requiring counseling, waiting periods, notification of parents, and the like prior to abortions).[30] Some contend that by these decisions, the Court has effectively nullified the *Roe* decision. Indeed, pro-choice forces have recently turned to the state courts to protect abortion rights under state constitutions. Whatever the future of *Roe,* it seems clear that Americans will continue to be at odds over the issue of abortion for some time to come.

The Rights of the Accused

The United States has one of the highest violent crime rates in the world. It is therefore not surprising that many Americans have extremely strong opinions about the rights of persons accused of criminal offenses. Indeed, some Americans complain that criminal defendants have too many rights.

Why do criminal suspects have rights? The answer is that all persons are entitled to the protections afforded by the Bill of Rights. If criminal suspects were deprived of their basic constitutional liberties, all people would suffer the consequences. In fact, these liberties take on added significance in the context of criminal law. After all, in a criminal case, a state official (such as the district attorney, or D.A.) prosecutes the defendant, and the state has immense resources that it can bring to bear against the accused person. By protecting the rights of accused persons, the Constitution helps to prevent the arbitrary use of power on the part of the government.

THE RIGHTS OF CRIMINAL DEFENDANTS

The basic rights, or constitutional safeguards, provided for criminal defendants are set forth in the Bill of Rights. These safeguards include the following:

PROBABLE CAUSE ● Cause for believing that there is a substantial likelihood that a person has committed or is about to commit a crime.

DOUBLE JEOPARDY ● To prosecute a person twice for the same criminal offense; prohibited by the Fifth Amendment in all but a few circumstances.

SELF-INCRIMINATION ● Providing damaging information or testimony against oneself in court.

EXCLUSIONARY RULE ● A criminal procedural rule requiring that any illegally obtained evidence will not be admissible in court. The rule is based on Supreme Court interpretations of the Fourth and Fourteenth Amendments.

***MIRANDA* WARNINGS** ● A series of statements informing criminal suspects, on their arrest, of their constitutional rights, such as the right to remain silent and the right to counsel; required by the Supreme Court's 1966 decision in *Miranda v. Arizona.*

- The Fourth Amendment protection from unreasonable searches and seizures.
- The Fourth Amendment requirement that no warrant for a search or an arrest be issued without **probable cause** (cause for believing that there is a substantial likelihood that a person has committed or is about to commit a crime).
- The Fifth Amendment requirement that no one be deprived of "life, liberty, or property, without due process of law." (As discussed earlier in this chapter, this requirement is also included in the Fourteenth Amendment, which protects persons against actions by state governments.)
- The Fifth Amendment prohibition against **double jeopardy** (being tried twice for the same criminal offense).
- The Fifth Amendment provision that no person can be required to be a witness against (incriminate) himself or herself. (This is often referred to as the constitutional protection against **self-incrimination.** It is the basis for a criminal suspect's "right to remain silent" in criminal proceedings.)
- The Sixth Amendment guarantees of a speedy trial, a trial by jury, a public trial, the right to confront witnesses, and the right to counsel at various stages in some criminal proceedings. (The right to counsel was established in 1963 in *Gideon v. Wainwright.*[31] The Supreme Court held that if a person is accused of a felony and cannot afford an attorney, an attorney must be made available to the accused person at the government's expense.)
- The Eighth Amendment prohibitions against excessive bail and fines and against cruel and unusual punishments.

THE EXCLUSIONARY RULE

Any evidence obtained in violation of the constitutional rights spelled out in the Fourth Amendment normally is not admissible at trial. This rule, which has been applied in the federal courts since at least 1914, is known as the **exclusionary rule.** The rule was extended to state court proceedings in 1961.[32] The reasoning behind the exclusionary rule is that it forces law enforcement personnel to gather evidence properly. If they do not, they will be unable to introduce the evidence at trial to convince the jury that the defendant is guilty.

THE *MIRANDA* WARNINGS

INFOTRAC°

**Origins of the
Fourth Amendment**

In the 1950s and 1960s, one of the questions facing the courts was not whether suspects had constitutional rights—that was not in doubt—but how and when those rights could be exercised. For example, could the right to remain silent (under the Fifth Amendment's prohibition against self-incrimination) be exercised during pretrial interrogation proceedings or only during the trial? Were confessions obtained from suspects admissible in court if the suspects had not been advised of their right to remain silent and other constitutional rights? To clarify these issues, in 1966 the Supreme Court issued a landmark decision in *Miranda v. Arizona.*[33] In that case, the Court enunciated the *Miranda* **warnings** that are now familiar to virtually all Americans:

> Prior to any questioning, the person must be warned that he has a right to remain silent, that any statement he does make may be used against him, and that he has a right to the presence of an attorney, either retained or appointed.

THE EROSION OF *MIRANDA*

As part of a continuing attempt to balance the rights of accused persons against the rights of society, the Supreme Court has made a number of exceptions to the *Miranda* ruling. In 1986, for example, the Court held that a confession need not be excluded even though the police failed to inform a suspect in custody that his attorney had tried to reach him by telephone.[34] In an important 1991 decision, the Court stated that a suspect's conviction will not be automatically overturned if the suspect was coerced into mak-

This police officer is reading the accused his *Miranda* warnings. Since the 1966 *Miranda* decision, the Supreme Court has relaxed its requirements in some situations, such as when a criminal suspect who is not under arrest enters a police station voluntarily.

ing a confession. If the other evidence admitted at trial was strong enough to justify the conviction without the confession, then the fact that the confession was obtained illegally can be, in effect, ignored.[35] In yet another case, in 1994, the Supreme Court ruled that a suspect must unequivocally and assertively state his right to counsel in order to stop police questioning. Saying, "Maybe I should talk to a lawyer" during an interrogation after being taken into custody is not enough. The Court held that police officers are not required to decipher the suspect's intentions in such situations.[36]

In 1999, the U.S. Court of Appeals for the Fourth Circuit stunned the nation's legal establishment by enforcing a long-forgotten provision, Section 3501, of the Omnibus Crime Control Act of 1968. Congress passed the act two years after the Supreme Court's *Miranda* decision in an attempt to reinstate a rule that had been in effect for 180 years before *Miranda*—namely, that statements by defendants can be used against them as long as they are voluntarily made. The Justice Department immediately disavowed Section 3501 as unconstitutional and continues to hold this position. The Fourth Circuit, however, could see no reason not to enforce the provision. After all, Congress has the "unquestioned power to establish the rules of procedure and evidence in federal courts," and there is no explicit constitutional requirement that defendants be told of their rights to counsel and to remain silent.[37]

The Fourth Circuit's ruling applies only to federal courts located within the states comprising its circuit (Maryland, North Carolina, South Carolina, Virginia, and West Virginia) and has no effect in state courts. Some legal scholars, however, believe that this decision may ultimately lead to a reconsideration of *Miranda*.[38]

Americans at Odds over Civil Liberties

Virtually every civil liberty discussed in this chapter has given rise to heated debate at one time or another in our history. Today, Americans are at odds over numerous issues concerning our civil liberties, including freedom of speech on the Internet, prayer in the schools, abortion, and the death penalty—to name but a few. Here we look first at the current controversy over whether criminal suspects have too many rights. Next we look at an issue that is currently percolating in the federal courts—whether college students must contribute, through mandatory student fees, to organizations that espouse causes that are contrary to some students' beliefs. Finally, we examine another topic over which Americans are at odds: whether Americans should have the "right to die."

Do Criminal Suspects Have Too Many Rights?

In the last decade or so, American society has become well acquainted with how procedural requirements can affect the outcome of criminal proceedings. TV crime series and live coverage of criminal trials (such as O. J. Simpson's trial in 1995) show us how difficult it is for criminal prosecutors to obtain evidence legally and to make sure that the evidence will be admissible in court. This remains true even though, as noted above, the courts have recently issued rulings that weaken *Miranda* and have also created exceptions to the exclusionary rule.

Do criminal suspects have too many rights? Many Americans believe that they do. Among this group is a New York state trial court judge, Harold Rothwax. Rothwax contends that the *Miranda* requirements and court interpretations of the Fourth and Fifth Amendments have resulted in the "collapse of criminal justice" in this country. If a criminal defendant can show that law enforcement officials violated a procedural requirement, the defendant will be permitted to go free—regardless of guilt. Among other things, Rothwax contends that the *Miranda* requirements should be eliminated.[39]

Law professor Paul Cassell has also concluded that the *Miranda* rules should be scrapped. Cassell estimates that each year the *Miranda* requirements cause prosecutors to lose cases against 30,000 violent criminal suspects, 90,000 property offenders (such as burglars), 62,000 drunk drivers, 46,000 drug dealers and users, and hundreds of thousands of others accused of less serious crimes. Cassell recommends that we do away with the *Miranda* warnings and, instead, require police to videotape all interrogations of criminal suspects. In Cassell's opinion, videotaping would be as effective as the *Miranda* requirements in preventing police misconduct, yet it would not have such a deterrent effect on voluntary confessions.[40] In fact, more and more law enforcement officials are now recording interrogations and confessions on videotape. Police officers in New Mexico, for example, carry tape recorders on their belts. Both Minnesota and Alaska require interrogations to be recorded. If this trend continues, the *Miranda* rules may indeed become unnecessary.

Other Americans, though they may agree that criminal procedures do sometimes get in the way of criminal justice, emphasize that these procedures play a vital role in securing citizens' rights. Procedural requirements help to ensure that state prosecutors do not infringe on the constitutional rights of defendants, particularly the right to due process of law. After all, a criminal prosecution brings the force of the state, with all its resources, to bear against the individual. The *Miranda* requirements, the exclusionary rule, and other procedural rules are designed to safeguard the rights of individuals against the immense power of the state.

Student Fees and Free Speech

Colleges and universities routinely require students to pay student activities fees. The bulk of these fees is used to support athletic programs, health services, concerts, and other events and programs that are not usually controversial. A small portion of the fees, though, is allocated to various student organizations to help cover their costs—and herein lies the problem.

What if a student objects to the idea of having to help pay for the promotional literature distributed by one or more of these groups? Does this violate the student's free speech rights?

In one case, for example, a small group of conservative Christian students at the University of Wisconsin in Madison sued the university and the state of Wisconsin over this issue. The students stated that they were opposed to abortion and homosexuality and that they supported the free enterprise system. Yet their fees went to support such campus organizations as the Lesbian, Gay, Bisexual Campus Center and the International Socialist Organization. They claimed that sixteen other campus organizations also engage in political and ideological activities that, to one degree or another, countered their views. Students on the University of Oregon campus in Eugene, Oregon, have also challenged the university's practice of using mandatory student fees to subsidize various campus organizations with political and ideological views different from their own.

There is fairly widespread support for both positions on this issue. Many have sided with the students, contending that no one should have to subsidize organizations that promote causes that are contrary to one's beliefs. Spokespersons for the universities and various other organizations, such as the Gay and Lesbian Alliance, look at the matter differently. They claim that using student activity fees to fund university grants to a broad variety of organizations gives students the opportunity to explore a wide range of ideas and policy issues. Essentially, the fees provide for a public forum for the expression of diverse thoughts. Just as a taxpayer cannot expect to obtain a tax refund when he or she objects to a group that uses the town square to conduct a demonstration, a student cannot expect to be able to opt out of helping to pay for a public forum on campus.

Clearly, this is a "nickel-and-dime" issue, as one observer commented, in the sense that the dollar stakes are not high. Yet the principle involved is a significant one, and the lower courts are in conflict on the topic. In the Wisconsin case, a federal appellate court held for the students, ruling that they could not be required to pay the portion of the fees that went to objectionable groups.[41] In the Oregon case, another federal court sided with the university administration.[42] The Wisconsin case is currently on appeal to the United States Supreme Court.

Should Americans Have the "Right to Die"?

INFOTRAC®

Severe Mercy in Oregon

Whether it is called euthanasia (mercy killing), assisted suicide, or a dignified way to leave this world, it all comes down to one basic question: Do terminally ill persons have, as part of their civil liberties, a right to die and to be assisted in the process by physicians or others? Phrased another way, are state laws banning physician-assisted suicide in such circumstances unconstitutional? This issue has received a lot of media publicity, particularly due to the activities of Dr. Jack Kevorkian ("Dr. Death"), who for years openly defied laws prohibiting assisted suicide and who only recently was convicted.

When the issue came before the United States Supreme Court in 1997, the Court characterized the question as follows: Does the liberty protected by the Constitution include a right to commit suicide, which itself includes a right to assistance in doing so? The Court's clear and categorical answer to this question was no. To hold otherwise, said the Court, would be "to reverse centuries of legal doctrine and practice, and strike down the considered policy choice of almost every State."[43] (Suicide, including attempts to aid or promote suicide, is defined as a crime in most, if not all, states.)

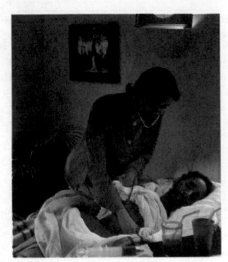

A physician listens to the lungs of an AIDS victim in a hospice center in Los Angeles, California. Whether terminally ill people should have the right to end their lives by physician-assisted suicide is one of today's most controversial issues.

Although the Court upheld the states' rights to ban such a practice, the Court did not hold that state laws *permitting* assisted suicide were unconstitutional. In 1997, Oregon became the first state—and so far, the only one—to implement such a law.

The debate has not ended, though, just because the Supreme Court has enunciated its opinion on the topic, just as the debate over abortion did not stop after the 1973 *Roe v. Wade* decision legalizing abortion. And Americans continue to be at odds over this issue.

WE HAVE A CONSTITUTIONAL RIGHT TO DIE

Those who are in favor of assisted suicide believe that the right to die is included in our constitutional privacy rights. This group argues that the right to die extends beyond simply refusing life support, or even food, to dying persons. The right also allows terminally ill persons to secure help from doctors who can chemically end their lives. Proponents of physician-assisted suicide also point out that there is little difference between turning off a life-support system (which is not necessarily illegal) and complying with a terminally ill patient's request to end his or her own life through assisted suicide. To treat the two acts differently violates the equal protection clause of the Constitution.

Those in favor of making assisted suicide legal also ask why terminally ill AIDS and cancer patients should be made to suffer the indignities that accompany the final stages of their illnesses. A state-enforced prohibition on hastening their deaths forces them to spend their last days in torture. The government has no business requiring the continuation of agony when death will certainly result.

For several thousand years, the predominant responsibility of a physician has been to serve the patient's needs while respecting that patient's dignity, not simply to preserve life at all costs. In fact, physician-assisted suicide goes on every day. A University of Massachusetts survey of oncologists (cancer specialists) found that 57 percent were asked by their terminally ill cancer patients for help in ending their lives. According to the survey, one in seven oncologists complied with these requests.[44]

WE HAVE NO RIGHT TO DIE

Opponents of assisted suicide argue that we live in a highly evolving technological world. Therefore, how can we know for certain that a person who seems terminally ill is truly beyond recovery? After all, a breakthrough in biomedical knowledge may allow a person who appears to be terminally ill to be cured. Possibly, too, the elderly and the financially "unfit" will be pressured into accepting assisted suicide if it is permitted. In any event, there is no implied constitutional right to death at the hands of another.

Moreover, most studies show that patients who seek euthanasia do so because of psychological factors such as depression, rather than unbearable physical suffering.[45] Pain appears to have been the sole motivating factor in only about 5 percent of euthanasia cases. Thus, the common perception of patients in pain asking to be put out of their misery does not fit the statistics. If our rights are expanded to include assisted suicide, then terminally ill patients with treatable pain or depression will be vulnerable and susceptible to influence by physicians, family members, and others on whom they depend.[46] A study of the assisted suicides that took place in Oregon during 1998 shows that of the fifteen terminally ill people who used the assisted-suicide law to end their lives, not one of them chose to do so because of intractable pain or suffering. Rather, they were firm believers in individual autonomy and chose suicide primarily because they feared becoming dependent on others for their care.[47]

Those who oppose assisted suicide argue that what we should be doing is improving the care we provide for those who are dying. We should develop better ways of alleviating pain. Instead of abandoning the terminally ill, we should increase their access to hospice care.

key terms

bill of attainder 83	*Lemon* test 89
civil liberties 83	libel 92
commercial speech 92	*Miranda* warnings 100
double jeopardy 100	obscenity 93
due process clause 84	probable cause 100
due process of law 84	sabotage 91
espionage 91	seditious speech 91
establishment clause 84	self-incrimination 100
ex post facto law 83	slander 92
exclusionary rule 100	symbolic speech 90
"fighting words" 92	treason 91
free exercise clause 84	writ of *habeas corpus* 83

chapter summary

1. The Bill of Rights (the first ten amendments to the Constitution) sets forth our civil liberties. Other civil liberties are specified in the Constitution itself. The Constitution provides that a writ of *habeas corpus* shall be available to all citizens. It also prohibits Congress and the state legislatures from passing bills of attainder or *ex post facto* laws.

2. Originally, the Bill of Rights limited only the power of the national government, not that of the states. Over time, the Supreme Court has interpreted the due process clause of the Fourteenth Amendment to mean that most of the liberties guaranteed by the national Constitution apply to state government actions as well.

3. The First Amendment prohibits government from passing laws "respecting an establishment of religion, or prohibiting the free exercise thereof." The first part of the amendment is referred to as the establishment clause; the second part is known as the free exercise clause.

4. Issues involving the establishment clause often focus on prayer in the schools and aid to parochial schools. The Supreme Court has ruled against officially sponsored prayer, meditation, or silent prayer in public schools. The Supreme Court has also struck down state laws prohibiting the teaching of evolution. The government can provide financial aid to religious schools if the aid is secular in aim, does not have the primary effect of advancing or inhibiting religion, and does not result in "an excessive government entanglement with religion."

5. No law or act of government may violate the constitutional right to the free exercise of religion. A distinction is made, however, between religious beliefs and religious practices. Although citizens have an absolute right to believe as they choose, their right to engage in religious practices may be limited if those practices violate the laws or threaten the health, safety, or morals of the community. Employers must accommodate the religious needs of employees unless to do so would cause the employer to suffer an "undue hardship."

6. The First Amendment also protects freedom of speech, including symbolic (nonverbal) speech. Although the Supreme Court has zealously safeguarded the right to free speech, at times it has imposed limits on speech in the interests of protecting other rights of society. Early restraints on speech were placed on seditious speech, which, since the 1960s, the Supreme Court has defined to mean only the advocacy of immediate and concrete acts of violence against the government. Certain restraints have also been placed on commercial speech (advertising). Some forms of speech—including libel and slander, "fighting words," and obscenity—are not protected by the First Amendment.

7. Another First Amendment freedom is the freedom of the press, which generally has the right to publish a wide range of opinions and information. Guidelines developed by the courts to decide whether freedom of expression can be restrained include the clear and present danger test, the bad-tendency test, the preferred-position doctrine, and a rule against prior restraint (censorship).

8. Since the 1960s, the justices of the Supreme Court have held that a right to privacy is implied by other constitutional rights set forth in the First, Third, Fourth, Fifth, and Ninth Amendments. The nature and scope of this right are not always clear, however. Whether this right encompasses a right to have an abortion or to commit assisted suicide are

two issues on which Americans have still not reached consensus.

9. The Fourth, Fifth, Sixth, and Eighth Amendments protect the rights of persons accused of crimes. Under the exclusionary rule, any evidence obtained in violation of the constitutional rights of criminal defendants normally is not admissible in court. In 1966, in *Miranda v. Arizona,* the Supreme Court required that certain warnings, known as the *Miranda* warnings, be given to criminal suspects to make sure that the suspects understand their constitutional rights. Failure to give the warnings prior to interrogation may mean that any confes-

sion or other evidence obtained from the suspect will not be admissible at trial. The *Miranda* rights have been significantly eroded in the last two decades, however.

10. Americans are at odds over numerous issues involving our civil liberties. Three currently contested issues have to do with whether criminal suspects have too many rights; whether college students should have to contribute, through their student fees, to groups whose values and beliefs are contrary to their own; and whether we have a right to commit physician-assisted suicide.

---

for critical analysis

1. If it is difficult to administer the death penalty fairly in a country such as the United States, which has more procedural protections for criminal defendants than any country in the world, can it be administered fairly in any nation?

2. Suppose that ninety-nine of the students in a small, rural elementary school were Christians and the remaining student was a Muslim. Further suppose that the school's Christmas program involved singing a number of Christmas carols reflecting Christian beliefs. If the school's practice were challenged in court, would the court hold that the school had violated the establishment clause? Should it?

3. A number of colleges and universities have created campus speech codes that prohibit various forms of "hate speech" against ethnic groups, disabled persons, and others. Those codes that have been challenged on constitutional grounds have uniformly been struck down by the courts as going too far in constraining speech. Do you agree with the courts on this issue? Why or why not?

4. The Supreme Court has held that the definition of what constitutes obscene speech or expression should be decided according to community standards. In effect, this means that persons in, say, a very conservative community will likely be more constrained in their speech than persons in a very liberal community will be. Is this a fair result?

5. In Britain, police officers, when arresting a suspect, must tell the suspect that he or she need not say anything, but "it may harm your defense if you do not mention when questioned something which you later rely on in court." In other words, silence may be used as evidence of guilt in Britain. Should the United States adopt this procedural approach with respect to the right to remain silent?

6. In your opinion, should terminally ill persons have the legal right to end their lives through physician-assisted suicide? Why or why not?

---

suggested readings

ARRIENS, Jan. *Welcome to Hell: Letters and Writings from Death Row.* Boston: Northeastern University Press, 1997. The author is one of the founders of LifeLines, a British group whose members correspond with prisoners on death row. He offers excerpts from prisoners' letters, along with brief commentaries, that provide brutal and shocking glimpses of life among the condemned.

LEO, Richard A., *et al.,* eds. *The Miranda Debate: Law, Justice, and Policing.* Boston: Northeastern University Press, 1998. This book presents an anthology of key writings on the 1966 *Miranda v. Arizona* ruling. The essays explore the pre-*Miranda* law governing confession as well as the legal and ethical dimensions of the *Miranda* decision.

SHEFFER, Martin S. *God versus Caesar: Belief, Worship, and Proselytizing under the First Amendment.* Albany, N.Y.: State University of New York Press, 1999. The author looks at how court interpretations of the free exercise clause have changed over time in response to changing social values and policies.

SHIELL, Timothy C., *Campus Hate Speech on Trial.* Lawrence, Kans.: University Press of Kansas, 1998. Shiell contends that American colleges and universities, which are ostensibly committed to free speech and the open exchange of ideas, betray this commitment when they implement hate-speech codes. The author believes that the principle of free speech must be upheld, even if it means tolerating hate speech.

politics
on the web

Almost three dozen First Amendment groups have launched the Free Expression Clearinghouse, which is a Web site designed to feature legislation updates, legal briefings, and news on cases of censorship in local communities. Go to

http://www.FREEExpression.org

The leading civil liberties organization, the American Civil Liberties Union (ACLU), can be found at

http://www.aclu.org

A group named the Liberty Counsel calls itself "a nonprofit religious civil liberties education and legal defense organization established to preserve religious freedom." You can access this organization's home page at

http://www.lc.org

Summaries and the full text of constitutional law decisions by the United States Supreme Court are included at the following site:

http://oyez.nwu.edu

For information on the effect of new computer and communications technologies on the constitutional rights and liberties of Americans, go to the Center for Democracy and Technology at

http://www.cdt.org

using
web resources

Vanderbilt University's Freedom Forum First Amendment Center Web site is an excellent source of information concerning civil liberties. Go to

http://www.freedomforum.org/first/welcome.asp

1. Select the "Outrage of the Week" and open the page. What First Amendment right is involved in this issue?

2. How and why did the issue arise? (Summarize briefly the "facts" of the "outrage.")

3. How do you feel about this issue? Is it one that is protected by the First Amendment? Should the federal government be involved?

4. Return to the main page and select one of the news stories. Summarize the story as it relates to the question of how the First Amendment should be interpreted.

notes

1. *The Economist,* May 15, 1999, p. 97.

2. Not everyone agrees that such a separation has benefited the United States. See, for example, Stephen Carter, *The Culture of Disbelief* (New York: Basic Books, 1993). Carter argues that politics and law in America have suffered from the exclusion of religion from public discourse.

3. 330 U.S. 1 (1947).

4. 370 U.S. 421 (1962).

5. 449 U.S. 39 (1980).

6. *Wallace v. Jaffree,* 472 U.S. 38 (1985).

7. 393 U.S. 97 (1968).

8. *Edwards v. Aguillard,* 482 U.S. 578 (1987).

9. 403 U.S. 602 (1971).

10. 473 U.S. 402 (1985).

11. 521 U.S. 203 (1997).

12. 98 U.S. 145 (1878).

13. *The National Law Journal,* March 16, 1998, p. A19.

14. *Schenck v. United States*, 249 U.S. 47 (1919).

15. 341 U.S. 494 (1951).

16. *Brandenburg v. Ohio*, 395 U.S. 444 (1969).

17. *Liquormart v. Rhode Island*, 517 U.S. 484 (1996).

18. 413 U.S. 15 (1973).

19. *Reno v. American Civil Liberties Union*, 521 U.S. 844 (1997).

20. *American Civil Liberties Union v. Reno*, 31 F.Supp.2d 473 (E.D.Pa. 1999).

21. 249 U.S. 47 (1919).

22. 268 U.S. 652 (1925).

23. 403 U.S. 713 (1971).

24. 484 U.S. 260 (1988).

25. *Smith v. Collin*, 439 U.S. 916 (1978).

26. Brandeis made this statement in a dissenting opinion in *Olmstead v. United States*, 277 U.S. 438 (1928).

27. *City of Chicago v. Morales*, 119 S.Ct. 1849 (1999).

28. *Gallo v. Acuna*, 14 Cal.4th 1090 (1997).

29. 410 U.S. 113 (1973). Jane Roe was not the real name of the woman in this case. It is a common legal pseudonym used to protect a party's privacy.

30. See, for example, the Supreme Court's decision in *Lambert v. Wicklund*, 520 U.S. 1169 (1997). The Court held that a Montana law requiring a minor to notify one of her parents before getting an abortion was constitutional.

31. 372 U.S. 335 (1963).

32. *Mapp v. Ohio*, 367 U.S. 643 (1961).

33. 384 U.S. 436 (1966).

34. *Moran v. Burbine*, 475 U.S. 412 (1986).

35. *Arizona v. Fulminante*, 499 U.S. 279 (1991).

36. *Davis v. United States*, 512 U.S. 452 (1994).

37. *United States v. Dickerson*, 166 F.3d 667 (4th Cir. 1999).

38. William Glaberson, "*Miranda* Ruling Faces Its Most Serious Challenge," *The New York Times*, February 11, 1999, pp. A1 and A25.

39. Harold J. Rothwax, *The Collapse of Criminal Justice* (New York: Random House, 1996).

40. Paul G. Cassell, "How Many Criminals Has *Miranda* Set Free?" *The Wall Street Journal*, March 1, 1995, p. A17.

41. *Southworth v. Grebe*, 151 F.3d 717 (7th Cir. 1998).

42. *Rounds v. Oregon State Board of Higher Education*, 166 F.3d 1032 (9th Cir. 1998).

43. *Washington v. Glucksberg*, 521 U.S. 702 (1997).

44. "Assisted Suicide Is a Fact: Now States Need Standards," *USA Today*, January 9, 1997, p. 12A.

45. Ezekiel J. Emanuel, *The End of Human Life* (Cambridge, Mass.: Harvard University Press, 1991).

46. This argument, among others, was set forth in briefs filed with the Supreme Court by Solicitor General Walter Dellinger in support of the effort by New York and Washington to defend their criminal prohibitions against physician-assisted suicide.

47. Wesley J. Smith, "Dependency or Death? Oregonians Make a Chilling Choice," *The Wall Street Journal*, February 25, 1999, p. A18.

Affirmative Action: Has It Run Its Course?

Ever since the Civil Rights Act of 1964, the federal government (and many state and local governments as well) has applied the concept of affirmative action to such diverse areas as employment, college admissions, and the awarding of government contracts. Affirmative action involves giving preferences to groups that have suffered from discriminatory treatment in the past. In reality, any program that involves preferences necessarily means that some people will be aggrieved. So, non-Hispanic whites resent preferences being given to African Americans and Hispanics. Men resent being displaced by women. Today, affirmative action is on the defensive. Has it run its course?

Go to CD-ROM

It's Time to Put an End to Affirmative Action

A growing number of Americans argue that we should put an end to affirmative action. Affirmative action programs have created a legal system in which different groups have different rights and thus violate the constitutional mandate that all Americans should be equally protected by the laws. Americans should enjoy a level playing field, but affirmative action prevents that. When employment and college admissions policies are based on preferences rather than merit, all society suffers. Moreover, the end result of such government meddling is a vast bureaucracy in both the public and the private sectors.

Critics of affirmative action also stress that racial and gender preferences do not equate to the empowerment of minorities and women. In fact, preferences inject a dose of poison into the body politic. In particular, minorities resent being stereotyped by "white" society as having "gotten their jobs only because of affirmative action, not because of ability." The racial divide that separates Americans is thereby increased.

Finally, opponents of affirmative action point out that it should be abandoned because it simply hasn't worked. Black male college graduates still make significantly less than their white counterparts, and the gap has increased since 1980. Racial and gender bias continues to exist in society, but this is a social problem that the government should not—and cannot, as witnessed by the failure of affirmative action—handle.

Affirmative Action Is Still Justified

Many other Americans, including those who have benefited from affirmative action, have come to its defense. They argue that affirmative action programs are still necessary to combat the effects of past discrimination. They point out that minorities and women have made great strides in both education and the work force in the last thirty years, in large part because of the effectiveness of affirmative action programs in countering racial and gender bias.

True, racial and gender bias still exists, but this is less a reason to abandon affirmative action than to continue it. To do away with affirmative action would destroy everything that we've accomplished in the last several decades. Without affirmative action, we would never attain the goal of equal opportunity. We must continue to require government agencies and employers to give preferences to minority applicants and to women in their hiring and promoting policies. If affirmative action preferences were eliminated, minorities and women would find it even more difficult to obtain jobs and advance in their careers. College administrators must continue to give preferences to minority applicants; otherwise, the number of minorities in the entering classes at many universities would be greatly reduced.

In sum, just because some affirmative action programs have had undesirable consequences does not mean the programs should be scrapped. Rather, they should be redesigned to minimize unwanted side effects. For example, if affirmative action is coupled with other efforts designed to extend opportunities to everybody, preferences in college admissions or employment may not necessarily hurt other groups—specifically, white males.

Where Do You Stand?

1. If it were up to you to decide whether affirmative action should be continued or abandoned, what would your decision be? Why?

2. If the government, by means of affirmative action, cannot end racial and gender bias in American institutions, who can?

On the Web

You can find a plethora of articles on the Web supporting either side of the debate on affirmative action. Simply go to any search engine, such as Yahoo at **www.yahoo.com**, and key in "affirmative action."

Introduction

CIVIL RIGHTS ● The rights of all Americans to equal treatment under the law, as provided for by the Fourteenth Amendment to the Constitution.

EQUAL PROTECTION CLAUSE ● Section 1 of the Fourteenth Amendment, which states that no state shall "deny to any person within its jurisdiction the equal protection of the laws."

INFOTRAC®

W's preferences

Affirmative action programs are part of an ongoing debate over the nature of our civil rights. We often lump civil rights together with civil liberties (discussed in the previous chapter), and many Americans use the terms interchangeably. Still, some scholars make a distinction between the two. They point out that whereas civil liberties are limitations on government action, setting forth what the government *cannot* do, civil rights specify what the government *must* do. Generally, though, the term **civil rights** refers to the rights of all Americans to equal treatment under the law, as provided for by the Fourteenth Amendment. One of the functions of our government is to ensure—through legislation or other actions—that this constitutional mandate is upheld.

Although the democratic ideal is for all people to have equal rights and equal treatment under the law, and although the Constitution guarantees those rights, this ideal has often remained just that—an ideal. It is people who put ideals into practice, and as James Madison once pointed out (and as we all know), people are not angels. As you will read in this chapter, the struggle of various groups in American society to obtain equal treatment has been a long one, and it still continues today.

In a sense, the history of civil rights in the United States is a history of discrimination against various groups. Discrimination against women, African Americans, and Native Americans dates back to the early years of this nation, when the framers of the Constitution refused to grant these groups rights that were granted to others (that is, to white, property-owning males). During our subsequent history, our nation became known as a "melting pot" of different cultures and traditions, as peoples from around the globe immigrated to this country at various times and for various reasons. Each of these immigrant groups has faced discrimination in one form or another. More recently, other groups, including older Americans, persons suffering from disabilities, and gay men and lesbians, have had to struggle for equal treatment under the law.

Central to any discussion of civil rights is the interpretation of the equal protection clause of the Fourteenth Amendment to the Constitution. For that reason, we look first at that clause and how the courts, particularly the Supreme Court, have interpreted it and applied it to civil rights issues.

The Equal Protection Clause

Equal in importance to the due process clause of the Fourteenth Amendment is the **equal protection clause** in Section 1 of that amendment, which reads as follows: "No State shall . . . deny to any person within its jurisdiction the equal protection of the laws." Section 5 of the amendment provides a legal basis for federal civil rights legislation: "The Congress shall have power to enforce, by appropriate legislation, the provisions of this article."

The equal protection clause has been interpreted by the courts, and especially the Supreme Court, to mean that states must treat all persons in an equal manner and may not discriminate *unreasonably* against a particular group or class of individuals unless there is a sufficient reason to do so. The task of distinguishing between reasonable discrimination and unreasonable discrimination is difficult. Generally, in deciding this question, the Supreme Court balances the constitutional rights of individuals to equal protection against government interests in protecting the safety and welfare of citizens. Over time, the Court has developed various tests, or standards, for determining whether the equal protection clause has been violated.

RATIONAL BASIS TEST ● A test (also known as the "ordinary scrutiny" standard) used by the Supreme Court to decide whether a discriminatory law violates the equal protection clause of the Constitution. Few laws evaluated under this test are found invalid.

FUNDAMENTAL RIGHT ● A basic right of all Americans, such as all First Amendment rights. Any law or action that prevents some group of persons from exercising a fundamental right will be subject to the "strict scrutiny" standard, under which the law or action must be necessary to promote a compelling state interest and must be narrowly tailored to meet that interest.

SUSPECT CLASSIFICATION ● A classification based on race, for example, that provides the basis for a discriminatory law. Any law based on a suspect classification is subject to strict scrutiny by the courts—meaning that the law must be justified by a compelling state interest.

THE RATIONAL BASIS TEST (ORDINARY SCRUTINY)

One test used to decide whether a discriminatory law violates the equal protection clause is the **rational basis test.** When applying this test to a law that classifies or treats people or groups differently, the justices ask whether the discrimination is rational. In other words, is it a reasonable way to achieve a legitimate government objective? Few laws tested under the rational basis test—or the "ordinary scrutiny" standard, as it is also called—are found invalid, because few laws are truly unreasonable. A municipal ordinance that prohibits certain vendors from selling their wares in a particular area of the city, for example, will be upheld if the city can meet this rational basis test. The rational basis for the ordinance might be the city's legitimate government interest in reducing traffic congestion in that particular area.

STRICT SCRUTINY

If the law or action prevents some group of persons from exercising a **fundamental right** (such as all First Amendment rights), however, the law or action will be subject to the "strict scrutiny" standard. Under this standard, the law or action must be necessary to promote a *compelling state interest* and must be narrowly tailored to meet that interest. A law based on a **suspect classification,** such as race, is also subject to strict scrutiny by the courts, meaning that the law must be justified by a compelling state interest.

INTERMEDIATE SCRUTINY

Because the Supreme Court had difficulty deciding how to judge cases in which men and women were treated differently, a third test was developed—the "intermediate scrutiny" standard. Under this standard, laws based on gender classifications are permissible if they are "substantially related to the achievement of an important governmental objective." For example, a law punishing males but not females for statutory rape is valid because of the important governmental interest in preventing teenage pregnancy in those circumstances and because virtually all of the harmful and identifiable consequences of teenage pregnancy fall on the young female.[1] A law prohibiting the sale of "nonintoxicating" beer to males under twenty-one years of age and to females under eighteen years is not valid, however.[2]

Generally, since the 1970s, the Supreme Court has scrutinized gender classifications closely, and many gender-based laws have been declared unconstitutional. In 1979, the Court held that a state law allowing wives to obtain alimony judgments against husbands but preventing husbands from receiving alimony from wives violated the equal protection clause.[3] In 1982, the Court declared that Mississippi's policy of excluding males from the School of Nursing at Mississippi University for Women was unconstitutional.[4] In a controversial 1996 case, *United States v. Virginia,*[5] the Court held that Virginia Military Institute, a state-financed institution, violated the equal protection clause by refusing to accept female applicants. The Court said that the state of Virginia had failed to provide a sufficient justification for its gender-based classification. Nonetheless, the goal of equal treatment for women, which dates back to the Constitution, has yet to be fully achieved.

Equal Treatment for Women

In 1776, Abigail Adams, anticipating that new laws would probably be necessary after the Declaration of Independence was issued, wrote the following words to her husband, John Adams:

> I desire you would remember the ladies. . . . If particular care and attention is not paid to the ladies, we are determined to foment a rebellion and will not hold ourselves bound by any laws in which we have no voice or representation.[6]

SUFFRAGE ● The right to vote; the franchise.

Despite this request, women, although considered citizens in the early years of the nation, had no political rights. Of course, neither did women in other countries—but the United States was different. Americans were not bound as tightly to age-old traditions and laws that allowed only men to participate fully in the political arena. In fact, in the New World "frontier," women had assumed far more responsibilities than their European counterparts. During the revolutionary era, women had played a significant political role, particularly in organizing boycotts against British imports and making substitute goods.

In this context, Abigail Adams's request is not all that surprising. The failure of the framers of the Constitution to give women political rights was viewed by many early Americans as an act of betrayal. Not only did the Constitution betray the Declaration of Independence's promise of equality, but it also betrayed the women who had contributed to the making of that independence during the Revolutionary War. Nonetheless, not until the 1840s did women's rights groups begin to form.

THE STRUGGLE FOR VOTING RIGHTS

In 1848, Lucretia Mott and Elizabeth Cady Stanton organized the first woman's[7] rights convention in Seneca Falls, New York. The three hundred people who attended approved a Declaration of Sentiments: "We hold these truths to be self-evident: that all men *and women* are created equal." In the following years, other women's groups held conventions in various cities in the Midwest and the East. With the outbreak of the Civil War, though, women's rights advocates devoted their energies to the war effort.

The movement for political rights again gained momentum in 1869, when Susan B. Anthony and Elizabeth Cady Stanton formed the National Woman Suffrage Association. Women's **suffrage**—the right to vote—became their goal. For members of the National Woman Suffrage Association, suffrage was only one step on the road toward greater social and political rights for women. Lucy Stone and other women, who had founded the American Woman Suffrage Association, thought that the right to vote should be the only goal. By 1890, the two organizations had joined forces, and the resulting National American Woman Suffrage Association had only one goal—the enfranchisement of women. When little progress was made, small, radical splinter groups took to the streets. Parades, hunger strikes, arrests, and jailings soon followed.

World War I (1914–1918) marked a turning point in the battle for women's rights. The war offered many opportunities for women. Thousands of women

Abigail Adams (left), Lucretia Mott (center), and Elizabeth Cady Stanton (right).

In 1996, Madeleine K. Albright was named secretary of state, the first woman to hold that office. In all, only fourteen women have been appointed to cabinet posts.

Table 5–1

Years, by Country, in Which Women Gained the Right to Vote

1893: New Zealand

1902: Australia

1913: Norway

1918: Britain

1918: Canada

1919: Germany

1920: United States

1930: South Africa

1932: Brazil

1944: France

1945: Italy

1945: Japan

1947: Argentina

1950: India

1952: Greece

1953: Mexico

1956: Egypt

1963: Kenya

1971: Switzerland

1984: Yemen

served as volunteers, and about a million women joined the work force, holding jobs vacated by men who entered military service. After the war, President Woodrow Wilson wrote to Carrie Chapman Catt, one of the leaders of the women's movement, that "it is high time that part of our debt should be acknowledged." Two years later, in 1920, seventy-two years after the Seneca Falls convention, the Nineteenth Amendment to the Constitution was ratified: "The right of citizens of the United States to vote shall not be denied or abridged by the United States or by any State on account of sex." Although the United States may seem slow in having given women the vote, it was really not far behind the rest of the world (see Table 5–1).

WOMEN IN AMERICAN POLITICS TODAY

More than ten thousand members have served in the U.S. House of Representatives. Only 1 percent of them have been women. No woman has as yet held any major leadership position in either the House or the Senate. Women continue to face a "men's club" atmosphere in Congress, although elections during the 1990s brought more women to Congress than either the Senate or the House had seen before. In the 106th Congress, 13 percent of the 435 members of the House of Representatives and 9 percent of the 100 members of the Senate were women. Considering that there are 97.1 million eligible female voters, as compared to 88.6 million eligible male voters, women are vastly underrepresented in the U.S. Congress.

The same can be said for the number of women receiving presidential appointments to federal offices. Franklin Roosevelt (1933–1945) appointed the first woman to a cabinet post—Frances Perkins, who was secretary of labor from 1933 to 1945. In recent administrations, several women have held cabinet posts. In addition, Ronald Reagan (1981–1989) appointed the first woman ever to sit on the Supreme Court, Sandra Day O'Connor. Bill Clinton appointed Ruth Bader Ginsburg to the Supreme Court, and, in his second term, he appointed Madeleine Albright as secretary of state, the first woman to hold that position.

Women have made greater progress at the state level, and the percentage of women in state legislatures has been rising steadily. Women now constitute about 22 percent of state legislators. Notably, in the 1998 elections gender seemed to be less of an issue than it had been in the past. In fact, in that year women won races for each of the top five offices in Arizona, the first such occurrence in U.S. history. Generally, women have been more successful politically in the western states than elsewhere. In Washington, 41 percent of the state's legislative seats are now held by women. At the other end of the spectrum, though, are states such as Alabama. In that state, less than 8 percent of the lawmakers are women.

Do women in other countries fare better than U.S. women in terms of gaining positions of political leadership? This issue is discussed in the feature entitled *Comparative Politics: The Political Participation of Women throughout the World.*

WOMEN IN THE WORKPLACE

An ongoing challenge for American women is to obtain equal pay and equal opportunity in the workplace. In spite of federal legislation and programs to promote equal treatment of women in the workplace, women continue to face various forms of discrimination.

Wage Discrimination

In 1963, Congress passed the Equal Pay Act. The act requires employers to pay equal pay for substantially equal work—males cannot be paid more than females who perform essentially the same job. The following year, Congress passed the Civil Rights Act of 1964, Title VII of which prohibits employment discrimination on the basis of race, color, national origin, gender, and religion. Women, however, continue to face wage discrimination.

comparative politics

The Political Participation of Women throughout the World

Women fare better in other countries than in the United States. This is particularly true in the Scandinavian countries. For example, women hold nearly 50 percent of the seats in Sweden's national legislature. In Norway, Finland, and Denmark, women hold between 34 and 41 percent of the legislative seats. In Austria, the Netherlands, Germany, and Spain, the percentage of national lawmakers who are women is somewhat lower, but it is still higher than the percentage of women in today's U.S. Congress.

Women in certain countries have not made great strides, though. In France, for example, when women were given the vote a half-century ago, 6 percent were elected to the French Parliament. That percentage remains the same today.

In addition, women in several European countries apparently face a problem that many American women encounter. Despite their relatively high rate of political participation, women in Europe's private sector are often denied access to high-level corporate positions.

For Critical Analysis

Why do you think women in Scandinavian countries have such a high degree of participation in government?

It is estimated that for every dollar earned by men, women earn about 75 cents. Although the wage gap has narrowed significantly since 1963, when the Equal Pay Act was enacted (at that time women earned 58 cents for every dollar earned by men), it still remains. Moreover, since 1993 the gap has begun to widen slightly. There also continues to be a correlation between the number of women in an occupation and the wages that are commanded in that occupation.

Additionally, even though an increasing number of women now hold business and professional jobs once held by men, few of these women are able to rise to the top of the career ladder in their firms due to the lingering bias against women in the workplace. This bias is reflected in the so-called **glass ceiling**—the often subtle obstacles to advancement that professional women encounter on the job.

Sexual Harassment

Title VII's prohibition of gender discrimination has been extended to also prohibit sexual harassment. **Sexual harassment** occurs when job opportunities, promotions, salary increases, or even the ability to retain one's job depends on whether an employee complies with demands for sexual favors. A special form of sexual harassment, called hostile-environment harassment, occurs when an employee is subjected to sexual conduct or comments in the workplace that interfere with the employee's job performance or that create an intimidating, hostile, or offensive environment.

The Supreme Court has upheld the right of persons to be free from sexual harassment on the job on a number of occasions. In 1986, the Court indicated that creating a hostile environment by sexual harassment violates Title VII, even when job status is not affected, and in 1993 the Court held that to win damages in a suit for sexual harassment a victim did not need to prove that the harassment caused psychological harm.[8] In 1998, the Court made it clear that sexual harassment includes harassment by members of the same sex.[9] In the same year, the Court held that employers

GLASS CEILING ● The often subtle obstacles to advancement faced by professional women in the workplace.

SEXUAL HARASSMENT ● Unwanted physical contact, verbal conduct, or abuse of a sexual nature that interferes with a recipient's job performance, creates a hostile environment, or carries with it an implicit or explicit threat of adverse employment consequences.

SEPARATE BUT EQUAL DOCTRINE
● A Supreme Court doctrine holding that the equal protection clause of the Fourteenth Amendment did not forbid racial segregation as long as the facilities for blacks were equal to those provided for whites. The doctrine was overturned in the *Brown v. Board of Education of Topeka* decision of 1954.

are liable for the harassment of employees by supervisors in their workplaces *unless* they can show that (1) reasonable care in preventing such problems (by implementing antiharassment policies and procedures, for example) had been exercised and (2) the employees failed to take advantage of any corrective opportunities provided by the employers.[10] Additionally, the Civil Rights Act of 1991 greatly expanded the remedies available for victims of sexual harassment. The act specifically states that victims can seek damages in addition to back pay, job reinstatement, and other remedies previously available.

African Americans

The equal protection clause was originally intended to protect the newly freed slaves after the Civil War (1861–1865). In the early years after the war, the U.S. government made an effort to protect the rights of blacks living in the former states of the Confederacy. The Thirteenth Amendment (which granted freedom to the slaves), the Fourteenth Amendment (which guaranteed equal protection under the law), and the Fifteenth Amendment (which stated that voting rights could not be abridged on account of race) were part of that effort. By the late 1870s, however, southern legislatures began to pass a series of segregation laws—laws that separated the white community from the black community. Such laws were commonly called "Jim Crow" laws (from a song that was popular in black minstrel shows). Some of the most common Jim Crow laws involved the use of public facilities such as schools and, later, buses. They also affected housing, restaurants, hotels, and many other facilities.

SEPARATE BUT EQUAL

In 1892, a group of Louisiana citizens decided to challenge a state law that required railroads to provide separate railway cars for African Americans. A man named Homer Plessy, who was seven-eighths Caucasian and one-eighth African, boarded a train in New Orleans and sat in the railway car reserved for whites. When Plessy refused to move at the request of the conductor, he was arrested for breaking the law.

Four years later, in 1896, the Supreme Court provided a constitutional basis for these segregation laws. In *Plessy v. Ferguson*,[11] the Court held that the law did not violate the equal protection clause because *separate* facilities for blacks were *equal* to those for whites. The lone dissenter, Justice John Marshall Harlan, disagreed: "Our Constitution is color-blind, and neither knows nor tolerates classes among citizens." The majority opinion, however, established the **separate but equal doctrine**, which was used to justify segregation in many areas of American life for nearly sixty years.

In the late 1930s and 1940s, the Supreme Court gradually moved away from this doctrine. The major breakthrough, however, did not come until 1954, in a case involving an African American girl who lived in Topeka, Kansas.

THE *BROWN* DECISIONS AND SCHOOL INTEGRATION

In the 1950s, Topeka's schools, like those in many cities, were segregated. Mr. and Mrs. Oliver Brown wanted their daughter, Linda Carol Brown, to attend a white school a few blocks from their home instead of an all-black school that was twenty-one blocks away. With the help of lawyers from the National Association for the Advancement of Colored People (NAACP), Linda's parents sued the Board of Education to allow their daughter to attend the nearby school.

In *Brown v. Board of Education of Topeka*,[12] the Supreme Court reversed *Plessy v. Ferguson*. The Court unanimously held that segregation by race in

Signs such as the one shown here were commonplace in the South from the 1870s to the 1960s. The "separate but equal" doctrine, enunciated by the Supreme Court in 1896, justified "Jim Crow" laws that permitted racial segregation.

DE JURE SEGREGATION ● Racial segregation that is legally sanctioned—that is, segregation that occurs because of laws or decisions by government agencies.

DE FACTO SEGREGATION ● Racial segregation that occurs not as a result of deliberate intentions but because of past social and economic conditions and residential patterns.

public education was unconstitutional. Chief Justice Earl Warren wrote as follows:

> Does segregation of children in public schools solely on the basis of race, even though the physical facilities and other "tangible" factors may be equal, deprive the children of the minority group of equal educational opportunities? We believe that it does . . . . [Segregation generates in children] a feeling of inferiority as to their status in the community that may affect their hearts and minds in a way unlikely ever to be undone. . . . We conclude that in the field of public education the doctrine of "separate but equal" has no place. Separate educational facilities are inherently unequal.

The following year, in *Brown v. Board of Education*[13] (sometimes called *Brown II*), the Supreme Court ordered desegregation to begin "with all deliberate speed," an ambiguous phrase that could be (and was) interpreted in a variety of ways.

Reactions to School Integration

The Supreme Court ruling did not go unchallenged. Bureaucratic loopholes were used to delay desegregation. Another reaction was "white flight." As white parents sent their children to newly established private schools, some formerly white-only public schools became 100 percent black. Arkansas's Governor Orval Faubus used the state's National Guard to block the integration of Central High School in Little Rock in 1957, which led to increasing violence in the area. The federal court demanded that the troops be withdrawn. Only after President Dwight D. Eisenhower federalized the Arkansas National Guard and sent in paratroopers to help quell the violence did Central High finally become integrated.

By 1970, school systems with *de jure* **segregation**—segregation that is legally sanctioned—had been abolished. That is not to say that *de facto* **segregation** (actual segregation, produced by circumstances even though no law requires it) was eliminated. It meant only that no public school could legally identify itself as being reserved for all whites or all blacks.

The process of achieving complete desegregation, in fact, is still under way and will continue wherever *de facto* segregation exists. Housing patterns are one of the major reasons for school segregation. Your community may have concentrations of ethnic groups in certain geographical areas. Such patterns create school districts that are largely black, Hispanic, white, and so on.

President Clinton and Arkansas governor Mike Huckabee comfort Minnijean Brown Trickey as she enters Central High School in Little Rock, Arkansas, on the fortieth anniversary of Central High's integration. Trickey, awash with emotion, and Thelma Mothershed-Wair (standing behind Trickey) were both members of the "Little Rock Nine." In his remarks, President Clinton lamented that although "segregation is no longer the law, . . . too often separation is still the rule."

BUSING ● The transportation of public school students by bus to schools physically outside their neighborhoods to eliminate school segregation based on residential patterns.

I N F O T R A C °

Integration dilemmas in a racist culture

Busing

Busing

Attempts to eliminate *de facto* segregation have included redrawing school district lines and reassigning pupils. **Busing**—the transporting of students by bus to schools physically outside their neighborhoods—to achieve racially desegregated schools has also been tried. The Supreme Court first sanctioned busing in 1971 in a case involving the school system in Charlotte, North Carolina.[14] Following this decision, the Court upheld busing in several northern cities, as well as in Denver, Colorado.[15]

In 1974, however, the Supreme Court rejected the idea of busing black children from the city to the suburbs and white children from the suburbs to the city.[16] In 1986, the Court refused to hear an appeal in a case in which the lower court had approved, in a 1984 decision, the end of a fifteen-year-old desegregation plan in the public school system in Norfolk, Virginia.[17] By the 1990s, some large-scale busing programs were either being cut back or terminated. In *Missouri v. Jenkins*[18] in 1995, the Supreme Court ruled that the state of Missouri could stop spending money to attract a multiracial student body through major educational improvements.

Busing has been unpopular with many groups. Parents and children complain that they lose the convenience of neighborhood schools. Local governments and school boards resent having the courts tell them what they must do. Some black parents argue that busing disrupts their children's lives and forces their children to face the hostility of white students in the schools to which they are bused. Some blacks also resent the implication that minority children can learn only if they sit next to white children. Others, however, believe that busing improves the educational and career opportunities of minority children and also enhances the ability of children from different ethnic groups to get along with each other.

THE CIVIL RIGHTS MOVEMENT

In 1955, one year after the first *Brown* decision, an African American woman named Rosa Parks boarded a public bus in Montgomery, Alabama. When it became crowded, she refused to move to the "colored section" at the rear of the bus. She was arrested and fined for violating local segregation laws. Her refusal and arrest spurred the local African American community to organize a year-long boycott of the entire Montgomery bus

In the left-hand photo, you see a police escort of buses carrying African American students to South Boston High in 1974. Busing was initiated in the late 1960s and early 1970s as a means to integrate public schools. A more common sight today is a public school bus transporting children of different racial and ethnic backgrounds, as in the photo on the right.

This is a photo of National Guard members blocking the entrance to Beale Street in Memphis, Tennessee, on March 29, 1968. Many of the civil rights advances made in the 1960s resulted from peaceful demonstrations such as the one shown here.

CIVIL RIGHTS MOVEMENT ● The movement in the 1950s and 1960s, by minorities and concerned whites, to end racial segregation.

system. The protest was led by a twenty-seven-year-old Baptist minister, Dr. Martin Luther King, Jr. During the protest period, he was jailed and his house was bombed. Despite the hostility and the overwhelming odds, the protesters were triumphant.

In 1956, a federal court prohibited the segregation of buses in Montgomery, and the era of the **civil rights movement**—the movement by minorities and concerned whites to end racial segregation—had begun. The movement was led by a number of diverse groups and individuals, including Dr. Martin Luther King and his Southern Christian Leadership Conference (SCLC). Other groups, such as the Congress of Racial Equality (CORE) and the NAACP, also sought to secure equal rights for African Americans.

This photo shows Martin Luther King, Jr., shaking hands with President Lyndon B. Johnson at the White House on July 2, 1964. Johnson had just signed into law the Civil Rights Act, the most comprehensive civil rights law of our country's modern era. At the signing, Johnson asked all Americans to join in his effort "to bring justice and hope to all of our people and to bring peace to our land."

CIVIL DISOBEDIENCE ● The deliberate and public act of refusing to obey laws thought to be unjust.

Civil disobedience, which is the deliberate and public act of refusing to obey laws thought to be unjust, was one tactic used to gain civil rights. For example, in 1960, in Greensboro, North Carolina, four African American students sat at the lunch counter at Woolworth's and ordered food. The waitress refused to serve them, but they stayed and were eventually arrested. Nonviolent sit-ins, freedom marches, freedom rides, boycotts, lawsuits, and occasional violent confrontations were all tactics used by the civil rights movement to heighten awareness and bring about change.

CIVIL RIGHTS LEGISLATION IN THE 1960S

As the civil rights movement demonstrated its strength, Congress began to pass civil rights laws. It became clear that while the Fourteenth Amendment prevented the *government* from discriminating against individuals or groups, the private sector—businesses, restaurants, and so on—could still freely refuse to employ and serve nonwhites.

The Civil Rights Act of 1964 was the first and most comprehensive civil rights law. It forbade discrimination on the basis of race, color, religion, gender, and national origin. The major provisions of the act were as follows:

- It outlawed discrimination in public places of accommodation, such as hotels, restaurants, snack bars, movie theaters, and public transportation.
- It provided that federal funds could be withheld from any federal or state government project or facility that practiced any form of discrimination.
- It banned discrimination in employment.
- It outlawed arbitrary discrimination in voter registration.
- It authorized the federal government to sue to desegregate public schools and facilities.

Other significant laws passed by Congress during the 1960s included the Voting Rights Act of 1965, which made it illegal to interfere with anyone's right to vote in any election held in this country (see Chapter 9 for a discussion of the historical restrictions on voting that African Americans faced), and the Civil Rights Act of 1968, which prohibited discrimination in housing. (The 1968 act authorized the use of "discrimination testers," or "bias testers," to see if particular landlords or other property owners engage in housing discrimination. Recently, bias testers have been used to test employers for discriminatory practices—see this chapter's feature, *A Question of Ethics: Does Employment-Bias Testing Constitute Fraud?*, for a discussion of this issue.)

Hispanics

In addition to African Americans, other minority groups in American society have had to deal with the effects of traditional cultural beliefs and social perceptions in their struggle for equal treatment. Hispanics, or Latinos, as they are often called, constitute by far the largest of these groups. Hispanics are now the second-largest minority group in the United States, representing about 11 percent of the U.S. population. If current trends continue, this figure will rise to nearly 19 percent by the year 2030 (see Figure 5-1). It is expected that by the end of 2004, Hispanics will overtake African Americans as the nation's largest minority group. Each year, the Hispanic population grows by nearly one million people, one-third of whom are newly arrived legal immigrants.

To classify Hispanics as a single minority group is misleading. Spanish-speaking individuals do not refer to themselves as Hispanics but rather identify themselves by their country of origin. The largest Hispanic group consists of Mexican Americans, who constitute slightly over 60 percent of the Hispanic population living in the United States. About 15 percent of Hispanics are Puerto Ricans, and approximately 6 percent are Cuban Americans. Other,

a question of ethics

Does Employment-Bias Testing Constitute Fraud?

For some time, civil rights organizations have hired bias testers to check for discrimination in housing. In a bias-testing operation, two persons—one white and one African American, for example—seek to rent or purchase the same property. Both persons tell the housing agency or owner roughly the same story with respect to their credit history, employment status, family size, and so on. If the housing agency or owner refuses to rent or sell the property to the African American, it indicates bias—in violation of the 1968 Civil Rights Act prohibiting discrimination in housing.

Although discrimination testing is permitted under the 1968 fair housing law, no law or court decision authorizes this practice in the employment context. Yet in recent years bias testers have been hired to identify businesses that discriminate against job appli-

cants. In one case, Lolita Pierce, an African American woman, applied for a job as a receptionist for Guardian Security Services, Inc., in Chicago. After a job interview, she was told selected applicants would be called later for second interviews. A few hours later, Eve Loftman, a white woman who had similar credentials was tested, interviewed, and offered the job. Neither woman really wanted the job—they had both been hired by the Legal Assistance Foundation of Chicago as bias testers.

Are such "sting" operations against employers fair? Civil rights advocates claim that they are—using bias testers to investigate employers is necessary to help curb employment discrimination. Some employers, including Guardian Security, argue that discrimination testing is not only unfair but also illegal. In essence,

presenting fake job qualifications and pretending interest in a job amount to fraud. The issue is now coming before the courts. A federal judge recently dismissed the action brought against Guardian Security by the bias testers, concluding that there were no grounds for the lawsuit—the bias testers were not really seeking a job and had suffered no harm. The decision may or may not be upheld on appeal. In the meantime, Guardian Security has sued the bias testers for fraud.

For Critical Analysis

Fraud, or fraudulent misrepresentation, is defined as a **tort** *(wrongful act) in our legal system, and victims of fraud can sue for damages. Should an exception to this legal principle be made for bias testers?*

---

smaller groups consist of individuals who have fled from Latin American countries for political reasons, hoping to find refuge in the United States.

ECONOMIC WELFARE

Hispanic households seem to have become entrenched as this country's working poor. The latest census data show that the poverty rate among Hispanics in the United States has surpassed that of African Americans. Hispanic residents constitute about 24 percent of the country's official

Figure 5–1
Hispanic Population, 1970–2030

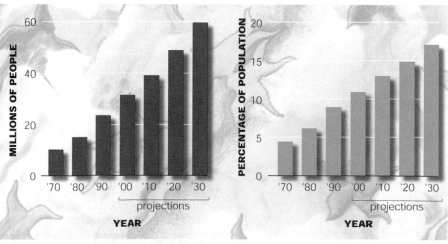

SOURCE: U.S. Bureau of the Census, 1999.

The fastest-growing minority in the United States consists of Hispanics, many of whom prefer to speak Spanish. Signs similar to those shown above appear in many parts of Los Angeles, Denver, New York City, San Antonio, and Miami.

poor, and their economic situation is worsening. Just since 1992, their median income has fallen by nearly 8 percent.

Researchers have found it difficult to pinpoint any reasons for this decline in income among Hispanics.[19] Hispanic leaders, however, tend to attribute this decline to language problems, lack of job training, and continuing immigration (which disguises statistical progress).

POLITICAL PARTICIPATION

Hispanics in the United States generally have a comparatively low level of political participation. When comparing citizens of equal incomes and educational backgrounds, however, Hispanic citizens' participation rate is higher than average. Even poor Hispanics are more likely to vote than poor whites. Given their increasing numbers, the demographic electoral importance of Hispanics cannot be denied.

Hispanics are indeed gaining power in some states. By the mid-1990s, more than 5 percent of the members of the state legislatures of Arizona, California, Colorado, Florida, New Mexico, and Texas were of Hispanic ancestry. By the 1970s, Hispanics had five representatives in Congress. By 1999, in the 106th Congress, the number of Hispanics had risen to eighteen. Also, President Bill Clinton appointed two Hispanics, Henry Cisneros and Federico Peña, to cabinet posts during his first term.

Cuban Americans have been notably successful in gaining local political power, particularly in Dade County, Florida, and Mexican Americans have also gained some clout in local politics. Puerto Ricans have had few political successes on the mainland, however. Generally, voting turnout by Puerto Ricans is low (only about 30 percent of them are registered to vote), and although they represent 10 percent of New York City's population, only a small percentage of that city's administrators are Puerto Rican.

Asian Americans

Asian Americans have also suffered, at times severely, from discriminatory treatment. The Chinese Exclusion Act of 1882 prevented persons from China and Japan from coming to the United States to prospect for gold or to work on the railroads or in factories in the West. After 1900, immigration continued to be restricted—only limited numbers of persons from China and Japan were allowed to enter the United States. Those who were allowed into the country faced racial prejudice by Americans who had little respect for their customs and culture. In 1906, after the San Francisco earthquake, Japanese American students were segregated into special schools so that white children could use their buildings.

The Japanese bombing of Pearl Harbor in 1941, which launched the entry of the United States into World War II, intensified Americans' fear of the Japanese. Actions taken under an executive order issued by President Franklin Roosevelt in 1942 subjected many Japanese Americans to curfews, excluded them from certain "military areas," and evacuated them to internment camps (also called "relocation centers").[20] In 1988, Congress provided funds to compensate former camp inhabitants—$1.25 billion for approximately 60,000 people.

Japanese Americans and Chinese Americans now lead other ethnic groups in median income and median education, however. Indeed, Asians who have immigrated to the United States since 1965 represent the most highly skilled immigrant group in American history. Nearly 40 percent of Asian Americans over the age of twenty-five have college degrees.

More recently, immigrants from Asia, particularly from Southeast Asia, have faced discrimination. Over a million Indochinese war refugees, most of them from Vietnam, have immigrated to the United States since the 1970s. Like their predecessors, the newer immigrants quickly increased

In what many consider to be one of America's low points, 120,000 Japanese Americans were moved to "internment camps" during World War II. Shown here are Japanese Americans from Bainbridge Island (off the coast of Washington) marching under Army escort at a Seattle dock. Their ultimate destination is Manzanar Camp in California. The internees suffered property losses estimated at over $400 million (several billion in today's dollars). The last camp was closed in March 1946.

their median income. Most came with relatives and were sponsored by American families or organizations. Thus, they had good support systems to help them get started.

Native Americans

Of all of the groups that have suffered discriminatory treatment in the United States, Native Americans stand out because of the unique nature of their treatment. In the 1600s, there were about ten million Native Americans, or "Indians," in the New World. Today, fewer than two million people in the United States identify themselves as Native Americans. Most Native Americans live in Oklahoma, New Mexico, Arizona, and California; about half of them live on reservations.

In 1789, Congress designated the Native American tribes as foreign nations so that the government could sign land and boundary treaties with them. As members of foreign nations, Native Americans had no civil rights under U.S. laws. This situation continued until 1924, when citizenship rights were extended to all persons born in the United States.

EARLY POLICIES TOWARD NATIVE AMERICANS

The Northwest Ordinance, passed by the Congress of the Confederation in 1787, stated that "the utmost good faith shall always be observed towards the Indians; their lands and property shall never be taken from them without their consent; and in their property, rights, and liberty, they shall never be invaded or disturbed, unless in just and lawful wars authorized by Congress." Over the next hundred years, many agreements were made with the Indian tribes; many were also broken by Congress, as well as by individuals who wanted Indian lands for settlement or exploration.

In the early 1830s, the government followed a policy of separation. To prevent conflicts, boundaries were established between lands occupied by Native Americans and those occupied by white settlers. In 1830, Congress

Here, young men from a variety of tribes pose for a photograph in 1872 on their arrival at the Hampton Institute in Virginia, a boarding school for Native Americans. Later, they will don school uniforms, and another photo will be taken (to be used for "before and after" comparisons). This was a typical practice at Native American boarding schools.

instructed the Bureau of Indian Affairs (BIA), which had been established in 1824 as part of the War Department, to remove all tribes to lands (reservations) west of the Mississippi River in order to free land east of the Mississippi for white settlement.

As white settlers continued to push westward, beyond the Mississippi, it became clear that the policy of separation could no longer effectively divide Native Americans from whites—there simply wasn't enough room on the continent for both groups to have separate lands. Thus, in the late 1880s, the U.S. government changed its policy. The goal became the "assimilation" of Native Americans into American society. Each family was given a parcel of land within the reservation to farm. The remaining acreage was sold to whites, thus reducing the number of acres in reservation status from 140 million to about 47 million acres. Tribes that would not cooperate with this plan lost their reservations altogether. To further the goal of cultural assimilation, agents from the BIA, which runs the Indian reservation system with the tribes, set up Native American boarding schools for the children to remove them from their parents' influence. In these schools, Native American children were taught how to speak the English language, instructed in the Christian religion, and encouraged to dress like white Americans.

The Foxwoods Casino in Ledyard, Connecticut, is owned by the Mashantucket Pequot Native American tribe. Today, many Native American tribes run lucrative gambling operations. Some critics of such institutions argue that these operations are wrongfully transforming the traditional Native American way of life.

NATIVE AMERICANS STRIKE BACK

Native Americans have always found it difficult to garner political power. In part, this is because they have no official representation. Additionally, the tribes are small and scattered, making organized political movements difficult. Today, Native Americans remain a fragmented political group, because large numbers of their population live off the reservations. Nonetheless, by the 1960s, Native Americans succeeded in forming organizations to strike back at the U.S. government and to reclaim their heritage, including their lands.

The first militant organization was called the National Indian Youth Council. In the late 1960s, a small group of persons identifying themselves as Indians occupied Alcatraz Island, claiming that the island was part of their ancestral lands. Other militant actions followed. For example, in 1973, supporters of the American Indian Movement took over Wounded Knee, South Dakota, where about 150 Sioux Indians had been killed by the U.S. Army in 1890.[21] The siege was undertaken to protest the government's policy toward Native Americans and to call attention to the injustices they had suffered.

As more Americans became aware of the concerns of Native Americans, Congress started to compensate them for past injustices. In 1990, Congress passed the Native American Languages Act, which declared that Native American languages are unique and serve an important role in maintaining Indian culture and continuity. Under the act, the government and the Indian community share responsibility for the survival of native languages and native cultures. Courts, too, have shown a greater willingness to recognize Native American treaty rights. For example, in 1985, the Supreme Court ruled that three tribes of Oneida Indians could claim damages for the use of tribal land that had been unlawfully transferred in 1795.[22]

The Indian Gaming Regulatory Act of 1988 allows Native Americans to have gambling operations on their reservations. The act has had a significant effect on the economic and social aspects of reservation life.

Securing Rights for Other Groups

In addition to those groups already discussed, other groups in American society have faced discriminatory treatment. Older Americans have been victims of discrimination. So have persons with disabilities and gay and lesbian groups. (See this chapter's *Politics on the Far Side* for another special group of Americans that claims to suffer from discrimination.)

PROTECTING OLDER AMERICANS

Today, over 34 million Americans (13 percent of the population) are aged sixty-five or over. By the year 2035, it is estimated that this figure will have reached 73.4 million. Clearly, as the American population grows older, the problems of aging and retirement will become increasingly important national issues. Because many older people rely on income from Social Security, the funding of Social Security benefits continues to be a major issue on the national political agenda, as you will read in Chapter 17.

Many older people who would like to work find it difficult because of age discrimination. Some companies have unwritten policies against hiring, retaining, or promoting people they feel are "too old," making it impossible for some older workers to find work or to continue with their careers. At times, older workers have fallen victim to cost-cutting efforts by employers. To reduce operational costs, companies may replace older, higher-salaried employees with younger workers who are willing to work for less pay.

As part of an effort to protect the rights of older Americans, Congress passed the Age Discrimination in Employment Act (ADEA) in 1967. This act prohibits employers, employment agencies, and labor organizations from discriminating against individuals over the age of forty on the basis of age. To succeed in a suit for age discrimination, an employee must prove that the employer's action, such as a decision to fire the employee, was motivated at least in part by age bias. Proof that qualified older employees are generally discharged before younger employees or that a younger person was hired for a job instead of an older, better qualified applicant may be enough. In 1996, the Supreme Court held that even when an employee over the age of forty is replaced by a younger employee who is also over the age of forty, the older person is entitled to bring a suit under the ADEA. The Court said that the issue in all ADEA cases is whether age discrimination has in fact occurred, regardless of the age of the replacement worker.[24]

politics on the far side

Should Bikers Be a Protected Class?

Groups defined by such characteristics as race, color, ethnic origin, gender, religion, age, or disability are regarded as "protected classes" under federal and state laws prohibiting discrimination. Recently, the United Bikers of Maine asked the Maine legislature to include motorcyclists as a protected class under the state Human Rights Act, because bikers are frequently victims of discrimination. They are turned away from bars, restaurants, and hotels simply because they have multiple ear piercings or look tough in their black leather jackets covered in "colors," or patches representing bike clubs. The bill's future is not too promising. Very likely, most legislators will agree with Robert Howe, of the Maine Innkeepers Association, who doubts whether bikers really need the kind of protection given to other groups under the law. After all, states Howe, "People cannot change their skin color or their religion, but a biker can change his clothes."[23]

For Critical Analysis: Which Americans are not members of a protected class?

OBTAINING RIGHTS FOR PERSONS WITH DISABILITIES

Like age discrimination, discrimination based on disability crosses the boundaries of race, ethnicity, gender, and religion. Persons with disabilities, especially physical deformities or severe mental impairments, have to face social bias against them simply because they are "different." Although attitudes toward persons with disabilities have changed considerably in the last several decades, persons with disabilities continue to suffer from discrimination in all its forms.

Persons with disabilities first became a political force in this country in the 1970s, and in 1973, Congress passed the first legislation protecting this group of persons—the Rehabilitation Act. This act prohibited discrimination against persons with disabilities in programs receiving federal aid. In 1975, Congress passed the Education for All Handicapped Children Act, which guarantees that all children with disabilities will receive an "appropriate" education. Further legislation in 1978 led to regulations for ramps, elevators, and the like in all federal buildings. The Americans with Disabilities Act (ADA) of 1990, however, is by far the most significant legislation protecting the rights of this group of Americans.

The ADA requires that all public buildings and public services be accessible to persons with disabilities. The act also mandates that employers "reasonably accommodate" the needs of workers or job applicants with disabilities who are otherwise qualified for particular jobs unless to do so would cause the employer to suffer an "undue hardship." The ADA defines persons with disabilities as persons who have physical or mental impairments that "substantially limit" their everyday activities. Health conditions that have been considered disabilities under federal law include blindness, alcoholism, heart disease, cancer, muscular dystrophy, cerebral palsy, paraplegia, diabetes, and acquired immune deficiency syndrome (AIDS). The ADA, however, does not require employers to hire or retain workers who, because of their disabilities, pose a "direct threat to the health or safety" of their co-workers.

GAY MEN AND LESBIANS

Until the late 1960s and early 1970s, gay men and lesbians tended to keep quiet about their sexual preferences because to expose them usually meant facing harsh consequences. This attitude began to change after a 1969

INFOTRAC®

The costly compassion of the ADA

Americans with disabilities demonstrate in Washington, D.C., in support of the Americans with Disabilities Act (ADA), which was signed into law by President Bush in 1990. The ADA requires that all public buildings and public services be accessible to persons with disabilities. The act also prohibits discrimination against a "qualified individual with a disability" with regard to job application and hiring procedures, training, compensation, fringe benefits, advancement, and other terms or conditions of employment. The ADA requires that employers "reasonably accommodate" the needs of employees or job applicants with disabilities.

EQUAL EMPLOYMENT OPPORTUNITY ● A goal of the 1964 Civil Rights Act to end employment discrimination based on race, color, religion, gender, or national origin and to promote equal job opportunities for all individuals.

INFOTRAC®

We the 50 peoples

incident in New York City, however. When the police raided the Stonewall Inn—a bar popular with gay men and lesbians—on June 27 of that year, the bar's patrons responded by throwing beer cans and bottles at the police. The riot continued for two days. The Stonewall Inn incident, which was later referred to as "the shot heard round the homosexual world," launched the gay power movement. By the end of the year, gay men and lesbians had formed fifty organizations, including the Gay Activist Alliance and the Gay Liberation Front.

The number of gay and lesbian organizations has grown from fifty in 1969 to several thousand today. These groups have exerted significant political pressure on legislatures, the media, schools, and churches. Since the 1970s, twenty-five states plus the District of Columbia have repealed their sodomy laws—laws that prohibited homosexual conduct. Such laws have been invalidated by the courts in seven other states. The Civil Service Commission eliminated its ban on the employment of gay men and lesbians, and in 1980, the Democratic Party platform included a gay rights plank.

Today, at least one hundred cities (the number is quickly increasing) throughout the United States have laws prohibiting discrimination against homosexuals in housing, education, banking, labor union employment, and public accommodations. In a landmark case in 1996, *Romer v. Evans*,[25] the Supreme Court held that a Colorado amendment, which would have invalidated all state and local laws protecting homosexuals from discrimination, violated the equal protection clause of the Constitution. The Court stated that the amendment would have denied to homosexuals in Colorado—but to no other Colorado residents—"the right to seek specific protection from the law."

Laws and court decisions protecting the rights of gay men and lesbians reflect social attitudes that are much changed from the days of the Stonewall incident. The issue of gay rights, though, continues to be divisive. In fact, a recent Gallup poll[26] indicates that despite the enormous social changes that have taken place in this country since 1977, Americans' views on gay rights have not really changed dramatically over the years.

For example, the percentage of Americans who think homosexual relations between consenting adults should be legal rose only seven percentage points between 1977 and 1999—from 43 percent to 50 percent. And the percentage of Americans who feel that homosexual relations between consenting adults should *not* be legal remained identical over that same time period—at 43 percent. When it comes to the issue of whether gay men and lesbians should be discriminated against in the employment context, however, a strong majority of Americans (83 percent) say "No."

Perhaps the most controversial issue with respect to gay rights is whether gay marriages should be legalized. The Gallup poll just mentioned indicates that about two-thirds of Americans believe that such marriages should not be recognized as valid by law. (For a further discussion of this issue, see this chapter's feature entitled *The American Political Spectrum: Should Same-Sex Couples Have the Legal Right to Marry?* on the next page.)

Beyond Equal Protection— Affirmative Action

One provision of the Civil Rights Act of 1964 called for prohibiting discrimination in employment. The federal government began to legislate programs of **equal employment opportunity.** Such programs require that employers' hiring and promotion practices guarantee the same opportunities to all individuals. Experience soon showed that minorities often had fewer opportunities to obtain education and relevant work experience than did whites. Because of this, they were still excluded from many jobs. Even though discriminatory practices were made illegal, the change in the law did not make up for the results of years of discrimination. Consequently, a new strategy was developed.

Should Same-Sex Couples Have the Legal Right to Marry?

Should gay and lesbian couples be allowed to marry? The controversy over this issue was fueled in 1993 when the Hawaii Supreme Court ruled that by denying the right of gay couples to marry, the state of Hawaii had violated the state constitution's equal protection clause.

The reaction to this decision was immediate. Bills to prohibit same-sex marriages were introduced in at least thirty-two state legislatures (sixteen of the bills were enacted into law by 1999). In 1996, President Clinton signed into law the federal Defense of Marriage Act, which allows states to refuse to recognize same-sex marriages. In 1998, residents of Hawaii voted for an amendment to the state constitution empowering the state legislature to ban same-sex marriages.

Conservatives Say No to Same-Sex Marriages

A large number of Americans, predominantly those with conservative political and social views, strongly oppose same-sex mar-

riages. Generally, this group does not support any laws designed to protect gay rights.

The strongest opposition to same-sex marriages comes, of course, from the Christian Right. From the outset, the gay rights movement has challenged Christian beliefs because, according to the Bible, homosexual conduct is sinful. Its purpose is not procreation (the reason marriage was sanctioned by the Catholic Church and eventually made a sacrament) but carnal pleasure. Leaders endorsed by the Christian Right, such as Pat Buchanan, argue that to allow homosexuals to marry would pervert the purpose of marriage. It would also further erode traditional American family values. These values are what has made this country great, and they must be protected if we are to sustain our polity.

Furthermore, the government has no authority to give legal sanction to conduct that violates the values of a large portion of American society and the princi-

ples and religious beliefs of the founders of this nation.

Liberals Say, "Why Not?"

Those with liberal social and political views have by and large supported gay rights. They tend to support the concept of homosexual marriage so that homosexual couples can have all of the legal rights of married couples. Already, homosexual partners have been given certain rights traditionally given only to spouses.

For example, some cities, including San Francisco, have passed city ordinances requiring companies receiving city contracts to offer the same health insurance and other benefits to employees' domestic partners, whether they be heterosexual or homosexual, as are offered to spouses. A number of leading companies also have nondiscriminatory benefits policies.

Why not allow homosexuals to marry? Doing so would resolve a number of issues, including questions about entitlement to benefits. It would also facilitate gay couples' attempts to adopt children, allow them to assume legal guardianship status when one partner is seriously ill, and so on. More important, nothing in the U.S. Constitution says homosexual couples cannot marry. To deprive these couples of marital rights is to deprive them of rights granted to all other citizens.

For Critical Analysis

Laws allowing homosexual marriages should be supported because they would help to create family values and more stable relationships among homosexuals. Analyze this argument.

Gay citizens demonstrate for the freedom to marry.

AFFIRMATIVE ACTION ● A policy calling for the establishment of programs that involve giving preference, in jobs and college admissions, to members of groups that have been discriminated against in the past.

REVERSE DISCRIMINATION ● The assertion that affirmative action programs that require preferential treatment for minorities discriminate against those who have no minority status.

QUOTA SYSTEM ● A policy under which a specific number of jobs, promotions, or other types of selections, such as university admissions, must be given to members of selected groups.

Initiated by President Lyndon B. Johnson (1963–1969), the new strategy came to be called **affirmative action,** a policy that requires employers to take positive steps to remedy *past* discrimination. Affirmative action programs involve giving preference, in jobs and college admissions, to members of groups that have been discriminated against in the past. All public and private employers who receive federal funds, until recently, have been required to adopt and implement these programs. Thus, the policy of affirmative action has been applied to all agencies of the federal, state, and local governments and to all private employers who sell goods to or perform services for any agency of the federal government. In short, it has covered nearly all of the nation's major employers and many of its smaller ones.

AFFIRMATIVE ACTION TESTED

The Supreme Court first addressed the issue of affirmative action in 1978 in *Regents of the University of California v. Bakke.*[27] Allan Bakke, a white male, had been denied admission to the University of California's medical school at Davis. The school had set aside sixteen of the one hundred seats in each year's entering class for applicants who wished to be considered as members of designated minority groups. Many of the students admitted through this special program had lower test scores than Bakke. Bakke sued the university, claiming that he was a victim of **reverse discrimination**—discrimination against whites. Bakke argued that the use of a **quota system,** in which a specific number of seats was reserved for minority applicants only, violated the equal protection clause.

The Supreme Court was strongly divided on the issue. Some justices believed that Bakke had been denied equal protection and should be admitted. A majority on the Court, however, concluded that both the Constitution and the Civil Rights Act of 1964 allow race to be used as a factor in making admissions decisions, although race could not be the *sole* factor. Because the university's quota system was based solely on race, it was unconstitutional.

One year later, a major test of the constitutionality of affirmative action programs in private employment came in *United Steelworkers of America v. Weber.*[28] An employer had created training programs in which half of the positions were reserved for African Americans. Brian Weber, a white worker, was not selected for the training program on three occasions, even though he had more seniority than several of the African American

employees chosen. The Supreme Court upheld the company's affirmative action program. It ruled that the Civil Rights Act of 1964 did not prohibit voluntary affirmative action programs in private industry.

REJECTING SOME AFFIRMATIVE ACTION

In the 1980s, the Supreme Court issued a string of rulings that rejected some affirmative action programs. In a 1984 case, for example, the Court ruled that layoffs of Memphis firefighters had to be done on the basis of seniority unless African American employees could prove that they were victims of racial bias.[29] In 1989, the Court rejected a minority set-aside program for city government contracts in Richmond, Virginia. The city had provided that any company awarded a city construction contract had to subcontract, or set aside, at least 30 percent of the work to minority businesses. The Court ruled that the set-aside program denied white contractors their Fourteenth Amendment right to equal protection.[30]

In another 1989 case, the Supreme Court ruled that white firefighters in Birmingham, Alabama, could challenge a minority hiring and promotion plan even after city officials and African Americans had agreed to the plan.[31] In still another 1989 decision, the Supreme Court made it harder for minority workers to succeed in lawsuits for discrimination. The case involved Alaskan cannery workers who charged their employers with employment bias. The Supreme Court ruled that statistical evidence was not enough proof to support the employees' claim of racial discrimination. The employees also had to show that the conditions they challenged were not the result of some legitimate business necessity.[32]

In response to these and other Supreme Court decisions, civil rights activists pressured Congress into taking action to protect discrimination victims from the Supreme Court's more conservative approach. The result was the Civil Rights Act of 1991, which effectively overturned the conservative rulings and made it easier for workers to sue their employers. The act also broadened the remedies available for employment discrimination. The act did *not,* however, decide on the constitutionality of affirmative action programs. Nor could it—that is the Supreme Court's job.

AFFIRMATIVE ACTION IS UNDER ATTACK

Although the *Bakke* case and later court decisions alleviated the harshness of the quota system, today's courts seem to be going even further in questioning the constitutional validity of affirmative action. Affirmative action is also being attacked at the ballot box.

The Courts Retrench

In 1995, the Supreme Court issued a landmark decision in *Adarand Constructors, Inc. v. Peña*.[33] The Court held that any federal, state, or local affirmative action program that uses racial classifications as the basis for making decisions is subject to "strict scrutiny" by the courts. As discussed earlier in this chapter, this means that, to be constitutional, a discriminatory law or action must be narrowly tailored to meet a *compelling* government interest.

The strict scrutiny standard has a reputation for being "strict in theory, but fatal in fact." After the Court's *Adarand* decision, some doubted whether any affirmative action program would survive strict scrutiny analysis. Justice Sandra Day O'Connor tried to stall off such an interpretation by stating in the *Adarand* opinion that the "unhappy persistence of both the practice and the lingering effects of racial discrimination against minority groups in this country is an unfortunate reality, and government is not disqualified from acting in response to it." In effect, though, the *Adarand* decision narrowed the application of affirmative action programs. An affirmative action program can no longer make use of quotas or preferences for less qualified persons and cannot be maintained simply to rem-

Nowhere has the backlash against affirmative action been more obvious than in California. In 1996, voters in that state approved Proposition 209, a ballot initiative that called for the elimination of affirmative action in public employment, education, and contracting. A court battle over the new law immediately ensued. A federal appellate court held that the law was constitutional and could be implemented. The Supreme Court decided not to review the case.

edy past discrimination by society in general. It must be narrowly tailored to remedy actual discrimination that has occurred, and once the program has succeeded, it must be changed or dropped.

Lower courts have followed the Supreme Court's lead—and some have even gone further. For example, in a 1996 case, *Hopwood v. State of Texas,*[34] two white law school applicants sued the University of Texas School of Law in Austin, claiming that they had been denied admission because of the school's affirmative action program. The program allowed admissions officials to take racial and other factors into consideration when determining which students would be admitted. A federal appellate court held that the program violated the equal protection clause because it discriminated in favor of minority applicants. In its decision, the court directly challenged the *Bakke* decision by stating that the use of race even as a means of achieving diversity on college campuses "undercuts the Fourteenth Amendment." In other words, race could never be a factor, even though it was not the sole factor, in such decisions. The Supreme Court declined to hear the case, thus letting the lower court's decision stand. During the term ending in 1998, the Court declined to review other cases involving other types of affirmative action programs.

State Initiatives

On November 5, 1996, the citizens of California voted on a Civil Rights Initiative to amend their state constitution. That initiative, which appeared on the ballot as Proposition 209, read in part as follows:

> The state shall not discriminate against, or grant preferential treatment to, any individual or group on the basis of race, sex, color, ethnicity, or national origin in the operation of public employment, public education, or public contracting.

Of the nearly 9 million Californians casting ballots, over 4.7 million (54 percent) voted in favor of the initiative.

The ink was barely dry on the new constitutional amendment when several groups and individuals filed a lawsuit in a federal court to prevent the amendment from being enforced. These groups claimed that the law was unconstitutional because, among other things, it denied to racial minorities and women the equal protection of the laws guaranteed by the Fourteenth Amendment. The federal judge granted the groups' request for a temporary restraining order, which meant that the law could not be enforced until further proceedings. On appeal, however, the federal appellate court reversed the lower court's decision.[35] The case was appealed to the United States Supreme Court, but the Court declined to review the case.

In 1997, the instigator and leader of the movement to pass Proposition 209, Ward Connerly, launched the American Civil Rights Institute. Its purpose is to lobby for federal legislation to ban affirmative action and to help garner support for measures similar to Proposition 209 that are on other states' ballots. Soon after the organization was started, a dozen states had asked for help in putting anti–affirmative action propositions on their ballots. In 1998, voters in one of these states, Washington, approved a ballot measure ending all state-sponsored affirmative action in that state.

AFFIRMATIVE ACTION— THE DEBATE CONTINUES

The latter half of the 1990s saw a growing backlash across the country against affirmative action. Nonetheless, a large group of Americans, including President Clinton, favor the continuation of affirmative action programs. Without such programs, they claim, minorities will have difficulty competing in university admissions and in the workplace.

Indeed, at the University of Texas Law School, three years after racial preferences were effectively banned by the *Hopwood* decision mentioned earlier, only eight of a first-year class of 455 students were African Americans, a smaller percentage than in 1950.[36] There has also been a

INFOTRAC®

Civil rights groups avoid taking cases

Students at the Berkeley Campus of the University of California demonstrate in favor of affirmative action outside a hall in which the university's Board of Regents were meeting. By voter initiatives, both California (in 1996) and Washington (in 1998) ended state-sponsored affirmative action in their states.

notable decline in minority admissions to the University of California at Berkeley. In the first year after the ban on affirmative action went into effect, freshman minority enrollment at Berkeley was cut in half. Without affirmative action, only a few Latinos and even fewer African Americans have been able to qualify for admission.

Opponents of affirmative action look at the issue from a different perspective. For example, they point out that Berkeley is an elite school within the California system—to be admitted there, students must be among the top 4 percent of students in the state. Those who are not admitted to Berkeley still have the option of attending other universities in the California state system. In fact, admission figures for all nine campuses of the University of California system show that, overall, the drop in admission rates for minorities has been relatively insignificant—less than two percentage points. Critics also stress that only about 20 percent of the nation's universities—the prestigious ones whose names are familiar to everyone—even use preferences to any significant extent. The vast majority of other four-year colleges and universities admit a significantly higher proportion of applicants, and in the past decade or so, the number of minority admissions has been climbing steadily.[37]

Essentially, what is at stake in the affirmative action controversy is not whether minorities get into college. Rather, it is whether they have an opportunity to enroll in the nation's leading educational institutions—and later, to move into the top echelons of the business or professional world. Whether this opportunity should be extended to minorities through preferential admissions policies is a question that continues to divide Americans.

Americans at Odds over Civil Rights

Throughout this nation's history, groups have been at odds over civil rights. Even at the Constitutional Convention, there was a strong division of opinion over the issue of civil rights for African Americans. Today, Americans continue to be at odds over a number of civil rights issues, including many touched on in this chapter, such as affirmative action. Here we look at two other controversial issues.

The Trend toward Resegregation

Fighting segregation in the schools seems to be a losing battle, and many Americans today are at odds over whether it's a battle worth continuing. Busing, once thought to be a solution, clearly hasn't had the desired result. In fact, during the 1990s, segregation in American schools has experienced a resurgence. According to a report of the National School Boards Association entitled "The Growth of Segregation in American Schools," the Northeast has the most segregated schools in the country and the South, the most integrated. But even in the South, the trend is toward more segregation.

By the late 1990s, less than 40 percent of African American students attended predominantly white schools, compared with 44 percent in 1987. Nationwide, one out of every three African American and Hispanic students goes to a school with more than 90 percent minority enrollment. In the largest U.S. cities, fifteen out of sixteen African American and Hispanic students go to schools with almost no whites.

A study by Harvard University's Civil Rights Project showed similar results. The study also showed that whites, too, are racially segregated. The average white student now attends a school that is 81 percent white.[38]

Many Americans contend that the cause of this resegregation is racism and that busing is necessary to counter the effect of racial bias on educational opportunities. Others argue that changing social and economic cir-

Two teenagers do chin-ups at a public junior high school in Texas. In spite of attempts to desegregate America's schools, today one out of three African American and Hispanic students attends a school with more than 90 percent minority enrollment.

cumstances are the major cause of increasing segregation. This group points to the rapid decline in the relative proportion of whites living in big cities. Many whites have left the cities for the suburbs, while immigration and high minority birthrates have increased the minority presence in urban areas. Increasingly, Americans holding the latter view are becoming a majority, and the segregation issue is focusing less on racism and more on improving conditions in urban schools generally. The goal of racially balanced schools, envisioned in the *Brown v. Board of Education of Topeka* decision in 1954, seems to be giving way to the goal of better educated children, however that goal is attained.

Sexual Harassment versus Free Speech

One of the issues over which Americans are at odds today is whether protection against sexual harassment has caused employers and others to lose sight of other rights, particularly free speech rights. During the last three decades, the number of sexual-harassment suits against companies has climbed dramatically. And just one successful suit for harassment against a small company can bankrupt that firm. Even if a worker does not succeed in the suit, the legal fees incurred by defending against the claim—and the possible harm to the firm's reputation—could be devastating for the firm's profits.

Not surprisingly, most employers have tried to curb liability for sexual harassment in their workplaces by establishing fairly comprehensive harassment policies and procedures, including policies governing Internet use. As mentioned earlier, the Supreme Court has recently ruled that in some cases, having such policies and procedures in place may help employers avoid liability for harassment.

ONLINE HARASSMENT

Today's "wired" workplace has made it even more difficult for employers to protect themselves against liability for sexual harassment. Employees who access Web sites containing sexually explicit materials, racist cartoons, and pornographic images can create a hostile environment for their co-workers. For example, a woman may walk by a co-worker's desk and see some images on that worker's computer that she finds objectionable. An employee may download materials from a pornographic site to the company's computer system, and another employee accidentally views them. A worker might print out a sexually explicit image and forget to remove it from the printer before a co-worker happens to see it.

Racial jokes, ethnic slurs, or other comments contained in e-mail may also be the basis for a claim of hostile-environment harassment or other form of discrimination. In one case, for example, Chevron Corporation had to pay $2.2 million to four female employees who claimed that they had been sexually harassed by e-mail messages.[39]

To ward off potential lawsuits for sexual harassment, some companies use special software to block employees' access to certain Web sites. Others prohibit their employees from using the Internet at all or allow employees to use it only for business purposes. A number of companies also monitor their employees' use of the Internet, including their e-mail, in an attempt to increase worker productivity as well as to minimize the risk of lawsuits for harassment.

WHAT ABOUT FREEDOM OF SPEECH?

Are employers going too far in controlling speech in the workplace? Walter Olson, an expert in employment law at the Manhattan Institute, believes that some employers' policies are so stern that even trifling remarks are banned. He would like to see Congress pass a comprehensive harassment bill that would narrow the conception of what constitutes harassing speech. "Unless the comment is a threat or a promise," he suggests, "the law should take no notice."[40]

In a few cases, the courts have also pointed to the need to balance the concept of harassment against free speech rights. In one case, a federal appellate court noted, "Where pure expression is involved, Title VII steers into the territory of the First Amendment. . . . [W]hen Title VII is applied to sexual-harassment claims based solely on verbal insults or pictorial or literary matter, the statute imposes content-based . . . restrictions on speech."[41]

key terms

affirmative action 129
busing 118
civil disobedience 120
civil rights 111
civil rights movement 119
de facto segregation 117
de jure segregation 117
equal employment
    opportunity 127
equal protection clause 111

fundamental right 112
glass ceiling 115
quota system 129
rational basis test 112
reverse discrimination 129
separate but equal doctrine 116
sexual harassment 115
suffrage 113
suspect classification 112

chapter summary

1. Civil liberties limit the government by stating what the government cannot do. Civil rights, in contrast, are constitutional provisions and laws specifying what the government must do. Generally, civil rights refer to the right to equal treatment under the laws, as guaranteed by the Fourteenth Amendment to the Constitution.

2. The struggle of women for equal treatment initially focused on gaining the franchise—voting rights. In 1920, the Nineteenth Amendment, which granted voting rights to women, was ratified. Today, women remain vastly underrepresented in Congress and political offices, even though eligible female voters outnumber male voters. In the workplace, women continue to face discrimination in the form of sexual harassment and wage discrimination.

3. The Fourteenth Amendment was added in 1868 to protect the newly freed slaves from discriminatory treatment. Soon, however, southern states began to pass segregation ("Jim Crow") laws that required separate facilities for blacks and whites in housing, restaurants, hotels, schools, buses, and other areas. In 1896, in *Plessy v. Ferguson*, the Supreme Court upheld these laws, concluding that "separate but equal" treatment of the races did not violate the equal protection clause. The separate but equal doctrine justified segregation for the next sixty years.

4. In the landmark case of *Brown v. Board of Education of Topeka*, the Supreme Court held that segregation in the schools violated the equal protection clause. Forced integration of the schools was begun, and court-ordered busing of schoolchildren from white to black schools and vice versa was undertaken in an attempt to integrate the schools. By the 1980s and 1990s, the courts were allowing cities and states to discontinue busing efforts.

5. The civil rights movement was a movement by minorities and concerned whites to end racial segregation. Led by Martin Luther King, Jr., and civil rights organizations, the members of the movement engaged in nonviolent sit-ins, freedom marches, freedom rides, boycotts, lawsuits, and other tactics to arouse public awareness and bring about change. In response, Congress passed a series of civil rights laws, the most comprehensive of which was the Civil Rights Act of 1964. The Voting Rights Act of 1965 and the Civil Rights Act of 1968 attempted to ensure African American voting rights and to prohibit discrimination in housing, respectively.

6. Hispanics, or Latinos, constitute the second-largest minority group in the United States, and their numbers are climbing. The largest Hispanic groups are Mexican Americans, Puerto Ricans, and

Cuban Americans. Economically, the situation of Hispanics is worsening. Politically, Hispanics have been gaining power in some states, and more than 5 percent of the state legislators in several states are Hispanic.

7. Asian Americans have suffered from racial bias and discrimination since they first began to immigrate to this country in the late 1800s. The worst treatment of Japanese Americans occurred during World War II, when they were placed in "internment camps." Economically, Asian Americans have the highest median income and median education of any ethnic group in the United States.

8. Initially, U.S. policy toward Native Americans was one of separation—removing them to lands separate from those occupied by whites. As settlers pushed westward and the frontier "filled up," the government undertook a policy of "assimilation." Each family was given acreage within the reservation to farm, and the rest was sold to whites. Beginning in the 1960s, Native Americans formed organizations to protest federal policy and reclaim their lands. By the late 1980s and 1990s, federal policy had changed, and legislation was passed that allowed gambling on reservation lands and encouraged the survival of Native American languages.

9. Other groups that have suffered discrimination and unequal treatment in American society include older Americans, persons with disabilities, and gay men and lesbians. The Age Discrimination in Employment Act of 1967 was passed in an attempt to protect Americans over the age of forty from age discrimination in employment. The Americans with Disabilities Act of 1990 provided significant protection for Americans who, although they suffer from disabilities, are otherwise qualified to work. Since 1969, gay rights groups have become a significant political force, and social attitudes toward these groups are changing. Many states and cities now have laws specifically protecting the rights of gay men and lesbians. Whether same-sex couples should be allowed to marry is an issue that has divided society.

10. Affirmative action programs were usually upheld by the courts until the 1980s when the Supreme Court, in a series of cases, held that particular affirmative action programs violated the equal protection clause. In 1995, the Supreme Court held that affirmative action programs that use racial classifications as their basis for making decisions would be subject to "strict scrutiny," meaning that a program must be narrowly tailored to meet a compelling government interest. In 1996, a federal appellate court held that race could never be a factor in making university admissions decisions. Both California and Washington have banned, by voter initiatives, state-sponsored affirmative action programs in their states.

11. Americans are at odds over numerous civil rights issues, including the resegregation that is occurring in the schools and the limitations on free speech in the workplace created by employers' harassment policies.

for critical analysis

1. The debate over affirmative action is essentially a debate over how "equal protection of the laws" can best be achieved. In your opinion, does the "end" of equal protection justify the "means" of affirmative action, which calls for unequal treatment? Why or why not?

2. Why is the "glass ceiling" faced by women in today's corporate world so difficult to penetrate? Is there anything the government should—or can—do to remedy this problem?

3. Assuming that women will continue to gain more seats in state legislatures and in Congress than they have in the past, how might this affect policymaking? In other words, do women have a different political agenda than men? What might be some policies that women would be more likely to promote than men?

4. Because of the high rate of intermarriage among so many different ethnic groups, is the concept of ethnic classifications used by the government—in obtaining census data as well as in other programs, such as affirmative action—becoming unrealistic? Should such classifications be abandoned?

5. Do you think that special laws to protect gay males and lesbians are necessary? Do they violate the Fourteenth Amendment's guarantee of "equal protection of the laws"?

6. Several states have passed "hate crime" statutes that are designed to give special protection to minority groups who have been victimized by crimes simply because of their race, ethnic origin, or sexual orientation. Many Americans think that these laws are necessary and that more states should have them.

Others claim that such statutes undermine the concept of equal treatment for all. In your opinion, should these laws be upheld by the courts? Why or why not?

7. Can you think of any ways, other than those mentioned in the final section of this chapter, in which Internet use in the workplace could create a hostile environment?

suggested readings

ANDREWS, Marcellus. *The Political Economy of Hope and Fear: Capitalism and the Black Condition in America.* New York: New York University Press, 1999. The author contends that there has been an aggressive conservative assault on liberal racial reform generally and on black well-being in particular. Yet appeals to fairness and justice, no matter how heartfelt, are bound to fail because the economic foundations of the civil rights movement have been destroyed by the combined forces of globalization, technology, and tight government budgets.

BAILEY, Robert W. *Gay Politics, Urban Politics: Identity and Economics in the Urban Setting (Power, Conflict, and Democracy).* New York: Columbia University Press, 1999. This exploration and analysis of gay male and lesbian politics in urban settings includes insightful case studies of how gay issues play out in contemporary urban political struggles.

BOWEN, William G., and Derek C. Bok. *The Shape of the River: Long-Term Consequences of Considering Race in College and University Admissions.* Ewing, N.J.: Princeton University Press, 1998. Two former university presidents shed significant light on the affirmative action debate by examining the admissions policies of several institutions and the effects of those policies on the future lives of minority graduates.

BROWN, Dee. *Bury My Heart at Wounded Knee.* New York: Holt, Rinehart & Winston, 1971. This is an important examination of the treatment of Native Americans as the frontier pushed westward.

TOBIAS, Sheila. *Faces of Feminism: An Activist's Reflections on the Women's Movement.* Boulder, Colo.: Westview Press, 1997. This book summarizes the history of the women's movement. The author believes that the patriarchy that existed up until the current women's movement still remains in place, but it has been badly shaken.

WOODWARD, C. Vann. *The Strange Career of Jim Crow.* New York: Oxford University Press, 1957. This is the classic study of segregation in the southern United States.

politics on the web

Stanford University's Web site contains secondary documents written about Martin Luther King, Jr., as well as primary documents written during King's life. The URL for the "Martin Luther King Directory" is

http://www.stanford.edu/group/King

If you are interested in learning more about the Equal Employment Opportunity Commission (EEOC), the laws it enforces, how to file a charge with the EEOC, and general information about this agency, go to

http://www.eeoc.gov

The home page for the National Association for the Advancement of Colored People (NAACP), which contains extensive information about African American civil rights issues, is

http://www.naacp.org

For information on Hispanics in the United States, Latino Link is a good source. You can find it at

http://www.latinolink.com

The most visible and successful advocacy group for older Americans is the American Association of Retired Persons (AARP). Its home page contains helpful links and much information. Go to

http://www.aarp.org

The home page of the National Organization for Women (NOW) has links to numerous resources containing information on the rights and status of women both in the United States and around the world. You can find NOW's home page at

> **http://www.now.org**
>
> For information on the Americans with Disabilities Act (ADA) of 1990, including the text of the act and related resources, access the Americans with Disabilities Act Document Center at
>
> **http://janweb.icdi.wvu.edu/kinder**
>
> The Lesbian and Gay Alliance against Defamation has an online News Bureau. To find this organization's home page, go to
>
> **http://www.glaad.org/**

using web resources

The diversity of the American population enhances our culture, but at the same time it can lead to conflicts between different racial or ethnic groups. One of the problems faced on many university campuses is the "hate speech" that is exchanged between certain ethnic groups. Go to the Web site of the American Civil Liberties Union at

http://www.aclu.org

On the right side you will find a list of issues. Select "Students' Rights" and open "Hate Speech on Campus."

1. Describe the issues involved in campus hate speech.

2. What is the ACLU's position on these issues?

3. How would the ACLU combat hate speech on campus?

4. Does your institution have a policy on hate speech? Do you believe that the ACLU would support your campus's policy?

notes

1. *Michael M. v. Superior Court,* 450 U.S. 464 (1981).

2. *Craig v. Boren,* 429 U.S. 190 (1976).

3. *Orr v. Orr,* 440 U.S. 268 (1979).

4. *Mississippi University for Women v. Hogan,* 458 U.S. 718 (1982).

5. 518 U.S. 515 (1996).

6. As quoted in Lewis D. Eigen and Jonathan P. Siegel, *The Macmillan Dictionary of Political Quotations* (New York: Macmillan, 1993), p. 324.

7. Early women's rights conventions were usually referred to as "woman's rights" conventions.

8. See *Meritor Savings Bank, FSB v. Vinson,* 477 U.S. 57 (1986) and *Harris v. Forklift Systems, Inc.,* 510 U.S. 17 (1993).

9. *Oncale v. Sundowner Offshore Services,* 523 U.S. 75 (1998).

10. *Faragher v. City of Boca Raton,* 524 U.S. 775 (1998).

11. 163 U.S. 537 (1896).

12. 347 U.S. 483 (1954).

13. 349 U.S. 294 (1955).

14. *Swann v. Charlotte-Mecklenburg Board of Education,* 402 U.S. 1 (1971).

15. *Keyes v. School District No. 1,* 413 U.S. 189 (1973).

16. *Milliken v. Bradley,* 418 U.S. 717 (1974).

17. *Riddick v. School Board of City of Norfolk,* 627 F.Supp. 814 (E.D.Va. 1984).

18. 515 U.S. 70 (1995).

19. Carey Goldberg, "Hispanic Households' Struggle as the Poorest of the Poor in the U.S.," *The New York Times,* National Edition, January 30, 1997, p. 1.

20. The Supreme Court upheld these actions in *Hirabayashi v. United States,* 320 U.S. 81 (1943); and *Korematsu v. United States,* 323 U.S. 214 (1944).

21. This siege was the subject of Dee Brown's best-selling book, *Bury My Heart at Wounded Knee* (New York: Holt, Rinehart, & Winston, 1971).

22. *County of Oneida, New York v. Oneida Indian Nation,* 470 U.S. 226 (1985).

23. "Hog Heaven Maine Ain't," *The National Law Journal,* February 22, 1999, p. A28.

24. *O'Connor v. Consolidated Coin Caterers Corp.,* 517 U.S. 308 (1996).

25. 517 U.S. 620 (1996).

26. Released on March 10, 1999.

27. 438 U.S. 265 (1978).

28. 443 U.S. 193 (1979).

29. *Firefighters Local Union No. 1784 v. Stotts,* 467 U.S. 561 (1984).

30. *City of Richmond v. J. A. Croson Co.,* 488 U.S. 469 (1989).

31. *Martin v. Wilks,* 490 U.S. 755 (1989).

32. *Wards Cove Packing Co. v. Atonio,* 490 U.S. 642 (1989).

33. 515 U.S. 200 (1995).

34. 84 F.3d 720 (5th Cir. 1996).

35. *Coalition for Economic Equity v. Wilson,* 110 F.3d 1431 (9th Cir. 1997).

36. "Affirmative Action: Living without It," *The Economist,* March 13, 1999, p. 34.

37. James Traub, "The Class of Proposition 209," *The New York Times Magazine,* May 2, 1999, pp. 44–51.

38. "A New Divide between Black and White," *Newsweek,* June 21, 1999, p. 64.

39. Tamar Lewin, "Chevron Settles Sexual-Harassment Charges," *The New York Times,* February 21, 1995, p. A14.

40. As quoted in John Leo, "The Law That Bit Clinton," *U.S. News & World Report,* January 18, 1999, p. 14.

41. *De Angelis v. El Paso Municipal Police Officers Association,* 51 F.3d 591 (5th Cir. 1995).

POLITICAL CULTURE AND IDEOLOGY

Contents

English Only: Worthy of Legislation?

A few years ago, a bill called the English Entitlement Act was introduced in Congress. Had it passed, the act would have required the federal government to conduct most of its business only in English.

Therefore, English has not been yet declared America's "official" language, although about half of the states have enacted laws requiring official speech to be in English. The majority of Americans speak English. Though 40 million Americans speak another language at home, only about 14 million do not speak English well or at all.[1] The major foreign language spoken in the United States is Spanish. Thus, some critics of English-only laws argue that such laws actually constitute a thinly veiled form of discrimination against Hispanics.

America's Strength Is Its One Language— English

Proponents of English-only laws argue that what made this country great was its ability to assimilate large numbers of foreigners—all speaking different languages—very quickly. This group argues that assimilation requires the ability to understand and speak English, and learning English should be encouraged, not discouraged. After all, language is the glue of any culture, and if we are to have an "American" culture, we must have a common language. Without English-only laws, say these proponents, immigrants remain isolated and are unable to fully participate in "the American dream."

They also point out that the courts have generally upheld English-only rules established by private corporations for their employees. In one case, for example, a federal court held that an employer's English-only rules did not violate any federal laws prohibiting employment discrimination. The court also stated that an employee does not have a "right" to express his or her cultural heritage on the job by speaking a foreign language.[2]

English-only legislation, according to its proponents, should be applied to all public schooling. They argue that bilingual programs have been a failure. Studies show that the longer students remain in such programs, the less successful they are in schoolwork later on. For example, the dropout rate for Latino students remains the highest in the country despite the nearly thirty-year history of bilingual school programs.

Recently, a group of Latino parents in California joined with conservative backers of a voter initiative that abolished bilingual education in that state. The parents said that they send their children to school to learn English, not Spanish.

According to Ohio University economist Lowell Gallaway, low English proficiency costs the economy money, too—over $175 billion a year in lost productivity.[3]

Don't Worry, English Predominates in the United States and in the World

Those who are at odds with English-only laws point out what they consider to be obvious: we simply do not need such laws. To be sure, numerous American residents now speak Spanish, but the growing hegemony of Spanish over other languages simply reflects the uninterrupted flow of Spanish-speaking immigrants to the United States. There is no reason to fear that Spanish will take over the country. Most native Spanish speakers want to learn English because they realize that knowing English will help them advance socially and economically.

Additionally, English is fast becoming the common language of the modern world. It already is so in finance, trade, technology, diplomacy, and mass entertainment. In a world of six billion people, one-third of all books printed are in English, and three-quarters of the world's secondary school students study English. In particular, young people of the world realize that knowing English is the key to understanding most of today's movies and pop music.

Furthermore, the Internet is quickly making English so dominant that no other language even has a chance. Other countries, particularly France, are complaining that Web sites using the English language are so numerous that Americans are trying to impose English and American culture everywhere. So, according to the opponents of "official" English, it is almost a joke to think that there is a need for an English-only policy.

Where Do You Stand?

1. Would your reaction to English-only legislation be different if you were a recently arrived immigrant?

2. Which educational approach is better for teaching children who do not speak English— education in the English language or education in the children's native languages?

On the Web

For other arguments supporting English-only laws, access the home page of "English First" at http://www.englishfirst.org. You can find arguments against English-only laws and in favor of bilingual education at James Crawford's "Language Policy Web Site and Emporium," the URL for which is http://ourworld.compuserve.com/homepages/JWCRAWFORD.

Introduction

POLITICAL CULTURE ● The set of ideas, values, and attitudes about government and the political process held by a community or nation.

AMERICAN CREED ● The principles set forth in a document written by William Tyler Page in 1917 and based on the Declaration of Independence.

INFOTRAC®

Conventional politics takes center stage

By now, you have probably decided that Americans are at odds over every possible issue, including whether English should be declared the official language of this country. You may be wondering whether there is anything on which Americans *do* agree. In fact, despite the geographic and ethnic diversity of this country and the wide range of interests voiced by its population, Americans agree on many issues.

One of the forces that unites Americans is a common **political culture,** which can be defined as a patterned set of ideas, values, and ways of thinking about government and politics. Despite the flaws and weaknesses of the American political system, most Americans are proud of their country and support it with their obedience to its laws, their patriotism, and their votes.

Certainly, Americans are at odds over some of the most pressing political issues, and they will continue to be so until some acceptable compromise is reached. But as you read in Chapter 1, conflicts over what society's priorities should be are natural and inevitable, and resolving those conflicts is what politics is all about. What is important is that Americans *are* able to reach acceptable compromises—because of their common political heritage.

American Political Values

I believe in the United States of America as a government of the people, by the people, and for the people; whose just powers are derived from the consent of the governed; a democracy in a Republic; a sovereign Nation of many sovereign States; a perfect Union, one and inseparable; established upon those principles of freedom, equality, justice, and humanity for which American patriots sacrificed their lives and fortunes.

I therefore believe it is my duty to my country to love it; to support its Constitution; to obey its laws; to respect its flag; and to defend it against all enemies.

This **American Creed,** written by William Tyler Page (1868–1942) in 1917, echoes the sentiments of many Americans. It represents a set of shared political beliefs that are based on the ideals and standards set forth in the Declaration of Independence. These ideals and standards, which go to the heart of American political culture, include natural rights (to life, liberty, and the pursuit of happiness), equality under the law, government by the consent of the governed, and limited government powers. In some

The American flag symbolizes not only our independence, but also such ideals as equality, liberty, and limited government. The original Stars and Stripes came about as a result of a resolution offered by the Marine Committee of the Second Continental Congress in Philadelphia on June 14, 1777. The current fifty-star flag of the United States was raised for the first time officially at 12:01 A.M. on July 4, 1960, at Fort McHenry National Monument in Baltimore, Maryland.

A controversial form of protest in modern times has been flag burning. On June 21, 1989, the United States Supreme Court ruled that burning the American flag in public to protest government policies is a protected form of speech under the First Amendment. President George Bush immediately asked for a constitutional amendment to prohibit flag burning, but none has ever been passed.

ways, the Declaration of Independence defines Americans' sense of right and wrong. It presents a challenge to anyone who might wish to overthrow our democratic processes or deny our citizens their natural rights.

Because of the importance of these basic values, Americans also attach great meaning to national symbols. The American flag, for example, represents not only independence, but also everything that Americans fought for during the Revolutionary War, including liberty, equality, and limited government. For this reason, flag burning as a gesture of protest does not sit well with many Americans. Indeed, in 1989, Congress even passed an act prohibiting such actions.[4] The Supreme Court, however, held that the act was unconstitutional because it violated the freedom of expression protected by the First Amendment.[5] Today, those who display the Confederate flag elicit hostility from many Americans who view that flag as a symbol of slavery—part of the political culture of the Old South (see the feature entitled *Politics on the Far Side: Flying the Rebel Flag*).

politics on the far side

Flying the Rebel Flag

Although the Civil War was fought and won by the Union more than 130 years ago, some southerners still fly the Confederate flag today. Many Americans are offended by any display of the Confederate flag because to them it represents the worst of the Old South—slavery.

The members of the Maryland chapter of the Sons of Confederate Veterans view the matter differently. They believe that the Confederate flag represents an important part of American history and that its display preserves the good names of their ancestors. In that vein, the Maryland Vehicle Administration has issued seventy-eight members of the group special license plates with the Confederate "Stars and Bars" prominently displayed.

For Critical Analysis: What cultural traditions—besides slavery—might the Confederate flag symbolize for southerners?

LIBERTY, EQUALITY, AND PROPERTY

A fundamental political value shared by most Americans is a belief in democracy—government of, by, and for the people. Other values that are deeply rooted in American political culture include liberty, equality, and property. These values provide a basic framework for American political discourse and debate because they are shared by most Americans, yet individual Americans often interpret their meaning quite differently.

Liberty

The term **liberty** refers to a state of being free from external controls or restrictions. In the United States, the Bill of Rights sets forth our civil liberties. These liberties include the freedom to practice whatever religion we choose and to be free from any state-imposed religion. They also include the freedom to speak freely on any topics and issues, including government actions. Because people cannot govern themselves unless they are free to

LIBERTY ● The freedom of individuals to believe, act, and express themselves freely so long as doing so does not infringe on the rights of other individuals in the society.

This Atlanta couple is proud of their heritage and the Confederate "Stars and Bars" that symbolizes it. Others believe that the Confederate flag should not be displayed, because it is too closely tied to the institution of slavery.

voice their opinions, freedom of speech is a basic requirement in a true democracy. The Bill of Rights gives us numerous other liberties as well.

Clearly, though, if we are to live together with others, there have to be some restrictions on individual liberties. If people were allowed to do whatever they wished, without regard for the rights or liberties of others, pandemonium would result. Hence, a more accurate definition of liberty would be as follows: *liberty is the freedom of individuals to believe, act, and express themselves freely so long as doing so does not infringe on the rights of other individuals in the society.*

Equality

The goal of **equality** has always been a central part of American political culture. Many of the first settlers came to this country to be free of unequal treatment and persecution. They sought the freedom to live and worship as they wanted. They believed that anyone who worked hard could succeed, and America became known as the "land of opportunity." The Declaration of Independence confirmed the importance of equality to early Americans by stating, "We hold these Truths to be self-evident, that all Men are created equal." Because of the goal of equality, the Constitution prohibited the government from granting titles of nobility. Article I, Section 9, of the Constitution states, "No Title of Nobility shall be granted by the United States." (The Constitution did not prohibit slavery, however—see Chapter 2.)

But what, exactly, does equality mean? Does it mean simply political equality—the right to vote and run for political office? Does it mean that individuals should have equal opportunities to develop their talents and skills? What about those who are poor, suffer from disabilities, or are otherwise at a competitive disadvantage? Should it be the government's responsibility to ensure that these groups also have equal opportunities? Although most Americans believe that all persons should have the opportunity to fulfill their potential, few contend that it is the government's responsibility to totally eliminate the economic and social differences that lead to unequal opportunities.

Property

The English philosopher John Locke (1632–1704) asserted that people are born with "natural" rights and that among these rights are life, liberty, and *property.* The Declaration of Independence makes a similar assertion:

EQUALITY ● A concept that holds, at a minimum, that all people are entitled to equal protection under the law.

The relationship between religious beliefs and political ideology sometimes can be taken to extremes.

people are born with certain "unalienable" rights, including the right to life, liberty, and the *pursuit of happiness*. For Americans, property and the pursuit of happiness are closely related. Americans place a great value on land ownership, on material possessions, and on the monetary value of their jobs. Property gives its owners political power and the liberty to do whatever they want—within limits.

"THE AMERICAN STORY"—WHAT VALUES AND IDEALS SHOULD BE INCLUDED?

You can tell a lot about a nation's political values by reading its history books. As you will learn in Chapter 9, our schools play an important part in the process of political socialization—the passing on of political values from one generation to the next. You can also tell a lot about a person's political ideals and values by asking her or him which themes should be stressed in the teaching of American history.

What themes should be stressed in teaching "the American story" to schoolchildren? To learn the answer to that question, the Roper Center conducted a survey, the results of which are shown in Table 6–1. The answers show that the respondents clearly place a high value on such ideals as democracy, limited government, liberty, and equality. The results also indicate that a majority of Americans want their children to know that this nation "was founded upon biblical principles" and that "America has a special place in God's plan for history." The inclusion of religious values in the American story should not come as a surprise, for Americans continue to express a high degree of association with religion and religious groups—more than that expressed by the citizens of any other Western nation. According to a poll by the National Opinion Research Center, 84 percent of Americans believe in God, and 58 percent of Americans pray at least once a day.[6]

Table 6–1

The Teaching of American History

Question: In teaching the American story to children, how important is the following theme . . . ?

	ESSENTIAL/VERY IMPORTANT	SOMEWHAT IMPORTANT	SOMEWHAT UNIMPORTANT/ VERY UNIMPORTANT/LEAVE IT OUT OF THE STORY
With hard work and perseverance, anyone can succeed in America.	83%	14%	4%
American democracy is only as strong as the virtue of its citizens.	83	14	4
Our founders limited the power of government, so government would not intrude too much into the lives of its citizens.	74	19	8
America is the world's greatest melting pot in which people from different countries are united into one nation.	73	21	5
America's contribution is one of expanding freedom for more and more people.	71	22	6
From its start, America had a destiny to set an example for other nations.	65	22	13
Our nation betrayed its founding principles by cruel mistreatment of blacks and American Indians.	59	24	17
Our nation was founded upon biblical principles.	58	26	15
Ours has been a history of war and aggression—our expansion occurred at the cost of much suffering.	58	26	16
America has a special place in God's plan for history.	50	22	29
Our founders were part of a male-dominated culture that gave important roles to men while keeping women in the background.	38	28	35

SOURCE: *The Public Perspective,* April/May 1999, p. 16.

The schools play an important role in the process of political socialization. Reciting the Pledge of Allegiance in school is one way that American children learn about their political heritage and values.

INFOTRAC®

Changing the face of kids TV

> **MULTICULTURALISM** ● The belief that the many cultures that make up American society should remain distinct and be protected and even encouraged by our laws.

Figure 6–1

Racial and Ethnic Composition of the U.S. Population

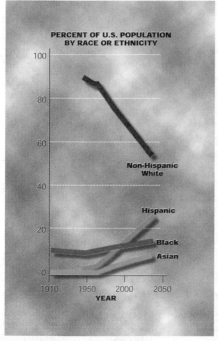

PERCENT OF U.S. POPULATION BY RACE OR ETHNICITY

Non-Hispanic White

Hispanic

Black

Asian

YEAR

SOURCE: U.S. Bureau of the Census, 1999.

Political Values in a Multicultural Society

The United States is a nation of immigrants. Except for a small number of Native Americans, all Americans are either recent immigrants or descendants of past immigrants. During the 1990s, more immigrants entered the United States than at any time since the 1910s. The face of immigration is changing, however. During the 1910s, the greatest number of immigrants were Europeans, whereas today they are Asians and Latin Americans. The ethnic makeup of the United States is changing accordingly, and quite rapidly (see Figure 6–1). Already, whites are close to being a minority in California. For the nation as a whole, non-Hispanic whites will be in the minority by the year 2060 or shortly thereafter.

As immigration rates increased during the 1990s, some Americans feared that rising numbers of immigrants would threaten traditional American political values and culture. Among other things, this fear led to growing criticism of multiculturalist goals and policies.

MULTICULTURALISM

From the earliest British and European settlers to the numerous cultural groups who today call America their home, American society has always been a multicultural society. Until recently, most Americans viewed the United States as the world's melting pot. They accepted that American society included numerous ethnic and cultural groups, but they expected that the members of these groups would abandon their cultural distinctions and assimilate the language and customs of Americans. One of the outgrowths of the civil rights movement of the 1960s, however, was an emphasis on **multiculturalism**—the belief that the many cultures that make up American society should remain distinct and be protected—and even encouraged—by our laws.

Supporters of Multiculturalism

Supporters of multiculturalist policies, who are mostly liberals, believe that Americans must be tolerant of other cultures and ways of life. According to multiculturalists, what has made this country great is its rich multicultural background. It will continue to be great only if we have increased tolerance for its diverse cultural elements.

Beginning in the 1960s, Spanish-English bilingual education programs became widespread, particularly in the southwestern states. Here, immigrant children in an elementary school in Austin, Texas, learn about the three branches of American government. By the 1990s, critics of bilingual programs (including many Hispanic parents) claimed that such programs prevented children from mastering English at an early age. In 1998, California voters ended bilingual education in that state by a ballot initiative.

Those in favor of multiculturalism argue that in the past, too much of what was taught in our educational institutions about history, art, and literature dealt with the achievements of "dead white men." Consequently, they have supported the elimination of standard Western civilization requirements at colleges and universities in favor of more emphasis on American minority groups and non-Western cultures. Since the 1960s, American universities have included in their curriculums courses and programs focusing on the culture and achievements of African Americans, women, other minority groups, and non-Western civilizations generally.

Multiculturalists have also been among the strongest supporters of bilingual education, arguing that immigrant groups, such as Hispanics, have a right to be educated in their own language. In 1974, the Supreme Court affirmed this right when it required a school district in California to provide special programs for Chinese students with language difficulties if a substantial number of such children were attending the schools in that district.

Bilingual education programs first appeared in the late 1960s, and Spanish-English bilingual programs became especially widespread in California, with its large Spanish-speaking population. By the 1990s, these programs were increasingly coming under attack, not only by white conservative groups but also by many Hispanic parents, who felt that their children were suffering academically because bilingual programs prevented their early mastery of the English language. In 1998, large numbers of Hispanics voted for a ballot initiative calling for the replacement of bilingual programs with short-term "English-immersion" programs.

Opponents of Multiculturalism

Opponents of multiculturalism, who are mostly conservatives, argue against the institutionalization of multiculturalist policies. In particular, they believe that English should be the language of schools and government, and they have backed efforts at both the state and federal levels to pass English-only laws. Today, about half of the states do have laws requiring all official speech to be in English, as mentioned in this chapter's opening feature. Attempts to pass such a law at the national level have not as yet been successful.

Critics of multiculturalism also point out that multiculturalist laws and policies promote moral relativism by implying that no one group's values are superior to those of another. Many conservatives argue that all groups should accept certain fundamental American values, including individual freedom and independence, liberty, equality among men and women, the freedom to voice unpopular opinions, the freedom of religion, and so on. Interestingly, conservatives' fears about moral relativism seem to be unfounded. According to Martha Minow, a Harvard Law School professor who specializes in family and education issues, the tolerance for immigrant groups' cultural practices typically extends only to those practices that are consistent with mainstream American values. She cites examples of cultural traditions (such as parent-child co-sleeping arrangements, rituals and ceremonies of initiation involving physical mutilation, and so on) that even the most extreme proponents of cultural diversity will not tolerate.[7]

Finally, many conservatives argue that multiculturalism is anti-individualistic. It expects individuals to conform to the perspective generally assumed to be that of a particular group. Hence, all women must share a so-called female perspective. All African Americans must share a so-called African American perspective. This leads to conformist attitudes that work against individualism. Classifying people by race, gender, or ethnic identity leads to a kind of "groupthink" that is hostile to individualism.

ARE THE "TIES THAT BIND THE NATION" REALLY WEAKENING?

Despite the fears that cultural diversity and increased tolerance for different cultural groups will destroy American values, there is no real evidence

An Asian immigrant and his toddler daughter arrive at a ceremony for U.S. citizenship in San Jose, California. Since the beginning of this nation, American culture has been enriched time and again by immigrants from different nations. Assertions that cultural diversity may be destroying the unity of American culture are largely unfounded, according to recent studies.

that these fears are being realized. Indeed, if patriotism is any indicator of the strength of a nation's political culture, Americans show a strong commitment to American political values (see this chapter's *Comparative Politics* for details).

In fact, the ties that bind the nation may be stronger than is often thought. According to a recent poll by Public Agenda, a nonpartisan research group in New York, over 80 percent of all groups in this country (whites, blacks, Hispanics, and so on) felt that it is "absolutely essential" for schools to teach students that "whatever their ethnic or racial background, they are all part of one nation." Overall, about 65 percent of the parents polled believed that immigrant children should learn English as quickly as possible, and an even higher percentage of recent immigrants supported that goal. Similarly, a large majority of respondents, regardless of their ethnic backgrounds or whether they were recent immigrants, believed that "to graduate from high school, students should be required to show they understand the common history and ideas that tie all Americans together."

What emerges from this report and similar studies is that American values are not being threatened by the increasing diversity of American society. Nevertheless, there is some concern that the intensity with which American political values are held is declining. For example, 60 percent of the parents polled in the Public Agenda survey believed that "America is losing its identity—its beliefs and values." According to Deborah Wadsworth, Public Agenda's president, the study suggests that the real threats to America "come not from immigrants but from taking our freedoms—and our success as a nation—for granted."[8] Another recent study by Public Agenda shows an increasing concern over whether today's teenagers will be capable of sustaining our political values and culture in the future.[9]

comparative **politics**

Patriotism: A Cross-National Comparison

According to a study of patriotism by the National Opinion Research Center at the University of Chicago, Americans are prouder of their country than are people in any other country in the world.[10] The survey, which compared patriotism in twenty-three nations, revealed that nearly 90 percent of Americans would rather be citizens of the United States than of any other country. The United States was followed on the list by Austria, Canada, Ireland, and New Zealand. At the bottom of the list were the nations that were formerly part of the Soviet Union or were dominated by the Soviet bloc—Hungary, Slovakia, Poland, Russia, and Latvia.

According to the director of the survey project, Tom Smith, "While America's position as the remaining superpower and world's largest economy clearly plays an important role in this top ranking, an important element of idealism also spurs pride in the U.S." Smith also noted that unlike most nations, which were "built up around a primordial tribe," the United States was from the outset a nation "based on a set of shared ideals."

For Critical Analysis

Can you think of any factors that would explain why the countries with the least amount of national pride, according to the above-cited survey, are those that formerly belonged to, or were dominated by, the Soviet Union?

The Spectrum of Political Attitudes

LIBERAL ● One who subscribes to a set of political beliefs that includes the advocacy of active government, government intervention to improve the welfare of individuals, support for civil rights, and political change.

CLASSICAL LIBERALISM ● Liberalism in its traditional form. Like modern liberalism, classical liberalism stressed political democracy, constitutionally guaranteed civil liberties, political equality, free political competition, and separation of church and state. Unlike modern liberalism, classical liberalism opposed government intervention in the economy and stressed free enterprise, individual initiative, and free trade.

MODERN LIBERALISM ● A political ideology that stresses political democracy, constitutionally guaranteed civil liberties, political equality, free political competition, and separation of church and state. Unlike classical liberalism, modern liberalism supports the notion that the national government should take an active role in solving the nation's domestic problems and in protecting the interests of poor and disadvantaged groups in society.

INFOTRAC®

A liberal country, after all

Americans clearly have much in common concerning basic political ideals and values. Yet they differ significantly on how best to attain those ideals or preserve American values. Generally, Americans fall into two broad camps with respect to political ideology: conservatives or liberals. Indeed, politicians frequently identify themselves as either liberals or conservatives, or they are identified as such by the media. The meanings of the terms *liberal* and *conservative* have changed over the years, however, and will continue to change as political attitudes and ideologies evolve. Although these terms may be hard to define, we know that they fall within a political spectrum that ranges from the far left (extremely liberal) to the far right (extremely conservative).

Look at Figure 6–2, which shows the spectrum of political attitudes and its relationship to the two major American political parties—Democrats and Republicans. As you can see, those with liberal views tend to identify with the Democratic Party, whereas those with conservative views tend to identify with the Republican Party.

LIBERALS AND LIBERALISM

Liberals usually believe in such ideals as political democracy, constitutionally guaranteed civil liberties, political equality, free political competition, and separation of church and state. **Classical liberalism**—liberalism in its traditional form—also stressed free enterprise, individual initiative, and free trade and opposed government intervention in the economy.

In the United States, classical liberalism gave way during the twentieth century to **modern liberalism,** or *progressive liberalism*. While modern liberalism retains the political and civil rights agenda of classical liberalism, it has modified classical liberalism's approach to social and economic issues. In contrast to classical liberalism, modern liberalism generally supports the notion that the national government should take an *active* role in solving the nation's domestic problems. Further, today's liberals feel that the national government must look out for the interests of the individual against the majority. Thus, they generally support social welfare programs that assist the poor and the disadvantaged.

You have probably noted that several elements characteristic of classical liberalism (free enterprise, individual initiative, and so on) are today more descriptive, at least in the United States, of the conservative political philosophy espoused by many Republicans. Thus, contemporary Republicans argue that they are classical liberals and that Democrats are "modern" liberals.

As Figure 6–2 illustrates, there is a close relationship between those holding liberal views and those identifying themselves politically as Democrats. For example, in a recent poll 72 percent of the Democrats surveyed agreed that the national government should give more help to the poor, whereas only 39 percent of the Republicans polled agreed with this

Figure 6–2
The Political Spectrum

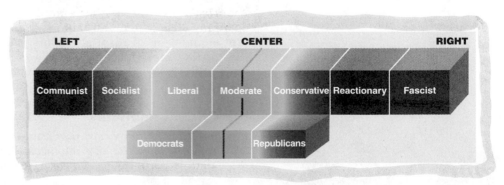

CONSERVATIVE ● One who subscribes to a set of political beliefs that includes a limited role for government, support for traditional values, and a preference for the status quo.

CONSERVATISM ● A set of beliefs that includes a limited role for the national government in helping individuals, support for traditional values and lifestyles, and a cautious response to change.

MODERATE ● With regard to the political spectrum, a person whose views fall in the middle of the spectrum.

VITAL CENTER ● The center of the political spectrum, or those who hold moderate political views. The center is vital because, without it, it may be difficult, if not impossible, to reach the compromises that are necessary to a political system's continuity.

proposition. Similarly, 92 percent of the Democrats felt that "more needs to be done to close the gap between the rich and poor" in this country. Only 66 percent of Republicans shared this sentiment.[11] Keep in mind, though, that not all Democrats share all of the liberal views just discussed. Rather, those with liberal views simply tend to find that *on the whole* the Democratic Party's positions on issues are more acceptable than those of the Republican Party.

CONSERVATIVES AND CONSERVATISM

Conservatives, as the term implies, seek to conserve tradition and the ways of the past. **Conservatism**, as a political philosophy, thus defends traditional institutions and practices. It places a high value on the principles of community, continuity, law and order, and—in some countries—the preservation of rule by the privileged classes.

In the United States, today's conservatives seek to preserve such traditions as states' rights, family values, individual initiative, and free enterprise. They want to minimize government interference in the business life of the nation. They believe that the federal government is already too big and should not be expanded further. They think that the nongovernment sectors of society—businesses and consumers—should be left alone more than they have been in the past few decades. Many conservatives also decry multiculturalism.

One politician has said that the "central liberal truth is that politics can change a culture and save it from itself." In contrast, the "central conservative truth is that it is culture, not politics, that determines the success of a society."[12] Today, American society appears to be leaning in the direction of the "central conservative truth." There is certainly a good deal of support for decentralization and a devolution of power (see Chapter 3). Decentralization of schools has started in earnest, as evidenced by the growing popularity across the country of school choice and school voucher programs. The welfare reform legislation passed in 1996 is often pointed to as evidence of the movement toward decentralization and the devolution of power, as well as of an emphasis on self-reliance—all conservative values.

In terms of party affiliation, conservatives tend to identify with the Republican Party. Again, however, you need to be careful about associating the term *conservative* with the Republican Party. Republicans do not constitute a cohesive group that is consistently in favor of an array of political, social, and economic policy prescriptions. In fact, today's Republican Party is becoming increasingly splintered by factions. At a minimum, the party consists of the factions outlined in Table 6-2 on the next page.

THE POLITICAL CENTER

People whose views fall in the middle of the political spectrum are generally called **moderates.** Moderates rarely classify themselves as either liberal or conservative. As you saw in Figure 6-2 on the previous page, the political center includes some Democrats and some Republicans.

In 1949, historian Arthur Schlesinger, Jr., described the position between communism and fascism on the political spectrum as the **vital center.** The center is vital because, without it, reaching the compromises that are necessary to a political system's continuity may be difficult, if not impossible. Hence, the declining number of political moderates in Congress in the mid-1990s caused some alarm. President Bill Clinton, after experiencing little success with his liberal agenda during his first term, began to look for the vital center during his second term. So too, did the former speaker of the House, Newt Gingrich, who, in the words of pundit William Safire, seemed to have learned the virtues of "slow dancing toward major change."[13]

Table 6–2

Major Republican Party Factions

FACTION	WHAT IT STANDS FOR
Economic Conservatives	In favor of free markets, less government bureaucracy, and lower taxes.
Moral Conservatives	In favor of prayer in schools; against abortion, gay marriages, and gay men and lesbians in the military.
America Firsters	Isolationists; in favor of English-only laws and protectionist measures to preserve American jobs; against multiculturalism.
Old-Fashioned Conservatives	In favor of family values, virtue, hard work, some national government involvement in the economy, a balanced budget (even if it means not lowering taxes); against any great change.

RADICAL LEFT ● Persons on the extreme left side of the political spectrum who would like to significantly change the political order, usually to promote egalitarianism. The radical left includes socialists, communists, and, often, populists.

RADICAL RIGHT ● Persons on the extreme right side of the political spectrum. The radical right includes reactionaries (who would like to return to the values and social systems of some previous era), fascists (who pursue strongly nationalistic policies), and libertarians (who believe in no regulation of the economy and individual behavior, except for defense).

IDEOLOGUE ● An individual who holds very strong political opinions.

THE EXTREME LEFT AND RIGHT

On both ends of the political spectrum are those who espouse radical views. The **radical left** consists of those who would like to significantly change the political order, usually to promote egalitarianism. Often, members of the radical left do not wish to work within the established political processes to reach their goals. They may even accept or advocate the use of violence or overthrowing the government in order to obtain those goals. The radical left includes socialists, communists, and, often, populists.

Socialists believe in equality and, usually, active government involvement in the economy to bring about this goal. Socialism covers a broader ideological spectrum than communism. *Communists* believe in total equality and often base their beliefs on the political philosophy of Karl Marx (1818–1883) or on communist ideology as developed in other nations. *Populists* also have socialist leanings, but they are generally less radical than socialists and communists in their aims. Populists generally advocate a more equitable distribution of wealth and power to accommodate the needs of the common people.

The **radical right** includes reactionaries and fascists. *Reactionaries* strongly oppose liberal and progressive politics and resist political and social change. They usually want to return to the values and social systems of some previous era. *Fascists* believe in a strong national government, usually headed by a dictator, that often pursues a belligerently nationalistic policy. Like those on the radical left of the political spectrum, members of the radical right may even advocate the use of violence to achieve their goals. A less extreme right-wing ideology is libertarianism. *Libertarians* believe in total political and economic liberty for individuals and no government regulation of the economy and individual behavior (except for defense).

The Average American versus the Ideologues

Many Americans consider individuals who are extremely liberal or extremely conservative to be **ideologues**—people who hold very strong political opinions. Most Americans, however, are not interested in *all* political issues and have a mixed set of opinions that do not fit under a conservative or liberal label. Research shows that only about 10 percent of Americans could conceivably be classified as ideologues. The rest of the population looks at politics more in terms of party lines—Democratic or Republican— or from the viewpoint of their own experiences as they relate to a particular issue, such as unemployment or crime.

THE POLITICAL SPECTRUM AND THE AMERICAN PUBLIC

In contrast to members of Congress, more Americans identify themselves as moderates than as either liberals or conservatives. The Gallup polling organization routinely conducts polls asking individuals what their ideological self-identification is. The combined results of twenty-two Gallup polls taken during 1997 and 1998 reveal that 42 percent of Americans consider themselves to be moderates, 20 percent identify themselves as liberals, and 38 percent consider themselves to be conservatives.[14]

Surprisingly, most Americans do not see a relationship between today's issues and political ideology. For example, polling data show that only a small fraction—about 2 percent—of Americans identify a conservative or liberal position with either side of the abortion debate. Additionally, the average American does not seem to adhere strictly to one ideology or another. Rather, he or she may identify more with one ideology in youth, another in middle age, and yet another later on in life. Winston Churchill once said, "If you are not a liberal at twenty, you have no heart, and if you are not a conservative at forty, you have no head."

IDEOLOGY VERSUS SELF-INTEREST

Public opinion polls reveal that political issues are not as important to Americans as the problems they face daily. In other words, a person who is poor is more likely to support aid to the poor than is a person who is extremely well-off. A bedridden elderly person is more likely to support increased government funding for long-term medical care than is a young, healthy person earning a high income.

Some researchers have determined that self-interest is a great generator of public opinion. Crime victims often express strong opinions about issues such as capital punishment or building more prisons. The recently unemployed frequently express negative opinions about the current president's ability to manage the economy.

The evidence suggests that the majority of Americans hold the strongest political convictions about issues that have a direct effect on their own lives. For example, a survey of views on immigration clearly showed that the views of those surveyed were largely driven by their station in life and their economic outlook, not by their party affiliations. Generally, the Republican Party has embraced an anti-immigration position, while the Democratic Party has been more supportive of immigrants. According to the survey, however, those Americans who are better off (disproportionately Republicans) tended to be more tolerant of immigration, while those at the lower end of the socioeconomic scale (disproportionately Democrats) tended to feel more threatened by immigration.[15]

This disparity between the position of the party leadership on an issue and the position of rank-and-file party identifiers should come as no surprise. The Republican leadership, by taking an anti-immigration stance, may attract some votes from working-class Democrats. The Democratic leadership, in turn, can argue that the Republicans' position on immigration disregards the needs of a growing portion of the American electorate—Hispanics.

A Political Typology

Liberal or conservative? Republican or Democrat? Socialist or capitalist? For years, political scientists and others have used these labels in describing American political culture and values. Typically, a typology of the American electorate ranges from those on the political right

the american political spectrum

A Typology of the American Electorate

The Pew Research Center for the People and the Press has created a typology of the American electorate based on surveys. The typology divides the electorate into ten groups based on three major elements: personal values and attitudes, party affiliation, and political participation. The percentage of the electorate falling into each group is indicated in parentheses after each subheading.

The Political Right: Republicans or Mostly Republicans

Enterprisers (12 percent) — Classic Republicans who are affluent, well educated, and predominantly white, and whose attitudes are pro-business, antigovernment, and antiwelfare.

Moralists (15 percent) — Middle-aged persons in the middle-income range who are predominantly white and religious (mostly evangelicals).

Libertarians (7 percent) — Highly educated, affluent, and predominantly white males who are pro-business, antigovernment, antiwelfare (but highly tolerant), very low on religious faith (and uncomfortable with the religious right), and cynical about politicians.

In the Center: Independents

New Economy Independents (14 percent) — Mostly young to middle-aged females with an average income. They have many conflict-ing values: they are strongly environmentalist but not believers in government regulation; they are pro-welfare but not very sympathetic to blacks; and they are inclined to fundamentalist religious beliefs but highly tolerant of homosexuals.

Bystanders (10 percent) — Very young, poorly educated persons with low income, many of whom are Hispanics. They opt out of politics or are ineligible to vote. Their only claimed commitment is to environmentalism.

Embittered (6 percent) — Middle-aged persons with low income and little education. One in five is black, and four in ten have children under the age of eighteen. Their old ties to the Democrats are gone, but they feel unwelcome in the Republican Party. They distrust government, politicians, and corporations; they are religious and socially intolerant; and they strongly blame discrimination for the lack of black progress, although they are not strongly pro-welfare.

On the Left: Democrats or Mostly Democrats

Seculars (7 percent) — Highly educated, sophisticated, affluent, mostly white baby boomers and Generation Xers. They embrace the "liberal" label and are highly tolerant, driven by social issues, very low in religious faith, highly pro-environment, moderately pro-government, and distrusting of business.

New Democrats (12 percent) — Mostly females with average income and education. They are religious, and the group divides equally between evangelical Protestants and Catholics. They are not intolerant, but they reject discrimination as a major barrier to black progress; they are more pro-business than other Democratic groups, but they are also pro-government and pro-environment.

New Dealers (8 percent) — Predominantly persons over the age of sixty-five with an average education and low income. They were once a part of Franklin Roosevelt's New Deal coalition, are beneficiaries of government programs, and are now turned off by politics and politicians. They are strongly conservative with respect to race and welfare, strongly religious, moderately tolerant, pro-American, and distrusting of business.

Partisan Poor (9 percent) — Very poor, disadvantaged, and predominantly southern, nonwhite persons living in households that earn under $20,000 a year. This oldest typology group, rooted in the New Deal coalition, wants more government spending on the poor. They are very religious and socially intolerant.

For Critical Analysis

Which of these groups comes closest to representing your views on politics?

(Republicans or mostly Republicans) to those on the political left (Democrats or mostly Democrats). One such typology is set forth above in this chapter's feature, *The American Political Spectrum: A Typology of the American Electorate.*

Americans at Odds over Political Culture and Ideology

As we have seen in this chapter, Americans are at odds not so much over basic political values but over how those values can best be translated into specific policies. Making such decisions involves attaching priorities to various values and ranking them in a value system. Value systems, of course, vary not only from group to group along the political spectrum but also from individual to individual within each group. Thus, Americans will always be at odds over ideological issues, some of which we look at here.

The Tension between Individual Liberty and Social Equality

One of the underlying values in American culture is individual liberty. In fact, from early times one of the distinguishing characteristics of this country was the focus on individualism—the right of Americans to pursue their own goals in their own way. American history and folklore are full of stories of the achievements of individual Americans—from the early settlers and pioneers to the founders of today's leading corporations. (See the *Perception versus Reality* feature on the next page for an example of how American history has sometimes been distorted to fit the individualist ideal.)

Yet there has always been an underlying tension between the ideal of individual liberty and another important American value: equality. For example, both individualism and egalitarianism call for equality of opportunity. Equality of opportunity, though, often leads to a meritocracy based on individual talent and effort. Therefore, equal opportunity does not necessarily promote social equality. Rather, those who have the advantage of more education, more money to invest in an enterprise, greater talent, and higher levels of energy will have a competitive edge and come out the winners. Those without such advantages will not. While equal opportunity promotes individualism and self-reliance, it also leads to an unequal result.

Enter affirmative action. As you read in Chapter 5, the goal of affirmative action programs is to level the playing field by giving preferences to minorities and other groups to make up for past discrimination. Yet such programs have been criticized because they also result in unequal treatment. Generally, those opposed to affirmative action reflect the spirit of individualism. Those who favor affirmative action demonstrate the ideal of egalitarianism.

As noted earlier, one of the criticisms of multiculturalist policies is that they lump Americans into groups defined by racial or ethnic characteristics in an effort to promote equality among these groups. Not surprisingly, this approach to equality has caused opponents of multiculturalism to claim that such policies violate the fundamental American principle of individualism.

The Clash of Civilizations

For Americans who grew up after World War II (1941–1945), the major conflicts in the world were between nations, particularly between the Western nations (including the United States and Europe) and the communist countries (such as the Soviet Union, its satellites, and the People's Republic of China). Much of our political ideology has been

perception **versus reality**

The Lonely American in the Wilderness of Yore

Countless movies, television shows, novels, and stories have dealt with American pioneers and frontier life. Through these media, Americans have acquired a very special view of how their ancestors lived hundreds of years ago.

The Perception

We tend to think of the United States as a country settled by solitary pioneers who cleared the forests, planted corn, and lived by barter. The French observer Alexis de Tocqueville (1805–1859) reinforced this image when he said, "The citizen of the United States is taught from infancy to rely upon his own exertions. . . . He looks upon the social authority with an eye of mistrust and anxiety and he claims its assistance only when he is unable to do without it." In other words, we view Americans of the past as being sovereigns over their own lives. Indeed, the solitary pioneer has been an important symbol of liberty.

The Reality

Most of our notions of the solitary pioneer turn out to be fanciful. In the 1830s, only a tiny fraction (0.05 percent) of the people living on the Appalachian frontier were living alone. Virtually no one could live alone and survive; that is why communities were formed. Even Henry David Thoreau, during his sojourn in the wilderness, was forced to go to a store and spend money to buy Indian meal and molasses.

You Be the Judge

Why do Americans cling to the notion that this country was settled by many solitary pioneers?

The romanticized image of the lone pioneer in the American wilderness.

formed by these conflicts and by the Cold War between the Western nations and communist countries that followed World War II and lasted until the early 1990s.

Today, in contrast, certain scholars believe that conflicts between nations are giving way to conflicts based on the *cultural lines* separating civilizations. According to Samuel Huntington, a professor of international politics at Harvard and the chairman of the Institute of Strategic Planning, a major cultural fault line now exists between the Christian West and Islam, Confucianism, Hinduism, and other belief systems in East Asia, Japan, Africa, and Latin America. Future conflicts will be less between *governments* than between *political cultures*. Huntington believes that as the influence of culture is rising, the influence of government is decreasing: "Peoples and countries with similar cultures are coming together. Peoples in countries with different cultures are coming apart."[16]

A counterforce to this clashing of cultures is, of course, the communications technology that is bringing the peoples of the globe closer together— in the world of cyberspace. Electronic networks are spreading different ideas throughout the world and linking together members of different cultures. The world's political and cultural divisions are rooted in age-old customs and belief systems, however, and whether electronic linkages and shared information among cultural groups can overcome these divisions remains to be seen.

key terms

American Creed 141
classical liberalism 148
conservatism 149
conservative 149
equality 143
ideologue 150
liberal 148
liberty 142

moderate 149
modern liberalism 148
multiculturalism 145
political culture 141
radical left 150
radical right 150
vital center 149

chapter summary

1. A political culture can be defined as a patterned set of ideas, values, and ways of thinking about government and politics. The political culture of the United States is a set of shared political beliefs based on ideals and standards set forth in the Declaration of Independence. These ideals include natural rights (to life, liberty, and the pursuit of happiness), equality under the law, government by the consent of the governed, and limited government powers.

2. Three deeply rooted values in American political culture are liberty, equality, and property. Liberty is the freedom of individuals to believe, act, and express themselves freely as long as doing so does not infringe on the rights of other individuals in the society. Since the beginning of this nation, Americans have disagreed over the meaning of equality and over what public policies should be formed and implemented to promote equality. The right to own property is closely connected to the right to the pursuit of happiness. Property rights give their owners political power and the liberty to do as they wish—within limits.

3. Americans seem to be in agreement as to what the basic political values of this country are. Polls show that Americans continue to place a high value on such ideals as democracy, limited government, individual liberty, and equality. Polls also show that Americans continue to express a high degree of association with religion and religious groups. Although many Americans, particularly conservatives, have expressed fears that multiculturalist policies and programs tend to erode American political values, there is no evidence that this has really happened.

4. The spectrum of political attitudes, beginning on the far left, includes the radical left, liberals, moderates, conservatives, and the radical right. Political attitudes are often labeled as either liberal or conservative. Liberals tend to believe in such ideals as political democracy, constitutionally guaranteed civil liberties, political equality, free political competition, and separation of church and state. Modern (progressive) liberalism generally supports the notion that the national government should take an active role in solving the nation's domestic problems and in protecting the interests of the individual against the majority.

5. Conservatives seek to conserve tradition and the ways of the past. Conservatism, as a political philosophy, thus defends traditional institutions and practices. In the United States, conservatism emphasizes community, continuity, law and order, family values, individual initiative, free enterprise, and minimal government interference in the business life of the nation.

6. At the center of the political spectrum are the moderates. At the far left of the spectrum is the radical left, which includes those who hold extreme egalitarian views, such as socialists or communists. At the far right of the spectrum is the radical right, which includes reactionaries and fascists. Groups on both the radical left and the radical right may accept or advocate the use of violence to achieve their goals.

7. In contrast to members of Congress, more Americans (currently, about 42 percent) identify themselves as moderates than as liberals or conservatives. Evidence suggests that most Americans hold the strongest political convictions about issues that have a direct effect on their own lives. Americans' views on political issues appear to be driven less by ideology or party affiliation than by self-interest and their economic station in life.

8. Americans are at odds not so much over basic political values but over how those values can best be translated into specific policies. Reaching agreement on such issues is difficult because policymaking involves deciding on priorities and ranking various political values into a system—and value systems differ from group to group as well as from individual to individual. One issue concerning political culture and ideology over which Americans are currently at odds involves the tension between liberty and equality. Clashes among different cultural groups on a global level are also of growing concern for many Americans.

for critical analysis

1. Most bilingual programs in the United States have been Spanish-English programs. Why haven't other languages received as much attention? Is it simply a matter of numbers? If so, is this fair?

2. Name three political beliefs that you think would be agreed to by all American citizens. Name three others on which Americans, in your opinion, would likely disagree.

3. Why is multiculturalism such a contentious issue in America today?

4. Should the cultural practices and traditions of immigrant groups be tolerated if they conflict with mainstream American values? Why or why not?

5. "Americans, while they may promote cultural diversity within the United States, are cultural imperialists with respect to the global community." Do you agree with this observation? What does it say about American political culture and values?

6. Is the concept of a political spectrum or of a political typology really very useful in understanding American political values?

7. No matter how sophisticated our society may be, many Americans are influenced—rightly or wrongly—by stereotypes. For example, many older people believe that they know where the young person is "coming from" if the person has multiple body piercings (nose rings, eyebrow rings, and so on) or spiked hair. Is it fair to assume that people who express similar fashion preferences have similar beliefs?

suggested readings

BRINKLEY, Alan. *Liberalism and Its Discontents*. Cambridge, Mass.: Harvard University Press, 1998. In this history of liberalism since the 1930s, a distinguished historian describes what liberalism is, why it emerged, and why it has weakened as a political ideology in recent years.

DIONNE, E. J. *They Only Look Dead: Why Progressives Will Dominate the Next Political Era*. New York: Simon & Schuster, 1996. This *Washington Post* reporter believes that the so-called Republican revolution will fail because Americans do not really want small-government conservatism.

ETZIONI, Amitai. *The New Golden Rule: Community and Morality in a Democratic Society*. New York: Basic Books, 1997. The author, a leading sociologist, searches for a new golden mean that can help resolve disputes over order versus liberty, individual versus group interests, cultural diversity versus universal rights, and other American values. He calls for a new balance between individual rights and social responsibility.

HIMMELFARB, Gertrude. *The De-Moralizing of Society: From Victorian Virtues to Modern Times*. New York: Vintage Books, 1996. The author, a leading intellectual historian, is appalled, as are many other Americans, by crime, drug trafficking and addiction, illiteracy, juvenile delinquency, and other problems that seem to be increasingly endemic to American life. She feels that Americans should espouse the concept of moral responsibility and proposes that we can learn much from the values of the Victorian era. These values include respectability, self-help, and self-discipline.

PELTON, Leroy H. *Doing Justice: Liberalism, Group Constructs, and Individual Realities*. Albany, N.Y.: State University of New York Press, 1999. The author contends that the liberal, group-based ideals that pervade public policy today are essentially discriminatory because they provide protection for Americans based on such criteria as race, ethnicity, or gender.

SCHWARZMANTEL, J. J. *The Age of Ideology: Political Ideologies from the American Revolution to Postmodern Times*. New York: New York University Press, 1998. This work offers a broad-ranging overview of modern political and social thought. The author examines nationalism, liberalism, socialism, and conservatism over the past two and a half centuries.

politics
on the web

The Pew Research Center for the People and the Press offers survey data online on numerous issues, many of which show how various groups identify themselves on the political spectrum. You can even answer a series of questions about your views on different issues and find out where you fit on the spectrum. The URL for the center's site is

http://www.people-press.org

For insights into a liberal approach to political and economic issues, you can explore the Democratic Party's site at

http://www.democrats.org

Similarly, you can explore predominantly conservative views on a number of issues by accessing the Republican National Committee's Web offerings at

http://www.rnc.org

Socialism has always found support among some Americans, and socialist third parties have put forth candidates in a number of elections, as you will read in Chapter 8. To learn more about socialist views, you can access the Socialist Party's Web site at

http://sp-usa.org

For a libertarian view of politics, you can visit the site of the Libertarian Party at

http://www.lp.org/lp.html

using
web resources

There is a great deal of dissatisfaction with using the terms *left*, *right*, *moderate*, and others to describe a person's political beliefs. Nevertheless, many continue to use these terms.

1. Access the following Web site:

http://www.ccnet.com/ ~ suntzu75/parties.htm

Read the brief analysis highlighting the problems associated with political labels and then go to one of the U.S. political party links. What is it about that political party that makes it either "left" or "right" wing?

2. Now go to the following Web site:

http://www.self-gov.org/quiz.html

Take the "World's Smallest Political Quiz." What was your ideology?

---

notes

1. U.S. Census Bureau.

2. *Garcia v. Spun State Co.*, 998 F.2d 1480 (9th Cir. 1993).

3. As cited in *USA Today*, February 28, 1997, p. 8A.

4. Congress passed the Flag Protection Act of 1989 after the Supreme Court had ruled in *Texas v. Johnson*, 491 U.S. 397 (1989), that a state law prohibiting the burning of the American flag was unconstitutional.

5. *United States v. Eichman*, 496 U.S. 310 (1990).

6. *The Public Perspective,* February/March 1997, p. 22.

7. Barbara Crossette, "Testing the Limits of Tolerance as Cultures Mix," *The New York Times,* March 6, 1999, p. A15.

8. As quoted in David Broder, "The Unity among Us," *The Washington Post,* November 25, 1998, p. A21.

9. The Public Agenda studies just cited, as well as a number of other recent surveys, can be accessed at Public Agenda's Web site: **http://www.publicagenda.org**.

10. A summary of this study is available at the National Opinion Research Center's Web site. Go to **http://www.norc.uchicago.edu/new/pats.htm**.

11. *Wall Street Journal*/NBC News poll, as reported in *The Wall Street Journal,* June 27, 1997, p. R2.

12. Daniel Patrick Moynihan, as quoted in *U.S. News & World Report,* October 21, 1996, p. 52.

13. William Safire, "After the Second Honeymoon, Let the Law Take Its Course," *International Herald Tribune,* November 8, 1996, p. 9.

14. *The Public Perspective,* April/May 1998, p. 7.

15. Albert R. Hunt, "On Immigration, Party Leaders Aren't Necessarily in Sync with Feelings of Rank and File," *The Wall Street Journal,* June 27, 1997, p. R2.

16. Samuel Huntington, *The Clash of Civilizations and the Remaking of the World Order* (New York: Simon & Schuster, 1996).

chapter

7

INTEREST GROUPS

Gun Control: Do We Need an Armed Citizenry?

One of the most successful interest groups in American history has been the National Rifle Association (NRA). Partly because of the Second Amendment to the U.S. Constitution, which guarantees the right to bear arms, and partly because of the effectiveness of NRA lobbying, the United States has the laxest gun-control laws in the developed world.

Go to CD-ROM

To some extent, the general public is at odds with the very effective lobbying results of the NRA. The cry for more gun-control legislation became increasingly loud after the killings in Columbine High School in Littleton, Colorado, in 1999, which followed a number of other high school shootings around the country. Recent polls show that about 80 percent of Americans want gun-control laws tightened.[1]

Yes, It Is Time to Stop Killing—We Need More Control on Guns

Let there be no doubt about it, contend those in favor of more gun control, the United States has the most heavily armed population in the world. The result, they say, is the highest murder rate in the developed world. The Constitution's Second Amendment, which guarantees the right to bear arms, was never meant to allow private citizens to keep firearms in their homes but only to allow citizens to bear firearms in the event that they were called to be part of a state-sponsored militia.[2]

The massive amount of firepower that criminals have in the United States is a direct result of our lax gun-control laws. Under what circumstances, ask those in favor of more gun control, would any American need a semiautomatic weapon for protection? Under what circumstances would individuals use automatic or semiautomatic weapons in sport shooting?

Most gun-control proponents don't argue in favor of an outright ban on all guns. They do admit that in certain situations, individuals should have a right to bear arms.

In any event, a gun in the home is many times more likely to kill a family member than to stop a criminal. Armed citizens are just not a deterrent to crime. The gun-control lobby has had some striking successes in its fight against the opponents of gun control, such as the NRA. For example, in 1993 the gun-control lobby was an effective force in convincing Congress to pass the Brady Handgun Violence Prevention Act (although the Supreme Court declared key provisions of the act unconstitutional in 1997[3]). In 1994, Congress also passed a ban on nineteen types of semiautomatic weapons.

We Have a Constitutional Right to Bear Arms, Says the NRA

The NRA is the most outspoken interest group in the United States with respect to fighting gun-control laws. The NRA claims a membership of nearly three million target shooters, hunters, gun collectors, gunsmiths, police, and others interested in firearms. The NRA includes the following statement in its "Ten Myths about Gun Control":

> The Second Amendment contains no qualifiers, no "buts," or "excepts." It affirms people's right to possess firearms.[4]

The Second Amendment is one of the most powerful arguments that opponents of gun control can muster. The right to bear arms is not only a constitutional right in the United States but it was also a traditional right in England.[5]

Those who are against further gun control also argue that the registration and licensing of guns will have no effect on crime. After all, criminals, by definition, do not obey laws. Furthermore, convicted felons are prohibited by law from possessing firearms, so they would not register anyway.

A recent study on gun control by John R. Lott, Jr., a professor at the University of Chicago Law School, offers some support for gun-control opponents. Lott's study showed that when states allowed concealed weapons, murders were reduced by 8.5 percent, rapes by 5 percent, robberies by 3 percent, and aggravated assaults by 7 per-cent. The decline in murder rates was greatest in counties with populations of more than 200,000 people in the states that allowed concealed handguns.[6]

In any event, more than 99 percent of all privately owned handguns in the United States are not used for criminal purposes. At least half of the handgun owners in the United States keep guns for protection and security. A handgun at home is an insurance policy, according to the NRA.

Where Do You Stand?

1. Do you agree that gun-control laws should be stricter in the United States? Why or why not?

2. "If guns are outlawed, only criminals will have guns." Do you accept this reasoning? Explain.

On the Web

For more information on how the American public feels about gun control, go to the Web site of the National Opinion Research Center at http://www.norc.uchicago.edu. For more information on the NRA's position on this issue, go to http://www.nra.org.

BEWARE! ARMED CITIZENRY

Introduction

INTEREST GROUP ● An organized group of individuals sharing common objectives who actively attempt to influence policymakers in all three branches of the government and at all levels.

INFOTRAC®

Target practice
Republicans

The groups supporting and opposing gun control provide but one example of how Americans form groups to pursue or protect their interests. All of us have interests that we would like to have represented in government: farmers want higher prices for their products; young people want good educational opportunities; environmentalists want clean air and water; and the homeless want programs that provide food and shelter.

The old adage that there is strength in numbers is certainly true in American politics. The right to organize groups is even protected by the Constitution, which guarantees people the right "peaceably to assemble, and to petition the Government for redress of grievances." The Supreme Court has defended this important right over the years.

Special interests significantly influence American government and politics. Some Americans think that this influence is too great and jeopardizes representative democracy. Others maintain that interest groups are a natural consequence of democracy. After all, throughout our nation's history, people have organized into groups to protect special interests. Because of the important role played by interest groups in the American system of government, in this chapter we focus solely on such groups. We look at what they are, why they are formed, and how they influence policymaking.

Interest Groups and American Government

An **interest group** is an organization of people sharing common objectives who actively attempt to influence government policymakers through direct and indirect methods. Whatever their goals—more or fewer social services, higher or lower prices—interest groups pursue these goals on every level and in every branch of government.

On any given day in Washington, D.C., you can see national interest groups in action. If you eat breakfast in the Senate dining room, you might see congressional committee staffers reviewing testimony with representatives from women's groups. Later that morning, you might visit the Supreme Court and watch a civil rights lawyer arguing on behalf of a client in a discrimination suit. Lunch in a popular Washington restaurant might

One of the most successful interest groups in the United States is the gun lobby. This gun dealer at a show in Orlando, Florida, is a member of the National Rifle Association (NRA), which has been in existence for more than 125 years. It is estimated that there are over 180 million long guns (rifles and shotguns) in Americans' possession today. The number of pistols in existence may even exceed that. It is not surprising that the NRA has been a very successful lobbying group, particularly with respect to preventing stringent gun-control laws in this country.

Alexis de Tocqueville (1805–1859) was a well-known French political scientist and historian. His best-known work is *Democracy in America*, which was published in 1835. In that book, he stated, "If men are to remain civilized or to become civilized, the art of association must develop and improve among them at the same speed as equality of conditions spreads." (Vol. 2, Part II, Chapter 5)

PLURALIST THEORY ● A theory that views politics as a contest among various interest groups—at all levels of government—to gain benefits for their members.

Table 7–1

Percentage of Americans Belonging to Various Groups

Health organizations	16%
Social clubs	17
Neighborhood groups	18
Hobby, garden, and computer clubs	19
PTA and school groups	21
Professional and trade associations	27
Health, sport, and country clubs	30
Religious groups	61

SOURCE: American Association of Retired Persons (AARP), 1999.

find you listening in on a conversation between an agricultural lobbyist and a congressional representative.

That afternoon you might visit an executive department, such as the Department of Labor, and watch bureaucrats working out rules and regulations with representatives from a labor interest group. Then you might stroll past the headquarters of the NRA, the American Association of Retired Persons (AARP), or the National Wildlife Federation.

THE AMERICAN PENCHANT FOR JOINING GROUPS

The French political observer and traveler Alexis de Tocqueville wrote in 1835 that Americans have a tendency to form "associations" and have perfected "the art of pursuing in common the object of their common desires." "In no other country of the world," said Tocqueville, "has the principle of association been more successfully used or applied to a greater multitude of objectives than in America."[7] Of course, de Tocqueville could not foresee the thousands of associations that now exist in this country. Surveys show that over 85 percent of Americans belong to at least one group. Table 7–1 shows the percentage of Americans who belong to various types of interest groups today.

HOW INTEREST GROUPS FUNCTION IN AMERICAN POLITICS

Despite the bad press that interest groups tend to get in the United States, they do serve several purposes in American politics:

■ Interest groups help bridge the gap between citizens and government and enable citizens to explain their views on policies to public officials.

■ Interest groups help raise public awareness and inspire action on various issues.

■ Interest groups often provide public officials with specialized and detailed information that might be difficult to obtain otherwise. This information may be useful in making policy choices.

■ Interest groups serve as another check on public officials to make sure that they are carrying out their duties responsibly.

Access to Government

In a sense, the American system of government invites the participation of interest groups by offering many points of access for groups wishing to influence policy. Consider the possibilities at just the federal level. An interest group can lobby members of Congress to act in the interests of the group. If the Senate passes a bill opposed by the group, the group's lobbying efforts can shift to the House of Representatives. If the House passes the bill, the group can try to influence the new law's application by lobbying the executive agency that is responsible for implementing the law. The group might even challenge the law in court, directly (through filing a lawsuit) or indirectly (by filing a brief as an *amicus curiae*,[8] or "friend of the court").

Pluralist Theory

The participation of groups in a decentralized structure of government that offers many points of access to policymakers describes the **pluralist theory** of American democracy. According to the pluralist theory, politics is a contest among various interest groups. These groups vie with each other—at all levels of government—to gain benefits for their members. Pluralists maintain that the influence of interest groups on government is not undemocratic. This is because individual interests are represented in the policymaking process, but indirectly, through groups. Although not every American belongs to an interest group, inevitably some group will represent each individual's interests. Each interest is satisfied to some extent through the compromises made in settling conflicts among competing interest groups.[9]

Pluralists also contend that because of the extensive number of interest groups vying for political benefits, no one group can dominate the political process. Additionally, because most people have more than one interest, conflicts among groups do not divide the nation into hostile camps.

HOW DO INTEREST GROUPS DIFFER FROM POLITICAL PARTIES?

Although interest groups and political parties are both groups of people joined together for political purposes, they differ in several important ways. As you will read in Chapter 8, a political party is a group of individuals outside government who organize to win elections, operate the government, and determine policy. Interest groups, in contrast, do not seek to win elections or operate the government. Clearly, though, they do seek to influence policy. Other ways in which interest groups differ from political parties include the following:

- Interest groups are often policy *specialists,* whereas political parties are policy *generalists.* Political parties are broad-based organizations that must attract the support of many opposing groups and consider a large number of issues. Interest groups, in contrast, have only a handful of key policies to push. An environmental group will not be as concerned about the economic status of Hispanics as it is about polluters. A manufacturing group is more involved with pushing for fewer regulations than it is with inner-city poverty.
- Interest groups are usually more tightly organized than political parties. They are often financed through contributions or dues-paying memberships. Organizers of interest groups communicate with members and potential members through conferences, mailings, newsletters, and electronic formats, such as e-mail.
- A political party's main sphere of influence is the electoral system; parties run candidates for political office. Interest groups try to influence the outcome of elections, but unlike parties, they do not compete for public office. Although a candidate for office may be sympathetic to—or even be a member of—a certain group, he or she does not run for election as a candidate of that group.

The American Association of Retired Persons (AARP) has become one of the most powerful interest groups in America. The AARP has approximately 33 million members and an annual budget of about $322 million. This group has lobbied for higher minimum wages, rent-control laws, the Family and Medical Leave Act, and higher taxes on gas. Certainly, the AARP will increase in importance when the big jump in the elderly population occurs between 2005 and 2030, as the baby boomers reach retirement age. It is not surprising that politicians, such as President Clinton in this photo, frequently seek the support of the AARP.

Different Types of Interest Groups

American democracy embraces almost every conceivable type of interest group, and the number is increasing rapidly. No one has ever compiled a *Who's Who* of interest groups, but you can get an idea of the number and variety by looking through the annually published *Encyclopedia of Associations*. Look at Figure 7-1 to see profiles of some selected important interest groups.

Figure 7-1
Profiles of Selected Interest Groups

Name: American Association of Retired Persons (AARP)
Founded: 1958
Membership: 33,000,000 working or retired persons 50 years of age or older.
Description: The AARP strives to better the lives of older people, especially in the areas of health care, worker equity, and minority affairs. The AARP sponsors community crime prevention programs, research on the problems associated with aging, and a mail-order pharmacy.
Budget: $322,000,000
Address: 601 E St. N.W., Washington, DC 20049
Phone: (202) 434–3741

Name: League of Women Voters of the United States (LWVUS)
Founded: 1920
Membership: 130,000 members and supporters.
Description: The LWVUS promotes active and informed political participation. It distributes candidate information, encourages voter registration and voting, and takes action on issues of public policy. The group's national interests include international relations, natural resources, and social policy.
Budget: $3,000,000
Address: 1730 M St. N.W., Washington, DC 20036
Phone: (202) 429–1965

Name: National Education Association (NEA)
Founded: 1857
Membership: 2,300,000 elementary and secondary school teachers, college and university professors, academic administrators, and others concerned with education.
Description: The NEA's committees investigate and take action in the areas of benefits, civil rights, educational support, personnel, higher education, human relations, legislation, minority affairs, and women's concerns.
Budget: $119,000,000
Address: 1201 16th St. N.W., Washington, DC 20036
Phone: (202) 833–4000

Name: National Rifle Association (NRA)
Founded: 1871
Membership: 2,800,000 persons interested in firearms.
Description: The NRA promotes rifle, pistol, and shotgun shooting, as well as hunting, gun collecting, and home firearm safety. It educates police firearm instructors and sponsors teams to participate in international competitions.
Budget: $156,500,000
Address: 11250 Waples Mill Road, Fairfax, VA 22030
Phone: 1–800–NRA–3888

Name: The Sierra Club (SC)
Founded: 1892
Membership: 650,000 persons concerned with the interrelationship between nature and humankind.
Description: The Sierra Club endeavors to protect and conserve natural resources, save endangered areas, and resolve problems associated with wilderness, clean air, energy conservation, and land use. Its committees are concerned with agriculture, economics, environmental education, hazardous materials, the international environment, Native American sites, political education, and water resources.
Budget: $45,000,000
Address: 85 2d St., 2d Floor, San Francisco, CA 94105
Phone: (415) 977–5500

PUBLIC-INTEREST GROUP ● An interest group formed for the purpose of working for the "public good"; examples of public-interest groups are the American Civil Liberties Union and Common Cause.

TRADE ORGANIZATION ● An association formed by members of a particular industry, such as the oil industry or the trucking industry, to develop common standards and goals for the industry. Trade organizations, as interest groups, lobby government for legislation or regulations that specifically benefit their groups.

Some interest groups have large memberships. The American Association of Retired Persons (AARP), for example, has about thirty-three million members. Others, such as the Tulip Growers Association, have as few as fourteen members. Some, such as the NRA, are household names and have been in existence for many years, while others crop up overnight. Some are highly structured and run by professional, full-time staffs, while others are loosely structured and informal.

The most common interest groups are private-interest groups, which seek public policies that benefit the economic interests of their members and work against policies that threaten those interests. Other groups, sometimes called **public-interest groups,** are formed with the broader goal of working for the "public good"; the American Civil Liberties Union and Common Cause are examples.

BUSINESS INTEREST GROUPS

Business has long been well organized for effective action. Hundreds of business groups are now operating in Washington, D.C., in the fifty state capitals, and at the local level across the country. Two umbrella organizations that include most corporations and businesses are the U.S. Chamber of Commerce and the National Association of Manufacturers (NAM). In addition to its more than two hundred thousand individual business members, the Chamber has four thousand local, state, and regional affiliates. It has become a major voice for the nation's thousands of small businesses. The NAM chiefly represents big business and has thirteen thousand members.

The hundreds of **trade organizations** are far less visible than the Chamber of Commerce and the NAM, but they are also important in seeking policy goals for their members. Trade organizations usually support policies that benefit specific industries. For example, people in the oil industry work for policies that favor the development of oil as an energy resource. Other business groups have worked for policies that favor the development of coal, solar power, and nuclear power. Trucking companies would work for policies that would result in more highways being built. Railroad companies would, of course, not want more highways built because that would hurt their business.

Traditionally, business interest groups have been viewed as staunch supporters of the Republican Party. This is because Republicans are more likely to promote a "hands-off" government policy toward business. In the

President Bill Clinton and Vice President Al Gore both have received support from trade groups representing the high-tech industry. Here, they are seen visiting the headquarters of Silicon Graphics, a successful software company located in "Silicon Valley," California.

LABOR FORCE ● All of the people over the age of sixteen who are working or actively looking for jobs.

INFOTRAC®

Labor's big bet

1990s, however, donations from corporations to the Democratic National Committee more than doubled. Why would business groups make contributions to the Democratic National Committee? Fred McChesney, a professor of law and business at Emory University's School of Law, offers an interesting answer to this question. He proposes that campaign contributions are often made not for political favors but rather to avoid political disfavor. Just as government officials can take away wealth from citizens (in the form of taxes, for example), politicians can extort from private parties payments *not* to expropriate private wealth.[10]

LABOR INTEREST GROUPS

Interest groups representing labor have been some of the most influential groups in our country's history. They date back to at least 1886, when the American Federation of Labor (AFL) was formed. The largest and most powerful labor interest group today is the AFL-CIO (the American Federation of Labor–Congress of Industrial Organizations), an organization that includes nearly ninety unions representing more than 16.1 million workers. Several million additional workers are members of other unions (not affiliated with the AFL-CIO), such as the International Brotherhood of Teamsters.

Like labor unions everywhere, American labor unions press for policies to ensure improved working conditions and better pay for their members. On some issues, however, unions may take opposing sides. For example, separate unions of bricklayers and carpenters may try to change building codes to benefit their own members even though the changes may hurt other unions. Unions may also compete for new members. In California, for example, the Teamsters, the AFL-CIO, and the United Mine Workers have vied to organize farm workers. Today, these unions are competing to organize farm workers in Texas, Florida, and other states. Also, organized labor does not represent all of American workers. It represents only 15 percent of the **labor force,** or all of the people over the age of sixteen who are working or actively looking for a job.

Although unions were highly influential in the late 1800s and the early 1900s, their strength and political power have waned in the last two decades. Nonetheless, they are still a powerful lobbying force and continue to work in support of their members' interests.

While organized labor groups represent a declining percentage of the American labor force, they are still very active. In the late summer of 1997, the Teamsters Union convinced workers at United Parcel Service (UPS) to go on strike. This strike, which was eventually settled, was regarded by some as an indication that the labor movement in America may be on the rise again.

Labor Unions Show Their Muscle in the 1996 Elections

AFL-CIO president John Sweeney declared at the beginning of 1996 that his group would amass a war chest of $35 million to defeat Republican candidates who were opposed to labor's interests. Sweeney targeted thirty-two Republican seats. To raise the $35 million, the AFL-CIO assessed an extra set of dues on its members. This was one of the largest special interest drives in the history of the United States. By comparison, the Christian Coalition raised only $1.4 million.

The much-publicized $35 million war chest was actually only a small part of labor's political efforts in 1996. It is estimated that the total cost of labor's phone banks, mailings, and get-out-the-vote drives was closer to $500 million, or more than four times the combined budgets for the Dole and Clinton campaigns.

What if some labor union members do not want a portion of their dues to go toward political activities? For a discussion of this issue, see the feature on the next page entitled *The American Political Spectrum: The Use of Union Dues for Political Activities*.

Unions in the Face of the Global Economy

Whether the AFL-CIO and other union groups can effectively expand their membership is in doubt because of the increased globalization of our economy. Throughout the world, in the face of high-wage union industries, manufacturers are "outsourcing" their work to nonunionized businesses, often in developing countries. Even when multinational companies come to the United States, they are often successful in setting up nonunion manufacturing plants. Witness the numerous nonunion auto-assembly plants—stretching from Tennessee to southern Ohio—that are largely Japanese owned. Even German auto manufacturers are trying to widen this nonunion "belt" by opening plants in states that have a history of hostility toward unions. BMW opened one such plant in South Carolina; Daimler-Benz (Mercedes-Benz autos) did so in Alabama.

AGRICULTURAL INTEREST GROUPS

Many groups work for general agricultural interests at all levels of government. Three broad-based agricultural groups represent over five million American farmers, from peanut farmers to dairy producers to tobacco growers. They are the American Farm Bureau Federation, the National Grange, and the National Farmers' Union. The Farm Bureau, with over 4.7 million members, is the largest and generally the most effective of the three. Founded

To save on labor costs, American manufacturers commonly "outsource" production work to factories in other countries. Shown here are Indonesian workers at a Reebok shoe factory located in the outskirts of Jakarta.

The Use of Union Dues for Political Activities

On average, each of the millions of private-sector union members in the United States pays about $400 in dues each year. Much of this money is used to support political causes and issues of interest to the labor movement. In fact, though, in 1988 the Supreme Court declared that current labor law cannot force workers to subsidize anything but the actual work of unions. In *Communications Workers of America v. Beck,*[11] Justice William Brennan wrote that the law allowed "the exaction of only those fees and dues necessary to 'performing the duties of an exclusive representative of the employees in dealing with the employer on labor-management issues.'"

In the last days of his administration, Republican president George Bush and his Labor Department put through the regulations that followed from the *Beck* decision. These regulations required unions to issue public reports breaking down their spending so that union workers would know what portion of their dues was going for political activities. The Bush administration issued an executive order that required federal contractors to inform workers that they could keep any union dues allocated to political activities.

What the Political Left Thinks of the *Beck* Decision

There is not much doubt as to how President Bill Clinton and his administration have regarded the Supreme Court's ruling in the *Beck* case. Within weeks of his inauguration, Clinton signed an executive order that nullified the regulations of the Bush administration, thus effectively gutting the *Beck* deci-

sion. In February 1997, the National Labor Relations Board (NLRB) held that a former member of the Oklahoma Carpenters and Joiners Union Local 943 was not entitled to a refund of the portion of his monthly union dues that went to the AFL-CIO's Washington headquarters for political action. The NLRB argued that the amount in question was too small to worry about (it was indeed only 70 cents a month). The AFL-CIO has about thirteen million members who pay dues twelve times a year, though, so the 70 cents per month paid by each member adds up to more than $100 million a year.

The unions, of course, are typically on the political left and support Democratic candidates. The unions are against the *Beck* decision because they want to be able to obtain the funds necessary to support their agenda. Political activists, such as John J. Sweeney, are now running the AFL-CIO and other leading unions. Such groups are spending large amounts of money on major organizational drives to bring in new members.

The View from the Political Right

Thomas Jefferson once said, "To compel a man to furnish contributions of money for the propagation of opinions which he disbelieves is sinful and tyrannical." This statement about sums up the views of most political conservatives on the use of union dues to support political activities. They point out that 40 percent of union members vote Republican, whereas virtually 100 percent of union support is for Democratic candidates at all levels of government.

Political conservatives tend to support the *Beck* decision and castigate Clinton for his administration's overt flouting of that ruling. For example, constitutional scholar Roger Pilon claimed that President Clinton has violated the obligation laid out in Article II, Section 3, of the Constitution that the president must take care that "the Laws be faithfully executed."[12] The generally politically conservative *Wall Street Journal* published the results of a poll taken in January 1997 showing that 63 percent of those polled opposed the use of union membership dues to support political causes.[13]

Certainly, it is not surprising that political conservatives, particularly Republicans, are against the use of union dues to support political activities. In 1998, a group of Republicans and other union foes sponsored an initiative in California that would have required employers and unions to obtain each worker's permission before withholding wages or using union dues or fees for political contributions. The initiative failed to pass, however, probably because of the effective countercampaign launched by its opponents.

For Critical Analysis

Conservative critics of President Bush point out that his administration took four years to implement regulations in support of the Supreme Court's decision in the Beck *case. What political considerations might have motivated Bush to delay the implementation of these regulations for four years?*

in 1919, the Farm Bureau achieved one of its greatest early successes when it helped to obtain government guarantees of "fair" prices during the Great Depression of the 1930s.[14] The Grange, founded in 1867, is the oldest group. It has a membership of about 300,000 farm families. The National Farmers' Union comprises approximately 310,000 smaller farmers.

politics on the far side

Let the Water (in Dollars) Flow

The Bureau of Reclamation undertook a study of the benefits of a water project called Animas–La Plata, in southwestern Colorado. The study concluded that the economic benefits of the project would be less than half of what it would cost taxpayers.

Nonetheless, Congress appropriated funds to begin construction of the multimillion-dollar project. Who benefited? A small handful of farmers who would pay $20 million for the water that would cost taxpayers $517 million to provide.

For Critical Analysis: Would this nation be better off if there were no interest groups to lobby Congress for special benefits?

Like special interest labor groups, producers of various specific farm commodities, such as dairy products, soybeans, grain, fruit, corn, cotton, beef, sugar beets, and so on, have formed their own organizations. These specialized groups, such as the Associated Milk Producers, Inc., also have a strong influence on farm legislation. Like business and labor groups, farm organizations sometimes find themselves in competition. In some western states, for example, barley farmers, cattle ranchers, and orchard owners may compete to influence laws concerning water rights—see the feature *Politics on the Far Side: Let the Water (in Dollars) Flow* for a discussion of one water project. Different groups also often disagree over the extent to which the government should regulate farmers.

CONSUMER INTEREST GROUPS

Groups organized for the protection of consumer rights were very active in the 1960s and 1970s. Some are still active today. The best known and perhaps the most effective are the public-interest consumer groups organized under the leadership of consumer activist Ralph Nader. Another well-known consumer group is Consumers Union, a nonprofit organization started in 1936. In addition to publishing *Consumer Reports,* Consumers Union has been influential in pushing for the removal of phosphates from detergents, lead from gasoline, and pesticides from food. Consumers Union strongly criticizes government agencies when they act against consumer interests.

In each city, consumer groups have been organized to deal with such problems as poor housing, discrimination against minorities and women, discrimination in the granting of credit, and business inaction on consumer complaints.

SENIOR CITIZEN INTEREST GROUPS

While the population of the nation as a whole has tripled since 1900, the number of elderly has increased eightfold. Persons over the age of sixty-five account for 13 percent of the population, and many of these people have united to call attention to their special needs and concerns. Interest groups formed to promote the interests of the elderly have been very outspoken and persuasive. As pointed out before, the AARP has about thirty-three million members. With 1,300 employees and eighteen lobbyists, it has become a potent political force.

ENVIRONMENTAL INTEREST GROUPS

With the current concern for the environment, the membership of established environmental groups has blossomed, and many new groups have formed. They are becoming some of the fastest-growing and most powerful interest groups in Washington, D.C. The National Wildlife Federation grew from 4.5 million members to approximately 5.6 million members in the last five years. Table 7–2 on the next page lists some of the major environmental groups and the number of members in each group.

Environmental groups have organized to support pollution controls, wilderness protection, and clean-air legislation. They have opposed strip-mining, nuclear power plants, logging activities, chemical waste dumps, and many other environmental hazards.

PROFESSIONAL INTEREST GROUPS

Most professions that require advanced education or specialized training have organizations to protect and promote their interests. These groups

Table 7-2

Selected Environmental Interest Groups

NAME OF GROUP	YEAR FOUNDED	NUMBER OF MEMBERS
Environmental Defense Fund	1967	300,000
Greenpeace USA	1971	2,500,000
Izaak Walton League of America	1922	50,000
League of Conservation Voters	1970	9,000,000
National Audubon Society	1905	550,000
National Wildlife Federation	1936	4,100,000
The Nature Conservancy	1951	900,000
The Sierra Club	1892	650,000
The Wilderness Society	1935	500,000
The World Wildlife Fund	1948	1,500,000

SOURCE: Foundation for Public Affairs, 1996; plus authors' update.

are concerned mainly with the standards of their professions, but they also work to influence government policy.

Four major professional groups are the American Medical Association, representing physicians; the American Bar Association, representing lawyers; and the National Education Association and the American Federation of Teachers, both representing teachers. In addition, there are dozens of less well known and less politically active professional groups, such as the Screen Actors Guild, the National Association of Social Workers, and the American Political Science Association.

How Interest Groups Shape Policy

Interest groups operate at all levels of government and use a variety of strategies to steer policies in ways beneficial to their interests. They some-

Environmental groups have become increasingly militant in recent years. Greenpeace was founded in 1971 to oppose U.S. nuclear testing in Alaska. It has fought to protect endangered species and to stop the dumping of hazardous waste. The *Rainbow Warrior* is a Greenpeace ship that was used, among other things, to protest French atmospheric nuclear weapons testing.

LOBBYING ● All of the attempts by organizations or by individuals to influence the passage, defeat, or contents of legislation or to influence the administrative decisions of government.

LOBBYIST ● An individual who handles a particular interest group's lobbying efforts.

times attempt to directly influence the policymakers themselves, while at other times they try to indirectly influence policymakers by shaping public opinion. The extent and nature of the groups' activities depend on their goals and their resources.

DIRECT TECHNIQUES

Lobbying and providing election support are two important direct techniques used by interest groups to influence government policy.

Lobbying

Today, **lobbying** refers to all of the attempts by organizations or individuals to influence the passage, defeat, or contents of legislation or to influence the administrative decisions of government. (The term *lobbying* arose because, traditionally, individuals and groups interested in influencing government policy would gather in the foyer, or lobby, of the legislature to corner legislators and express their concerns.) A **lobbyist** is an individual who handles a particular interest group's lobbying efforts. Most of the larger interest groups have lobbyists in Washington, D.C. These lobbyists often include former members of Congress or former employees of executive bureaucracies who are experienced in the methods of political influence and who "know people." Many lobbyists also work at state and local levels. In fact, lobbying at the state level has increased in recent years as states have begun to play a more significant role in policymaking. Table 7–3 on the next page summarizes some of the basic methods by which lobbyists directly influence legislators and government officials.

politics on the far side

Special Interest Groups Are Effective at the State Level, Too

At the New York state legislature, there is something called the "member item." It is the most secretive and least regulated way of satisfying special interest groups. Each year more than one hundred "member items" are added to the state's spending bills.

For example, when the private White Otter Fish and Game Club in the southern Adirondacks needed $150,000 for a new clubhouse, its members turned to a former president who still belonged to the club—state senator William R. Sears. Tucked away in Sears's $1 million in appropriations for his "member item" projects was an allocation of $150,000 for the private club.

For Critical Analysis: What checks the influence that can be wielded by specific interest groups?

The Effectiveness of Lobbying

Lobbying is one of the most widely used and effective ways to influence legislative activity. For example, Mothers Against Drunk Driving has had many lobbying successes at both the state and federal levels. The NRA has successfully blocked most proposed gun-control laws, even though a majority of Americans are in favor of such laws. An NRA brochure describes its lobbying operation as "the strongest, most formidable grassroots lobby in the nation." As mentioned in the chapter-opening feature, the NRA has occasionally been defeated in its lobbying efforts by interest groups that support gun control. (For a comparison of the U.S. and British approaches to gun control, see the feature on page 173 entitled *Comparative Politics: Gun Control in Britain and the United States—A Tale of Two Lobbies.*)

As another example of how effective lobbying can help special interest groups, consider the minimum wage bill passed in 1996. (For an example of how special interests can affect state legislation, see the feature, *Politics on the Far Side: Special Interest Groups Are Effective at the State Level, Too.*) Virtually everyone was certain that Clinton would sign the bill; therefore, any special interest legislation attached to the bill would be passed along with it. So lobbyists went to work in the Senate and succeeded in getting the following provisions tacked on to the minimum wage bill:

■ A provision that shielded insurance companies from new, costly lawsuits.
■ Larger tax write-offs for small businesses.
■ Tax deductions for Alaskan fisheries (for example, the ability to claim deductions on the cost of all meals the fishers eat while at sea).
■ Extension of tax credits for companies that hire disadvantaged people.

Table 7–3

Direct Lobbying Techniques

TECHNIQUE	DESCRIPTION
Making Personal Contacts with Key Legislators	A lobbyist's personal contacts with key legislators or other government officials—in their offices, in the halls of Congress, or on social occasions, such as dinners, boating expeditions, and the like—are one of the more effective direct lobbying techniques. The lobbyist provides the legislators with information on a particular issue in an attempt to convince the legislators to support the interest group's goals.
Providing Expertise and Research Results for Legislators	Lobbyists often have knowledge and expertise that are useful in drafting legislation, which is a major strength for an interest group. Because many harried members of Congress cannot possibly be experts on everything they vote on and therefore eagerly seek information to help them make up their minds, some lobbying groups conduct research and present their findings to those legislators.
Offering "Expert" Testimony before Congressional Committees	Lobbyists often provide "expert" testimony before congressional committees for or against proposed legislation. A bill to regulate firearms, for example, might concern several interest groups. The NRA would probably oppose the bill, and representatives from the interest group might be asked to testify. Groups that would probably support the bill, such as law enforcement personnel or wildlife conservationists, might also be asked to testify. Each side would offer as much evidence as possible to support its position.
Providing Legal Advice or Assistance to Legislators and Bureaucrats	Many lobbyists assist legislators or bureaucrats in drafting legislation or prospective regulations. Lobbyists are a source of ideas and sometimes offer legal advice on specific details.
Following Up on Legislation	Because executive agencies responsible for carrying out legislation can often increase or decrease the power of the new law, lobbyists may also try to influence the bureaucrats who implement the policy. For example, beginning in the early 1960s, regulations outlawing gender discrimination were broadly outlined by Congress. Both women's rights groups favoring the regulations and interest groups opposing the regulations lobbied for years to influence how those regulations were carried out.

- Deductions for companies that underwrite their employees' college education, plus a second credit to employees attending graduate school.
- A provision to reduce the excise tax on hard-cider producers.
- A provision backed by the securities industry that would allow all homemakers to deposit $2,000 annually, tax free, into an individual retirement account.
- A renewal of the 20 percent tax credit for corporate research and development.

Lobbying can be directed not only at the legislative branch of government but also at administrative agencies and even at the courts. For example, individuals stricken with AIDS formed a strong lobby in the early 1990s to force the Food and Drug Administration to allow patients to use experimental drugs to treat AIDS before the drugs were fully tested. Lobbying can also be directed at changing international policies. For example, after political changes had opened up Eastern Europe to business in the late 1980s and early 1990s, intense lobbying by Western business groups helped persuade the United States and other industrial powers to reduce controls on the sale of high-technology products, such as personal computers, to Eastern European countries.

comparative politics

Gun Control in Britain and the United States—A Tale of Two Lobbies

In March 1995, a former Boy Scout leader named Thomas Hamilton acquired four high-powered rifles and took them to a primary school in a peaceful Scottish village named Dunblane. There he methodically slaughtered sixteen small children and their teacher. Gun violence was no longer something the British could dismiss as a uniquely American problem.

Less than a year and a half later, the government in London responded by banning virtually all handguns except .22 caliber and smaller guns, which were later also banned. Under the new laws, which are said to be among the toughest gun-control laws in the world, British residents face the prospect of up to ten years in prison if they fail to give up their weapons.

Two Different Gun Cultures

The United States has experienced many "slaughters" similar to the one in Dunblane, Scotland, and yet our gun-control laws do not come close to those of Britain. As Table 7–4 shows, the United States and Britain also differ considerably in both the number of guns owned and the number of murders committed with guns.

Table 7–4

Ownership of Firearms and Number of Murders in the United States versus Britain

	UNITED STATES	BRITAIN
Total firearms	222,000,000	409,000
Firearms per capita	0.853	0.006
Total firearm murders	14,000	80
Firearm murders per 100,000 people	5.25	0.116

SOURCES: Bureau of Justice Statistics (United States); Home Office (Britain). Data are for 1996.

A Different Mentality or Just Different Lobbying?

The British have had a long history of stringent gun-control laws. In the past, anyone seeking a gun in Britain had to obtain a certificate from the police and demonstrate a need for the weapon. Whereas 50 percent of private citizens in the United States have guns in their homes, fewer than 5 percent of British citizens do.

Prior to the ban on guns in Britain, an opinion poll showed that British citizens favored such a ban by 81 percent to 15 percent.[15] Similarly, in the United States a majority of citizens would like stricter gun-control laws; yet such laws have not been passed in this country. Why not?

The answer to this question, at least in part, has to do with the effective lobbying efforts of the NRA, which, as mentioned at the beginning of this chapter, strongly opposes any gun-control legislation. In contrast, the most important gun lobby in Britain is primarily concerned with protecting the group's interest in sports shooting. Sports shooting in Britain is not something just anyone can do. Rather, it is associated with landowning. Apparently, joining a good shooting club is a big step

(continued)

up the social ladder in the British countryside. Those who shoot typically use shotguns, which have escaped bans in Britain (at least so far). So the gun lobby in Britain has been effective, but only in protecting what is important to the most powerful classes—the free use of shotguns in the countryside.

For Critical Analysis

Opponents of the British handgun ban argued that in 1996, 41 percent of homicides were from knives; 29 percent were from blunt objects, hitting, and kicking; and 18 percent were from strangulation. That leaves only 12 percent from guns.[16] Do these statistics represent a valid argument against the British handgun ban? Explain.

POLITICAL ACTION COMMITTEE (PAC) ● A committee that is established by a corporation, labor union, or special interest group to raise funds and make contributions on the establishing organization's behalf.

I N F O T R A C ®
PAC plays

Providing Election Support

Interest groups often become directly involved in the election process. Many interest group members join and work with political parties in order to influence party platforms and the nomination of candidates. Interest groups provide campaign support for legislators who favor their policies and sometimes urge their own members to try to win posts in party organizations. Most important, interest groups urge their members to vote for candidates who support the views of the group. They can also threaten legislators with the withdrawal of votes. No candidate can expect to have support from *all* interest groups, but if the candidate is to win, she or he must have support (or little opposition) from the most powerful ones.

As you will read in Chapter 10, since the 1970s federal laws governing campaign financing have allowed corporations, labor unions, and special interest groups to raise funds and make campaign contributions through **political action committees (PACs).** In recent years, both the number of PACs and the amount of money they spend on elections have grown astronomically. There were about 1,000 PACs in 1976; by the mid-1990s, there were more than 4,600 PACs. The total amount of spending by PACs grew from $19 million in 1973 to an estimated $450 million in 1995–1996.[17]

Lobbyists often line up in the "lobbies," or halls, of Congress while awaiting their turns to consult with members of Congress. The term *lobby* comes from the medieval Latin *lobia,* which signified a monastic cloister. The word began to be used in U.S. politics in the 1830s, when agents gathered in the lobbies of both Congress and state legislatures to press their causes.

RATING SYSTEM ● A system by which a particular interest group evaluates (rates) the performance of legislators based on how often the legislators have voted consistently with the group's position on particular issues.

Although campaign contributions do not guarantee that officials will vote the way the groups wish, contributions usually do ensure that the groups will have the ear of the public officials they have helped to elect. PACs have also succeeded in bypassing campaign-contribution limits, thereby obtaining the same type of "vote-buying" privileges that wealthy individual contributors enjoyed in the past.

INDIRECT TECHNIQUES

Interest groups also try to influence public policy indirectly through third parties or the general public. Such indirect techniques may appear to be spontaneous, but they are generally as well planned as the direct lobbying techniques just discussed. Indirect techniques can be particularly effective because public officials are often more impressed by contacts from voters than from lobbyists.

Shaping Public Opinion

Public opinion weighs significantly in the policymaking process, so interest groups cultivate their public images carefully. If public opinion favors a certain group's interests, then public officials will be more obligated to listen and more willing to pass legislation favoring that group. To cultivate public opinion, an interest group's efforts may include television publicity, newspaper and magazine advertisements, mass mailings, and the use of public-relations techniques to improve the group's public image.

For example, environmental groups run television ads to dramatize threats to the environment. Oil companies respond to criticism about increased gasoline prices with advertising showing their concern for the public welfare. The goal of all these activities is to convince both the public and the policymakers that the public overwhelmingly supports the interest group's position. Through such activities, interest groups attempt to bring grassroots pressure to bear on officials.

Some interest groups also try to indirectly influence legislators through **rating systems.** A group selects legislative issues that it feels are important to its goals and rates legislators according to the percentage of times they vote favorably on that legislation. For example, a score of 90 percent on the Americans for Democratic Action (ADA) rating scale means that the legislator supported that group's position to a high degree (see Table 7–5 on the next page). Other groups tag members of Congress who support (or fail to support) their interests to a significant extent with telling labels. For instance, the Communications Workers of America refer to policymakers who take a position consistent with their own views as "Heroes" and those who take the opposite position as "Zeroes." Needless to say, such tactics can be an effective form of indirect lobbying, particularly with legislators who do not want to earn a low ADA score or be placed on the "Zeroes" list.

One of the most effective indirect lobbying techniques used by interest groups is to enlist public support for their products or causes through advertising. Shown here is a magazine ad promoting a campaign for milk products sponsored by American dairy farmers. Ron Howard (and other celebrities) make such ads especially popular and appealing.

Mobilizing Constituents

Interest groups sometimes urge members and other constituents to contact government officials—by letter, e-mail, or telephone—to show their support for or opposition to a certain policy. Large interest groups can generate hundreds of thousands of letters, e-mail messages, and calls. Interest groups often provide form letters or postcards for constituents to fill out and mail. The NRA has successfully used this tactic to fight strict federal gun-control legislation by delivering half a million letters to Congress within a few weeks. Policymakers recognize that the letters were initiated by an interest group, but they are still made aware of an issue that is important to that group.

Fighting It Out in the Courts

Achieving policy goals through the legal system offers another avenue for influencing the political process. Civil rights groups paved the way for

Table 7-5

ADA Ratings for 1998

Americans for Democratic Action (ADA), a liberal political organization, tracks the votes of all senators and representatives on the issues that the ADA thinks are most important. The "score" for each senator listed below is the percentage of "correct" votes from the ADA's point of view. Not surprisingly, the senators with the highest ratings are all Democrats, and those with the lowest ratings are all Republicans.

SENATOR	HIGHEST RATING
Bumpers, D. (D., Ark.)	100%
Wellstone, P. (D., Minn.)	100
Wyden, R. (D., Ore.)	100
Boxer B. (D., Calif.)	95
Durbin, R. (D., Ill.)	95
Harkin, T. (D., Iowa)	95

SENATOR	LOWEST RATING
Brownback, S. (R., Kans.)	0%
Burns, C. (R., Mont.)	0
Cochran, T. (R., Miss.)	0
Coverdale, P. (R., Ga.)	0
Grams, R. (R., Minn.)	0
Kyl, J. (R., Ariz.)	0
Lugar, R. (R., Ind.)	0
Mack, C. (R., Fla.)	0
McConnell, M. (R., Ky.)	0
Nickles, D. (R., Okla.)	0
Roberts, P. (R., Kans.)	0
Sessions, J. (R., Ala.)	0

SOURCE: Americans for Democratic Action, 1999.

interest group litigation in the 1950s and 1960s with major victories in cases concerning equal housing, school desegregation, and employment discrimination. Environmental groups, such as the Sierra Club, have also successfully used litigation to protect their interests. For example, an environmental group might challenge in court an activity that threatens to pollute the environment or that will destroy the natural habitat of an endangered species. The legal challenge forces those engaging in the activity to bear the costs of defending themselves and possibly delays their project. In fact, much of the success of environmental groups has been linked to their use of lawsuits.

Demonstration Techniques

Some interest groups stage protests to make a statement in a dramatic way. The Boston Tea Party of 1773, in which American colonists dressed as Native Americans and threw tea into Boston Harbor to protest British taxes, is testimony to how long this tactic has been around. Over the years, many groups have organized protest marches and rallies to support or oppose such issues as legalized abortion, busing, gay and lesbian rights, government assistance to farmers, the treatment of Native Americans, and the increasing restrictions on the use of federally owned lands in the West.

Today's Lobbying Establishment

Without a doubt, interest groups and their lobbyists have become a permanent feature in the landscape of American government. The major interest groups all have headquarters in Washington, D.C., close to the center of government. Professional lobbyists and staff members of various interest groups move freely between their groups' headquarters and congressional offices and committee rooms. Interest group representatives are routinely consulted when Congress drafts new legislation. As already mentioned, interest group representatives are frequently asked to testify before congressional committees or subcommittees on the effect or potential effect of particular legislation or regulations. In a word, interest groups have become an integral part of the American government system.

As interest groups have become a permanent feature of American government, lobbying has developed into a profession. A professional lobbyist—one who has mastered the techniques of lobbying discussed earlier in this chapter—is a valuable ally to any interest group seeking to influence government. Professional lobbyists can and often do move from one interest group to another.

INFOTRAC®
Letters we get letters

A lobbyist talks with a member of Congress outside the congressperson's office.

THE "REVOLVING DOOR" BETWEEN INTEREST GROUPS AND GOVERNMENT

The door between private interests and government is often characterized as a "revolving door" because of the back-and-forth movement between government personnel and private-interest groups. Increasingly, those who leave positions with the federal government become lobbyists or consultants for the private-interest groups they helped to regulate. Former government officials, particularly those who held key positions in Congress or the executive branch, have little difficulty finding work as lobbyists. For one thing, they often have inside information that can help an interest group's efforts. More important, they normally have an established network of personal contacts, which is a great political asset.

In spite of legislation and regulations that have been passed in an attempt to reduce the "revolving door" syndrome, it is still functioning quite well. When Representative Sam Gibbons (D., Fla.) retired, he went to work as a lobbyist on the same tax and trade issues he had handled as a member of the House Ways and Means Committee. Representative Bill Brewster (D., Okla.) stated that when he retired, he planned to work on the same health-care and energy issues he worked on in Congress. Even though current law requires former lawmakers and aides to wait a year before directly lobbying their former colleagues, the restrictions have had little discernible effect. On average, about one in four former lawmakers becomes a lobbyist.

WHY DO INTEREST GROUPS GET BAD PRESS?

Despite their importance to democratic government, interest groups, like political parties, are sometimes criticized by both the public and the press. Our image of interest groups and their special interests is not very favorable. You may have run across political cartoons depicting lobbyists prowling the hallways of Congress, briefcases stuffed with money, waiting to lure representatives into a waiting limousine.

These cartoons are not entirely factual, but they are not entirely fictitious either. President Richard Nixon was revealed to have yielded to the campaign contributions of milk producers by later authorizing a windfall increase in milk subsidies. In 1977, "Koreagate," a scandal in which a South Korean businessman was accused of offering lavish "gifts" to several members of Congress, added to the view that politicians were too easily susceptible to the snares of special interests. In the early 1990s, it was revealed that a number of senators who received generous contributions

"A very special interest to see you, Senator."

from one particular savings and loan association turned around and supported a "hands off" policy by savings and loan regulators. The savings and loan association in question later got into financial trouble, costing the taxpayers billions of dollars to bail it out.

In the wake of numerous scandals over the years, Congress passed a set of rules in both the House and the Senate in 1996 that banned members of Congress from accepting free trips, meals, and gifts from interest group lobbyists. Although congresspersons and lobbyists have found ways to get around these rules, a few bad apples do not spoil the whole interest group barrel. For every dishonest action, hundreds of honest transactions take place between interest group leaders and public officials. For every lobbyist who attempts to bribe a public official, there are hundreds who try only to provide public officials with solid facts that support the goals of their groups.

★ The Regulation of Interest Groups

In an attempt to control lobbying, Congress passed the Federal Regulation of Lobbying Act in 1946. This act is the only major law regulating interest groups, and it applies only to groups that lobby Congress. The major provisions of the act are as follows:

- Any person or organization that receives money to be used principally to influence legislation before Congress must register with the clerk of the House and the secretary of the Senate.
- Any group or persons registering must identify their employer, salary, amount and purpose of expenses, and duration of employment.
- Every registered lobbyist must give quarterly reports on his or her activities, which are to be published in the *Congressional Quarterly*.
- Anyone failing to satisfy the specific provisions of this act can be fined up to $10,000 and be imprisoned for up to five years.

The act is very limited and has not regulated lobbying to any great degree for several reasons. First, the Supreme Court has restricted the application of the law to only those lobbyists who seek to influence federal legislation *directly*.[18] Any lobbyist seeking to influence legislation indirectly through public opinion does not fall within the scope of the law. Second, the act requires that only persons or organizations whose principal purpose is to influence legislation need register. Any interest groups or individuals claiming that their principal function is something else need not register. Many groups can avoid registration in this way. Third, the act does not cover lobbying directed at agencies in the executive branch or lobbyists who testify before congressional committees. Fourth, the public is almost totally unaware of the information in the quarterly reports, and Congress has created no agency to oversee interest group activities.

The problem, of course, is that any stricter regulation of lobbying may run into constitutional problems because of the potential abridgment of First Amendment rights. As long as the Supreme Court views indirect lobbying as falling outside the scope of the law, lobbying will be difficult to control.

Americans at Odds over Interest Groups

Because we live in a democracy, we will always have interest groups. Very likely, too, Americans will always be at odds over the extent to which interest groups influence government policymaking and the ways in which this influence is wielded.

The "Mischiefs of Factions"

Interest groups were a cause of concern even before the Constitution was ratified. Recall from Chapter 2 that those opposed to the Constitution (the Anti-Federalists) claimed that a republican form of government could not work in a country this size because there would be too many factions—interest groups—contending for power. The eventual result would be anarchy and chaos.

James Madison attempted to allay these fears in *Federalist Paper* No. 10 (see Appendix F) by arguing that the "mischiefs of factions" could be controlled. Madison pointed out that factions would be inevitable if we wanted a democratic form of government. After all, different groups in society have different interests, and all citizens have the right to express their views and petition the government for redress. Yet precisely because of the large size of the United States, there would be so many diverse interests and factions that no one faction would be able to gain control of the government. Small factions could simply be outvoted, thus eliminating the possibility that they could impose the will of a minority on the majority. Large factions would be neutralized by other large factions, which would emerge in a large republic. What Madison did not foresee is that small, intensely focused interest groups can indeed affect policymaking in the United States. As you have seen in this chapter, so-called pork-barrel legislation—legislation benefiting only a small group of persons—is not all that unusual in American government.

One of the reasons why Americans are at odds over interest groups is that our democracy really cannot survive without them, yet, at the same time, many feel that they threaten democracy and the principle of representative government. In fact, the significant role played by interest groups in shaping national policy has caused many Americans to question whether we really have a democracy at all. (See, for example, the feature entitled *Perception versus Reality: Interest Groups and Representative*

Democracy.) The most powerful groups—those with the most resources and political influence—are primarily business, trade, or professional groups. In contrast, public-interest groups and civil rights groups make up only a small percentage of the interest groups lobbying the government.

The results of lobbying efforts, however, do not always favor the interests of the most powerful groups. Although the National Chamber of Commerce may be accepted as having a justified interest in the question of business taxes, many legislators might feel that the group should not engage in the debate over the size of the federal budget deficit. In other words, groups are seen as having a legitimate concern in the issues closest to their interests but not necessarily in broader issues. This may explain why some of the most successful interest groups are those that focus on very specific issues—such as tobacco farming, funding of abortions, or handgun control—and do not get involved in larger conflicts.

---

perception versus reality

Interest Groups and Representative Democracy

As you have read, even before the Constitution was ratified, many Americans were concerned about the potential threat to democracy posed by interest groups. Madison's argument that there would be so many interest groups that no one group could become dominant seems to have been validated by history. Today, interest groups continue to vie for influence and political favors at all levels of American government. Do these groups really reflect the interests of a broad spectrum of Americans, however?

The Perception

Remember that the pluralist theory of American politics views politics as a struggle among various interest groups to gain benefits for their members. The pluralist approach views compromise among various competing interests as the essence of political decision making. Underlying the pluralist view is the perception that we do have a democracy, even though it may be a democracy in which the interests of groups, rather than individuals, are represented. Ultimately, though, the thousands of interest groups lobbying government at all levels do represent the interests of the broad American citizenry. A large number of Americans share this view.

The Reality

In reality, interest groups are not necessarily representative of the broad array of American interests. Most interest groups have a middle-class or upper-class bias. Members of interest groups can afford to pay the membership fees, are generally fairly well educated, and normally participate in the political process to a greater extent than the "average" American can. Also, leaders of interest groups tend to constitute an "elite within an elite." The leaders usually are from a higher social class than their members, and their views do not necessarily reflect those of the members.

Consider just one interest group—the National Education Association (NEA). Combined fed-

eral, state, and local dues for NEA members range from $300 to $700 per year. These dues pay for, among other things, the salaries of the NEA staff. More than two thousand officials of the group and its state affiliates make an annual salary of over $100,000, which is three times the salary of the average NEA member. During the 1996 campaigns, the NEA gave 99 percent of its campaign funds to Democratic candidates, yet a survey by the National Center for Education Information disclosed that only 42 percent of public school teachers identify themselves as Democrats.

You Be the Judge

What factors, other than those discussed in this feature, might help to explain the elitist bias in interest groups?

Issue Advocacy

One of the hottest political issues with respect to interest groups is the way in which they are able to skirt campaign funding laws. As you will read in Chapter 10, interest groups can get around such laws in several ways. One way is by making contributions to a political party for "independent expenditures"—that is, expenditures that are not targeted for specific political candidates. An interest group may make it clear, however, that these independent expenditures should support candidates who have been outspoken about a particular issue.

Issue-advocacy money can have a clear effect on the outcome of elections. Both parties have been helped by such interest group spending. Republicans receive help from organizations that favor making abortions illegal (such as the Christian Coalition) and from organizations that favor term legislative limits (such as Americans for Tax Reform). The AFL-CIO spent millions of dollars on issue advertising that benefited Democratic candidates.

Money for issue advocacy can come directly from corporate or union treasuries. There are no limits or reporting requirements. Such freedom, according to the Supreme Court, is mandated by the First Amendment guarantee of free speech. The Federal Election Commission (FEC) has tried to stop issue advocacy when it became too blatant, but the FEC has lost in court on numerous occasions. Indeed, according to election lawyer Jan Baran, "The FEC has spent twenty years trying to stamp this out. They're like a dog that refuses to be house-trained and gets beaten over the nose with a rolled-up newspaper by the courts."[19] Currently, several such cases are still pending in the courts.

key terms

interest group 161
labor force 166
lobbying 171
lobbyist 171
political action
   committee (PAC) 174

pluralist theory 162
public-interest group 165
rating system 175
trade organization 165

chapter summary

1. An interest group is an organization of people sharing common objectives who actively attempt to influence government policymakers through direct and indirect methods. Interest groups pursue their goals at every level and in every branch of government. Interest groups differ from political parties in that interest groups pursue more specialized interests and are more tightly organized than parties. Also, interest groups do not compete for public office, as parties do.

2. Interest groups serve several purposes in American politics, including the following: (1) they help bridge the gap between citizens and government; (2) they help raise public awareness and inspire action on various issues; (3) they often provide pub-

lic officials with specialized and detailed information, which helps officials to make informed public-policy choices; and (4) they help to ensure that public officials are carrying out their duties responsibly. Pluralist theory explains American politics as a contest among various interest groups that compete at all levels of government to gain benefits for their members.

3. The most common interest groups are private groups that seek government policies that will benefit (or at least, not harm) their members' interests. Many major interest groups are concerned about issues relating to the following areas or groups of persons: business, labor, agriculture, consumers, senior citizens, the environment, and professionals.

4. Direct techniques used by interest groups include lobbying efforts and providing election support, particularly through the use of political action committees (PACs). Indirect techniques include advertising and other promotional efforts to cultivate public opinion, thus bringing public pressure to bear on government officials; mobilizing constituents to work for a particular cause by contacting their representatives in Congress; bringing lawsuits to obtain legal protection for their interests; and organizing demonstrations and protests to make the public aware of their goals.

5. Interest group representatives play an important role in government policymaking by serving as information sources for members of Congress and congressional committees. Government policymakers, in turn, often serve as political consultants or lobbyists for interest groups on leaving government office. Legislation and regulations have attempted to curb this interplay between interest group representatives and government officials, which has been characterized as the "revolving door" syndrome, but the door continues to revolve.

6. Interest groups have often received bad press because of several scandals involving political favors given to special interest groups by government officials who benefited from those groups' campaign contributions. The image of political corruption fostered by these incidents, though, disguises the fact that for every lobbyist who attempts to bribe a public official, there are hundreds who try only to provide public officials with solid facts that support the goals of their groups.

7. The Federal Regulation of Lobbying Act of 1946 attempted to regulate the activities of lobbyists, but it has not regulated lobbying to any great degree for the following reasons: (1) it applies only to lobbyists who seek to influence federal legislation *directly;* (2) it imposes registration requirements only on persons or organizations whose principal purpose is to influence legislation; (3) it does not cover lobbying directed at agencies in the executive branch or lobbyists who testify before congressional committees; and (4) the public is in large part unaware of the information contained in the quarterly reports that lobbyists regulated by the act must submit and that are published in *Congressional Quarterly.*

8. Americans will probably always be at odds over the extent to which interest groups influence policymaking. Concerns over the potential harm that can be caused by interest groups, or factions, date back to the beginning of the nation. The contest among interest groups to influence Congress through ever-increasing campaign contributions has generated widespread concern over the need for campaign reform. Interest group contributions for "issue advocacy" present a particularly thorny challenge because free speech issues are necessarily involved.

for critical analysis

1. Does an individual have any real voice in the American political system, or must one become a member of an interest group to influence political decision making?

2. Has the proliferation of interest groups in recent years led to a situation in which there is now so much "noise" in our political system that the influence of interest groups is likely to be diminished?

3. What other factors, besides interest groups and their campaign dollars, influence legislators' views and decisions?

4. Why has Mothers Against Drunk Driving (MADD) been such a successful interest group?

5. Is there anything wrong with foreigners forming interest groups and using their clout to influence American politics?

6. If all lobbying were banned, how would Americans influence government?

7. Should issue-advocacy groups be banned? Why or why not?

suggested readings

BIERSACK, Robert. Ed. *After the Revolution: PACs, Lobbies, and the Republican Congress.* New York: Allyn & Bacon, 1999. This collection of essays examines the way in which special interests have worked since the Republicans took control of Congress in 1995. Included are analyses of business groups (such as AT&T), labor groups (such as the AFL–CIO), and environmental groups (such as the Sierra Club).

DEKIEFFER, Donald E. *The Citizen's Guide to Lobbying Congress.* Chicago: Chicago Review Press, 1997. This book is an excellent reference for political activists who seek to make changes in government policy. According to the author, a group must first understand how political alliances are built and then learn how to organize and get the most from letter-writing campaigns. He also discusses the importance of government resources, seminars, and Web sites for interest groups seeking to affect government policy.

HEINZ, John P., *et al. The Hollow Core: Private Interests in National Policy Making.* Cambridge, Mass.: Harvard University Press, 1997. The authors test the proposition that private-interest groups exert too much influence on the decisions of government. Their results, which are based on interviews with more than three hundred interest groups, eight hundred lobbyists, and three hundred government officials, show how interest groups influence federal policy in four areas—agriculture, energy, health, and labor policy.

LEWIS, Charles. *The Buying of the Congress: How Special Interests Have Stolen Your Right to Life, Liberty, and the Pursuit of Happiness.* New York: Avon, 1998. The author, the executive director of the Center for Public Integrity, examines how powerful, monied groups influence members of Congress. According to the author, there is a direct link between monied interests and bad legislation—which works to the detriment of most Americans.

McCHESNEY, Fred S. *Money for Nothing: Politicians, Rent Extraction and Political Extortion.* Cambridge, Mass.: Harvard University Press, 1997. McChesney argues that interest groups pay (make campaign contributions) not so much to obtain political favors as to avoid political disfavor. He contends that interest groups make contributions to prevent lawmakers from enacting laws that would adversely affect the groups' interests. Thus, according to McChesney, such contributions are a form of "rent extraction," or "political extortion."

politics on the web

The Public Interest Research Group offers a host of lobbying and public-interest activities. Its home page can be accessed at

http://www.igc.apc.org/pirg

You can access the home page of the NRA at

http://www.nra.org

The home page for the AARP can be found at

http://www.aarp.org

If you are interested in the NEA, its home page can be found at

http://www.nea.org

Generally, you can find lists of interest groups operating at the local, state, and federal levels by simply going to a search engine, such as Yahoo, and keying in

interest groups

using web resources

X-PAC is a nonpartisan political action committee (PAC) dedicated to representing the economic and political needs of Generation X. This PAC is interested in a wide variety of political issues but currently focuses on Social Security reform.

Go to X-PAC's Web site at

http://www.x-pac.org

1. Select "Leadership" to determine who the "movers and shakers" of X-PAC are. Whom do they represent? What are their political affiliations?

2. Return to the main page and review the various links and information. Do you believe that X-PAC will have much influence on the Social Security debate in Congress? Why or why not?

3. In your opinion, what could be done to make X-PAC more successful?

notes

1. See, for example, the National Opinion Research Center's survey released May 6, 1999.

2. In recent years, constitutional scholars have been reexamining the theory that only state militias have the right to bear arms, concluding that the founders may have intended individuals to have this right. See, for example, William Glaberson, "The Right to Bear Arms: A Second Look," *The New York Times,* May 30, 1999, p. 3.

3. *Printz v. United States,* 521 U.S. 898 (1997).

4. Taken from the NRA Web site: **http://www.nra.org**.

5. For an interesting discussion of the evolution of the right to bear arms in England, see Joyce Lee Malcolm, *To Keep and Bear Arms: The Origins of an Anglo-American Right* (Cambridge, Mass.: Harvard University Press, 1996).

6. John R. Lott, Jr., "Crime, Deterrence, and Right-to-Carry Concealed Handguns," *The Journal of Legal Studies,* Vol. 26, No. 1 (January 1997). For a discussion of Lott's more recent research on this issue, see Jacob Sullum, "Gun Shy," *Reason,* April 1998, p. 20.

7. *Democracy in America,* Vol. 1, ed. by Phillip Bradley (New York: Knopf, 1980), p. 191.

8. Pronounced ah-*mee*-kus *kure*-ee-eye.

9. David Truman, *The Governmental Process* (New York: Knopf, 1951); and Robert Dahl, *Who Governs?* (New Haven, Conn.: Yale University Press, 1961).

10. Fred McChesney, *Money for Nothing: Politicians, Rent Extraction and Political Extortion* (Cambridge, Mass.: Harvard University Press, 1997).

11. 487 U.S. 735 (1988).

12. "Exempt from Reform," *The Wall Street Journal,* February 10, 1997, p. A18.

13. *Ibid.*

14. The Agricultural Adjustment Act of 1933 (declared unconstitutional) was replaced by the 1937 Agricultural Adjustment Act, which later was changed and amended several times.

15. "A Tale of Two Lobbies," *The Economist,* October 19, 1996, p. 20.

16. "Overboard on Gun Control," *The Wall Street Journal Europe,* October 23, 1996, p. 6.

17. Norman Ornstein et al., *Vital Statistics on Congress, 1995–1996* (Washington, D.C.: Congressional Quarterly Press, 1996), p. 95.

18. *United States v. Harriss,* 347 U.S. 612 (1954).

19. As quoted in Ruth Marcus, "Taking Issue with Advocacy: A Loophole in the Election Law Allows Interest Groups to Spend Unlimited Amounts," *The Washington Post,* National Weekly Edition, April 15–21, 1996, p. 13.

POLITICAL PARTIES

Contents

The Rise of the Independent Voter: Is the Party Over?

America's political system is a two-party system. After all, the Democrats and the Republicans are basically the only games in town for candidates who want to be elected. In the voters' minds, however, party identification has been slipping. Since 1960, the number of voters willing to identify themselves as Republicans or Democrats has dropped. At the same time, a growing number of voters regard themselves simply as independents—people who are not committed to any political party. In the 1940s, independents accounted for only 20 percent of voters. In 1999, however, 38 percent of Americans identified themselves as independent or having no party affiliation—more than identified themselves as Democrats (34 percent) or Republicans (28 percent).[1]

Go to CD-ROM

Party Regulars Decry the Rise of the Independent Voter

Certainly, the members of the "old guard" in the two major political parties are not in favor of the rise of the independent voter. This is not surprising, for independents weaken the effectiveness of the two major political parties. Today, voters seem to be less willing than they were in the past to vote a *straight ticket*—that is, to vote for all of the candidates of one party. *Split-ticket* voting, such as voting for a Democratic presidential candidate and for a Republican congressional candidate, has shown a big increase.

Democratic and Republican Party regulars are dismayed by the rise of the independent voter for another reason: independent voters pay less attention to party agendas. Therefore, candidates are less dependent on party organizations.

Finally, those in favor of maintaining the strength of the two major parties argue that only a strong party in office has a chance of effecting serious policy changes. In other words, a party in power needs a mandate so that it can deal from strength when it has to make new policies to respond to changing social, economic, and political conditions in the United States and abroad. If parties continue to lose the loyalty of their voters, the end result will be disastrous—those who serve in government will be less and less committed to effecting important policy changes.

More Independents Reflect a Changing America

Those in favor of the on-going increase in independents and the subsequent decline in Republican and Democratic voter identification are certain of one thing: today's parties are parties of the past; they have not kept up with the changing times. People who see the increase in independent voters in a positive light contend that being a member of the Democratic or Republican Party means virtually nothing today anyway. Party leaders, time and again, have adopted planks from the opposing party's platform to gain popular support. No clear-cut distinctions between the two parties exist, so why should American voters associate with one or the other?

Furthermore, claim the critics of the major parties, both parties seem to be dominated by special interest groups. These groups do not necessarily represent the wishes of the party identifiers—or even the views of the interest groups' rank-and-file membership.

In any event, media consultants and public-relations specialists have taken over many of the functions parties traditionally performed for political candidates. Candidates no longer depend on their parties because they make their own arrangements for television spots, undertake direct-mail advertising, and hire professional campaign managers. If candidates do not really need the political party apparatus, why do voters?

This is particularly true, say these critics of the two-party system, in today's cyber world. Developments in communications technology have led to a situation in which political candidates can communicate directly with the voters and vice versa. The mediating function of the party is no longer necessary, at least to the extent it has been in the past.

Today, it is hard to imagine a person working her or his way up the traditional party bureaucracy, being rewarded by a political candidacy, and then winning an election. Obtaining office in that manner just does not happen anymore.

Where Do You Stand?

1. If you belong to a political party, what is your reason for doing so?

2. If independents are becoming so important, why couldn't you start an independent party?

On the Web

You can find information on independent voters at the following Web site: http://www.cuip.org/index.htm.

Introduction

POLITICAL PARTY ● A group of individuals outside the government who organize to win elections, operate the government, and determine policy.

TWO-PARTY SYSTEM ● A political system in which two strong and established parties compete for political offices.

CONSENSUS ● A general agreement among the citizenry (often defined as an agreement among 75 percent or more of the people) on matters of public policy.

I N F O T R A C ®

A warming trend for third parties

The rise of the independent voter and the waning influence of the two major parties have led many to speculate that the party is indeed over. Nonetheless, the two major political parties have a long history in this country, and traditionalists are not convinced that the Republican and Democratic parties will be replaced in the future by an alternate party system.

A **political party** can be defined as a group of individuals *outside the government* who organize to win elections, operate the government, and determine policy. Political parties were an unforeseen development in American political history. The founders defined many other important institutions, such as the presidency and Congress, and described their functions in the Constitution. Political parties, however, are not even mentioned in the Constitution. In fact, the founders decried factions and parties. Thomas Jefferson probably best expressed the founders' antiparty sentiments when he declared, "If I could not go to heaven but with a party, I would not go there at all."[2]

If the founders did not want political parties, who was supposed to organize political campaigns and mobilize supporters of political candidates? Clearly, there was a practical need for some kind of organizing group to form a link between citizens and their government. Even our early national leaders, for all their antiparty feelings, realized this: several of them were active in establishing or organizing the first political parties.

Political parties continue to serve as major vehicles for citizen participation in our political system. It is hard to imagine democracy without political parties. Political parties provide a way for the public to choose who will serve in government and which policies will be carried out.

America's Two-Party System

In the United States, we have a **two-party system.** This means that two major parties—the Democrats and the Republicans—dominate national politics. (For alternative party systems, see this chapter's *Comparative Politics* on the next page.)

REASONS FOR THE AMERICAN TWO-PARTY SYSTEM

Why has the two-party system become so firmly entrenched in the United States? According to some scholars, the first major political division in this country—between the Federalists and the Anti-Federalists—established a precedent that ultimately resulted in the domination of the two-party system. A number of factors help to explain this phenomenon. For example, today's established institutions, particularly the news media, do not encourage third parties. Typically, the media do not spend much time covering third party activities, but tend to focus almost exclusively on the Democrats and Republicans. The consensus among Americans on important principles of government and our elective process also contribute to the two-party system.

National Consensus and Moderate Views

A **consensus** is a general agreement among citizens, sometimes defined as an agreement among 75 percent or more of the people, on matters of public policy. In the United States, most citizens generally agree on certain broad social and economic issues. For example, most of us believe in the basic principles of government as outlined in the U.S. Constitution. We believe that people have a right to own private property and the right to freedom of religion. We also believe that people should be free to choose where they live and work. Our differences usually lie more in *how* to attain the goals, rather than in the goals themselves.

comparative politics

Alternative Party Systems

Unlike the United States, which has a two-party system, many of the world's nations have one-party or multiparty political systems. In a *one-party system,* a single party monopolizes the organization of governmental power and the positions of authority. The single party's functions are controlled by party leaders, and even if elections are held, party members, once on the ballot, have no competition. In most dictatorships, such as Iraq and the People's Republic of China, only one party is officially allowed to exist. Until the early 1990s, this was also true of many countries in Eastern and Central Europe, including the former Soviet Union.

Another alternative is a *multiparty system,* in which more than two political parties compete for power and electoral offices. This type of system exists in most European democracies, including France and Germany. In a multiparty system, parties are usually organized around different beliefs or interests, such as religion, occupation, or political ideology. For example, Italy has nine national parties and several regional parties, including the Christian Democrats, the Socialists, the Radicals, the Liberals, and the Proletarian Unity Party. Israel has more than twenty parties. In one recent election, the Czech Republic had twenty-two political parties including the Communist Party, the Socialist Party, the "Public Against Violence" Party, and a party called the "Alliance of Farmers and the Countryside." In multiparty systems, much of the work of party leaders involves building coalitions with other parties to vote for (or not vote for) certain proposals in the legislature.

For Critical Analysis

What are some of the advantages of having a multiparty system? Are there any disadvantages?

Because of this general political consensus, the United States does not have the conditions that would lead to numerous, strong parties vying for power. Certainly, during our history Americans have disagreed over many issues. We were deeply divided during such times as the Civil War in the 1860s and the Great Depression in the 1930s. We were also divided during the 1960s and 1970s over such issues as civil rights and the war in Vietnam. Nevertheless, unlike many other countries, we have not seen prolonged and intense conflicts based on religious beliefs, ethnic identity, language, class, or social status. Perhaps for this reason, there are no significant, permanent groups in this country that support radical government policies.

Political consensus and moderation in the United States have had another effect on our parties. They have given us two parties that look very much alike. Despite the perceived differences in their positions on political issues, both tend to be moderate, middle-of-the-road parties built on compromise. (See the feature *Perception versus Reality: What Do the Two Parties Really Stand For?*) The parties' similarities have often led to criticism; their sternest critics think of them as "tweedledee" and "tweedledum."[3]

Our Elective Process

Our elective process also supports the two-party system. In most elections, only one candidate can win the election to each office under what is called the **single-member district system.** The candidate who gets the *most* votes obtains a **plurality** and wins the election, even if he or she receives less than 50 percent of the total votes cast.

SINGLE-MEMBER DISTRICT SYSTEM ● A method of election in which only one candidate can win election to each office.

PLURALITY ● A situation in which a candidate wins an election by receiving more votes than the others but does not necessarily win a majority (over 50 percent of the votes). Most federal, state, and local laws allow for elections to be won by a plurality vote.

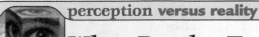

What Do the Two Parties Really Stand For?

The United States has two major political parties, the Republicans and the Democrats. Everybody knows that, and just about everybody thinks that he or she has a pretty good idea of the differences between the two parties.

The Perception

The Democratic Party is known for the following traits:

- It is the party of the little people.
- It is the party of the working class.
- It is in favor of social legislation to help the underclass.
- It protects individual liberties and rights, including privacy rights.
- It is for big government, deficits, and a lot of spending.

In contrast, the Republican Party is known for the following traits:

- It supports family values.
- It is against abortion.
- It is in favor of a strong military.
- It is against much social legislation and welfare and stresses self-reliance.
- It is in favor of big business.
- It is against unions.
- It is fiscally conservative.

The Reality

Although these perceptions of the differences between the Republicans and the Democrats might be true generally, party identifiers are often surprised at the contrasts between these perceptions and what party members do in Washington, D.C.

Consider a full-page political ad that recently appeared in *USA Today*. The ad, which was titled "An Open Letter to the American People," stated that it was time to "move on" to an agenda that includes "saving Social Security," improving education, and easing the tax burden for "working people." It would be easy for those reading this ad to assume that it was created by liberals in Congress. In fact, the signatures at the bottom of the ad were those of Republicans Dennis Hastert (speaker of the House of Representatives) and Trent Lott (Senate majority leader).[4]

Consider also that in 1996 a Democratic president signed a major reform bill that fundamentally changed welfare as we knew it. The bill did what everyone would expect Republicans—not Democrats—to do. Consider also that the Democrats are known to side with labor unions, yet a Democratic president, Bill Clinton, approved the North American Free Trade Agreement—despite the bitter public denunciations from most of the nation's unions.

Now let's talk about fiscal conservatives. The Republicans have always claimed that fiscal conservatism is their domain, yet the reality is somewhat different. The stingiest president in modern history is none other than Democrat Bill Clinton. That is to say, the rate of growth of various federal government spending programs will have increased less under Bill Clinton than under any other modern president, including several so-called fiscally conservative Republicans. Indeed, some of the most fiscally profligate administrations (ignoring the defense budget completely) have been those of Republican presidents, including George Bush and Richard Nixon.

Perhaps the moral of the story is that party labels do not necessarily tell you what candidates are going to do when they take office. It may also be that, as one veteran of American politics has stated, solutions to political issues are found not on the sides of the political spectrum but in the "sensible center."[5]

You Be the Judge

In spite of the inconsistencies between the perceived party positions and the political actions of party members, do you think that there is a significant difference between Democrats and Republicans? If so, what is it?

The single-member district system makes it very difficult for a third party candidate to win. Most Americans realize this and therefore usually vote for either a Democrat or a Republican, which discourages third party candidates from running. Our elective system makes it difficult for third party candidates to win elections, and without election victories, parties tend to fade fast. Third parties do not have the numbers, recognition, or financial resources to endure or to win most elections.

American election law also discourages third party candidates. In most states, the established major parties need only a relatively few signatures to place their candidates on the ballot, while a third party must get many more signatures. The criterion is often based on the total party vote in the last election, which penalizes a new party that did not enter that election.

ELECTORATE ● All of the citizens eligible to vote in a given election.

PARTY PLATFORM ● The document drawn up by each party at its national convention that outlines the policies and positions of the party.

PARTY IDENTIFIER ● A person who identifies himself or herself as being a member of a particular political party.

PARTY ELITE ● A loose-knit group of party activists who organize and oversee party functions and planning during and between campaigns.

COMPONENTS OF THE TWO MAJOR AMERICAN PARTIES

The two major American political parties are sometimes described as three-dimensional entities. This is because each party consists of three components: (1) the party in the electorate, (2) the party organization, and (3) the party in government.

The Party in the Electorate

The party in the **electorate** is the largest component, consisting of all of those people who describe themselves as Democrats or Republicans. There are no dues, no membership cards, and no obligatory duties. Members of the party in the electorate never need to work on a campaign or attend a party meeting. They may register as Democrats or Republicans, but registration is not legally binding and can be changed at will.

The Party Organization

Each major party has a national organization with national, state, and local offices. As will be discussed later in this chapter, the party organizations are made up of several levels of people who maintain the party's strength between elections, make its rules, raise money, organize conventions, help with elections, and recruit candidates.

The Party in Government

The party in government consists of all of the candidates who have won elections and now hold public office. Even though members of Congress, state legislators, presidents, and all other officeholders almost always run for office as either Democrats or Republicans, the individual candidates do not always agree on government policy. The party in government helps to organize the government's agenda by coaxing and convincing its own party members to vote for its policies. If the party is to translate its promises into public policies, the job must be done by the party in government.

Party Affiliation

What does it mean to belong to a political party? In many European countries, being a party member means that you actually join a political party. You get a membership card to carry around in your wallet, you pay dues, and you vote to select your local and national party leaders. In the United States, becoming a member of a political party is far less involved. To be a member of a political party, an American citizen has only to think of herself or himself as a Democrat or a Republican (or a member of a third party, such as the Libertarian Party or the American Independent Party). Members of parties do not have to pay dues, work for the party, or attend party meetings. Nor must they support the **party platform**, which is the party's declaration of beliefs and positions on major issues.[6]

Generally, the party in the electorate consists of **party identifiers** (those who identify themselves as being a member of one of the parties) and the **party elite**, active party members who choose to work for the party and even become candidates for office. Political parties need year-round support from the latter group to survive. During election campaigns in particular, candidates depend on active party members or volunteers to mail literature, answer phones, conduct door-to-door canvasses, organize speeches and appearances, and, of course, donate money. Between elections, parties also need active members to plan the upcoming elections, organize fund raisers, and keep in touch with party leaders in other communities to keep the

SOLIDARITY ● Mutual agreement with others in a particular group.

PATRONAGE ● A system of rewarding the party faithful and workers with government jobs or contracts.

party strong. Generally, the major functions of American political parties are carried out by the party elite, who have been described as a small, relatively loose-knit group of party activists.[7]

WHY PEOPLE JOIN POLITICAL PARTIES

Generally, in the United States people belong to a political party because they agree with many of its main ideas and support some of its candidates. In a few countries, such as the People's Republic of China, people belong to a political party because they are required to do so, regardless of whether they agree with the party's ideas and candidates.

People join political parties for a multitude of reasons. One reason is that people wish to express their **solidarity,** or mutual agreement, with the views of friends, loved ones, and other like-minded people. People also join parties because they enjoy the excitement of politics. In addition, many believe they will benefit materially from joining a party, through better employment or personal career advancement. The traditional institution of **patronage**—rewarding the party faithful with government jobs or contracts—lives on, even though it has been limited to prevent abuses.[8] Finally, some join political parties because they wish to actively promote a set of ideas and principles that they feel are important to American politics and society.

Generally, people join political parties because of their overall agreement with what the party stands for. Thus, when interviewed, people may make the following remarks when asked why they support the Democratic Party: "It seems that the economy is better when the Democrats are in control." "The Democrats are for the working people." People might say about the Republican Party: "The Republicans help the small businessperson more than the Democrats." "The Republicans deal better with foreign policy issues."

DEMOGRAPHIC FACTORS AND PARTY IDENTIFICATION

Regardless of how accurate or inaccurate these stereotypes are, individuals with similar characteristics do tend to align themselves more often with one or the other major party. Factors such as race, age, income, education, and marital status all influence party identification.

As Table 8–1 on the next page shows, slightly more men than women identify with the Republican Party, while more women than men identify themselves as Democrats. In regard to race, while slightly more whites identify with the Republican Party, people in the other categories (nonwhite, black, and Hispanic) overwhelmingly classify themselves as Democrats. As to age, the most notable differences in party preferences are found in those over age sixty-five: a significantly larger number of people in this group identify themselves as Democrats (42 percent) than as Republicans (29 percent). As stated, other factors, such as income, religion, and marital status, also seem to influence party preference.

Although there is clearly a link between these factors and party preference, each party encompasses diverse interests and activities. Both political parties welcome various groups and strive to attract as many members as possible.

What Do Political Parties Do?

As noted earlier, the Constitution does not mention political parties. Historically, though, political parties have played a vital role in our democratic system. Their main function has been to link the people's policy preferences to actual government policies. Political parties also perform many other functions.

Table 8-1

Demographic Factors and Party Preferences

	PERCENT REPUBLICAN	PERCENT DEMOCRAT	PERCENT INDEPENDENT
TOTAL	30	31	39
GENDER			
Male	31	26	43
Female	28	37	35
RACE			
White	33	28	39
Nonwhite	9	56	35
Black	6	64	30
Hispanic	21	37	42
AGE			
Under 30	29	26	45
30–49	30	29	41
50–64	30	33	37
65+	29	42	29
EDUCATION			
College Graduate	35	28	37
Some College	31	29	40
High School Graduate	29	32	39
Less than High School Graduate	22	38	40
FAMILY INCOME			
$75,000+	42	24	34
$50,000–$74,999	37	27	36
$30,000–$49,999	32	29	39
$20,000–$29,999	27	33	40
Less than $20,000	22	38	40
RELIGIOUS PREFERENCE			
Total White Protestant	38	25	37
White Protestant Evangelical	42	25	33
White Protestant Nonevangelical	34	26	41
White Catholic	30	32	38
MARITAL STATUS			
Married	33	29	38
Divorced/Separated	22	35	43
Widowed	27	44	29
Never Married	26	30	44

SOURCE: The Pew Research Center for the People and the Press, 1997; based on surveys conducted in 1996.

SELECTING CANDIDATES

One of the most important functions of the two political parties is to recruit and nominate candidates for political office. This function simplifies voting choices for the electorate. Political parties take the large number of people who want to run for office and narrow the field to one candidate. They accomplish this by the use of the **primary,** which is a preliminary election to choose a party's final candidate. The party chooses the best-qualified member to be the party candidate. It is much easier for voters to choose between two candidates who have been selected by established political parties than to choose among many candidates.

PRIMARY ● A preliminary election held for the purpose of choosing a party's final candidate.

MINORITY PARTY ● The political party that has fewer members in the legislature than does the opposing party.

MAJORITY PARTY ● The political party that has more members in the legislature than does the opposing party.

I N F O T R A C ®

Changes to the presidential primary election system

INFORMING THE PUBLIC

Political parties help educate the public about currently important political issues. In recent years, these issues have included defense and environmental policies, our tax system, welfare reform, crime, education, and Social Security. Each party presents its view of these issues through television announcements, newspaper articles or ads, campaign speeches, rallies, debates, and pamphlets. These activities help citizens learn about the issues, consider proposed solutions, and form opinions.

Through these activities, political parties also help to stimulate citizens' interest and participation in public affairs. They seek people to work at party headquarters or to help with door-to-door canvasses, which involve distributing campaign literature and asking people to vote for the party's candidate. Political parties also ask volunteers to work at polling places where people cast their votes during elections and to drive voters to the polling places. Through such pursuits, citizens can participate in the political process.

COORDINATING POLICYMAKING

In our complex government, parties are essential for coordinating policy among the various branches of the government. The political party is usually the major institution through which the executive and legislative branches cooperate with each other. Each president, cabinet member, and member of Congress is normally a member of the Democratic or the Republican Party. The party with fewer members in the legislature is the **minority party.** The party with the most members is the **majority party.** The president works through party leaders in Congress to promote the administration's legislative program. Parties also act as the glue of our federal structure by connecting the various levels of government with a common bond. (For a more detailed discussion of the role played by political parties in Congress, see Chapter 13.)

CHECKING THE POWER OF THE PARTY IN GOVERNMENT

The party that does not control Congress or a state legislature, or the presidency or a state governorship, also plays a vital function in American politics. The "out party" acts as a watchdog and keeps an eye on the activities

Drawing by Dana Fradon; © 1987 The New Yorker Magazine, Inc.

"My God! I went to sleep a Democrat and I've awakened a Republican."

> **COALITION ●** An alliance of
> individuals or groups with a variety of
> interests and opinions who join
> together to support all or part of a
> political party's platform.

of the party in power. The out party thus provides a check on the activities of the party in government. Such monitoring by the loyal opposition encourages the party in power to heed the public's wishes and to remain responsive.

BALANCING COMPETING INTERESTS

Political parties are often described as vast umbrellas under which Americans with diverse interests can gather. Political parties are essentially **coalitions**—individuals and groups with a variety of interests and opinions who join together to support the party's platform, or parts of it.

The Republican Party, for example, includes a number of groups with many different views on the issue of abortion. The role of party leaders in this situation is to adopt a broad enough view on the issue so that the various groups will not be alienated. In this way, different groups can hold their individual views and still come together under the umbrella of the Republican Party. Leaders of both the Democratic Party and the Republican Party modify contending views and arrange compromises among different groups. In so doing, the parties help to unify, rather than divide, their members.

RUNNING CAMPAIGNS

Through their national, state, and local organizations, parties coordinate campaigns. Political parties take care of a large number of small and routine tasks that are essential to the smooth functioning of the electoral process. They work at getting party members registered and at conducting drives for new voters. They sometimes staff the polling places.

A Short History of American Political Parties

Political parties have been a part of American politics since the early years of our nation. Throughout the course of our history, many parties have formed, and many have disappeared. Even today, although we have only two major political parties, numerous other parties are also contending for power, as will be discussed later in this chapter.

THE FIRST POLITICAL PARTIES

The founders reacted negatively to the idea of strong political parties because they thought the power struggles that would occur between small economic and political groups would eventually topple the balanced democracy they wanted to create. Nonetheless, two major political factions—the Federalists and Anti-Federalists—were formed even before the Constitution was ratified. Remember from Chapter 2 that the Federalists pushed for the ratification of the Constitution because they wanted a stronger national government than the one that had existed under the Articles of Confederation. The Anti-Federalists argued against ratification. They supported states' rights and feared a too-powerful central government.

These two national factions continued, in somewhat altered form, after the Constitution was ratified. Alexander Hamilton, the first secretary of the Treasury, became the leader of the Federalist Party, which supported a strong central government that would encourage the development of commerce and manufacturing. The Federalists generally thought that a democracy should be ruled by its wealthiest and best-educated citizens. Opponents of the Federalists and Hamilton's policies referred to themselves not as Anti-Federalists, but as Democratic Republicans. The Democratic Republicans were more sympathetic to the "common man" and favored a more limited role for government. They believed that the nation's welfare would be best served if the states had more power than the central government. In their view, Congress should dominate the government, and gov-

ernment policies should help the nation's shopkeepers, farmers, and laborers. The Democratic Republicans later became the Democratic Party.

FROM 1796 TO 1860

The nation's first two parties clashed openly in the elections of 1796, in which John Adams, the Federalists' candidate to succeed Washington as president, defeated Thomas Jefferson. Over the next four years, Jefferson and James Madison worked to extend the influence of the Democratic Republican Party. In the presidential elections of 1800 and 1804, Jefferson won the presidency under the Democratic Republican banner. His party also won control of Congress. The Federalists never returned to power and thus became the first (but not the last) American party to go out of existence. (See the time line of American political parties in Figure 8–1.)

The Democratic Republicans dominated American politics for the next twenty years. Jefferson was succeeded in the White House by two other Democratic Republicans—James Madison and James Monroe. In the mid-1820s, however, the Democratic Republicans split into two groups.

Figure 8–1
A Time Line of U.S.
Political Parties

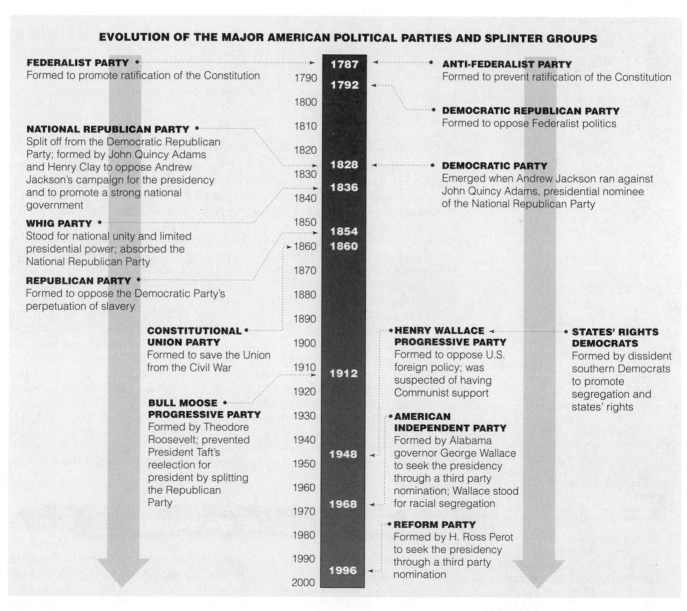

EVOLUTION OF THE MAJOR AMERICAN POLITICAL PARTIES AND SPLINTER GROUPS

FEDERALIST PARTY
Formed to promote ratification of the Constitution

ANTI-FEDERALIST PARTY
Formed to prevent ratification of the Constitution

DEMOCRATIC REPUBLICAN PARTY
Formed to oppose Federalist politics

NATIONAL REPUBLICAN PARTY
Split off from the Democratic Republican Party; formed by John Quincy Adams and Henry Clay to oppose Andrew Jackson's campaign for the presidency and to promote a strong national government

DEMOCRATIC PARTY
Emerged when Andrew Jackson ran against John Quincy Adams, presidential nominee of the National Republican Party

WHIG PARTY
Stood for national unity and limited presidential power; absorbed the National Republican Party

REPUBLICAN PARTY
Formed to oppose the Democratic Party's perpetuation of slavery

CONSTITUTIONAL UNION PARTY
Formed to save the Union from the Civil War

HENRY WALLACE PROGRESSIVE PARTY
Formed to oppose U.S. foreign policy; was suspected of having Communist support

STATES' RIGHTS DEMOCRATS
Formed by dissident southern Democrats to promote segregation and states' rights

BULL MOOSE PROGRESSIVE PARTY
Formed by Theodore Roosevelt; prevented President Taft's reelection for president by splitting the Republican Party

AMERICAN INDEPENDENT PARTY
Formed by Alabama governor George Wallace to seek the presidency through a third party nomination; Wallace stood for racial segregation

REFORM PARTY
Formed by H. Ross Perot to seek the presidency through a third party nomination

1790, 1800, 1810, 1820, 1830, 1840, 1850, 1860, 1870, 1880, 1890, 1900, 1910, 1920, 1930, 1940, 1950, 1960, 1970, 1980, 1990, 2000

1787, 1792, 1828, 1836, 1854, 1860, 1912, 1948, 1968, 1996

Andrew Jackson (1767–1845) was the greatest military hero of his time and became associated with increased popular participation in government. The National Republican Party, a split-off from the Democratic Republican Party, was formed by John Q. Adams and Henry Clay to oppose Jackson's 1828 campaign for the presidency. Jackson won the election, nonetheless.

Andrew Jackson, who was elected president in 1828, aligned himself with the group that called themselves the Democrats. The Democrats were mostly small farmers, debtors, and slaveholders. The other group, the National Republicans (later the Whig Party), was led by the well-known Henry Clay and the great orator Daniel Webster. It was a coalition of bankers, business-persons, and southern planters.

As the Whigs and Democrats competed for the White House throughout the 1840s and 1850s, the two-party system as we know it today emerged. Both parties were large, with well-known leaders and supporters across the nation. They both had grassroots organizations of party workers commit-ted to winning as many political offices (at all levels of government) for the party as possible. Both the Whigs and the Democrats remained vague on the issue of slavery, and the Democrats were divided into northern and southern camps. By the mid-1850s, the Whig coalition fell apart, and most Whigs were absorbed into the new Republican Party, which opposed the extension of slavery into new territories. Campaigning on this platform, the Republicans succeeded in electing Abraham Lincoln as the first Republican president in 1860.

FROM THE CIVIL WAR TO THE GREAT DEPRESSION

By the end of the Civil War in 1865, the Republicans and the Democrats were the most prominent political parties. From the election of Abraham Lincoln in 1860 until the election of Franklin Roosevelt in 1932, the Republican Party, sometimes referred to as the Grand Old Party, or the GOP, remained the majority party in national politics, winning all but four presidential elections.

AFTER THE GREAT DEPRESSION

The social and economic impact of the Great Depression of the 1930s destroyed the majority support that the Republicans had enjoyed for so long and contributed to a realignment in the two-party system. In a **realigning election,** the popular support for and relative strength of the parties shift so that the minority (opposition) party emerges as the major-ity party. (A realigning election can also reestablish the majority party in power, albeit with a different coalition of supporters.) The landmark realigning election of 1932 brought Franklin Delano Roosevelt to the presi-dency and the Democrats back to power at the national level. Realigning elections also occurred in 1860 and 1896.

Roosevelt was reelected to the presidency in 1936, 1940, and 1944. When he died in office in 1945, his vice president, Harry Truman, assumed the presidential office. Truman ran for the presidency in 1948 and won the election. A Republican candidate, Dwight D. Eisenhower, won the presi-dential elections of 1952 and 1956. From 1960 through 1968, the Democrats, headed by John F. Kennedy and Lyndon B. Johnson, respec-tively, held power. The Republicans came back into power in 1968 and, except for Jimmy Carter's one term (1977–1981), retained the presidency until Bill Clinton was elected in 1992.

In Congress, the Democrats were the dominant party from the Great Depression until 1994. The 1994 election resulted in a Republican major-ity in Congress.

REALIGNING ELECTION ● An election in which the popular support for and relative strength of the parties shift so that either (1) the minority (opposition) party emerges as the majority party or (2) the majority party is reestablished with a different coalition of supporters.

THIRD PARTY ● In the United States, any party other than one of the two major parties (Republican and Democratic) is considered a minor party, or third party.

Third Parties and American Politics

Throughout American history, smaller minor parties, sometimes called **third parties,**[9] have competed for power in the nation's two-party system. Indeed, third parties have been represented in most of our national elec-tions. Although third parties have found it difficult—if not impossible—to gain credibility within the two-party–dominated American system, they play an important role in our political life.

THE MANY KINDS OF THIRD PARTIES

Third parties are as varied as the causes they represent, but all of these parties have one thing in common: their members and leaders want to challenge the major parties, because they believe that certain needs and values are not being properly addressed. Third parties name candidates who propose to remedy the situation.

Some third parties have tried to appeal to the entire nation; others have focused on particular regions of the country, states, or local areas. Most third parties have been short lived. A few, however, including the Socialist Labor Party (founded in 1891) and the Social Democrats (founded in 1901) have lasted for a long time. The number and variety of third parties make them difficult to classify, but most fall into one of the general categories discussed in the following subsections.

Issue-Oriented Parties

An issue-oriented third party is formed to promote a particular cause or timely issue. For example, the Free Soil Party was organized in 1848 to oppose the expansion of slavery into the western territories. The Prohibition Party was formed in 1869 to advocate prohibiting the use and manufacture of alcoholic beverages. The U.S.A. Green Party was founded in 1972 to raise awareness of environmental issues. Most issue-oriented parties fade into history as the issue that brought them into existence fades from public attention, is taken up by a major party, or is resolved.

Ideological Parties

As discussed in Chapter 6, an *ideology* is a comprehensive set of beliefs about human nature and government institutions. An ideological party supports a particular set of beliefs or political doctrine. For example, a party such as the Socialist Workers Party may believe that our free enterprise system should be replaced by one in which government or workers own all of the factories in the economy. The party's members may feel that competition should be replaced by cooperation and social responsibility so as to secure an equitable distribution of income. In contrast, an ideological party such as the Libertarian Party may oppose virtually all forms of government interference with personal liberties and private enterprise.

Splinter or Personality Parties

A splinter party develops out of a split within a major party. Often this split involves the formation of a party to elect a specific person. For example, when Theodore Roosevelt did not receive the Republican Party's nomination in 1912, he created the Bull Moose Party (also called the Progressive Party) to promote his platform. From the Democrats have come Henry Wallace's Progressive Party and the States' Rights (Dixiecrat) Party, both formed in 1948. In 1968, the American Independent Party was formed to support George Wallace's campaign for president.

Most splinter parties have been formed around a leader with a strong personality, which is why they are sometimes called personality parties. When that person steps aside, the party usually collapses. A good example of a personality party is the Reform Party, which was formed in 1996 mainly to provide a campaign vehicle for H. Ross Perot.

THE EFFECT OF THIRD PARTIES ON AMERICAN POLITICS

Although most Americans do not support third parties or vote for their candidates, third parties have influenced American politics in several ways, some of which we examine here.

INFOTRAC®

Should conservatives start their own party

**Figure 8–2
The Effect of Third Parties on Vote Distribution**
In eight presidential elections, a third party's candidate received more than 10 percent of the popular vote—in six of those elections, the incumbent party lost. As shown here, only in 1856 and 1924 did the incumbent party manage to hold onto the White House in the face of a significant third party showing.

Third Parties Bring Issues to the Public's Attention

Third parties have brought many political issues to the public's attention. They have exposed and focused on unpopular or highly debated issues that major parties have preferred to ignore. Third parties are in a position to take bold stands on issues that are avoided by major parties because third parties are not trying to be all things to all people. Progressive social reforms such as the minimum wage, women's right to vote, railroad and banking legislation, and old-age pensions were first proposed by third parties. The Free Soilers of the 1850s, for example, were the first true antislavery party, and the Populists and Progressives put many social reforms on the political agenda.

Some people have argued that third parties are often the unsung heroes of American politics, bringing new issues to the forefront of public debate. Some of the ideas proposed by third parties were never accepted, while others were taken up by the major parties as they became more popular.

Third Parties Can Affect the Vote

Third parties can influence not only voter turnout but also election outcomes. On occasion, third parties have taken victory from one major party and given it to another, thus playing the "spoiler role."

For example, in 1912, when the Progressive Party split off from the Republican Party, the result was three major contenders for the presidency: Woodrow Wilson, the Democratic candidate; William Howard Taft, the regular Republican candidate; and Theodore Roosevelt, the Progressive candidate. The presence of the Progressive Party "spoiled" the Republicans' chances for victory and gave the election to Wilson, the Democrat. Without Roosevelt's third party, Taft might have won. A significant showing by a minor party also reduces an incumbent party's chances of winning the election, as you can see in Figure 8–2. In 1992, for example, third party candidate H. Ross Perot captured about 19 percent of the vote. Had those votes been distributed between the candidates of the major parties, incumbent George Bush and candidate Bill Clinton, the outcome of the election might have been different.

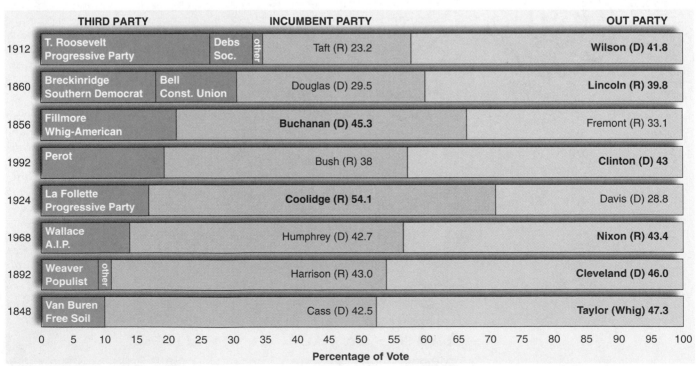

SOURCE: *Congressional Quarterly Weekly Report*, June 13, 1992, p. 1729.

Jesse Ventura, governor of Minnesota. One of the most surprising results of the 1998 elections was Ventura's victory in the Minnesota gubernatorial race. Few thought that Reform Party candidate Ventura (a former professional wrestler known as Jesse "The Body," who was dubbed Jesse "The Mind" during the campaign) had even a slim chance to win the governorship.

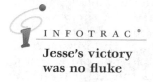

INFOTRAC®

Jesse's victory was no fluke

Third Parties Provide a Voice for Dissatisfied Americans

Third parties also provide a voice for voters who are frustrated with and alienated from the Republican and Democratic parties. Americans who are unhappy with the two major political parties can still participate in American politics through third parties that reflect their opinions on political issues. Certainly, young Minnesota voters turned out in record numbers during the 1998 elections to vote for Jesse Ventura, a Reform Party candidate for governor in that state (see this chapter's feature, *The American Political Spectrum: Third Parties,* on the next page for further details on Ventura's surprising victory).

WHY DO THIRD PARTIES ALMOST ALWAYS FAIL TO WIN ELECTIONS?

Third parties fail to win elections mainly because of low membership, lack of financial resources, and the public's traditional habit of voting within the major parties. The American people have always had a two-party system and are accustomed to selecting only from the nominees of those parties.

One major problem for third parties is raising enough money for a modern campaign. Most Americans have come to believe that a third party candidate could never win, and they are consequently unwilling to contribute to an underdog candidate's campaign. A 1974 law does, however, decrease the severity of this problem for third party candidates in presidential elections. The law states that presidential candidates who receive over 5 percent of the vote will be partially repaid for their campaign expenses by the federal government.

Another problem for third parties is getting candidates on the ballot in all fifty states. Before 1968, some state laws forced candidates to gather a considerable number of signatures in a short period of time before being listed on the state ballot. In 1968, third party candidate George Wallace went to the Supreme Court to have such a law in Ohio ruled unconstitutional.[10] States have since relaxed these requirements, but laws in some states still make the task of getting a new party on the ballot very complicated, thus favoring the two major parties and working against minor parties.

Finally, any third party that succeeds in winning the support of a significant number of voters will soon fall victim to its own success. After all, the two major parties can easily adopt additional planks in their platforms to attract those individuals who are supporting the third party. In this way, the two major parties can undermine any successful third party campaign. Suppose, for example, that a third party is in favor of imposing a federal tax on all businesses, to be used for cleaning up air pollution. If that third party succeeds in gaining considerable voter support, then the major parties can simply endorse the tax as part of their own party platforms. (For a discussion of yet another stumbling block faced by third party candidates, see the feature *A Question of Ethics: Should Third Party Candidates Be Let in on the Great Debates?* on page 201.)

How American Political Parties Are Structured

In theory, each of the major American political parties has a standard, pyramid-shaped organization (see Figure 8–4 on page 201). This theoretical structure is much like that of a large company, in which the bosses are at the top and the employees are at various lower levels.

Actually, neither major party is a closely knit or highly organized structure. Both parties are fragmented and *decentralized*, which means there is no central power with a direct chain of command. If there were, the national chairperson of the party, along with the national committee, could simply dictate how the organization would be run, just as if it were

the american political spectrum

Third Parties

The image of a political spectrum going from "left" to "right" does not fully capture American politics, particularly the wide-ranging concerns expressed by third parties. Look at Figure 8–3. There you see only a few of the parties that ran candidates in the 1996 presidential elections. Other third parties fielding candidates during the 1996 election cycle included the following:

- The American Conservative Party
- The Creators Rights Party
- Democratic Socialists of America
- International Socialists Organization
- The League of Revolutionaries for a New America
- The New Party
- The Pansexual Peace Party
- The Socialist Equality Party

If They Can't Win, Why Do Third Parties Run for Election?

Typically, third parties run to influence the electorate, rather than to win the election. They can bring substantial pressure to bear on the major parties. Ralph Nader's Green Party in California, for example, was created as an effort to push the Democrats to the left. In 1992, H. Ross Perot succeeded in arousing real concern about the federal budget deficit.

Sometimes, They Do Win . . .

One of the great surprises of the 1998 elections was the stunning victory of Jesse Ventura, a candidate running for governor in Minnesota on the Reform Party ticket. No one expected the former professional wrestler to defeat his respected opponents—Democrat Hubert ("Skip") Humphrey III, state attorney general and son of the late vice president, and Republican Norman Coleman, mayor of St. Paul.

During the campaign, Ventura downplayed his wealth, often wearing faded jeans and sneakers. He spoke bluntly against government meddling, promised that he would not increase taxes and would return all future state budget surpluses to the taxpayers, and generally struck an antiestablishment pose. He declared that he wanted to be the governor "who destroys the property-tax system as we know it." Few thought he would succeed in the election. Indeed, his campaign was viewed by the press and his opponents as, at most, providing some comic relief from the campaigns of the other two, much less colorful candidates.

After the votes were in, however, many Minnesotans were shocked at how wrong they could be. Ventura had succeeded in becoming Minnesota's governor. He was the first candidate of Perot's Reform Party to gain a statewide office. Ventura's campaign galvanized younger voters, who appeared at the polls in record numbers on election day. In fact, due to the new voters, Minnesota's 61 percent election turnout was the highest in the nation. In Ventura's eyes, his victory is a wake-up call to the major parties. "If these parties don't wake up from their bipartisan bickering, there will be more Jesse Venturas on the horizon," he said a few months after the election.[11]

For Critical Analysis

In your opinion, was Ventura's victory an anomaly in American politics or, as he believes, a warning sign to the major parties?

Figure 8–3
Selected Third Parties and Their Candidates in the 1996 Presidential Election

JOHN HAGELIN
Candidate for the Natural Law Party

Advocated transcendental meditation and "Yogic Flying" for all American voters; supported government-provided health care as long as alternative medicine was used.

RALPH NADER
Candidate for the Green Party

Fought against the self-perpetuation of the two-party system; advocated ecological positions.

HOWARD PHILLIPS
Candidate for the U.S. Taxpayers Party

Called for the elimination of all direct taxes, the elimination of the civil service, and the end of U.S. participation in the United Nations, NATO, and the International Monetary Fund.

HARRY BROWNE
Candidate for the Libertarian Party

Supported the legalization of drugs and prostitution, along with the elimination of the Central Intelligence Agency, the Environmental Protection Agency, the Internal Revenue Service, and the Federal Bureau of Investigation.

Should Third Party Candidates Be Let in on the Great Debates?

Only twice since 1960, when the first televised presidential debate was held, have American TV viewers and radio listeners been able to hear the voice of a third party candidate. The first third party candidate to participate in the debates was John Anderson in 1980, and the second was H. Ross Perot in 1992. Before the 1996 presidential debates occurred, two important third party candidates, H. Ross Perot of the Reform Party and John Hagelin of the Natural Law Party, asked to be participants. The Commission for Presidential Debates chose not to allow them on the air. When taken to court, the Federal Election Commission and the Commission for Presidential Debates won, and Perot and Hagelin lost.[12]

The ethical question here is whether it was right to deny these important third party candidates "their day in the TV sun." After all, when Congress created the Federal Election Commission, it defined a presidential candidate as one who qualified in ten or more states. Perot had qualified in all fifty states, and Hagelin had qualified in forty-five. The Commission for Presidential Debates decided that only candidates who had a "reasonable" chance of success could participate. The founders had strong feelings about the right of people to govern themselves through free elections. Free elections mean little, however, if minor party candidates do not have realistic access to public forums, such as television.

For Critical Analysis

What arguments might supporters of the two major parties make against allowing third parties to participate in televised debates between presidential candidates?

Microsoft or Netscape. In reality, state party organizations are all very different and are only loosely tied to the party's national structure. Local party organizations are often quite independent from the state organization. There is no single individual or group who gives orders to all party members. Instead, a number of personalities, frequently at odds with one another, form loosely identifiable leadership groups.[13]

STATE AND LOCAL PARTY ORGANIZATIONS

In both the Democratic and Republican parties, state and local party organizations are separate from the national party organizations. Most

Figure 8–4
The Theoretical Structure of the American Political Party
The relationship between state and local parties varies from state to state. Further, some state parties resist national party policies.

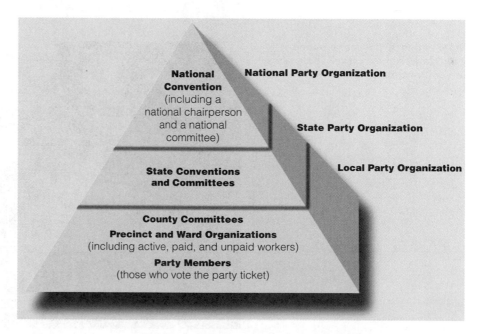

National Convention (including a national chairperson and a national committee)

State Conventions and Committees

County Committees
Precinct and Ward Organizations (including active, paid, and unpaid workers)
Party Members (those who vote the party ticket)

National Party Organization

State Party Organization

Local Party Organization

WARD ● A local unit of a political party's organization, consisting of a division or district within a city.

PRECINCT ● A political district within a city (such as a block or a neighborhood) or a portion of a rural county; the smallest voting district at the local level.

NATIONAL CONVENTION ● The meeting held by each major party every four years to select presidential and vice presidential candidates, to write a party platform, and to conduct other party business.

state and local parties work closely with their national organization only during major elections.

State Organizations

The powers and duties of state party organizations differ from state to state. In general, the state party organization is built around a central committee and a chairperson. The committee works to raise funds, recruit new party members, maintain a strong party organization, and help members running for state offices.

The state chairperson is usually a powerful party member chosen by the committee. In some cases, however, the chairperson is selected by the governor or a senator from that state.

Local Organizations

Local party organizations differ greatly, but generally there is a party unit for each district in which elective offices are to be filled. These districts include congressional and legislative districts, counties, cities and towns, wards, and precincts.

A **ward** is a political division or district within a city. A **precinct** can be either a political district within a city, such as a block or a neighborhood, or a portion of a rural county. The local, grassroots foundations of politics are formed within voting precincts. Polling places are located within the precincts. Political parties elect or appoint precinct captains or chairpersons who organize the precinct, assist new members, register voters, and take care of party business.

THE NATIONAL PARTY ORGANIZATION

On the national level, the party's presidential candidate is considered to be the official leader of the party. In some cases, well-known members of Congress are viewed as national party leaders. In addition to the party leaders, the structure of both major parties includes four major elements: the national convention, the national committee, the national chairperson, and the congressional campaign committees.

The National Convention

Most of the public attention that the party receives comes at the **national convention,** which is held every four years during the summer before the

State and local parties help their candidates run for office. These signs in Ventura County, California, are typical.

Every four years, each major party holds a national convention to nominate the party's presidential and vice presidential candidates. This 1996 Democratic National Convention was held in Chicago. The first Democratic National Convention was held in 1832 in Baltimore, where it was held every four years thereafter through 1852. The first Republican National Convention was held in 1856 in Philadelphia. Chicago has hosted more national party conventions than any other city.

presidential election. The news media cover these conventions extensively, and as a result, they have become quite extravagant. They are often described as the party's national voice and are usually held in major cities.

The national conventions are attended by delegates chosen by the states in various ways. The delegates' most important job is to choose the party's presidential and vice presidential candidates, who together make up the **party ticket.** The delegates also write the party platform, which, as mentioned, sets forth the party's positions on national issues. Essentially, through its platform, the party promises to initiate certain policies if it wins the presidency. Despite the widespread perception that, once in office, candidates can and do ignore these promises, in fact, many of them become law.[14]

The National Committee

Each state elects a number of delegates to the **national party committee.** The Republican National Committee and the Democratic National Committee direct the business of their respective parties during the four years between national conventions. The committees' most important duties, however, are to organize the next national convention and to plan how to obtain a party victory in the next presidential election.

The National Chairperson

The party's national committee elects a **national party chairperson** to serve as administrative head of the national party. The chairperson is chosen by the party's presidential candidate at a meeting of the national committee right after the national convention.[15] The duties of the national chairperson are to direct the work of the national committee from party headquarters in Washington, D.C. The chairperson is involved in raising funds, providing for publicity, promoting party unity, recruiting new voters, and other activities. In presidential election years, the chairperson's attention is focused on the national convention and the presidential campaign.

The Congressional Campaign Committee

Each party has a campaign committee, made up of senators and representatives, in each chamber of Congress. Members are chosen by their colleagues and serve for two-year terms. The committees work to help reelect party members to Congress.

PARTY TICKET ● A list of a political party's candidates for various offices.

NATIONAL PARTY COMMITTEE ● The political party leaders who direct party business during the four years between the national party conventions, organize the next national convention, and plan how to obtain a party victory in the next presidential election.

NATIONAL PARTY CHAIRPERSON ● An individual who serves as a political party's administrative head at the national level and directs the work of the party's national committee.

Americans at Odds over Political Parties

Some issues relating to our political parties have, in a sense, just begun to surface. As pointed out at the beginning of this chapter, the rise of the independent voter certainly has caused concern in both the Democratic and the Republican parties. Here we look at some of the issues facing the American electorate (and party leaders) today.

Can the Major Parties Survive?

As pointed out in this chapter's opening feature, in the last fifty years the number of independent voters has increased significantly. Figure 8–5 graphically illustrates this trend. The growing importance of independent voters and the declining support for the two major parties have led many to speculate that the traditional two-party system may be giving way to the needs of a new era. Indeed, some contend that we have reached the end of the industrial age and that the institutions that supported that period, including the traditional two-party system, are dying.[16]

Few doubt that the coming decades will see a transformation of the American party system. Traditionalists tend to believe that the Republican and Democratic parties will survive by realigning themselves to recapture the voters' support. This may be difficult, especially for the Republican Party, which has suffered from intraparty disputes between social and economic conservatives.[17] Others, including political scientist David Gillespie, have suggested that a centrist, people-centered party may replace one of the major parties. This suggestion is premised on the

Figure 8–5
Party Identification in Presidential Election Years

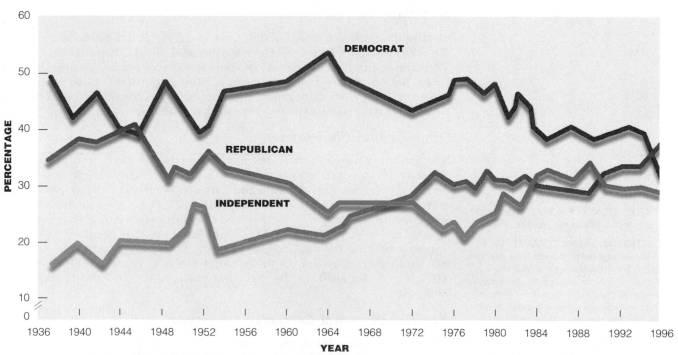

SOURCES: *The Gallup Opinion Index*, July 1979; *The Gallup Report*, December 1981; *The Gallup Report*, 1983; *The Gallup Report*, May 1987; *The Gallup Report*, May 1990; *The Public Perspective*, July/August 1992; *The Gallup Report*, August 1995; Pew Center for the People and the Press, August 1996.

assumption that voters have become increasingly frustrated over the influence wielded by special interest groups on both of today's major parties.[18]

Split-Ticket Voting and Divided Government

Not only have ties to the two major parties weakened in the last three decades, but voters are also less willing to engage in straight-ticket voting—that is, to vote for all of the candidates of one party. The percentage of voters who engage in ticket splitting has increased from 12 percent in 1952 to more than 38 percent in the presidential elections of 1996. In part, this trend reflects the increase in the number of independent voters, who are more likely to split their ballots and less likely to trust one of the parties to control both branches of government.

Americans have a long tradition of distrusting government at every level. In recent years, this trend seems to be manifested by the voters' preferences for divided government—that is, a government in which the legislative branch is controlled by one major party and the executive branch by another. Polls taken during 1996 showed that the American people were willing and able to use the ballot to maintain a government that they trusted—that is, one that balanced power between a Republican Congress and a Democratic presidential administration. In late October 1996, a *New York Times* poll asked whether voters would prefer a Democratic or Republican Congress if Bill Clinton was reelected. Only 41 percent preferred a Democratic Congress, while 48 percent preferred a Republican Congress to "limit the power of President Clinton." Voters in the 1998 elections expressed a preference for moderate policymaking, and the compromises necessitated by divided government will likely tend to reflect those preferences.

Is a True Third Party on the Horizon?

Some political commentators, such as journalist David Broder, believe that a permanent third party, one that will break the two-party system, may be in our nation's future.[19] He has argued that the public's dissatisfaction with the Democrats and Republicans has become too great to be ignored. He agrees with former senator Sam Nunn, who believes that the two-party system has served our nation well for years, but that we are in a new period. They both argue that the Reform Party, started by Perot, may end up being the true permanent third party in the United States.

From data collected by a 1996 *Time*/CNN poll, it is clear that Americans are willing to consider alternatives to the current two-party system. When asked whether they favored a third party that would run candidates for president, Congress, and state offices against Republicans and Democrats, 54 percent of those questioned answered that they would support such a party.

E. J. Dionne, Jr., a journalist for the *Washington Post*, also finds potential for a new party. Dionne suggests that a new reform movement will find supporters and believes that the seeds for a remodeled political movement are planted in the voters' tremendous discontent with the current two major political parties.[20]

key terms

coalition 194
consensus 187
electorate 190
majority party 193
minority party 193
national convention 202
national party chairperson 203
national party committee 203
party elite 190
party identifier 190
party platform 190
party ticket 203

patronage 191
plurality 188
political party 187
precinct 202
primary 192
realigning election 196
single-member district
   system 188
solidarity 191
third party 196
two-party system 187
ward 202

chapter summary

1. A political party is a group of individuals outside the government who organize to win elections, to operate the government, and to determine policy. In the American system, political parties provide citizens with a way to participate in the system and to choose who will serve in government and which policies will be adopted.

2. In the United States, we have a two-party system in which two major parties, the Democrats and the Republicans, vie for control of the government.

3. Some of the factors that help to explain why the two-party system has become entrenched in the United States include (1) a general agreement, or consensus, among American citizens on broad social and economic issues; and (2) our elective process, which makes it difficult for third parties to compete successfully against the major parties.

4. Each of the two major parties consists of three components: the party in the electorate, the party organization, and the party in government.

5. To become a party member, one need only identify oneself with the party. A large number of party members, known as party identifiers, are not actively involved in party politics and may do nothing more than vote occasionally for some of the party's candidates. A smaller, relatively loose-knit group of actively involved party members, the party elite, carry out the major functions of the party, such as planning elections, organizing fund raisers, and keeping in touch with party leaders in other communities.

6. People join political parties for a variety of reasons, including the desire to express their solidarity, or mutual agreement, with the views of others;

to benefit materially from party membership by obtaining a better job or personal advancement; and to promote political ideas and principles that they feel are important.

7. The main function of political parties is to link the people's policy preferences to actual government policies. Other important functions of parties include selecting candidates to run for political office, informing the public about important political issues, coordinating policymaking among the various branches and levels of government, checking the power of the party in government (a function of the "out party"), balancing competing interests and effecting compromises, and running campaigns.

8. In the early years of the nation, the Federalists (who advocated a strong central government under the control of the wealthiest and best-educated citizens) and the Democratic Republicans (who favored a more limited central government in which the "common man" played a greater role) vied for power. In the mid-1820s, the Democratic Republicans split into the Democrats (who became the Democratic Party) and the National Republicans (later, the Whig Party). In the mid-1850s, the Whig Party fell apart, and most Whigs were absorbed into the new Republican Party, which elected Abraham Lincoln as the first Republican president in 1860. Since that time, the Democrats and Republicans have been the major parties controlling American government.

9. There are many different kinds of minor parties, or third parties. Some are issue oriented while others are based on ideology. Some third parties form as splinter parties as a result of a split within a

major party. Third parties have an impact on American politics because they bring political issues to the public's attention, alter election outcomes by gaining votes that would otherwise go to one of the major parties, and provide a voice for voters who are frustrated with or alienated from the major parties. Third parties usually fail to win elections, mainly because of low membership, lack of financial resources, and the public's preference for major party candidates. Additionally, major parties can easily undermine the third party by adopting additional planks in their platforms.

10. In theory, both of the major political parties have a pyramid-shaped organization, with the national committee and national chairperson at the top of the organization and the local party units at the bottom. In practice, the parties are decentralized, and the state and local party organizations work closely with the national organization only during major elections. The state central committee, which directs the state party organization, works to raise funds, recruit new party members, maintain a strong party organization, and help members running for state offices. Party units at the local level include wards and precincts.

11. At the national level, the most public event is the party's national convention, which is held every four years. Delegates from each state choose the party's presidential and vice presidential candidates and write the party platform. The national party committee, headed by the national party chairperson, plans the national convention and directs party affairs between conventions. The national party chairperson is involved in fund raising, publicity, promoting party unity, recruiting new voters, and other activities. Each major party also has a campaign committee in each house of Congress, which works to help reelect party members to congressional seats.

12. Americans are at odds over many issues relating to political parties. Increasingly, the two major parties are losing support among American voters, and over one-third of the voters classify themselves as independents. Many speculate that unless the two parties can realign themselves significantly to recapture the support of the voters, the existing two-party system may give way to one involving a permanent third party.

for critical analysis

1. Does the current political party system work to exclude members of minority groups from the political process?

2. Would your vote have more influence in a local election than a national election? Why or why not?

3. Would the outcome of local elections be any different if all the students in your college or university formed a political party and voted?

4. Is it fair to describe the Republican Party as the party of the rich?

5. If you are not impressed with the achievements or directions taken by the Republican and Democratic parties, should you identify yourself as an independent or join one of the two major parties anyway? What factors would influence your decision?

6. Do you see any major differences between the two major parties, or do they exist primarily to elect candidates?

7. Would you ever vote for a candidate fielded by a third party? Why or why not?

suggested readings

BROOKS, David. Ed. *Backward and Upward: The New Conservative Writing.* New York: Vintage Books, 1996. This is a collection of combative, often funny essays from the political right. The authors hold nothing sacred, and their lampooning of various liberal beliefs shows that conservatism is as much about personality as ideology.

FAUX, Geoffrey P. *The Party's Not Over: A New Vision for the Democrats.* New York: Basic Books, 1996. The author, who is the president of the Economics Policy Institute, argues that President Clinton's focus on balancing the federal budget caused him to lose his core constituency on the left wing of the party. Faux's stories of Americans who lost their jobs as a result of Clinton's policies give the book a human dimension.

FRYMER, Paul. *Uneasy Alliances: Race and Party Competition in America.* Ewing, N.J.: Princeton University Press, 1999. The author, a political scientist at the University of California at Los Angeles, examines the relationship between the two major political parties and African Americans. He concludes that two-party competition for white voters has the effect of excluding African Americans and other minorities from participation in the political process.

GREENBERG, Stanley B. *Middle Class Dreams: The Politics and Power of the New American Majority*. New York: Times Books, 1995. President Clinton's adviser looks at the radical shape of American politics today and contends that both political parties have betrayed the middle class.

SORENSEN, Theodore C. *Why I Am a Democrat*. New York: Henry Holt & Co., 1996. In this work, one of John F. Kennedy's key advisers tells why he chose to become a Democrat. The book offers useful insights into the linkages between personal values and party preference. At one point, he says, "I am a Democrat, by conviction as well as affiliation, not by birth but by choice, not because of my parents or neighbors or spouse but because of my basic values and beliefs. . . . I am simply one of millions who find the Democratic Party's candidates, principles, and positions consistently preferable to those of Republicans."

politics
on the web

For a list of political sites available on the Internet, sorted by country and with links to parties, organizations, and governments throughout the world, go to

http://www.agora.stm.it/politic/home.htm

The Democratic Party is online at

http://www.democrats.org

The Republican National Committee is at

http://www.rnc.org

The Libertarian Party has a Web site at

http://www.lp.org/lp/lp.html

The Socialist Party's Web site can be accessed at

http://sp-usa.org

Last but (perhaps) not least, for a change of political pace visit Jesse Ventura's Web site at

http://www.presidentventura.com

using
web resources

The Green Parties of North America use both electoral politics and direct action to work for the issues most important to their ideology: peace, environmental sanity, democracy, and social justice. They are building political parties that seek consensus rather than passing down orders from the top.

Go to the "Green Parties of North America" Web site at

http://www.greens.org

1. What are the values of the Green Parties? Do these values resonate with you?

2. How successful have Greens been in recent elections in the United States?

3. Is there a Green organization in your state?

4. Would you support the Green Parties? Why or why not?

notes

1. *The Gallup Report,* April 9, 1999.

2. Letter to Francis Hopkinson written from Paris while Jefferson was minister to France, as cited in John P. Foley, ed., *The Jeffersonian Cyclopedia* (New York: Russell & Russell, 1967), p. 677.

3. From the names of the twins in Lewis Carroll's *Through the Looking Glass.*

4. *USA Today*, February 23, 1999, p. 6A. See also Albert R. Hunt, "The Me-Too—Or Yes-But—Republicans," *The Wall Street Journal*, February 25, 1999, p. A19.

5. Richard Darman, *Who's in Control? Polar Politics and the Sensible Center* (New York: Simon & Schuster, 1996).

6. In most states, a person must declare a preference for a particular party before voting in that state's primary election (discussed in Chapter 10). This declaration is usually part of the voter registration process.

7. See, for example, Leon D. Epstein, *Political Parties in Western Democracies* (New Brunswick, N.J.: Transaction, 1980).

8. For an interesting discussion of the pros and cons of patronage from a constitutional perspective, see the majority opinion versus the dissent in the Supreme Court case, *Board of County Commissioners v. Umbehr*, 518 U.S. 668 (1996).

9. The term *third party*, although inaccurate (because sometimes there have been fourth parties, fifth parties, and so on), is commonly used in reference to a minor party.

10. *Williams v. Rhodes*, 393 U.S. 23 (1968).

11. "Ventura Muscles Up a Warning," *Tulsa World*, February 23, 1999, p. 5.

12. *Perot v. Federal Election Commission*, 97 F.3d 553 (D.C.Cir. 1996).

13. Malcolm E. Jewell and David M. Olson, *American State Political Parties and Elections*, rev. ed. (Homewood, Ill.: Dorsey Press, 1982), p. 73.

14. Gerald M. Pomper and Susan S. Lederman, *Elections in America: Control and Influence in Democratic Politics*, 2d ed. (New York: Longman, 1980).

15. If that candidate loses, however, the chairperson is often changed.

16. Gerald Celente, *Trends 2000: How to Prepare for and Profit from the Changes of the Twenty-First Century* (New York: Warner Books, 1997).

17. Carolyn Barta, "A Bridge to Where? Third Party Could Emerge or Major Parties Could Realign," *Dallas Morning News*, December 15, 1996.

18. J. David Gillespie, *Politics at the Periphery: Third Parties in Two-Party America* (Columbia, S.C.: University of South Carolina Press, 1993).

19. David S. Broder, "There's a Third Party in America's Near Future," *International Herald Tribune*, August 13, 1996, p. 11.

20. E. J. Dionne, Jr., *They Only Look Dead: Why Progressives Will Dominate the Next Political Era* (New York: Simon & Schuster, 1995).

Contents

Voter Apathy: Is This the End of Our Democracy?

As we enter into a new century, many Americans—including political scientists, journalists, politicians, and others—are concerned about voter apathy. In the 1960s, over 60 percent of the voting-age population participated in the three presidential elections held during that decade. In the 1970s and 1980s, voter turnout dropped to between 50 and 55 percent in presidential elections. In 1996, only 49 percent of eligible voters cast their votes at the polls—the lowest turnout since 1924.

Remember from the *America at Odds* feature at the beginning of Chapter 1 that some scholars use low voter turnouts to bolster their argument that Americans no longer care about government. Here we look solely at the controversy over the implications of low voter turnouts for the future of our democracy.

Voter Apathy May Kill Our System

Those who are concerned about lack of public participation in our elections make an obvious point: a democracy depends on the ability of the people to elect political candidates who will represent the people's views in our governing institutions. If fewer and fewer Americans participate in elections, how can we ensure that the wishes of the people are carried out?

If the people do not determine government policy through voting, then that policy will be determined by the influence of powerful interest groups. What we will see is the dominance of the "intensely interested," says Curtis Gans, head of the Nonpartisan Committee for the Study of the American Electorate. According to Gans and other scholars, it is the ideologically moderate voters who stay home. That allows the "intensely interested" to elect candidates from the extreme right and the extreme left of the political spectrum. If this trend continues, claims Gans, we will have an electorate consisting only of the most strongly motivated voters and "the ideologically zealous."[1]

Senior citizens are a case in point. It is not surprising that they often succeed in getting Congress to pass legislation in their favor. Two-thirds of those aged sixty-five and older vote, whereas only one-third of those between the ages of eighteen and twenty-five go to the polls on election day. Young constituents may complain loudly about too many government benefits going to older Americans, but unless younger groups start voting in greater numbers, politicians will continue to be more responsive to the special interests of senior citizens.

Voter apathy is the enemy of representative democracy. As long as it persists, government policy will continue to steer benefits to the more vocal, better organized, and wealthier groups in our society at the expense of other deserving groups. Moreover, because those who vote tend to have stronger partisan attachments than those who do not, the result will be a polarized Congress. Certainly, the voting in the House of Representatives on whether President Clinton should be impeached was strongly partisan. According to Gans and others, this suggests that the House members were listening more closely to the wishes of their voting constituents than to the opinion polls indicating that a significant majority of Americans did not want the president to be impeached.[2]

Voter Apathy Is Not a Significant Problem

Other Americans, including some political scientists, are not convinced that a decrease in voter turnout is cause for worry. Indeed, this group argues that low voter turnouts essentially mean that things are going all right and there is no need to go to the polls to "change things." Also, this group points out that low voter turnout has little to do with lack of faith in government, as is often alleged. A recent League of Women Voters survey[3] showed that voters and nonvoters have nearly identical levels of mistrust in government. Thus, distrust in government is not a factor in nonvoting.

Factors that do play an important role in voter turnout, according to this

same survey, are the ability of the voters to relate the consequences of elections and voting to their personal lives, such as their jobs and personal security; voters' fears that they do not have access to accurate and unbiased information on the candidates; and whether potential voters had been contacted by people in get-out-the-vote drives. What is needed, this survey suggests, is more emphasis on voter education and more effective attempts to communicate with the voters prior to elections.

Those who do not seem to worry about voter apathy make another point. Voting is voluntary. Whatever Americans choose to do is, by definition, acceptable because they are exercising their right to do as they wish. Is that not the essence of a democracy? Would it not be antithetical to our democratic principles to coerce people to vote and perform their "civic duties"?

Where Do You Stand?

1. In 1876, 82.4 percent of adult men voted. In modern times, the highest voter participation rate was in 1960, when 62.8 percent of voting-age Americans went to the polls. Do these statistics mean that we were a more democratic society in 1876, somewhat less so in 1960, and much less so today?

2. Do you think that the extensive media coverage given to the low voter turnout in the 1996 elections may, in itself, contribute to even lower voter turnouts in future presidential elections?

On the Web

You can find more information on voter turnout, as well as on a number of other issues, at **www.policy.com**.

Introduction

PUBLIC OPINION ● The individual attitudes or beliefs about politics, public issues, and public policies that are shared by a significant portion of adults; a complex collection of opinions held by many people on issues in the public arena.

POLITICAL SOCIALIZATION ● A learning process through which most people acquire their political attitudes, opinions, beliefs, and knowledge.

AGENTS OF POLITICAL SOCIALIZATION ● People and institutions that influence the political views of others.

INFOTRAC®

Americans' political apathy

Many Americans are naturally concerned about the dwindling number of citizens who have turned out to vote during recent elections. After all, if people do not vote, how can their opinions affect public policy? In a democracy, at a minimum the public must form opinions and openly express them to their elected public officials. Only when the opinions of Americans are communicated effectively to elected representatives can those opinions form the basis of government action. As President Franklin D. Roosevelt once said, "A government can be no better than the public opinion that sustains it."

What exactly is "public opinion"? How do we form our opinions on political issues? How can public opinion be measured accurately? What factors affect voter participation? Researchers and scholars have addressed these questions time and again. They are important questions because the backbone of our democracy has always been civic participation—taking part in the political life of the country.

What Is Public Opinion?

People hold opinions—sometimes very strong ones—about a variety of issues, ranging from the ethics of capital punishment to the latest trends in fashion. In this chapter, however, we are concerned with only a portion of those opinions. For our purposes here, we define **public opinion** as the individual attitudes or beliefs about politics, public issues, and public policies that are shared by a significant portion of adults. Public opinion is the sum total of a complex collection of opinions held by many people on issues in the public arena, such as taxes, health care, Social Security, clean-air legislation, unemployment, and so on.

When you hear a news report or read a magazine article stating that "a significant number of Americans" feel a certain way about an issue, you are probably hearing that a particular opinion is held by a large enough number of people to make government officials turn their heads and listen. For example, in the 1990s, as public opinion surveys began showing that Americans were concerned about environmental problems, many politicians began taking strong public stances on environmental issues.

How Do People Form Political Opinions?

When asked, most Americans are willing to express an opinion on political issues. Not one of us, however, was born with such opinions. Most people acquire their political attitudes, opinions, beliefs, and knowledge through a learning process called **political socialization.** This complex process begins early in a person's childhood and continues throughout that person's life.

Most political socialization is informal, and it usually begins during early childhood, when the dominant influence on a child is the family. Although parents normally do not sit down and say to their children, "Let us explain to you the virtues of becoming a Democrat," their children nevertheless come to know the parents' feelings, beliefs, and attitudes. Words such as *acquire, absorb,* and *pick up* perhaps best describe the informal process of political socialization.

The strong early influence of the family later gives way to the multiple influences of school, peers, television, co-workers, and other groups. People and institutions that influence the political views of others are called **agents of political socialization.**

Political socialization starts at a very young age, usually within the family unit. Children also learn about politics and government through such school activities as reciting the Pledge of Allegiance and displaying the American flag.

THE IMPORTANCE OF FAMILY

Most parents or guardians do not deliberately set out to form their children's political ideas and beliefs. They are usually more concerned with the moral, religious, and ethical values of their offspring. Yet a child first sees the political world through the eyes of his or her family, which is perhaps the most important force in political socialization. Children do not "learn" political attitudes the same way they learn to master in-line skating. Rather, they learn by hearing their parents' everyday conversations and stories about politicians and issues and by observing their parents' actions. They also learn from watching and listening to their siblings, as well as from the kinds of situations in which their parents place them.

The family's influence is strongest when children clearly perceive their parents' attitudes. For example, in one study, more high school students could identify their parents' political party affiliation than their parents' other attitudes or beliefs. In most situations, the political party of the parents becomes the political party of the children.

Students learn about the political process early on when they participate in class elections.

MEDIA ● Newspapers, magazines, television, radio, the Internet, and any other printed or electronic means of communication.

POLITICAL AGENDA ● The issues that politicians will address; often determined by the media.

THE SCHOOLS AND EDUCATIONAL ATTAINMENT

Education also strongly influences an individual's political attitudes. From their earliest days in school, children learn about the American political system. They say the Pledge of Allegiance and sing patriotic songs. They celebrate national holidays, such as Presidents' Day and Veterans Day, and learn about the history and symbols associated with them. In the upper grades, young people acquire more knowledge about government and democratic procedures through civics classes and through student government and various clubs. They also learn citizenship skills through school rules and regulations. Generally, those with more education have more knowledge about politics and policy than those with less education. The level of a person's education also influences his or her political values, as will be discussed later in this chapter.

THE MEDIA

The **media**—newspapers, magazines, television, radio, and the Internet— also have an impact on political socialization. The most influential of these media is, of course, television. Children in the elementary grades spend an average of thirty-two hours per week watching television—more time than they spend in academic classes. Television does not necessarily decrease the level of information about politics. It is the leading source of political and public affairs information for most people.

The Agenda-Setting Function of the Media

The media can determine what issues, events, and personalities are in the public eye. When people hear the evening's top news stories, they usually assume automatically that these stories concern the most important issues facing the nation. In actuality, the media decide the relative importance of issues by publicizing some issues and ignoring others and by giving some stories high priority and others low priority. By helping to determine what people will talk and think about, the media set the **political agenda**—the issues that politicians will address. In other words, to borrow from Bernard Cohen's classic statement on the media and public opinion, the media may not be successful in telling people what to think, but they are "stunningly successful in telling their audience what to think about."[4]

For example, television played a significant role in shaping public opinion about the Vietnam War (1964–1975), which has been called the first "television war." Part of the public opposition to the war in the late 1960s

The media often help set the political agenda, but much of that agenda can be managed by astute politicians. Here, photographers attempt to cover the movements of President Bill Clinton.

PEER GROUP ● Associates, often those close in age to oneself; may include friends, classmates, co-workers, club members, or church group members. Peer group influence is a significant factor in the political socialization process.

came about as a result of the daily portrayal of the war's horrors on TV news programs. Film footage and narrative accounts of the destruction, death, and suffering in Vietnam brought the war into living rooms across the United States. The war to free Kuwait from Iraqi occupation in 1991 also received extensive media coverage, although some critics feel that this coverage may have shown only the better side of the United States' efforts.

How Extensive Is the Media's Influence?

Clearly, the media play an important role in shaping public opinion. The *extent* of that role, however, is often debated. Some contend that the media's influence is increasing to the point where the media are as influential as the family in shaping public opinion, particularly among high school students. For example, in her analysis of the media's role in American politics, media scholar Doris A. Graber points out that high school students, when asked where they obtain the information on which they base their attitudes, mention the mass media far more than their families, friends, and teachers.[5]

Other studies have shown that the media's influence on people's opinions may not be so great as was once thought. Generally, people watch television and read articles with preconceived ideas about the issues. These preconceived ideas act as a kind of perceptual screen that blocks out information that is not consistent with those ideas. For example, if you are already firmly convinced that daily meditation is beneficial for your health, you probably will not change your mind if you watch a TV show that asserts that those who meditate live no longer on average than people who do not. (Apparently, many people refuse to alter their opinions on issues even in the face of contrary statistical evidence. For an example of this phenomenon, see the feature entitled *Perception versus Reality: Those Pesky Numbers about the State of America.*)

Generally, the media tend to wield the most influence over the views of persons who have not yet formed opinions about certain issues or political candidates. (See Chapter 11 for a more detailed discussion of the media's role in American politics.)

OPINION LEADERS

Every state or community has well-known citizens who are able to influence the opinions of their fellow citizens. These people may be public officials, religious leaders, teachers, or celebrities. They are the people to whom others listen and from whom others draw ideas and convictions about various issues of public concern. These opinion leaders play a significant role in the formation of public opinion. Martin Luther King, Jr. (1929–1968), for example, was a powerful opinion leader during the civil rights movement.

More recently, Jesse Jackson has been a widely respected leader on the issue of human rights. Other opinion leaders include well-known talk-show hosts and media personalities, such as Oprah Winfrey. Winfrey's statements on various issues influence a broad spectrum of TV viewers. Certainly, her status as an opinion leader was recognized by cattle ranchers when she said on one of her shows that the fear of "mad cow" disease "stopped her cold from eating a hamburger." (A group of Texas cattle ranchers immediately sued her for defaming their product, beef, but the court held that the ranchers failed to make their case.)

PEER GROUPS

Once children enter school, the views of friends begin to influence their attitudes and beliefs. From junior high school on, the **peer group**—friends, classmates, co-workers, club members, or church group members—becomes a significant factor in the political socialization process. Most of this socialization occurs when the peer group is actively involved in political activities. For example, your political beliefs might be influ-

Oprah Winfrey greets the press following the court ruling in her favor in the defamation lawsuit brought against her by a group of Texas cattle ranchers. Because of her status as an opinion leader, the ranchers feared that a comment Winfrey made on one of her talk shows (specifically her statement that the fear of "mad cow" disease "stopped her cold from eating a hamburger") would be detrimental to the reputation and sale of their product—beef.

perception **versus** reality

Those Pesky Numbers about the State of America

Americans are constantly bombarded by statistics about the United States. In particular, they cannot help reading, seeing, or hearing about changes in the unemployment rate, the rate of inflation, the stock market, and crime. Do these data influence Americans' perception of the world around them? The answer turns out to be "not really." This disregard for statistics is not because Americans cannot do the arithmetic. The *Washington Post* gave a math quiz to selected Americans and found out that in general they understood concepts related to percentages, changes in percentages, and the like.[6]

The Perception

An extensive poll conducted before the 1996 elections by the Kaiser Family Foundation, Harvard University, and the *Washington Post* found that Americans had the following views on the economy:[7]

- *Unemployment.* According to the poll's respondents, 21 percent of American adults were unemployed and looking for work; 51 percent thought that the unemployment rate was the same as or higher than it had been five years earlier. (One in four respondents thought that the number of unemployed topped 25 percent, the rate of unemployment during the Great Depression.)
- *The federal budget deficit.* According to 70 percent of the poll's respondents, the federal budget deficit was larger in 1996 than it had been five years earlier; 17 percent of those polled said that it was the same.
- *Inflation.* On average, those polled thought that the rate of inflation was 13.5 percent; 80 percent said that it was the same as or higher than it had been five years earlier.

The Reality

The reality was starkly different from the perceived state of the American economy. At the time the poll was taken, unemployment had dropped dramatically during the previous five years and was only about 5.5 percent. The annual federal budget deficit had fallen from almost $300 billion to a little above $100 billion (it has since disappeared). The rate of inflation had dropped from around 6 percent per year to a little less than 3 percent per year.

You Be the Judge

Many of those polled, when told the real statistics, simply responded that they did not believe them. What are the implications of this phenomenon for policy formulation in the United States?

enced by a peer group with which you are working on a common political cause, such as preventing the clear-cutting of old-growth forests or saving an endangered species. Your political beliefs probably would not be as strongly influenced by peers with whom you ski regularly or listen to jazz.

Some Americans worry that peer influence, particularly at the high school level, may be a negative agent in the political socialization process because of the increasing hostility among teens to traditional American values and political culture. For example, a recent poll indicates that 35 percent of teens believe that they are under a "great deal" or "some" pressure from their peers to "break the rules." Additionally, 48 percent of teens say they "like to live dangerously"; 48 percent say they like to "shock people"; and 54 percent say that one usually cannot trust people who are in power.[8]

Polls also indicate that a significant number of high school students blame peer influence for the "bad things" that are happening in America, such as school killings. In a survey taken of views on the Littleton, Colorado, high school killings, for example, about 40 percent of the teenaged respondents placed the blame on peer influence, and only 4 percent thought that parents or family were responsible for the violence. (Interestingly, 45 percent of the adults surveyed in the same poll felt that the responsibility for the shootings lay with the parents and family, and none of the parents considered peer influence to be a cause.[9])

PUBLIC OPINION POLL ● A numerical survey of the public's opinion on a particular topic at a particular moment.

SAMPLE ● In the context of opinion polling, a group of people selected to represent the population being studied.

STRAW POLL ● A nonscientific poll; a poll in which there is no way to ensure that the opinions expressed are representative of the larger population.

ECONOMIC STATUS AND OCCUPATION

A person's economic status may influence her or his political views. For example, poorer people are more likely to favor government assistance programs than wealthier people are. On an issue such as abortion, lower-income people are likely to be more conservative—that is, to be against abortion—than are higher-income groups (of course, there are many exceptions). In general, people in lower economic classes tend to identify with and vote for the Democratic Party.

Where a person works will also affect her or his opinion. Individuals who spend a great deal of time working together tend to be influenced by their co-workers. For example, labor union members working together for a company will tend to have similar political opinions, at least on the issue of government involvement in labor. Individuals working for a nonprofit agency that depends on government funds will tend to support government spending in that area. Business managers are more likely to favor tax shelters and aid to businesses than are people who work in factories. People who work in factories are more likely to favor a government-sponsored, nationwide health-care program than are business executives.

Measuring Public Opinion

If public opinion is to affect public policy, then public officials must be made aware of it. They must know which issues are of current concern to Americans and how strongly people feel about those issues. They must also know when public opinion changes. Of course, public officials most commonly learn about public opinion through election results, personal contacts, interest groups, and media reports. The only *relatively* precise way to measure public opinion, however, is through the use of public opinion polls.

A **public opinion poll** is a numerical survey of the public's opinion on a particular topic at a particular moment. The results of opinion polls are most often cast in terms of percentages: 62 percent feel this way, 27 percent do not, and 11 percent have no opinion. Of course, a poll cannot survey the entire U.S. population. Therefore, public opinion pollsters have devised scientific polling techniques for measuring public opinion through the use of **samples**—groups of people who are typical of the general population.

EARLY POLLING EFFORTS

During the 1800s, one way to spice up a magazine or newspaper article was by conducting a **straw poll,** or mail survey, of readers' opinions. Straw polls try to read the public's collective mind by simply asking a large number of people the same question. Straw polls are still used today. For example, some newspapers have interviewers who ask adults in shopping centers and other central locations to "cast ballots" on certain issues. Also, many newspapers and magazines still run "mail-in" polls. Increasingly, though, this type of polling makes use of telephone technology and "900" telephone numbers.

The major problem with straw polls is that there is no way to ensure that the opinions expressed are representative of the larger population. Indeed, as a general rule, such opinions usually represent only a small portion of the population. Opinions gathered on a particular issue at a yacht club, for example, might differ significantly from opinions on the same issue gathered at a thrift store. Similarly, a survey of readers of the *Wall Street Journal* will likely have different results than a survey of readers of the *Reader's Digest*.

The most famous of all straw-polling errors was committed by the *Literary Digest* in 1936. The magazine sent out millions of postcard ballots

INFOTRAC®
Polling pitfalls

BIASED SAMPLE ● A poll sample that does not accurately represent the population.

RANDOM SAMPLE ● In the context of opinion polling, a sample in which each person within the entire population being polled has an equal chance of being chosen.

for the purpose of predicting the presidential election outcome. The *Digest* predicted that Alfred Landon would easily defeat incumbent Franklin D. Roosevelt. Instead, Roosevelt won by a landslide.

Why was the magazine's prediction so erroneous? The answer is that the *Digest* had drawn a **biased sample**, one that did not accurately represent the population. Its editors had sent mail-in cards to citizens whose names appeared in telephone directories, to its own subscribers, and to automobile owners—in all, to a staggering 2,376,000 people. In the mid-Depression year of 1936, however, people who owned a car or a telephone or who subscribed to the *Digest* were certainly not representative of the majority of Americans. The vast majority of Americans were on the opposite end of the socioeconomic ladder. Despite the enormous number of people surveyed, the sample was unrepresentative and consequently inaccurate.

Several newcomers to the public opinion poll industry, however, did predict Roosevelt's landslide victory. These organizations are still at the forefront of the polling industry today: the Gallup poll, started by George Gallup; and Roper Associates, founded by Elmo Roper and now known as the Roper Center.

SAMPLING

How can interviewing a small sample of between 1,500 and 2,000 voters possibly indicate what *millions* of voters think? Clearly, to be representative of all the voters in the population, a sample must consist of a group of people who are *typical* of the general population. If the sample is properly selected, the opinions of those in the sample will be representative of the opinions held by the population as a whole. If the sample is not properly chosen, then the results of the poll may not reflect the ideas of the general population.

The most important principle in sampling is randomness. A **random sample** means that each person within the entire population being polled has an equal chance of being chosen. For example, if a poll is trying to measure how women feel about an issue, the sample should include respondents from all groups within the female population in proportion to their percentage of the entire population. If the sample is properly drawn, all segments of the relevant population will be included among the

Polling has become commonplace throughout America. More and more Americans are getting used to being asked by pollsters their opinions on a variety of subjects, such as who they plan to vote for and how they feel about the state of the economy. There is even a "poll on polls," in which respondents are asked to indicate how they feel about polls.

SAMPLING ERROR ● In the context of opinion polling, the difference between what the sample results show and what the true results would have been had everybody in the relevant population been interviewed.

respondents. A properly drawn random sample, for example, would include appropriate numbers of women in terms of age, racial and ethnic characteristics, occupation, and so on.

Polls can be remarkably accurate when they are conducted properly. In the last twelve presidential elections, Gallup polls conducted early in September predicted the eventual winners in ten out of the twelve races. Even polls several months in advance of elections have been able to predict the eventual winner quite well. Not surprisingly, politicians, the news media, and the public traditionally have placed a great deal of faith in the accuracy of poll results. Policymakers use polls to determine how the majority of Americans stand on given issues. Supporters of polling argue that it is a tool for democracy. In contrast, critics of polling think that the widespread use of opinion polls makes politicians reactors rather than leaders. Others argue that polls can discourage voters from voting if the numbers predict that their candidates will lose.

PROBLEMS WITH POLLS

The methods used by public opinion pollsters have improved dramatically since the days of the *Literary Digest,* but they are not entirely without limitations or faults. One problem with polls is that how a question is phrased can significantly affect how people answer the question. For example, consider a question about whether high-speed hookups to the Internet should be added to the school library's computer center. One way to survey opinions on this issue is simply to ask, "Do you believe that the school district should provide high-speed hookups to the Internet?" Another way to ask the same question is, "Are you willing to pay higher property taxes so that the school district can have high-speed hookups to the Internet?" Undoubtedly, the poll results will differ depending on how the question is phrased.

Another criticism of polls is that they often reduce complex issues to questions that call for simple "yes" or "no" answers. For example, a survey question might ask respondents whether they favor giving aid to foreign countries. A respondent's opinion on the issue might vary, depending on the recipient country or the purpose and type of the aid. The poll would nonetheless force the respondent to give a "yes" or "no" answer that does not necessarily reflect his or her true opinion. Quite simply, opinion polls can be biased and must be interpreted with care.

Public opinion polls can also be misused. Instead of measuring public opinion, they can end up creating it. For example, to gain popularity, a candidate might claim that all the polls show that he is ahead in the race. People who want to support the winning candidate (rather than the candidate of their choice) may support this candidate despite their true feelings. The media also sometimes misuse polls. Many journalists take the easy route during campaigns and base their political coverage almost exclusively on poll findings, with no mention of any evidence of gross errors.

Some people also question the reliability of opinion polls. After all, drawing accurate random samples is a difficult process. Additionally, the answers given to pollsters may not be reliable. Those interviewed may be influenced by the interviewer's personality or tone of voice. They may answer without having any information on the issue, or they may give the answer that they think will please the interviewer. Additionally, any opinion poll contains a **sampling error,** which is the difference between what the sample results show and what the true results would have been had everybody in the relevant population been interviewed. Another problem with opinion polls of voter preferences is that such polls cannot reflect rapid shifts in public opinion unless they are taken frequently.

OPINION POLLS AND THE 1998 ELECTIONS

Perhaps the greatest surprise of the 1998 elections was how well the Democrats fared, relative to expectations. Since 1934, the party of the president had lost seats in Congress as a result of midterm elections. During the months prior to the 1998 elections, polling organizations predicted that this trend would continue. Only in the last few days before the elections did the polls suggest that the Democrats were faring better than the polls had earlier predicted.

The Democrats' success in reversing the historical trend in midterm elections in 1998 was attributed to their willingness to listen to the polls and act accordingly. Relying on preelection polls indicating that African Americans were among the president's strongest supporters, the Democrats turned their efforts to increasing African American turnout on election day. Polls also indicated that Americans were tired of hearing about the Clinton-Lewinsky affair and did not think that Congress should impeach the president. The Democrats therefore concentrated on issues, such as education, during their campaigns. The Republicans, in contrast, focused on President Clinton's behavior and impeachment proceedings. Election commentators believed that the Republican Party's last-minute ads evoking the Lewinsky affair hindered, rather than helped, Republicans' chances at the polls.

Factors Affecting Voter Turnout

The factors that affect public opinion also affect voter turnout and behavior. Of course, a major factor affecting voting behavior in the past was the fact that many groups of Americans were simply not entitled to vote in elections. Legal restraints on the right to vote are now largely a thing of the past for all citizens over the age of eighteen, yet certain requirements must still be met before a person can vote.

WHO CAN VOTE?

In the United States today, all citizens who are at least eighteen years of age have the right to vote. This was not always true, however. Recall from Chapter 5 that restrictions on suffrage, the legal right to vote, have existed since the founding of our nation. Expanding the right to vote has been an important part of the gradual democratization of the American electoral process. Table 9–1 on the next page summarizes the major amendments, Supreme Court decisions, and laws that extended the right to vote to various American groups.

Historical Restrictions on Voting

Those who drafted the Constitution left the power to set suffrage qualifications to the individual states. Most states limited suffrage to adult white males who owned property. There were also voting restrictions based on religious beliefs and payment of taxes. The logic behind restricting voting rights to property owners was seriously questioned by Thomas Paine in his pamphlet *Common Sense:*

> Here is a man who today owns a jackass, and the jackass is worth $60. Today the man is a voter and goes to the polls and deposits his vote. Tomorrow the jackass dies. The next day the man comes to vote without his jackass and cannot vote at all. Now tell me, which was the voter, the man or the jackass?[10]

By 1810, religious restrictions on the right to vote were abolished in all states. Next, with the growth of democratic sentiment and the expansion of the western frontier, property ownership and tax payment requirements gradually began to disappear. By 1850, all white males were allowed to vote. Restrictions based on race and gender continued, however. As you read in Chapter 5, women finally obtained the right to vote in 1920, with the ratification of the Nineteenth Amendment. The most recent extension of the franchise occurred in 1971 when the voting age was reduced to eighteen by the Twenty-sixth Amendment.

Here an African American does his part to "get out the vote" prior to an election. African Americans faced significant restrictions on voting until the 1950s and 1960s, when new laws and policies helped to end both formal and informal barriers to voting for this group. Today, although voter turnout among African Americans is increasing, they remain underrepresented at the polls.

Table 9-1

Extension of the Right to Vote

YEAR	ACTION	IMPACT
1870	Fifteenth Amendment	Discrimination based on race outlawed.
1920	Nineteenth Amendment	Discrimination based on gender outlawed.
1924	Congressional Act	All Native Americans given citizenship.
1944	*Smith v. Allwright*	Supreme Court prohibits white primary.
1957	Civil Rights Act of 1957	Justice Department can sue to protect voting rights in various states.
1960	Civil Rights Act of 1960	Courts authorized to appoint referees to assist voter registration procedures.
1961	Twenty-third Amendment	Residents of District of Columbia given right to vote for president and vice president.
1964	Twenty-fourth Amendment	Poll tax in national elections outlawed.
1965	Voting Rights Act of 1965	Literacy tests prohibited; federal voter registrars authorized in seven southern states.
1970	Voting Rights Act Amendments of 1970	Voting age for federal elections reduced to eighteen years; maximum thirty-day residency requirement for presidential elections; state literacy tests abolished.
1971	Twenty-sixth Amendment	Minimum voting age reduced to eighteen for all elections.
1975	Voting Rights Act Amendments of 1975	Federal voter registrars authorized in ten more states; bilingual ballots to be used in certain circumstances.
1982	Voting Rights Act Amendments of 1982	Extended provisions of Voting Rights Act amendments of 1970 and 1975; allows private parties to sue for violations.

Literacy Tests. The Fifteenth Amendment, added in 1870 five years after the Civil War had ended, guaranteed suffrage to African American males. Yet for most of the next century, African Americans were effectively denied the ability to exercise their voting rights. Groups of white southerners obstructed black Americans from voting through methods ranging from mob violence to economic restrictions. States sometimes required voters to pass **literacy tests** to ensure that voters could read and write and thus evaluate political information. Such tests sometimes required those who wished to register to vote to interpret complicated written passages. Most African Americans, many of whom had been denied an education, were functionally illiterate and so were not allowed to vote. These tests were not evenly applied to whites and African Americans, however, and many illiterate whites were allowed to vote.

Poll Taxes and Grandfather Clauses. The **poll tax,** a fee of several dollars, was another device used to prevent African Americans from voting. At the time, this tax was often a sizable portion of a working person's monthly income. It was a burden not only for most blacks but also for immigrants, small farmers, many working-class citizens, and many poor whites in general. Another popular restriction was the **grandfather clause,** which restricted the franchise to those whose grandfathers had voted. This practice gave rise to the current phrase that something has been "grandfathered" in.

The Voting Rights Act of 1965

The civil rights movement of the 1950s and 1960s and the consequent policy changes (see Chapter 5) helped to end both formal and informal barri-

---

LITERACY TEST ● A test given to voters to ensure that they could read and write and thus evaluate political information; a technique used in many southern states to restrict African American participation in elections.

POLL TAX ● A fee of several dollars that had to be paid in order to vote; a device used in some southern states to prevent African Americans from voting.

GRANDFATHER CLAUSE ● A clause in a state law that restricted the franchise to those whose grandfathers had voted; one of the techniques used in the South to prevent African Americans from exercising their right to vote.

Voting is a right, but not everyone exercises this right. These volunteers are trying to register citizens to vote in an upcoming election.

ers to African American suffrage. The Voting Rights Act of 1965 made it illegal to interfere with anyone's right to vote in any election held in this country, whether federal, state, or local. It suspended the use of literacy tests and sent federal voter registrars into states and counties where less than 50 percent of the people of voting age were registered. It also stipulated that no new election laws could go into effect without the approval of the U.S. Department of Justice.

The 1965 act was amended several times and now covers other minorities, including Hispanics, Asians, Native Americans,[11] and Native Alaskans. The act thus serves as a basic protection for minority voting rights. For example, states must provide bilingual ballots in counties where 5 percent or more of the population speaks a language other than English.

Voting in America is private and secret. Sometimes it is done electronically, sometimes it is done with mechanical voting machines, and sometimes it is done manually with a pen or pencil.

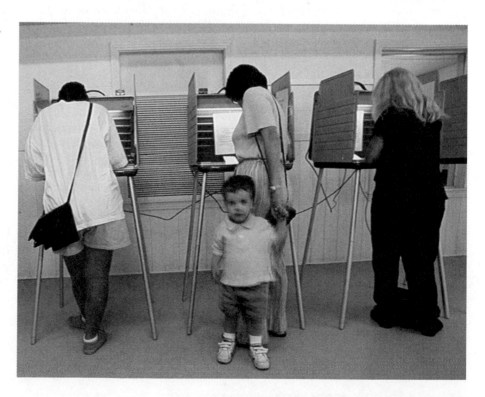

Current Requirements for Voting

Although today all citizens over the age of eighteen are entitled to vote, there are still some restrictions on this right. Every state except North Dakota requires voters to register with the appropriate state or local officials before voting. Generally, a person must register well in advance of an election, but in some states, people can register up to and on election day. Registration provides officials with lists of eligible voters and is intended to prevent fraudulent voting.

In the past, many states expected people to appear in person at an official building during normal working hours in order to register. In 1993, however, Congress passed the National Voter Registration Act (often referred to as the Motor Voter Law), which made registration easier. (See the feature entitled *The American Political Spectrum: The Motor Voter Law* for a discussion of this act.)

---

the american political spectrum

The Motor Voter Law

President Clinton signed the National Voter Registration Act into law in 1993. Also known as the Motor Voter Law, the act requires states to provide all eligible citizens with the opportunity of registering to vote when they apply for or renew a driver's license. The law also requires that states allow mail-in registration, with forms given out at certain public-assistance agencies. Since the law took effect on January 1, 1995, it has facilitated millions of registrations.

The law has been controversial, however. The battle lines were drawn prior to the bill's passage and are still there.

Most Republicans Are against the Act

Many Republicans fought the Motor Voter Law originally and are continuing to fight it. Their reasoning is that the majority of individuals who sign up will vote for Democratic candidates. In particular, they note that the law's requirement that states allow mail-in registration, with forms provided at certain public-assistance agencies, effectively is biased against Republicans. After all, those on public assistance typically vote for Democrats and for bigger government.

The main resistance to the law has come from Republican gover-

nors. For example, Pete Wilson of California refused to implement the law, arguing that it was unconstitutional and would cost the state $18 million. A federal judge ordered California state agencies to implement the law, which they did not do. Wilson also lost on appeal,[12] and the United States Supreme Court refused to hear the case. At the same time, six other states also tried to block the law.

Congressional Republicans have introduced bills in the House and the Senate to end the implementation of the Motor Voter Law until Congress antes up the money to pay for it. Political observers contend that, had Bob Dole won the 1996 election, he would have pushed Congress to repeal the law entirely.

Republicans (as well as some Democrats) now believe that states have done such a great job of attracting so many new voters that they have no way of confirming whether the new voter registrations are legitimate. Consequently, the Motor Voter Law may have led to increased voting fraud.

The Democrats Fought Long and Hard for Passage of the Law

When Clinton signed the Motor Voter Law, he said that "voting is an empty promise unless people vote." Democrats have realized that peo-

ple who do not register typically are disproportionately young and disproportionately poor. When they do vote, these groups vote more heavily for Democratic candidates. One of the purposes of the Motor Voter Law was to increase voter participation among these groups. As evidence of the law's benefits, the Democrats point out that between January 1, 1995, when the law went into effect, and the 1996 elections, new registrants were signed up at a rate of about 680,000 per month. Those in favor of the Motor Voter Law argue that its critics want to retain "screening devices" similar to the literacy tests and poll taxes that were used in the past.

Furthermore, some supporters of the act contend that the law appears to have helped the Republicans gain strength, so Republicans should not worry so much. Supporters also point out that studies have shown that, in general, increased voter registration has increased the number of independent voters.[13]

For Critical Analysis

Can you think of any reason why all voters in all states shouldn't be able to register to vote at the polling places on election day?

Residency requirements are also usually imposed for voting. In most states, a person must live within the state for a specified period of time in order to qualify to vote. The length of time a person must reside in a state or district varies widely from state to state, but since 1972 no state can impose a residency requirement of more than thirty days. Twenty-five states require that length of time, while the other twenty-five states require fewer or no days. Another voting requirement is citizenship. Aliens may not vote in any public election held anywhere in the United States. Most states also do not permit prison inmates, mentally ill people, convicted felons, and election-law violators to vote.

WHO ACTUALLY VOTES?

Just because an individual is eligible to vote does not necessarily mean that the person will actually go to the polls on election day and vote. Why do some eligible voters go to the polls while others do not? Although nobody can answer this question with absolute conviction, certain factors, including those discussed here, appear to affect voter turnout.

Educational Attainment, Income Level, and Age

Among the factors affecting voter turnout, education appears to be the most important. The more education a person has, the more likely it is that she or he will be a regular voter. People who graduated from high school vote more regularly than those who dropped out, and college graduates vote more often than high school graduates. Differences in income also lead to differences in voter turnout. Wealthier people tend to be overrepresented among regular voters.

Generally, older voters turn out to vote more regularly than younger voters do, although participation tends to decline among the most elderly. Participation likely increases with age because older people tend to be more settled, are already registered, and have had more experience with voting.

Minority Status

Racial and ethnic minorities traditionally have been underrepresented among the ranks of voters. In several recent elections, however, participation by these groups, particularly African Americans and Hispanics, has increased.

In the 1996 elections, the percentage of eligible African American male voters who turned out at the polls increased by 17 percent. African American male voting turnout jumped from 8.2 million in 1992 to 9.6 million in 1996. Political analysts have linked this increase in black male voter participation to the Million Man March organized by Black Muslim leader Louis Farrakhan in Washington, D.C., on October 16, 1995. Farrakhan told African American males who participated in the march that it was up to them to take more responsibility for their lives. One way to do this was by voting.[14]

Hispanics are also going to the polls in greater numbers. In the 1992 elections, 62 percent of registered Hispanic voters cast their votes at the polls; in 1996, voter turnout among registered Hispanics increased to 72 percent. The total number of Latino voters increased by more than 23 percent—from 4.24 million to 5.25 million—between 1992 and 1996. Of course, in absolute terms, the number of Hispanics in the United States has also increased. Between 1992 and 1996, the majority of newly naturalized citizens in the United States were of Hispanic origin.

Although voter participation by African Americans and Hispanics has increased, these groups remain underrepresented at the polls. For a discussion of the consequences of this in California, where ethnic minorities constitute a significant percentage of the population, see the feature entitled *Politics on the Far Side: Electoral Apartheid in California?* on page 226.

A voter casts her vote at the polling place. Generally, older Americans turn out to vote in far greater numbers than do younger Americans.

I N F O T R A C °

Republicans aim to drive down voter turnout

These are participants in the Million Man March in Washington, D.C., which took place on October 16, 1995. Actually, only around a half-million African American males showed up for the march, but this still represented well over 4 percent of the total group of African Americans over the age of eighteen. One of the messages from the march's organizer, the controversial Louis Farrakhan, was that African Americans should assume more responsibility for their lives and their communities. Many claim that the increased voter participation by African American males in the following year's elections resulted from the march and Farrakhan's messages.

Why People Vote as They Do

What prompts some citizens to vote Republican and others to vote Democratic? What persuades voters to choose certain kinds of candidates? Clearly, more is involved than measuring one's own position against the candidates' positions and then voting accordingly. Voters choose candidates for many reasons, some of which are explored here. These questions cannot be answered with absolute certainty, but because of the technology of opinion polling, researchers have collected more information on voting than on any other form of political participation in the United States. These data shed some light on why people decide to vote for particular candidates.

PARTY IDENTIFICATION

Many voters have a standing allegiance to a political party, or a party identification, although the proportion of the population that does so is shrinking. For established voters, party identification is one of the most prominent and lasting predictors of how a person will vote. Party identification is an emotional attachment to a party that is influenced by family, age, peer groups, and other factors that play a role in the political socialization process discussed earlier.

Increasingly, there are indications that party identification has lost some of its impact. As we saw in Chapter 8, split-ticket voting—voting for candidates of both parties in the same election—has increased. Also, a growing number of voters now call themselves independents. Despite this label, though, many independents actually do support one or the other of the two major parties quite regularly. Figure 9–1 shows how those who identified themselves as Democrats, Republicans, and independents voted in the most recent presidential elections.

politics on the far side

Electoral Apartheid in California?

In a study of Mexican politics and democracy,[15] Jorge Castañeda looked at voter turnout in California and drew some disturbing conclusions. Castañeda found that although Asian Americans represent 10 percent of the California population, they cast only 4 percent of the votes. Latinos, who constitute 26 percent of the population, cast only 10 percent of the votes.

Furthermore, foreigners are not allowed to vote, and 55 percent of that state's six million Latinos do not have citizenship. According to Castañeda, "only a minority participates in elections, and that minority is white, Anglo, middle or upper-middle class, and elderly."[16] In effect, concludes Castañeda, a small, privileged group of Californians that uses fewer and fewer of the social programs financed by state taxes, such as public education—is deciding policy for the state.[17]

For Critical Analysis: What factors might help to explain the relatively low Asian American and Latino voter turnout in California?

Figure 9–1
**Party Identification
and Voting Behavior in
the Last Presidential Election**

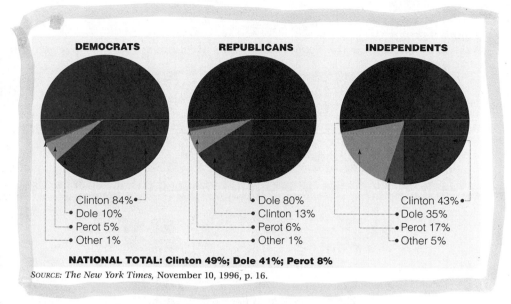

DEMOCRATS · REPUBLICANS · INDEPENDENTS

Clinton 84%
Dole 10%
Perot 5%
Other 1%

Dole 80%
Clinton 13%
Perot 6%
Other 1%

Clinton 43%
Dole 35%
Perot 17%
Other 5%

NATIONAL TOTAL: Clinton 49%; Dole 41%; Perot 8%

SOURCE: *The New York Times*, November 10, 1996, p. 16.

PERCEPTION OF THE CANDIDATES

Voters' choices also depend on their image of the candidates. Voters often base their decisions more on their *impression* of the candidates than on the candidates' *actual* qualifications.

To some extent, voter attitudes toward candidates are based on emotions rather than on any judgment about experience or policy. In 1996, voters' decisions were largely guided by their perceptions of which party they could trust to run the economy. Bob Dole tried to reduce the voters' trust in Democratic candidate Bill Clinton but failed to make an impact. Many contend that the increase in split-ticket voting and the voters' apparent comfort with divided government indicate that the voters generally do not trust either party to control government.

POLICY CHOICES

When people vote for candidates who share their positions on particular issues, they are engaging in policy voting. If a candidate for senator in your state opposes gun-control laws, for example, and you decide to vote for her for that reason, you have engaged in policy voting.

Historically, economic issues have had the strongest influence on voters' choices. When the economy is doing well, it is very difficult for a challenger, particularly at the presidential level, to defeat the incumbent. In contrast, when there is increasing inflation, rising unemployment, or high interest rates, the incumbent will likely be at a disadvantage. Studies of how economic conditions affect voting choices differ in their conclusions, however. Some studies indicate that people vote on the basis of their personal economic well-being, whereas other studies seem to show that people vote on the basis of the nation's overall economic health.

Some of the most heated debates in American political campaigns involve social issues, such as abortion, gay and lesbian rights, the death penalty, and religion in the schools. In general, presidential candidates prefer to avoid taking a definite stand on these types of issues, because voters who have strong opinions about such issues are likely to be offended if a candidate does not share their views.

SOCIOECONOMIC FACTORS

Some of the factors that influence how people vote can be classified as socioeconomic factors. These factors include a person's educational attainment, income level, age, gender, religion, and geographic location. Some of these factors have to do with the families and circumstances into which individuals are born; others have to do with choices made later in life. Figure 9–2 on the next page indicates how various groups voted in the 1996 presidential elections.

Figure 9–2

Voting by Groups in the 1996 Presidential Elections

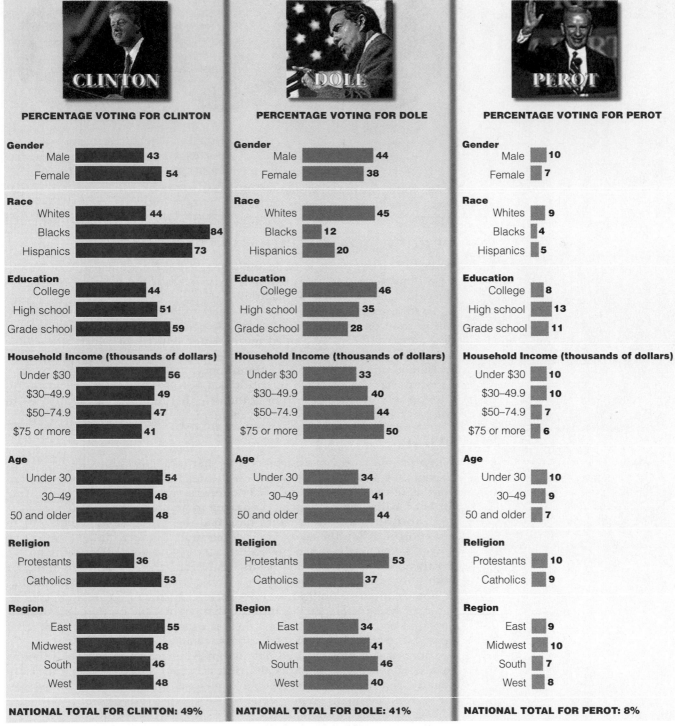

PERCENTAGE VOTING FOR CLINTON

Gender
- Male — 43
- Female — 54

Race
- Whites — 44
- Blacks — 84
- Hispanics — 73

Education
- College — 44
- High school — 51
- Grade school — 59

Household Income (thousands of dollars)
- Under $30 — 56
- $30–49.9 — 49
- $50–74.9 — 47
- $75 or more — 41

Age
- Under 30 — 54
- 30–49 — 48
- 50 and older — 48

Religion
- Protestants — 36
- Catholics — 53

Region
- East — 55
- Midwest — 48
- South — 46
- West — 48

NATIONAL TOTAL FOR CLINTON: 49%

PERCENTAGE VOTING FOR DOLE

Gender
- Male — 44
- Female — 38

Race
- Whites — 45
- Blacks — 12
- Hispanics — 20

Education
- College — 46
- High school — 35
- Grade school — 28

Household Income (thousands of dollars)
- Under $30 — 33
- $30–49.9 — 40
- $50–74.9 — 44
- $75 or more — 50

Age
- Under 30 — 34
- 30–49 — 41
- 50 and older — 44

Religion
- Protestants — 53
- Catholics — 37

Region
- East — 34
- Midwest — 41
- South — 46
- West — 40

NATIONAL TOTAL FOR DOLE: 41%

PERCENTAGE VOTING FOR PEROT

Gender
- Male — 10
- Female — 7

Race
- Whites — 9
- Blacks — 4
- Hispanics — 5

Education
- College — 8
- High school — 13
- Grade school — 11

Household Income (thousands of dollars)
- Under $30 — 10
- $30–49.9 — 10
- $50–74.9 — 7
- $75 or more — 6

Age
- Under 30 — 10
- 30–49 — 9
- 50 and older — 7

Religion
- Protestants — 10
- Catholics — 9

Region
- East — 9
- Midwest — 10
- South — 7
- West — 8

NATIONAL TOTAL FOR PEROT: 8%

SOURCES: *The New York Times,* November 10, 1996, p. 16; *The Washington Post,* National Weekly Edition, November 11–17, 1996, p. 11.

Educational Attainment

As a general rule, people with more education are more likely to vote Republican. Typically, those with less education are more inclined to vote for the Democratic nominee.

GENDER GAP • A term used to describe the difference between the percentage of votes cast for a particular candidate by women and the percentage of votes cast for the same candidate by men.

Occupation and Income Level

Professionals and businesspersons tend to vote Republican. Manual laborers, factory workers, and especially union members are more likely to vote Democratic. The higher the income, the more likely it is that a person will vote Republican. Conversely, a much larger percentage of low-income individuals vote Democratic. But there are no hard and fast rules. Some very poor individuals are devoted Republicans, just as some extremely wealthy persons are supporters of the Democratic Party.

Age

Although one might think that a person's chronological age would determine political preferences, apparently age does not matter very much. Some differences can be identified, however: young adults tend to be more liberal than older Americans on most issues, and young adults tend to hold more progressive views than older persons on such issues as racial and gender equality.

Although older Americans tend to be somewhat more conservative than younger groups, their greater conservatism may be explained simply by the fact that individuals maintain the values they learn when they first became politically aware. Forty years later, those values may be considered relatively conservative. Additionally, people's attitudes are sometimes shaped by the events that unfolded as they grew up. Individuals who grew up during an era of Democratic Party dominance will likely remain Democrats throughout their lives. The same will hold true for those who grew up during an era of Republican Party dominance.

In elections from 1952 through 1980, voters under the age of thirty clearly favored the Democratic presidential candidates. This trend reversed itself in 1984 when voters under thirty voted heavily for Ronald Reagan. George Bush maintained that support in 1988. In 1992, however, Bill Clinton won back the young voters by 10 percentage points, a margin that expanded to 20 percentage points in 1996.

Gender

Until relatively recently, there seemed to be no fixed pattern of voter preferences by gender in presidential elections. One year, more women than men would vote for the Democratic candidate; another year, more men than women would do so. Some political analysts believe that a **gender gap** became a major determinant of voter decision making in the 1980 presidential elections. In that year, Ronald Reagan outdrew Jimmy Carter by 16 percentage points among male voters, whereas women gave about an equal number of votes to each candidate. Although the gender gap has varied since 1980, it reappeared in force in 1996, when President Clinton received 54 percent of women's votes and only 43 percent of men's votes.

The gender gap in the 1996 elections was clearly evident among working women, with 57 percent of that group voting for Clinton and 34 percent voting for Dole. The gender gap was even wider among single and divorced women, who gave Clinton 60 percent of their votes and Dole, 28 percent. In contrast, the votes of married women were split more or less evenly between the two candidates.[18]

What is happening here? For one thing, divorced women are concerned about having the government provide a social safety net. About one-third of all divorced women spend some time on welfare. Additionally, of the twenty-four million Americans who work for the government or for nonprofit institutions, more than fourteen million are

Different groups of Americans often have dissimilar traditions, interests, and goals, and these differences are reflected in their voting choices. While generalizations often fail to reflect the complexity of our society, we have seen that African Americans have voted principally for Democrats. As another example, in recent elections a larger percentage of women voted for Democrats than for Republicans.

women. These women tend to vote more often for Democrats than Republicans.

Religion and Ethnic Background

Traditionally, the majority of Protestants have voted Republican, while Catholics and Jews have tended to be Democrats. Voters of Italian, Irish, Polish, Eastern European, and Slavic descent have generally supported Democrats, while those of British, Scandinavian, and French descent have voted Republican.

African Americans vote principally for Democrats. They have given the Democratic presidential candidate a clear majority of their votes in every election since 1952, although this majority began to weaken in the 1980s. Democratic presidential candidates have received, on average, more than 80 percent of the African American vote since 1956.

Geographic Region

Where a voter lives also influences his or her preferences. For more than one hundred years after the Civil War, most southerners, regardless of background or socioeconomic status, were Democrats. In large part, this is because the Republicans were in power when the Civil War broke out, and many southerners thus blamed the Republicans for that conflict and its results for the South. Known as the **Solid South,** this strong coalition has recently crumbled in the presidential elections, although the rural vote in the South still tends to be Democratic.

Although the Solid South is no more, it appears that something like a Solid Northeast may be emerging, with a strong Democratic majority.[19] Republicans continue draw much of their strength from the western states. Except for the elections in 1964, 1992, and 1996, the Republicans have held the edge in western states in every presidential election since 1956.

SOLID SOUTH ● A term used to describe the tendency of the southern states to vote Democratic after the Civil War.

PUSH POLL ● A poll intended to push the voter to the candidate whose campaign sponsored the poll.

Americans at Odds over Public Opinion and Voting

In the last several decades, public opinion polls have become part of the American political landscape. In 1996, for example, from September 1 through November 4, almost three hundred national pre-election polls asked the question, "How would you vote if the presidential election were being held today?" In 1992, only half that number of polls were conducted to learn how voters would answer this question. In 1968, there were only ten such polls. This plethora of polls and the percentages they contain may be one of the reasons why many Americans do not give much credence to statistics in general (as discussed earlier in this chapter in the *Perception versus Reality* feature). Americans seem to be at odds not only over polling techniques and poll results but also about the meaning and causes of low voter turnout.

Problems with Polls—Revisited

There are many problems with public opinion polls, as discussed earlier in this chapter. Pollsters have long known that the wording of questions can influence the response that a person gives. In recent years, a far more deliberate misuse of question wording has surfaced in election campaigns. In early 1996, for example, voters were interviewed in what seemed to be legitimate polls. One or more of the questions in these polls, however, gave the respondents false or misleading information about the opposing candidates in an effort to influence the respondents' votes. Such surveys became known as **push polls,** because they were intended to push the voter to the candidate whose campaign sponsored the poll.

ARE AMERICANS LOSING CONFIDENCE IN POLLS?

Some scholars speculate that Americans are losing confidence in polls because poll samples are becoming smaller, thus calling the polls' reliability into question. The Survey Research Center at the University of Michigan often tells its graduate school students that a good national survey should have between 1,200 and 1,500 respondents. In addition, the questions should be carefully worded. There should be systematic callbacks to reach people who were not at home when the initial calls were made. Finally, careful mechanisms should be used to ensure that the samples were reliably representative of the population.

Today, we regularly read about survey results in which the samples consisted of only five or six hundred—or even fewer—potential voters. Many of these surveys are done by phone because telephone polls are less expensive than surveys involving face-to-face interviewing. Now there are even focus groups, which bring together twenty-five to thirty voters to talk with an interviewer. Although those who organize such groups do not intend them to be substitutes for broader opinion surveys, some journalists use the results from focus groups as if they were full-blown surveys, even giving percentages. It is not surprising that daily reports on the status of public opinion prior to elections mean less and less.

THE PUBLIC STILL BELIEVES IN POLLS, NONETHELESS

In spite of the growing criticism of polls, the majority of Americans still believe in them, according to the Gallup poll's annual poll on polls. In effect, this poll asks the public to give its opinion on polling and polling results. In 1975, the Gallup people asked an important question: "Would the nation be better off if leaders followed the views of the public?" In response to the question, 67 percent of those polled said yes. In 1996, the same question elicited a positive response from 80 percent of the respondents. Even when the question was changed to read "Would the nation be better off if leaders followed the views of public opinion polls?" almost 75 percent of the respondents said the country would be better off. That is to say, they want the nation's leaders to follow public opinion polls more closely.

Has Negative Campaigning Caused the Decline in Voter Turnout?

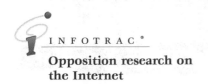

Opposition research on the Internet

The Motor Voter Law facilitated the registration of fifteen million new voters in 1995 and 1996. Additionally, one million immigrants became naturalized citizens in the twelve months prior to the 1996 elections. In view of these developments, why did fewer voters go to the polls in 1996 than in 1992? As you found out in this chapter's opening feature, voter turnout in the United States in 1996 was the lowest it has been since 1924 (when only 50.1 percent of eligible voters voted). Figure 9–3 shows what has happened since the 1960s.

What has caused the drop in the overall percentage of eligible voters who turn out on election day? Among other reasons that have been suggested for decreasing voter turnout is the effect on the voters of negative campaigning.

The barrage of negative ads, especially on TV, prior to the 1996 presidential elections may have simply turned voters off. Indeed, in 1996 the three presidential candidates—Bill Clinton, Bob Dole, and H. Ross Perot— had the highest negative voter ratings in history: Clinton, 45 percent; Dole, 55 percent; and Perot, 70 percent. Obviously, negative advertising worked. The idea behind negative advertising, of course, is to turn voters away from an opposing candidate (see Chapters 10 and 11). Instead, such advertising may have turned voters away from the process completely. If the candidates are all such nasty people, why vote for any of them?[20] (For a discussion of a new type of research spawned by negative campaigning, see the feature entitled *A Question of Ethics: Is It Ethical for Candidates to Use Opposition Researchers?*)

Figure 9–3
Voter Turnout since 1960

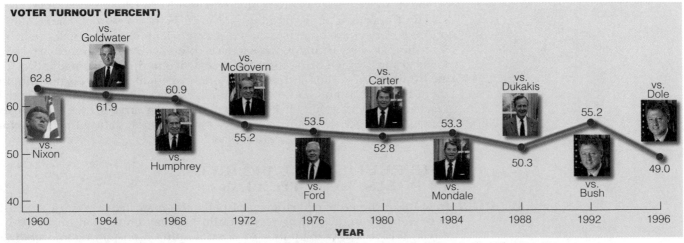

SOURCES: *Statistical Abstract of the United States*, various issues; and the Committee for the Study of the American Electorate.

a question of ethics

Is It Ethical for Candidates to Use Opposition Researchers?

A small but growing number of groups in the United States are engaged in one of the darker sides of politics—opposition research. The task of "oppo" is to dig up dirt on political rivals. Of course, no politician or candidate would ever condone such activity. Political candidates all publicly deplore "dishing dirt" on their opponents. Nonetheless, every serious politician, when running for office or reelection, has a seasoned oppo research team. Oppo pioneer Ken Khachician even claims that elections are "won in the library."

Actually, elections are probably won in the storerooms where public records are filed. Oppo researchers scour through these records to find out whether an opposing candidate has ever had a tax lien filed on his or her property. They seek to learn whether a candidate has ever failed to vote in a recent election. They look for embarrassing political events that occurred while an opposing candidate was in office. The best example was when George Bush's oppo team discovered that Bush's opponent in the 1988 presidential race, Michael Dukakis (who was then governor of Massachusetts), had supported a furlough program from state prisons. Willie Horton, an African American prisoner released under the program, committed murder and rape while on furlough.

Currently, more than sixty oppo firms are listed in *Campaigns & Elections* magazine. The editor of that magazine, Ron Faucheux, estimated that candidates spent up to $30 million on oppo research in the 1996 election cycle, compared to $10 million in 1992.

For Critical Analysis

Is it possible that truthful opposition research results can actually help voters make better choices? If so, would this result have a bearing on the question of whether opposition research is ethical?

key terms

agents of political
   socialization 213
biased sample 219
gender gap 229
grandfather clause 222
literacy test 222
media 215
peer group 216
political agenda 215
political socialization 213

poll tax 222
public opinion 213
public opinion poll 218
push poll 231
random sample 219
sample 218
sampling error 220
Solid South 230
straw poll 218

chapter summary

1. Public opinion is the sum total of the individual attitudes or beliefs about politics, public issues, and public policies shared by a significant portion of adults. The most common ways in which public officials learn about public opinion are through election results, personal contacts, interest groups, media reports, and public opinion polls.

2. Most people acquire their political views through a complex learning process called political socialization, which begins early in a person's childhood and continues throughout that person's life. The family is one of the most important influences in the political socialization process. Other important influences in shaping a person's political opinions include the schools and educational attainment, the media, opinion leaders, peer groups, and economic status and occupation.

3. A public opinion poll is a numerical survey of the public's opinion on a particular topic at a particular moment. The results of opinion polls are most often cast in terms of percentages. Because a poll cannot survey the entire U.S. population, public

opinion pollsters have devised scientific polling techniques for measuring public opinion through the use of samples—groups of people who are typical of the general population.

4. Early opinion polling efforts often were inaccurate because the samples were biased—they were not representative of the entire population. To achieve more accurate results, pollsters now use random samples, in which each person within the entire population being polled has an equal chance of being chosen.

5. There are many problems with polls for the following reasons: (1) how a question is worded can affect the poll's results; (2) polls often reduce complex issues to questions calling for "yes" or "no" answers; (3) polls are often misused by politicians and the press; (4) polls are not always reliable, because respondents' answers may be influenced by the interviewer's attitudes or conduct and because of sampling errors; and (5) polls cannot reflect rapid shifts in public opinion unless they are taken frequently.

6. In the early days of this nation, an important factor affecting voter turnout was, of course, the existence of numerous restrictions on voting. These restrictions were based on property, race, gender, religious beliefs, and payment of taxes. Over time, these restrictions were removed (refer back to Table 9–1). Women only achieved the right to vote (in 1920, with the ratification of the Nineteenth Amendment) after a long, historic struggle.

7. African Americans were effectively deprived of the ability to exercise their voting rights (given to them in 1870 by the Fifteenth Amendment) until the civil rights legislation of the 1960s. State requirements, including literacy tests and poll taxes, prevented a majority of black Americans from voting, while groups of white southerners used methods ranging from mob violence to economic restrictions to effectively keep African Americans from the polling places.

8. Currently, there are still some voting restrictions in the form of registration, residency, and citizenship requirements. Even those who meet these requirements do not always turn out at the polls, however. Although the reasons why some people vote and others do not cannot be known with certainty, indications are that voter turnout is affected by specific factors, including educational attainment, income level, age, and minority status.

9. Extensive research on voting behavior indicates that the following factors all influence voters' preferences: party identification, perception of the candidates, policy choices, and socioeconomic factors. The latter include educational attainment, occupation and income level, age, gender, religion and ethnic background, and geographic region.

10. Americans are at odds over certain issues concerning public opinion and voting. Some of these issues relate to polling techniques, such as "push polling," and inaccurate poll results. Although some argue that Americans are losing confidence in polls for these and other reasons, a recent Gallup poll on opinion polls revealed that the majority of Americans think that the leaders of this nation should follow public opinion polls more closely and that polls are "a good thing for the country." Other significant issues of concern to many Americans today include declining voter turnout and the effects of negative advertising on voter turnout.

for critical analysis

1. Who played the most significant role in shaping your views of politics and government? Why?

2. What is the most important political issue to you? Do major national candidates address this issue to your satisfaction?

3. In Australia, where voting is mandatory, voter turnout is very high. Should voting be made mandatory in the United States? Why or why not?

4. Should voters have to be able to read the ballot to be able to vote?

5. Should ballots be printed only in English? If not, in how many languages should ballots be printed for voters in areas such as Los Angeles, where over one hundred languages are spoken?

6. To what extent, if any, do your peers influence your political attitudes?

7. Which do you think is most important in determining how a person will vote—race, wealth, or gender?

suggested readings

Amato, Paul R., and Alan Booth. *A Generation at Risk: Growing Up in an Era of Family Upheaval.* Cambridge, Mass.: Harvard University Press, 1997. This book, by two leading sociologists, gives a clear, close-up picture of how the young Americans who have been dubbed "Generation X" have been affected by the changes that have taken place in American society over the past few decades.

Delli Carpini, Michael X., and Scott Keeter. *What Americans Know about Politics and Why It Matters.* New Haven, Conn.: Yale University Press, 1996. The authors conclude that the proportion of Americans who know a lot about politics has remained about the same over the past fifty years. They also conclude that whites, men, older Americans, and wealthier groups are more informed and more likely to participate in politics than blacks, women, young Americans, and those who are less well off financially.

Miller, Warren E., and J. Merrill Shanks. *The New American Voter.* Cambridge, Mass.: Harvard University Press, 1996. These political scientists analyze voting patterns from 1952 through the early 1990s. Among other things, they find that long-lasting cultural and ideological predispositions play a major role in determining voters' choices for president and that the personalities of presidential candidates and their positions on campaign issues tend to matter far less than is often claimed.

Mitchell, Michele. *A New Kind of Party Animal.* New York: Simon & Schuster, 1998. The author focuses on the importance of young people in American politics. Generally, her text counteracts the general impression that young people are not interested in politics.

Nye, Joseph S., *et al.* Eds. *Why People Don't Trust Government.* Cambridge, Mass.: Harvard University Press, 1997. For three decades, Americans' confidence in their government has been declining. This collection of essays by leading Harvard University scholars blames the news media for the public's increasing disaffection from the political process.

Sharp, Elaine B. *The Sometime Connection: Public Opinion and Social Policy.* Albany, N.Y.: State University of New York Press, 1999. This book focuses on public opinion on six policy topics: abortion, affirmative action, welfare, Social Security, corrections, and pornography. The book provides complete policy histories, information on trends in public opinion, and an analysis of the role that public opinion has played in the development of policy for each of the six topics discussed.

politics
on the web

Recent polls conducted and analyzed by the Roper Center for Public Opinion Research can be found at

http://www.ropercenter.uconn.edu

According to its home page, the mission of the National Election Studies (NES) "is to produce high-quality data on voting, public opinion, and political participation that serves the research needs of social scientists, teachers, students, and policymakers concerned with understanding the theoretical and empirical foundations of mass politics in a democratic society." The NES is a good source of information on public opinion. To reach this site, go to

http://www.umich.edu/~nes

At the Gallup organization's Web site, you can find the results of recent polls as well as an archive of past polls and information on how polls are conducted. Go to

www.gallup.com

You can find further links to poll data and other sources on public opinion at the following site:

www.publicagenda.org

using
web resources

The Pew Research Center for the People and the Press is an independent opinion research group that studies attitudes toward the press, politics, and public-policy issues. It is best known for regular national surveys that measure public attentiveness to major news stories and for polls that chart trends in values and fundamental political and social attitudes.

Access the center's Web site at

http://www.people-press.org/index.htm

1. Select "Recent Survey Reports" and review one of the entries. What does the survey information add to your knowledge of the topic?

2. Return to the main page and select the "News Interest Index." Scan the list of titles from top to bottom. In what kinds of news stories are Americans interested? Why do you think these are popular?

3. Return to the main page and select "Poll Analysis." Scroll down to "GOOD TIMES TRUMP CLINTON TROUBLES," dated November 4, 1998. What do the exit polls say about the 1998 elections?

notes

1. As cited in Owen Ullman, "Why Voter Apathy Will Make a Strong Showing," *Business Week,* November 4, 1996.

2. Jackie Calmes, "Why U.S. Congress Toes Party Lines," *The Wall Street Journal,* December 17, 1998, p. 14.

3. As reported in *U.S. News & World Report,* June 10, 1996, p. 11.

4. Bernard Cohen, *The Press and Foreign Policy* (Princeton, N.J.: Princeton University Press, 1963), p. 81.

5. See Doris A. Graber, *Mass Media and American Politics,* 5th ed. (Washington, D.C.: Congressional Quarterly Books, 1996).

6. Richard Morin, "You Figure It Out: The People Can Do the Arithmetic, but They Have a Hard Time Believing the Numbers," *The Washington Post,* National Weekly Edition, January 6, 1997, p. 38.

7. As reported in Richard Morin and John M. Berry, "Economic Anxieties: What Americans Don't Know Helps Explain Their Suspicious Mood," *The Washington Post,* National Weekly Edition, November 4–10, 1996, p. 6.

8. *The Gallup Report,* April 28, 1999.

9. *The Gallup Report,* May 21, 1999.

10. Thomas Paine, *Common Sense* (London: H. D. Symonds, 1792), p. 28.

11. All Native Americans were granted the right to vote in 1924 when they were granted full U.S. citizenship.

12. *Voting Rights Coalition v. Wilson,* 60 F.3d 1411 (9th Cir. 1995).

13. *CQ Weekly Report,* January 27, 1996, p. 6.

14. David A. Bositis, "The Farrakhan Factor: Despite the Decline in Voter Turnout, There Has Been an Increase in Black Men at the Ballot Box," *The Washington Post,* National Weekly Edition, December 16–22, 1996, p. 24.

15. Jorge G. Castañeda, *The Mexican Shock: Its Meaning for the U.S.* (New York: New Press, 1995).

16. *Ibid.,* p. 22.

17. *Ibid.,* p. 23.

18. *Los Angeles Times* poll; Voters News Service exit poll; and Werthlin worldwide poll.

19. See Adam Nagourney, "For G.O.P., Northeast Is Becoming Foreign Turf," *The New York Times,* National Edition, November 14, 1996, p. B12.

20. This is the thesis put forth by Stephen Ansolabehere and Shanto Iyengar in *Going Negative: How Attack Ads Shrink and Polarize the Electorate* (New York: Free Press, 1996), based on their extensive survey of voters' opinions on negative ads.

chapter

10

CAMPAIGNS AND ELECTIONS

Contents

Negative Advertising: To Trash or Not to Trash?

Negative political campaigning has been an integral part of American politics for a long time. As far back as 1796, John Adams's supporters labeled Adams's opponent, Thomas Jefferson, "an Atheist, anarchist, demagogue, coward, . . . [and] trickster" whose followers were "cutthroats who walk in rags and sleep among filth and vermin." One ardent supporter of Adams declared that if Jefferson were to be elected, "We may see our wives and daughters the victims of legal prostitution."

Go to CD-ROM

Today's candidates certainly have continued the tradition of gratuitous character assassination, albeit less blatantly. Crafters of today's TV ads use a variety of techniques to get their message across, including dim lighting, ominous music (such as the theme from *Jaws*), the voice of what could pass for a news announcer, slow motion, patriotic music, and rapid sequences of images making close scrutiny impossible. Showing one's opponent in black and white also seems to be a favorite technique.

Just because negative political campaigning has been around for two hundred years does not mean that everybody likes it, however.

It's Time to Put an End to Negative Politicking

The 1996 campaign season was accentuated by a variety of negative adertisements. Indeed, opponents of negative political advertising argued that it was responsible for the lowest voter participation in over seven decades. The average American voter, this group contends, is sick of hyperbole and partisanship.

In the 1998 congressional campaigns, negative advertising also was very visible. Notable in 1998 were the number of "issue ads" sponsored by various interest groups. The ads, in essence, attacked incumbents in Congress who opposed the interests of particular groups.

Consider the ad campaign against Democrat Frank Pallone, Jr., a six-term U.S. representative from New Jersey. In 1998, just before the November elections, Pallone was the target of a negative advertising campaign sponsored by an interest group called Americans for Job Security, which was basically a front group for large insurance companies that were concerned over Pallone's endorsement of managed health-care reform. The organization waged a $2 million campaign against Pallone to keep him from being reelected. Among other things, TV ads accused Pallone of voting to use Social Security funds to pay for welfare. "Call Congressman Pallone," the ad announcer said, "and tell him to . . . stop gambling with our futures." Pallone maintained that the ad was misleading, but that didn't really matter—he still had to defend himself against the allegations.[1]

Critics of such tactics believe that they impose unnecessary costs on candidates, who are forced to defend themselves against allegations that are often baseless. According to these critics, negative advertising is essentially an exhausted political art form that usually ends up being a big waste of resources.

Negative Advertising Is Good for Democracy

Not everyone is against negative advertising. Those who support negative ads point out that negative campaigning has an honored history in American politics. Negative advertising enables a candidate to expose an opposing candidate who really is dishonest, unethical, or inappropriate for political office.

Those who use negative advertising believe that no challenger can hope to win

against an incumbent without attention-grabbing, memorable negative ads. Why shouldn't a candidate make the public aware of her opponent's shortcomings and broken promises? The only relevant criticism of a negative ad is that it is irrelevant or untrue.

Supporters of negative ads do accept that such ads discourage a small percentage of the electorate from voting. On balance, though, they argue, attack ads are good for democracy because they educate the voters, make politicians more accountable, and counteract biases of the media. Moreover, even negative advertising addresses substantive issues, such as crime, education, and taxes.

Finally, those who support negative advertising make the important point that this is a free country. If someone or some group wants to voice an opinion about a political candidate, that person or group has a right to freely express that opinion. To hold otherwise would violate our constitutional right to free speech.

Where Do You Stand?

1. Do you think that most people believe the messages conveyed by negative ads—or by any political ads, for that matter?

2. How could you change the rules about negative advertising without infringing on freedom of speech?

On the Web

For more information on free TV time for politicians, go to Vote Smart's Web site at http://www.vote-smart.org.

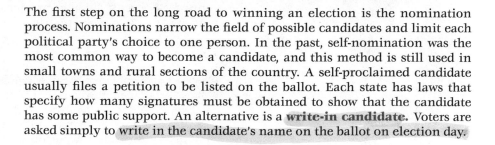

Introduction

WRITE-IN CANDIDATE ● A candidate whose name is written on the ballot by the voter on election day.

CAUCUS ● A meeting held by party leaders to choose political candidates. The caucus system of nominating candidates was eventually replaced by nominating conventions and, later, by direct primaries.

NOMINATING CONVENTION ● An official meeting of a political party to choose its candidates. Nominating conventions at the state and local levels also select delegates to represent the people of their geographical areas at a higher-level party convention.

DELEGATE ● A person selected to represent the people of one geographical area at a party convention.

I N F O T R A C ®
Advertising battles

Political advertising is just one of the weapons available to candidates in their struggles to become elected representatives of the people. The population of the United States now exceeds 272 million. Clearly, all voting-age citizens cannot gather in one place to make laws and run the government. We have to choose representatives to govern the nation and act on behalf of our interests. We accomplish this through popular elections. Campaigning for election has become an arduous task for every politician. As you will see in this chapter, American campaigns are long, complicated, and very expensive undertakings.

How We Nominate Candidates

The first step on the long road to winning an election is the nomination process. Nominations narrow the field of possible candidates and limit each political party's choice to one person. In the past, self-nomination was the most common way to become a candidate, and this method is still used in small towns and rural sections of the country. A self-proclaimed candidate usually files a petition to be listed on the ballot. Each state has laws that specify how many signatures must be obtained to show that the candidate has some public support. An alternative is a **write-in candidate.** Voters are asked simply to write in the candidate's name on the ballot on election day.

THE PRECURSOR OF THE NATIONAL CONVENTION—THE PARTY CAUCUS

The Constitution gives no instructions for nominating candidates for the presidency and vice presidency. Thus, in 1797 the leaders of the two parties decided to keep political power in their hands by holding congressional conferences, later called **caucuses.**[2] In these early meetings, the party leaders, who were wealthy and influential members of the community, would choose the candidates in secret. The voters at large played no part in choosing the nominees.

By the presidential race of 1824, the caucus method of nomination had become a controversial issue. Andrew Jackson and other presidential candidates who felt that the caucus was undemocratic derisively referred to the system as "King Caucus." Faced with rising opposition, party leaders were forced to find other methods of nominating candidates. As the caucus system faded away in presidential politics, its use diminished at the state and local levels as well.

THE PARTY NOMINATING CONVENTION

As the use of the caucus method diminished around the country, it was replaced in many states by party conventions. A **nominating convention** is an official meeting of a political party to choose its candidates and to select **delegates**—persons sent to a higher-level party convention to represent the people of one geographical area. For example, delegates at a local party convention would nominate candidates for local office and would also choose delegates to represent the party at the state convention. By 1840, the convention system had become the most common way of nominating candidates for government offices at every level.

Little by little, criticism of the corruption in nominating conventions at the state level caused state legislatures to disband most of them. They are still used in some states, including Connecticut, Delaware, Michigan, and Utah. At the national level, the convention is still used to select presidential and vice presidential candidates.

DIRECT PRIMARY ● An election held within each of the two major parties—Democratic and Republican—to choose the party's candidates for the general election.

CLOSED PRIMARY ● A primary in which only party members can vote to choose that party's candidates.

OPEN PRIMARY ● A primary in which voters can vote for a party's candidates regardless of whether they belong to the party.

BLANKET PRIMARY ● A "wide open" primary in which each voter receives a single ballot listing each party's candidates for each nomination.

THE DIRECT PRIMARY

In most states, direct primaries gradually replaced nominating conventions. A **direct primary** is an election held within each of the two major parties—Democratic and Republican—to pick its candidates for the general election. This is the method most commonly used today to nominate candidates for office.

Although the primaries are *party* nominating elections, they are now closely regulated by the states. The states set the dates and conduct the primaries. The states also provide polling places, election officials, registration lists, and ballots, in addition to counting the votes.

Most state laws require the major parties to use a primary to choose their candidates for the U.S. Senate and the House, for the governorship and all other state offices, and for most local offices as well. A few states, however, use different combinations of nominating conventions and primaries to pick candidates for the top offices.

Because state laws vary, several types of primaries are used throughout the country. Generally, though, primaries fall into two broad categories: closed primaries and open primaries.

Closed Primaries

In a **closed primary,** only party members can vote to choose that party's candidates, and they may vote only in the primary of their own party. Thus, only registered Democrats can vote in the Democratic primary to select candidates of the Democratic Party. Only registered Republicans can vote for the Republican candidates. A person usually establishes party membership when he or she registers to vote. Some states have a *semiclosed* primary, which allows voters to register with a party or change their party affiliations on election day.

Regular party workers favor the closed primary because it promotes party loyalty. Independent voters oppose it because it excludes them from the nominating process.

Open Primaries

An **open primary** is a direct primary in which voters can vote for a party's candidates regardless of whether they belong to the party. In most open primaries, all voters receive both a Republican ballot and a Democratic ballot. Voters then choose either the Democratic or the Republican ballot in the privacy of the voting booth. In a *semiopen* primary, voters request the ballot for the party of their choice.

A different version of the open primary is used in Alaska, California, and Washington. These states have a "wide open" primary, or **blanket primary,** in which each voter receives a single ballot listing each party's candidates for each nomination. Voters may choose candidates from different parties. Thus, a voter may choose a Democratic candidate for one office and a Republican candidate for another office. For example, a voter could select a Democratic candidate for governor but a Republican candidate for senator. Louisiana is unique in that all candidates run in the same, nonpartisan primary election. Figure 10–1 shows which states have closed (or semiclosed), open (or semiopen), blanket, or nonpartisan primaries.

Typically, candidates for most offices have to win only a plurality of the votes (more votes than the opposing candidates), rather than a majority (over 50 percent). In some states, a majority vote is required, so if no candidate receives more than 50 percent of the votes, there is a run-off election between the two candidates who won the most votes in the first primary election.

NOMINATING PRESIDENTIAL CANDIDATES

In some respects, being nominated for president is more difficult than being elected. The nominating process narrows a very large number of hopefuls down to a single candidate from each party. Choosing a presidential candi-

Figure 10–1
Types of Direct Primaries

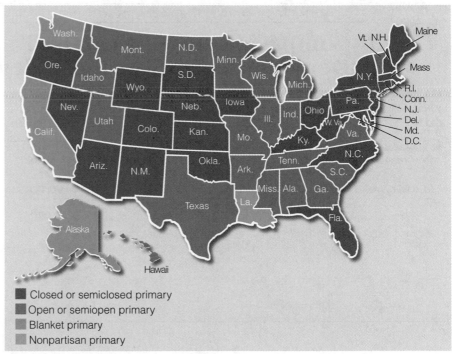

Closed or semiclosed primary
Open or semiopen primary
Blanket primary
Nonpartisan primary

SOURCE: Thomas R. Dye, *Politics in States and Communities,* 9th ed. (Upper Saddle River, N.J.: Prentice Hall, 1997), p. 135; and authors' update.

date is unlike nominating candidates for any other office. One reason for this is that the nomination process combines several different methods.

State Primaries

The majority of the states hold presidential primaries, beginning early in the election year. For a candidate, a good showing in the early primaries results in plenty of media attention as television networks and newspaper reporters play up the results. Subsequent state primaries tend to serve as contests to eliminate unlikely candidates.

State legislatures and state parties make the laws that determine how the primaries are set up, who may enter them, and who may vote in them. Several different methods of voting are used in presidential primaries. In some states, primary voters only select delegates to a party's national convention and do not know which candidates the delegates intend to vote for at the convention. In other states, the ballot lists the delegates' names along with the names of the candidates they support. In still other states, the names of the candidates for the nomination and the delegates appear separately. Voters may then cast separate votes for candidates and for delegates. This is known as a **preference poll.**

Some states, Texas among them, use a form of the preference poll in which delegates are selected at a state convention. The voters then cast ballots for candidates, and the delegates must vote for the winning candidate at the national convention. This method is called a **mandatory preference poll.**

In some states, delegates to the national convention are chosen through caucuses or conventions instead of through presidential primaries. Iowa, for example, holds caucuses to choose delegates to local conventions. These delegates, in turn, choose those who will attend the state and national conventions. Other states use a combination of caucuses and primaries.

Do the views of Democratic delegates differ significantly from those of Republican delegates? How closely do the delegates to either party's national convention represent the people's views? These questions are explored in the feature on the next page entitled *The American Political Spectrum: Comparing Republican and Democratic Convention Delegates.*

PREFERENCE POLL ● A method of voting in a primary election in which the names of the candidates for the nomination and the delegates appear separately, and voters cast separate votes for candidates and for delegates.

MANDATORY PREFERENCE POLL ● A form of the preference poll in which delegates to the national party convention are selected at a state convention, and the delegates must vote for the candidate chosen by the voters.

the american political spectrum

Comparing Republican and Democratic Convention Delegates

Do the people who go to the national party conventions really differ? That is to say, is there much of a difference between the "grassroots" in the two different parties? Look at Table 10–1, which shows the personal characteristics of Republican delegates versus Democratic delegates in 1996.

Clearly, Republican delegates were skewed toward white males. As could be expected, a larger percentage of Democratic delegates were from unions (34 percent versus 4 percent). The percentage of delegates who were college graduates did not differ significantly, however. Nor was there much difference in the distribution of income.

Of course, as could also be expected, there *were* huge differences with respect to political ideology. Those who characterized themselves as very liberal or somewhat liberal constituted 43 percent of the Democratic delegates, but zero percent of the Republican delegates. At the other end of the spectrum, 66 percent of the Republican delegates classified themselves as very or somewhat conservative versus only 5 percent of the Democrats.

Now look at Table 10–2, which shows the attitudes of the different delegates. As you can see, the Republican delegates did not think the government should do much to solve the nation's problems or regulate businesses. At the same time, Republicans did think that the government should promote traditional values. The table also shows that, compared to Republicans, Democratic delegates are about six times more likely to be in favor of abortion, about three times more likely to favor a nationwide ban on assault weapons, and nine times more likely to be in favor of continuing affirmative action.

For Critical Analysis

In what personal characteristics and attitudes listed in the two tables in this feature did convention delegates differ greatly from all voters?

Table 10–1

Personal Characteristics of Republican and Democratic Delegates

PERCENTAGE OF . . .	REPUBLICAN DELEGATES	DEMOCRATIC DELEGATES	ALL VOTERS
Men	64%	47%	46%
Women	36	53	54
White	91	71	84
Black	3	17	11
Age			
18 to 29 years old	2	6	17
30 to 44 years old	26	27	32
45 to 64 years old	53	55	30
65 and older	17	11	21
Political ideology			
Very liberal	0	15	4
Somewhat liberal	0	28	12
Moderate	27	48	42
Somewhat conservative	31	4	24
Very conservative	35	1	8
Member of a labor union	4	34	11
College graduate	73	69	23
Family income			
Under $50,000	23	29	71
$50,000 to $75,000	18	22	14
Over $75,000	47	46	11

SOURCE: *The New York Times*, August 26, 1996, p. A12.

Table 10–2

Attitudes of Republican and Democratic Delegates

PERCENTAGE OF . . .	REPUBLICAN DELEGATES	DEMOCRATIC DELEGATES	ALL VOTERS
SCOPE OF GOVERNMENT			
Government should do more to			
—solve the nation's problems.	4%	76%	36%
—regulate the environment and safety practices of businesses.	4	60	53
—promote traditional values.	56	27	42
SOCIAL ISSUES			
Abortion should be permitted in all cases.	11	61	27
A nationwide ban should be imposed on assault weapons.	34	91	72
Laws are necessary to protect racial minorities.	30	88	51
Affirmative action programs should be continued.	9	81	45

SOURCE: *The New York Times*, August 26, 1996, p. A12.

National party conventions held by both Democrats and Republicans occur every four years. The first national convention was held by the Anti-Masonic Party in Baltimore in 1831. In 1832, the Democrats held their first national convention and nominated Andrew Jackson. The Republicans held their first convention in 1856. Today, national conventions ratify front-runner candidates who won the primaries and state caucuses.

Primaries—The Rush to Be First

In an effort to make their primaries prominent in the media and influential in the political process, many states have moved the date of their primary to earlier in the year. This "front-loading" of the primaries started after the 1968 Democratic National Convention in Chicago, which appeared to be ruled by a few groups. Then, in 1988, southern states created "Super Tuesday" by holding most of their primaries on the same day in early March. Recently, many states in the Midwest, New England, and the Pacific West (including California) decided to move their primaries to an earlier date, too.

Consider that in 1968 there were only fifteen primaries, all of which were held after March except for New Hampshire's. By 1996, there were primaries in forty states, twenty-nine of which were held by the end of March within a six-week period. In the 2000 presidential elections, at least thirty-seven primaries and caucuses will be held by the end of March, and roughly three-fourths of all party convention delegates will be chosen between the end of January and the middle of March (see Figure 10–2). If this trend continues, we will eventually have a one-day national primary.

Figure 10–2
Front-Loading the Delegate-Selection Process

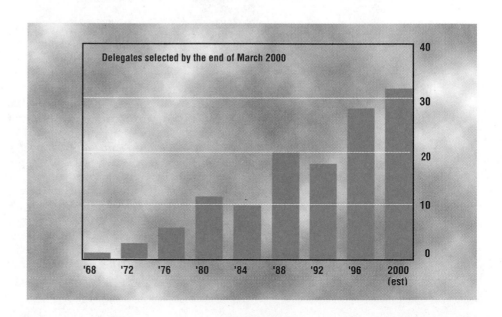

The 1996 Republican Convention.

Some Americans worry that with a shortened primary season, long-shot candidates will no longer be able to propel themselves into serious contention by doing well in small, early-voting states, such as New Hampshire or Iowa. Traditionally, for example, a candidate who had a successful showing in the New Hampshire primary had time to obtain enough financial backing to continue in the race. The candidate also had time to become known to the voters through political advertising, TV appearances, and campaign speeches along the campaign trail. With the shortened primary system, the winners will be those candidates who can start their fund-raising early and load up on national TV spots. The fear is that an accelerated schedule of presidential primaries will likely favor the richest candidates.

National Party Conventions

Born in the 1830s, the American national political convention has been and continues to be in one sense a true political circus. It is also unique in Western democracies. Elsewhere, candidates for prime minister or chancellor are chosen within the confines of party councils. That is actually the way the framers wanted it done—nowhere in the Constitution is there any mention of a nominating convention. Indeed, Thomas Jefferson loathed the idea. He feared that if the presidential race became a popularity contest, it would develop into "mobocracy." That is why presidential candidates were supposed to simply "stand" for election, rather than run for office. Instead of shaking hands and making speeches, they were supposed to stay on their farms and wait for the people's call, just as George Washington did.

Party nominating conventions have been described as giant pep rallies. Despite the hats, signs, and blaring horns and sirens, each convention's task is a serious one—to adopt the official party platform and decide who will be the party's presidential and vice presidential candidates. In late July or early August, the two or three thousand delegates at each convention theoretically represent the wishes of the voters and political leaders of their home states.

INFOTRAC®

Where America is heading

On the first day of the convention, delegates hear the reports of the **Credentials Committee,** which inspects each prospective delegate's claim to be seated as a legitimate representative of his or her state. When the eligibility of delegates is in question, the committee decides who will be seated. In the evening, there is usually a keynote speaker to whip up enthusiasm among the delegates. The second day includes committee reports and debates on the party platform. Of course, other things are happening on an unofficial agenda: backers of certain candidates are seeking to influence uncommitted delegates and change the minds of those pledged to other candidates.

State delegations also are meeting to discuss strategies and how they will vote. The third day is devoted to nominations and voting. Balloting begins with an alphabetical roll call in which states and territories announce their votes. By midnight, the convention's real work is over and the presidential candidate has been selected. The vice presidential nominations and the acceptance speeches occupy the fourth day.

Do National Conventions Serve Any Real Purpose Today?

During the 1996 conventions, journalists complained that the conventions had become giant infomercials that were scripted, managed, and prepackaged. Even so-called impromptu moments seemed to have been well prepared.

In view of this development, do conventions really serve any useful purpose today? Yes, at least according to one political commentator, George F. Will. Will argues that a well-scripted political convention is "the meticulous expression of a party's thinking." Conventions are therefore part of the "process of persuasion that is the essence of the ethic of democracy."[3] Will also points out that less is at stake in politics today than previously. After all, the Cold War is over, and there are no issues of great proportion threatening the nation. Audiences for conventions would be shrinking even if the conventions remained as unscripted and unpredictable as they were in the past.

CREDENTIALS COMMITTEE ● A committee of each national political party that evaluates the claims of national party convention delegates to be the legitimate representatives of their states.

CAMPAIGN MANAGER ● The person who coordinates and plans a political candidate's campaign and the strategy that will be used for it.

POLITICAL CONSULTANT ● A person who, for a large fee, devises a political candidate's campaign strategies, monitors the campaign's progress, plans all media appearances, and coaches the candidate for debates.

Conventions Reward Party Supporters and Stimulate Donations

However dull conventions may appear to be, they remain singularly important for the parties themselves. They give parties a chance to reward major contributors and to ask for more money. Interest groups—corporations and lobbyists—are the first ones asked to pay for the whole convention. Then these interest groups are asked to pay for private fund-raising parties. Then, at the private parties, other interest groups are asked to donate money. Many congressional candidates hold their own fund raisers at the conventions. The National Association of Manufacturers, for example, may throw a $1,500-per-person fund raiser for a specific congressional candidate. Some of these events are labeled as parties to "honor" a specific member of Congress.

The combined campaign "takes" for the 1996 conventions were estimated to be at least $50 million. Critics of these party-sponsored fund raisers argue that they provide tangible evidence of how unregulated the campaign-finance system really is. Everything that goes on at such conventions is considered "party building" and therefore exempt from regulations (campaign-financing regulations will be discussed shortly).

The Modern Political Campaign

Once nominated, candidates focus on their campaigns. The term *campaign* originated in the military context. Generals mounted campaigns, using their scarce resources (soldiers and materials) to achieve military objectives. Using the term in a political context is apt. In a political campaign, candidates also use scarce resources (time and money) in an attempt to defeat their adversaries in the battle to win votes.

To run a successful campaign, the candidate's campaign staff must be able to raise funds for the effort, get media coverage, produce and pay for political ads, schedule the candidate's time effectively with constituent groups and potential supporters, convey the candidate's position on the issues, conduct research on the opposing candidate, and get the voters to go to the polls. When party identification was stronger and TV campaigning was still in its infancy, a strong party organization on the local, state, or national level could furnish most of the services and expertise that the candidate needed. Less effort was spent on advertising a single candidate's position and character, because the party label communicated that information to many of the voters.

Today, party labels are no longer as important as they once were. In part, this is because fewer people identify with the major parties, as evidenced by the rising number of independent voters (see Chapter 8). Instead of relying so extensively on political parties, candidates now turn to professionals to manage their campaigns.

THE PROFESSIONAL CAMPAIGN ORGANIZATION

Look at Figure 10–3, which shows a typical presidential campaign organization. The **campaign manager** coordinates and plans the campaign strategy, while other staff members provide leadership in specific areas, such as tracking public opinion through polls, preparing the candidate's speeches, researching policy issues, and the like. Increasingly, campaigns rely on the expertise of professional political consultants. The **political consultant,** for a large fee, devises campaign strategies, monitors the campaign's progress, plans all media appearances, and coaches the candidate for debates. As Figure 10–3 also indicates, the political party continues to play an important role in campaigns, particularly in recruiting and directing volunteers to help with various tasks, such as distributing campaign literature.

A major development in contemporary American politics is the rise of a new style of campaigning based mainly on reaching the voters through the effective use of the media, particularly television. Information based on public opinion polls becomes a major part of campaign strategy. Poll

TRACKING POLL ● Polls that are taken almost every day toward the end of a political campaign to find out how well the candidates are competing for votes.

taking is widespread during the primaries. Typically, presidential candidates also have private polls taken to make sure that there is at least some chance that they could be nominated and, if nominated, elected. Increasingly, nominees depend on polls to fine-tune their campaigns, and during the presidential campaign itself, continual polls are taken both by the regular pollsters (such as Gallup and Roper) and by each candidate's campaign organization. As election day nears, many candidates use **tracking polls,** which are polls taken almost every day, to find out how well they are competing for votes.

WHAT IT COSTS TO WIN

The modern political campaign is an expensive undertaking. Huge sums must be spent for professional campaign managers and consultants, television and radio ads, the printing of campaign literature, travel, office rent, equipment, and other necessities. To get an idea of the cost of waging a campaign for Congress today, look at Table 10–3 on the next page, which lists the top spenders in the 1998 congressional campaigns. The average campaign expenditures of congressional candidates in 1998 were, of course, much lower, but still extraordinarily high compared to campaign costs in previous elections. Today, a candidate who cannot put together a war chest of at least $500,000 has little chance of being elected.

Presidential campaigns are even more costly. In 1992, Americans were stunned to learn that about $550 million had been spent in the presidential

Figure 10–3
A Typical Presidential Campaign Organization

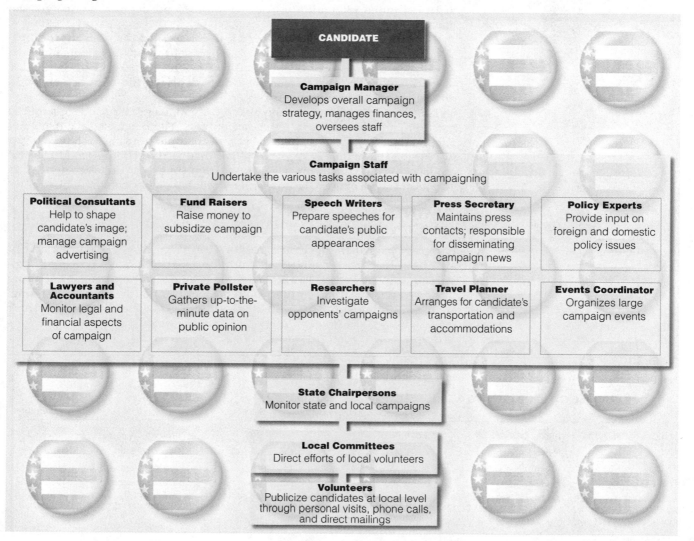

President Bill Clinton seeks the support of these Texans for his reelection to the presidency in 1996. Presidential campaigns have become increasingly expensive. The estimate for the 1996 campaign was about $600 million.

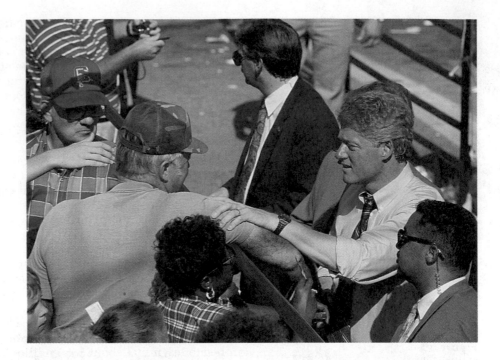

campaigns. In 1996, presidential campaign expenditures rose even higher, to an estimated $600 million, making the 1996 presidential campaigns the most expensive in history.

Clearly, money matters in determining success at the polls. In the 1998 elections, for example, candidates who outspent their opponents emerged victorious in 95 percent of the House races and 94 percent of the Senate races. In more than 60 percent of House districts, the winner's expenditures were ten times those of the loser.[4]

The connection between money and campaigns gives rise to some of the most difficult challenges in American politics. The biggest fear is that campaign contributors may be able to influence people running for office by giving large gifts or loans. Another possibility is that some special interest groups will try to buy favored treatment from those who are elected to office. To prevent these abuses, the government regulates campaign financing.

REGULATIONS GOVERNING CAMPAIGN FINANCING

Congress passed the Federal Election Campaign Act (FECA) of 1971[5] in an effort to curb irregularities and abuses in the ways political campaigns were financed. The 1971 act placed no limit on overall spending but restricted the amount that could be spent on mass-media advertising, including television. It limited the amount that candidates and their

Table 10-3

Top Spenders in the 1998 Congressional Campaigns

HOUSE OF REPRESENTATIVES				SENATE			
Party	State	Candidate	Expenditures	Party	State	Candidate	Expenditures
D	New Mex.	Phillip Maloof	$8,020,643	R	N.Y.	Alfonse D'Amato	$24,195,287
R	Ga.	Newt Gingrich	7,578,716	R	Ill.	Peter Fitzgerald	17,677,698
D	Mass.	Christopher Gabrieli	5,283,156	D	N.Y.	Charles Schumer	16,671,877
R	Wash.	Linda Smith	5,159,527	D	Calif.	Barbara Boxer	13,737,548
R	Wisc.	Mark Neumann	4,373,953	R	Calif.	Darrell Issa	13,549,659

SOURCE: Federal Election Commission, 1999.

LOOPHOLE ● A legal way of evading a certain legal requirement.

families could contribute to their own campaigns and required disclosure of all contributions and expenditures in excess of $100. In principle, the 1971 act limited the role of labor unions and corporations in political campaigns. Also in 1971, Congress passed a law that provided for a $1 checkoff on federal income tax returns for general campaign funds to be used by major-party presidential candidates. This law was first applied in the 1976 campaign. (Since then, the amount of the checkoff has been raised to $3.)

The 1971 act did not go far enough, however. Amendments to the act passed in 1974 essentially did the following:

■ *Created the Federal Election Commission (FEC) to administer and enforce the act's provisions.*

■ *Provided public financing for presidential primaries and general elections.* Presidential candidates who raise some money on their own in at least twenty states can get funds from the U.S. Treasury to help pay for primary campaigns. For the general election campaign, presidential candidates receive federal funding for almost all of their expenses *if* they are willing to accept campaign spending limits.

■ *Limited presidential campaign spending.* Any candidate accepting federal support must agree to limit expenditures to amounts set by federal law.

■ *Required disclosure.* Candidates must file periodic reports with the FEC that list who contributed to the campaign and how the money was spent.

■ *Limited contributions.* Individuals can contribute up to $1,000 to each candidate in each federal election or primary. The total limit for any individual in one year is $25,000. Groups can contribute a maximum of $5,000 to a candidate in any election.

In a significant 1976 case, *Buckley v. Valeo*,[6] the Supreme Court declared unconstitutional the provision in the 1971 act that limited the amount each individual could spend on his or her own campaign. The Court held that a "candidate, no less than any other person, has a First Amendment right to engage in the discussion of public issues and vigorously and tirelessly to advocate his own election."

THE RISE OF PACS

The FECA, as further amended in 1976, allows corporations, labor unions, and special interest groups to set up political action committees (PACs) to raise money for candidates. For a PAC to be legitimate, the money must be raised from at least fifty volunteer donors and must be given to at least five candidates in the national elections. PACs can contribute up to $5,000 per candidate in each election, but there is no limit on the total amount of PAC contributions during an election cycle. As discussed in Chapter 7, the number of PACs has grown significantly since the 1970s, as have their campaign contributions. (PACs are even used in some judicial elections, as described in the feature on the next page entitled *A Question of Ethics: Should PACs Be Allowed to Influence Judicial Elections?*)

SKIRTING THE CAMPAIGN-FINANCING RULES

Given the restrictions imposed by campaign-financing laws, how is it possible that candidates can raise funds to the degree they did during the 1996 presidential campaigns? Consider the approximately $600 million spent by presidential candidates during their campaigns prior to the 1996 elections. Only $86 million, or about 14 percent, came from the federal government. Where did the remaining $514 million come from? The answer is that individuals and corporations have found **loopholes**—legal ways of evading certain legal requirements—in the federal laws limiting campaign contributions.

a question of ethics

Should PACs Be Allowed to Influence Judicial Elections?

One tends to think of our judiciary as beyond the realm of partisan politics. In fact, judges in many states have to campaign to get elected. Consider the example of North Carolina. Candidates for the state supreme court have to wage extensive and expensive campaigns to get elected. Judicial candidates in North Carolina increasingly have sought contributions from political action committees (PACs). Since 1986, PAC contributions to North Carolina Supreme Court candidates have increased by over 30 percent.[7]

Not surprisingly, PACs that donate to judicial candidates are heavily sponsored by trial lawyers. Business PACs are also important and have been particularly active in Texas in recent years.[8]

For Critical Analysis

What are the ethical implications of trial lawyers' groups and business groups supporting PACs that contribute to the campaigns of judicial candidates?

Soft Money

The biggest loophole in federal campaign laws is that they do not prohibit individuals or corporations from contributing to political *parties*. Today, many contributors make donations to the national parties to cover the costs of such activities as registering voters, printing brochures and fliers, advertising in the media (which often means running candidate-oriented ads), campaigns to "get out the vote," and fund-raising events—such as the Democratic Party's $10,000-a-ticket fiftieth-birthday dinner for President Bill Clinton in August 1996. Contributions to political parties, instead of to particular candidates, are referred to as **soft money** because, as one observer said, it is "so squishy." Although soft money clearly is used to support the candidates, it is difficult to track exactly where the money goes.

Although this loophole has existed since the passage of a 1979 amendment to the federal election laws, it was little known or used until the 1990s. Today, soft-money contributions allow parties to raise millions of dollars from corporations and individuals. Corporations such as Seagram & Sons and Walt Disney gave more than half a million dollars to the Democratic National Committee in 1996, while Philip Morris, the tobacco company, contributed more than a million dollars to the Republican Party.[9]

SOFT MONEY ● Campaign contributions that are made to political parties, instead of to particular candidates.

In 1997, the Senate opened an investigation of Democratic campaign-financing irregularities. The chairman of the committee, Senator Fred Thompson (R., Tenn.), is shown here in the center of the photo. Flanking him are Senator John Glenn (D., Ohio) on the left and Michael Madigan (chief Republican counsel) on the right. After much anticipation, the investigation came and went without any real damage being done to the Democrats.

INDEPENDENT EXPENDITURE ● An expenditure for activities that are independent from (not coordinated with) those of a political candidate or a political party.

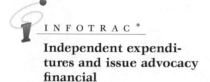

INFOTRAC®

Independent expenditures and issue advocacy financial

During the 1998 election cycle, the national party committees raised $193.2 million in soft money—double the amount raised in 1994, the last nonpresidential election cycle.[10] According to Federal Election Commission data, business PACs alone contributed nearly $105.6 million to the party committees ($33.5 million to the Democrats and $72.1 million to the Republicans).[11]

Soft dollars have become the main source of campaign money in the presidential race, far outpacing PAC contributions and federal campaign funds. In fact, soft-money donations in 1996 were more than twice what they were in the 1992 presidential elections. The Republicans raised close to $300 million in soft dollars, and the Democrats received somewhere over $200 million. The political parties and their interest group allies went to great lengths to evade the laws that were put on the books in the 1970s. (Whether most Americans are truly concerned about this issue is another story. See the feature entitled *Perception versus Reality: Are Americans Really All That Concerned about the Democrats' Fund-Raising Tactics?*)

Increasingly, the message for interest groups is that if money buys access, more money buys more access. This principle is clearly expressed in Table 10–4 on the next page, which shows each national party committee's list of what donors receive in return for contributions in various dollar amounts.

Independent Expenditures

Another major loophole in campaign-financing laws is that they do not prohibit corporations, labor unions, and special interest groups from making **independent expenditures** in an election campaign. Independent

---

perception versus reality

Are Americans Really All That Concerned about the Democrats' Fund-Raising Tactics?

In the wake of the 1996 election cycle, the Republicans hurled a number of devastating accusations at the Democratic Party. Among other things, the Republicans accused Clinton and the Democrats of breaking campaign-finance laws and degrading the White House by using access to the president to raise political funds. Republicans contended that Clinton personally rewarded top donors by selling overnight stays at the White House and meting out other awards. How did these accusations and the investigations they spawned affect Americans?

The Perception

The media's intense focus on improper and possibly illegal fund-raising activities of the Democratic Party during the 1996 elections led to a fairly widespread perception that a majority of Americans were up in arms over the matter. They were aghast that President Clinton

could use the power of his office to dole out favors to contributors. They were shocked that campaign funds from foreign sources helped him win a second term. They were convinced that politics is dirtier than ever.

The Reality

In reality, Americans did not appear to be all that concerned about the Democrats' fund-raising tactics in the 1996 elections. In a December 1996 poll asking Americans to rank fourteen problems facing the country, respondents rated campaign-finance reform as number fourteen on the list—giving it the lowest priority. Despite the alleged fund-raising scandals, the polls showed that a majority of Americans still supported President Clinton—his approval ratings continued to be in the 50 to 60 percent range.

If Americans are disillusioned by the campaign money machine,

their disillusionment is with the system, not with the Democrats or President Clinton. More than six out of ten respondents to a *USA Today*/CNN/Gallup poll conducted in the spring of 1997 viewed Clinton's fund-raising practices as typical of both parties. Over half of the respondents rated Clinton's ethics as typical of White House occupants. Even back in 1943, when public trust in our leaders seemed to be at its highest level, a Gallup poll found that nearly half of the respondents thought that it was almost impossible to go into politics and stay honest.

You Be the Judge

Did the media overplay the Democratic fund-raising excesses during the 1996 elections and downplay the fact that political survival today depends on increasingly larger war chests? Is there any way around this problem?

Table 10-4

National Party Committee Donor Programs

REPUBLICAN NATIONAL COMMITTEE

Program	What You Pay	What You Get
Team 100	$100,000	—Special relationship with party leaders —Meetings in exclusive locations —Benefits of either program below
Republican Eagles	$20,000	—Four national meetings in Washington —Regional directors to address Eagles' needs —Attendance on international trade missions —Two invitations to an annual gala —Golf and tennis with key legislators
Majority Fund	$15,000	—Quarterly dinners with key GOP legislators —Monthly meetings with key GOP legislators —Golf with key legislators —Two invitations to an annual gala —Issues briefings and weekly faxes

DEMOCRATIC NATIONAL COMMITTEE

Program	What You Pay	What You Get
Jefferson Trust	$100,000	—Weekend retreats with party leaders —Dinners with the president or vice president —Issue briefings and regular faxes
Major Supporter	$50,000	—Small events with the president or vice president —"Very high" attention from the committee staff
Democratic Business Council	$15,000*	—Dinners with the president or vice president —An event with the president —Annual Democratic Business Council retreat —Staff contact assigned especially to you

*For PACs; $10,000 for individuals.

SOURCE: Jeffrey H. Birnbaum, "Capitol Clout: A Buyer's Guide," *Fortune,* October 26, 1998, pp. 177–184.

expenditures, as the term implies, are expenditures for activities that are independent from (not coordinated with) those of the candidate or a political party. In other words, groups can wage their own "issue" campaigns as long as they do not go so far as to say "Vote for Candidate X." The problem is, where do you draw the line between advocating a position on a particular issue, such as abortion (which a group has a right to do under the First Amendment's guarantee of freedom of speech), and contributing to the campaign of a candidate who endorses that position?

In addressing this thorny issue, the United States Supreme Court has developed two bright-line tests. Under the first test, a group's speech is a campaign "expenditure" only if it explicitly calls for the election of a particular candidate. Using this test, the courts repeatedly have held that interest groups have the right to advocate their positions. For example, the Christian Coalition has the right to publish voter guides informing voters of candidates' positions. The second test applies when a group or organization has made expenditures explicitly for the purpose of endorsing a candidate. Such expenditures are permissible unless they were made in "coordination" with a campaign. According to the Supreme Court, an issue-oriented group has a First Amendment right to advocate the election of its preferred candidates as long as it acts independently.

In 1996, the Supreme Court held that these guidelines apply to expenditures by political parties as well. Parties may spend money on behalf of candidates if they do so independently—that is, if they do not let the candidates know how, when, or for what the money was spent.[12] As critics of this decision have pointed out, parties generally work closely with candidates, so establishing the "independence" of such expenditures is problematic.

GENERAL ELECTION ● A regularly scheduled election to elect the U.S. president, vice president, and senators and representatives in Congress; general elections are held in even-numbered years on the first Tuesday after the first Monday in November.

SPECIAL ELECTION ● An election that is held at the state or local level when the voters must decide an issue before the next general election or when vacancies occur by reason of death or resignation.

AUSTRALIAN BALLOT ● A secret ballot that is prepared, distributed, and counted by government officials at public expense; used by all states in the United States since 1888.

PARTY-COLUMN BALLOT ● A ballot (also called the Indiana ballot) that lists all of a party's candidates under the party label; voters can vote for all of a party's candidates for local, state, and national offices by making a single "X" or pulling a single lever.

Foreign Contributions

It is against federal law for political parties or candidates in the United States to accept money from foreign sources. Nevertheless, various loopholes in the law allowed literally tens of millions of dollars to be funneled, through various means, from foreign sources to U.S. candidates and political parties during the 1996 election cycle.

A major loophole in the federal campaign laws permits legal U.S. residents, even if they have foreign citizenship, to make contributions. Another loophole allows U.S. subsidiaries of foreign companies to contribute campaign funds (provided the funds were earned in the United States). In numerous instances, when campaign contributions during the 1996 election cycle were scrutinized, it became obvious that the funds were generated offshore and not in the United States. One case unearthed by *New York Times* columnist William Safire involved the fund-raising activities of John Huang. Huang once worked for the Lippo Group, an Indonesian-based banking and real estate conglomerate. Later, he was appointed by President Clinton to a position in the Commerce Department, after which he moved to full-time fund raising for the Democratic Party. Huang obtained $427,000 from an Indonesian couple living in Virginia. The man, a legal resident but not an American citizen, worked as a landscaper; the woman, though, was connected to Indonesian business interests. (See the feature on the following page entitled *A Question of Ethics: Why Was All That Foreign Money Donated?*)

Despite the media attention given to the questionable fund-raising tactics of the Democratic Party, one should realize that Republicans have also benefited from funds from foreign sources. Reporters for *Time* magazine discovered that Hong Kong businessman Ambrous Tung Young put up $2 million to help finance Republican campaigns in 1994 and 1996. The funds were channeled to the Republican Party through a small U.S. firm that was quietly backed by an investment company controlled by Hong Kong and Taiwanese businessmen.[13]

How We Elect Candidates

The ultimate goal of the political campaign and the associated fund-raising efforts is, of course, winning the election. The most familiar kind of election is the **general election,** which is a regularly scheduled election held in even-numbered years on the first Tuesday after the first Monday in November. During general elections, the voters decide who will be the U.S. president, vice president, and senators and representatives in Congress. The president and vice president are elected every four years, senators every six years, and representatives every two years. General elections are also held to choose state and local government officials, often at the same time as those for national offices. A **special election** is held at the state or local level when the voters must decide an issue before the next general election or when vacancies occur by reason of death or resignation (see Chapter 20 for further details on state elections).

TYPES OF BALLOTS

Since 1888, all states in the United States have used the **Australian ballot**—a secret ballot that is prepared, distributed, and counted by government officials at public expense. Two variations of the Australian ballot are used today. Most states use the **party-column ballot** (also called the Indiana ballot), which lists all of a party's candidates together in a single column under the party label. In some states, the party-column ballot allows voters to vote for all of a party's candidates for local, state, and national offices by making a single "X" or pulling a single lever. The major parties favor this ballot form because it encourages straight-ticket voting.

a question of ethics

Why Was All That Foreign Money Donated?

Republican presidential nominee Bob Dole, when touting campaign reform in 1996, said, "We simply cannot allow the political influence of any American to be outweighed by foreign money." Dole, of course, was referring to the millions of dollars that found their way from foreign sources into the coffers of the Democratic Party during the 1996 campaign, even though federal law prohibits foreign contributions to American campaigns.

What Was John Huang Selling?

At one fund raiser prior to the 1996 elections, President Clinton said, "I'd like to thank my long-time friend John Huang for being so effective." The president was referring to Huang's success in soliciting soft-money contributions for the U.S. Democratic Party from large numbers of Asian businesses and individuals.

There is no way of knowing exactly what Huang was "selling" when he raised millions of dollars from Asian Americans for the Democratic campaign. Papers released by the Democratic Party

clearly show that there was a specific strategy called the "National Asian Pacific American Campaign Plan." Its goal was to raise $7 million from the Asian American communities. The records surrounding Huang's efforts indicate that the *quid pro quo* promised in exchange for large donations was, at a minimum, a face-to-face meeting with President Clinton.

Some argue that a direct link can be established between large contributions and public-policy changes. As an example, they point out that the Lippo Group owns immense coal mines and reserves in Indonesia. Hence, the Lippo Group was pleased when President Clinton designated 1.7 million acres of Utah wilderness as a national monument, thereby removing 62 billion tons of coal reserves in the region from possible mining by a British-owned company. In essence, the Lippo Group, which was in competition with U.S.–based coal companies, benefited from the elimination of a serious competitor in Utah. The White House claimed that such

speculations about its policies were preposterous.[14]

Why Are Foreigners So Concerned about U.S. Politics?

The Lippo Group is just one of a number of foreign business groups that are interested in influencing U.S. politics. According to the Center for Public Integrity, Japanese interest groups are even more important than Indonesian interests. Japanese interest groups apparently spend $100 million a year both monitoring and trying to influence U.S. policy, mainly with respect to trade and other business issues. Additionally, British interest groups and companies have donated heavily to American political campaigns. British companies, such as Brown & Williamson Tobacco and British Petroleum, routinely donate to the Republican Party. In general, Europeans spend tens of millions of dollars a year on big-name law firms and consultants to influence such issues as the tax treatment of American subsidiaries of foreign companies.

Why are foreign companies so concerned about influencing U.S. policy? There are two main reasons: (1) the United States is a huge market for other countries' exports, and (2) the American military can promote stability or wreak destruction virtually anywhere. So, because the U.S. government influences the lives of foreigners, foreigners have a real stake in U.S. political affairs. Small countries can be dramatically affected by what happens in Washington, D.C. Consequently, the only way to get a hearing in the United States is for those countries to "buy their way in."

For Critical Analysis

To what extent should U.S. subsidiaries of foreign companies be restricted in their lobbying efforts, compared to their U.S.–owned competitors?

John Huang's fund-raising efforts for the Democrats prior to the 1996 elections put him in the public spotlight. After the elections, Huang agreed to cooperate with the Justice Department in its investigation of campaign-financing irregularities.

OFFICE-BLOCK BALLOT ● A ballot that lists together all of the candidates for each office.

POLL WATCHER ● A representative from one of the two major political parties who is allowed to monitor a polling place to make sure that the election is run fairly and to avoid fraud.

ELECTOR ● A member of the electoral college.

ELECTORAL COLLEGE ● The group of electors who are selected by the voters in each state to officially elect the president and vice president. The number of electors in each state is equal to the number of that state's representatives in both chambers of Congress.

WINNER-TAKE-ALL SYSTEM ● A term used to describe the electoral college system, in which the candidate who receives the largest popular vote in a state is credited with all that state's electoral votes—one vote per elector.

Other states use the **office-block ballot,** which lists together all of the candidates for each office. Politicians tend to dislike the office-block ballot because it places more emphasis on the office than on the party and thus encourages split-ticket voting.

CONDUCTING ELECTIONS AND COUNTING THE VOTES

Recall from Chapter 9 that local units of government, such as cities, are divided into smaller voting districts, or precincts. State laws usually restrict the size of precincts, and local officials set their boundaries. Within each precinct, voters cast their ballots at one polling place.

A precinct election board supervises the polling place and the voting process in each precinct. The board sets hours for the polls to be open according to the laws of the state and sees that ballots or voting machines are available. In most states, the board provides the list of registered voters and makes certain that only qualified voters cast ballots in that precinct. When the polls close, the board counts the votes and reports the results, usually to the county clerk or the board of elections. Representatives from each party, called **poll watchers,** are allowed at each polling place to make sure the election is run fairly and to avoid fraud.

PRESIDENTIAL ELECTIONS AND THE ELECTORAL COLLEGE

The framers of the Constitution argued long and hard about the method of electing the president. Many did not want the president to be elected directly by the people because the framers did not trust the average person's judgment. They feared that citizens scattered across the new country would have a hard time learning enough about the candidates to make informed choices. They wanted the president to be elected by the nation's elite—wealthy, powerful, and presumably reasonable leaders. The result was the electoral college.

The Electoral College

Many voters who vote for the president and vice president think that they are voting directly for a candidate. Actually, they are voting for **electors** who will cast their ballots in the **electoral college.** The electors are selected during each presidential election year by the states' political parties, subject to the laws of the state. Each state has as many electoral votes as it has U.S. senators and representatives. In addition, there are three electors from the District of Columbia. The electoral college system is a **winner-take-all system,** in which the candidate who receives the largest popular vote in a state is credited with all that state's electoral votes—one vote per elector. The winner gets all the electoral votes no matter what the margin of victory was.

In December, after the general election, electors (either Democrats or Republicans, depending on which candidate won the state's popular vote) meet in their state capitals to cast their votes for president and vice president. When the Constitution was drafted, the framers intended for the electors to use their own discretion in deciding who would make the best president. Today, however, the electors usually vote for the candidates who won popular support in their states. The electoral college ballots are then sent to the Senate, which counts and certifies them before a joint session of Congress held early in January. The candidates who receive a majority of the electoral votes are officially declared president and vice president.

To be elected, a candidate must receive more than half of the 538 electoral votes available. Thus, a candidate needs 270 votes to win. If no candidate gets an electoral college majority (which has happened twice—in 1800 and 1824), the House of Representatives votes on the candidates, with each state delegation casting only a single vote. The vice president is chosen by the Senate, with each senator casting one vote.

Most voting is done at the precinct level, even for national elections. A precinct election board supervises the polling place. At virtually all polling places, there are poll watchers. They make certain that only qualified voters cast their ballots in that precinct.

Pros and Cons of the Electoral College

The electoral college system has been criticized as being out of date and undemocratic. A major criticism is that the winner-take-all system makes possible the election of a candidate who lost the total popular vote but won the electoral vote. Three times in the 1800s, the electoral college system gave Americans a president who had not won the popular vote.[15] In 1968, a shift of only sixty thousand votes to third party candidate George C. Wallace would have thrown the race into the House. Again in 1976, a shift of only a few thousand votes would have produced an electoral victory for Gerald Ford despite a popular majority vote for Jimmy Carter.

One of the major arguments in favor of keeping the electoral college is that it helps give the appearance that the winning candidate has received a "mandate." Even if the popular vote is relatively close, typically the electoral college vote is skewed heavily toward the winning candidate. Most often this occurs because successful candidates typically spend a lot of their campaign resources in states that have the most electoral college votes. (See the distorted map in Figure 10–4, which shows the relative importance of states in terms of electoral votes.)

According to Alan Natapoff of the Massachusetts Institute of Technology, the electoral college offers yet another benefit: the current state-by-state, winner-take-all system makes close elections more likely, so voters in states where the electoral vote looks close get wooed more. Candidates have to appeal for every last vote, so each voter's influence increases. If presidents were elected by a simple nationwide popular ballot, presidential candidates might not fight so hard because a trailing candidate would find it more difficult to come from behind under such a system. According to Natapoff, the electoral college system forces candidates to reach beyond their core constituencies to other interest groups and organizations.[16]

Figure 10–4
How Electoral Votes Are
Apportioned among the States
This map shows the relative importance of
the states in terms of the number of electoral
votes apportioned to each state.

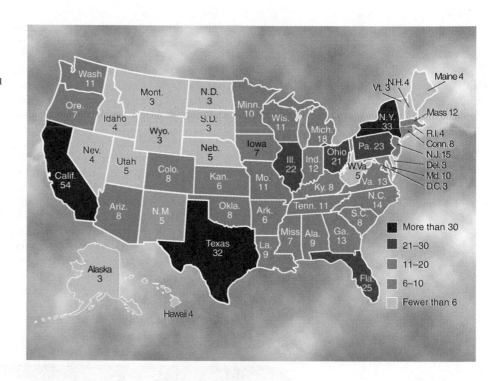

Americans at Odds over Campaigns and Elections

Americans are at odds over several aspects of campaigns and elections. One problematic issue has to do with campaign money and representative democracy. Can the "people" really rule the United States if our leaders are beholden to special interest groups for the money that helped them get elected? As you read in Chapter 7, the influence of interest groups on government and policymaking is not a new concern. It has become more intense in recent years, though, as campaign costs have mounted. Would-be political leaders, unless they are extraordinarily wealthy, are forced, in a sense, to "play the game" and work closely with interest groups to obtain campaign funds.

Another troubling issue facing Americans today is the apparent willingness of both parties in recent years to skirt federal campaign-financing regulations. During the 1996 and 1998 campaigns, an escalating money war was waged by interest groups and political candidates beyond the limits set by law. The cry is for campaign-financing reform. The issue is, how can such reform be achieved?

Campaign Contributions and Policy Decisions

As might be expected, business interest groups donate more to campaigns than any other type of group. After all, businesses can more easily see from their bottom lines whether they benefit or lose from a particular political candidate or policy decision. According to the Center for Responsive Politics, businesses raised around $250 million in the 1996 election cycle. Much of that included "soft money" that went to the national parties, particularly the Republicans. Because the Republicans won control of both chambers in Congress in the 1994 elections, Republican candidates now get three times more PAC money than do Democratic candidates.

Do these donations influence government policymaking? Clearly, there is no reason to conclude that a member of Congress who received X amount of dollars from a certain business group while campaigning for Congress will vote differently on policy issues than she or he would otherwise vote. After all, many groups make contributions not so much to influence a candidate's views as to ensure that a candidate whose views the group supports will win the election. Other groups routinely donate to candidates from both parties so that, regardless of who wins the race, the groups will have access to the officeholder. Money does matter, however, and those who succeed in gaining seats in Congress with the help of campaign funds from certain groups will likely take those groups' interests into consideration when making policy decisions—particularly if they want to retain their seats in the next election.

In an attempt to correlate campaign contributions with policy choices, the Center for Responsive Politics analyzed fourteen heavily lobbied issues. The center concluded that campaign contributions are made for very practical business reasons. Simply put, you need money to play and be heard. One example the center used was the sugar industry, which wanted to keep a sugar subsidy in place. The sixty-one senators who voted to continue the subsidy received an average of $13,473 each in campaign contributions from the industry. The thirty-five senators who voted against the industry's subsidy received an average of $1,461. In the House, the difference was $5,994 versus $853.[17]

Campaign Reform—The Real Issues

After the 1996 election cycle, many political commentators argued that campaign-financing reform was a must. The general public also wants campaign-financing reform. In a *Wall Street Journal*/NBC News poll, 92 percent of Americans said that too much money was being spent on campaigns; 51 percent said they opposed unlimited giving and spending even with full disclosure.[18] There is little consensus, however, on what should be done. In fact, a recent poll indicates that 63 percent of Americans agreed with the statement, "No matter what new laws are passed, special interests will always find a way to maintain their power in Washington."[19] Nonetheless, several proposals have been put forth, including those discussed here.

BAN OR AT LEAST STRICTLY LIMIT PACS

Many liberal public-interest groups (often associated with Ralph Nader), President Bill Clinton, former senator and 1996 presidential candidate

After numerous campaign-funding irregularities were made public in 1997, President Clinton and Vice President Gore repeatedly recommended campaign-finance reform legislation. As of 1999, no such legislation has been passed.

Bob Dole, and others would like to strictly limit or ban completely money that comes from PACs. One of the reasons for limiting or banning PAC money is that PAC campaign contributions are biased toward incumbents.

Critics of placing more restrictions on PACs—or banning them completely—argue that such an action would further concentrate power in the hands of government, particularly those already in office. Campaign contributions can be viewed as "protection" money, according to these observers. Individuals, businesses, and unions should be able to avail themselves of this one method they have of protecting themselves from legislators, agencies, and bureaucrats.

BAN OR LIMIT FOREIGN CONTRIBUTIONS

Americans are seriously at odds over the possible influence foreign business interests may have on our government. Clearly, the way foreign contributions were obtained during the 1996 election cycle raises ethical issues. Not so clear is how these issues can be resolved.

Is the way out of the problem simply to ban foreign gifts? The Federal Election Commission considered such a possibility as recently as 1991. Then it rejected a proposal to prohibit companies that were more than 50 percent foreign owned from establishing corporate PACs. The reason the commission rejected the proposal is that as business has become more and more global, it is no longer easy to decide whether a company is foreign or domestic. American companies may have ownership in a foreign company, which then has a U.S. subsidiary. Is that a foreign or domestic company?

There is also a constitutional question. U.S. citizens working for a foreign subsidiary in the United States presumably are entitled to equal participation in the U.S. political process relative to their colleagues working for a similar company that is 100 percent U.S. owned. To take an example, workers at a Ford plant in Ohio are not much different than workers at a Honda plant in the same state. On the other side of the coin, American companies with foreign operations donate to foreign elections. Should

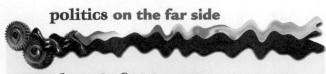

politics on the far side

Outlaw Soft Money—
Are You Kidding?

That Congress finds it difficult to achieve consensus on outlawing soft money should not really be surprising. All one needs to ask is the following question: "Who benefits from soft money?" The answer, of course, is incumbent members of Congress. To expect a member of Congress to vote for reform legislation that would jeopardize his or her chances of reelection is unrealistic. Mitch McConnell, a Republican senator from Kentucky, made this clear at a recent meeting with Republican state party chairpersons in April 1999. "Take away 'soft money' and we wouldn't be in the majority in the House and the majority in the Senate and couldn't win back the White House," McConnell remarked. "Hell's going to freeze over before we get rid of soft money."[20]

For Critical Analysis: Can you think of any other types of reform that would require members of Congress to act against their self-interest?

INFOTRAC®

Political influence of advocacy groups

that be prevented, too? Thus, even though both the Republicans and the Democrats support the proposal to bar contributions from U.S. subsidiaries of foreign companies, eliminating such contributions would raise an issue of fairness.

OUTLAW SOFT MONEY COMPLETELY

Perhaps the major issue in campaign-financing reform has to do with soft money. During the 1996 and 1998 election cycles, U.S. corporations and unions flooded the political market with unprecedented amounts of soft-money contributions. At the same time, the Federal Election Commission has had its budget cut. In effect, it has had to stand by helplessly as the national party committees have skirted the campaign-financing laws during recent elections.

A number of groups, including Common Cause, support President Clinton's suggestion that soft money be eliminated or restricted dramatically. In fact, Congress has been considering various bills over the last few years that would outlaw soft money, but to date no legislation has been enacted. (See the feature *Politics on the Far Side: Outlaw Soft Money—Are You Kidding?* for one reason why legislators find it hard to do this.)

REPEAL LIMITS ON CAMPAIGN CONTRIBUTIONS

A small group of election watchers have come up with a different idea about reforming campaign contributions. They argue that there should be no limits on campaign contributions. Rather, there should simply be a full disclosure of all funding sources. Politicians would have to document on a daily basis the source and size of every contribution—including donated labor and equipment.

There is a privacy issue here, to be sure. The privacy of donors would be compromised. Because we are dealing with the purchase of political access or influence, however, it is not clear that this is a serious concern. More serious is the record-keeping problem that would arise. Documenting all contributions would cost time and money. The requirement would be particularly hard on smaller groups that could not afford to hire expensive legal advisers to help them and that would not have the computing power to fill out the reports easily. One way around the problem would be to limit reporting to contributions in excess of some threshold, say, $5,000.

THE FREE SPEECH ISSUE

Any type of campaign reform would involve a larger issue—freedom of speech. Pursuant to several Supreme Court decisions, individuals can spend as much money as they want on their own campaigns. Recently, a group of constitutional scholars started a campaign to overturn the Supreme Court's decision in *Buckley v. Valeo*, which, as mentioned earlier in the chapter, was the precedent-setting case on this free speech issue.[21] Interestingly enough, because of all of the campaign restrictions in place and because of the free speech right of candidates to pay for their own elections, Congress has more millionaires than ever before. They are the only ones who apparently can overcome the restrictions on individual, corporate, and union donations to specific candidates.

key terms

Australian ballot 253
blanket primary 240
campaign manager 246
caucus 239
closed primary 240
Credentials Committee 245
delegate 239
direct primary 240
elector 255
electoral college 255
general election 253
independent expenditure 251
loophole 249

mandatory preference poll 241
nominating convention 239
office-block ballot 255
open primary 240
party-column ballot 253
political consultant 246
poll watcher 255
preference poll 241
soft money 250
special election 253
tracking poll 247
winner-take-all system 255
write-in candidate 239

chapter summary

1. In the early years of this nation's history, candidates were nominated for political offices by elite political leaders who held secret congressional meetings, or caucuses, for that purpose. The caucus system was gradually replaced (in most states) by the nominating convention, which in turn was replaced by the direct primary (although national conventions are still used by both parties to nominate presidential and vice presidential candidates). The direct primary is a statewide election held within each party to pick its candidates for the general election. In a closed primary, only party members can vote to choose the party's candidates, and they may vote only in the primary of their own party. In an open primary, voters can vote for a party's candidates regardless of the voters' party affiliations.

2. The majority of the states hold presidential primaries to elect delegates to the parties' national conventions. The primary campaign recently has been shortened to the first few months of the year. In July or August, each political party holds a national convention during which the convention delegates, among other things, adopt the official party platform and decide who will be the party's presidential and vice presidential candidates.

3. American political campaigns are lengthy and extremely expensive. In recent years, they have become more candidate centered than party centered in response to technological innovations and declining party identification among the voters. Candidates rely less on the party and more on paid professional campaign managers and political consultants. The campaign organization devises a campaign strategy to maximize the candidate's chances of winning. Candidates use public opinion polls,

both private and public, to gauge their popularity among the voters.

4. The amount of money spent in financing campaigns has increased dramatically in the last two elections. Federal legislation instituted major reforms in the 1970s by limiting spending and contributions. The laws allowed corporations, labor unions, and interest groups to set up political action committees, or PACs, to raise money for candidates. Increasingly, the parties are skirting the federal campaign regulations limiting donations. The channeling of soft money, independent expenditures, and foreign contributions to parties and candidates in recent elections is a cause of growing concern in this country and underscores the need for campaign-finance reform.

5. General elections are regularly scheduled elections held in even-numbered years on the first Tuesday after the first Monday in November. During general elections, the voters decide who will be the U.S. president, vice president, and senators and representatives in Congress. State general elections, which may occur at the same time, are held to elect state and local government officials.

6. Since 1888, all states in the United States have used the Australian ballot—a secret ballot that is prepared, distributed, and counted by government officials at public expense. Two variations of the Australian ballot are the party-column ballot (which lists all of a party's candidates in a single column under the party label) and the office-block ballot (which lists together all of the candidates for each office).

7. Elections are held in voting precincts (districts within each local government unit). Precinct officials supervise the polling place and the voting

process. Poll watchers from each of the two major parties typically monitor the polling place as well to ensure that the election is conducted fairly and to prevent voting fraud.

8. In the presidential elections, citizens do not vote directly for the president and vice president; instead, they vote for electors who will cast their ballots in the electoral college. Each state has as many electoral votes as it has U.S. senators and representatives; there are also three electors from the District of Columbia. The electoral college is a winner-take-all system because the candidate who receives the largest popular vote in a state takes all of that state's electoral votes. In December, after the general election, members of the electoral college meet in their state capitals to cast their votes for president and vice president. Ultimately, the U.S. Senate counts and certifies the electoral college votes before a joint session of Congress held in early January.

9. Americans are at odds over several issues relating to campaigns and elections. One major issue has to do with campaign-financing abuses and the need for campaign-financing reform. Another significant issue concerns the extent to which campaign contributions influence government policymaking.

for critical analysis

1. What is the most memorable negative ad you have ever seen? Why was it so effective?

2. If you could change one thing about the funding of political campaigns, what would it be?

3. Do you see any problems with allowing foreigners to contribute to American presidential campaigns?

4. Do you agree with those who feel that the Supreme Court's opinion in *Buckley v. Valeo* should be overturned? Why or why not?

5. Should the American government be allowed to influence foreign elections in order to elect officials friendly to the United States?

6. Some Americans think that the electoral college should be abolished. What would be some of the advantages of abolishing the electoral college? What would be some of the disadvantages?

7. Would voter participation increase if candidates for the U.S. Senate in your state stuck to debating the issues during the campaign and avoided personal attacks?

suggested readings

ANSOLABEHERE, Stephen, and Shanto Iyengar. *Going Negative: How Attack Ads Shrink and Polarize the Electorate.* New York: Free Press, 1996. These two political scientists, based on a six-year study of political advertising, have joined others who claim that political ads have become a cancer in American society. The authors describe how the entire campaign season has become filled with political ads that are not only extremely costly but also negative and nasty attacks on the opposing candidates. The effect of the ads, according to the authors, is to turn off voters from the whole political process.

KING, Anthony Stephen. *Running Scared: Why America's Politicians Campaign Too Much and Govern Too Little.* New York, Free Press, 1997. The author contends that U.S. politicians have become vulnerable to the permanent campaign and, as a result, are no longer able to make independent decisions that may jeopardize their chances for success in the next election. According to the author, all major policies and features of our political system are now under the sway of the effects of the permanent campaign.

ROZELL, Mari, and Clyde Wilcox. *Interest Groups in American Campaigns: The New Face of Electioneering.* Washington, D.C.: Congressional Quarterly Press, 1998. The authors examine the influence of interest groups on modern political campaigns at the local, state, and national levels. The work is based on research gathered from interviews, surveys, and campaign-financing reports.

SABATO, Larry. Ed. *Toward the Millennium: The Elections of 1996.* Englewood Cliffs, N.J.: Prentice Hall, 1997. This collection of essays, three of which are by Sabato, focuses on the 1996 elections. Each essay provides an insightful look into some aspect of the elections, including the candidates, the front-loaded primaries, the media's performance, and campaign financing (the latter under the title "The Law of the Jungle"). One essay looks at the 1996 elections to state offices.

politics on the web

You can find out exactly what the letter of the law is with respect to campaign financing by accessing the Federal Election Commission's Web site. The commission has provided an online "Citizen's Guide" that spells out exactly what is and is not legal. You can also download actual data on campaign donations from the site. Go to

http://www.fec.gov

If you want to look at the data available from the Federal Election Commission in a more user-friendly way, you can access the following nonpartisan independent site that allows you to type in an elected official's name and receive large amounts of information on contributions to that official. There is also a detailed section on soft-money contributions:

http://www.tray.com/FECInfo

The Document Center of the University of Michigan offers a comprehensive collection of government documents, related news stories, and links to other sites. Among other things, you can find information on campaign financing and reform at this site. Go to

http://www.lib.umich.edu/libhome/Documents.center/docnews.html

Another site that offers information on campaign financing, as well as voting, can be accessed at

http://www.vote-smart.org

using web resources

Go to the "FECInfo" Web site at

http://www.tray.com/FECInfo

1. Select the name of a presidential candidate for the 2000 elections and study the contributions to his or her campaign. Who has given the most money to the candidate?

2. Return to the main page and scroll down to "US House/Senate Campaign Money Info" and select the most recent election for your representative in the House. What categories of people and PACs gave money to the winning candidate? Did money play too large a role in the election of your representative?

3. What percentage of the money given to your representative was from out of state? Do you believe this has a detrimental effect on the electoral process? Why or why not?

notes

1. Romesh Ratnesar, "The New Money Game," *Time,* November 2, 1998, pp. 49–50.

2. This word apparently was first used in the name of a men's club, the *Caucus Club* of colonial Boston, sometime between 1755 and 1765. (Many early political and government meetings took place in pubs.) The origin of the word is unknown, but some scholars have concluded it is of Algonquin origin.

3. George F. Will, "Conventional Journalism," *Newsweek,* September 2, 1996.

4. Center for Responsive Politics, 1999. These data and other information on campaign expenditures are available at the center's Web site at **www.crp.org.**

5. This act is sometimes referred to as the Federal Election Campaign Act of 1972, because it became effective in that year. The official date of the act, however, is 1971.

6. 424 U.S. 1 (1976).

7. Traciel V. Reid, "PAC Participation in North Carolina Supreme Court Elections," *Judicature,* Vol. 80, No. 1 (July/August 1996), p. 22, Table 1.

8. *Ibid.*, pp. 26–27.

9. Paul Allen Beck, *Party Politics in America,* 8th ed. (New York: Longman Publishers, 1996), pp. 293–294.

10. *The Wall Street Journal,* March 30, 1999, p. A28.

11. These and other data on soft-money contributions to the parties are available at FECInfo's user-friendly Web site at **www.tray.com/fecinfo.**

12. *Colorado Republican Federal Campaign Committee v. Federal Election Commission,* 518 U.S. 604 (1996).

13. Michael Weisskopf and Michael Duffy, "The G.O.P.'s Own China Connection," *Time,* May 5, 1997, pp. 45–46.

14. Karen Gullo, "Set-Aside of Utah Coal Reserve Question: Some See Connection to Indonesian Concern," *USA Today,* December 26, 1996, p. 4A.

15. John Quincy Adams in the 1824 election (he was selected by the House of Representatives), Rutherford B. Hayes in 1876, and Benjamin Harrison in 1888.

16. As cited in Peter Coy, "Electoral College, Hail to Thee," *Business Week,* November 4, 1996, p. 42.

17. Leslie Wayne, "Lobbyists' Gifts to Politicians Reap Benefits, Study Shows," *The New York Times,* National Edition, January 23, 1997, p. A11.

18. *The Wall Street Journal,* December 13, 1996, p. 1.

19. *The Gallup Report,* March 20–22, 1998.

20. Fred Wertheimer, "The Hypocrisy of the Foreign Money Uproar," *The Washington Post,* April 25, 1999, p. B4.

21. These scholars include Professor Ronald Dworkin and Professor Burt Neuborne, both of the New York University Law School, and twenty-five others who signed a statement calling on the Supreme Court to reconsider and reverse the decision.

POLITICS AND THE MEDIA

Contents

Free TV Time for Politicians: Will Anybody Watch?

There is a very good reason why campaign costs tripled during the 1990s: the quantity of TV airtime purchased for political advertising by the parties, the candidates, and the candidates' supporters and detractors skyrocketed during those years. One important campaign-reform idea is to give free airtime to those candidates who raise a minimum amount of money on their own or who get a minimum number of signatures on a petition.

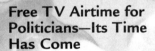

Free TV Airtime for Politicians—Its Time Has Come

Those in favor of a specified amount of free TV time, at least for presidential candidates, argue that its time has come. After all, one of the reasons the 1996 campaign became so "sleazy" is that so much money was needed to buy televised political advertising. It is not surprising that the candidates in 1996 were willing to bend federal campaign rules to obtain money from contributors, including foreign sources (see Chapter 10), to pay for this advertising.

Supporters of free TV time for politicians also argue that it would allow the candidates to engage in more issues-centered dialogues. With free TV time, the candidates would have more time to communicate their views to the voters. They would not have to rely on thirty-second negative ads or ten-second "sound bites" delivered by network news channels.

One group in favor of free airtime for political candidates is the Free TV for Straight Talk Coalition. This group, headed by a former newspaper reporter, Paul Taylor, convinced three of the four major networks, plus PBS and CNN, to give away quite a few minutes of prime-time television to the presidential candidates in 1996. Although the free-time statements did not garner a very large audience, they were noteworthy for other reasons. Each candidate devoted a smaller proportion of time to attacking his opponent during the free-time statements than during paid political advertisements. The free-time state-

ments were also more factually accurate than were the candidates' comments during the presidential debates. Finally, the candidates addressed a broader range of topics than they did during the debates or in their paid political ads.

Proponents of free airtime suggest that scheduling free TV slots for the candidates is the only way we can reduce the need for the candidates to raise so much money for television commercials. As long as political candidates need to raise extensive funds to pay for costly TV time, they will remain dependent on special interest groups for campaign financing.

A Nice Idea, but It Won't Work

Another group is at odds with the concept of offering free TV time for candidates. This group first points out that the experiment during the last elections was, in a word, a disaster. Only about 22 percent of registered voters were aware that the candidates were given any free TV time.[1] In any event, the only reason the TV networks, PBS, and CNN offered the deal is because Fox Network had announced that it would give each candidate ten free one-minute slots during prime time and a free half-hour on the eve of the election.

Those who oppose free TV time also argue that there is no guarantee that it would result in a meaningful, informative dialogue among the candidates. More than likely, they would continue to make the same inane and sometimes offensive remarks in their free airtime as they currently do in their paid campaign ads.

Opponents of free TV do not feel that it is the only solution to the problem of high campaign costs. They suggest that the way to get better and cheaper political coverage is to simply have more news competition. In their view, the federal government should open up the entire electromagnetic spectrum for as many new digital TV stations and high-speed Internet accesses as is physically possible. Speech over the electromagnetic spectrum would be cheaper, and debate would become more robust.

Finally, those against free TV airtime raise a significant question: What would be the *quid pro quo* for this alleged benefit to the candidates? Would the amount of money a candidate can spend on all TV advertising be restricted? But wouldn't such restrictions violate the candidates' First Amendment right to freely express their opinions?

Where Do You Stand?

1. Does what a candidate says on TV at any time necessarily affect how you are going to vote anyway?

2. Who ends up paying for "free" TV political time?

On the Web

For more information on free TV time for politicians, go to Vote Smart's Web site at **http://www.vote-smart.org**.

Introduction

MASS MEDIA ● Communication channels, such as newspapers and radio and television broadcasts, through which people can communicate to mass audiences.

PRINT MEDIA ● Communication channels that consist of printed materials, such as newspapers and magazines.

ELECTRONIC MEDIA ● Communication channels that involve electronic transmissions, such as radio, television, and, to an extent, the Internet.

I N F O T R A C®
Free TV time for politicians

The debate over free TV airtime for political candidates underscores the importance of media exposure for any successful political campaign. Strictly defined, the term *media* means communication channels. It is the plural form of *medium of communication*. In this strict sense, any method used by people to communicate—including the telephone—is a communication medium. What we look at in this chapter, though, is the **mass media**—communication channels through which people can communicate to mass audiences. These channels include the **print media** (newspapers and magazines) and the **electronic media** (radio, television, and, to an increasing extent, the Internet).

The media have a wide-ranging influence on American politics. As discussed in Chapter 9, the media play an important role in shaping public opinion, both as agents of political socialization and as agenda setters—determining what issues will get on the political agenda. The exact nature of the media's influence is hard to determine because of the intricate interplay between the media and politics. Clearly, what the media say and do has an impact on what Americans think about political issues. But just as clearly, the media also reflect what Americans think about politics. Scholars who try to analyze the relationship between American politics and the media inevitably confront the chicken-and-egg conundrum: Do the media cause the public to hold certain views, or do the media merely reflect views that are formed independently of the media's influence?

Although the media's influence cannot be measured precisely, we do know that the media have an impact on politics and that their most significant impact is during campaigns and elections. Politicians and political candidates have learned—often the hard way—that positive media exposure and news coverage are essential to winning votes.

The Candidates and Television

Of all the media, television has the greatest impact. Television reaches into every pocket of the United States. More homes have televisions (98 percent) than have telephones (94 percent). Even outside their homes, Americans can watch television. There are TVs in airports, shopping mall food courts, bowling lanes, golf clubhouses, and dentists' offices. According to a recent study conducted by the Pew Research Center for the People and the Press, television is the primary news source for 72 percent of Americans. Figure 11–1 on the next page clearly shows the prominence of television among the media.

The electronic media, particularly television, have come to dominate virtually all campaigns. Here, 1996 presidential candidate Bob Dole and his wife, Elizabeth Dole, are shown on *Larry King Live*. For the last several years, virtually all presidential candidates have been interviewed frequently by Larry King. Elizabeth Dole later launched her own campaign for the presidency, running as a Republican candidate in the 2000 presidential race.

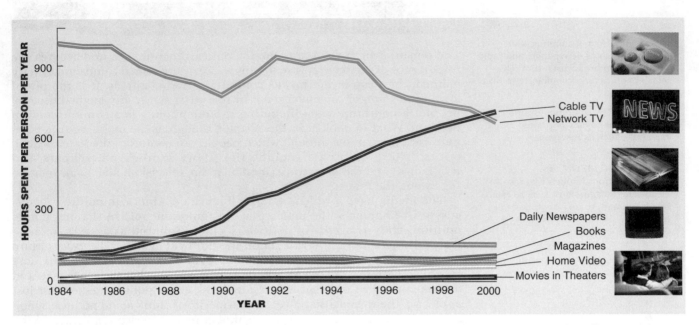

SOURCE: U.S. Department of Commerce, *Statistical Abstract of the United States, 1998* (Washington, D.C.: U.S. Government Printing Office, 1998), p. 572. Data for 1998 and 2000 are projections.

Figure 11–1
Media Usage by
Consumers, 1984 to 2000

Given the TV-saturated environment in which we live, it should come as no surprise that candidates spend a great deal of time—and money—obtaining TV coverage through political ads, debates, and general news coverage. Candidates and their campaign managers realize that such time and money are well spent because television has an important impact on the way people see the candidates, understand the issues, and cast their votes.

POLITICAL ADVERTISING

Today, televised **political advertising** consumes at least half of the total budget for a major political campaign. According to one estimate, in 1996 the Clinton/Gore campaign and the National Democratic Committee spent more than $70 million between April 1 and the elections on November 4, while the Dole/Kemp campaign and the Republican National Committee spent about $60 million. These millions of dollars allowed the candidates and the two major parties to broadcast about fourteen hundred hours of TV ads, most of which were thirty-second announcements. That is the equivalent of fifty-eight days of commercials in the seventy-five major media markets.[2] Fourteen hundred hours of TV ads may seem like a lot, but it is less than 20 percent of the 750,000 political TV commercials that were broadcast from April 1 to November 4, 1996. Table 11–1 shows how many spots were broadcast by the two parties in the top ten markets in which all campaign ads were aired.

Heavy TV advertising by a candidate carries no guarantees, as the Republicans learned in California. The Dole/Kemp campaign and the Republican National Committee placed 3,543 ads in Los Angeles, 2,635 ads in Sacramento, and 2,056 ads in San Diego. Nonetheless, the Republican ticket lost by a large margin in that state.

The Emergence of Televised Political Advertising

Political advertising first appeared on television during the 1952 presidential campaign. At that time, there were only about fifteen million television sets; today, there are well over one hundred million. Initially, political TV commercials were more or less like any other type of advertising.

POLITICAL ADVERTISING ●
Advertising undertaken by or on behalf of a political candidate to familiarize voters with the candidate and his or her views on campaign issues.

Table 11-1

Spots Aired by the Parties in the Top Ten Media Markets

CLINTON AND THE DEMOCRATS		DOLE AND THE REPUBLICANS	
MARKET	NUMBER OF SPOTS	MARKET	NUMBER OF SPOTS
1. Albuquerque, N.M.	3,079	1. Los Angeles	3,543
2. Lexington, Ky.	2,681	2. Denver	2,727
3. Sacramento, Calif.	2,535	3. Sacramento, Calif.	2,635
4. Tampa, Fla.	2,446	4. Cleveland	2,284
5. Denver	2,397	5. Nashville	2,244
6. Louisville, Ky.	2,392	6. Albuquerque, N.M.	2,216
7. Flint, Mich.	2,384	7. Tampa, Fla.	2,161
8. Cincinnati	2,381	8. Cincinnati	2,131
9. Cleveland	2,345	9. Atlanta	2,097
10. Detroit	2,316	10. San Diego	2,056

SOURCE: *New York Times*, November 13, 1996, p. D20.

Instead of focusing on the positive qualities of a product, thirty-second or sixty-second ads focused on the positive qualities of a political candidate. Within the decade, however, **negative political advertising** began to appear in the TV medium.

Negative Political Ads

Despite the barrage of criticism levied against the candidates' use of negative political ads during the 1996 election cycle, such ads are not new. Indeed, **attack ads**—advertising that attacks the character of an opposing candidate—have a long tradition in this country. In 1800, an article in the *Federalist Gazette of the United States* described Thomas Jefferson as having a "weakness of nerves, want of fortitude, and total imbecility of character."[3]

Candidates also use **issue ads**—ads that focus on flaws in the opponents' positions on issues. For example, in the 1996 presidential campaigns, rarely did the candidates attack each other personally.[4] Rather, they leveled criticisms at each other's stated positions on various issues, such as balancing the federal budget, and previous actions with respect to those issues. Candidates also try to undermine their opponents' credibility by pointing to discrepancies between what the opponents say in their campaign speeches and their political records, such as voting records, which are available to the public and thus can be easily verified. As noted in Chapters 7 and 10, issue ads are also used by interest groups to gather support for candidates who endorse the groups' causes.

Issue ads can be even more devastating than personal attacks—as Barry Goldwater learned in 1964 when his opponent in the presidential race, President Lyndon Johnson, aired the "daisy girl" ad. This ad, which set new boundaries for political advertising, showed a little girl standing quietly in a field of daisies. She held a daisy and pulled off the petals, counting to herself. Suddenly, a deep voice was heard counting: "10, 9, 8, 7, 6 . . . ." When the countdown hit zero, the unmistakable mushroom cloud of an atomic bomb filled the screen. Then President Johnson's voice was heard saying, "These are the stakes: to make a world in which all of God's children can live, or to go into the dark. We must either love each other or we must die." A message on the screen then read: "Vote for President Johnson on November 3." The implication, of course, was that Goldwater would lead the country into a nuclear war.

TELEVISION DEBATES

Televised debates have been a feature of presidential campaigns since 1960, when presidential candidates Republican Richard M. Nixon and Democrat

NEGATIVE POLITICAL ADVERTISING
● Political advertising undertaken for the purpose of discrediting an opposing candidate in the eyes of the voters; attack ads and issue ads are forms of negative political advertising.

ATTACK AD ● A negative political advertisement that attacks the character of an opposing candidate.

ISSUE AD ● A negative political advertisement that focuses on flaws in an opposing candidate's position on a particular issue.

When presidential television debates started in 1960, they were a major media event. By the time of the 1996 Clinton-Dole debates shown here, the public had lost some of its enthusiasm. Some argue that presidential debates oversimplify the issues in order to reach a wider audience.

John F. Kennedy squared off in the first great TV debate. Television debates provide an opportunity for voters to find out how candidates differ on issues. They also allow candidates to capitalize on the power of television to improve their image or point out the failings of their opponents.

The presidential debates of 1992 included a third party candidate, H. Ross Perot, along with the candidates from the two major parties, Republican George Bush, the incumbent president, and Democrat Bill Clinton. In 1996, two third party candidates, H. Ross Perot and John Hagelin, sought to participate in the TV debates but were prevented from doing so by the Commission for Presidential Debates.[5] (For a further discussion of third party candidates and presidential debates, see the feature in Chapter 8 entitled *A Question of Ethics: Should Third Party Candidates Be Let in on the Great Debates?*) Of the three debates held in 1996, two were between presidential candidates Bill Clinton and Bob Dole, and one was between the vice presidential candidates, Al Gore and Dole's Republican running mate, Jack Kemp.

Many contend that a candidate's performance in a televised debate is perhaps equal in importance to political advertising in shaping the outcome of the elections. Others doubt that these televised debates have ever been taken very seriously. Political commentator William Plass has concluded that presidential debates, by their very nature, oversimplify the issues in order to reach a wider audience.[6]

THE CANDIDATES AND NEWS COVERAGE

Whereas political ads are expensive, coverage by the news media is free. Accordingly, the candidates try to take advantage of the media's interest in campaigns to increase the quantity and quality of news coverage. In recent years, candidates' campaign managers and political consultants have shown increasing sophistication in creating newsworthy events for journalists and TV camera crews to cover, an effort commonly referred to as **managed news coverage.** As one scholar points out, "To keep a favorable image of their candidates in front of the public, campaign managers arrange newsworthy events to familiarize potential voters with their candidates' best aspects."[7]

Besides becoming aware of how camera angles and lighting affect a candidate's appearance, the political consultant plans political events to accommodate the press. The campaign staff attempts to make what the candidate is doing appear interesting. The staff also knows that journalists

MANAGED NEWS COVERAGE ●
News coverage that is manipulated (managed) by a campaign manager or political consultant to gain media exposure for a political candidate.

News reporters love to catch candidates in embarrassing or compromising situations. Not surprisingly, when presidential candidate Bob Dole fell off a platform during a campaign rally in Chico, California, on September 18, 1996, photographers captured the moment on film. The event made the evening news. Some said that the media were exploiting Dole.

INFOTRAC®

Kick out the image makers

SPIN DOCTOR ● A political candidate's press adviser who tries to convince reporters to give a story or event concerning the candidate a particular "spin" (interpretation, or slant).

SPIN ● A reporter's slant on, or interpretation of, a particular event or action.

and political reporters compete for stories and that they can be manipulated by granting favors, such as an exclusive personal interview with the candidate. Each candidate's press advisers, often called **spin doctors,** also try to convince reporters to give the story or event a **spin,** or interpretation, that is favorable to the candidate.

Overall, television has created a new kind of political candidate—one who must be at ease with the camera and ever conscious of the image that is being conveyed to the public via the TV. Almost every decision that consultants make about a candidate's activities—where to eat dinner, what to wear, and what to say about particular issues—is calculated according to its potential media impact. In a word, television dictates how the campaign is run.

This photo of President Bill Clinton campaigning in Liberty City (Miami) in 1996 helped him capture the African American vote. Some people accused Clinton of exploiting the media.

WHO BENEFITS FROM EXPENSIVE CAMPAIGNS?

Who benefits the most from expensive TV ads and news coverage during political campaigns? The answer is political consultants and TV stations. The complex relationship that exists between political consultants and the media during political campaigns has sometimes been described as a **symbiotic relationship.** (The phrase stems from the biological term *symbiosis*, which refers to a relationship of two or more different organisms in a close association that may be—but is not necessarily—of benefit to each.) Political consultants depend on the media to get their candidates' names and images before the voters through managed news coverage and political ads. The media need news to cover, and during campaigns, the news is what the candidates are doing. The media must also stay in business, and revenues from advertising help them to do this.

Today, there are about seven thousand full-time professional political consultants. In an election year, their fees total over a billion dollars. These are the individuals behind the sometimes tasteless, but often entertaining, political ads. At the 1997 convention of the American Association of Political Consultants, *Washington Post* columnist David Broder accused them of "filling the airways with trash."[8] In response, the former chairman of the association pointed out that compared to movies, most TV shows, and everything else in the media, political ads seem pretty bland. "There is no sex and no violence in our ads," he said.

The TV industry also profits handsomely from campaign expenditures. Indeed, the National Association of Broadcasters has fought heavily to squelch any true reform that would allow free political TV airtime. Local stations benefit the most when there is a hotly contested campaign. The "trash" ads start appearing fast and furiously. Take as an example Raleigh, North Carolina. Because of several heavily contested races in 1996, including the races for the governorship and a Senate seat, politicians aired more than eighteen thousand commercials, which cost more than $9 million for airtime. Total revenues for the Raleigh TV stations increased by about 7 percent as a result.

THE MEDIUM DOES AFFECT THE MESSAGE

Although research undertaken by the Pew Research Center for the People and the Press shows an increase in radio and Internet usage for news, TV remains the primary news source for most Americans, as mentioned earlier. Does the TV medium alter in any way the presentation of the news? If you compare how an important political issue is covered in the print media with how the same issue is covered by the TV networks, you will note some striking differences. For one thing, the print media (particularly leading newspapers such as the *Washington Post*, the *New York Times*, and the *Wall Street Journal*) treat the issue in much more detail. In addition to news coverage based on reporters' research, you will find editorials taking positions on the issue and arguments supporting those positions. Television news, in contrast, is often criticized as being too brief and too superficial.

Time Constraints

The medium of television necessarily imposes constraints, particularly with respect to time, on how the news is presented. News stories must be reported quickly, in only a few minutes or occasionally in only a **sound bite,** a brief comment lasting for just a few seconds that captures a thought or a perspective and has an immediate impact on the viewers. News stories must also rely extensively on visual elements, rather than words, to capture the viewers' attention. Inevitably, the photos or videos selected to depict a particular political event have exaggerated importance. Those watching the news presentation do not know what portions of a video being shown have been deleted, what other photos may have been taken, or whether other records of the event exist.

James Carville, President Clinton's top defender and former campaign manager. Carville has been active in "exporting" U.S. campaign strategy to other nations as well. In 1998, he helped Israeli Labor Party leader Ehud Barak in an effort to oust Benjamin Netanyahu, who was then prime minister of Israel. In 1999, Carville advised one of the candidates in the Argentinian presidential race.

The Prevalence of the Remote Control

Most Americans have a remote control in hand while watching TV,[9] and the prevalence of the remote control allows channel surfers to have their way under virtually all circumstances. Consequently, even when an in-depth political discussion is available, such as during the free TV spots given to the presidential candidates by several of the major networks in 1996, the viewership can be abysmal.

The Popularity of TV News Magazines

To stay in business, TV stations need viewers, and to attract viewers to their programs the "channel-flipping factor," as one reporter called it, must be considered. More and more, an "infotainment" news industry is emerging. Witness the recent growth in the number of TV "news magazines," which include CNN's *Impact* and *NewsStand*, ABC's *PrimeTime Live* and *Turning Point*, and CBS's *60 Minutes* and *48 Hours*. According to NewsTV Reports, a company that tracks the networks, the number of news magazine hours airing in July 1998 was 142 percent above the number for the same month in 1996.[10] These programs, which are popular with viewers, offer an added benefit: they are inexpensive to produce.

According to a recent survey of journalists,[11] most of those surveyed fear the influence these programs are having on the delivery of the news. Generally, news magazines tend to focus on personality, crime, health, and consumer news to the exclusion of education, economics, government, foreign affairs, and most of the traditional subjects of public debate.

Talk Radio—A New Force in Politics?

On the night of November 2, 1920, KDKA-Pittsburgh transmitted the first scheduled radio program in the United States: the presidential election race between Warren G. Harding and James M. Cox. A few thousand people tuned in to listen on very primitive radio sets. From that time on, radio quickly became a fixture in American homes. Today, about 100 million homes have radios. Another 220 million radios are found outside the home, including those in offices and, of course, in that true fixture of American society, the automobile.

President Franklin D. Roosevelt (1933–1945) was the first president to use radio broadcasts to send messages to the American people. Roosevelt gave twenty-eight "fireside chats," the first of which was on the bank crisis and was transmitted on Sunday, March 12, 1933. It lasted for thirteen minutes and forty-two seconds. He transmitted his last fireside chat on Monday, June 12, 1944.

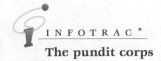

INFOTRAC°
The pundit corps

Ever since Franklin D. Roosevelt started his "fireside chats" on radio, politicians have realized the power of radio. Today, talk radio is a political force to be reckoned with. In 1988, there were 200 talk-show radio stations. Today, there are over 1,200, and that number is growing.[12] The most recent estimates are that one in six Americans listens to talk radio regularly.

TALK RADIO'S "ARRIVAL" IN 1994

When President Clinton called talk-radio station KMOX in St. Louis directly from *Air Force One*, talk radio had arrived. The time was 1994, during the congressional elections. Clinton had placed the call to complain about the criticism he had been receiving from syndicated talk-show host Rush Limbaugh. Ever since Clinton's inauguration in 1993, Limbaugh, an ultra-conservative Republican and a powerful political force in 1994, had relentlessly attacked Clinton's policies and those of the Democratic Congress. Limbaugh's show, with its audience of about 20 million listeners on 660 radio stations, definitely was influential, and the president wanted equal time. Today, politicians routinely appear as guests on talk-radio shows.

THE NEW WILD WEST OF THE MEDIA

According to journalism professor Ruth D. Smith, talk radio has become the "last public forum." She points out that talk radio conveys a certain intimacy that does not exist with other forms of mass communication. People feel that the announcers are talking to them personally.

In many respects, talk radio is indeed a public forum—one that is sometimes characterized as the Wild West of the media. Journalistic conventions do not exist. Political ranting and raving are common. Many popular talk shows do seem to have a conservative bent, but their supporters argue that talk radio has been a good way to counter the liberal bias in the print and TV media.

Some people are uneasy because talk shows empower fringe groups, perhaps magnifying their rage. Clearly, a talk show is not necessarily a democratic forum in which all views are aired. Talk-show hosts such as Limbaugh and Don Imus do not attempt to hide their political biases; if anything, they exaggerate them for effect. Supporters of the sometimes outrageous, sometimes reactionary remarks broadcast during talk-radio shows reply that such shows are simply a reply to consumer demand. Furthermore, those who think that talk radio is good for the country argue that talk shows, taken together, provide a great populist forum for political debate. They maintain that in a sense, talk radio has become an equalizer because it is relatively inexpensive to start up a rival talk show.

Talk-show hosts Rush Limbaugh (caricatured on left) and Don Imus (right).

Those who claim that talk-show hosts go too far in their rantings and ravings ultimately have to deal with the constitutional issue of free speech. After all, as First Amendment scholars point out, there is little the government can do about the forces that shape the media. The courts have always protected freedom of expression to the fullest extent possible, although, for many reasons, the government has been able to exercise some control over the electronic media—see the discussion of freedom of the press in Chapter 4.

The Print Media—Can They Survive?

Prior to the advent of TV and radio broadcasting, the print media were, of course, the major news sources. Indeed, a few printed publications stand out as being instrumental in changing the fate of the nation. As pointed out in Chapter 2, Thomas Paine's *Common Sense* played a key role in unifying American sentiment against the British on the eve of the American Revolution. Later, *The Federalist Papers* were instrumental in creating the atmosphere necessary for the ratification of the Constitution.

Television's impact has been felt by the publishers of evening newspapers. From 1950 to 1997, the number of evening newspapers being published fell from 1,450 to 816.[13] Nonetheless, the print media continue to be important sources of news. Currently, there are more than sixteen thousand newspapers in circulation. Although the number of daily papers is declining, the number of weekly newspapers is increasing, probably due to the growth of the suburbs and the need for local news outlets there. The newspaper industry on the whole, however, is "flat" in terms of growth, while the television industry continues to expand. Use of the Internet, with its enormous capacity to deliver information to the home, is also increasing. These developments have led some observers to speculate that newspapers may eventually disappear—or at least decline significantly in importance—as we become an increasingly "wired" society.

" INTERESTING.....IT'S LIKE A PORTABLE 500K FILE *and* YOU DON'T HAVE TO WAIT FOR IT TO DOWNLOAD.... AND YOU SAY IT'S CALLED A NEWSPAPER ?"

Have Americans Lost Faith in the Mass Media?

The American people today are less interested in political news than they once were. In the early 1990s, interest in political campaigns was already slipping. A study of the 1992 campaign by the University of Michigan's Center for Political Studies discovered the following:

- Fifty percent of voters paid no attention to newspaper articles about the campaign.
- Seventy-seven percent paid no attention to magazine articles.

In 1996, the public's interest in the mass media's coverage of the elections reached a modern all-time low. The lack of interest was reflected in the dramatic reduction of campaign coverage by the news media. According to the Media Study Center, the 1996 election was the least-covered presidential campaign in recent years. On average, television network coverage was down 43 percent compared to 1992 and down 52 percent compared to 1988. (It is difficult to know the extent to which the 1998 elections might have been covered, because throughout 1998 the media were preoccupied not with the elections but with the Clinton-Lewinsky scandal—see the feature *Politics on the Far Side: Elections 1998—Where Were the Media?*)

Some observers speculate that many of today's citizens are simply unwilling to undertake the task of acquiring political information and critically evaluating the candidates' positions on important issues. Others suggest that the declining interest in news reflects a growing lack of faith in the media's ability to report the news accurately and meaningfully, without bias and distortion. Still others claim that Americans' lack of confidence in the media is due to an erosion of the media's values. Perhaps this mistrust of the media also helps to explain why President Clinton's job approval ratings remained high in 1998, even while the media frenzy over the Lewinsky affair raged.

MEDIA BIAS

Since the media first appeared on the American political landscape, they have been criticized by one group or another as being biased (see the feature *The American Political Spectrum: The Question of Media Bias* for examples of some of these criticisms). The many studies that have been undertaken on the subject of media bias, however, have reached different conclusions.

INFOTRAC*

Three wishes and public faith in the media

politics on the far side

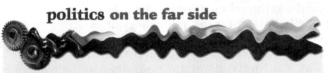

Elections 1998—Where Were the Media?

Normally, the national media play a key role in election contests for highly visible offices. In 1998, however, the national media largely ignored the real issues of the campaign. From the beginning of the year, the media's focus was on the Clinton-Lewinsky scandal. As the elections neared, the impeachment process and other aspects of the affair continued to dominate the media. Little attention was given to the candidates' issue positions in key races for Congress, and several election outcomes took the nation by surprise. For example, little national media attention was given to third party candidate Jesse Ventura, a former professional wrestler running for governor in Minnesota on the Reform Party ticket, yet he turned out to be the winner.

For Critical Analysis: Why were the media focusing on the Clinton-Lewinsky scandal rather than other issues in the 1998 campaigns?

Studies on Media Bias

In a significant study conducted in the 1980s, the researchers found that the media producers, editors, and reporters (the "media elite") showed a notably liberal bias in their news coverage.[14] Other studies, however, have concluded that the overall stance of newspapers and major TV networks has a pro-Republican and pro-conservative bias. Still other researchers assert that the press is largely apolitical. Calvin F. Exoo, in his study of the media and politics, suggests that journalists are neither liberal nor conservative. Rather, they are constrained by both the pro-American bias of the media ownership and the journalists' own code of objectivity. Most are

the american political spectrum

The Question of Media Bias

Ever since the media first became a reporting vehicle, there have been cries that, in general, news coverage in magazines, newspapers, and television broadcasts is biased. Indeed, every time a political party loses an election, at least some of its members attribute the election outcome to media bias.

The Media Are Too Liberal, Say the Conservatives

For years now, conservatives have been calling the media liberal. Some evidence seems to support their claim. A majority of Washington-based political reporters have voted Democratic for quite some time. Both the Freedom Forum Media Study Center and the Roper Center discovered that 89 percent of Washington journalists voted for Bill Clinton during his first election, which stands in stark contrast to the 43 percent of the popular vote that he received. Results of studies conducted by the Center for Media and Public Affairs, a research group headed by S. Robert Lichter, appear to confirm this bias. Lichter and his colleagues tracked coverage by ABC, CBS, and NBC during the last two presidential elections. They found that 50 percent of the stories about Clinton were positive in tone, whereas only 33 percent of the stories about Dole were posi-

tive. According to Lichter, Clinton got better press on issue positions as well as on campaign performance. The center had released almost identical findings when Clinton ran against Republican George Bush in 1992.

Conservatives argue that the media's liberal political bias taints the news and often distorts Republicans' messages to the voting public. It is not surprising that current polls show that the media suffer from a crisis of credibility. Most Americans surveyed ranked journalists and politicians just above tax collectors.

The Media Are Fairly Neutral, Say the Liberals

Liberals do not believe the argument that the media distort Republicans' messages and play favorites with Democratic candidates and elected officials. Liberals point out that the survey of Washington journalists mentioned above had a sample size of only 139, whereas there are thousands of professional reporters and editors throughout the United States. Moreover, who is to say that there is any real correlation between personal voting and political coverage?

Also, political liberals point out that television and the print media were merciless during Clinton's first year and a half in office. During that time, 62 per-

cent of all major news stories about the White House were negative. In contrast, during Bush's first eighteen months in office, only 51 percent of network stories had a negative tone.

Liberals also observe that the so-called liberal press, including such allegedly liberal icons as the *Washington Post* and the *New York Times*, continues to "tell it like it is." These media have consistently criticized Clinton and his administration, even in their editorials. Who was it, ask the liberals, that broke all of the damaging stories about the Clintons? It was the *New York Times* that uncovered the Whitewater scandal as well as Hillary Clinton's financial windfall in commodities trading. It was the *Los Angeles Times* that dug deeply enough to discover the Indonesian campaign contributions scandal and bring it to the public's attention.

Some liberals maintain that, if anything, the press holds a conservative bias. Press coverage tends to support established political institutions and their representatives while ignoring the voices of the unorganized and unenfranchised.

For Critical Analysis

Do you think that media bias is more apparent in the choice of what news to cover or in how that news is covered?

more interested in improving their career prospects than in discussing public policies.[15]

The Bias toward Bad News

Political scientist Thomas Patterson says that the real bias of the news media is toward bad news and cynicism rather than any partisan position. It appears that a large number of Americans would agree with Patterson's assertion. In a *Time*/CNN poll, 63 percent of the respondents stated that the news media are too negative, and 73 percent were skeptical about the accuracy of news.[16] Although Americans complain about the media's bias toward bad news, in some other countries, even bad news goes unreported. (See the feature on the following page entitled *Comparative Politics: Not All Countries Allow Free Expression in the Media.*)

comparative politics

Not All Countries Allow Free Expression in the Media

People complain that the media, at least in the United States, concentrate on reporting bad news—airplane crashes, major automobile wrecks, famines, floods, fires, earthquakes, tornadoes, cyclones, and ethnic wars. Some countries, however, still severely restrict media coverage of any news within their borders, either by their own citizens or by foreigners. Such restrictions may have grave consequences.

No Media Coverage of North Korea's Famine

One such country is North Korea, which remains one of the most closed societies in the world today. For several years now, North Korea has been faced with a devastating famine. Not much is mentioned in the U.S press about this subject, however. Strange, you may say, because when Somalia and Ethiopia suffered food shortages, American newspapers covered the problem and TV stations showed numerous pictures of emaciated children. Americans responded by sending millions of dollars, both from Washington, D.C., and from the heartland, to help alleviate the suffering.

But no funds were forthcoming when North Korea's years of hunger started at least as early as 1995. One of the major problems in generating sympathy for North Korea is that Americans and the rest of the world have been unable to see the suffering on television or in newspaper and magazine pictures. North Korea's borders are in effect sealed to foreign journalists, especially foreign TV crews. Some relief workers have described emaciated children in the streets, but there have been no photos—and the West in particular has not reacted very much.

China Uses TV to Pitch the Government Line

The Chinese government controls all television transmission and programming. Just before Taiwan's first democratic presidential elections in the spring of 1996, China's state-controlled television blanketed the airwaves with footage of Chinese military exercises in the Taiwan straits. The latest weaponry and the roar of missiles were seen and heard in mainland China, Hong Kong, and Taiwan. Chinese central television uses the same heavy-handed tactics when it shows films on Japan's military aggression against China in the 1930s and World War II. One former U.S. ambassador to China, James Lilley, said that Chinese television depicts the Japanese as "monsters."[17]

The Rest of the World

The truth remains that although the number of TV sets in the world has tripled in the last two decades, most of the world's governments keep a tight control over local broadcasting networks. In almost half of the countries in the world, the government owns the entire television broadcasting infrastructure. In another seventy or so countries, the government has part ownership.

For Critical Analysis

Are countries with state-controlled television better or worse off than they were when there was no TV at all?

Table 11-2

The Erosion of Media Values

BEST DESCRIBES NEWS MEDIA?	1985 %	1999 %
Moral	54	40
Immoral	13	38
Helps democracy	54	45
Hurts democracy	23	38
Professional	72	52
Unprofessional	11	32

SOURCE: Pew Research Center for the People and the Press survey, February 18–21, 1999.

THE EROSION OF MEDIA VALUES

Some observers suggest that Americans are less concerned about media bias than about a perceived erosion in media values—the ethical standards that guide the news profession. Consider the results of a survey conducted in 1999 by the Pew Research Center for the People and the Press. The center compared the results from the 1999 survey with the results from a similar survey taken in 1985. As you can see in Table 11–2, attitudes toward the media changed significantly during that period. Notably, the number of Americans who concluded that the news media are "immoral" nearly trebled during those years, as did the number of respondents who felt that the media were "unprofessional."

Journalists are also concerned about what is happening in their profession. The Pew Research Center survey found that a large majority of news professionals believe that the culture of news is changing. The traditional respect for facts and factual verification is giving way to a news culture characterized by argument, opinion, haste, and news as entertainment. According to the survey, 69 percent of journalists believe that the distinction between reporting and commentary has seriously eroded.

Americans at Odds over Politics and the Media

Americans are at odds over a number of issues concerning politics and the media. Here we look at just a few of these issues.

The Expanding Media Universe

INFOTRAC®

Building growing with HGTV

The cable-TV competitive news wars that transpired during the last few years will seem rather quaint to us in the future. The advances in wiring, digitization, compression, and transmission are going to allow full-time, full-motion video on the Web. Literally millions of channels will be available. The question, of course, is whether anybody will be watching. Research concerning most products shows that consumers choose among about seven interchangeable brands (assuming there are that many) and virtually ignore all others. Will they do the same with the product called news, particularly political news? No one knows.

What is certain is that the big media players are trying to establish themselves as quickly as possible, before the hundreds or thousands or millions of news outlets become available on the Web. They believe that they have to become major players today to distinguish themselves from the huge number of other choices that are going to be available. According to some, the expansion of television programming seems unfortunately to be more of the same. Even the newest TV channels for news do not look much different than the old ones.

NARROWCASTING ON THE RISE

With more and more information outlets available, so-called **narrowcasting**—catering media programming to the specialized tastes and preferences of targeted audiences—is on the rise. One perhaps unintended result of narrowcasting is that individuals are abandoning traditional broadcast and mass-market information vehicles for information that is more tailored to their personal interests. The community suffers because people who get news only on topics that interest them no

NARROWCASTING ● Catering media programming to the specialized tastes and preferences of targeted audiences.

News reporters who attain celebrity status are often themselves in the news. Here, Ed Bradley, the "star" of CBS's *60 Minutes,* was pressed into double duty as a correspondent in covering the 1996 Republican convention.

longer share a common pool of information with the community. Perhaps as a result, rumors and innuendo are less likely to be countered, at least in many people's minds, by solid community-based news stories and outlets.

NEWS COMMENTARY VERSUS INFORMATION

One would think that with the explosion of news sources, the total cost of news gathering would have increased concomitantly. In fact, the opposite has occurred. The networks and many major newspapers have engaged in serious cost-cutting efforts. In particular, the number of correspondents has been reduced. The result is not more news, but more talk *about* news—commentary versus information. Every viewpoint gets aired, without any particular sense of a need to do the research to back up these viewpoints. Some commentators believe that what we are now hearing and viewing is simply cocktail party conversation that is labeled journalism. Certainly, the media's relentless coverage in 1998 of the issues surrounding President Clinton's relationship with Monica Lewinsky illustrates this point.

★ Are Americans Really Less Interested in Political News?

Paradoxically, at the same time that Americans are being inundated with more news than ever before, they seem to be less interested in news. Even though more than 70 percent of voters get their information from TV, the audience for network news has dropped steadily from about 40 percent in 1980 to about 26 percent today.

Why are today's citizens less interested in political news than citizens were in the past? This issue, which was discussed earlier in this chapter, is of major concern to many Americans. Some observers link this disinterest to the public's disdain for managed news and a perceived lack of credibility on the part of the news media. Others have voiced the fear that the disinterest masks an inability of voters to think critically. The worry is that

American culture, and the educational system in particular, may not be producing citizens who can understand complex political issues. It could also be argued that the contemporary American family lifestyle does not afford as much time for watching the nightly news or reading the daily newspaper as the lifestyle of a generation ago did. In any event, the increasing disinterest in political news, combined with decreased voter turnout in recent years (see Chapter 9), has caused some Americans to be concerned about the future of our democracy.

Some observers claim that what we are witnessing is less a decline in the level of interest in news than a change in the type of news coverage desired by Americans and in the way in which Americans follow the news. According to a survey conducted in 1998,[18] Americans were reading, watching, and listening to the news just as often in 1998 as they were in 1996. Although interest in national and international news is on the wane, there is strong interest in news closer to home—local TV stations thrive. Also, more Americans are turning to cable news channels for their news. Between 40 and 60 percent of Americans now regularly watch one of the cable news networks instead of network news programs.

There also seems to be a generation gap in the way in which Americans are responding to the "information explosion." Whereas 68 percent of Americans aged sixty-five and older "enjoy keeping up with the news a lot," only 33 percent of Americans between the ages of eighteen and twenty-nine make that claim. At the same time, the survey indicated that far more younger Americans (77 percent) than seniors (33 percent) liked "having so many information sources to choose from."

Additionally, Internet use has soared. In 1995, 4 percent of adults went online to get news once a week; now 20 percent of adults do so. It is difficult to predict how evolving communications technologies, including the Internet, will affect Americans' appetite for news, but clearly it is already having some effect.

Do Media Conglomerates Lead to Less Aggressive Journalism?

Five companies now dominate the television industry:

- General Electric, owner of NBC.
- Walt Disney Company, owner of ABC.
- Viacom, owner of CBS.
- Time/Warner, owner of CNN.
- Rupert Murdoch's News Corporation, owner of the Fox News Network.

The print media are similarly characterized by large chains, such as those owned by the Gannett Company, Knight-Ridder, Inc., the E. W. Scripps Company, the Los Angeles Times-Mirror Company, and Dow Jones & Company.

Some worry that the domination of the media by a few huge conglomerate enterprises means that citizens will no longer have access to multiple points of view from the media. Others maintain that media concentration, even though it reduces competition in the news marketplace, does not necessarily reduce the quality of news coverage: as long as news corporations seek profits, those companies will vie for coverage of breaking news to sell to the public. Perhaps the more important question here is whether there will be enough buyers. Given the decreasing demand for substantive news coverage among the American public, whether the news available reflects multiple points of view may be a moot issue.

key terms

attack ad 269
electronic media 267
issue ad 269
managed news coverage 270
mass media 267
narrowcasting 279
negative political
   advertising 269

political advertising 268
print media 267
sound bite 272
spin 271
spin doctor 271
symbiotic relationship 272

chapter summary

1. The mass media include the print media (newspapers and magazines) and the electronic media (radio, television, and, to an extent, the Internet). The media have a wide-ranging effect on American politics. The impact of the media, particularly television, is greatest during political campaigns.

2. According to the Pew Research Center for the People and the Press, television is now the primary source of news for 72 percent of Americans. Because we live in a TV-saturated environment, political candidates spend a great deal of time and money obtaining TV exposure, through political ads, debates, and general news coverage. The biggest campaign expense today is for political TV ads. Although today's political campaigns are characterized by extensive negative political advertising, the candidates tend to refrain from blatant personal attack ads and focus instead on attacking their opponents' positions on the issues.

3. Television debates have been a feature of presidential campaigns since the first debate was held in 1960. In the 1992 debates, third party candidate H. Ross Perot was allowed to join the contenders from the major parties, incumbent Republican George Bush and Democratic challenger Bill Clinton. In 1996, however, Perot and another third party candidate, John Hagelin, were denied access to the debates, a decision upheld by a federal court.

4. The candidates try to take advantage of the media's interest in campaigns to increase the quantity and quality of news coverage they receive. In recent years, candidates' campaign managers and political consultants have shown increasing sophistication in creating newsworthy events for journalists and TV camera crews to cover. Overall, television has created a new kind of political candidate—one who must be at ease with the camera and ever conscious of the image that he or she is conveying to the public via the TV.

5. Two groups benefit the most from expensive campaigns: political consultants and TV stations. Political consultants make millions of dollars during each campaign by shaping effective political ads and managing news coverage for candidates. Television stations profit from the sale of political ads as well as from access to breaking news about the candidates.

6. Although most Americans look to TV news programs for their political information, the time constraint and visual format required by the TV medium significantly alter the scope and depth of news coverage on TV relative to coverage in the print media. As a result, the majority of Americans acquire relatively little information on most significant political issues.

7. Ever since Franklin Roosevelt broadcast his "fireside chats," politicians have realized the power of radio. Today, talk radio is becoming a political force. Talk radio has been subject to criticism because of its "Wild West" character—the usual journalistic conventions do not exist, and political ranting and raving are common.

8. The print media have played a significant role in this nation's history, and they continue to provide the most thorough and detailed analyses of political issues. Nonetheless, growth in the newspaper industry is "flat," while the TV industry and Internet use continue to expand. Recent polls indicate that confidence in news coverage by the print media is on the wane.

9. Americans' interest in news coverage also seems to be waning. In 1996, the public's interest in the mass media's coverage of the elections reached a modern all-time low. Some observers attribute this declining interest in the news to an unwillingness on the part of today's citizens to acquire political information and critically evaluate the candidates' positions on the issues. Others suggest that the declining interest in news reflects a growing lack of faith in the media due to media bias and distortion. Still others credit changing media habits for the apparent decline in news interest.

10. Americans are at odds over a number of issues concerning politics and the media. These issues include concerns over the effect of an expanding media universe on news presentation; the public's changing news-viewing habits, which may have implications for democracy; and the consequences of media concentration for the delivery of the news.

for critical analysis

1. In your opinion, should negative political ads (attack ads) be banned? Why or why not?

2. It is often said that an incumbent president has an advantage in televised debates. Why might this be?

3. Would it be fair to limit political advertising to two weeks before an election? Why or why not?

4. In your opinion, should third party presidential candidates be allowed to participate in televised debates?

5. Recently, radio has made a comeback as an important political voice. Is it likely to remain so?

6. To what extent do local newspaper endorsements have an effect on local political races? Do they have a similar effect on national political races?

7. Does the fact that older Americans are more interested in "keeping up with news" than younger Americans disturb you? Are there news interests of younger Americans that may offset this finding?

suggested readings

CAPPELLA, Joseph N., and Kathleen Hall Jamieson. *Spiral of Cynicism: The Press and the Public Good.* New York: Oxford University Press, 1997. The authors contend that the media are responsible for much of the political apathy and cynicism that characterize today's voters. The media, by putting form over substance and emphasizing sound bites rather than an objective treatment of the issues, have helped to create a political climate that resembles a traveling circus, full of talk and glitter but low on content or real-life relevance.

COOK, Timothy E. *Governing with the News: The News Media as a Political Institution.* Chicago, Ill.: University of Chicago Press, 1998. The author analyzes the implications of a press that no longer consists of a diverse range of individual outlets but is instead the result of a collective institution that exercises collective power over news coverage.

IGGERS, Jeremy. *Good News, Bad News: Journalism, Ethics, and the Public Interest.* Boulder, Colo.: Westview Press, 1998. The author argues that the dissatisfaction with the news media lies, in part, with the standards of journalists themselves, and that these standards need to be redefined in response to the changes in ownership and organization of the news media that are taking place today.

JAMIESON, Kathleen Hall. *Packaging the Presidency: A History and Criticism of Presidential Campaign Advertising.* 3d ed. New York: Oxford University Press, 1996. In this third edition of her classic work, campaign analyst Jamieson presents an insightful and informing discussion of presidential campaign advertising. She looks at how campaign ads have evolved over time from printed handbills to television coverage of carefully orchestrated events.

NYE, Joseph S., *et al.* Eds. *Why People Don't Trust Government.* Cambridge, Mass.: Harvard University Press, 1997. For three decades, Americans' confidence in their government has been declining. This collection of essays by leading Harvard University scholars explores the various explanations that have been offered for this growing distrust in government and concludes that none of the explanations addresses the real reasons: the cultural and political conflicts stirred up by the news media.

politics on the web

Literally thousands of new sources, including newspapers, news magazines, and television and radio stations, are now online. Total News Now offers a directory of more than a thousand news sources, including Fox News, MSNBC, CBS, ABC, and *USA Today.* To find Total News Now, go to

http://totalnews.com

Another site for news sources is the Ultimate Collection of News Links. This site provides links to more than six thousand news sources, ranging from daily newspapers to business magazines, and subject-specific weekly or monthly publications. You can access this site at

http://pppp.net/links/news/NA.html

If you are interested in news stories covered by ABC, CBS, and NBC television since 1968, you can find abstracts of these stories at Vanderbilt University's Television News Archive, which is online at

http://tvnews.vanderbilt.edu

To find out what newspapers are online and whether your own local paper may be on the Web, you can access Newspapers Online at

http://www.newspapers.com

using web resources

The Media Research Center (MRC) was, according to information on its Web site, "founded in 1987 with the mission of bringing political balance to the nation's news media and responsibility to the entertainment media." Also, as stated on its Web site, "The MRC tapes over 150 hours a week of news and entertainment shows aired on the broadcast networks and cable news channels. With over 160,000 hours on more than 25,000 videotapes, the MRC is the only organization with a complete tape library of network news and entertainment shows back to the late 1980s."

Go to the MRC's Web site at

http://www.mediaresearch.org

1. Examine two of the links on the main page. What is the focus of the MRC's Web site? In what ways is its focus different from the mainstream news services?

2. Return to the main page and select "Conservative News Service." What is the lead story? Why was the story selected? What are the MRC's objections to the mainstream news coverage of this story?

3. Return to the main page and select the "Parents Television Council" link. Read one of the reviews on the site. Do you find it informative? Is it a fair review? Why or why not?

notes

1. Opinion poll taken by the Public Center of the Annenberg School of Communication, based on a national random sample of 1,031 persons with a margin of error of plus or minus 3.2 percent.

2. Competitive media reporting tracks only the top seventy-five markets.

3. For an excellent description and analysis of political advertising, including the techniques used in attack ads, see Kathleen Hall Jamieson, *Dirty Politics: Deception, Distraction, and Democracy* (New York: Oxford University Press, 1992).

4. Note that Dole's decision to hold back was criticized by many Republicans, including some in his campaign organization. Clinton's lead in the race meant that he did not need negative ads.

5. The commission's action was upheld by a federal court. See *Perot v. Federal Election Commission,* 97 F.3d 553 (D.C.Cir. 1996).

6. William Plass, "Not Just Simplistic But Dishonest, Too," *International Herald Tribune,* October 10, 1996, p. 13.

7. Doris Graber, *Mass Media and American Politics,* 5th ed. (Washington, D.C.: Congressional Quarterly Press, 1996), p. 59.

8. *U.S. News & World Report,* March 10, 1997, p. 32.

9. According to a survey conducted by the Pew Research Center for the People and the Press from April 24 to May 11, 1998.

10. As reported in Richard Huff, "July Was Bustin' Out All Over with Newsmags," *The New York Daily News,* August 4, 1998, p. 66.

11. The survey was conducted by the Committee of Concerned Journalists in conjunction with the Pew Research Center for the People and the Press between November 20, 1998, and February 11, 1999.

12. Based on a *Talkers* magazine survey conducted in the fall of 1998.

13. Robert J. Samuelson, "Down with the Media Elite!?" *Newsweek,* July 13, 1998, p. 47.

14. S. Robert Lichter, Stanley Rothman, and Linda S. Lichter, *The Media Elite* (New York: Adler & Adler, 1986).

15. Calvin F. Exoo, *The Politics of the Mass Media* (St. Paul: West Publishing Co., 1994), pp. 49–50.

16. *Time,* October 21, 1996, p. 63.

17. *U.S. News & World Report,* November 11, 1996, p. 48.

18. Pew Research Center for the People and the Press survey conducted between April 24 and May 11, 1998.

POLITICS IN CYBERSPACE

Contents

News on the Web: Who Should Be Accountable?

When TWA Flight 800, filled with 230 people flying from New York to Paris, exploded shortly after takeoff on July 17, 1996, the world was stunned. Immediately, conspiracy theories started flying, particularly on the Web. A few months later, former ABC news correspondent Pierre Salinger announced that he had "evidence" that Flight 800 crashed after a "friendly fired" U.S. missile hit it. The mainstream press carried the story. Salinger's source was—you guessed it—the Internet. He had uncovered a supposedly secret document from a "foreign intelligence agency" on the Web. There was just one problem: the document had been published on the World Wide Web months earlier as a joke. Immediately, two groups were at odds, and they continue to be so. One group wants to "force" news-providing information services on the Web to be accountable for what they publish. The other group believes that the Web should remain free of any restrictions.

If It Cannot Be Verified, Don't Use It

Those who want responsible Web-generated news point out that Salinger's weak Web sources for his friendly fire theory of the crash of TWA Flight 800 represent merely the tip of an iceberg. The fact is, the Internet is completely unedited. This means that a fraudulent or unethical organization can post materials on the Web as easily as a reputable company, news organization, or government agency can. If news content can be taken directly from unaccountable sources on the Web, then all news is fit to print, no matter how unreliable, unfounded, damaging, or nonsensical.

Therefore, maintain those who argue for news accountability on the Web, it is up to news-providing services to verify Web-generated information. If such information cannot be verified, it should not be used. More specifically, this group argues that news must be associated with reliable, accountable, standard news sources, such as the *Washington Post*, the *Wall Street Journal*, *MSNBC 24-Hour News*, and CNN/Time's *AllPolitics*. Standard fact-substantiating techniques make these news sources reliable, whereas others are not.

Even the White House is afraid of unsubstantiated news on the Web. One internal memo issued by the office of the White House Counsel was entitled "Communications Stream of Conspiracy Commerce." The memo reported that fringe, right-wing publications placed bogus stories on the Internet. The stories then spread rapidly around the world and resurfaced in "right-of-center mainstream papers."

Leave the Web Alone

Those who are not worried about Web-generated news believe that we are entering a new era of information in which everything on the Internet should be read with care. In other words, we cannot just scroll through Internet sources uncritically; we must act as our own editors. After all, there is a big difference between the news you find in the *National Enquirer* and that in the *Washington Post*.

Why should the Web be any different?

Electronic journalism, to be sure, has no clear authorship. Many news sites on the Web have multiple authors and really are just editorial perspectives. When the source or credibility of news on the Web is unclear, you should proceed with care. Indeed, one of the reasons that the Internet has become such a popular forum is precisely because it is unregulated—free speech reigns. If an external authority, such as a government agency, forced everyone to be accountable for what news they reported on the Web, the value of the Internet as a news forum would be diminished.

It is up to the mainstream news media to verify any news they pick up from the Web.

Where Do You Stand?

1. How might standard news organizations be held more accountable for "information" from the Web that they reuse in their own stories?

2. Is there any difference between a standard printed article that quotes "anonymous sources" and a Web article offered by a multi-authored Web site?

On the Web

For more information on news accountability on the Web, go to http://www.fair.org.

Introduction

INFOTRAC®
Persistent Pierre

James Madison once said that "knowledge will forever govern ignorance, and people who mean to be their own governors must arm themselves with the power which knowledge gives." Enter the Internet. People can get information on just about any topic they want. Whether the information is reliable is another issue, as discussed in the chapter-opening feature.

Will the Internet change politics as we know it? Very likely. As you will read in this chapter, the Internet is already changing the American political landscape. No doubt, these changes will continue into the future. John Perry Barlow, the co-founder of the Electronic Frontier Foundation, announced in the September 1996 issue of *Wired* that we will see an era in which the Internet "will have changed so radically the structure of every system (economic and political) that the United States Senate will be as obsolete as the House of Lords in Great Britain. The interactive world is already in the process of creating systems of government that are better adapted to the global information economy than those of the nation state from the industrial era." Barlow may be right, but as yet, no one can say for certain just how the Internet will reshape American politics and political institutions.

A Short History of the Internet

In the 1960s, when the Cold War was perhaps at its peak, government officials were worried. What would happen to the military communications network in time of war? In 1969, to solve the problem, the U.S. Department of Defense created the Advanced Research Projects Agency Network, or ARPANET. The department's goal was to establish a survivable communications network for all organizations involved in defense-related research. In case of a nuclear attack, information could still be rerouted because the network was implemented using a **store and forward procedure.** That is to say, each piece of information was split up into packets and transmitted from one network node to another. The packets ultimately ended up at their destinations and then could be reunited to form the initial piece of information. Thus, if one part of a network was damaged, the network could resend the packets over an alternate path and still get them delivered.

An important step in developing the Internet occurred in 1982, when university researchers, under the guidance of the National Science Foundation (NSF), expanded this rudimentary network into what was called the Computerized Science Network. By 1983, all U.S. military sites were linked on this expanded network, and it became fully functional.

ACADEMIC USE OF THE INTERNET

Another important step was taken in 1988, when the NSF helped to create a new, high-speed area network that could be used by all educational and research facilities, both in the United States and worldwide, and by government employees. This development marked the real birth of the Internet and its widespread use by academics, especially graduate students, who began to use the Internet for other purposes, such as exchanging Star Trek trivia with invisible friends around the globe.

THE WORLD WIDE WEB

The World Wide Web (or, more simply, the Web) is the leading information retrieval service of the Internet. The Web gives Internet users access to literally millions of documents, photos, videos, and other information.

The Web was begun in 1989 by Tim Berners-Lee and his colleagues at an international scientific organization called CERN, based in Geneva, Switzerland. They created a system that standardized communications between server computers and people trying to access information within those computers.

The real impetus for the growth of the Internet and the Web was the creation of the first **Web browser,** called *Mosaic,* which was released in September 1993. Mark Andreessen, the developer of *Mosaic,* co-founded Netscape Communications Corporation, whose *Netscape Navigator* has become one of the dominant Web browsers in the world today.

CURRENT INTERNET USE

The growth of Internet use in the United States has been explosive. As you can see in Figure 12–1, over 50 percent of American households now have personal computers (PCs), and over 60 percent of those computers are connected to the Internet.

If you have an interest, there is an Internet chat group you can join. During campaigns, numerous candidates start up chat groups to elicit more interest in their views. Such chat groups are not quite the same thing as face-to-face communication, however.

To get an idea of the tremendous growth rate in Internet use, consider that in 1994, only 3 million people were connected to the Internet. Today, more than 100 million people worldwide are using it. In the United States alone, the number of adults who had ever been on the Web increased by 10 million—from 80 million to 90 million—in just one two-month period in early 1999.[1] Also consider that radio existed for thirty-eight years before it had 50 million listeners, and television took thirteen years to reach that mark. The Internet, however, crossed the line in just four years.[2]

What do people do with the Internet? The most important use of the Internet, of course, is for sending e-mail. In 1994, 776 billion messages were sent. In 1997, the number of messages sent had climbed to 2.6 trillion. By the year 2000, an estimated 6.6 trillion e-mail messages will move through U.S.–based computer networks.[3] Another major use of the Internet is to obtain information. Millions of home pages offer information—or links to information—on every imaginable topic. At least one American is asking whether we should be creating, for historical purposes, some kind of repository of the information available today on the Web—see the feature entitled *Politics on the Far Side: Creating a "Library of Congress" for the Internet.* Business use of the Internet, or e-commerce, is also growing rapidly. An increasing number of Americans now make online purchases of goods ranging from airline tickets to books to automobiles.

Figure 12–1
U.S. Households with Personal Computers and Internet Connections

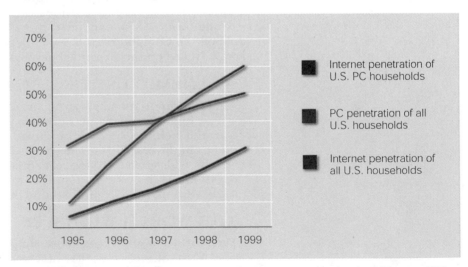

■ Internet penetration of U.S. PC households

■ PC penetration of all U.S. households

■ Internet penetration of all U.S. households

SOURCE: Technology User Profile by InfoBeads, a Ziff Davis, Inc., organization, issued January 1999.

The Internet is quickly becoming a source of news for Americans as well. Look at Figure 12–2. Although most Americans still turn to television, newspapers, and magazines for news, fully 25 percent of American adults are now going online to obtain news, and 20 percent do so regularly—at least once a week. In contrast, in 1995, only 4 percent of American adults went online at least once a week to get news.

Cyberspace and Political Campaigns

Today's political parties and candidates are beginning to realize the benefits of using not only computers and computer databases to communicate with voters but also of using the Internet to conduct online campaigns and raise funds. Voters also are increasingly using the Internet to access information about parties and candidates, promote political goals, and obtain political news.

In a sense, the use of the Internet is the least costly way for candidates to contact, recruit, and mobilize supporters, as well as disseminate information on their positions on issues. In effect, the Internet can replace brochures, letters, and position papers. Individual voters or political-party supporters can use the Internet to avoid having to go to special meetings or to a campaign site to do volunteer work or obtain information on a candidate's position.

That the Internet is now a viable medium for communicating political information and interacting with voters was made clear in the 1996 presidential election cycle. According to a postelection survey by the Werthlin Worldwide polling organization, approximately 9 percent of the voters surveyed (about 8.5 million Americans) indicated that information on the Internet had influenced their vote. The Internet became even more significant as a campaign vehicle in the 2000 presidential races, as you will read shortly.

politics on the far side

Creating a "Library of Congress" for the Internet

The Library of Congress is the official keeper of books in the United States. If a book has ever been printed, you can almost be sure you will find it there. But what about everything "printed" in cyberspace? A hundred years from now, will there be a Library of Congress in cyberspace? The answer is probably no, at least not a library operated by the U.S. government.

To remedy the situation, Brewster Kahle has become perhaps the world's first electronic historian. Kahle, a multimillionaire computer scientist and the founder of Thinking Machines Corporation, believes that there is real value in our early Internet history, and he wants to save it. He has purchased with his own funds computers and collection devices to surf the Web and save everything being produced today.

For Critical Analysis: Does the relative transcience of Web sites (they tend to come and go) affect the value of material published on the Web?

Figure 12–2
Where Americans Get Their News

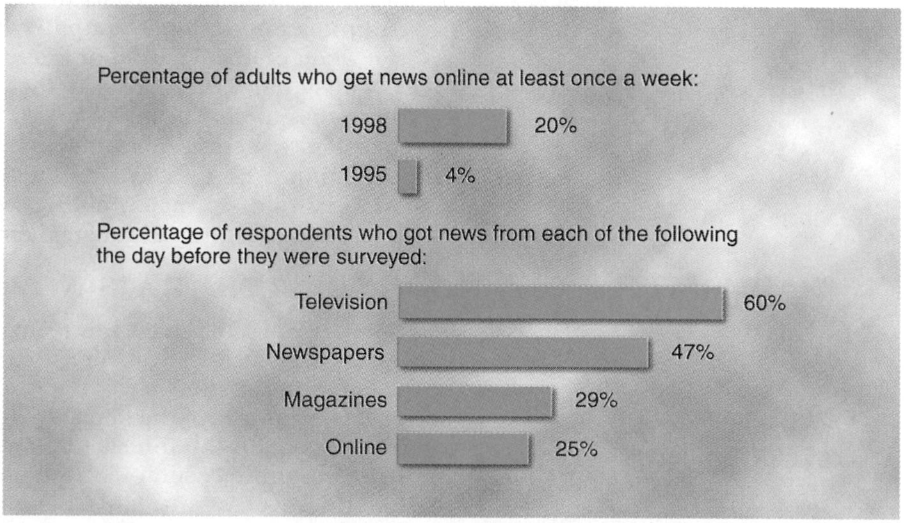

Percentage of adults who get news online at least once a week:

1998	20%
1995	4%

Percentage of respondents who got news from each of the following the day before they were surveyed:

Television	60%
Newspapers	47%
Magazines	29%
Online	25%

SOURCE: *The New York Times,* July 27, 1998, p. C9; based on data obtained by the Pew Research Center for the People and the Press in a survey conducted April 24 to May 11, 1998.

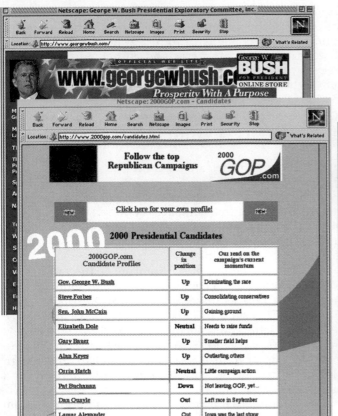

COMPUTERS AS POLITICAL CAMPAIGN TOOLS

There is no question that computers have changed the way politicking occurs in the United States. Without computers, grassroots lobbying would be extremely expensive and time consuming. In the past, mailing lists were compiled manually from paper directories. Now they are purchased as computer files or on CD-ROMs. Thanks to computers, important voting information can now be mailed to literally millions of people at a reduced cost.

Politicians can "narrowcast" their requests for funds, all thanks to the sophistication of current computer programs. These programs ferret out potential donors on the basis of information acquired from numerous files, all processed in large computers.

Even when political parties or interest groups want to do a "walk"—go door-to-door—they don't do it the way they used to do. They obtain information about the "best doors" to knock on via the same type of computer programs that tell them where to mail requests for political campaign contributions. CompuMentor, a nonprofit organization based in the San Francisco Bay area, has one key role—to match political organizations with technology-savvy mentors who are willing to donate their services to a cause they support.

ONLINE FUND RAISING

Today's political candidates are realizing that the Internet can be an effective—and inexpensive—way to raise campaign funds. The leading candidates in the 2000 presidential race all engaged in online fund raising, as did the national committees of the Republican and Democratic parties.

Fund raising on the Internet by presidential campaign candidates began in earnest after the Federal Election Commission decided, in June 1999, that the federal government could distribute matching funds for credit-card donations received by candidates via the Internet. By the end of the following month, Democratic presidential contender Bill Bradley had already garnered $312,000 in online contributions; Democrat Al Gore and Republican George W. Bush had received $70,000 and $41,572, respectively; and the Republican National Committee had raised $200,000 from donations made online. The success of fund raising via the Internet, and particularly the ability of the candidates to broaden their appeals to "low-dollar" donors online, led one campaign analyst to conclude that the Internet is "the ultimate grassroots fund-raising mechanism."[4]

Of course, voters can also use the Internet to raise funds in order to launch their own campaigns against specific candidates. For example, in the fall of 1998 Joan Blades and Wes Boyd, a husband-and-wife team who develop software in Silicon Valley, thought that Congress was paying too little attention to public opinion in deciding whether to impeach President Clinton. They used their Web page to protest the impeachment, and within days they had generated some 500,000 electronic petitions from voters to their congresspersons. When they asked for campaign donations to help defeat members of Congress who were in favor of impeaching the president, they received $13 million in pledges for the coming year.[5]

THE RISE OF THE INTERNET CAMPAIGN STRATEGIST

Increasingly, candidates are facing the need for professionals who can create well-designed, informative, and user-friendly campaign Web sites to attract viewers, hold their attention, and generally manage their e-mail and track credit-card contributions from supporters. Enter the Internet campaign strategist—a professional consultant who manages a candidate's Web site.

For example, Democratic presidential candidate Bill Bradley hired Lynn Reed (who ran the Clinton/Gore Web site in 1996) to manage his Web site for the 2000 campaign. For a monthly consulting fee of $4,000, Reed agreed to screen position papers and other campaign materials before they were posted on the site, to offer suggestions on how to improve the site to make it easier to navigate, to handle incoming e-mail and credit-card campaign contributions, and generally to integrate the Web site into the overall campaign strategy developed by Bradley's political advisers.[6]

Although candidates have used Web site strategists in the past, particularly in the 1996 and 1998 elections, the trend toward Web site competition was clearly evident in the 2000 presidential campaigns. According to one commentator, the 2000 campaigns may go down in history as the first ones in which candidates widely competed via the Internet.[7]

WILL THE INTERNET CHANGE POLITICAL CAMPAIGNING AS WE KNOW IT?

Although some observers claim that Internet use will fundamentally change the way in which political candidates conduct their campaigns, others are not so sure. For one thing, to reach out to large numbers of voters, candidates need a mass medium, such as television, and the Internet is not that kind of medium—at least, not yet. Certainly, Democratic candidate Bill Bradley was aware of the Internet's limited reach when he announced his candidacy on his Web site in 1999. Before he made the announcement, he had his campaign staff call reporters from the major media to alert them to go online to see the announcement.

Another problem with using the Internet for campaigning is that the user has to be motivated to access the information. As Mark Mellman, a political consultant in Washington, D.C., notes, "The problem is, not many people want political information. When you go on the Web, you have to want to go to a political site."[8] Finally, those who are the most likely to use computers are younger Americans, and, as you learned in Chapter 9, members of this group are the least likely to vote. In the 1996 presidential elections, fewer than one-third of computer users between the ages of

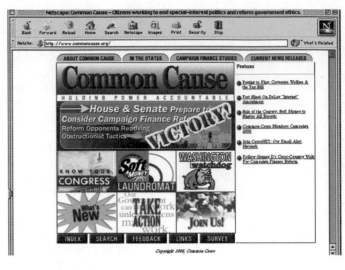

eighteen and twenty-nine went to the polls. In contrast, nearly two-thirds of computer users over the age of fifty voted.[9]

TRACKING CAMPAIGN CONTRIBUTIONS

The Internet has become an efficient way for citizens to track campaign contributions. Although the Federal Election Commission (FEC) has its own Web site (at **http://www.fec.gov**), it is not very manageable. Enter Tony Raymond, a former manager at the FEC. He developed FECInfo, a nonpartisan, independent site containing FEC data (the URL for this site is **http://www.tray.com/FECInfo**).

If you want to find out who sent contributions to a particular candidate in recent election cycles, you can do so easily at the FECInfo site. You can also find out to whom particular individuals, organizations, or corporations contributed and the size of their contributions simply by typing in their names.

Currently, FECInfo is most frequently accessed by journalists, who obtain information from the site for their articles. Political scientists are also starting to use the site to find data that are useful for political analyses and speech making.

You can find similar information from the site of Common Cause at **http://www.commoncause.org**. Common Cause describes itself as a nonprofit, nonpartisan citizens' lobbying organization dedicated to promoting honest and accountable government. From its Web site, you can obtain an extensive amount of information on campaign financing, including details on which industries and interest groups made the largest contributions to the parties during recent campaigns. You can also find out who the biggest campaign spenders in Congress are.

Political News on the Web

As mentioned earlier, Americans increasingly are turning to the Web for political news. Certainly, news generated for the Web is becoming more and more important, but, at least as yet, online news coverage has not been responsible for a decline in the use of traditional news sources (see the feature on the next page entitled *Perception versus Reality: Does Online Information Really Mean the Death of Traditional News?*). Traditional news sources are now taking the Internet seriously, however.

perception versus reality

Does Online Information Really Mean the Death of Traditional News?

News on the Web is, in fact, itself news. Numerous articles appear in the traditional press discussing how much news is being transmitted on the Internet.

The Perception

A broad sampling of traditional news articles about online information sources gives the impression that people are turning to their information appliance—the personal computer—when they need news. Because this perception is becoming more widespread, the traditional news media, including TV networks, are spending large amounts of resources to establish a "presence" on the Internet.

The Reality

Clearly, the number of Americans who go online to obtain news is rising rapidly. Recent studies suggest, though, that those who obtain news online are also those who view news programs on TV and who read daily newspapers. In other words, there is no evidence that going online for news leads to less reading or viewing of more traditional news sources. Also, despite the dramatic growth in online news consumption, cable television's impact remains far greater. About 40 percent of Americans now regularly watch one of the cable news networks, compared to 57 percent who regularly view network news broadcasts, including news magazine shows. The size of the cable TV audience rises to 60 percent, however, when specialty programming, such as the Weather Channel, is factored in.[10]

You Be the Judge

Do you believe that the Internet will ever replace traditional news sources (TV broadcasts, newspapers, and news magazines)?

Not only do most major newspapers and news magazines now have online versions, but many of the standard TV news sources have started to spread the TV wars to cyberspace. NBC teamed up with Bill Gates's Microsoft to provide twenty-four-hour-a-day news on the Web at a site called MSNBC (all relevant URLs can be found at the end of this chapter). CNN developed CNN Interactive and joined with other news services to create *AllPolitics*. During the presidential elections, Fox News created a home page for a site called "Tail of the Tape," dealing with presidential candidates. The CNN and MSNBC sites have their own staff. MSNBC even has its own political online newspaper called *Slate*.

These sites are crammed with news service stories and other information. On election night in 1996, the Internet even had some scoops that other news sources did not have. For example, CBS's projection that Republican senator Mitch McConnell of Kentucky was going to win reelection was posted on the Web well before CBS News anchor Dan Rather got around to mentioning it on the air.

As one indication that an increasingly large number of people are turning to the Web for their news, consider the following: When the United States fired cruise missiles at Iraq in November 1996, traffic at CNN Interactive tripled within minutes. During that week, 18 million pages of information were transferred from the site. This number climbed even higher—to 20.4 million pages—on the evening of August 17, 1998, when President Clinton gave his speech admitting to a relationship with Monica Lewinsky.

In September 1998, the nation witnessed an unprecedented use of the Internet by the government, when the House of Representatives released for online publication Independent Counsel Kenneth Starr's report of his investigation of President Clinton. An estimated 5.9 million people read the report within two days after it was posted on the Internet.

TABLOID JOURNALISM ON THE INTERNET

Matt Drudge, creator of the Web's Drudge Report, has become widely known for his tabloid-type journalism. Critics refer to him as a "cybergossip" who is

Here is Matt Drudge, who has become the Web's tabloid-type–news rumor monger. He has already been sued for libel.

PUSH TECHNOLOGY ● Software that enables Internet users to customize the type of information they receive from Web sources. The information is "pushed" to the user automatically as it is put on the Web.

Grudge begrudged

not all that concerned about distinguishing between fact and fiction in his "news" reports. For example, in January 1998, he "reported" that President Clinton had had an affair with White House intern Monica Lewinsky. The allegation was unsubstantiated and apparently had been taken from a *Newsweek* article that was never printed. Nonetheless, it set the media wheels in motion. Within days, the *Washington Post* had investigated the allegation and published an article based on documented facts. The other major media quickly followed suit, and the details of the "Lewinsky scandal" unfolded before the American public.

In one sense, what happened here was not really new. After all, printed tabloids have often been the first to mention breaking scandals or other news items, which then find their way into the more "respectable" news media. What is striking about the events following the Drudge Report's story about Monica Lewinsky is how quickly the story was investigated and reported on by the leading print and electronic news sources. Indeed, some journalists claim that the Internet has not only increased the amount of tabloid "reporting" but also accelerated the pace of publication. Thus, online tabloids could dramatically increase the potential impact of tabloid journalism on mainstream journalism.

The accelerated pace of publication has also had another effect: an increased pressure on news publishers to compete for top stories within a short period. Even respected, mainstream news organizations have occasionally posted inaccurate stories on their Web sites.[11]

"NARROWCASTING" THE NEWS

Technology is quickening the pace at which news is replacing the "one size fits all" standard with highly specialized "packets." The Internet is the ultimate "narrowcasting" vehicle. If you are interested in UFOs, you can direct your Web browser to give you just news on UFOs.

The latest in news systems further enhances the narrowcasting of news. Using so-called **push technology,** Web users can totally customize their daily supply of information. The best-known provider of this type of service is PointCast Network. You decide which type of news you want, and PointCast and its competitors will "push" this news through your Internet hookup. How do you decide what type of news you really want? You first use one of the search engines typically located in your *Netscape Navigator* or *Internet Explorer* Web browser. Then you start "surfing" the Web to find the sites that you like most. Then you tell the "push" software which sites to go to and how many times a day. One of the problems with such narrowcasting is that users do not get different views on a particular subject.

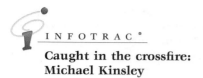

**Caught in the crossfire:
Michael Kinsley**

CYBER PUNDITS BECOME MORE EVIDENT

The number of political commentators on the Web is also increasing. We are not talking about fringe-group activists and extremist groups, but rather highly respected mainstream political pundits, such as Michael Kinsley, a former *New Republic* columnist and TV personality, and David Broder of the *Washington Post*. Kinsley is the editor of Microsoft Corporation's online magazine *Slate*. Even James Carville, the well-known political campaign manager who was credited with President Clinton's victory in 1992, has his "Swamp Fever" column in the online magazine *Salon*.

The Internet—A Boon to Interest Groups

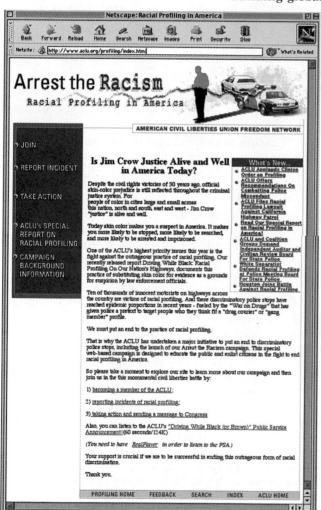

For interest groups with few resources, the Internet offers the possibility of building global networks at a very low cost. For example, Earth Trust is a worldwide organization dedicated to resolving transnational environmental problems. With very few resources, Earth Trust organized a global network. All it did was equip volunteers in remote areas with inexpensive computer hookups and e-mail accounts. The use of e-mail allowed Earth Trust to knit together a widely dispersed but highly effective organization. The organization was put together in less than two years, something unthinkable prior to inexpensive Internet access.

Today, a group of nongovernmental organizations that have such diverse missions as saving the wilderness, liberating political prisoners, and stopping hunger have formed the Econ-Net/Peace Net, otherwise known as the "Global Civil Society." Throughout this network, technology-savvy activists provide expertise and training. Native American activists have linked themselves together through NativeNet and INDIANnet.

Additionally, of course, existing interest groups can use their Web sites to gain public support for specific issues. For example, when the American Civil Liberties Union (ACLU) recently became concerned about the practice of "racial profiling" by police officers (using skin color as a ground for suspicion in making traffic stops), it launched a new Web site dealing with the issue (at **http://www.aclu.org/ profiling/index.html**). The site included a report documenting the practice as well as a complaint form that drivers can use to report improper police stops to the ACLU.[12]

LABOR DISCOVERS THE POWER OF THE WEB

Cyber demonstrations came to the Web in a big way when Bridgestone-Firestone Tire was facing a strike in 1996. After Bridgestone-Firestone fired and replaced 2,300 striking employees, the International Federation of Chemical Workers Unions decided it needed to do something. In July, it sent out a message via the Internet to all of its members throughout the world. The message asked the members to inundate Bridgestone-Firestone management with e-mail protesting what had happened. The federation also had its members send e-mail messages describing Bridgestone's actions to management personnel at automobile tire resale outlets, as well as at the banks and other corporations that did business with Bridgestone. With the simple click of a mouse, supporting members in various unions around the world could e-mail their thoughts on the management at Bridgestone.

Vic Thorp, the general secretary of the federation, stated, "From now on, it is possible that all those who have access to the Web can participate in a

CYBER DEMONSTRATION ● A labor protest, or demonstration, organized and executed by the use of e-mail communications among labor union members.

focused campaign against a multinational."[13] In the past, such campaigns were conducted using faxes. The difference between the two types of campaigns is remarkable. Sending one fax to 150 unions associated with the federation took several hours and resulted in a huge phone bill. Today, sending an e-mail message via the Internet takes a minute and costs almost nothing.

When unions want to put pressure on a particular employer, they can also enlist consumers in their fight through individual e-mail messages and specially created Web pages. An example occurred in 1997 when dockers were on strike in Liverpool, England. They created their own Web home page, which they claimed was useful in countering media indifference to their cause. Their Web site declared, "The world is our picket line!" The dockers were effective at linking their Web site to the various **search engines,** such as Yahoo, WebCrawler, Excite, and Lycos. They linked themselves to discussion forums at numerous sites dealing with union activities. One result was a sympathy cyber strike against Drake International, one of the two companies providing replacement workers for the striking Liverpool dockers. This cyber strike was organized by Canadian union members.

THE INTERNET—HOME TO HUMAN RIGHTS GROUPS

Today, as a result of the Internet, human rights activists and other interest groups concerned with human rights violations no longer have to spend years getting organized and soliciting funds to pay for their operating expenses, for distributing literature, and for costly media ads exposing human rights violations. They can plead their causes on the Internet. They can publish online, at virtually no cost, reports about what governments or businesses are doing thousands of miles away.

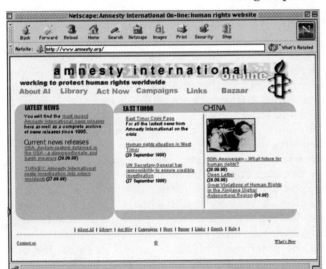

Governments around the globe are feeling the power wielded by these online interest groups. For example, in 1998 reports of atrocities committed against Indonesia's minority Chinese population, allegedly carried out by an elite military unit, were disseminated worldwide via the Internet. The Chinese in Indonesia are a small, relatively defenseless minority that controls a good deal of the country's wealth. The group has often been subject to brutal treatment, especially in times of trouble, but in the past their suffering has gone largely unnoticed.

In 1998, however, the world was quickly made aware of what was happening in Indonesia. Human rights groups spread the news via their Web sites and in e-mail to various groups, while Chinese people living in other countries orchestrated anti-Indonesian rallies in Boston, Chicago, Houston, Los Angeles, New York, and Washington, D.C., as well as in Hong Kong, Singapore, Kuala Lumpur, and Manila. The pressure brought by these groups and their demands for a full accounting prompted the Indonesian Army to launch an investigation.[14]

Similar pressure was placed on the Mexican government after forty-five Native villagers were killed in late 1997 in a village in the state of Chiapas, Mexico. Support groups all over the world sent hundreds of e-mail messages and posted communications on the Internet to denounce the attack and call for action. This helped to foster two weeks of demonstrations targeting U.S. and Mexican consulates, oil companies with interests in Chiapas, and the stock exchange in Mexico.[15]

Note that, unlike in the United States, some countries severely limit access to the Internet. (See, for example, the feature entitled *Comparative Politics: Limiting Access to the Internet.*)

comparative **politics**

Limiting Access to the Internet

The United States has few, if any, restrictions on how, when, and where citizens may access the Internet. While policymakers wrestle with numerous controversial issues, such as pornography and privacy, access to the Internet is virtually unrestricted. For citizens in some other countries, however, access to the Internet is highly restricted. These countries include the People's Republic of China, Indonesia, Saudi Arabia, Iraq, and Iran. It is instructive to examine how one country, Iran, is "tiptoeing" to the Internet.

The Islamic theocracy in Iran wishes to propagate its message to the rest of the world and wants to become a source for the answers to questions on Islamic law. The Internet would seem a perfect vehicle for Iran's purposes, except that the Internet works both ways. If Iran opens itself up to questions and tries to proselytize online, then its citizens will also have access to Western political views and cultural beliefs, the views of those who supported the deposed Shah of Iran, and a barrage of information on virtually every topic under the sun. In 1989, Salman Rushdie's novel *The Satanic Verses* was deemed so offensive to Islam that the Iranian government put out a worldwide call to kill its author. Certainly, a number of sites now on the Web would be much more offensive to the Iranian clergy than whatever was deemed blasphemous in *The Satanic Verses*.

When the government of Iran decided it could not control what came in via satellite TV, it simply banned satellite dishes. In 1996, the most extreme members of the clergy asked for an outright ban on the Internet as well.

The Iranian government has decided that one way to control access to the Internet is by centralizing all access through its Ministry of Posts and Telecommunications. The government now screens thousands of sites for their appropriateness. Many sites are banned—and not just the "spicy" ones, such as Playboy.com. A Web site operated by Mujahedeen Khalq, an Iranian opposition group based in Iraq, has also been banned.

For Critical Analysis

Is it possible for any nation to maintain control over the flow of electronically transmitted information?

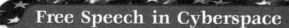

Free Speech in Cyberspace

Virtually instantaneous transmission of large amounts of information—including black-and-white and color photos, animations, and, by the time you read this book, perhaps full-motion videos—is now possible because of the Internet. Understandably, this new medium of communication presents new legal issues. We have already discussed some of these issues in Chapters 2 and 4. Others will continue to arise in the future. Here we look at three significant issues that have come before the courts: online obscenity, electronic junk mail, and online protests containing threatening speech.

ONLINE OBSCENITY

One of the most discussed issues today concerns obscene and pornographic materials. Such materials are easily accessed by anyone of any age almost anywhere in the world via numerous Web sites. Recall from Chapter 4 that in 1996, in the interest of protecting children from potentially harmful materials, Congress passed the Communications Decency Act. The act made it a crime to transmit "indecent" and "patently offensive" speech to minors (those under the age of eighteen) or to make such speech available online to minors. In 1997, however, the Supreme Court ruled that the act was unconstitutional; it violated the First Amendment because it suppressed a large amount of constitutionally protected adult speech.[16]

In 1998, Congress again attempted to regulate speech on the Internet when it passed the Child Online Protection Act (COPA). The law imposed criminal penalties on persons who distribute, via the Internet, material that is "harmful to minors" without using an age-verification system to separate adult and minor Web users. Like the CDA of 1996, the COPA was immediately challenged in court, and a federal court issued a preliminary injunction temporarily blocking the act's enforcement.[17] (Compare the U.S. approach to Internet regulation with that in the countries discussed in the feature entitled *Comparative Politics: High-Tech Vice Squads in Other Countries.*)

An important question here, at least in the eyes of many Americans, is whether the courts should be passing judgment on the extent to which the government can regulate the Internet. Even one of the justices of the United States Supreme Court, David Souter, has acknowledged doubts about making such decisions. In a 1996 case concerning the regulation of cable TV, Souter wrote, "I have to accept the real possibility that 'if we had

I N F O T R A C *
Get serious on security

---

comparative politics

High-Tech Vice Squads in Other Countries

Some European nations are getting serious about patrolling the Internet. Most major European police authorities have high-tech vice squads that comb the Internet for "illegal" materials, mostly Web sites involving child pornography. The police department in Munich, Germany, for example, has a five-member Internet "patrol team." Of course, when a German police department discovers an "illegal" Web site originating in another country, there is little that it can do. About one-third of the cases discovered do involve Germans, however, and they are prosecuted.

Some countries, including Germany, are now prosecuting service providers, such as CompuServe. In April 1997, CompuServe's general manager, Felix Somm, was charged with criminally allowing the dissemination of pornography. In another case, Austrian police raided one of Austria's service providers that was being investigated for disseminating child pornography.

In Britain, Scotland Yard works with that country's main Internet service provider, which assists the police in ferreting out "smut" on home pages. In addition, the British Internet industry has set up the Internet Watch Foundation, which is backed by the government, the police, and the industry itself. The foundation has a hotline that callers can use to report illegal materials on the Internet. Then, a team of "surfers" checks out the complaints and forwards any questionable materials to appropriate authorities.

For Critical Analysis

Is there a difference between "ferreting out" smut on the Internet and doing the same thing in the print media?

to decide today . . . just what the First Amendment should mean in cyberspace, . . . we would get it fundamentally wrong.'"[18]

DOES FREE SPEECH INCLUDE THE RIGHT TO TRANSMIT ELECTRONIC JUNK MAIL?

Increasingly, individuals with e-mail addresses are being flooded by junk e-mail, known in Internet jargon as "spam." America Online (AOL), one of the largest online service providers, attempted to stop Cyber Promotions, Inc., from sending mass commercial mailings to all of AOL's millions of subscribers.

Cyber Promotions claimed that it had a First Amendment right to communicate junk e-mail via the Internet to whomever it wished. A federal district court disagreed, ruling that Cyber Promotions did not have a constitutional right, under the First Amendment, to send unsolicited e-mail advertisements to AOL subscribers and that AOL was entitled to block such transmissions.[19] In a 1997 case brought against Cyber Promotions by another online service provider, CompuServe, a federal court similarly ruled that Cyber Promotions had no right to send junk e-mail to CompuServe subscribers.[20]

FREE SPEECH VERSUS CRIMINAL THREATS— THE CASE OF THE NUREMBERG FILES

In 1999, a federal court faced a significant question with respect to online speech: At what point does information on a Web site cross the line between protected speech and speech that illegally incites violence? The case involved a Web site sponsored by an antiabortion group called "The Nuremberg Files."

The site showed simulated blood dripping from fetus parts, referred to those who performed abortions as "baby butchers," and listed the names of dozens of physicians and clinic workers around the country who provided abortion services. The site not only gave their names but also included their photographs, home addresses, license plate numbers, and the names of their spouses and children. Some of the physicians had a line through their names, indicating that they had been killed. Those who had been wounded had their names listed in gray. At protests staged near abortion clinics, the group would hand out "wanted-style" posters offering rewards to anyone who successfully "persuaded" the physicians to stop their "child killing."

Planned Parenthood and several of the physicians who had been targeted by the group sued the site's sponsors, claiming that the Web site and the group's actions constituted illegal threats. A federal court jury in Portland agreed, and the court ordered the sponsors of the Web site to close it down.[21] On the evening of the court's decision, the site's Internet service provider refused to furnish the group with further online services.

The Question of Privacy in Cyberspace

Nowhere is the issue of privacy a hotter topic than in cyberspace—the Internet. We touched on some issues involving privacy in cyberspace in Chapter 2. Other issues concern the amount of personal information that is gathered and stored electronically by various organizations, including the government, and the development of encryption software to protect the privacy of online transmissions.

HOW MUCH DO "THEY" KNOW ABOUT YOU?

Here is a partial listing of the information about you that is already stored in government and corporate computer files:

- Your health, credit, marital, educational, and employment history.
- Your magazine subscriptions and the books that you borrow from the library.

■ All of your cash withdrawals from ATMs and all of your purchases by credit card or check.

■ Your e-mail and telephone messages (usually at work).

■ Everything you see on the World Wide Web (obtained from "cookies" installed in your computer by virtually every commercial Web site that you access).

Decades ago, Americans were sufficiently alarmed by the accumulation of personal information in government files that they pressured Congress to pass laws permitting individuals to access their files. Congress responded in 1966 with the Freedom of Information Act, which allows any person to request copies of any information on her or him contained in government files. In 1974, Congress passed the Privacy Act, which also gives persons the right of access to such information.

Although Americans have a right to see this information, it is not all that easy to get the government to respond to requests (see the feature entitled *Politics on the Far Side: Finding Out What Is in Your Government File*). To make matters worse, as we move into the world of cyberspace, the rules are changing: How can we even know what kind of information on our personal lives and preferences is being collected by Internet users and online merchants? How can we know how that information will be used?

Of course, the "information highway" is a two-way street. Just as the government has access to personal information on U.S. citizens, so do those citizens also have access to information about U.S. government officials. Americans can now quickly learn, through online resources, who contributed what amount of money to which member of Congress, how particular members of Congress voted on certain issues, and the like.

THE THORNY ENCRYPTION ISSUE

A lot of people would like to make sure that anything they send on the Internet is "secure" from the prying eyes of others, including the government. It is easy to eavesdrop on Internet communications. The wrong person might learn your credit-card number when you enter it to make an online purchase. Your Social Security number might be revealed when it is passed through cyberspace. Details of your business transactions or your private life might be revealed to persons to whom you would not otherwise give such information. One way to make Internet communications secure is by using **encryption software**.

Encryption is the process by which a message (plaintext) is transformed into something (ciphertext) that the sender and receiver intend third parties not to understand. Decryption is the process of transforming ciphertext into plaintext. An encryption code is a program used in encryption software to transform plaintext into ciphertext and vice versa. This software includes source codes, object codes, applications software, and system software.

Law enforcement authorities are afraid that the wrong persons, including international terrorists, will take advantage of Internet security to engage in illegal activities. For this reason, U.S. Department of Commerce regulations have prohibited the export of encryption code. This prohibition has been challenged in a few cases on the ground that an encryption code is speech and therefore protected by the First Amendment. That would mean that the regulations banning its export are unconstitutional.[22] In a recent case, however, a federal district court held that an

politics on the far side

Finding Out What Is in Your Government File

The Federal Bureau of Investigation (FBI) alone has more than ten million files on individuals, organizations, and criminal investigations. The empty 9-by-11½-inch folders alone, if stacked one on top of the other, would create a paper tower extending twenty miles into the sky.

The Freedom of Information and Privacy Acts give you the right to access government documents. Even if you fill out the required forms correctly, though, do not expect to get much information back very soon. The typical wait today is between two and four years, because you will be placed at the bottom of a waiting list containing at least fifteen thousand names. If you still want to make a request, contact the FBI's Freedom of Information/Privacy Act Section at 202-324-3000. Alternatively, you can call the Freedom of Information Act clearinghouse at 202-588-1000.

For Critical Analysis: Do online merchants who collect information from their customers pose a greater privacy threat than government information-gathering activities do?

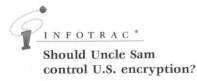

INFOTRAC®

Should Uncle Sam control U.S. encryption?

ENCRYPTION SOFTWARE ●
Computer programs that enable the user to encode ("encrypt") data to prevent access to the data by unauthorized persons.

More and more students have access to computers in their primary, middle, and high schools. Increasingly, public schools will be wired to the Internet because of recently legislated lower phone charges for such hookups.

encryption code is not speech, because its purpose is to "transfer functions, not to communicate ideas."[23] The controversy over this issue was eased somewhat in the fall of 1999, when the Clinton administration relaxed some of the prohibitions on exporting encryption code.

The Wiring of American Schools

During Clinton's 1992 presidential campaign, vice presidential candidate Al Gore's favorite buzz words were "the information superhighway." Although that phrase is now considered passé, Clinton and Gore continue to be concerned with the "wiring" of American schools. In a speech in Knoxville, Tennessee, on October 10, 1996, President Clinton asked that every public school and library be given basic Internet service for free. He called this the "E-rate," or educational rate. The administration estimated that the cost of linking schools and libraries to the Internet would be about $2.5 billion annually for five years.

Tucked away in the Telecommunications Act of 1996 was a measure to give libraries and schools special treatment with respect to "enhanced services." That term has been taken to mean Internet access. An eight-person board, including three members of the Federal Communications Commission (FCC), attempted to design the basis for the final rule.

In the final rule, which was issued in May 1997, the FCC declared that there would be "universal" access to the Internet for schools and libraries. Starting in 1998, more than 100,000 (mainly public) schools benefited from a "supertariff" for accessing the Internet. They received reductions, ranging from 20 to 90 percent, for all costs associated with setting up online connections and subscribing to Internet service providers. The discount depended on the economic condition of each school's student body—the lower the average income, the greater the discount. These discounts were financed by a fund that will reach $4.6 billion annually. To raise monies for this fund, every household or business with more than one telephone number has to pay a monthly tax of $3.50 to $5.00 for each additional telephone number.

Critics of the federal government's mandate to the telecommunications industry to "wire" public schools point out the obvious: the cost of hooking up to the Internet is becoming cheaper every year. With the advent of the digital wireless connections currently being used in numerous locations by AT&T, the concept of "wiring" becomes a nonissue. All that will be required to hook up to the Internet is a wireless phone with a modem connection, and the price of such equipment will steadily fall—perhaps becoming as cheap as a standard telephone is today.

Americans at Odds over Politics in Cyberspace

Americans and indeed the rest of the world confront a host of issues in cyberspace. In previous chapters in this text, you have already been exposed to a number of them. We have treated others within this chapter. We look next at an issue that simply will not go away: the threat of cyber warfare. We then consider how the Internet may affect American politics in the years to come.

Can a Country Cyber-Bury the United States?

The setting: The United Nations General Assembly. The date: September 27, 1956. The statement: "We will bury you." The speaker: Nikita Khrushchev, then the head of the Soviet Union. Khrushchev took his shoe off and pounded on the table as he screamed his challenge to the American people.

Well, history has obviously shown that the Soviet Union did not bury the United States. Today, though, there is evidence that Russia, the largest of the fifteen "republics" of the former Soviet Union, may be trying to figure out a way to cyber-bury the United States.

PREPARING FOR CYBER WAR

From the outside, Russia's military looks like an empty shell. It was unable to defeat a ragtag militia in Chechnya in 1996–1997. Its approximately 1.7 million troops are ill paid and ill fed. Yet U.S. intelligence has discovered that Russia is spending serious money to focus its limited resources on "information warfare." It is working on viruses and other high-tech "wrecking" systems that could attack U.S. civilian computers. In 1997, the Russian parliament doubled its defense research and development appropriations to $2 billion. Some people fear that it will increase its appropriations even more whenever the Russian economy improves. If Russia waged a successful cyber war against the United States, our utility grids, telephone systems, and financial systems could be seriously impaired.

In preparation for cyber war, the U.S. government's National Defense University in Washington, D.C., has been playing cyber games to see what would happen if a computer worm started to corrupt files from the Pentagon's top-secret force-deployment database. Such games also examine the possibility of "sniffer" programs running amuck in the Bank of England's electronic funds transfer system.

WILL CYBER WAR EVER BECOME A REALITY?

Clearly, information warfare has reached the game-playing stage. Will it ever become a reality? For some time, several high-level defense and intelligence officials in the United States thought that the probability of actual information warfare was low. By the mid-1990s, however, attitudes toward this new national security threat were changing.

In 1996, Howard Frank, director of the Information Technology Office at the Defense Department's Advanced Research Projects Agency had the following to say about information warfare: "A couple of years ago, no one took information warfare seriously. But the more you learn about it, the more concerned you bcome."[24] In the same year, President Clinton created the Commission on Critical Infrastructure Protection to devise a coordinated policy to deal with cyber warfare threats. Congress also ordered the Pentagon to commission a study of the problem. The National Research Council, which conducted the study, reported in 1999 that the military's key communications infrastructure was dangerously vulnerable to cyberspace attacks. According to the council, the Defense Department should give cyber warfare threats higher priority than it has in the past.[25]

The fact is that even a relatively poor country has the ability to obtain the programmers, expertise, and computer hardware necessary to conduct cyber warfare.

Cyber Politics—What's Ahead?

Already, citizens and their government officials are communicating with each other electronically. Cyber villages are also becoming a reality. For example, electronic villages in Sylvania, Ohio, and Farmington, Michigan, allow citizens to interact with their governments via the Internet. They can access online library-circulation services, public officials, and civic announcements; they can even make tax payments electronically. The specter of even more electronic interactions between citizens and their governments suggests a future that is characterized by very different patterns of political behavior than those to which we are now accustomed.

In the future, when virtually everyone is connected to the Internet, electronic voting may become a reality. As mentioned in Chapter 1, some people envision a truly *electronic democracy,* in which the entire population, via online voting forums, will vote on important policy matters as they arise. Of course, one of the reasons that electronic democracy may be possible in the United States is the low cost of Internet usage. (For a comparison of the cost of Internet access in the United States and in other countries, see the feature on the next page entitled *Comparative Politics: The Cost of Internet Use.*)

Although we cannot foresee the future, it is clear that certain developments—made possible by the Internet—will have an impact on politics in the years to come. For one thing, the ability to organize interest groups online at relatively low cost may mean more pressure on government by poorer classes in the United States—who in the past have been greatly underrepresented in legislative lobbies at all levels of government.

Additionally, civic participation in an electronic democracy will be affected by the extent to which different population segments have access to, and use, the Web for political purposes. For example, traditionally, the highest voter turnout has been among older Americans—those over the age of fifty. Yet according to recent polls, only a small—if growing—number of Internet users fall within this age group. Other factors that have affected voting behavior in the past include income, education, and geography. The point here is that differential access to the Internet among various groups in the population could have a substantial effect on politics.

comparative **politics**

The Cost of Internet Use

It goes without saying that if the Internet is to have real political use, access has to be cheap. It certainly is economical in the United States. In the first place, the required hardware has become relatively inexpensive. One can access the Internet with a Web TV system for $300 or with a used computer and modem setup for $500 or $600. More important, as a result of significant competition, some online service providers have brought the cost of unlimited usage down to as little as $10 a month. Then there is the phone service. At least as of the writing of this text, most people paid no additional charge for local calls, no matter how long they were online.

This is not the situation in the rest of the world, however. Ignoring for the moment the nations that impose severe political limitations on Internet access, Internet use comes with a much higher price tag in most other countries (with the exception of Canada) than in the United States. As Figure 12–3 shows, the cost of Internet access for twenty hours per month of daytime online use can be dramatically higher abroad.

Why is using the Internet so costly in other countries? Basically, the reason is the lack of competition in the telecommunications arena. In virtually all of the countries surveyed, government monopolies control telephone rates. Once a telecommunications treaty and agreements are negotiated within the European Union, we can expect to see more competition in the telecommunications industry worldwide and, as a consequence, falling prices for Internet access. Thus, the rest of the world may catch up with the United States before long in the extent to which the Internet is used in campaigning and for other political purposes.

For Critical Analysis

It has been estimated that between 80 and 90 percent of the home pages on the Internet are in English. Could this be another reason why Internet use is relatively low in countries whose native tongue is not English? Will this change?

I N F O T R A C °

Non U.S.-centric international Internet

Figure 12–3
Comparative Cost of Internet Use

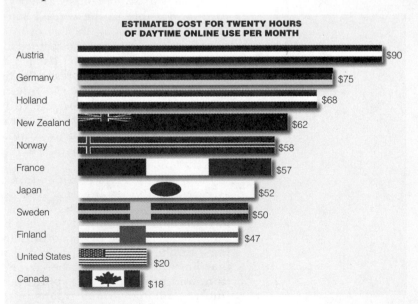

ESTIMATED COST FOR TWENTY HOURS
OF DAYTIME ONLINE USE PER MONTH

Austria	$90
Germany	$75
Holland	$68
New Zealand	$62
Norway	$58
France	$57
Japan	$52
Sweden	$50
Finland	$47
United States	$20
Canada	$18

Source: Organization for Economic Cooperation and Development, 1996.

key terms

cyber demonstration 295

encryption software 300

push technology 294

search engine 296

store and forward procedure 287

Web browser 288

chapter summary

1. The Internet evolved from a network of interconnected computer systems, called ARPANET, which was established by the U.S. Defense Department to make military communications possible should nuclear war break out. Academicians began to use the ARPANET for research not related to defense. In 1982, this rudimentary network was further developed and expanded. In the 1980s, the Internet was born, initially connecting about six hundred computers. The World Wide Web is the leading information retrieval service of the Internet. A major impetus for the explosive growth of the Internet and the Web was the creation of the first Web browser, released in 1993. Today, more than 100 million people worldwide are using the Internet.

2. Today's political parties and candidates realize the benefits of using computers and, increasingly, the Internet as campaign tools. Sophisticated computer programs allow politicians to target potential donors and "narrowcast" their requests for funds. The Internet provides an inexpensive way for candidates to contact, recruit, and mobilize their supporters; to disseminate information on the issues; and to raise funds. Some of the problems with using the Internet for campaigning is that it cannot reach mass audiences, as TV can; users have to be motivated to access the information; and those who are most likely to access information on the Web (younger Americans) are the least likely to vote.

3. The Internet is becoming more important as a news source. Most major newspapers and news magazines now have online versions, and many of the standard TV news sources are creating news sites on the Internet. An increasing number of political commentators are appearing on the Web, including highly respected mainstream political pundits. The Internet is the ultimate "narrowcasting" vehicle in the sense that users can direct their Web browsers to find only sites of interest to the users. Using push technology, users can totally customize their daily supply of information.

4. The Internet is a boon for interest groups because it offers the possibility of building global networks among those who share common interests at very low cost. It also offers existing interest groups a way to inexpensively promote their causes. Labor unions are finding that the Internet allows them to quickly mobilize their members and gain support for strikes, protests, and the like. Human rights activists and other interest groups have found the Internet to be an effective tool in the struggle against governments that, in the eyes of these groups, violate the human rights of their citizens.

5. Understandably, the new medium of communication that is the Internet presents new legal issues. A significant issue has to do with online obscenity and whether the Internet should be regulated to prevent children from being exposed to pornographic materials. Other legal issues concern the transmission of electronic junk mail and Web sites that incite violence.

6. One of the challenges presented by the Internet is how privacy rights can be protected in cyberspace. Although federal laws give individuals the right to access information collected in government files, it is sometimes difficult to obtain that information. Furthermore, there is often no way of knowing what information on our personal lives is being collected by Internet users and how that information will be used. One way to protect the privacy of communications is by encrypting messages, using encryption software. The U.S. government, however, concerned that drug traffickers, terrorists, and others may use such software to their advantage, has placed restrictions on the export of such software.

7. According to a provision in the Telecommunications Act of 1996 and a subsequent rule issued by the Federal Communications Commission in May 1997, there will be "universal" access to the Internet for schools and libraries. Schools will receive discounts depending on the economic condition of each school's student body. This federal mandate has come under criticism because the cost of Internet access is becoming lower each year, and new technology will continue to reduce the price of Internet access and use.

8. Americans are at odds over a number of issues regarding politics in cyberspace. One issue that will not go away is the threat of cyber warfare. Another issue concerns how the Internet will affect American politics in the future.

for critical analysis

1. One of the practical problems in regulating the Internet is that it is a global medium. What is offensive in Moscow, Idaho, might not be in Moscow, Russia. Who should decide what types of speech should and should not be allowed online? Is it even possible to regulate the Internet?

2. Do you believe that people are any more likely to access online information on candidates' positions during political campaigns than they have accessed such information in the past from other sources?

3. Some analysts have concluded that the people who are using the Internet to obtain news are the same people who traditionally have kept up with current events. Does this mean that the Internet will have little impact in the future on the percentage of people who are interested and involved in the political process?

4. Do your news viewing and reading habits differ from those of your parents? If so, in what ways?

5. If you heard a rumor that a giant meteor was approaching the earth, where would you go to get accurate information? Is one source just as good as another?

6. Do you believe the Internet makes it easier for the federal government to snoop in your affairs, or is "Big Brother" about the same size as he was a couple of decades ago?

7. Will "wired" schools improve students' awareness of political issues?

suggested readings

ALEXANDER, Cynthia J., and Leslie A. Pal. Eds. *Digital Democracy: Policy and Politics in the Wired World.* New York: Oxford University Press, 1998. This is a collection of twelve essays by Canadian and American scholars on the impact of cyberspace on politics and the implications of this impact for our future as private citizens.

DAVIS, Richard. *The Web of Politics: The Internet's Impact on the American Political System.* New York: Oxford University Press, 1999. The author shows how current political players, including candidates, public officials, and media representatives, are adapting to the Internet and assuring that this new medium benefits them in their struggle for power.

DERTOUZOS, Michael L. *What Will Be: How the New World of Information Will Change Our Lives.* San Francisco: HarperEdge, 1997. The author, an Internet pioneer and the head of the computer science laboratory at the Massachusetts Institute of Technology, sets forth his vision of how technology and the Internet will affect our lives and institutions in the future.

DIFFIE, Whitfield, and Susan Landau. *Privacy on the Line: The Politics of Wiretapping and Encryption.* Cambridge, Mass.: MIT Press, 1999. The authors examine national security, law enforcement, commercial, and civil liberties issues. They discuss the social function of privacy, how it underlies a democratic society, and what happens when it is lost.

KATZ, Jon. *Virtuous Reality: How America Surrendered Discussion of Moral Values to Opportunists, Nitwits, and Blockheads like William Bennett.* New York: Random House, 1997. The author, the media critic for *Wired* magazine, explores the "cultural civil war" between the old media (now owned by a few conglomerates) and the new (including the Internet, MTV, live radio, and cable TV talk shows).

OWEN, Bruce M. *The Internet Challenge to Television.* Cambridge, Mass.: Harvard University Press, 1999. Television technology has begun to change at the same dizzying pace as computer software. What this will mean—for television, for computers, and for the popular culture in which these video media reign supreme—is the subject of this book.

politics
on the web

You can obtain news tailored to your personal interests by using the PointCast Network (described in the text of this chapter), which you can find at

http://www.pointcast.com

After downloading and installing the free software provided by PointCast, your computer will connect to the Internet, at any interval you choose, and download the most recent news about topics that interest you.

The Claremont Institute is an interactive community on the Internet that aims to bring Internet users together with public-policy organizations under "the broad umbrella of 'conservative' thoughts, ideas, and actions." It can be found at

http://www.townhall.com

In the United States, the AFL-CIO's Web page can be accessed through

http://www.aflcio.org

Or, you can go directly to

http://www.paywatch.org

Called Pay Watch, this Web page has a wealth of information about the pay of the heads of Disney, Apple, Coca-Cola, and other companies. The program included on the Pay Watch site allows you to calculate the number of years a regular employee would have to work to pay an executive's salary for one year. The site also has information on the antilabor actions of the corporations in question. Visitors to this site are asked to boycott those multinationals that engage in antilabor practices.

For those of you who want to find news on the Web, refer to the *Politics on the Web* feature at the end of Chapter 11.

using web resources

The New Zealand Electronic Electoral Trial is a pilot project to increase awareness of electronic voting as a means of enhancing citizen participation in the democratic process.

Access the pilot project's Web site at

http://www.polemic.net/nzeet.html

1. Scan through the information on the page. Describe the two phases of the trial project, called "alpha trial" and "beta trial."

2. What do you believe are the main advantages to electronic voting? What are the main disadvantages?

3. Generally, what are the goals of the project?

notes

1. E-Commerce Study conducted by InfoBeads, a Ziff Davis, Inc., organization, between February 14 and April 20, 1999 and reported on InfoBeads's Web site at **http://www.infobeads.com**.

2. "Numbers," *Time*, July 27, 1998, p. 19.

3. S. C. Gwynne and J. E. Dickerson, "Lost in the E-Mail," *Time*, April 21, 1997, p. 89.

4. N. Rebecca Donatelli, as quoted in Amy Borrus, *Business Week*, August 30, 1999, p. 54.

5. Jim Drinkard, "One Click Can Reach Millions," *USA Today*, p. 1A.

6. John Simons, "Inside U.S. Presidential Campaign 2000: The Internet Is the New Battleground," *The Wall Street Journal Europe*, May 25, 1999, p. 10.

7. *Ibid.*

8. As quoted in Rebecca Fairley Raney, "Politicians Woo Voters on the Web," *The New York Times*, July 30, 1998, p. D1.

9. David Shribman, "www.SomeThingsNeverChange.gov," *Fortune*, May 10, 1999, p. 34.

10. Pew Research Center for the People and the Press survey, April 24 to May 11, 1998.

11. Brigid McMenamin, "Humbled by the Internet," *Forbes*, July 27, 1998.

12. "ACLU Targets Profiling by Police in Traffic Stops," *The Internet Newsletter*, July 1999, p. 12.

13. *Libération*, April 25, 1997, Multimedia Section, p. ii.

14. Joseph L. Galloway, "Internet Fuels Human-Rights Protests," *U.S. News & World Report*, August 31, 1998, p. 6.

15. Karine Granier-Deferre, "Radical Politics Embrace the Internet," *International Herald Tribune*, September 28, 1998, p. 13.

16. *Reno v. American Civil Liberties Union*, 521 U.S. 844 (1997).

17. *American Civil Liberties Union v. Reno*, 31 F.Supp.2d 473 (E.D.Pa. 1999).

18. *Denver Area Educational Telecommunications Consortium, Inc. v. Federal Communications Commission*, 518 U.S. 727 (1996).

19. *Cyber Promotions, Inc. v. America Online, Inc.*, 948 F.Supp. 436 (E.D.Pa. 1996).

20. *CompuServe, Inc. v. Cyber Promotions, Inc.*, 962 F.Supp. 1015 (S.D.Ohio 1997).

21. *Planned Parenthood of Columbia/Willamette, Inc. v. American Coalition of Life Activists*, 41 F.Supp.2d 1130 (D.Or. 1999).

22. See, for example, *Bernstein v. U.S. Department of Justice*, 176 F.3d 1132 (9th Cir. 1999).

23. *Junger v. Daley*, 8 F.Supp.2d 708 (N.D.Ohio 1998).

24. *The International Herald Tribune*, October 1, 1996, p. 6.

25. Joseph Schuman, "Report: Military Computers Vulnerable to Cyberspace Attack," *The Ann Arbor News*, March 22, 1999, p. A1.

CONGRESS

Contents

America at Odds

Term Limits: Forcing Members of Congress to Go Back Home

A little over a hundred years ago, the average length of service in the House of Representatives was four years. During our nation's first century, turnover averaged 43 percent; but by the 1980s, 99.3 percent of congressional and state legislative incumbents won reelection. Actually, for years there was greater turnover in the former Soviet Union's Communist Party leadership and in Britain's House of Lords than there was in the U.S. Congress.

Go to CD-ROM

The idea of limiting the time that members can serve in Congress is not new. Indeed, members of the first Congress suggested term limitations, but the idea was rejected. Self-imposed limits on officeholders were previously a part of this country's public-service ethic. Members would voluntarily return to private life after only a couple of terms. By 1995, twenty-three states had passed laws limiting the time that senators and representatives from their states could serve in Congress. The Supreme Court, however, declared that such laws were unconstitutional.[1] The Court stated that because the Constitution was silent on the issue of term limits, such limits could only be established by a constitutional amendment.

A constitutional amendment was subsequently introduced in Congress, but it never got out of the Senate. Most proposals for term limits would restrict House members to six two-year terms and Senate members to two six-year terms. Clearly, given that twenty-three states had already voted for term limits, there is a sizable group of Americans who favor them. Some Gallup polls show that term limits are favored by a 2 to 1 ratio. Indeed, one study found that 83 percent of survey respondents favored mandatory rotation in office for elected officials.[2] Nonetheless, Americans are at odds about this issue.

Leave Well Enough Alone

Apart from the old saw, "If it ain't broke, don't fix it," a number of serious scholars and laypersons alike are adamantly against the imposition of term limits on the service of members of Congress. They argue that such limits would restrict voters' choices and are undemocratic. Perhaps more significantly, opponents of term limits argue that the result would be a Congress filled with inexperienced legislators, who might be unduly influenced by veteran congressional staff members (who are not elected to their jobs).

Opponents of term limits also argue that they would make members of Congress much less responsive to the wishes of their constituents. After all, elected officials in their final terms cannot be reelected, so voters have no way of punishing them.

Send Them Packing

Perhaps equally compelling are the arguments of those in favor of term limits. They point out that limiting congressional terms could free members of Congress from their concern over being reelected. With term limits, senators and representatives could tackle the business of government more objectively and with less concern over how their votes would affect their constituents. Of course, if more than one term is allowed, this argument would apply only to legislators serving their final terms in Congress.

Proponents of term limits do not buy the "experience" argument mentioned above. They believe that the expertise learned—the art of logrolling, putting deals together, and other political activities—is something that the nation could well do without.

The main argument in favor of term limits is that they would eliminate the professional politician. After all, the power of incumbency is so great that most incumbents win reelection and careerists dominate public policy. We end up with individuals who have spent a significant portion of their lives as politicians and are out of touch with the nongovernment world in which most of us live. As Thomas Jefferson once said, "Whenever a man has cast a longing eye on [political office], a rottenness begins in his conduct."[3] Power and influence tend to corrupt, as the old argument goes, and with seniority comes too much power and influence.

Where Do You Stand?

1. If term limits were imposed, would the demographic characteristics of those who run for political office change? If so, how?

2. What are some of the weaknesses in the arguments put forth by both the supporters and the opponents of term limits?

On the Web

For arguments on both sides of this issue, go to **http://www.ustermlimits.org** (for) and **http://www.epn.org/prospect/24/24schr.html** (against).

310

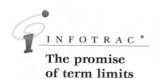

INFOTRAC®

**The promise
of term limits**

Introduction

In the 1980s, the U.S. Congress was racked with numerous ethical problems and scandals, ranging from videotaped payoffs to members of Congress, to publicly recorded meetings between prostitutes and members of Congress, to check-kiting scandals involving the House bank . . . (the list goes on and on). Surveys of Americans consistently showed that Congress was the least respected governmental institution.

In 1994, perhaps because the sitting Congress was held in such low esteem, the so-called Republican revolution occurred. The Democrats were no longer in the majority. In 1996, the Republican Party retained control of both chambers of Congress for the first time in more than seventy years. The Republicans remained in the majority after the 1998 elections. Still, the public's assessment of the job Congress is doing remains, for the most part, unfavorable.

Some argue that one way to improve Congress's performance is to limit the terms of all congresspersons, a topic discussed in this chapter's opening feature. Whether term limits should be imposed is a significant issue because members of Congress perform such an important job in the American political system. When someone says, "There ought to be a law," at the federal level it is Congress that will make that law, for Congress is the lawmaking branch of government. The framers of the Constitution established Congress as the first branch of government. The framers had a strong suspicion of a powerful executive authority. They also were aware of how ineffective the Congress had been under the Articles of Confederation. Consequently, the framers intended Congress to be the central institution of American government.

The Origin, Structure, and Make-Up of Congress

The framers agreed that the Congress should be the "first branch of the government," as James Madison said, but they did not agree on its organization.

Citizens demonstrate in favor of term limits, budget reform, and lower taxes.

INFOTRAC°

Supreme Court gets lessons in enumeration

Ultimately, they decided on a bicameral legislature—a Congress consisting of two chambers. This was part of the Great Compromise, which you read about in Chapter 2. The framers favored a bicameral legislature so that the two chambers, the House and the Senate, might serve as checks on each other's power and activity. The House was to represent the people as a whole, or the majority. The Senate was to represent the states and would protect the interests of small states by giving them the same number of senators (two per state) as the larger states. (For a discussion of the differences between the U.S. Congress and the British Parliament, see the feature *Comparative Politics: How the British Parliament Differs from the U.S. Congress.*)

APPORTIONMENT OF HOUSE SEATS

The Constitution provides for the **apportionment** (distribution) of House seats among the states on the basis of their respective populations. As the population changes, the number of House seats is reapportioned accordingly, based on census results. (Figure 13–1 shows the number of seats that were gained by some states and lost by others following the 1990 census.) Because representation in the House is based on population, the more people a state has, the more representatives it will send to the House. California, for example, with an estimated 2000 population of 34.8 million, has fifty-two representatives. North Carolina, with an estimated 2000 population of 7.8 million, has twelve representatives. Wyoming, with an estimated 2000 population of 522,000, has one representative.

Each state is guaranteed at least one seat, no matter what its population. Today, seven states have only one representative.[4] The District of Columbia, American Samoa, Guam, and the U.S. Virgin Islands all send nonvoting delegates to the House. Puerto Rico, a self-governing possession of the United States, is represented by a nonvoting resident commissioner.

Because the number of legislators each state has in the House of Representatives is vital to that state's political interests, the results of the U.S. census are extremely significant. How accurate are these results? That

Figure 13–1
Reapportionment of House Seats following the 1990 Census

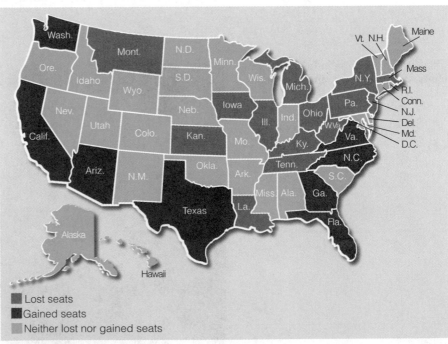

SOURCE: U.S. Bureau of the Census.

How the British Parliament Differs from the U.S Congress

The framers of the U.S. Constitution, for the most part, were used to the British form of government in which the central institution is the national legislature, known as Parliament. Like our own Congress, Parliament is a bicameral body: it is made up of the House of Commons and the House of Lords. Unlike Congress, however, the British Parliament (as in all parliamentary systems) is based on the *fusion* of powers rather than the *separation* of powers. It manages both the legislative and the executive powers of the nation. Parliament's legislative powers include passing and changing laws; its executive powers include choosing the prime minister, who is the leader of the majority party in the House of Commons, and the cabinet that will serve the prime minister.

The House of Commons

The House of Commons is the legislative branch that consists of elected officials. This lower house, known as "the Commons," is the more powerful of the two houses. Its members, known as Members of Parliament, or MPs, are popularly elected from geographic districts. Any MP is allowed to introduce legislation, but most measures are introduced by the government, which is made up of the prime minister and the cabinet collectively. The bill is then debated and sent to one of the eight standing committees that review bills and prepare them for final consideration by the full chamber. Unlike congressional committees, which specialize in areas such as agriculture or the armed forces, committees in the House of Commons are general committees that consider bills on a wide variety of subjects.

The House of Lords

The upper chamber of Parliament, known as the House of Lords, is a body of aristocratic persons who have mostly inherited their titles. Seven hundred fifty are hereditary peers (members of the nobility who became so by birth) with titles such as *baron, viscount, earl,* and *duke.* (In 1998, the British government announced that it plans to abolish these 750 hereditary seats.) The five hundred other members are appointed for life by the queen. They include twenty-six bishops of the Church of England, nine specially appointed *law lords* (the British equivalent of our Supreme Court), and individuals honored for their careers in arts, politics, science, or business. Usually, only about one hundred members are in attendance at sessions of the House of Lords.

The House of Lords was once a powerful branch of the British government, but today it has little real authority over legislation. If the House of Lords defeats a bill passed in the Commons, the Commons need only pass it a second time in the next session to make the bill become law. The House of Lords may amend legislation, but any changes it makes can be canceled by the Commons.

For Critical Analysis

What is one of the key differences between the upper chamber of the British Parliament and the U.S. Senate?

CONGRESSIONAL DISTRICT ● The geographical area that is served by one representative in Congress.

question is explored in this chapter's feature, entitled *Perception versus Reality: How Accurate Is the U.S. Census?*

CONGRESSIONAL DISTRICTS

Senators are elected to represent all of the people in the state, whereas representatives are elected by the voters of a particular area known as a **congressional district.** The Constitution makes no provisions for congressional districts, and in the early 1800s each state was given the right to decide whether to have districts at all. Most states set up single-member districts, in which voters in each district elected one of the state's representatives. In states that chose not to have districts, representatives were chosen at large, from the state as a whole. In 1842, however, Congress passed an act that required all states to send representatives to Congress from single-member districts.

In the early 1900s, the number of House members increased as the population expanded. In 1929, however, a federal law fixed House membership at 435 members. Today, the 435 members of the House are chosen by the voters in 435 separate congressional districts across the country. If a state's population allows it to have only one representative, as is the situation in a few states, the entire state is one congressional district. In contrast, states with large populations have numerous districts. California, for example, because its population entitles it to send fifty-two representatives to the House, has fifty-two congressional districts.

The lines of the congressional districts are drawn by the authority of state legislatures. States must meet certain requirements, though, in drawing district boundaries. To ensure equal representation in the House, districts must contain, as nearly as possible, an equal number of people. Additionally,

perception versus reality

How Accurate Is the U.S. Census?

The U.S. Constitution requires that an "actual Enumeration" of the nation's population be made every ten years, beginning with the year 1791, "in such Manner as [Congress] shall by Law direct." The census count is important in American politics because, as mentioned elsewhere in this chapter, the number of seats in the House of Representatives apportioned to each state is based on the state's population. Additionally, the determination of income levels and other data concerning the population are important in allocating federal funds under various programs (see Chapter 17). Thus, the question of whether census figures are accurate is extremely significant.

The Perception

Most Americans think very little about the actual logistics of how the U.S. Census Bureau collects

information on the number of people living in this country and other demographic data. Most citizens know that the Census Bureau hires people to go door-to-door or to mail out questionnaires to learn such information. But other than that, Americans give little thought to the methods. Generally, the perception is that all heads are counted in the process and that census results are accurate.

The Reality

In reality, the Census Bureau typically misses a significant number of U.S. residents, particularly migrant workers and people who live in inner-city areas. The latter group, for one reason or another, are typically difficult to reach. The last census, conducted in 1990, missed the mark by about ten million people. During the 1990s, the Census Bureau issued updates on

population and other demographic data using sampling techniques similar to those used by pollsters.

(For the 2000 census, it was proposed that statistical sampling techniques be used, in addition to the traditional physical head count, to make the census more accurate. In 1999, however, the United States Supreme Court ruled that the use of such techniques violates the Census Act of 1954, which was enacted to carry out the constitutional requirement of an "actual enumeration."[5])

You Be the Judge

Who do you think would be more likely to support sampling techniques to supplement traditional methods of conducting the census, Democrats or Republicans?

MALAPPORTIONMENT ● A condition that results when, based on population and representation, the voting power of citizens in one district becomes more influential than the voting power of citizens in another district.

"ONE PERSON, ONE VOTE" RULE ● A rule, or principle, requiring that congressional districts must have equal population so that one person's vote counts as much as another's vote.

GERRYMANDERING ● The drawing of a legislative district's boundaries in such a way as to maximize the influence of a certain group or political party.

each district must have contiguous boundaries and must be "geographically compact."

The Requirement of Equal Representation

If congressional districts are not made up of equal populations, the value of people's votes is not the same. In the past, state legislatures often used this knowledge to their advantage. For example, traditionally, many state legislatures were controlled by rural areas. By drawing districts that were not equal in population, rural leaders attempted to curb the number of representatives from growing urban centers. At one point in the 1960s, in many states the largest district had twice the population of the smallest district. In effect, this meant that a person's vote in the largest district had only half the value of a person's vote in the smallest district.

For some time, the Supreme Court refused to address this problem. In 1962, however, in *Baker v. Carr,*[6] the Court ruled that the Tennessee state legislature's **malapportionment** was an issue that could be heard in the federal courts because it affected the constitutional requirement of equal protection under the law. Two years later, in *Wesberry v. Sanders,*[7] the Supreme Court held that congressional districts must have equal population. This principle has come to be known as the **"one person, one vote" rule.** In other words, one person's vote has to count as much as another's vote.

Gerrymandering

Although the Supreme Court, in the 1960s, established the requirement that congressional districts must be equal in population, it continued to be silent on the issue of gerrymandered districts. **Gerrymandering** occurs when a district's boundaries are drawn to maximize the influence of a certain group or political party. This can be done by drawing the boundaries in such a way as to include as many of the political party's voters as possible. In another form of gerrymandering, the lines are drawn so that the opponent's supporters are spread across two or more districts, thus diluting the opponent's strength.

The term *gerrymandering* was originally used in reference to the tactics used by Elbridge Gerry, governor of Massachusetts, prior to the 1812 elections. The Massachusetts legislature divided up Essex County in a way that favored Gerry's party; the result was a district that looked like a salamander (see Figure 13–2 on the next page). A news editor of the time referred to it as a "gerrymander," and the name stuck.

Political gerrymandering has a long history in this country, and only in 1986 did the Supreme Court finally rule, in *Davis v. Bandemer,*[8] that redistricting for the political benefit of one group could be challenged on constitutional grounds. In the early 1990s, however, the U.S. Department of Justice instructed state legislatures to undertake another type of gerrymandering: drawing district lines to maximize the voting power of minority groups. In effect, the government required the states to engage in racial and ethnic gerrymandering. We will look at this issue, and the controversy it has generated, later in the chapter.

CONGRESSIONAL ELECTIONS

The U.S. Constitution requires that congressional representatives be elected every second year by popular vote. Senators are elected every six years, also (since the ratification of the Seventeenth Amendment) by popular vote. Under Article I, Section 4, of the Constitution, state legislatures control the "Times, Places and Manner of holding Elections for Senators and Representatives." Congress, however, "may at any time by Law make or alter such Regulations." As you read in Chapter 10, control over the process of nominating congressional candidates has shifted from party conventions to direct primaries in which the party identifiers in the electorate select the candidates who will carry that party's endorsement into the actual election.[9]

Figure 13–2
The First "Gerrymander"

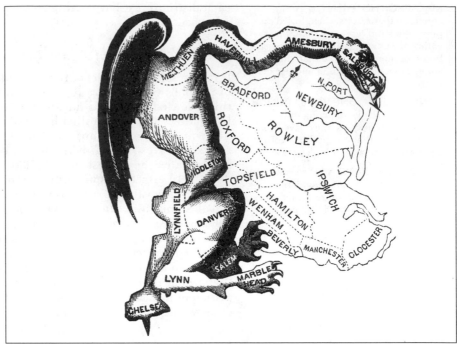

SOURCE: *Congressional Quarterly's Guide to Congress*, 3d ed. (Washington, D.C.: Congressional
Quarterly Press, 1982), p. 695.

Who Can Be a Member of Congress?

The Constitution sets forth only a few qualifications that those running for
Congress must meet. To be a member of the House, a person must be a citizen of the United States for at least seven years prior to his or her election, a legal resident of the state from which he or she is to be elected, and
at least twenty-five years of age. To be elected to the Senate, a person must
be a citizen for at least nine years, a legal resident of the state from which
she or he is to be elected, and at least thirty years of age. The Supreme
Court has ruled that neither the Congress nor the states can add to these
three qualifications.[10]

Once elected to Congress, a senator or representative receives an annual
salary from the government. He or she also enjoys certain perks and
privileges. (See the feature entitled *Perception versus Reality: The Issue of
Congressional Pay* for more detail on congressional pay.) Additionally, if

Representative Loretta Sanchez (D.,
Calif.) attempts to solicit campaign
contributions at a private home. Every
two years there are congressional
elections for seats in the House of
Representatives. Consequently, our
representatives are constantly
campaigning and trying to raise funds.

perception versus reality

The Issue of Congressional Pay

At first blush, members of Congress do not seem to be paid very much.

The Perception

The current perception is that members of Congress are paid more than the average American to be sure, but certainly nowhere near as much as captains of industry and finance. After all, the annual pay for a senator or representative in the 106th Congress was $136,700. (In the fall of 1999, Congress passed a bill that, if signed by the president, would increase congressional salaries by $4,600 or more.)

The Reality

Congress takes care of its own. Consider former Senate majority leader and presidential candidate Bob Dole. Thirty-five years before his retirement, he entered Washington with virtually no savings. He left with a multimillion-dollar nest egg—all obtained perfectly legally. For example, he earned over $1.6 million in speaking fees, mainly from special interest groups (now the Senate has barred members from accepting such honoraria). He charged thousands of dollars a year in meals to leadership expense accounts and then to his campaign. He was also able to make significant profits from business deals in which he legally invested.

Although members of Congress work in the nation's capital, a special section of the Internal Revenue Code allows them to deduct expenses incurred while living in Washington, D.C. Of course, that is not all. Members of Congress have access to the private Capitol Hill gymnasium facilities, get low-cost haircuts, and receive free, close-in parking at Reagan National and Dulles airports. They eat in a subsidized dining room, get free medical care, and are given a generous pension plan that costs them very little. They can even avoid parking tickets.

You Be the Judge

If you attempted to live the lifestyle of a member of Congress, how much do you think your annual before-tax income would have to be?

the person wants to run for reelection in the next congressional elections, his chances will be greatly enhanced. As you can see in Table 13–1 on the following page, the overwhelming majority of incumbents who decide to run for reelection are successful.

Shakeups in 1992 and 1994

You can also see in Table 13–1 that the percentage of House incumbents who were reelected in presidential-year elections declined from 98.3 percent in 1988 to 88.9 percent in 1992. The hold of incumbents over the electorate also lost force to some extent in the 1994 midterm elections.

The shakeup of 1992 reflected the public's growing disgust with Congress, both because of the numerous scandals involving congresspersons and the stalemate ("gridlock") that existed between President George Bush and Congress over many issues. When the polls closed, forty-eight incumbents had been defeated. The term-limits legislation passed in many states reflected this critical attitude of the electorate toward their legislators in Washington, D.C. A record number of legislators who were up for reelection decided to retire rather than face bitter campaigns. For a few representatives, there was a financial incentive to retire as well: they belonged to the group that would be allowed to convert campaign funds to personal use if they left office before 1994.

The angry mood of the voters and Bill Clinton's unpopularity during his first years as president were reflected in another shakeup in 1994. The 1994 midterm elections ousted the Democratic majority that had controlled Congress for decades and brought in a Republican majority. The results of the election surprised and shocked the members of Congress and the parties themselves. According to exit polls taken on election day, Republican candidates for Congress won not only the votes of their own party identifiers but also the votes of a majority of independents and a few Democratic voters. In all, the Democrats lost 53 seats in the House, with 190 incumbents reelected and 35 defeated. All of the Republican incumbents in the House were reelected.[11]

Table 13-1

The Power of Incumbency

	PRESIDENTIAL-YEAR ELECTIONS						MIDTERM ELECTIONS						
	1976	1980	1984	1988	1992	1996	1974	1978	1982	1986	1990	1994	1998
House													
Number of incumbent candidates	384	398	409	409	368	382	391	382	393	393	407	382	401
Reelected	368	361	390	402	325	359	343	358	354	385	391	347	394
Percentage of total	95.8	90.7	95.4	98.3	88.9	93.4	87.7	93.7	90.1	98.0	96.1	90.8	98.2
Defeated	16	37	19	7	43	23	48	24	39	8	16	35	7
In primary	3	6	3	1	19	2	8	5	10	2	1	1	1
In general election	13	31	16	6	24	21	40	19	29	6	15	34	6
Senate													
Number of incumbent candidates	25	29	29	27	28	21	27	25	30	28	32	26	29
Reelected	16	16	26	23	23	19	23	15	28	21	31	24	26
Percentage of total	64.0	55.2	89.6	85.0	82.1	90.0	85.2	60.0	93.3	75.0	96.9	92.3	89.6
Defeated	9	13	3	4	5	2	4	10	2	7	1	2	3
In primary	0	4	0	0	1	1	2	3	0	0	0	0	0
In general election	9	9	3	4	4	1	2	7	2	7	1	2	3

SOURCES: Harold W. Stanley and Richard G. Niemi, *Vital Statistics on American Politics,* 5th ed. (Washington, D.C.: Congressional Quarterly, Inc., 1995); and authors' update.

The 1996 and 1998 Elections

By 1996, a Democratic president and a Republican Congress seemed to be working well together, and public approval ratings for Congress rose. The 1996 elections appeared to confirm the voters' approval of divided government, with Bill Clinton being reelected to the White House and Republican majorities being returned to Congress.

Typically, the party of the president loses seats in midterm elections, but this was not the case in 1998. Prior to the elections, the Republicans held significantly more seats (228) in the House of Representatives than the Democrats (206). After the elections, these figures were 223 and 211, respectively, representing a loss of five seats for the Republicans. The Senate partisan distribution of seats (55 to 45, in favor of the Republicans) remained unchanged.

The election outcomes, which Republicans regarded as a defeat for their party, posed some serious questions for the Republican Party leaders in Congress: What had gone wrong? Why had the Republicans lost seats, rather than gained additional seats, as expected? Several Republicans in Congress suggested that the party needed new leadership. The conservative wing of the Republican Party was clearly disappointed in the failure of the party leaders to push forward the conservative agenda.

Facing challenges to his leadership, Newt Gingrich announced his resignation from his post as speaker of the House and from Congress three days after the election—largely to avoid a fight to maintain his position that he might not have won. Bob Livingston of Louisiana, who was expected to succeed Gingrich, also resigned. Ultimately, the choice for the new speaker of the House was Dennis Hastert, a Republican representative from Illinois.

Republican Dennis Hastert is speaker of the House for the 106th Congress. The speaker of the House holds a substantial amount of power.

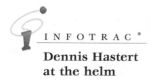

INFOTRAC®

Dennis Hastert at the helm

SPEAKER OF THE HOUSE ● The presiding officer in the House of Representatives. The speaker has traditionally been a long-time member of the majority party and is often the most powerful and influential member of the House.

Congressional Terms and Sessions

Each Congress lasts for a meeting period, or term, of two years. Each term is numbered consecutively, dating back to March 4, 1789. The date for the convening of each term was reset by the Twentieth Amendment in 1933; it is now January 3 of an odd-numbered year unless Congress sets another date.

Each term of Congress is divided into two regular sessions, or meetings—one for each year. Until about 1940, Congress remained in session for only four or five months, but the complicated rush of legislation and increased demand for services from the public in recent years have forced Congress to remain in session through most of each year.[12] Both chambers, however, schedule short recesses, or breaks, for holidays and vacations.

Congress remains in session until its members vote to adjourn. Neither house may adjourn a session without the consent of the other. Only the president may call Congress to meet during a scheduled recess. Such meetings are called *special sessions,* and only twenty-six such sessions have ever been held. As Congress now meets on nearly a year-round basis, a special session is unlikely to be needed.

CONGRESSIONAL LEADERSHIP

How each chamber of Congress is organized is largely a function of the two major political parties. The majority party in each chamber chooses the major officers of that chamber, controls debate on the floor, selects all committee chairpersons, and has a majority on all committees.

House Leadership

Both the House and the Senate have systems of leadership. Before Congress begins work, members of each party in each chamber meet to choose their leaders. The Constitution provides for the presiding officers of the House and Senate; Congress may choose what other leaders it feels it needs.

Speaker of the House. Chief among the leaders in the House of Representatives is the **speaker of the House.** This office is mandated by the Constitution and is filled by a vote taken at the beginning of each congressional term. The speaker has traditionally been a long-time member of the majority party who has risen in rank and influence through years of service in the House. The candidate for speaker is selected by the majority party caucus; other House members merely approve the selection.

As the presiding officer of the House and the leader of the majority party, the speaker has a great deal of power. In the early nineteenth century, the speaker had even more power and was known as the "king of the congressional mountain." Speakers known by such names as "Uncle Joe Cannon" and "Czar Reed" ruled the House with almost exclusive power. A revolt in 1910 reduced the speaker's powers and gave some of those powers to various committees. Today, the speaker still has many important powers, including the following:

■ The speaker has substantial control over what bills get assigned to which committees.
■ The speaker presides over the sessions of the House, recognizing or ignoring members who wish to speak.
■ The speaker votes in the event of a tie, interprets and applies House rules, rules on points of order (questions about procedures asked by members), puts questions to a vote, and determines the outcome of most of the votes taken.
■ The speaker plays a major role in making important committee assignments, which all members desire.
■ The speaker schedules bills for action.

The speaker may choose whether to vote on any measure. If the speaker chooses to vote, he appoints a temporary presiding officer (called a speaker *pro tempore*), who then occupies the speaker's chair.

The current House majority leader is Dick Armey (R., Tex.), shown on the left. The current House minority leader is Richard A. Gephardt (D., Mo.), shown on the right.

Under the House rules, the only time the speaker *must* vote is to break a tie, because otherwise a tie automatically defeats a bill. The speaker does not often vote, but by choosing to vote in some cases, the speaker can actually cause a tie and defeat a proposal that is unpopular with the majority party.

Majority Leader. The **majority leader** of the House is elected by the caucus of party members to act as spokesperson for the party and to keep the party together. The majority leader's job is to help plan the party's legislative program, organize other party members to support legislation favored by the party, and make sure the chairpersons on the many committees finish work on bills that are important to the party. The House majority leader makes speeches on important bills, stating the majority party's position.

Minority Leader. The House **minority leader** is the leader of the minority party. Although not as powerful as the majority leader, the minority leader has similar responsibilities. The primary duty of the minority leader is to maintain cohesion within the party. The minority leader persuades influential members of the party to follow its position and organizes fellow party members in constructive criticism of the majority party's policies and programs.

Whips. The leadership of each party includes assistants to the majority and minority leaders known as **whips.** Whips originated in the British House of Commons, where they were named after the "whipper in," the rider who keeps the hounds together in a fox hunt. The term was applied to assistant party leaders because of the pressure that they place on party members to follow the party's positions. Whips try to determine how each member is going to vote on certain issues and then advise the party leaders on the strength of party support. Whips also try to see that members are present when important votes are to be taken and that they vote with the party leadership. For example, if the Democratic Party strongly supports a child-care bill, the Democratic Party whip might meet with other Democrats in the House to try to persuade them to vote with the party.

MAJORITY LEADER ● The party leader elected by the majority party in the House or in the Senate.

MINORITY LEADER ● The party leader elected by the minority party in the House or in the Senate.

WHIP ● A member of Congress who assists the majority or minority leader in the House or in the Senate in managing the party's legislative preferences.

Senate majority leader Trent Lott (R., Miss.) is shown here on the steps of the Senate with other senators who support a balanced-budget amendment.

STANDING COMMITTEE ● A permanent committee in Congress that deals with legislation concerning a particular area, such as agriculture or foreign relations.

Senate Leadership

The Constitution makes the vice president of the United States the president of the Senate. As presiding officer, the vice president may call on members to speak and put questions to a vote. The vice president is not an elected member of the Senate, however, and may not take part in Senate debates. The vice president may cast a vote in the Senate only in the event of a tie. In practice, the vice president has little influence in the Senate and is rarely even present.

President *Pro Tempore.* Because vice presidents are rarely available to preside over the Senate, senators elect another presiding officer, the president *pro tempore* ("pro tem"), who serves in the absence of the vice president. The president pro tem is elected by the whole Senate and is ordinarily the member of the majority party with the longest continuous term of service in the Senate. In the absence of both the president pro tem and the vice president, a temporary presiding officer is selected from the ranks of the Senate, usually a junior member of the majority party.

Party Leaders. The real power in the Senate is held by the majority leader, the minority leader, and their whips. The majority leader is the most powerful individual and chief spokesperson of the majority party. The majority leader directs the legislative program and party strategy. The minority leader commands the minority party's opposition to the policies of the majority party and directs the legislative strategy of the minority party.

CONGRESSIONAL COMMITTEES

Thousands of bills are introduced during every session of Congress, and no single member can possibly be adequately informed on all the issues that arise. The committee system is a way to provide for specialization, or a division of the legislative labor. Members of a committee can concentrate on just one area or topic—such as agriculture or transportation—and develop sufficient expertise to draft appropriate legislation when needed. The flow of legislation through both the House and the Senate is determined largely by the speed with which the members of these committees act on bills and resolutions. The permanent and most powerful committees of Congress are called **standing committees;** their names are shown in Table 13–2. (For a

Table 13–2

Standing Committees in Congress

HOUSE COMMITTEES	SENATE COMMITTEES
Agriculture	Agriculture, Nutrition, and Forestry
Appropriations	Appropriations
Armed Services	Armed Services
Banking and Financial Services	Banking, Housing, and Urban Affairs
Budget	Budget
Commerce	Commerce, Science, and Transportation
Education and the Workforce	Energy and Natural Resources
Government Reform and House Administration	Environment and Public Works
International Relations	Finance
Judiciary	Foreign Relations
Resources	Governmental Affairs
Rules	Health, Education, Labor, and Pensions
Science	Indian Affairs
Small Business	Judiciary
Standards of Official Conduct	Rules and Administration
Transportation and Infrastructure	Small Business
Veterans' Affairs	Veterans' Affairs
Ways and Means	

This photo shows a Senate subcommittee at work. Subcommittees meet regularly in both chambers of Congress. There are over two hundred congressional subcommittees today. Each subcommittee specializes in a particular policy area.

SUBCOMMITTEE ● A division of a larger committee that deals with a particular part of the committee's policy area. Each of the standing committees in Congress has several subcommittees.

discussion of the interplay between standing committees and interest groups, see the feature entitled *A Question of Ethics: Do PACs Exercise Too Much Control over Standing Committees?*)

Before any bill can be considered by the entire House or Senate, it must be approved by a majority vote in the standing committee to which it was assigned. As mentioned, standing committees are controlled by the majority party in each chamber. Committee membership is generally divided between the parties according to the number of members in each chamber. Most House and Senate committees are also divided into **subcommittees,** which have limited areas of jurisdiction. Today, there are more than two hundred subcommittees. There are also other types of committees in Congress. Special, or select, committees, which may be either permanent

a question **of ethics**

Do PACs Exercise Too Much Control over Standing Committees?

It is illegal to bribe members of Congress. It is also quite against any ethical precepts that the American public harbors about the way Congress should work. The most that special interest groups can do is to make large contributions, typically through political action committees (PACs), to give us "the best Congress that money can buy." Specialized standing committees, however, offer unique opportunities for repeated interaction between special interest groups

and legislators. Members of such committees who do not please their campaign contributors can be punished. They can be denied campaign contributions in the next election cycle.

Take an example—the House Banking and Financial Services Committee. The members of that committee obtain three to six times more election and reelection money from banks and investment firms than other members of Congress. Moreover, in contrast to other members of

Congress, members of the committee receive specialized contributions—either from bank PACs or from investment PACs, but rarely from both. Additionally, the more senior the committee member, the more the PACs contribute to her or his reelection.

For Critical Analysis

Why don't banks give campaign contributions equally to all members of the House Banking and Financial Services Committee?

or temporary, are formed to study specific problems or issues. Joint committees are formed by the concurrent action of both chambers of Congress and consist of members from each chamber. Joint committees have dealt with the economy, taxation, and the Library of Congress. There are also conference committees, which include members from both the House and the Senate. They are formed for the purpose of achieving agreement between the House and the Senate on the exact wording of legislative acts when the two chambers pass legislative proposals in different forms. No bill can be sent to the White House to be signed into law unless it first passes both chambers in identical form.

Most of the actual work of legislating is performed by the committees and subcommittees (the "little legislatures"[13]) within Congress. In creating or amending laws, committee members work closely with relevant interest groups and administrative agency personnel. (For more detail on the interaction among these groups, see the discussion of "iron triangles" in Chapter 15.)

The Differences between the House and the Senate

The major differences between the House and the Senate are listed in Table 13–3. To understand what goes on in the chambers of Congress, we need to look at the effects of bicameralism. Each chamber of Congress has developed certain distinct features.

SIZE MATTERS

Obviously, with 435 members, the House cannot operate the same way that the Senate can with only 100 members. (There are also nonvoting delegates from the District of Columbia, Guam, American Samoa, Puerto Rico, and the U.S. Virgin Islands in the House.) With its larger size, the House needs both more rules and more formal rules; otherwise no work would ever get done. The most obvious formal rules that are required have to do with debate on the floor.

Table 13–3

Major Differences between the House and the Senate

HOUSE*	SENATE*
Members chosen from local districts	Members chosen from an entire state
Two-year term	Six-year term
Originally elected by voters	Originally (until 1913) elected by state legislatures
May impeach (accuse, indict) federal officials	May convict federal officials of impeachable offenses
Larger (435 voting members)	Smaller (100 members)
More formal rules	Fewer rules and restrictions
Debate limited	Debate extended
Floor action controlled	Unanimous consent rules
Less prestige and less individual notice	More prestige and media attention
Originates bills for raising revenues	Power of "advice and consent" on presidential appointments and treaties
Local or narrow leadership	National leadership

*Some of these differences, such as term of office, are provided for in the Constitution, while others, such as debate rules, are not.

politics on the far side

The Important Game Called "Room Draw"

What happens every two years in Washington, D.C., that can be compared to the National Football League's college draft? The answer is Room Draw—the vying for offices on Capitol Hill. The newly elected freshmen in the House have last pick. They fight over cramped offices that are sometimes about the size of a large broom closet. In general, selection is based on seniority.

Prior to the first day of Room Draw, office managers for the various representatives develop a scouting report that includes the probabilities of obtaining particular offices for their bosses. During the first day of Room Draw, office managers use their cellular phones frequently to confer with their bosses. Each representative has twenty minutes to decide (measured to the second with a digital clock). The Senate also has a Room Draw, but because it has fewer members, the process is much less formal.

Some etiquette is involved here. It is considered bad form to survey a retiring legislator's office prior to election day. If a member of Congress dies in office, "it's vulture city, with everyone looking over the office. It gets a little morbid when people come by to look."[14]

For Critical Analysis: If the decision were yours to make, would you continue the seniority rule in Congress—in Room Draw as well as in other matters?

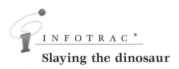

INFOTRAC°

Slaying the dinosaur

RULES COMMITTEE ● A standing committee in the House of Representatives that provides special rules governing how particular bills will be considered and debated by the House. The Rules Committee normally proposes time limitations on debate for any bill, which are accepted or modified by the House.

FILIBUSTERING ● The Senate tradition of unlimited debate, undertaken for the purpose of preventing action on a bill.

CLOTURE ● A method of ending debate in the Senate and bringing the matter under consideration to a vote by the entire chamber.

The Senate normally permits extended debate on all issues that arise before it. In contrast, the House uses an elaborate system: the House **Rules Committee** normally proposes time limitations on debate for any bill, which are accepted or modified by the House. Despite its greater size, as a consequence of its stricter time limits on debate, the House is often able to act on legislation more quickly than the Senate. (Another difference between the House and the Senate is apparent when senators and representatives vie for office space on Capitol Hill—see the feature, *Politics on the Far Side: The Important Game Called "Room Draw."*)

IN THE SENATE, DEBATE CAN JUST KEEP GOING AND GOING

At one time, both the House and the Senate allowed unlimited debates, but the House ended this practice in 1811. In the Senate, the tradition of unlimited debate, called **filibustering,** dates back to 1790 and continues today. The longest filibuster was waged by Senator Strom Thurmond (R., S.C.), who held forth on the Senate floor for twenty-four hours and eighteen minutes in an attempt to thwart the passage of the 1957 Civil Rights Act.

Today, under Senate Rule 22, debate may be ended by invoking **cloture**—a method of closing debate and bringing the matter under consideration to a vote in the Senate. Sixteen senators must sign a petition requesting cloture, and then, after two days have elapsed, three-fifths of the entire membership must vote for cloture. Once cloture is invoked, each senator may speak on a bill for no more than one hour before a vote is taken. Additionally, a final vote must take place within one hundred hours after cloture has been invoked.

THE SENATE WINS THE PRESTIGE RACE, HANDS DOWN

Because of the large number of representatives, few can garner the prestige that a senator enjoys. Senators have relatively little difficulty in gaining access to the media. Members of the House, who run for reelection every two years, have to survive many reelection campaigns before they can obtain recognition for their activities. Usually, a representative has to become an important committee leader before she or he can enjoy the consistent attention of the national news media.

The Legislative Process

Look at Figure 13–3, which shows the basic elements of the process through which a bill becomes law at the national level. Not all of the complexities of the process are shown, to be sure. For example, the schematic does not indicate the extensive lobbying and media politics that are often involved in the legislative process. There is also no mention of the informal negotiations and "horse trading" that go on to get a bill passed.

The steps in the process are as follows:

1. *Introduction of legislation.* Most bills are proposed by the executive branch, although individual members of Congress or its staff can come up with ideas for new legislation; so, too, can private citizens or lobbying groups. Only a member of Congress can formally introduce legislation,

Figure 13–3
How a Bill Becomes a Law
This illustration shows the most typical way in which proposed legislation is enacted into law. The process is illustrated with two hypothetical bills, House bill No. 100 (HR 100) and Senate bill No. 200 (S 200). Bills must be passed by both chambers in identical form before they can be sent to the president. The path of HR 100 is traced by an orange line, and that of S 200 by a purple line. In practice, most bills begin as similar proposals in both chambers.

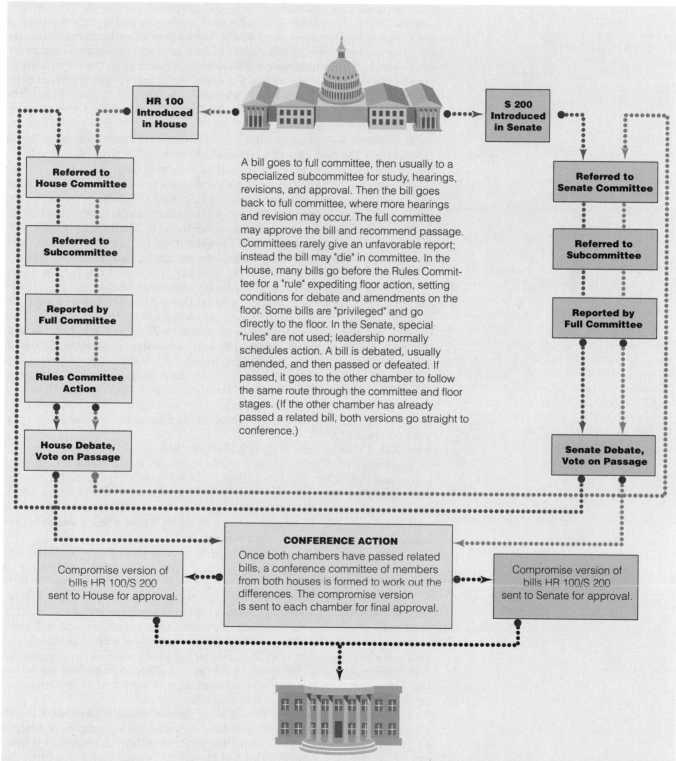

A bill goes to full committee, then usually to a specialized subcommittee for study, hearings, revisions, and approval. Then the bill goes back to full committee, where more hearings and revision may occur. The full committee may approve the bill and recommend passage. Committees rarely give an unfavorable report; instead the bill may "die" in committee. In the House, many bills go before the Rules Committee for a "rule" expediting floor action, setting conditions for debate and amendments on the floor. Some bills are "privileged" and go directly to the floor. In the Senate, special "rules" are not used; leadership normally schedules action. A bill is debated, usually amended, and then passed or defeated. If passed, it goes to the other chamber to follow the same route through the committee and floor stages. (If the other chamber has already passed a related bill, both versions go straight to conference.)

CONFERENCE ACTION
Once both chambers have passed related bills, a conference committee of members from both houses is formed to work out the differences. The compromise version is sent to each chamber for final approval.

Compromise version of bills HR 100/S 200 sent to House for approval.

Compromise version of bills HR 100/S 200 sent to Senate for approval.

A compromise bill approved by both chambers is sent to the president, who can sign it, veto it, or let it become law without the president's signature. Congress may override a veto by a two-thirds majority vote in each chamber.

MARKUP SESSION ● A meeting held by a congressional committee or subcommittee to approve, amend, or redraft a bill.

however. In reality, an increasing number of bills are proposed, developed, and often written by the White House or an executive agency. Then a "friendly" senator or representative introduces the bill in Congress. Such bills are rarely ignored entirely, although they are often defeated.

2. *Referral to committees.* As soon as a bill is introduced and assigned a number, it is sent to the appropriate standing committee. In the House, the speaker assigns the bill to the appropriate committee. In the Senate, the presiding officer assigns bills to the proper committees. For example, a farm bill in the House would be sent to the Agriculture Committee; a gun-control bill would be sent to the Judiciary Committee. A committee chairperson will typically send the bill on to a subcommittee. For example, a Senate bill concerning additional involvement in NATO in Europe would be sent to the Senate Foreign Relations Subcommittee on European Affairs. Alternatively, the chairperson may decide to put the bill aside and ignore it. Most bills that are pigeonholed in this manner receive no further action.

If a bill is not pigeonholed, committee staff members go to work researching the bill and sometimes hold public hearings during which people who support or oppose the bill may express their views. Committees also have the power to order witnesses to testify at public hearings. Witnesses may be executive agency officials, experts on the subject, or representatives of interest groups concerned about the bill.

The subcommittee must meet to approve the bill as it is, add new amendments, or draft a new bill. This meeting is known as the **markup session.** If members cannot agree on changes, a vote is taken. When a subcommittee completes its work on a bill, it goes to the full standing committee, which then meets for its own markup session. The committee may hold its own hearings, amend the subcommittee's version, or simply approve the subcommittee's recommendations.

3. *Reports on a bill.* Finally, the committee will report the bill back to the full chamber. It can report the bill favorably, report the bill with amendments, or report a newly written bill. It can also report a bill unfavorably, but usually such a bill will have been pigeonholed earlier instead. Along with the bill, the committee will send to the House or Senate a written report that explains the committee's actions, describes the bill, lists the major changes made by the committee, and gives opinions on the bill.

4. *The Rules Committee and scheduling.* Scheduling is an extremely important part of getting a bill made into law. A bill must be put on a calendar. Typically, the House Rules Committee plays a major role in the scheduling process. This committee, along with the House leaders, regulates the flow of the bills through the House. The Rules Committee will also specify the amount of time to be spent on debate and whether amendments can be made by a floor vote.

In the Senate, a few leading members control the flow of bills. The Senate brings a bill to the floor by "unanimous consent," a motion by which all members present on the floor set aside the formal Senate rules and consider a bill. In contrast to the procedure in the House, individual senators have the power to disrupt work on legislation.

5. *Floor debate.* Because of its large size, the House imposes severe limitations on floor debate. The speaker recognizes those who may speak and can force any member who does not "stick to the subject" to give up the floor. Normally, the chairperson of the standing committee reporting the bill will take charge of the session during which it is debated. You can often watch such debates on C-SPAN.

Only on rare occasions does a floor debate change anybody's mind. The written record of the floor debate completes the legislative history of the proposed bill in the event that the courts have to interpret it later on. Floor debates also give the full House or Senate the opportunity to consider amendments to the original version of the bill.

CONFERENCE COMMITTEE ● A temporary committee that is formed when the two chambers of Congress pass separate versions of the same bill. The conference committee, which consists of members from both the House and the Senate, works out a compromise form of the bill.

CONFERENCE REPORT ● A report submitted by a congressional conference committee after it has drafted a single version of a bill.

POCKET VETO ● A special type of veto power used by the chief executive after the legislature has adjourned. Bills that are not signed by the president die after a specified period of time and must be reintroduced if Congress wishes to reconsider them.

6. *Vote.* In both the House and the Senate, the members present generally vote for or against the bill. There are several methods of voting, including voice votes, standing votes, and recorded votes (also called roll-call votes). Since 1973, the House has had electronic voting. The Senate does not have electronic voting, however.

7. *Conference committee.* To become a law, a bill must be passed in identical form by both chambers. When the two chambers pass separate versions of the same bill, the measure is turned over to a special committee called a **conference committee**—a temporary committee with membership from the two chambers.

   Most members of the committee are drawn from the standing committees that handled the bill in both chambers. In theory, the conference committee can consider only those points in a bill on which the two chambers disagree; no proposals are supposed to be added. In reality, however, the conference committee sometimes makes important changes in the bill or adds new provisions.

   Once the conference committee members agree on the final compromise bill, a **conference report** is submitted to each house. The bill must be accepted or rejected by both houses as it was written by the committee, with no further amendments made. If the bill is approved by both chambers, it is ready for action by the president.

8. *What the president can do.* All bills passed by Congress have to be submitted to the president for approval. The president has ten days to decide whether to sign the bill or veto it. If the president does nothing, the bill goes into effect unless Congress has adjourned before the ten-day period expires. In that case, the bill dies in what is called a **pocket veto.**

The Budgeting Process

The Constitution makes it very clear that Congress has the power of the purse. Only Congress can impose taxes, and only Congress can authorize expenditures. To be sure, the president submits a budget, but all final decisions are up to Congress.

Congress exercises its "power of the purse" through a budgeting process, in which the executive branch also plays a key role. Here President Bill Clinton and Vice President Al Gore discuss the federal budget with White House staff members during a meeting held in the Oval Office of the White House on October 14, 1998.

AUTHORIZATION ● A part of the congressional budgeting process that involves the creation of the legal basis for government programs.

APPROPRIATION ● A part of the congressional budgeting process that involves determining how many dollars will be spent in a given year on a particular set of government activities.

ENTITLEMENT PROGRAM ● A government program (such as Social Security) that allows, or entitles, a certain class of people (such as the elderly) to receive special benefits. Entitlement programs operate under open-ended budget authorizations that, in effect, place no limits on how much can be spent.

FISCAL YEAR ● A twelve-month period that is established for bookkeeping or accounting purposes. The government's fiscal year runs from October 1 through September 30.

FIRST BUDGET RESOLUTION ● A budget resolution, which is supposed to be passed in May, that sets overall revenue goals and spending targets for the next fiscal year, which begins on October 1.

SECOND BUDGET RESOLUTION ● A budget resolution, which is supposed to be passed in September, that sets "binding" limits on taxes and spending for the next fiscal year, which begins on October 1.

AUTHORIZATION AND APPROPRIATIONS

The budgeting process involves a two-part procedure. **Authorization** is the first part. It involves the creation of the legal basis for government programs. In this phase, Congress passes authorization bills outlining the rules governing the expenditure of funds. Limits may be placed on how much money can be spent and for what period of time.

Appropriation is the second part of the budgeting process. In this phase, Congress determines how many dollars will actually be spent in a given year on a particular set of government activities. Appropriations must never exceed the authorized amounts, but they can be less.

Many **entitlement programs** operate under open-ended authorizations that, in effect, place no limits on how much can be spent. The government is obligated to provide benefits to persons who qualify under entitlement laws, such as Social Security, veterans' benefits, and the like. The remaining federal programs are subject to discretionary spending and can be altered at will by Congress. National defense is the most important item in the discretionary-spending part of the budget.

THE ACTUAL BUDGETING PROCESS

Look at Figure 13–4, which is a schematic outlining the lengthy budgeting process. The process runs from January, when the president submits a proposed federal budget for the next **fiscal year,** to the start of that fiscal year on October 1. In actuality, about eighteen months prior to October 1, the executive agencies submit their requests to the Office of Management and Budget (OMB), and the OMB outlines a proposed budget. If the president approves it, the budget is officially submitted to Congress.

The legislative budgeting process comprises eight to nine months before the start of the fiscal year. The **first budget resolution** is supposed to be passed in May. It sets overall revenue goals and spending targets and, by definition, the size of the federal budget deficit or surplus. The **second budget resolution,** which sets "binding" limits on taxes and spending, is supposed to be passed in September, prior to the beginning of the fiscal year on October 1. Whenever Congress is unable to pass a complete budget

Figure 13–4
The Budgeting Process

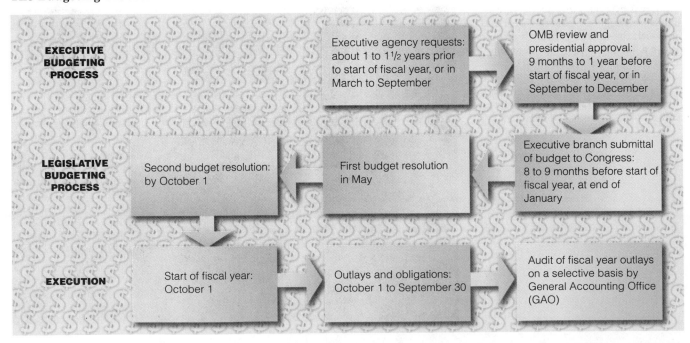

EXECUTIVE BUDGETING PROCESS	Executive agency requests: about 1 to 1½ years prior to start of fiscal year, or in March to September	OMB review and presidential approval: 9 months to 1 year before start of fiscal year, or in September to December
LEGISLATIVE BUDGETING PROCESS	Second budget resolution: by October 1 / First budget resolution in May	Executive branch submittal of budget to Congress: 8 to 9 months before start of fiscal year, at end of January
EXECUTION	Start of fiscal year: October 1 / Outlays and obligations: October 1 to September 30	Audit of fiscal year outlays on a selective basis by General Accounting Office (GAO)

CONTINUING RESOLUTION ● A resolution, which Congress passes when it is unable to pass a complete budget by October 1, that enables the executive agencies to keep on doing whatever they were doing the previous year with the same amount of funding.

MINORITY-MAJORITY DISTRICT ● A congressional district whose boundaries are drawn in such a way as to maximize the voting power of a minority group.

INFOTRAC®

Cynthia McKinney
black member

by October 1, it passes **continuing resolutions,** which enable the executive agencies to keep on doing whatever they were doing the previous year with the same amount of funding. Even continuing resolutions have not always been passed on time.

Americans at Odds over Congress

Americans are often at odds over issues relating to the U.S. Congress. Here we look at the controversial practice of racial gerrymandering, which has not only divided American citizens but has also pitted one branch of government (the courts) against an agency (the Justice Department) of the executive branch. We also revisit the issue touched on in this chapter's opening feature: congressional "careerism" and the perception that congressional behavior is dictated less by the needs of the nation and the next generation than by the pursuit of reelection to office.

Racial Gerrymandering

As mentioned earlier in this chapter, in the early 1990s the U.S. Department of Justice required the states to draw the boundaries of congressional districts in such a way as to maximize the voting power of minority groups. As a result, several so-called **minority-majority districts** were created, many of which took on bizarre shapes. For example, North Carolina's newly drawn Twelfth Congressional District was 165 miles long—a narrow strip that, for the most part, followed Interstate 85. Georgia's new Eleventh District stretched from Atlanta to the Atlantic, splitting eight counties and five municipalities.

THE BATTLE LINES ARE DRAWN

Immediately, Americans were at odds over the constitutionality of such "racial" or "ethnic" gerrymandering. On the one side were those who contended that minority-majority districts were necessary to ensure equal representation of minority groups, as mandated by the Voting Rights Act of 1965.

On the other side were those who felt that such race-based districting was unconstitutional because it violated the equal protection clause. The practice also countered the "one person, one vote" principle and questionably violated the traditional principle of geographical compactness. Opponents of racial gerrymandering also pointed to what they considered a basic flaw in the underlying rationale for such a practice: racial gerrymandering assumed that people of a particular race, merely because of their race, think alike, share the same political interests, and will prefer the same candidates at the polls.

THE SUPREME COURT TAKES A STAND

In a series of cases, the Supreme Court sided with the opponents of racial gerrymandering. First, in a 1993 decision, the Court declared that racially gerrymandered districts were subject to strict scrutiny under the equal protection clause, meaning that they can be justified only by a compelling state interest and must be narrowly tailored by the state to serve that interest.[15] Then, in 1995, the Court even more aggressively attacked the concept of race-based redistricting by declaring that Georgia's Eleventh District was unconstitutional. It noted that the district had been

Figure 13–5
The Twelfth District of New York

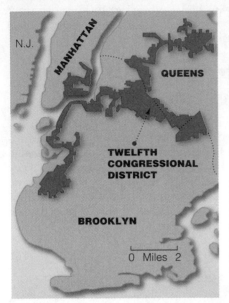

N.J.

MANHATTAN

QUEENS

TWELFTH
CONGRESSIONAL
DISTRICT

BROOKLYN

0 Miles 2

SOURCE: *The New York Times,* February 27, 1997, p. A12.

called a "monstrosity" that linked "widely spaced urban centers that have absolutely nothing to do with each other." The Court also said that assigning voters on the basis of race was offensive and demeaning to racial minorities. The Court chastised the Justice Department for concluding that race-based districting was mandated under the Voting Rights Act of 1965: "When the Justice Department's interpretation of the Act compels race-based districting, it by definition raises a serious constitutional question, and should not receive deference."[16]

The next year, the Supreme Court reinforced its position that when race is the dominant factor in the drawing of congressional district lines, the districts are unconstitutional. In two cases decided in 1996, the Court ruled that the Twelfth District in North Carolina and three Texas districts were unconstitutional for this reason.[17]

Court challenges continue to be brought against other minority-majority districts created in the 1990s. In 1997, for example, the New York legislature was taken to task in a federal district court for the way it redrew the lines of that state's Twelfth Congressional District. According to one commentator, the district (shown in Figure 13–5) resembled "ink splotches from a Rorschach test."[18] Its boundary changed direction 813 times. The federal court, following the Supreme Court's guidelines, held that the district was unconstitutional because race and ethnicity were the dominant factors used to draw it.[19] Nevertheless, despite the Supreme Court's ruling on the issue, the debate continues.

Term Limits: A Cure for Congressional Careerism?

For decades, Gallup polls have asked Americans to indicate how much confidence they have in various institutions (including the military, organized religion, the United States Supreme Court, banks and banking, public schools, Congress, business, labor, the media, and so on). Polls taken during the 1990s suggested that Americans' confidence in Congress had reached an all-time low.

Certainly, Congress came under attack during the 1990s. In part, this was because of Congress's intransigence and refusal to work cooperatively with a president from the opposing political party. In addition, the many ethical scandals that have plagued Congress in the last decade or so have not helped to boost its image in the eyes of the public, nor did Congress's impeachment and trial of President Clinton. Many Americans are also bothered by another problem, which is reflected in the cry for term limits: political careerism.

The complaint is that, in contrast to congressional representatives and senators in the past, today's legislators often view holding congressional office as a career in itself. As a result, the argument goes, our political leaders make decisions less on the basis of any perceived national interest than on how their decisions will affect their chances for reelection. One of the arguments in favor of term limits is that they would remove the element of careerism from politics. Term limits would allow legislators to exercise independent judgment, and Congress could assume the role envisioned for it by the Constitution's framers: that of a deliberative body whose foremost concern is to maintain a carefully crafted balance of power among competing interests.

Although polls show that a majority of Americans support the idea of term limits, it may be difficult—if not impossible—to enact them. As journalist and political commentator George Will pointed out, "term limits for Congress may become one of the few exceptions to the rule that when Americans want something, and want it intensely and protractedly, they get it. Only the political class can enact limits, and limits would be unnecessary if that class were susceptible to self-restraint."[20] Furthermore, according to some scholars, the reason that Congress has become an enemy of the public is precisely because it is itself so public and does reflect public interests. In a sense, then, Americans who are at odds with Congress are essentially at odds with themselves.[21]

Whose Interests Should Members of Congress Represent?

The debate over term limits involves, to some extent, conflicting views over the nature of congressional representation. Suppose that in supporting constituents' goals, a member of Congress wins the continued support (votes) of those constituents in an upcoming bid for reelection. To be sure, that politician's political career will be enhanced, but representing the interests of constituents is part of the congressperson's job. After all, people elect representatives to Congress to do just that—represent their interests. Indeed, some Americans contend that the primary function of the congressperson is to act as an **instructed delegate**—that is, to mirror the views of the majority of the constituents who voted him or her into office. Only in such a way will the many competing interests in society be represented in Congress.

Others approach the issue from the opposite perspective, arguing that legislators should act as **trustees** of the broad interests of the entire society. If their perception of national needs dictates that they should vote against the narrow interests of their constituents, they should do so. If members of Congress were merely instructed delegates, there would be nothing for Congress to deliberate or discuss. As Edmund Burke (1729–1797), the British architect of political conservativism, once said, "Government and legislation are matters of reason and judgment. . . . What sort of reason is that in which the determination precedes the discussion?"

Clearly, a member of Congress does have an obligation to his or her constituents. Less clear is the extent to which broad national interests should play a role in congressional representation. Perhaps of greater significance in terms of Americans' hostility toward congressional careerism is the role played by interest groups and campaign contributions in determining congressional decision making (see Chapters 7 and 10 for further discussions of this issue).

INSTRUCTED DELEGATE ● A representative (such as a member of Congress) who is expected to mirror the views of those whom he or she represents (such as a congressional member's constituents).

TRUSTEE ● In regard to a legislator, one who acts according to his or her conscience and the broad interests of the entire society.

key terms

chapter summary

1. The U.S. Constitution established a bicameral legislature—a Congress consisting of two chambers, the House and the Senate. Each chamber could serve as a check on the other. The Senate was to represent the states and would protect the interests of small states by giving them the same number of senators (two per state) as the larger states. The House was to represent the people as a whole, and seats in the House are thus apportioned, or distributed, on the basis of each state's population.

2. Each representative to the House is elected by voters in a specific area, or congressional district. The lines of congressional districts are drawn by the authority of state legislatures, and in the past, districts of unequal population and the practice of gerrymandering (drawing district lines to maximize the control of a particular party or group) were common. Over time, as a result of Supreme Court decisions, state legislatures were required to ensure that voting districts had equal populations. In the early 1990s, the U.S. Justice Department directed the states to redraw district boundaries to maximize minority representation. In a series of decisions during the 1990s, the Supreme Court held that this "racial gerrymandering" was unconstitutional.

3. The U.S. Constitution requires that congressional representatives be elected every second year by popular vote. Senators are elected every six years, also (since the ratification of the Seventeenth Amendment) by popular vote. State legislatures control the times, places, and manner of holding congressional elections. Only a few qualifications—relating to citizenship, residency, and age—must be met to be a member of Congress. Public disgust with the behavior of Congress in the 1990s resulted in a dramatic change in the make-up of Congress, particularly in 1994, when for the first time in decades, the Republicans took control of both chambers. The 1996 elections seemed to confirm that Americans were satisfied with "divided government"—a president from one political party and a Congress dominated by the opposing party. Divided government continued after the 1998 elections.

4. Each Congress lasts for a two-year term, and terms are numbered consecutively, dating back to 1789. Each congressional term is divided into two regular sessions—one for each year. Currently, Congress remains in session through most of each year, with occasional recesses for holidays and vacations. The president may call a special session to meet during a scheduled recess, but such sessions are rare.

5. The organization of each chamber of Congress is largely a function of the two major political parties. The majority party in each chamber chooses the major officers of that chamber, controls debate on the floor, selects committee chairpersons, and has a majority on all committees. The speaker of the House is the chief leader in the House of Representatives. Other significant leaders in the House are the majority leader (who works to see that the party's legislative goals are met), the minority leader (who maintains cohesion within the minority party), and whips (assistants to the majority and minority leaders).

6. The Constitution makes the vice president the president of the Senate, but in practice the vice president is rarely present in the Senate. The president "pro tem" (pro tempore), an alternate presiding officer elected by the senators, serves in the absence of the vice president. The real power in the Senate is held by the majority leader (the chief spokesperson for the majority party), the minority leader (who commands the minority party's opposition to the majority party's policies), and their respective whips.

7. Most of the actual work of Congress is handled by committees and subcommittees. The permanent and most powerful committees are called standing committees. Before any bill can be considered by the entire House or Senate, it must be approved by a majority vote in the standing committee to which it was assigned. Most House and Senate committees are also divided into subcommittees, which have limited areas of jurisdiction.

8. Many of the differences between the House and the Senate are due to their different sizes. With its larger size, the House requires more formal rules, particularly with respect to debate on the floor. In the House, the Rules Committee places time limitations on debate for most bills. In the Senate, in contrast, the tradition of unlimited debate (which existed also in the House until 1811), or filibustering, continues. Debate in the Senate may be ended, however, if three-fifths of the senators vote for cloture (closing debate and bringing the issue being debated to a vote). Members of the Senate generally enjoy more prestige due to their positions than do members of the House.

9. There are several steps in the legislative process—the process by which a bill becomes a law. First, the bill is introduced in Congress. The bill is then referred to the appropriate standing committee,

which may pigeonhole the bill, place it on the committee agenda, or assign it to a subcommittee. Eventually, the committee reports the bill back to the full chamber, with or without modifications, and the bill is scheduled for debate. Following debate by the full House or Senate, the chamber votes on the bill. To become law, a bill must be passed in identical form by both chambers. Often, this means that the measure must be turned over to a conference committee, which works out a final compromise bill. If the bill is approved by both houses, it is submitted to the president, who can sign the bill, veto it, or do nothing (in which case the bill becomes law within ten days unless Congress adjourns before that ten-day period expires, effecting a pocket veto).

10. The Constitution provides that only Congress can impose taxes and authorize expenditures. The congressional budgeting process involves authorization (the creation of the legal basis for government programs) and appropriation (determining how much money will actually be spent in a given year on a particular program or project). The budgeting process begins in January, when the president submits a proposed budget for the next fiscal year, which begins on October 1. The first budget resolution of Congress, which sets overall revenue goals and spending targets, is supposed to be passed in May. The second budget resolution, which sets "binding" limits on taxes and spending, is supposed to be passed in September. Whenever Congress is unable to pass a complete budget by the beginning of the new fiscal year on October 1, it operates on the basis of continuing resolutions, which enable the executive agencies to keep on doing whatever they were doing the previous year with the same amount of funding.

11. Americans are often at odds over several issues relating to the U.S. Congress. One issue on which Americans have conflicting opinions concerns the practice of racial gerrymandering—redrawing the lines of congressional districts to maximize the representation of minority groups in Congress. Another issue perplexing today's electorate has to do with congressional "careerism" and the perception that congressional behavior is dictated less by the needs of the nation and the next generation than by the pursuit of reelection to office.

for critical analysis

1. Would imposing term limits on members of Congress reduce the influence of interest groups on American politics? Why or why not?

2. What advantages do incumbents have when running for reelection?

3. Do you think that political parties play too important a role in national politics by organizing the activities of Congress? Can you think of any alternative to this arrangement?

4. Do you think that the lack of long-term residence would hurt a candidate's chances of winning an election for the U.S. Senate in your state?

5. Why aren't there more women in Congress?

6. What arguments could you make in support of "racial gerrymandering"? How would you argue against this practice?

7. Do you expect your representatives in Congress to "vote their conscience" or vote in accordance with the views of the majority of their constituents?

suggested readings

KESSLER, Ronald. *Inside Congress: The Shocking Scandals, Corruption, and Abuse of Power behind the Scenes on Capitol Hill.* New York: Simon & Schuster, 1997. The author, an investigative reporter familiar to the readers of the *Wall Street Journal* as well as the *Washington Post,* adds Congress to his "inside" list—joining his *Inside the White House, Inside the CIA,* and other publications. In this book, as the title suggests, Kessler examines the political corruption and scandals of today's Congress. Based on interviews with more than 350 "insiders," Kessler reveals details of various scandals, including sex scandals and questionable fundraising tactics, of today's Congress.

LUBLIN, David. *The Paradox of Representation: Racial Gerrymandering and Minority Interests in Congress.* Princeton, N.J.: Princeton University Press, 1997. The author offers an objective appraisal of the problem of racial representation in Congress. He points out that racial redistricting is important as a means of ensuring that African Americans and other minorities are represented. He notes, however, among other things, that the concentration of minority populations into a small number of districts, particularly in the South, decreases the liberal influence in the remaining districts.

SHULL, Steven A., and Thomas C. Shaw. *Explaining Congressional-Presidential Relations: A Multiple Perspective Approach.* Albany, N.Y.: State University of New York Press, 1999. The authors analyze the interactions between presidents and Congress and the major factors that influence these interactions. The book encompasses presidential position taking on legislative votes, legislative support of presidents' positions, presidents' propensity to veto legislation, and budget agreement between the two branches, all of which are elements in the adoption of public policy.

WEISBERG, Jacob. *In Defense of Government: The Fall and Rise of Public Trust.* New York: Scribner, 1996. Weisberg, a political columnist for the *New York Magazine* and contributing editor of the *New Republic,* offers advice for liberals dealing with a Republican-dominated, devolutionary Congress. He contends that lack of trust in national institutions is a response to the failure of both Democrats and Republicans to define what government is supposed to do. He suggests that liberals should take the lead and aggressively advocate stronger central government in key areas to restore the public's confidence in government.

WHITBY, Kenny J. *The Color of Representation: Congressional Behavior and Black Interests.* Ann Arbor, Mich.: University of Michigan Press, 1998. The author examines the relationship of African Americans to the U.S. House of Representatives. The focus is on how well members of Congress represent the interests of African Americans. The topics covered include redistricting, voting, partisanship, and party affiliation.

politics on the web

There is an abundance of online information relating to Congress and congressional activities. The THOMAS site (named for Thomas Jefferson), maintained by the Library of Congress, provides a record of all bills introduced into Congress, information about each member of Congress and how they voted on specific bills, and other information. Go to

http://thomas.loc.gov

GPO Access on the Web offers information on Congress in session, bills pending and passed, and a history of the bills at

http://thorplus.lib.purdue.edu:80/gpo

To learn more about how a bill becomes a law, go to

http://www.vote-smart.org

Click on "Vote Smart Classroom," select "An Introduction to the U.S. Government," and then choose "How a Bill Becomes a Law."

You can find e-mail addresses and home pages for members of the House of Representatives at

http://www.house.gov

For e-mail addresses and home pages for members of the Senate, go to

http://www.senate.gov

using web resources

In 1976, African American members of Congress created the Congressional Black Caucus (CBC), and Hispanics established the Congressional Hispanic Caucus (CHC). Both work to promote legislation affecting their constituencies and to assist in developing future leaders.

Browse through the Web sites of the CBC and the CHC at

CBC: **http://www.cbcfonline.org/people**

CHC: **http://www.house.gov/roybal-allard/CHC.htm**

1. What states are represented on the CBC? What states are represented on the CHC? How many representatives are men? How many are women?

2. What are the legislative priorities of each caucus?

3. Generally, how are these two organizations similar? How do they differ?

notes

1. *U.S. Term Limits v. Thornton,* 514 U.S. 779 (1995).

2. Priscilla Southwell and David Waguespack, "Support for Term Limits and Voting Behavior in Congressional Elections," *Social Science Journal,* Vol. 34, No. 1 (January 1997).

3. Thomas Jefferson, "Letter to Tench Coke" (1799).

4. These states are Alaska, Delaware, Montana, North Dakota, South Dakota, Vermont, and Wyoming.

5. *Department of Commerce v. United States House of Representatives,* 525 U.S. 316 (1999).

6. 369 U.S. 186 (1962).

7. 376 U.S. 1 (1964).

8. 478 U.S. 109 (1986).

9. For a discussion of the role of political parties in the selection of congressional candidates, see Gary Jacobson, *The Politics of Congressional Elections,* 4th ed. (New York: Longman Publishers, 1997).

10. *Powell v. McCormack,* 395 U.S. 486 (1969).

11. For a perceptive analysis of the antigovernment sentiment that resulted in the shakeup of 1994, see Daniel J. Balz *et al., Storming the Gates: Protest Politics and the Republican Revival* (Boston: Little, Brown, 1996).

12. Some observers maintain that another reason Congress *can* stay in session longer is the invention of air conditioning. Until the advent of air conditioning, no member of Congress wanted to stay in session during the hot and sticky spring, summer, and fall months.

13. A term used by Woodrow Wilson in *Congressional Government* (New York: Meridian Books, 1956 [first published in 1885]).

14. Arlene Peterson, aide to Representative Joe Skeen (R., N.Mex.), as quoted in *The New York Times,* November 13, 1996, p. D20.

15. *Shaw v. Reno,* 509 U.S. 630 (1993).

16. *Miller v. Johnson,* 515 U.S. 900 (1995).

17. *Shaw v. Hunt,* 517 U.S. 899 (1996); *Bush v. Vera,* 517 U.S. 952 (1996).

18. Clifford Levy, "New York's 12th District Is Ruled Invalid," *The New York Times,* February 27, 1997, p. A12.

19. *Diaz v. New York* (E.D.N.Y. 1997); this decision is not reported in West's *Federal Supplement.*

20. George F. Will, "Save Us from the Purists," *Newsweek,* February 17, 1997, p. 78.

21. For an elaboration of this view, see John R. Hibbing and Elizabeth Theiss-Morse, *Congress as Public Enemy: Public Attitudes toward American Political Institutions* (New York: Cambridge University Press, 1996).

THE PRESIDENCY

Contents

Should a Sitting President Be Immune from Civil Lawsuits?

In 1994, when Paula Corbin Jones filed her sexual-harassment lawsuit against President Bill Clinton, she unleashed a debate over a significant constitutional question: Can a sitting president be sued for conduct that occurred before taking office? President Clinton argued that he should not have to deal with the suit as long as he was in office, and a lower federal court agreed. In 1997, however, the United States Supreme Court declared that the suit could go forward.[1]

The Court pointed out that executive privilege—a doctrine that grants presidents immunity from suits by those adversely affected by presidential decisions—applies only to *official* actions, or actions undertaken by a president while in office. (Of course, this immunity is limited when criminal actions are involved, as President Richard Nixon learned in 1974. In *United States v. Nixon,*[2] the Supreme Court held that the president had to turn over tapes of Oval Office conversations that could shed light on the Watergate affair. The Court held that executive privilege could not be used to prevent evidence from being heard in criminal proceedings.)

In the more than two hundred-year history of this nation, only three presidents have been subjected to suits for their private actions that occurred before they took office as president: Theodore Roosevelt (1901–1909), Harry Truman (1945–1953), and John F. Kennedy (1961–1963). In each case, the lawsuit was settled or dismissed after the defendant assumed the presidency.

Yes, Presidents Should Have Immunity

Those who claim that a sitting president should be immune from such lawsuits point out that the public interest demands the undivided time and attention of the president to public duties.

Furthermore, allowing persons to sue the president for unofficial conduct prior to taking office could lead to a spate of politically motivated suits against the nation's executive. The Supreme Court thought that its ruling probably would not have this result; the Court emphasized that until Jones's suit there had generally been an unofficial taboo against suing a sitting president. Those who argue for presidential immunity point out that times have changed. Many new rights have been created in recent years, including the right not to be sexually harassed, as alleged by Jones. Americans have also become more litigious generally.

Also, given today's political tactics, there is nothing to prevent political opponents from bringing frivolous, politically motivated suits against the president simply to mar the president's reputation. By the time the public learned that the charges were frivolous, the damage would already be done.

Even though Jones's lawsuit was not deemed frivolous, it was ultimately dismissed by a federal court, but not before testimony was taken from President Clinton concerning his relations with, among others, Monica Lewinsky. This testimony, in which the president denied having sexual relations with Monica Lewinsky, laid the groundwork for the investigation and ultimate impeachment of the president. Had the Supreme Court not allowed Jones's suit to go forward, both the president and Congress would have had much more time during 1998 and 1999 to focus on the business of government.

Finally, subjecting the head of the executive branch to the orders and schedules of the judicial branch may be contrary to the constitutional separation of powers envisioned by our nation's founders.

No, Presidents Should Not Have Immunity

There are also good arguments against presidential immunity from lawsuits based on unofficial conduct. For one thing, although having immunity for official presidential actions makes sense, the president should not be

above the laws with respect to private conduct. The notion that the "king is above the law" is long dead—it died with the birth of our republic. Presidents, like other people, should be held accountable for their actions.

Additionally, consider what might happen if a plaintiff like Paula Jones had to wait to commence a lawsuit until the president stepped down from office. The delay could jeopardize the plaintiff's chances of proving the case against the president. Key witnesses might have difficulty remembering specific details about what they saw or heard, and a party or a witness might even die before the suit could go forward.

Finally, this group argues (as did the Supreme Court in the *Jones* case) that the constitutional separation of powers is not really an issue here. On several occasions, the courts have used their power of judicial review to invalidate official actions of presidents.[3] The argument is that if *official* presidential actions are subject to judicial scrutiny, it stands to reason that the courts have the power to determine the legality of the president's *unofficial* conduct as well.

Where Do You Stand?

1. In your opinion, should a sitting president be subject to civil lawsuits for unofficial conduct?

2. Can you think of some additional arguments supporting either side of this debate?

On the Web

For a complete review of the *Clinton v. Jones* case, go to http://www.courttv.com/legaldocs/government/jones/staylor.html.

INFOTRAC®

Another chat with the lady

Introduction

One of the reasons that President Clinton wanted to delay the proceedings in *Clinton v. Jones* is that he did not want the litigation to interfere with his duties as president. This is understandable, given the busy schedule of the president of the United States. Former president Lyndon Johnson (1963–1969) stated in his autobiography[4] that "[o]f all the 1,886 nights I was President, there were not many when I got to sleep before 1 or 2 A.M., and there were few mornings when I didn't wake up by 6 or 6:30." President Harry Truman (1945–1953) once observed that no one can really understand what it is like to be president: there is no end to "the chain of responsibility that binds him," and he is "never allowed to forget that he is president." These responsibilities are, for the most part, unremitting. Unlike Congress, the president never adjourns.

Given the demands of the presidency, why would anyone seek the office? The answer is, of course, that some very special perks are associated with the presidency. Although the salary at $200,000[5] a year is peanuts compared to that of chief executive officers of private corporations, the president enjoys, among other things, the use of the White House. The White House has 132 rooms located on 18.3 acres of land in the heart of the nation's capital. At the White House, the president in residence has a staff of more than eighty persons, including chefs, gardeners, maids, butlers, and a personal tailor. Amenities also include a tennis court, a swimming pool, bowling lanes, and a private movie theater. The president also has at his disposal a fleet of automobiles, helicopters, and jets (including *Air Force One*, which costs $30,000 an hour to run). For relaxation, the presidential family can go to Camp David, a resort hideaway in the Catoctin Mountains of Maryland. Other perks include free dental and medical care.

No doubt, these amenities are part of the motivation for wanting to be president of the United States. The presidency, though, is also at the apex of the political ladder. It is the most powerful and influential political office that any one individual can hold. Presidents can help to shape not only domestic policy but also global developments. With the demise of the Soviet Union and its satellite communist countries, the president of the United States is regarded by many as the leader of the most powerful nation on earth. The president heads the greatest military force anywhere. It is not surprising, therefore, that many Americans aspire to attain this office.

Who Can Become President?

The notion that anybody can become president of this country has always been a part of the great American dream. Certainly, the requirements for becoming president set forth in Article II, Section 1, of the Constitution are not difficult to meet:

> No Person except a natural born Citizen, or a Citizen of the United States, at the time of the Adoption of this Constitution, shall be eligible to the Office of President; neither shall any Person be eligible to that Office who shall not have attained to the Age of thirty-five Years, and been fourteen Years a Resident within the United States.

It is true that modern presidents have included a haberdasher (Harry Truman), a peanut farmer (Jimmy Carter), and an actor (Ronald Reagan), although all of these men also had significant political experience before assuming the presidency. If you look at Appendix E, though, you will see that the most common previous occupation of U.S. presidents has been the legal profession. Out of forty-two presidents, twenty-six have been lawyers, and many presidents have been wealthy. Additionally, although the Constitution states that anyone who is thirty-five years of age or older can become president, the average age at inauguration has been fifty-four. The

Harry Truman became president after the death of Franklin D. Roosevelt on April 12, 1945. Certainly, at the beginning of Truman's life, it did not appear that he was destined to become a great political leader. His background was modest. His father was disapproving and abusive. The young Truman never went to college. He tried to be a concert pianist but failed. He tried to be a businessman but failed—both as a haberdasher and as an entrepreneur in oil drilling. He failed as a farmer. He was living proof that "anyone can become president."

youngest person elected president was John F. Kennedy (1961–1963), who assumed the presidency at the age of forty-three (the youngest person to hold the office was Theodore Roosevelt, who was forty-two when he became president after the assassination of William McKinley); the oldest was Ronald Reagan (1981–1989), who was sixty-nine years old when he became president.

To date, all U.S. presidents have been male, white, and (with the exception of John F. Kennedy, who was a Roman Catholic) Protestant. Polls indicate, though, that many Americans expect to see a woman or an African American assume the office in the not-too-distant future. According to one survey, 54 percent of respondents expect to live to see a woman elected to the presidency, and 75 percent expect to see an African American elected as president.[6]

Presidential Powers

The constitutional source for the president's authority is found in Article II of the Constitution, which states, "The executive Power shall be vested in a President of the United States of America." The Constitution then sets forth the president's relatively limited constitutional responsibilities. Just how much power should be entrusted to the president was debated at length by the framers of the Constitution. On the one hand, they did not want a king. On the other hand, they believed that a strong executive was necessary if the republic was to survive. The result of their debates was an executive who was granted enough powers in the Constitution to balance those of Congress.[7]

EXPLICIT CONSTITUTIONAL POWERS

Article II grants the president broad but vaguely described powers. From the very beginning, there were different views as to what exactly the "executive Power" clause enabled the president to do. Nonetheless, Sections 2 and 3 of Article II list the following specific presidential powers:

- To serve as commander in chief of the armed forces and the state militias.
- To appoint, with the Senate's consent, the heads of the executive departments, ambassadors, justices of the Supreme Court, and other top officials.
- To grant reprieves and pardons, except in cases of impeachment.
- To make treaties, with the advice and consent of the Senate.
- To deliver the annual State of the Union address to Congress and to send other messages to Congress from time to time.
- To call either house or both houses of Congress into special sessions.
- To receive ambassadors and other representatives from foreign countries.
- To commission all officers of the United States.
- To ensure that the laws passed by Congress "be faithfully executed."

INHERENT POWERS

The president also has inherent powers—powers that are necessary to carry out the specific responsibilities of the president as set forth in the Constitution. The presidency is, of course, an institution of government, but it is also an institution that consists, at any one moment in time, of one individual. That means that the lines between the presidential office and the person who holds that office often become blurred. Certain presidential powers that are today considered part of the rights of the office were simply assumed by strong presidents to be inherent powers of the presidency, and their successors then continued to exercise these powers.

President Woodrow Wilson (1913–1921) clearly indicated this interplay between presidential personality and presidential powers in the following statement:

> The President is at liberty, both in law and conscience, to be as big a man as he can. His capacity will set the limit; and if Congress be overborne by him, it will be no fault of the makers of the Constitution—it will be from no lack of constitutional powers on his part, but only because the President has the nation behind him, and Congress has not.[8]

In other words, because the Constitution is vague as to the actual carrying out of presidential powers, presidents are left to define the limits of their authority—subject, of course, to the other branches of government.

Many of the powers of the president are inherent to the office. Carrying out foreign policy is one such power. Here, President Bill Clinton sits with the leaders of Great Britain, France, and Russia. They are signing a North Atlantic Treaty Organization (NATO) expansion agreement to include former Soviet-bloc countries.

By the time the sixteenth president, Abraham Lincoln, gave his Inauguration Day speech, seven southern states had already seceded from the Union. Four more states seceded after he issued a summons to the militia. During the Civil War, Lincoln issued the Emancipation Proclamation in 1863. Some scholars believe that his skillful and vigorous handling of the Civil War increased the power and prestige of the presidency.

When Franklin D. Roosevelt assumed the presidency in 1933, he launched his "Hundred Days" (during March through June in 1933) of legislation to counter the effects of the Great Depression. Roosevelt's administration not only extended the role of the national government in regulating the nation's economic life but also, claim many analysts, further increased the power of the president.

As you will read in this chapter, Congress has sometimes allowed the president to exercise certain powers and sometimes limited presidential powers. Additionally, the Supreme Court, as the head of the judicial branch of the government and the final arbiter of the Constitution, can check the president's powers. The Court, through its power of judicial review, can determine whether a president, by taking a certain action, has exceeded the powers granted by the Constitution.

THE POWER TO PERSUADE

The president is also in a position of power simply because he has access to important information sources that are beyond the reach of most people. The president also has access to whomever he wishes to see, can determine who gets certain jobs, and can guide how federal money is spent. All of these factors make people highly responsive to the president's demands. Consider that a call from the president to a head of state, a senator, a military commander, or a television producer rarely goes unanswered.

The president's political skills and ability to persuade others play a large role in determining presidential success. According to Richard Neustadt, in his classic work entitled *Presidential Power,* "Presidential power is the power to persuade."[9] For all of the resources at the president's disposal, the president still must rely on the cooperation of others if the administration's goals are to be accomplished. After three years in office, President Harry Truman made this remark about the powers of the president:

> The president may have a great many powers given to him in the Constitution and may have certain powers under certain laws which are given to him by the Congress of the United States; but the principal power that the president has is to bring people in and try to persuade them to do what they ought to do without persuasion. That's what the powers of the president amount to.[10]

THE EXPANSION OF PRESIDENTIAL POWERS

The Constitution defined presidential powers in very general language, and even the founders were uncertain just how the president would perform the various roles. Only experience would tell. Thus, over the past two centuries, the powers of the president have been defined and expanded by the personalities and policies of various White House occupants.

For example, George Washington removed officials from office, interpreting the constitutional power to appoint officials as implying a power to remove them as well.[11] He established the practice of meeting regularly with the heads of the three departments that then existed. He set a precedent of the president acting as chief legislator by submitting proposed legislation to Congress. He also exercised the president's constitutional power to veto legislation. As commander in chief, he used troops to put down a rebellion in Pennsylvania, and as chief diplomat, he made foreign policy without consulting Congress. This latter action took Congress by surprise and laid the groundwork for our long history of the president's active role in the area of foreign policy.

Abraham Lincoln, confronting the problems of the Civil War during the 1860s, took several important actions while Congress was not in session. He suspended certain constitutional liberties, spent funds that Congress had not appropriated, blockaded southern ports, and banned "treasonable correspondence" from the U.S. mails. All of these actions were carried out in the name of his power as commander in chief and his constitutional responsibility to "take Care that the Laws be faithfully executed."

The greatest expansion of presidential powers occurred in the twentieth century, beginning with Franklin D. Roosevelt's administration. Roosevelt claimed the presidential power to regulate the economy during the Great Depression in the 1930s. Since that time, Americans have expected the president to be actively involved in economic matters and social programs.

The President's Many Roles

The president exercises numerous powers in the course of performing various presidential roles. For example, as commander in chief of the armed services, the president can exercise significant military powers, as will be discussed shortly. Which roles a president plays well usually depends on what is happening domestically and internationally as well as on the president's personality. Some presidents, including Bill Clinton during his first term, have shown much more interest in domestic policy than in foreign policy. Others, such as George Bush, were more interested in foreign affairs than in domestic policies. In particular, Bush seemed to show little interest in the economy.

Table 14–1 summarizes the major roles of the president. An important role is, of course, that of chief executive. Other roles include those of commander in chief, chief of state, chief diplomat, chief legislator, and political party leader.

CHIEF EXECUTIVE

According to the Constitution,

The executive Power shall be vested in a President of the United States of America . . . . [H]e may require the Opinion, in writing, of the principal Officer in each of

Table 14–1

The Roles of the President

ROLE	DESCRIPTION	SPECIFIC FUNCTIONS
Chief executive	Enforces laws and federal court decisions, along with treaties signed by the United States	• Can appoint, with Senate approval, and remove high-ranking officers of the federal government • Can grant reprieves, pardons, and amnesty • Can handle national emergencies during peacetime, such as riots or natural disasters
Commander in chief	Leads the nation's armed forces	• Can commit troops for up to 90 days in response to a military threat (War Powers Resolution) • Can make secret agreements with other countries • Can set up military governments in conquered lands • Can end fighting by calling a cease-fire (armistice)
Chief of state	Performs certain ceremonial functions, as personal symbol of the nation	• Throws out first baseball of baseball season • Lights national Christmas tree • Decorates war heroes • Dedicates parks and post offices
Chief diplomat	Directs U.S. foreign policy and is the nation's most important representative in dealing with foreign countries	• Can negotiate and sign treaties with other nations, with Senate approval • Can make pacts (executive agreements) with other heads of state, without Senate approval • Can accept the legal existence of another country's government (power of recognition) • Receives foreign chiefs of state
Chief legislator	Informs Congress about the condition of the country and recommends legislative measures	• Proposes legislative program to Congress in traditional State of the Union address • Suggests budget to Congress and submits annual economic report • Can veto a bill passed by Congress • Can call special sessions of Congress
Political party leader	Heads political party	• Chooses a vice president • Makes several thousand top government appointments, often to party faithful (patronage) • Tries to execute the party's platform • May attend party fund raisers • May help reelect party members running for office as mayors, governors, or members of Congress

CHIEF EXECUTIVE ● The head of the executive branch of government. In the United States, the president is the head of the executive branch of the federal government.

EXECUTIVE ORDER ● A presidential order to carry out a policy or policies described in a law passed by Congress.

COMMANDER IN CHIEF ● The supreme commander of the military forces of the United States.

the executive Departments, upon any Subject relating to the Duties of their respective Offices . . . and he shall nominate, and by and with the Advice and Consent of the Senate, shall appoint . . . Officers of the United States . . . . [H]e shall take Care that the Laws be faithfully executed.

This constitutional provision makes the president of the United States the nation's **chief executive,** or the head of the executive branch of the federal government. When the framers created the office of the president, they created a uniquely American institution. Nowhere else in the world at that time was there a democratically elected chief executive. The executive branch is also unique among the branches of government because it is headed by a single individual—the president.

As the nation's chief executive, the president is considered to have the inherent power to issue **executive orders,** which are presidential orders to carry out policies described in laws that have been passed by Congress. These orders have the force of law. Presidents have issued executive orders for a variety of purposes, including to establish procedures for appointing noncareer administrators, restructure the White House bureaucracy, ration consumer goods and administer wage and price controls under emergency conditions, classify government information as secret, implement affirmative action policies, and regulate the export of certain items. Presidents issue executive orders frequently, sometimes as many as one hundred a year.

COMMANDER IN CHIEF

The Constitution states that the president "shall be Commander in Chief of the Army and Navy of the United States, and of the Militia of the several States, when called into the actual Service of the United States." As **commander in chief** of the nation's armed forces, the president exercises tremendous power.

Under the Constitution, war powers are divided between Congress and the president. Congress was given the power to declare war and the power to raise and maintain the country's armed forces. The president was given the power to lead the armed forces as commander in chief. Although the president shares war powers with Congress, the president's position in military affairs is dominant.

Article II, Section 2, of the Constitution states that "The President shall be Commander in Chief of the Army and Navy of the United States." Today, that constitutional provision extends to all of the armed forces. Here, President Bill Clinton is shown with Navy personnel aboard the *U.S.S. Theodore Roosevelt.*

The ceremonial role of chief of state is taken seriously by many presidents, including President Clinton. Here, Clinton performs this role with gusto as he welcomes the 1997 NBA champions, the Chicago Bulls, to the White House.

Presidential Military Actions

George Washington first exercised the president's power as commander in chief when he called up the militia of several states and physically led the troops to crush the Whiskey Rebellion in 1794.[12] Since that time, American presidents have made military decisions that changed the course of history.

Consider that although Congress has declared war only five times in this nation's history, the United States has engaged in more than two hundred activities involving the armed services. In 1846, President James K. Polk provoked Mexico into a war. Before the United States entered World War II in 1941, Franklin D. Roosevelt ordered the Navy to "shoot on sight" any German submarine that appeared in the Western Hemisphere security zone. Without congressional approval, President Truman sent U.S. armed forces to Korea in 1950, thus involving American troops in the conflict between North Korea and South Korea.

The United States also entered the Vietnam War (1964–1975) without congressional approval, and President Lyndon Johnson personally selected targets and ordered bombing missions during that war. President Nixon personally made the decision to invade Cambodia in 1970. President Reagan sent troops to Lebanon and Grenada in 1983 and ordered American fighter planes to attack Libya in 1986 in retaliation for terrorist attacks on American citizens. No congressional vote was taken before President Bush sent troops into Panama in 1989. Bush did, however, obtain congressional approval to use American troops to force Iraq to withdraw from Kuwait in 1991. President Clinton made the decision to send troops to Haiti in 1994 and to Bosnia in 1995, and to bomb Iraq in 1998. In 1999, he also decided to send U.S. forces, under the command of NATO (the North Atlantic Treaty Organization), to bomb Yugoslavia.

As commander in chief, the president must also take responsibility for the most difficult of all military decisions—if and when to use nuclear weapons. In 1945, Harry Truman made the awesome decision to drop atomic bombs on the Japanese cities of Hiroshima and Nagasaki. "The final decision," he said, "on where and when to use the atomic bomb was up to me. Let there be no mistake about it." During the Cold War that followed World War II, several presidents shouldered the terrible responsibility of being the ultimate decision makers with respect to nuclear warfare.

The War Powers Resolution

As commander in chief, the president can respond quickly to a military threat without waiting for congressional action. This power to commit troops and to involve the nation in a war upset many members of Congress as the undeclared war in Vietnam dragged on for years into the 1970s. Criticism of the president's role in Vietnam led to the passage of the War Powers Resolution of 1973, which limits the president's war-making powers. The law, which was passed over Nixon's veto, requires the president to notify Congress within forty-eight hours of deploying troops. It also prevents the president from sending troops abroad for more than sixty days (or ninety days, if more time is needed for a successful withdrawal). If Congress does not authorize a longer period, the troops must be removed.

CHIEF OF STATE

Traditionally, a country's monarch has played the role of **chief of state**—the country's representative to the rest of the world. The United States, of course, has no king or queen to act as chief of state. Thus, the president of the United States fulfills this role. The president engages in many symbolic or ceremonial activities, such as throwing out the first baseball to open the baseball season and turning on the lights of the national Christmas tree. The president also decorates war heroes, dedicates parks and post offices, receives visiting chiefs of state at the White House, and goes on official state visits to other countries.

CHIEF OF STATE ● The person who serves as the ceremonial head of a country's government and represents that country to the rest of the world.

DIPLOMAT ● In regard to international relations, a person who represents one country in dealing with representatives of another country.

CHIEF DIPLOMAT ● The role of the president in recognizing and interacting with foreign governments.

TREATY ● A formal agreement between the governments of two or more countries.

Some argue that presidents should not perform such ceremonial functions because they take time that the president could be spending on "real work." (See the feature entitled *Comparative Politics: Having a Separate Chief of State* for more information on how other countries handle this issue.)

CHIEF DIPLOMAT

A **diplomat** is a person who represents one country in dealing with representatives of another country. In the United States, the president is the nation's **chief diplomat.** The Constitution did not explicitly reserve this role to the president, but since the beginning of this nation, presidents have assumed the role based on their explicit constitutional powers to recognize foreign governments and, with the advice and consent of the Senate, to appoint ambassadors and make treaties. As chief diplomat, the president directs the foreign policy of the United States and is its most important representative.

Proposal and Ratification of Treaties

A **treaty** is a formal agreement between two or more sovereign states. The president has the sole power to negotiate and sign treaties with other countries. The Senate, however, must approve the treaty by a two-thirds vote of the members present before it becomes effective. If the treaty is approved by the Senate and signed by the president, it becomes law.

Presidents have not always succeeded in winning the Senate's approval for treaties. Woodrow Wilson lost his effort to persuade the Senate to approve the Treaty of Versailles,[13] the peace treaty that ended World War I in 1918. Among other things, the treaty would have made the United States a member

comparative **politics**

Having a Separate Chief of State

In the seven Western European countries headed by royalty, the monarch is considered the chief of state and plays a ceremonial role. In the United Kingdom, for example, Queen Elizabeth represents the state at ceremonial occasions, such as the opening sessions of Parliament, the christening of ships, and receptions for foreign ambassadors.

In the monarchies of the Netherlands and Norway, the king or queen initiates the process of forming a government after national elections by determining which parties can combine to rule in a coalition. This process really depends on the results of the election and the desires of the political parties—yet the monarch must certify the results.

The majority of European states are not monarchies, but they nonetheless split the duties of government between a prime minister and a president. In Switzerland, for example, the president is elected indirectly by the legislature and assumes purely ceremonial duties.

Throughout Western Europe, the pattern is the same: presidents have ceremonial powers only. The single exception to this rule occurs in France, which has a presidential system in which the head of state has real political power, particularly in foreign affairs.

For Critical Analysis

What are the benefits of having a single person perform only chief-of-state activities? Are there any benefits to the American system, in which the duties of chief executive and chief of state are combined?

of the League of Nations. In contrast, Jimmy Carter convinced the Senate to approve a treaty returning the Panama Canal to Panama by the year 2000 (over such objections as that of Senator S. I. Hayakawa, a Republican from California, who said, "We stole it fair and square"). The treaty was approved by a margin of a single vote.

The Power to Make Executive Agreements

Presidential power in foreign affairs is enhanced by the ability to make **executive agreements,** which are pacts between the president and other heads of state. Executive agreements do not require Senate approval (even though Congress may refuse to appropriate the necessary funds to carry out the agreements), but they have the same legal status as treaties.

Presidents form executive agreements for a wide range of purposes. Some involve routine matters, such as promises of trade or assistance to other countries. Others concern matters of great importance. In 1940, for example, President Franklin D. Roosevelt formed an important executive agreement with Prime Minister Winston Churchill of Britain. The agreement provided that the United States would lend American destroyers to Great Britain to help protect that nation's land and shipping during World War II. In return, the British allowed the United States to use military and naval bases on British territories in the Western Hemisphere.

To prevent presidential abuse of the power to make executive agreements, Congress passed a law in 1972 that requires the president to inform Congress within sixty days of making any executive agreement. The law did not limit the president's power to make executive agreements, however, and they continue to be used far more than treaties in making foreign policy.

CHIEF LEGISLATOR

Nowhere in the Constitution do the words *chief legislator* appear. The Constitution, however, does require that the president "from time to time give to the Congress Information of the State of the Union, and recommend to their Consideration such Measures as he shall judge necessary and expedient." The president has, in fact, become a major player in shaping the congressional agenda—the set of measures that actually get discussed and acted on.

Legislative Programs

Congress has come to expect the president to develop a legislative program. Congress also receives from the president a suggested budget and the annual *Economic Report of the President.* The budget message suggests what amounts of money the government will need for its programs. The *Economic Report of the President* talks about the state of the nation's economy and recommends ways to improve it. From time to time, the president also submits special messages on certain subjects. These messages all call on Congress to enact laws that the president thinks are necessary.

Besides these formal legislative mechanisms, the president also works closely with members of Congress to persuade them to support particular programs. The president writes, telephones, and meets with various congressional leaders to discuss pending bills. The president also sends aides to lobby on Capitol Hill. In addition, the president may use the strategy known as "going public"[14]—that is, using press conferences, public appearances, and televised events to arouse public opinion in favor of certain legislative programs. The public will then pressure legislators to support the administration's programs. A president who has the support of the public can wield significant persuasive powers over Congress. Presidents who are voted into office through "landslide" elections have increased bargaining power because of their widespread popularity (but see the feature on the next page entitled *Perception versus Reality: Presidents and the "Popular Vote"*).

INFOTRAC®
Prompts media's alleluia

perception **versus reality**

Presidents and the "Popular Vote"

Every four years, American citizens go to the polls to cast their votes for the presidential candidate of their choice. Some presidential contests are close; others, less so. When a presidential candidate wins the race by a wide margin, we may hear the election referred to as a *landslide election* or a *landslide victory* for the winning candidate.

The Perception

A common perception is that the president is elected by a majority of eligible American voters. As the people's choice, the president is beholden to the wishes of the broad American electorate that voted him into office. A president who has been swept into office in a so-called landslide election may claim to have received a "mandate

from the people" to govern the nation. A president may assert that a certain policy or program he endorsed in campaign speeches is backed by popular support simply because he was elected to office by a majority of the voters.

The Reality

In reality, the "popular vote" is not all that popular, in the sense of representing the wishes of a majority of American citizens who are eligible to vote. In fact, the president of the United States has *never* received the votes of a majority of all adults of voting age. Lyndon Johnson, in 1964, came the closest of any president in history to gaining the votes of a majority of the voting-age public, and even he gained the votes of less than 40 percent of those who

were old enough to cast a ballot. Ronald Reagan, for all his popularity as president, received the votes of only 26.7 percent of the voting-age population in 1980, and 32.0 percent in 1984. About 23 percent of eligible voters voted for Bill Clinton both in 1992 and in 1996. It is useful to keep these figures in mind whenever a president claims to have received a mandate from the people. The truth is, no president has ever been elected with sufficient popular backing to make this a serious claim.

You Be the Judge

Does it matter whether a presidential candidate, once elected, received a relatively high (or low) percentage of the popular votes cast?

One study of the Washington agenda found that "no other single actor in the political system has quite the capability of the president to set agendas in given policy areas." As one lobbyist told a researcher, "Obviously, when a president sends up a bill [to Congress], it takes first place in the queue. All other bills take second place." At times, however, presidential attempts to set the policymaking agenda have been thwarted by a hostile Congress. In 1995, for example, the Republican-dominated 104th Congress balked at President Clinton's efforts to get legislation passed.

Thomas Jefferson refused to present the State of the Union address orally before Congress, preferring to send it in writing. In 1913, Woodrow Wilson broke with this precedent by personally delivering his first State of the Union address. Today, presidents—including President Clinton, as shown here—use the State of the Union address as a ceremonial way of reporting on the "health" of the nation and its concerns. It is also a speech in which the president lays out the administration's broad policies and makes legislative recommendations.

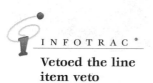

VETO ● A Latin word meaning "I forbid"; the refusal by an official, such as the president of the United States or a state governor, to sign a bill into law.

INFOTRAC®

Vetoed the line item veto

The Legislative Success of Various Presidents

Look at Figure 14–1, which shows the success record of presidents in getting their legislation passed. Success is defined as how often the president won his way on roll-call votes on which he took a clear position. As you can see, typically a president's success record is very high when he first takes office and then gradually declines. Interestingly, President Clinton's success rate, which was very high during his first two years in office, dropped to only 36.2 percent in 1995. We can attribute Clinton's lack of success in his third year to the new power that the Republicans obtained by taking control of both the House and the Senate for the first time in forty years during the 1994 midterm elections.

The President's Veto Power

The Constitution requires that any act of Congress be signed by the president before it can become law. The president thus can **veto** a bill by returning it unsigned to Congress with a veto message attached, setting forth objections. Congress can then change the bill and resubmit it to the president, or Congress can override the veto with a two-thirds vote by the members present in each chamber. If the president does not send a bill back to Congress after ten congressional working days, the bill becomes law without the president's signature. If the president refuses to sign the bill and Congress adjourns within ten working days after the bill has been submitted to the president, the bill is killed for that session of Congress. As mentioned in Chapter 13, this is called a *pocket veto.*

Presidents used the veto power sparingly until the administration of Andrew Johnson (1865–1869). Johnson vetoed twenty-one bills, and his successor, Ulysses Grant, vetoed forty-five. Franklin D. Roosevelt (1933–1945) vetoed more bills by far than any of his predecessors or successors in the presidency. During his administration, there were 372 regular vetoes, nine of which were overridden by Congress, and 263 pocket vetoes. By 1999, President Clinton had vetoed twenty-one bills.

Figure 14–1
Presidential Success Record

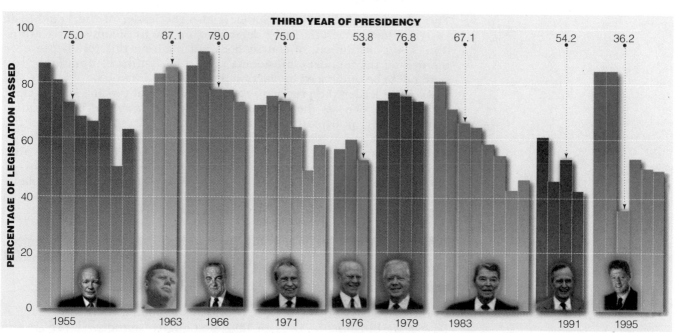

SOURCE: *Congressional Quarterly Weekly Report,* various issues.

Most presidents view press conferences as a way to obtain positive publicity. Recent presidents have learned to memorize the first names of virtually all important reporters who regularly attend such press conferences.

Many presidents have complained that they cannot control "pork-barrel" legislation—specifically, federal expenditures tacked on to bills to "bring home the bacon" to a particular congressional member's district. For example, specific expenditures on sports stadiums might be added to a bill involving crime. The reason is simple: without a line-item veto (the ability to veto just one item in a bill), to eliminate the "pork" in proposed legislation, the president would have to veto the entire bill—and that might not be feasible politically.

Forty-three state governors have had the line-item veto for years (see Chapter 20). After various attempts to give the president a line-item veto, Congress finally passed a line-item bill, which was signed into law by President Clinton in 1996. The Line-Item Veto Act, however, had a short life. When a lawsuit challenging the constitutionality of the act came before the Supreme Court in 1998, the Court concluded that it violated Article I, Section 7, of the Constitution, which stipulates the actions a president may take on bills that have been presented to him.[15]

THE PRESIDENT AS PARTY CHIEF

The president of the United States is also the leader of the Republican Party or the Democratic Party, depending on the president's party affiliation. The Constitution, of course, does not mention this role because, in the eyes of the founders, presidents (and other political representatives) were not to be influenced by "factional" (partisan) interests.

As party leader, the president exercises substantial powers. For example, the president chooses the national committee chairperson. The president can also exert political power within the party by using presidential appointment and removal powers. Naturally, presidents are beholden to party members who put them in office, and usually they indulge in the practice of patronage—appointing individuals to government or public jobs—to reward those who helped them win the presidential contest. Understandably, the appointment and removal powers of the president and the system of patronage give the president singular powers.

The Organization of the Executive Branch

In the early days of this nation, presidents answered their own mail, as George Washington did. Only in 1857 did Congress authorize a private secretary for the president, to be paid by the federal government. Even Woodrow Wilson (1913–1921) typed most of his correspondence, although by that

President Clinton signs a bill into law in the Oval Office. The only other way in which a bill passed by Congress becomes law is if the president does not return the bill to Congress after ten congressional working days. In this event, the bill becomes law without the president's signature.

time several secretaries were assigned to the president. When Franklin D. Roosevelt became president in 1933, the entire staff consisted of thirty-seven employees. Only after Roosevelt's New Deal and World War II did the presidential staff become a sizable organization.

THE PRESIDENT'S CABINET

The Constitution does not specifically mention presidential assistants and advisers. The Constitution only states that the president "may require the Opinion, in writing, of the principal Officer in each of the executive Departments." Since the time of our first president, presidents have had an advisory group, or **cabinet,** to turn to for counsel. Originally, the cabinet consisted of only four officials—the secretaries of state, treasury, and war and the attorney general. Today, the cabinet includes thirteen secretaries and the attorney general (see Table 14–2 for the names of today's cabinet members).

CABINET ● An advisory group selected by the president to assist with decision making. Traditionally, the cabinet has consisted of the heads of the executive departments and other officers whom the president may choose to appoint.

Table 14–2

The Cabinet as of 1999

DEPARTMENT	SECRETARY OR HEAD
Agriculture	Dan Glickman
Commerce	William Daley
Defense	William Cohen
Education	Richard Riley
Energy	Bill Richardson
Health and Human Services	Donna Shalala
Housing and Urban Development	Andrew Cuomo
Interior	Bruce Babbitt
Justice	Janet Reno
Labor	Alexis Herman
State	Madeleine Albright
Transportation	Rodney Slater
Treasury	Lawrence Summers
Veterans Affairs	Togo West, Jr.

KITCHEN CABINET ● The name given to a president's unofficial advisers. The term was coined during Andrew Jackson's presidency.

EXECUTIVE OFFICE OF THE PRESIDENT (EOP) ● A group of staff agencies that assist the president in carrying out major duties. Franklin D. Roosevelt established the EOP in 1939 to cope with the increased responsibilities brought on by the Great Depression.

Because the Constitution does not require the president to consult with the cabinet, its use is purely discretionary. Some presidents have relied on the counsel of their cabinets. Other presidents solicited the opinions of their cabinets and then did what they wanted to do anyway. After a cabinet meeting in which a vote was seven nays against his one aye, President Lincoln supposedly said, "Seven nays and one aye, the ayes have it."[16] Still other presidents have sought counsel from so-called kitchen cabinets. A **kitchen cabinet** is a very informal group of persons, such as Ronald Reagan's trusted California coterie, to whom the president turns for advice. The term *kitchen cabinet* originated during the presidency of Andrew Jackson, who relied on the counsel of close friends who often met with him in the kitchen of the White House.

In general, few presidents have relied heavily on the advice of the formal cabinet, and often presidents meet with their cabinet heads only reluctantly. To a certain extent, the growth of other components of the executive branch has rendered the formal cabinet less significant as an advisory board to the president. Additionally, the department heads are at times more responsive to the wishes of their own staffs or to their own political ambitions than they are to the president. They may be more concerned with obtaining resources for their departments than with helping presidents achieve their goals. As a result, there is often a conflict of interest between presidents and their cabinet members. It is likely that formal cabinet meetings are held more out of respect for the cabinet tradition than for their problem-solving value.

THE EXECUTIVE OFFICE OF THE PRESIDENT

In 1939, President Franklin D. Roosevelt set up the **Executive Office of the President (EOP)** to cope with the increased responsibilities brought on by the Great Depression. Since then, the EOP has grown significantly to accommodate the expansive role played by the national government, including the executive branch, in the nation's economic and social life.

The EOP is made up of the top advisers and assistants who help the president carry out major duties. Over the years, the EOP has changed, according to the needs and leadership style of each president. It has become an increasingly influential and important part of the executive branch. Table 14–3 lists the various offices within the EOP. We look at some of the key offices of the EOP in the following subsections.

Table 14–3

The Executive Office of the President

DEPARTMENT	YEAR ESTABLISHED
White House Office	1939
Council of Economic Advisers	1946
Council on Environmental Quality	1969
National Security Council	1947
Office of Administration	1977
Office of Management and Budget	1970
Office of National Drug Control Policy	1989
Office of Policy Development	1977
—Domestic Policy Council	1993
—National Economic Council	1993
Office of Science and Technology Policy	1976
Office of the U.S. Trade Representative	1963
Office of the Vice President of the United States	1939

Source: *United States Government Manual, 1997/98* (Washington, D.C.: U.S. Government Printing Office, 1997).

WHITE HOUSE OFFICE ● The personal office of the president. White House Office personnel handle the president's political needs and manage the media.

CHIEF OF STAFF ● The person who directs the operations of the White House Office and who advises the president on important matters.

PRESS SECRETARY ● A member of the White House staff who holds press conferences for reporters and makes public statements for the president.

PRESS CONFERENCE ● A scheduled interview with the media.

OFFICE OF MANAGEMENT AND BUDGET (OMB) ● An agency in the Executive Office of the President that assists the president in preparing and supervising the administration of the federal budget.

COUNCIL OF ECONOMIC ADVISERS (CEA) ● A three-member council created in 1946 to advise the president on economic matters.

The White House Office

Of all of the executive staff agencies, the **White House Office** has the most direct contact with the president. The White House Office is headed by the **chief of staff,** who advises the president on important matters and directs the operations of the presidential staff. The chief of staff, who is often a close, personal friend of the president, has been one of the most influential of the presidential aides in recent years. A number of other top officials, assistants, and special assistants to the president also aid him in such areas as national security, the economy, and political affairs. A **press secretary** meets with reporters and makes public statements for the president. The counsel to the president serves as the White House lawyer and handles the president's legal matters. The White House staff also includes speech writers, researchers, the president's physician, the director of the staff for the First Lady, and a correspondence secretary. Altogether, the White House Office has more than four hundred employees.

The White House staff has several duties. First, the staff investigates and analyzes problems that require the president's attention. Staff members who are specialists in certain areas, such as diplomatic relations or foreign trade, gather information for the president and suggest solutions. White House staff members also screen the questions, issues, and problems that people present to the president, so matters that can be handled by other officials do not reach the president's desk. The staff also provides public relations support. For example, the press staff handles the president's relations with the White House press corps and schedules **press conferences.** Finally, the White House staff ensures that the president's initiatives are effectively transmitted to the relevant government personnel. Several staff members are usually assigned to work directly with members of Congress for this purpose.

The Office of Management and Budget

The **Office of Management and Budget (OMB)** was originally the Bureau of the Budget. Under recent presidents, the OMB has become an important and influential unit of the Executive Office of the President. The main function of the OMB is to assist the president in preparing the proposed annual budget, which the president must submit to Congress in January of each year (see Chapter 13 for details on preparing the annual budget). The federal budget lists the revenues and expenditures expected for the coming year. It indicates which programs the federal government will pay for and how much they will cost. Thus, the budget is an annual statement of the public policies of the United States translated into dollars and cents. Making changes in the budget is a key way for presidents to try to influence the direction and policies of the federal government.

The president appoints the director of the OMB with the consent of the Senate. The director of the OMB has become at least as important as cabinet members and is often included in cabinet meetings. She or he oversees the OMB's work and argues the administration's position before Congress. The director also lobbies members of Congress to support the president's budget or to accept key features of it. Once the budget is approved by Congress, the OMB has the responsibility of putting it into practice. It oversees the execution of the budget, checking the federal agencies to ensure that they use funds efficiently.

Beyond its budget duties, the OMB also reviews new bills prepared by the executive branch. It checks all legislative matters to be certain that they agree with the president's own position.

The Council of Economic Advisers

The Employment Act of 1946 established a **Council of Economic Advisers (CEA),** consisting of three members, to advise the president on economic matters. For the most part, the function of the CEA has been to prepare the annual economic report to Congress. Each of the three members is appointed by the president and can be removed at will.

The National Security Council

The **National Security Council (NSC)** was established in 1947 to manage the defense and foreign policy of the United States. Its members are the president, the vice president, and the secretaries of state and defense; it also has several informal advisers. The NSC is the president's link to his key foreign and military advisers. The NSC has the resources of the National Security Agency (NSA) at its disposal in giving counsel to the president. (The NSA protects U.S. government communications, produces foreign intelligence information, and is also responsible for computer security.) The president's special assistant for national security affairs heads the NSC staff.

THE VICE PRESIDENCY AND PRESIDENTIAL SUCCESSION

As a rule, presidential nominees choose running mates who balance the ticket or whose appointment rewards or appeases party factions. For example, a presidential candidate from the South may solicit a running mate from the West. President Clinton ignored this tradition when he selected Senator Al Gore of Tennessee as his running mate in 1992 and in 1996. Gore, close in age and ideology to Clinton, also came from the mid-South. Despite these similarities, Clinton gained two advantages by choosing Gore: Gore's appeal to environmentalists and Gore's compatibility with Clinton.

The Role of Vice Presidents

Vice presidents play a unique role in the American political system. On the one hand, they are usually regarded as appendages to the presidency and can wield little power on their own—although Al Gore's vice presidential responsibilities are changing this somewhat. On the other hand, the vice president is in a position to become the nation's chief executive should the president die, be impeached, or resign the presidential office. Eight vice presidents have become president because of the death of the president.

Presidential Succession

Vice President Al Gore actively promotes the Clinton administration's environmental and educational policies.

One of the questions left unanswered by the Constitution is what the vice president should do if the president becomes incapable of carrying out necessary duties while in office. The Twenty-fifth Amendment to the Constitution, ratified in 1967, filled this gap. The amendment states that when the president believes that he is incapable of performing the duties of office, he must inform Congress in writing of this fact. Then the vice president serves as acting president until the president can resume his normal duties.

When the president is unable to communicate, a majority of the cabinet, including the vice president, can declare that fact to Congress. Then the vice president serves as acting president until the president resumes normal duties. If a dispute arises over the return of the president's ability to discharge the normal functions of the presidential office, a two-thirds vote of Congress is required to decide whether the vice president shall remain acting president or whether the president shall resume these duties.

The Twenty-fifth Amendment also addresses the question of how the president should fill a vacant vice presidency. Section 2 of the amendment states, "Whenever there is a vacancy in the office of the Vice President, the President shall nominate a Vice President who shall take office upon confirmation by a majority vote of both Houses of Congress."

In 1973, Gerald R. Ford became the first appointed vice president of the United States after Spiro Agnew was forced to resign. One year later, President Richard Nixon resigned, and Ford advanced to the office of president. President Ford named Nelson Rockefeller as his vice president. For the first time in U.S. history, neither the president nor the vice president was elected to his position.

What if both the president and the vice president die, resign, or are disabled? According to the Succession Act of 1947, then the speaker of the

House of Representatives will act as president on his resignation as speaker and as representative. If the speaker is unavailable, next in line is the president pro tem of the Senate, followed by members of the president's cabinet in the order of the creation of their departments (see Table 14–4).

Great versus Not-So-Great Presidents

Most experts agree that the strongest presidents have been George Washington, Thomas Jefferson, Andrew Jackson, Abraham Lincoln, Theodore Roosevelt, Woodrow Wilson, and Franklin D. Roosevelt. Each president ruled in difficult times and acted decisively, and each set a precedent by expanding the president's power to perform certain functions. Of course, there have also been presidents who were not so strong and far less memorable.

The game of ranking presidents has been a popular pastime among presidential scholars and historians for some time. It was started in 1948 by Arthur M. Schlesinger, Jr., a history professor at Harvard. In the Schlesinger poll, historians are asked to place each president in one of several categories ranging from "great" to "failure." The results of the latest poll are shown in Figure 14–2 on the next page. Not everybody agrees with the poll's results. For example, although the poll indicates that Richard M. Nixon was a failure (he was forced to resign to avoid impeachment proceedings), some of his supporters point out that this ranking overlooks his many achievements—including the establishment of diplomatic relations with the People's Republic of China.[17]

Americans at Odds over the Presidency

Americans are at odds over a number of issues concerning today's presidency, some of which have already been discussed in this chapter. For example, an ongoing issue has to do with the role of the president in engaging the nation in military actions. To what extent does the War Powers Resolution limit presidential action? What should be Congress's

Table 14–4

The Line of Succession to the U.S. Presidency

1. Vice president
2. Speaker of the House of Representatives
3. President pro tem of the Senate
4. Secretary of the Department of State
5. Secretary of the Department of the Treasury
6. Secretary of the Department of Defense
7. Attorney general
8. Secretary of the Department of the Interior
9. Secretary of the Department of Agriculture
10. Secretary of the Department of Commerce
11. Secretary of the Department of Labor
12. Secretary of the Department of Health and Human Services
13. Secretary of the Department of Housing and Urban Development
14. Secretary of the Department of Transportation
15. Secretary of the Department of Energy
16. Secretary of the Department of Education
17. Secretary of the Department of Veterans Affairs

Figure 14–2
How Do the Presidents Rate?

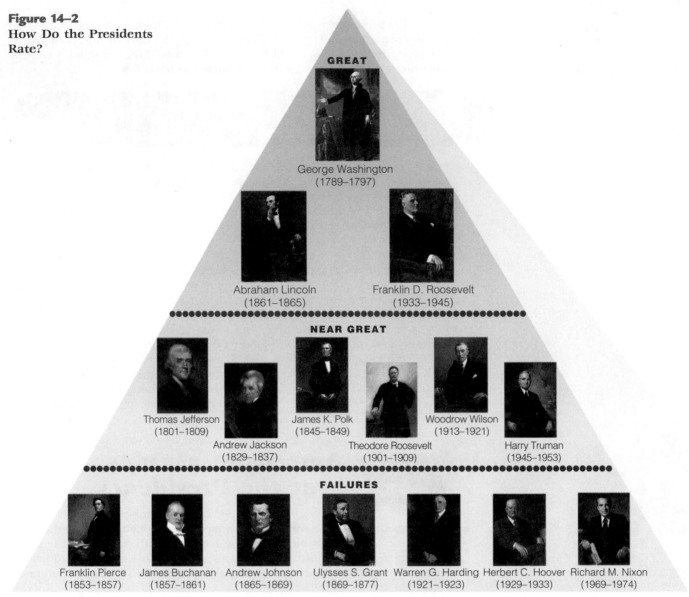

GREAT

George Washington
(1789–1797)

Abraham Lincoln
(1861–1865)

Franklin D. Roosevelt
(1933–1945)

NEAR GREAT

Thomas Jefferson
(1801–1809)

Andrew Jackson
(1829–1837)

James K. Polk
(1845–1849)

Theodore Roosevelt
(1901–1909)

Woodrow Wilson
(1913–1921)

Harry Truman
(1945–1953)

FAILURES

Franklin Pierce
(1853–1857)

James Buchanan
(1857–1861)

Andrew Johnson
(1865–1869)

Ulysses S. Grant
(1869–1877)

Warren G. Harding
(1921–1923)

Herbert C. Hoover
(1929–1933)

Richard M. Nixon
(1969–1974)

SOURCE: Arthur M. Schlesinger, Jr., "The Ultimate Approval Rating," *The New York Times Magazine,* December 15, 1993, pp. 48–49.

role in making critical war-related decisions? Combined with that concern is the uncertainty of many Americans about the role the United States should play in a world without any superpower competition. We look here at some other controversial issues involving today's presidency, particularly the ethical and legal issues surrounding the Clinton administration.

Ethics and the Clinton Administration

"The presidency is not merely an administrative office. That is the least of it. It is preeminently a place of moral leadership."[18] Most Americans would probably agree with these words by Franklin D. Roosevelt. In any event, a number of Americans seriously question the moral quality of President Clinton's leadership. Perhaps no other president—including Richard Nixon, who was forced to resign from office to avoid impeachment proceedings—has faced more ethical (and legal) challenges than Bill Clinton. (History tells us, though, that presidential perfidies have existed

politics on the far side

Scandals in the White House

President Clinton might take some comfort in knowing that White House scandals have a long history. Even that paragon of virtue, George Washington, did not escape being accused of immoral and illegal behavior. Contemporaries claimed that he had fathered dozens of illegitimate children, including his secretary of the Treasury, Alexander Hamilton (which is not true). Our first president was also accused of land theft—illegally taking Shenandoah Valley farmland and then evicting the families who farmed it. Additionally, Washington's secretary of the Treasury, Hamilton, was twice investigated by Congress on charges of pilfering the till.

The record of scandals does not stop there. Andrew Jackson was accused of immoral and illegal behavior because technically his wife was not divorced from her previous spouse at the time she married Jackson. A scandalous cloud descended over Ulysses S. Grant's White House after it was learned that his appointees took kickbacks and siphoned off federal whiskey taxes. Rutherford B. Hayes was said to have been put into office by Republican "kingmakers" who bribed electors to vote for Hayes. The list goes on and on.[20]

For Critical Analysis: As a result of the Clinton-Lewinsky scandal, the majority of Americans gave low ratings to President Clinton's moral leadership of the nation.[21] Yet throughout his impeachment and trial in 1998 and 1999, Clinton's job approval ratings remained high. How can you explain this?

since the beginning of the republic—see the feature entitled *Politics on the Far Side: Scandals in the White House.*)

Clinton's critics point out that during his first presidential campaign, he lambasted the Bush administration's low ethical standards. At one point, Clinton said that, if elected, he would conduct "the most ethical administration in the history of the Republic." By Clinton's second presidential campaign, his opponent, Bob Dole, was able to charge that more than thirty Clinton-era officials had been investigated, dismissed, or forced out of office because of unethical behavior. By early 1999, 74 percent of Americans believed that the phrase "honest and trustworthy" did not apply to Bill Clinton.[19]

In the latter part of the 1990s, an independent counsel, Kenneth Starr, conducted a criminal investigation of the Clintons for a wide array of possible crimes, including tax fraud, bank fraud, perjury, obstruction of justice, missing federal funds, and selling government jobs. In 1998, Starr was authorized by the Justice Department to investigate charges of obstruction of justice and perjury in regard to President Clinton's relationship with White House intern Monica Lewinsky.

Starr's investigation of these charges led to requests for testimony from members of the White House staff. Even the president was requested to testify before the grand jury, which he did on August 17, 1998. Shortly thereafter, Starr submitted his report on the Clinton-Lewinsky investigation to Congress. Starr concluded that there were several grounds, including perjury and obstruction of justice, for impeaching the president.

Following an impeachment inquiry conducted by the House Judiciary Committee, the full House voted on December 19, 1998, to impeach Clinton. As discussed in Chapter 2, the House approved two of the four impeachment articles drawn up by the Judiciary Committee. One of the two articles approved by the House charged

President Bill Clinton's videotaped testimony before the grand jury on August 17, 1998, was later released for public viewing. The testimony related to his widely publicized relationship with White House intern Monica Lewinsky and marked a low point in the nation's moral leadership.

Clinton with perjury; the other, with obstruction of justice. On February 12, 1999, the Senate voted to acquit the president.

The Starr Investigation—Did It Go Too Far?

Americans are clearly at odds over the investigations that ultimately led to the impeachment, if not the conviction, of President Clinton. Some contend that the investigations were politically motivated and were pursued mainly by the president's enemies. This group, as well as other Americans, are also concerned that the results of the investigations may not justify the high costs—which mounted to more than $40 million. Another group claims that a president's personal life should be off limits—to the media as well as special investigators, such as Starr. In his speech to the nation on August 17, 1998, following his appearance before the grand jury, President Clinton suggested that presidents, like other persons, have a right to privacy. Many Americans agreed and blamed Starr and the media for creating the national drama that surrounded Clinton's affair with Lewinsky and that led to the impeachment of the president. Additionally, a number of legal and political scholars worry that some of the precedents set during the course of Starr's investigation may have adverse effects on the institution of the presidency.

Other Americans, however, including Independent Counsel Starr and many Republicans in Congress, believe that Clinton's behavior violated the laws, including Article II, Section 3, of the Constitution, which states that the president "shall take Care that the Laws be faithfully executed."

Independent Counsel Kenneth Starr completed his investigation of the Clinton-Lewinsky affair in the fall of 1998 and submitted his report to the House Judiciary Committee. Shown here are the boxes full of supporting documents that were also delivered to the committee. Starr's ambitious investigation into President Clinton's affairs cost the nation more than $40 million.

key terms

cabinet 351
chief diplomat 346
chief executive 344
chief of staff 353
chief of state 345
commander in chief 344
Council of Economic Advisers (CEA) 353
diplomat 346
executive agreement 347
Executive Office of the President (EOP) 352

executive order 344
kitchen cabinet 352
National Security Council (NSC) 354
Office of Management and Budget (OMB) 353
press conference 353
press secretary 353
treaty 346
veto 349
White House Office 353

chapter summary

1. The Constitution sets forth relatively few requirements for becoming president. To be eligible for the presidency, a person must be a natural-born citizen, at least thirty-five years of age, and a U.S. resident for fourteen years. Most presidents have been well educated, and many have been wealthy. The average age of presidents at the time of their inauguration has been fifty-four. To date, all U.S. presidents have been male, white, and (with the exception of John F. Kennedy, who was a Roman Catholic) Protestant.

2. Article II of the Constitution makes the president the nation's chief executive and delineates the explicit constitutional powers of the president. The president also has certain inherent powers—powers necessary to fulfill the presidential responsibilities explicitly mentioned in the Constitution. Over time, strong presidents have defined the inherent powers of the president in such a way as to expand presidential powers. The greatest expansion occurred in the twentieth century, beginning with the administration of Franklin D. Roosevelt.

3. The president exercises these and other powers when performing the many presidential roles. As chief executive, the president exercises numerous powers, including the power to issue executive orders. As commander in chief, the president is the ultimate decision maker in military matters. As chief diplomat, the president directs the foreign policy of the United States, represents the United States in its relations with other nations, negotiates treaties, and signs executive agreements. As chief legislator, the president plays a major role in shaping the policymaking agenda. The president proposes legislation to Congress, lobbies Congress for its passage, approves laws, and exercises veto power. The president's annual State of the Union address communicates the president's legislative goals to Congress and to the American people. As chief of state, the president is the ceremonial head of the government. The president is also party chief.

4. The cabinet—advisers to the president—consists of the heads of the fourteen executive departments. The tradition of turning to the cabinet for advice was begun by George Washington. Generally, few presidents have relied heavily on the advice of the formal cabinet. Some presidents have preferred to rely on the counsel of close friends and associates (sometimes called a "kitchen cabinet").

5. The president also receives advice from members of the Executive Office of the President (including the White House Office, the Office of Management and Budget, the Council of Economic Advisers, and the National Security Council). Of the various offices and agencies within the EOP, the White House Office has the most direct contact with the president.

6. The vice president is next in line for the presidency if the president should die, be impeached, resign from office, or become incapacitated. The Twenty-fifth Amendment sets out procedures to be followed in the event the president becomes incapacitated. The Succession Act of 1947 established the line of succession to the presidency in the event that both the president and the vice president die or become unable to fulfill their responsibilities (see Table 14–4).

7. Many American presidents have been regarded as great or near-great leaders. Others have fared less well in the eyes of historians.

8. Americans are at odds over a number of issues concerning the presidency, including the ethical and legal challenges that have faced the Clinton administration and the president's impeachment.

for critical analysis

1. Do you know anyone who would *not* vote for a woman, African American, Jew, Latino, or Native American for president? What reasons might he or she give for not voting for a person from one of these groups?

2. How would you rate the presidency of Bill Clinton?

3. Do you think that President Clinton's impeachment trial would have turned out differently if the American economy had been weak at that time?

4. Does it make any difference whether a president has military experience?

5. Can a president select anyone to serve as a cabinet member?

6. Do you think the president will have more or less power twenty years from now? Why or why not?

7. Many parents tell their kids that they can grow up to be the president of the United States if they really want to do so. Are these parents telling the truth?

suggested readings

CRONIN, Thomas E., and Michael A. Genovese. *The Paradoxes of the American Presidency*. New York: Oxford University Press, 1998. The authors view the American presidency as a series of paradoxes that shape and define the office. They focus on the vagaries of the presidential selection process, the various relationships (with Congress, the public, and the courts) that all presidents must develop if they are to lead successfully, and the managerial side of the executive branch.

PIOUS, Richard M. *The Presidency*. Boston: Allyn & Bacon, 1996. In this comprehensive look at the presidency, the author uses examples from many presidencies, including the Clinton administration, to illustrate his discussions of presidential influence.

SHENKMAN, Richard. *Presidential Ambition: How the Presidents Gained Power, Kept Power, and Got Things Done*. New York: HarperCollins, 1999. The author looks at how presidents have come to power and how they have acted during their term of office. He concludes that presidents have been most successful when they molded the presidency to their talents and skills rather than trying to fit into a preconceived model of an "ideal president."

SKOWRONEK, Stephen. *The Politics Presidents Make: Leadership from John Adams to Bill Clinton*. Cambridge, Mass.: Harvard University Press, 1997. The author, winner of the Richard E. Neustadt Award for the best book on the presidency, contends that presidents are agents of change and that they continually disrupt and transform the political landscape. Skowronek views each president in terms of "political time"—that is, in relation to the preceding president. In the process, the author brings insights to each presidency discussed.

politics
on the web

The White House home page offers links to numerous sources of information on the presidency. You can access this site at

http://www.whitehouse.gov

The Library of Congress's White House page is another useful site that offers links to information related to the presidency. Go to

http://lcweb.loc.gov/global/executive/fed.html

If you are interested in reading the inaugural addresses of American presidents from Washington to Clinton, go to

http://www.bartleby.com/index.html

In addition to the full text of the inaugural addresses, this site provides biographical information on the presidents and a picture of each president.

If you would like to research documents and academic resources concerning the presidency, a good Internet site to consult is that provided by Texas A&M University at

http://www.tamu.edu/whitehouse

using
web resources

Each former president has a library administered by the National Archives and Records Administration. These libraries have Web sites that include a wide variety of information concerning the former presidents. President Jimmy Carter served from 1977 through 1981. Access the Jimmy Carter Library and Museum Web site at

http://carterlibrary.galileo.peachnet.edu

1. What is the National Archives and Records Administration?

2. Read about the "Faces of Time Exhibit" and take the "Faces of Time Quiz" by selecting the appropriate link on the main page.

3. What are three examples of documents found online at the Carter Web site?

notes

1. *Clinton v. Jones,* 520 U.S. 681 (1997). A federal court judge later dismissed the case, however, but Paula Jones appealed the court's decision. In November 1998, the suit was settled.

2. 418 U.S. 683 (1974).

3. See Chapter 16 for a discussion of this power of the courts.

4. Lyndon B. Johnson, *The Vantage Point: Perspectives of the Presidency, 1963–1969* (New York: Henry Holt & Co., 1971).

5. A bill passed by Congress in the fall of 1999, if signed into law by the president, will up the president's salary to $400,000 in 2001.

6. *Newsweek* poll, October 1996.

7. Forrest McDonald, *The American Presidency: An Intellectual History* (Lawrence, Kans.: University Press of Kansas, 1994), p. 179.

8. As cited in Lewis D. Eigen and Jonathan P. Siegel, *The Macmillan Dictionary of Political Quotations* (New York: Macmillan, 1993), p. 565.

9. Richard E. Neustadt, *Presidential Power: The Politics of Leadership* (New York: John Wiley, 1980), p. 10.

10. As quoted in Richard M. Pious, *The American Presidency* (New York: Basic Books, 1979), pp. 51–52.

11. The Constitution does not grant the president explicit power to remove from office officials who are not performing satisfactorily or who do not agree with the president. In 1926, however, the Supreme Court prevented Congress from interfering with the president's ability to fire those executive branch officials whom he had appointed with Senate approval. See *Myers v. United States,* 272 U.S. 52 (1926).

12. This rebellion, which was reminiscent of colonial protests against Britain and severely tested the national government's authority, occurred in response to a 1791 act of Congress that imposed a tax on whiskey. At that time, an American adult imbibed, on average, six gallons of hard liquor per year. See Paul S. Boyer *et al., The Enduring Vision: A History of the American People,* 3d ed. (Lexington, Mass.: D. C. Heath & Co., 1996), pp. 213–214.

13. Versailles, located about twenty miles from Paris, is the name of the palace built by King Louis XIV of France. It served as the royal palace until 1793 and was then converted into a national historical museum, which it remains today. The preliminary treaty ending the American Revolution was signed between the United States and Great Britain at Versailles in 1783.

14. A phrase coined by Samuel Kernell in *Going Public: New Strategies of Presidential Leadership,* 2d ed. (Washington, D.C.: Congressional Quarterly Press, 1992).

15. *Clinton v. City of New York,* 524 U.S. 417 (1998).

16. As quoted in Thomas E. Cronin, *The State of the Presidency,* 2d ed. (Boston: Little, Brown, 1980), p. 11.

17. The Nixon administration first encouraged new relations with the People's Republic of China by allowing a cultural exchange of Ping-Pong teams.

18. Franklin D. Roosevelt, as quoted in *The New York Times,* November 13, 1932.

19. According to a Gallup poll taken January 15–17, 1999.

20. See The Gallup poll taken September 14–15, 1998, for example.

21. For more examples of presidential scandals, see Suzanne Garment, *Scandal: The Culture of Mistrust in American Politics* (New York: Times Books, 1991).

THE BUREAUCRACY

Contents

Is Government Bureaucracy Running Amuck?

Even though government bureaucrats now constitute 15 percent of the American labor force, a larger percentage than ever before, the U.S. government bureaucracy is still one of the smallest in the industrialized world. For critics of the bureaucracy, however, it is not small enough. Those who are part of that bureaucracy believe that, although improvements could be made, the bureaucracy is functioning quite well. The critics are not so kind. They believe that bureaucrats, particularly federal bureaucrats, are out of control and trampling on citizens' rights. They go so far as to say the bureaucracy is a major threat to democracy.

Go to CD-ROM

What the Critics Say

Critics of the bureaucracy believe that ordinary citizens have lost touch with the federal government. The size of the federal bureaucracy has grown to immense proportions, and ordinary citizens have little control over what bureaucrats are allowed to do. There is a sense that "They" can do whatever they want. Just consider the Federal Bureau of Investigation (FBI). In 1992, the FBI ended up shooting and killing the wife and child of white supremacist Randy Weaver at Ruby Ridge, Idaho. The Bureau of Alcohol, Tobacco, and Firearms (BATF), along with the FBI, completely botched the raid on the Branch Davidian compound in Waco, Texas, in 1993, resulting in the fiery death of the members of the sect.

And that's not all. The bureaucrats representing the federal government seem to be insensitive to the needs of local land users. They continue to increase the restrictions on the use of federal lands, and they have "an attitude," to boot.

Finally, the federal bureaucracy seems to be rigid and slow. Just consider that in 1972 Congress told the Environmental Protection Agency (EPA) to research all six hundred existing pesticides to determine which ones should be banned because they posed unnecessary environmental or health risks. Almost three decades later, the EPA has evaluated only thirty pesticides. At this pace, the agency will finish its job in the year 2570.

The Bureaucracy Is Doing a Good Job, Say Its Defenders

According to its supporters, the bureaucracy, and particularly the federal bureaucracy, is doing a good—if not a great—job. First of all, every large-scale organization, including the government, needs a bureaucracy. After all, someone has to do the work of government. If we didn't have bureaucrats, who would see to it that the laws passed by Congress were carried out?

Furthermore, our country's citizens benefit from the existence of the federal bureaucracy. Just compare the United States in the nineteenth century with today. Federal government bureaucrats in the EPA have helped to ensure that our drinking water is safe. Bureaucrats in the federal Food and Drug Administration make sure that the food we eat and the drugs we take will not kill us. The Occupational Safety and Health Administration attempts to ensure that our working conditions are safe. The National Highway Traffic Safety Administration takes steps to reduce the dangers associated with driving on our nation's highways. Our savings are secure in our banks, thanks to the Federal Deposit Insurance Corporation.

Now contrast the U.S. bureaucracy with other government bureaucracies, particularly those in South America, eastern Europe,

mainland China, or even France or England. By any standard, the U.S. bureaucracy is many times more efficient and pleasant to deal with than the bureaucracies in those countries. Another point is also quite important: in general, bureaucrats in the United States do not expect "side payments"[read: bribes] to get the job done. We have a truly neutral bureaucracy as opposed to one that can be bought off.

Finally, although critics argue that government agencies indulge in overkill by creating overly long, detailed regulations, such regulations need to be very specific. If they were not, endless disputes would occur, resulting in nonstop agency hearings and litigation. Certainly, any bureaucratic system can be improved, but the bureaucracy we have today works—so let's not abandon it.

Where Do You Stand?

1. Top-ranking bureaucrats are not elected, but appointed. Does that mean that the bureaucracy is a threat to democracy?

2. Just because the U.S. government bureaucracy is relatively more efficient than bureaucracies in many other countries, does that necessarily mean we do not have a problem worth solving?

On the Web

For a critical view of the bureaucracy, go to http://www.cato.org.

BUREAUCRAT ● An individual who works in a bureaucracy; as generally used, the term refers to a government employee.

BUREAUCRACY ● A large, complex, hierarchically structured administrative organization that carries out specific functions.

Reducing government bureaucracy civil service reform

Introduction

Did you eat breakfast this morning? If you did, **bureaucrats**—individuals who work in the offices of government—had a lot to do with that breakfast. If you had bacon, the meat was inspected by federal agents. If you drank milk, the price was affected by rules and regulations of the Department of Agriculture. If you looked at a cereal box, you saw fine print about minerals and vitamins, which was the result of regulations made by several other federal agencies, including the Food and Drug Administration. If you ate leftover pizza for breakfast, bureaucrats made sure that the kitchen of the pizza house was sanitary and safe and that the employees who put together (and perhaps delivered) the pizza were protected against discrimination in the workplace.

Today, the word *bureaucracy* often evokes a negative reaction. For some, it conjures up visions of depersonalized automatons performing their chores without any sensitivity toward the needs of those they serve. For others, it is synonymous with the "red tape" involved in government work. A **bureaucracy,** however, is simply a large, complex administrative organization that is structured hierarchically in a pyramid-like fashion.[1] Government bureaucrats carry out the policies of elected government officials. Bureaucrats deliver our mail, clean our streets, teach in our public schools, and run our national parks. Life as we know it would be impossible without government bureaucrats to keep our governments—federal, state, and local—in operation.

Some critics think that the bureaucracy has grown too big, as we pointed out in this chapter's opening feature. Before we can examine the growth of the bureaucracy, though, we need first to look at its nature.

EPA agents run tests at a toxic clean-up site in Denver.

The Nature and Size of the Bureaucracy

The concept of a bureaucracy is not confined to the federal government. Any large-scale organization has to have a bureaucracy. In each bureaucracy, everybody (except the head of the bureaucracy) reports to at least one other person. For the federal government, the head of the bureaucracy is the president of the United States.[2]

A bureaucratic form of organization allows each person to concentrate on her or his area of knowledge and expertise. In your college or university, for example, you do not expect the basketball coach to solve the problems of the finance department. The reason that the bureaucracy exists is that Congress, over time, has delegated certain tasks to specialists. For example, in 1914, Congress passed the Federal Trade Commission Act, which established the Federal Trade Commission to regulate deceptive and unfair trade practices. Those appointed to the commission were specialists in this area. Similarly, in 1972, Congress passed the Consumer Product Safety Act, which established the Consumer Product Safety Commission to investigate the safety of consumer products placed on the market. (For a detailed discussion of how Congress creates administrative agencies, see Chapter 18.) The commission is one of many federal administrative agencies.

Another key aspect of any bureaucracy is that the power to act resides in the *position* rather than in the *person*. In your college or university, the person who is currently president has more or less the same authority as any other previous president. Additionally, bureaucracies usually entail standard operating procedures—directives on what procedures should be followed in specific circumstances. Bureaucracies normally also have a merit system, in which people are hired and promoted on the basis of demonstrated skills and achievements.

THE GROWTH OF BUREAUCRACY

The federal government that existed in 1789 was small. It had three departments, each with only a few employees: (1) the Department of State (nine employees); (2) the Department of War (two employees); and (3) the Department of the Treasury (thirty-nine employees). By 1798, the federal bureaucracy was still quite small. The secretary of state had seven clerks. His total expenditures on stationery and printing amounted to $500, or about $5,750 in 1999 dollars. The Department of War spent, on average, a grand total of $1.4 million each year, or about $15.8 million in 1999 dollars.

The times have changed, that is for certain. Look at Figure 15–1, which shows the growth in the size of the federal bureaucracy just since 1975, as well as the growth in state and local bureaucracies. All in all, the government employs about 15 percent of the civilian labor force. Currently, more Americans are employed by government (at all three levels) than by the entire manufacturing sector of the U.S. economy.

THE COSTS OF MAINTAINING THE BUREAUCRACY

The costs of maintaining the bureaucracy are high and growing. In 1929, government at all levels accounted for about 8.5 percent of the total national income in the United States. Today, that figure is about 40 percent. That means that you, as an average citizen, will spend about 40 percent of your income on maintaining the federal, state, and local governments. You do this by paying income taxes, sales taxes, property taxes, and many other types of taxes and fees. To fully understand the amount of money spent by federal, state, and local governments each year, consider that the same sum

Figure 15–1
Government Employment at Federal, State, and Local Levels

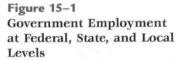

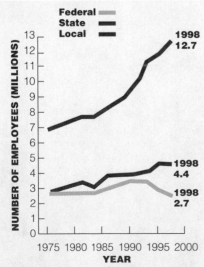

SOURCE: U.S. Department of Labor, Bureau of Labor Statistics, *Monthly Labor Review,* various issues.

The Role of the Bureaucracy in Our Political System

Government in the United States has certainly become "big government" by historical standards (but not necessarily in comparison with the relative size of governments in western Europe). Until World War II, government at all levels averaged about 5 percent of total employment and less than 15 percent of annual national income. Today, those numbers are about 15 percent and 40 percent, respectively. Clearly, there is no way to run massive welfare, retraining, and education programs, as well as other government projects and programs, without an enlarged bureaucracy. In this country, there are certainly two relatively distinct groups—those who believe that today's extensive government bureaucracy is beneficial to this country and those who don't.

What the Liberals Believe

Political liberals generally are in favor of maintaining government programs that help the poor and the disadvantaged in our society. They therefore see nothing wrong with keeping bureaucrats on the government payroll to administer

such programs. They believe that it is important to allocate payments to welfare recipients through the bureaucracy, rather than simply giving the payments directly to the recipients via some form of negative income tax or demographic grant. Liberals generally are in favor of public housing programs, which clearly require agencies and bureaucrats to administer them. They are in favor of expending resources to bring better health care to those who could not otherwise afford it. In short, liberals see an important role for government in transferring income from the wealthier classes of our society to the poorer classes, even though doing so requires an extensive bureaucracy.

What the Conservatives Believe

Many conservatives argue that the poor were not the reason for the expansion of the bureaucracy that started with the War on Poverty, which President Lyndon Johnson pushed through Congress in 1965. Rather, they view the expansion of the bureaucracy as the reason for the growing number of officially

defined poor. After all, the percentage of poor people was declining well before we had a federal bureaucracy to help the poor. Some conservatives claim that every time a program failed to reduce the official poverty rate, the failure was cited as a good reason to increase expenditures on the poor.

If we want to help the poor, why not give them income directly, without the layers of bureaucracy that necessarily siphon off some benefits to pay for salaries and consulting fees? Some studies show that direct transfers of money could lift every man, woman, and child in the United States above the official poverty level at less than half the cost of the government's antipoverty programs.[3] In short, conservatives believe that the large bureaucracy that disperses welfare benefits exists more to expand government than to put greater income into the hands of the poor.

For Critical Analysis

If we decided to give welfare benefits directly to the poor, how could we do this without employing bureaucrats to oversee the operation?

of money could be used to purchase all of the farmland in the United States plus all of the assets of the one hundred largest American corporations.

The bureaucracy is costly, to be sure, but it also provides numerous services for Americans. Cutting back on the size of the bureaucracy inevitably means a reduction in those services. (For a discussion of how the different ends of the political spectrum view the role of bureaucracy in today's political life, see the feature above entitled *The American Political Spectrum: The Role of the Bureaucracy in Our Political System*.)

DOWNSIZING THE FEDERAL BUREAUCRACY

During election time, politicians throughout the nation claim they will "cut big government and red tape" and "get rid of overlapping and wasteful bureaucracies." For the last several decades, virtually every president has campaigned of a platform calling for a reduction in the size of the federal bureaucracy. At the same time, candidates promise to establish programs

perception versus reality

Government Downsizing

Shortly after Bill Clinton was sworn in for his first four years as president, he and Vice President Al Gore set out on the road to "reinventing government." They claimed that they wanted to make government smaller and more efficient.

The Perception

Much press has been given to the numbers that the Clinton administration has put forth with respect to government downsizing. By 1997, his administration claimed that the federal work force had been cut by 250,000 employees, or by 11 percent, making the executive branch the smallest since John F. Kennedy was president.[4]

At the end of Clinton's first term, Vice President Gore issued an annual "reinventing government" report, claiming that about $120 billion in savings had been accrued

as a result of the administration's downsizing efforts. The general perception, consistent with these numbers, is that the federal government is indeed getting smaller.

The Reality

In the first place, of the 250,000 employees who have been cut, 212,000 came from defense jobs or from the winding down of the savings and loan bailout. Moreover, many federal employees who were let go were later rehired as private-sector consultants.

Consider one example—the downsizing of the U.S. Postal Service. Downsizing began in April 1993. By November 1995, postal employment had grown from 782,000 to 855,000![5] Labor costs remained about 80 percent of total postal service costs—the same percentage as in 1969.

The reality is that the number of people working on federal programs continues to increase, although some of those people are now private-sector employees. Indeed, Paul Light, a scholar at the Brookings Institution, maintains that in addition to the full-time employees of the federal government, an additional seventeen million people work in the "shadow government"—that is, these nonfederal employees work under federal contracts and grants, and provide the government with goods and services.[6]

You Be the Judge

Does it matter to you, as a taxpayer-citizen, whether the federal government "gets the job done" with federal government employees or with outside private-sector contractors?

that require new employees—even if they are "consultants" that are not officially counted as part of the bureaucracy. (During the first Clinton administration, the officially counted size of the federal bureaucracy did indeed fall, although the total dollars spent by the federal government increased—see the feature above entitled *Perception versus Reality: Government Downsizing.*)

Every day, hundreds of thousands of government employees report to work at various federal buildings across the country. In spite of recent attempts to downsize the federal bureaucracy, the total number of people working for the government continues to rise.

How the Federal Bureaucracy Is Organized

A complete organization chart of the federal government would cover an entire wall. A simplified version is provided in Figure 15–2. The executive branch consists of a number of bureaucracies that provide services to Congress, to the federal courts, and to the president directly. (For a comparison of the organization of the U.S. bureaucracy with that of other countries, see the feature on the next page entitled, *Comparative Politics: The U.S Bureaucracy Really Is Special.*)

Figure 15–2
The Organization of the Federal Government

THE GOVERNMENT OF THE UNITED STATES

THE CONSTITUTION

LEGISLATIVE BRANCH

THE CONGRESS
SENATE   HOUSE

Architect of the Capitol
United States Botanic Garden
General Accounting Office
Government Printing Office
Library of Congress
Congressional Budget Office

EXECUTIVE BRANCH

THE PRESIDENT
THE VICE PRESIDENT

Executive Office of the President

White House Office
Office of the Vice President
Council of Economic Advisers
Council on Environmental Quality
National Security Council
Office of Administration

Office of Management and Budget
Office of National Drug Control Policy
Office of Policy Development
Office of Science and Technology Policy
Office of the U.S. Trade Representative

JUDICIAL BRANCH

The Supreme Court of the United States

United States Courts of Appeals
United States District Courts
Territorial Courts
United States Court of International Trade
United States Court of Federal Claims
United States Court of Appeals for the Armed Forces
United States Tax Court
United States Court of Veterans Appeals
Administrative Office of the United States Courts
Federal Judicial Center
United States Sentencing Commission

| DEPARTMENT OF AGRICULTURE | DEPARTMENT OF COMMERCE | DEPARTMENT OF DEFENSE | DEPARTMENT OF EDUCATION | DEPARTMENT OF ENERGY | DEPARTMENT OF HEALTH AND HUMAN SERVICES | DEPARTMENT OF HOUSING AND URBAN DEVELOPMENT |

| DEPARTMENT OF THE INTERIOR | DEPARTMENT OF JUSTICE | DEPARTMENT OF LABOR | DEPARTMENT OF STATE | DEPARTMENT OF TRANSPORTATION | DEPARTMENT OF THE TREASURY | DEPARTMENT OF VETERANS AFFAIRS |

INDEPENDENT ESTABLISHMENTS AND GOVERNMENT CORPORATIONS

African Development Foundation
Central Intelligence Agency
Commodity Futures Trading Commission
Consumer Product Safety Commission
Corporation for National and Community Service
Defense Nuclear Facilities Safety Board
Environmental Protection Agency
Equal Employment Opportunity Commission
Export-Import Bank of the U.S.
Farm Credit Administration
Federal Communications Commission
Federal Deposit Insurance Corporation
Federal Election Commission
Federal Emergency Management Agency
Federal Housing Finance Board

Federal Labor Relations Authority
Federal Maritime Commission
Federal Mediation and Conciliation Service
Federal Mine Safety and Health Review Commission
Federal Reserve System
Federal Retirement Thrift Investment Board
Federal Trade Commission
General Services Administration
Inter-American Foundation
Merit Systems Protection Board
National Aeronautics and Space Administration
National Archives and Records Administration
National Capital Planning Commission
National Credit Union Administration
National Foundation on the Arts and the Humanities

National Labor Relations Board
National Mediation Board
National Railroad Passenger Corporation (AMTRAK)
National Science Foundation
National Transportation Safety Board
Nuclear Regulatory Commission
Occupational Safety and Health Review Commission
Office of Government Ethics
Office of Personnel Management
Office of Special Counsel
Panama Canal Commission
Peace Corps
Pension Benefit Guaranty Corporation
Postal Rate Commission
Railroad Retirement Board

Securities and Exchange Commission
Selective Service System
Small Business Administration
Social Security Administration
Tennessee Valley Authority
Trade and Development Agency
U.S. Arms Control and Disarmament Agency
U.S. Commission on Civil Rights
U.S. Information Agency
U.S. International Development Cooperation Agency
U.S. International Trade Commission
U.S. Postal Service

SOURCE: *United States Government Manual, 1997/98* (Washington, D.C.: U.S. Government Printing Office, 1997), p. 22.

comparative politics

The U.S. Bureaucracy Really Is Special

Americans are fond of believing that they are different, and with respect to the federal bureaucracy, they have a lot of facts to back them up. Consider that in the United States, the federal bureaucracy is controlled by several institutions. The president and Congress can exercise control over any agency. If you ever get appointed to a senior position in the federal bureaucracy, you will have to deal with two masters: the one who appointed you (the executive branch) and the one who pays you (Congress). Several congressional committees or subcommittees may also be able to nose around in your affairs.

Not so in Great Britain. In that country and in most parliamentary systems, the prime minister controls the cabinet ministers (the equivalent of our "secretaries") who appoint the bureaucrats. Most British and French bureaucrats, for example, have little or nothing to do with Parliament. Rather, they take orders only from the ministers in charge of their departments.

Because the U.S. political system is federal, as opposed to unitary (see Chapter 3), most agencies in the federal bureaucracy have counterparts at the state or local level. The federal agencies often work together with state and local agencies in performing certain government functions. Consider the Department of Health and Human Services. It is involved with numerous state and local government agencies, and it often reimburses state and local governments for money spent on health care for the nation's underclass. The Department of Labor provides funds to state and local agencies to help fund job-training programs.

In contrast, in any unitary system, by definition the number of subnational agencies is very limited. Local governments in France at the *département* (a unit of government somewhat like our county) and municipal levels have almost no control over housing, education, or health and employment programs. They are all run by the central government.

For Critical Analysis

Would a bureaucracy in a unitary system be more "efficient" than a bureaucracy in a federal system, such as the United States? Would a unitary or a federal system promote more responsiveness to citizens' needs?

The executive branch of the federal government includes four major types of bureaucratic structures:

- Executive departments.
- Independent executive agencies.
- Independent regulatory agencies.
- Government corporations.

Each type of bureaucratic structure has its own relationship to the president and its own internal workings.

THE EXECUTIVE DEPARTMENTS

You were introduced to the various executive departments in Chapter 14, when you read about how the president works with the cabinet and other close advisers. The fourteen executive departments, which are directly accountable to the president, are the major service organizations of the federal government. They are responsible for performing government functions, such as training troops (Department of Defense), printing money (Department of the Treasury), and enforcing federal laws setting minimum safety and health standards for workers (Department of Labor).

Each department was created by Congress as the perceived need for it arose, and each department manages a specific policy area. The head of each department is known as the secretary, except for the Department of Justice, which is headed by the attorney general. Each department head is appointed by the president and confirmed by the Senate. Table 15–1 on the next two pages provides an overview of each of the departments within the executive branch.

A TYPICAL DEPARTMENTAL STRUCTURE

Although there are organizational differences among the departments, each department generally follows a typical bureaucratic structure. The Department of Agriculture provides a model for how an executive department is organized (see Figure 15–3).

One aspect of the secretary of agriculture's job is to carry out the president's agricultural policies. Another aspect, however, is to promote and protect the department. The secretary will spend time ensuring that Congress allocates enough money for the department to work effectively. The secretary also makes sure that constituents, or the people the department serves—usually owners of major farming corporations—are happy. In general, the

Figure 15–3
The Organization of the Department of Agriculture

DEPARTMENT OF AGRICULTURE

SECRETARY
DEPUTY SECRETARY

- Chief Financial Officer
- General Counsel
- Inspector General
- Executive Operations
- Director of Communications

Under Secretary for Natural Resources and Environment
- Forest Service
- Natural Resources Conservation Service

Under Secretary for Farm and Foreign Agricultural Services
- Farm Service Agency
- Foreign Agricultural Service
- Risk Management Agency

Under Secretary for Rural Development
- Rural Utilities Service
- Rural Housing Service
- Rural Business Cooperative Service

Under Secretary for Food, Nutrition, and Consumer Services
- Food and Consumer Service

Under Secretary for Food Safety
- Food Safety and Inspection Service

Under Secretary for Research, Education, and Economics
- Agricultural Research Service
- Cooperative State Research, Education, and Extension Service
- Economic Research Service
- National Agricultural Statistics Service

Assistant Secretary for Congressional Relations
- Office of Congressional and Intergovernmental Relations

Assistant Secretary for Marketing and Regulatory Programs
- Agricultural Marketing Service
- Animal and Plant Health Inspection Service
- Grain Inspection, Packers and Stockyards Administration

Assistant Secretary for Administration
- Policy Analysis and Coordination Center
- Administrative Law Judges
- Judicial Officer
- Board of Contract Appeals

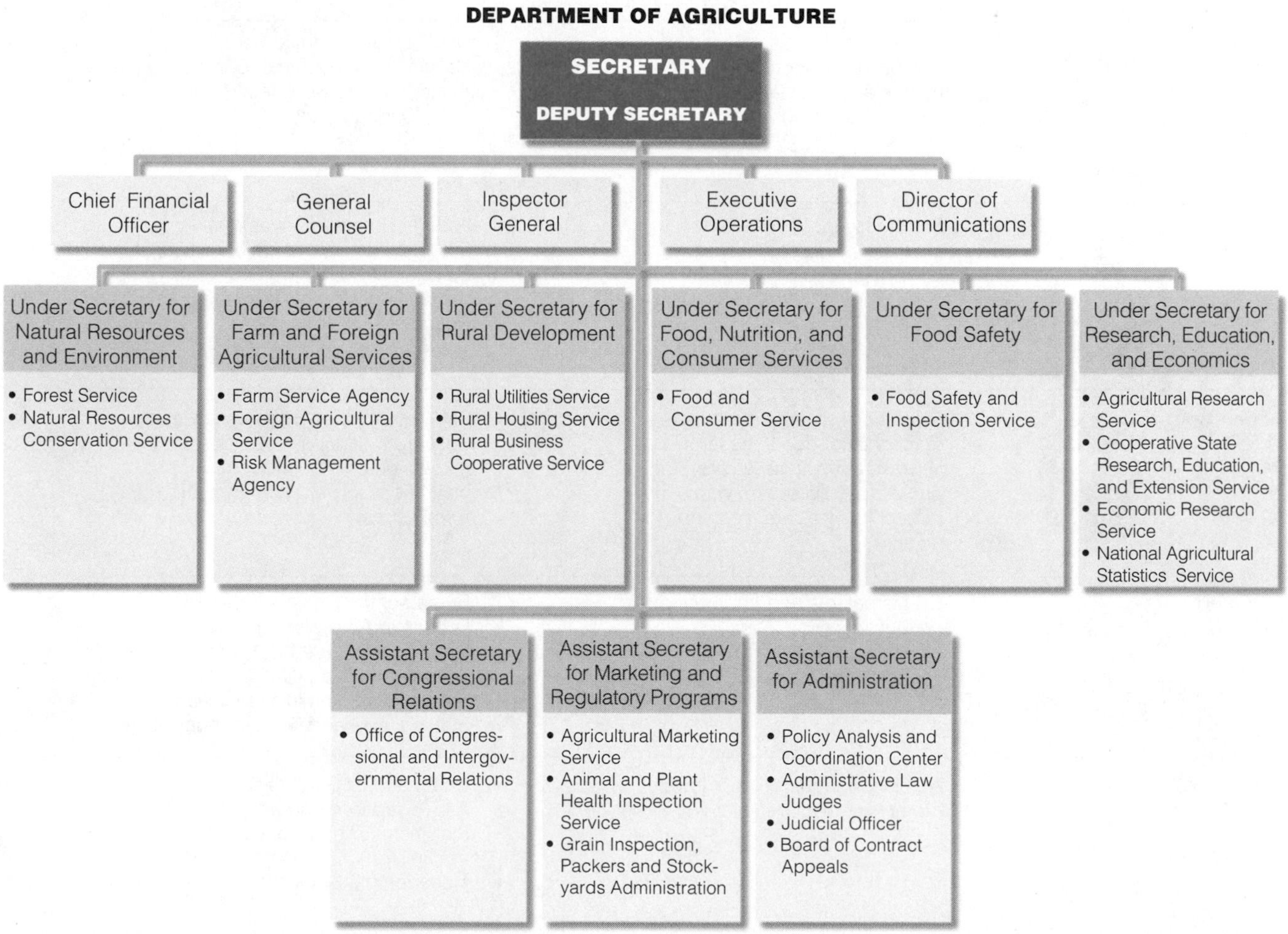

SOURCE: *United States Government Manual, 1997/98* (Washington, D.C.: U.S. Government Printing Office, 1997), p. 111.

secretary tries to maintain or improve the status of the department with respect to all of the other departments and units of the federal bureaucracy.

The secretary of agriculture is assisted by a deputy secretary and several assistant secretaries, all of whom are nominated by the president and put into office with Senate approval. The secretary and each assistant secretary have staff who help with all sorts of jobs, such as hiring new people and generating positive public relations for the Department of Agriculture.

Table 15-1
Executive Departments

DEPARTMENT (Year Established)		PRINCIPAL DUTIES	MOST IMPORTANT SUBAGENCIES
State (1789)		Negotiates treaties; develops our foreign policy; protects citizens abroad.	Passport Agency; Bureau of Diplomatic Security; Foreign Service; Bureau of Human Rights and Humanitarian Affairs; Bureau of Consular Affairs; Bureau of Intelligence and Research.
Treasury (1789)		Pays all federal bills; borrows money; collects federal taxes; mints coins and prints paper currency; operates the Secret Service; supervises national banks.	Internal Revenue Service; Bureau of Alcohol, Tobacco, and Firearms; U.S. Secret Service; U.S. Mint; Customs Service.
Interior (1849)		Supervises federally owned lands and parks; operates federal hydroelectric power facilities; supervises Native American affairs.	U.S. Fish and Wildlife Service; National Parks Service; Bureau of Indian Affairs; Bureau of Mines; Bureau of Land Management.
Justice (1870)		Furnishes legal advice to the president; enforces federal criminal laws; supervises the federal corrections system (prisons).	Federal Bureau of Investigation; Drug Enforcement Administration; Bureau of Prisons; United States Marshals Service; Immigration and Naturalization Service.
Agriculture (1889)		Provides assistance to farmers and ranchers; conducts research to improve agricultural activity and to prevent plant disease; works to protect forests from fires and disease.	Soil Conservation Service; Agricultural Research Service; Food and Safety Inspection Service; Federal Crop Insurance Corporation; Farmers Home Administration.
Commerce (1903)		Grants patents and trademarks; conducts national census; monitors the weather; protects the interests of businesses.	Bureau of the Census; Bureau of Economic Analysis; Minority Business Development Agency; Patent and Trademark Office; National Oceanic and Atmospheric Administration; United States Travel and Tourism Administration.
Labor (1913)		Administers federal labor laws; promotes the interests of workers.	Occupational Safety and Health Administration; Bureau of Labor Statistics; Employment Standards Administration; Office of Labor-Management Standards.

INDEND

INDEPENDENT EXECUTIVE AGENCY
● A federal bureaucratic agency that is not located within a cabinet department.

INDEPENDENT EXECUTIVE AGENCIES

Independent executive agencies are federal bureaucratic organizations that have a single function. They are independent in the sense that they are not located within a department; rather, independent executive agency heads report directly to the president who has appointed them. A new

Table 15–1

Executive Departments (Continued)

DEPARTMENT (Year Established)		PRINCIPAL DUTIES	MOST IMPORTANT SUBAGENCIES
Defense (1949)*		Manages the armed forces (Army, Navy, Air Force, Marines); operates military bases; responsible for civil defense.	National Guard; Defense Investigation Service; National Security Agency; Joint Chiefs of Staff; Departments of the Air Force, Navy, Army.
Health and Human Services (1979)†		Promotes public health; enforces pure food and drug laws; is involved in health-related research.	Food and Drug Administration; Public Health Service; Administration for Children and Families; Health Care Financing Administration.
Housing and Urban Development (1965)		Concerned with the nation's housing needs; develops and rehabilitates urban communities; promotes improvements in city streets and parks.	Office of Block Grant Assistance; Emergency Shelter Grants Program; Office of Urban Development Action Grants; Office of Fair Housing and Equal Opportunity.
Transportation (1967)		Finances improvements in mass transit; develops and administers programs for highways, railroads, and aviation; involved with offshore maritime safety.	Federal Aviation Administration (FAA); Federal Highway Administration; National Highway Traffic Safety Administration; U.S. Coast Guard; Federal Transit Administration.
Energy (1977)		Involved in conservation of energy and resources; analyzes energy data; conducts research and development.	Office of Civilian Radioactive Waste Management; Bonneville Power Administration; Office of Nuclear Energy, Science, and Technology; Energy Information Administration; Office of Conservation and Renewable Energy.
Education (1979)†		Coordinates federal programs and policies for education; administers aid to education; promotes educational research.	Office of Special Education and Rehabilitation Services; Office of Elementary and Secondary Education; Office of Postsecondary Education; Office of Vocational and Adult Education.
Veterans Affairs (1989)		Promotes the welfare of veterans of the U.S. armed forces.	Veterans Health Administration; Veterans Benefits Administration; National Cemetery System.

*Formed from the Department of War (1789) and the Department of the Navy (1798).
†Formed from the Department of Health, Education, and Welfare (1953).

PARTISAN POLITICS ● Political actions or decisions that are influenced by a particular political party's ideology.

INDEPENDENT REGULATORY AGENCY ● A federal bureaucratic organization that is responsible for creating and implementing rules that regulate private activity and protect the public interest in a particular sector of the economy.

I N F O T R A C *
U.S. intelligence failures

federal independent executive agency can be created only through joint cooperation between the president and Congress.

Prior to the twentieth century, the federal government did almost all of its work through the executive departments. In the twentieth century, in contrast, presidents have asked for certain executive agencies to be kept separate, or independent, from existing departments. Today, there are more than two hundred independent executive agencies.

Sometimes, agencies are kept independent because of the sensitive nature of their functions; at other times, Congress has created independent agencies to protect them from **partisan politics**—politics in support of a particular party's ideology. The Civil Rights Commission, which was created in 1957, is a case in point. Congress wanted to protect the work of the Civil Rights Commission from the influences not only of its own political interest groups but also of the president. The Central Intelligence Agency (CIA), which was formed in 1947, is another good example. Both Congress and the president know that the intelligence activities of the CIA could be abused if it were not independent. Finally, the General Services Administration (GSA) was created as an independent executive agency in 1949 to monitor federal government spending. To perform its function of overseeing congressional spending, it has to be an independent agency.

Among the more than two hundred independent executive agencies, a few stand out in importance either because of the mission they were established to accomplish or because of their large size. You can see some of the most important independent executive agencies in Table 15–2.

INDEPENDENT REGULATORY AGENCIES

Independent regulatory agencies are responsible for a specific type of public policy. Their function is to create and implement rules that regulate private activity and protect the public interest in a particular sector of the economy. They are sometimes called the "alphabet soup" of government, because most such agencies are known in Washington by their initials.

Table 15–2

Selected Independent Executive Agencies

NAME	DATE FORMED	PRINCIPAL DUTIES
Central Intelligence Agency (CIA)	1947	Gathers and analyzes political and military information about foreign countries so that the United States can improve its own political and military status; conducts covert activities outside the United States.
General Services Administration (GSA)	1949	Purchases and manages all property of the federal government; acts as the business arm of the federal government, overseeing federal government spending projects; discovers overcharges in government programs.
National Science Foundation (NSF)	1950	Promotes scientific research; provides grants to all levels of schools for instructional programs in the sciences.
Small Business Administration (SBA)	1953	Promotes the interests of small businesses; provides low-cost loans and management information to small businesses.
National Aeronautics and Space Administration (NASA)	1958	Responsible for U.S. space program, including building, testing, and operating space vehicles.
Federal Election Commission (FEC)	1974	Ensures that candidates and states follow the rules established by the Federal Election Campaign Act.

GOVERNMENT CORPORATION •
An agency of the government that is run as a business enterprise. Such agencies engage in primarily commercial activities, produce revenues, and require greater flexibility than that permitted in most government agencies.

One of the earliest independent regulatory agencies was the Interstate Commerce Commission (ICC), established in 1887. (This agency was abolished in 1995.) After the ICC was formed, other agencies were created to regulate aviation (the Civil Aeronautics Board, or CAB, which was abolished in 1985), communication (the Federal Communications Commission, or FCC), the stock market (the Securities and Exchange Commission, or SEC), and many other areas of business.

Table 15–3 lists some major independent regulatory agencies. You will read more about the administration of regulatory agencies in Chapter 18.

GOVERNMENT CORPORATIONS

The newest form of federal bureaucratic organization is the **government corporation,** a business that is owned by the government. Government corporations are not exactly like corporations in which you buy stock, become a shareholder, and share in the profits by collecting dividends. The U.S. Postal Service is a government corporation, but it sells no shares. If a government corporation loses money in the course of doing business, it is not shareholders but taxpayers who foot the bill.

Table 15–3

Selected Independent Regulatory Agencies

NAME	DATE FORMED	PRINCIPAL DUTIES
Federal Reserve System Board of Governors (Fed)	1913	Responsible for determining policy with respect to interest rates, credit availability, and the money supply.
Federal Trade Commission (FTC)	1914	Responsible for preventing businesses from engaging in unfair trade practices, for stopping the formation of monopolies in the business sector, and for protecting consumer rights.
Securities and Exchange Commission (SEC)	1934	Responsible for regulating the nation's stock exchanges, in which shares of stocks are bought and sold; requires full disclosure of the financial profiles of companies that wish to sell stocks and bonds to the public.
Federal Communications Commission (FCC)	1934	Responsible for regulating all communications by telegraph, cable, telephone, radio, and television.
National Labor Relations Board (NLRB)	1935	Responsible for protecting employees' rights to join unions and to bargain collectively with employers; attempts to prevent unfair labor practices by both employers and unions.
Equal Employment Opportunity Commission (EEOC)	1964	Responsible for working to eliminate discrimination that is based on religion, gender, race, color, national origin, or age; examines all claims of discrimination.
Environmental Protection Agency (EPA)	1970	Responsible for undertaking programs aimed at reducing air and water pollution; works with state and local agencies to help fight environmental hazards.
Nuclear Regulatory Commission (NRC)	1974	Responsible for ensuring that electricity-generating nuclear reactors in the United States are built and operated safely; regularly inspects operations of such reactors.
Defense Nuclear Facilities Safety Board	1988	Reviews and evaluates the construction and operation of defense nuclear facilities; investigates any practices at these facilities that may be harmful to the public.

Government corporations are like private corporations in that they provide a service that could be handled by the private sector. They are also like private corporations in that they charge for their services, though sometimes they charge less than what a consumer would pay for similar services provided by private-sector corporations. Table 15–4 lists some of the major government corporations.

How Bureaucrats Get Their Jobs

Since 1883, anybody who wants to work for the federal government normally must take a civil service exam.

As already noted, federal bureaucrats holding top-level positions are appointed by the president and confirmed by the Senate. These bureaucrats include department and agency heads, their deputy and assistant secretaries, and so on. The list of positions that are filled by appointments is published after each presidential election in a 260-page document called *Policy and Supporting Positions.* The booklet is more commonly known as the "Plum Book," because the eight thousand jobs it summarizes are known as "political plums." Normally, these jobs, which pay annual salaries of between $86,160 and $148,400, go to those who supported the winning presidential candidate—in other words, the patronage system is alive and well.[7]

The rank-and-file bureaucrats—the rest of the federal bureaucracy—obtain their jobs through the Office of Personnel Management (OPM), an agency established by the Civil Service Reform Act of 1978. The OPM recruits, interviews, and tests potential government workers and determines who should be hired. The OPM makes recommendations to the individual agencies as to which persons meet the standards (typically, the top three applicants for a position), and the agencies generally decide whom to hire. The 1978 act also created the Merit Systems Protection Board (MSPB) to oversee promotions, employees' rights, and other employment matters. The MSPB evaluates charges of wrongdoing, hears employee appeals from agency decisions, and can order corrective action against agencies and employees.

Table 15–4

Selected Government Corporations

NAME	DATE FORMED	PRINCIPAL DUTIES
Tennessee Valley Authority (TVA)	1933	Operates a Tennessee River control system and generates power for a seven-state region and for U.S. aeronautics and space programs; promotes the economic development of the Tennessee Valley region; controls floods and promotes the navigability of the Tennessee River.
Federal Deposit Insurance Corporation (FDIC)	1933	Insures individuals' bank deposits up to $100,000; oversees the business activities of banks.
Export/Import Bank of the United States (Ex/Im Bank)	1933	Promotes American-made goods abroad; grants loans to foreign purchasers of American products.
National Railroad Passenger Corporation (AMTRAK)	1970	Provides an integrated, balanced national and intercity rail passenger service network; controls over 20,000 miles of track with about 500 stations.
U.S. Postal Service (formed from the Postmaster General of the Treasury Department [1789])	1971	Delivers mail throughout the United States and its territories; is the largest government corporation, with over 850,000 employees.

CIVIL SERVICE ● Employees of the civil government, or civil servants.

NEUTRAL COMPETENCY ● The application of technical skills to jobs without regard to political issues.

The idea that the **civil service** (employees of the civil government, or civil servants) should be based on a merit system dates back more than a century. The Civil Service Reform Act of 1883 established the principle of government employment on the basis of merit through open, competitive examinations. Initially, only about 10 percent of federal employees were covered by the merit system. Today, more than 90 percent of the federal civil service is recruited on the basis of merit. (For some of the benefits enjoyed by federal employees, see the feature entitled *A Question of Ethics: Should Federal Employees Have More Protection than Private-Sector Employees?*)

Bureaucrats as Policymakers

Federal bureaucrats are expected to exhibit **neutral competency,** which means that they are supposed to apply their technical skills to their jobs without regard to political issues. In principle, they should not be swayed by the thought of personal or political gain. For example, a bureaucrat in the Department of Defense is not supposed to look the other way if she sees a company doing shoddy construction of a fighter jet. Even if this bureaucrat is hoping that the same company might offer her a job after she retires, she is supposed to apply her skills and attempt to solve the problem without letting her future aspirations interfere with her job performance.

In reality, each independent agency and each executive department is interested in its own survival and expansion. Each is constantly battling the others for a larger share of the budget. All agencies and departments wish to retain or expand their functions and staffs; to do this, they must gain the goodwill of both the White House and Congress.

HOW BUREAUCRATS ACT AS POLITICIANS

Bureaucratic agencies of the federal government are prohibited from directly lobbying Congress. Departments and agencies, nonetheless, have developed techniques to help them gain congressional support. Each organization maintains a congressional information office, which specializes in helping members of Congress by supplying any requested information and solving casework problems. For example, if a member of the House

a question of ethics

Should Federal Employees Have More Protection than Private-Sector Employees?

Firings from the federal government are few and far between. One reason for this is that federal employees have a strong union, the American Federation of Government Employees (AFGE), to protect their rights. When a long-time employee of the Labor Department told a young part-time worker that too much work was piling up, the subordinate broke her superior's jaw. Was the subordi-nate fired? No. The AFGE inter-vened. Rather than fight an uphill battle, the Labor Department decided not to fire the worker and transferred her instead. The lucky worker ended up with a perma-nent job and a raise of almost $4,000 a year.

Few workers in the private sec-tor have such job security. Although some claim that federal employees have too much protec-tion, others argue that private-sector employees should have more protection—equal to that of government employees.

For Critical Analysis

Should private-sector employees have as many rights as government workers normally enjoy? Why or why not?

of Representatives receives a complaint from a constituent that his Social Security checks are not arriving on time, that member of Congress may go to the Social Security Administration and ask that something be done. Typically, requests from members of Congress receive immediate attention.

The Department of Defense is an example of an organization that has earned a reputation for being able to generate publicity for itself to win support from Congress. When President Ronald Reagan wanted Congress to approve the sale of specialized spy planes to Saudi Arabia, the Department of Defense arranged for such a plane to be stationed near Washington. The department invited members of Congress and their staffs to take guided tours of the plane that explained the plane's complex technology. In this way, both the Defense Department and President Reagan got what they wanted from Congress.

HOW BUREAUCRATS MAKE POLICY—THE IRON TRIANGLE

Analysts have determined that one way to understand the bureaucracy's role in policymaking is to examine the **iron triangle,** which is the three-way alliance among legislators (members of Congress), bureaucrats, and interest groups. (Iron triangles are also referred to as subgovernments, policy communities, or issue networks.) Presumably, the laws that are passed and the policies that are established benefit the interests of all three sides of the iron triangle.

Agriculture as an Example

Consider the bureaucracy within the Department of Agriculture. It consists of about 100,000 individuals working directly for the federal government and thousands of other individuals who work indirectly for the department as contractors, subcontractors, or consultants. Now consider that various interest groups or client groups are concerned with what certain bureaus or agencies in the Agriculture Department do for agribusinesses. Some of these groups are the American Farm Bureau Federation, the National Cattleman's Association, the National Milk Producers Association, the Corn Growers Association, and the Citrus Growers Association.

Finally, take a close look at Congress and you will see that two major committees are concerned with agriculture: the House Committee on Agriculture and the Senate Committee on Agriculture, Nutrition, and Forestry. Each committee has several specialized subcommittees. The triangle is an alliance of bureaucrats, interest groups, and legislators who cooperate to create mutually beneficial regulations or legislation. Iron triangles, or policy communities, are well established in almost every part of the bureaucracy.

Congress's Role

The secretary of agriculture is nominated by the president (and confirmed by the Senate) and is the head of the Department of Agriculture. But that secretary cannot even buy a desk lamp if Congress does not approve the appropriations for the department's budget. Within Congress, the responsibility for considering the Department of Agriculture's request for funding belongs first to the House and Senate appropriations committees and then to the agriculture subcommittees under them. The members of those subcommittees, most of whom represent agricultural states, have been around a long time and have their own ideas about what is appropriate for the Agriculture Department's budget. They carefully scrutinize the ideas of the president and the secretary of agriculture.

The Influence of Interest Groups

Finally, the various interest groups—including producers of farm chemicals and farm machinery, agricultural cooperatives, grain dealers, and exporters—

WHISTLEBLOWER ● In the context of government employment, someone who "blows the whistle" on (reports to authorities) gross governmental inefficiency, illegal action, or other wrongdoing.

have vested interests in whatever the Department of Agriculture does and in whatever Congress lets the department do. Those interests are well represented by the lobbyists who crowd the halls of Congress. Many lobbyists have been working for agricultural interest groups for decades. They know the congressional committee members and Agriculture Department staff extremely well and routinely meet with them.

The Success of the Iron Triangle in Agriculture

For whatever reason, our nation's farmers have benefited greatly from the iron triangle in agriculture. According to the Organization for Economic Cooperation and Development, U.S. taxpayers paid more than $400 billion to farmers over a ten-year period.[8] Nevertheless, about 70 percent of the nation's farmers received no direct payment. That means that most taxpayer payments went to the wealthiest farmers and agribusinesses in the country.

Curbing Waste and Improving Efficiency

There is no doubt that our bureaucracy is costly. There is also little doubt that at times it can be wasteful (see, for example, the feature entitled *Politics on the Far Side: The Federal Bureaucracy Can Be Outrageous*) and inefficient. Over the years, Congress has made several attempts to reduce waste and inefficiency by, among other things, encouraging government employees to report to appropriate government officials any waste and wrongdoing that they observe.

politics on the far side

The Federal Bureaucracy Can Be Outrageous

Each year it is possible to cull through the budgets of the various federal agencies and discover quite outrageous examples of government waste. Here are some recent ones:

■ More than $11 million paid to psychics by the Pentagon and the Central Intelligence Agency to discover whether those psychics would offer insights about foreign threats to the United States.

■ Payments of more than $20 million a year to thousands of prisoners through the Social Security Administration's Supplemental Income Program.

■ A total of $10 million per year paid by the Department of Energy to its employees to encourage them to lose weight.

■ Payments to maintain 32 billion cubic feet of helium in Amarillo, Texas, pursuant to the federal helium program that started in 1925 to keep our blimps afloat.

According to researcher Robert Tollison, "You could multiply the famous examples by a factor of one-thousand and still not cover the wasteful and redundant government programs."[9]

For Critical Analysis: Is wasteful spending inevitable in any large bureaucracy?

HELPING OUT THE WHISTLEBLOWERS

The term **whistleblower**, as applied to the federal bureaucracy, has a special meaning: it is someone who blows the whistle, or reports, on gross governmental inefficiency, illegal action, or other wrongdoing. Federal employees are often reluctant to blow the whistle on their superiors, however, for fear of reprisals.

To encourage federal employees to report government wrongdoing, Congress has passed laws to protect whistleblowers. The 1978 Civil Service Reform Act included some protection for whistleblowers by prohibiting reprisals against whistleblowers by their superiors. The act also set up the Merit Systems Protection Board as part of this protection. The Whistle-Blower Protection Act of 1989 provided further protection for whistleblowers. That act authorized the Office of Special Counsel (OSC), an independent agency, to investigate complaints of reprisals against whistleblowers. Many federal agencies also have toll-free hotlines that employees can use to anonymously report bureaucratic waste and inappropriate behavior.

In spite of these laws, there is little evidence that whistleblowers are adequately protected against retaliation. According to a study conducted by the General Accounting Office, 41 percent of the whistleblowers who turned to the OSC for protection during a recent three-year period reported that they were no longer employed by the agencies on which they blew the whistle. Many other federal employees who have blown the whistle say that they would not do so again because it was so difficult to get help, and even when they did, the experience was a stressful ordeal.

Consider what happened to Frederic Whitehurst, a scientist-agent with the FBI, who informed the press that the FBI crime lab had been tainting evidence in favor of the prosecution in several high-profile cases. In early 1997, just days after FBI Director Louis Freeh learned about Whitehurst's actions, Whitehurst was suspended from his job and barred from entering any FBI building.

Creating more effective protection for whistleblowers remains an on-going goal of the government. The basic problem, though, is that most organizations, including federal government agencies, do not like to have their wrongdoings and failings exposed, especially by insiders.

IMPROVING EFFICIENCY AND GETTING RESULTS

The Government Performance and Results Act, which went into effect in 1997, has forced the federal government to change the way it does business. In seventy-one pilot programs throughout the federal government, agencies are experiencing a three-year shakedown. Beginning in October 1997, virtually every agency (except for the intelligence agencies) had to describe its new goals and a method for evaluating how well those goals are met. A results-oriented goal of an agency could be as broad as lowering the number of highway traffic deaths or as narrow as trying to reduce the number of times an agency's phone rings before it is answered.

As one example, consider the National Oceanic and Atmospheric Adminstration. It improved the effectiveness of its short-term forecasting services, particularly in issuing warnings of tornadoes. The warning time has increased from seven to nine minutes.[10] This may seem insignificant, but it provides additional critical time for those in the path of a tornado.

Supporters of the new law argue that it will go far toward improving bureaucratic efficiency. Others are less optimistic that it can overcome the inertia characteristic of any large-scale bureaucracy, including that of the U.S. government.

ANOTHER APPROACH — PAY-FOR-PERFORMANCE PLANS

For some time, the private sector has used pay-for-performance plans as a means to increase employee productivity and efficiency. About one-third of the major firms in this country use some kind of alternative pay system such as team-based pay, skill-based pay, profit-sharing plans, or individual bonuses. In contrast, workers for the federal government traditionally have received fixed salaries; and promotions, salary increases, and the like are given on the basis of seniority, not output.

Recently, though, the federal government has been experimenting with pay-for-performance systems. In 1996, the U.S. Postal Service implemented its Economic Value Added program, in which bonuses are tied to performance. In 1997, as part of a five-year test of a new pay system, three thousand scientists working in Air Force laboratories began getting salaries based on actual results. Also in 1997, the Department of Veterans Affairs launched a skill-based pay project at its New York regional office.

Many hope that by offering such incentives, the government will be able to compete more effectively with the private sector for skilled and talented employees. Additionally, according to some, pay-for-performance plans will go a long way toward countering the entitlement mentality that has traditionally characterized employment within the bureaucracy.

Americans at Odds over the Bureaucracy

In spite of claims to the contrary, the federal government bureaucracy is far from becoming truly efficient. Nor is it getting much smaller. Even the Office of the Vice President—occupied for most of the 1990s by a man (Al Gore) who wished to "reinvent government" by downsizing—has almost 50 percent more staff than it had during the previous vice president's term.

The bureaucracy is not about to disappear. Nor is it about to be "reinvented" so that it doesn't resemble what we've come to accept in the United States. Continuing attempts at changing it, though, are guaranteed. Every administration would like to make government more efficient. The problem is, different groups are at odds over how this can be done.

The Protection of Pet Agencies and Programs

Change will never come easily to the federal bureaucracy. Members of Congress who have been in office for many years often end up benefiting themselves and others by protecting "pet" agencies and programs. For example, soon after the Republicans took control of Congress in 1995, the House immediately barred any personnel cuts in the Veterans Health Administration. The GOP in Congress didn't even consider consolidating the one-hundred-plus job-training programs, because it knew that opposition by individual senators and representatives would be strong. Similarly, the electrification program authorized by the Rural Electrification Act of 1936, which is no longer necessary because the entire country has been wired for electricity, has not been touched.

Basically, reining in the federal bureaucracy will never become a major activity of Congress. After all, the iron triangle is strong.

What to Do about AMTRAK?

The National Railroad Passenger Corporation, popularly known as AMTRAK, was created in 1970 to take over the private sector's failing intercity rail passenger service. It controls over twenty thousand miles of track with some five hundred stations. When AMTRAK took over the private sector's money-losing intercity routes, the companies had lost $1.7 billion in the previous year. Twenty-five years after its inception, in spite of a $1 billion annual federal subsidy, AMTRAK was facing widening losses and dwindling ridership. AMTRAK's trains and facilities are generally old and unattractive. What, if anything, should be done to save AMTRAK?

On May 1, 1971, the National Railroad Passenger Corporation—AMTRAK—took over virtually all U.S. passenger railroad traffic. This federal government corporation consistently sustains losses. These losses, of course, are paid for with taxpayer dollars.

PRIVATIZATION • The replacement of government agencies that provide products or services to the public by private firms that provide the same products or services.

Starting with fiscal year 1997, AMTRAK's administration revealed a five-year plan to cut out its most unprofitable routes and simultaneously improve service on profitable ones. It claims it will reach self-sufficiency by the year 2002.

Many argue that AMTRAK should be sold to the private sector as part of a general federal government **privatization** program. Many observers predict that that will not happen, however. Government reform is difficult when the benefits from a specific government activity are concentrated among a small group of citizens and the costs are diffused across all taxpayers. After all, AMTRAK's $1-billion-a-year subsidy comes out to fewer than $10 per working American. This amount is not sufficient to motivate the average American worker to spend time trying to see AMTRAK privatized. Other people, though, will spend time to make sure AMTRAK is *not* privatized. These people are AMTRAK employees and suppliers, train buffs, and politicians who have constituents who live in sparsely populated areas currently serviced by AMTRAK. Additionally, some people argue that the government can improve surface public transportation along the lines of Japan and Europe. In the meantime, they want to keep AMTRAK alive as a minimal model for rail service.

The National Aeronautics and Space Administration—Still in Trouble

I N F O T R A C®

NASA's exploration projects to Mars

In 1984, President Ronald Reagan pledged that within ten years the United States would build an orbiting space station. Such a station would be capable of providing a base for missions to Mars as well as for servicing satellites. Ten years later, nothing close to this vision had been realized. By 1998, the federal government had spent almost half of the projected $27.5 billion on the project, yet only a trivial percentage of the 500,000 pounds of hardware necessary for the space station had been built. The National Aeronautics and Space Administration (NASA) has spent most of the money on redesigns.

Not everyone believes that the money has been wasted. Supporters of NASA and the space station argue that such expenditures allow the government to preserve crucial skills in a declining aerospace industry. In contrast, NASA's critics argue that to maintain congressional support for the program, NASA spreads its contracts across as many congressional dis-

The National Aeronautics and Space Administration (NASA) has had a checkered history. One of its most recent successes involved a project to explore Mars. This photo shows the Pathfinder vehicle that landed on Mars on July 4, 1997. The Pathfinder is a joint product of NASA and the Jet Propulsion Laboratory of the California Institute of Technology.

tricts as possible. That's why we have the Lyndon B. Johnson Space Center in Houston; the John F. Kennedy Space Center at Cape Canaveral, Florida; the George C. Marshall Space Flight Center in Huntsville, Alabama; and the Goddard Space Flight Center in Greenbelt, Maryland. This "spreading of the wealth" has necessarily resulted in a cumbersome and inefficient management system for putting together the space station.

In the meantime, the original satellite plan, called "Freedom," was redesigned and renamed "Alpha." As of several years ago, an estimated $5 billion had been spent on salaries, equipment, and blueprints for the old project—all of it completely wasted.[11] Congress must still decide whether to continue funding for a space station designed to service satellites (it now appears that there is no demand for that service) and a manned mission to Mars—which most people believe is totally "pie in the sky."

What to Do about the U.S. Postal Service?

The U.S. Postal Service has not taken a dime of taxpayers' money since 1982, but it still faces a problem: big losses in the first-class mail business. By 1997, it had lost over $2 billion in two years on first-class mail, and it was expected to lose another $2 billion by the year 2000.[12] Basically, the postal service has fared badly in its competition with phone calls, faxes, and electronic mail. Moreover, as mentioned in the feature entitled *Politics on the Far Side: The Federal Government Chooses FedEx over the U.S. Postal Service,* the Private Express Statutes prevent it from competing for new business by offering discounted or negotiated rates. As the Internet expands and as FedEx, UPS, and Airborne become more efficient, the U.S. Postal Service will continue to face a serious competitive threat in first-class mail. Indeed, it has already downgraded its own express-mail services in favor of two-day or priority delivery.

If the U.S. Postal Service were a private company, it would cut back on unprofitable and underused services. Under the current law, however, the postal service has to serve every household no matter where it is located, and it has to charge the same price for every letter regardless of whether the destination is twenty miles or two thousand miles away.

At the heart of the problem is the fact that delivery of first-class mail has traditionally been a government monopoly via the U.S. Postal Service. Consequently, the postal service has had no part in developing fax transmissions, interactive TV, or computer-based electronic mail. There likely will be increasing calls for the privatization of postal services. There is a precedent for this. The Netherlands has done so, and Sweden is allowing private companies to compete with the state-run system in delivering mail to its capital, Stockholm.

One thing is certain: the cyberworld of today will render traditional post office services less and less necessary.

politics on the far side

The Federal Government Chooses FedEx over the U.S. Postal Service

Recently, the General Services Administration (GSA)—the government's procurement agency—signed a $300 million contract with Federal Express because FedEx can deliver overnight mail $3 cheaper per letter than the U.S. Postal Service can. The new six-year contract with FedEx, the Memphis-based private mail and package carrier, followed one that was signed in 1990.

The GSA rejected the U.S. Postal Service's bid for delivery service. One of the reasons that the U.S. Postal Service was unable to beat FedEx is that laws (the Private Express Statutes) prohibit the U.S. Postal Service from offering volume-rate discounts or negotiated rates to individual customers. As a result, the postal service has less than a 15 percent market share for overnight letters and packages.

For Critical Analysis: Should the U.S. Postal Service be privatized?

Would Term Limits Reduce Government Spending?

It used to be that the Democrats were regarded as the "big spenders" in Congress. Now, the nation is not sure. Certainly, the Republican-dominated

Congress since 1995 has had little success in reducing the dollars spent by the federal government each year. In fact, just the opposite has occurred, as discussed in Chapter 3. Some scholars have added another dimension to the controversy over term limits (see Chapter 13) by suggesting that the imposition of term limits on members of Congress may help to curb government spending.

Aaron Steelman of the Cato Institute, for example, argues that partisanship has little to do with government spending today. Rather, it is length of service in Congress that is the determining factor. Steelman bases his conclusions on the results of a study in which the voting records of junior Republicans in Congress were compared with those of senior Republicans on thirty-one significant issues. Steelman noted that in nearly every one of the thirty-one votes, junior Republicans favored less federal spending in far greater numbers than did senior Republicans. In other words, the big spenders are long-time congressional Republicans. These findings, concludes Steelman, suggest that if the public wants Congress to reduce the size and scope of government, term limits may be a solution.[13]

key terms

bureaucracy 365	iron triangle 378
bureaucrats 365	neutral competency 377
civil service 377	partisan politics 374
government corporation 375	privatization 382
independent executive agency 373	whistleblower 379
independent regulatory agency 374	

chapter summary

1. A bureaucracy is a large, complex administrative organization that is structured hierarchically in a pyramid-like fashion. The federal bureaucracy is an administrative organization that carries out the policies of elected government officials.

2. In 1789, the federal bureaucracy had only about fifty civilian employees. Today, the federal government employs about 15 percent of the civilian labor force. The costs of maintaining the bureaucracy at all levels have grown from about 8.5 percent of total U.S. national income in 1929 to about 40 percent today.

3. There are four major types of bureaucratic structures within the executive branch of the federal government. The fourteen *executive departments* are directly accountable to the president and are responsible for performing certain government functions and managing specific policy areas. *Independent executive agencies* are special-function agencies. They are located outside the executive departments either because of the sensitive nature of their function or to shield them from the influence of partisan politics. *Independent regulatory agencies* are established to create and implement rules that regulate private activities and protect the public interest in particular

sectors of the economy. Like independent executive agencies, these agencies exist outside the executive departments. Government corporations are government-owned corporations, such as the U.S. Postal Service, that provide services that could be provided by the private sector.

4. Bureaucrats holding the top positions in the federal government are appointed by the president and confirmed by the Senate. Rank-and-file bureaucrats obtain their jobs through the Office of Personnel Management (OPM), which was created by the Civil Service Reform Act of 1978. The OPM recruits, interviews, and tests potential workers and determines who should be hired. Final decisions are made by the hiring agencies. The 1978 act also created the Merit Systems Protection Board to protect employees' rights. The civil service is based on the merit system, which was initiated in 1883 by the Civil Service Reform Act of that year.

5. Iron triangles, or policy communities, are at work throughout the bureaucracy. An iron triangle consists of legislators, bureaucrats, and interest groups that work together to create mutually beneficial legislation in a specific policy area, such as agriculture.

6. Over the years, Congress has made several attempts to curb bureaucratic waste and inefficiency. The 1978 Civil Service Reform Act prohibits reprisals against whistleblowers (those who blow the whistle [report] on gross governmental inefficiency, illegal action, or other wrongdoing) by their superiors, and the Merit Systems Protection Board was established as part of the act's protection. The Whistle-Blower Protection Act of 1989 provided further protection for whistleblowers and authorized the Office of Special Counsel to investigate complaints of reprisals against whistleblowers. Many federal agencies also have toll-free hotlines that employees can use to anonymously report wrongdoing in the bureaucracy.

7. The Government Performance and Results Act, which went into effect in 1997, requires federal agencies to describe their goals and establish methods for evaluating how well those goals are met.

Some believe that pay-for-performance plans, with which the government is now experimenting, will also help to improve efficiency.

8. The need to reform the bureaucracy is widely recognized, but different groups are at odds over how this can be done. The iron triangles throughout the bureaucracy make change difficult. Another reason bureaucratic reform is difficult is because members of Congress who have been in office for many years often find it beneficial for themselves and others to protect "pet" agencies or programs even though doing so results in an inefficient or wasteful use of resources. Still another reason why government reform is difficult is because those who have a stake in a certain program, such as AMTRAK, are strongly motivated to push for its continuation, while the great majority of Americans may be indifferent because of the relatively low per capita costs of the program.

for critical analysis

1. Why is it so difficult for Congress and the president to reduce the size of the bureaucracy?

2. What political incentives might explain the desire to foster the illusion that the national government is smaller than it really is?

3. Should the federal government continue to fund the National Aeronautics and Space Administration (NASA) or turn over the exploration of space to private industry?

4. Generally, should more of the services provided by government be privatized? What government services would you *not* like to see turned over to private contractors?

5. Would term limits for members of Congress help to reduce the effects of "iron triangles"? Why or why not?

6. How much federal funding is received by your college or university? Would you receive as good an education without the involvement of the federal government in educational programs?

7. How would you argue in favor of a privately run postal service? How would you argue against this idea?

suggested readings

BEKKE, Hans, *et al.* Eds. *Civil Service Systems in Comparative Perspective.* Bloomington, Ind.: Indiana University Press, 1996. This excellent collection of papers dealing with different civil service systems puts the U.S. bureaucracy in perspective relative to the rest of the world. Some of the papers present a history of civil service systems in other countries. This is an important work on a subject that touches all of us.

COOK, Brian J. *Bureaucracy and Self-Government: Reconsidering the Role of Public Administration in American Politics.* Baltimore: Johns Hopkins University Press, 1996. The author examines the tension between two traditional perceptions of the bureaucracy in American political life. One perception views bureaucrats as implementers of the orders given by elected officials. The other perception views bureaucrats as policymakers.

HOWARD, Philip K. *The Death of Common Sense: How Law Is Suffocating America.* New York: Warner Books, 1996. The author offers an extremely critical appraisal of the American bureaucracy, contending that we have created a nightmarish system of regulations implemented by ineffective and often corrupt bureaucrats. He argues that the regulatory system has worsened, not improved, the problems it was designed to solve—such as unsafe working conditions, environmental degradation, and the like. The strength of the book lies not in the author's proposed solutions to the problems he sees but in the many examples he offers concerning the ills of the bureaucracy.

LIGHT, Paul C. *The True Size of Government.* Washington, D.C.: Brookings Institution Press, 1999. Light's research on the number of workers in the "shadow government" (that contract to perform government services) indicates how large the federal government really is. He offers several suggestions for how the government can better manage this work force that it has built over the last half-century.

OSBORNE, David, and Peter Plastrik. *Banishing Bureaucracy: The Five Strategies for Reinventing Government.* Reading, Mass.: Addison-Wesley, 1997. In this book, David Osborne (co-author of *Reinventing Government,* a 1992 publication that put bureaucratic reform high on the popular agenda) and journalist Peter Plastrik argue that the government should trim all nonessential functions of the bureaucracy and find alternative ways, such as through privatization and contracting out, to handle the remaining functions.

politics on the web

The goal of the National Performance Review (NPR) is to "reinvent" the federal government—that is, transform it into a government that "works better and costs less." One way to keep abreast of this attempt is to go to

http://www.npr.gov

Once on this page, you can go to The Highlights Library, The News Room, The Customer Service Page, and The Reports Feature.

To learn more about the mission of the General Services Administration (GSA) and its role in managing the federal bureaucracy, go to

http://www.gsa.gov

Federal World is a government site that contains links to numerous federal agencies and government information. You can find this site at

http://www.fedworld.gov

Another source for information on federal agencies is the Federal Web Locator, which allows you to search for agency names and find links to information about the bureaucracy. You can find the locator at

http://www.law.vill.edu/Fed-Agency/fedwebloc.html

If you want to get an idea of what federal agencies are putting on the Web, you can go to the Department of Commerce's Web site at

http://www.doc.gov

The *Federal Register,* which is the official publication for executive branch documents, including the orders, notices, and rules of all federal administrative agencies, is online at

http://www.gpo.ucop.edu/search/fedfld.html

The *United States Government Manual* contains information on the functions, organization, and administrators of every federal department. You can now access the most recent edition of the manual online at

http://www.gpo.ucop.edu/catalog/govman.html

using web resources

The Project on Government Oversight (POGO) is a nonpartisan, nonprofit government watchdog. Its mission is "to investigate, expose, and remedy abuses of power, mismanagement, and government subservience to special interests by the federal government." Access POGO's Web site at

http://www.pogo.org

1. What are three issues of special interest to POGO?

2. Select one of the categories listed on the left side of the main page. What are POGO's criticisms of the industry? Do you find its complaints compelling?

3. How would you become an intern for POGO?

notes

1. This definition follows the classical model of bureaucracy put forth by German sociologist Max Weber. See Max Weber, *Theory of Social and Economic Organization,* Talcott Parsons, ed. (New York: Oxford University Press, 1974).

2. It should be noted that although the president is technically the head of the bureaucracy, the president cannot always control the bureaucracy—as you will read later in this chapter.

3. Thomas Sowell, "A Dishonest Slogan," *Forbes,* January 30, 1995, p. 81.

4. Stephen Barr, "Downsizing's Blurry Bottom Line: The Government Is Shrinking, but Is It Really More Efficient?" *The Washington Post,* Weekly Edition, September 30–October 6, 1996, p. 34.

5. Nick Gillespie, "Upside Downsizing," *Reason,* January 1997, p. 15.

6. Paul C. Light, *The True Size of Government* (Washington, D.C.: Brookings Institution Press, 1999).

7. "The Political Hacks' Ultimate Fantasy Book," *Fortune,* March 3, 1997, p. 46.

8. Anne B. Fisher, "One Welfare Program That Won't Die," *Fortune,* November 27, 1995, p. 40.

9. As quoted in Bob Norton, "Why Federal Programs Won't Die," *Fortune,* August 21, 1995, p. 35.

10. Douglas Stanglin, "What Are You Trying to Do? A New Law Demands That Bureaucrats Rethink Their Missions," *U.S. News & World Report,* March 3, 1997, pp. 36–37.

11. John Carey, "2002, a Space Oddity—Or Just Pork Pie in the Sky?" *Business Week,* August 15, 1994, p. 94.

12. Douglas Stanglin, "Don't Return to Sender: Can the Postal Service Change—And Still Deliver Your Mail for Thirty-two Cents?" *U.S. News & World Report,* October 7, 1996, p. 49.

13. Aaron Steelman, "Term Limits and the Republican Congress: The Case Strengthens," Cato Institute Briefing Paper No. 41, October 28, 1998.

THE JUDICIARY

EQUAL JUSTICE

Contents

Protecting the Accused: Has the Supreme Court Gone Too Far?

Through a series of decisions, particularly in the 1960s, the United States Supreme Court has definitely expanded the rights of the accused. In 1968, the Court granted the right to a jury trial in all criminal cases in which the penalty for a conviction is more than six months' imprisonment.[1] In a landmark decision in *Gideon v. Wainwright*[2] (1963), the Court provided that criminal defendants have a right to an attorney—and a right to have one provided for them at government expense if they cannot afford an attorney. In another landmark case, *Miranda v. Arizona*[3] (1966), the Supreme Court held that all suspects in criminal cases have a right to be informed of their constitutional rights, including the right to remain silent, the right to talk to a lawyer before answering questions, and the right to have counsel present during questioning.

The Supreme Court also developed the *exclusionary rule* in the interests of protecting accused persons. Under this rule, any evidence obtained from an illegal search and seizure is excluded (cannot be admitted at trial), even though it clearly indicates the guilt of the defendant. This principle was strengthened in the case of *Mapp v. Ohio*[4] (1961), in which the Court declared that "all evidence obtained by searches and seizures in violation of the Constitution is . . . inadmissible in a state court."

In these and other decisions, the Supreme Court has gone far to defend the constitutional rights of the individual against the immense power of the state in criminal proceedings. The question is, has it gone too far?

Yes, the Supreme Court Has Gone Too Far

Those who believe that the Supreme Court has gone too far in protecting the rights of the accused point out that the increase in crime in the United States since World War II has paralleled the increase in the rights of the accused. They argue that protecting these rights ties the hands of the police and public prosecutors, thereby reducing the effectiveness of the government's war against crime.

Furthermore, they argue that because the rights of the accused have been so well publicized, actual and potential criminals are aware of their ability to get off on a "technicality" (such as a procedural error) and thus are on the watch for any improper action on the part of law enforcement personnel. Consequently, the expected cost of committing crimes has fallen, leading to more crime.

By giving such extensive rights and protections to accused persons, the Supreme Court has placed the rights of criminal suspects above the rights of society as a whole. As a result, say the Court's critics, the scales of justice are out of balance. It's time for the Court to restore this balance by interpreting the Constitution less expansively where criminal rights are concerned.

No, the Supreme Court Has Not Gone Too Far

Others argue that the trend toward increasing the rights of accused persons was reversed in the 1980s, and now the rights of the accused, particularly under the exclusionary rule, are actually being jeopardized. For example, in an important case in 1984, *United States v. Leon*,[5] the Supreme Court allowed a conviction to stand even though a judge had issued a warrant without firmly establishing probable cause. In this case, the Court established the *good faith exception* to the exclusionary rule. The majority on the Court concluded that the exclusionary rule is not a right, but a remedy justified only by its ability to deter illegal police conduct. As long as the police are acting in good faith, there is little problem.

Additionally, the Supreme Court has slowly eroded the *Miranda* ruling through other decisions, as discussed in Chapter 4. Today, confessions are admissible even without clear evidence that they were voluntary. Even in cases that are not tried in federal court, confessions by criminal suspects who have not been fully informed of their legal rights may be taken into consideration. The Court has also ruled that when "public safety" requires action, police can interrogate a suspect before advising that person of his or her right to remain silent.[6]

Where Do You Stand?

1. In your opinion, has the Supreme Court gone too far in protecting the rights of accused persons?

2. Do you think that Supreme Court decisions have any effect on the crime rate?

On the Web

For examples of how constitutional protections apply in criminal cases, go to **http://courttv.com**.

Go to CD-ROM

JUDICIARY ● The courts; one of the three branches of the federal government in the United States.

COMMON LAW ● The body of law developed from judicial decisions in English and U.S. courts, not attributable to a legislature.

PRECEDENT ● A court decision that furnishes an example or authority for deciding subsequent cases involving identical or similar facts and legal issues.

STARE DECISIS ● A common law doctrine under which judges normally are obligated to follow the precedents established by prior court decisions.

Introduction

"The Judicial Department comes home in its effects to every man's fireside: it passes on his property, his reputation, his life, his all." So stated John Marshall, chief justice[7] of the United States Supreme Court from 1801 to 1835. If you reflect for a moment on these words, you will realize their truth. A single Supreme Court decision can affect the lives of millions of Americans. For example, in 1954 the Supreme Court held that state laws upholding racial segregation in public schools violated the Fourteenth Amendment and were thus invalid. As a result, the lives of millions of Americans were directly affected. Any Supreme Court decision concerning a constitutional right or liberty can have a widespread impact—as indicated in the chapter-opening feature.

When the Supreme Court renders an opinion on how the Constitution is to be interpreted, it is, necessarily, making policy on a national level. The exercise of policymaking powers always generates controversy, and this is certainly true with respect to today's courts, as you will read in this chapter. To understand the nature of this controversy, however, you need to first understand how the **judiciary** (the courts) functions in this country. We begin by looking at the origins and sources of American law. We then examine the federal (national) court system, at the apex of which is the United States Supreme Court.

The Origins and Sources of American Law

The American colonists brought with them the legal system that had developed in England over hundreds of years. To understand how the American legal system operates, we thus need to go back in time to the early English courts and the traditions they established.

THE COMMON LAW TRADITION

After the Normans conquered England in 1066, William the Conqueror and his successors began the process of unifying the country under their rule. One of the means they used to this end was the establishment of the "king's courts," or *curiae regis*. Before the Norman Conquest, disputes had been settled according to the local legal customs and traditions in various regions of the country. The law developed in the king's courts applied to the country as a whole. What evolved in these courts was the beginning of the **common law**—a body of general rules prescribing social conduct that was applied throughout the entire English realm.

The Rule of Precedent

The early English courts developed the common law rules from the principles underlying judges' decisions in actual legal controversies. Judges attempted to be consistent, and whenever possible, they based their decisions on the principles applied in earlier cases. They sought to decide similar cases in a similar way and considered new cases with care, because they knew that their decisions would make new law. Each interpretation became part of the law on the subject and served as a legal **precedent**—that is, a decision that furnished an example or authority for deciding subsequent cases involving similar legal principles or facts.

The practice of deciding new cases with reference to former decisions, or precedents, eventually became a cornerstone of the English and American judicial systems. The practice forms a doctrine called *stare decisis*[8] ("to stand on decided cases"). Under this doctrine, judges are

PRIMARY SOURCE OF LAW ● A source of law that establishes the law. Primary sources of law include constitutions, statutes, administrative agency rules and regulations, and decisions rendered by the courts.

CONSTITUTIONAL LAW ● Law based on the U.S. Constitution and the constitutions of the various states.

STATUTORY LAW ● The body of law enacted by legislatures (as opposed to constitutional law, administrative law, or case law).

obligated to follow the precedents established in their jurisdictions. For example, if the Supreme Court of Georgia holds that a state law requiring political candidates to pass drug tests is unconstitutional, that decision will control the outcome of future cases on that issue brought before the state courts in Georgia. Similarly, a decision on a given issue by the United States Supreme Court (the nation's highest court) is binding on all inferior courts. For example, if the Georgia case on drug testing is appealed to the Supreme Court and the Court agrees that the Georgia law is unconstitutional, the high court's ruling will be binding on *all* courts in the United States. In other words, similar drug-testing laws in other states would be invalid and unenforceable.

Departures from Precedent

Sometimes a court will depart from the rule of precedent if it decides that a precedent is simply incorrect or that technological or social changes have rendered the precedent inapplicable. Cases that overturn precedent often receive a great deal of publicity. For example, in 1954, in *Brown v. Board of Education of Topeka*,[9] the United States Supreme Court expressly overturned precedent when it concluded that separate educational facilities for African Americans, which had been upheld as constitutional in numerous prior cases under the "separate but equal" doctrine[10] (see Chapter 5), were inherently unequal and violated the equal protection clause. The Supreme Court's departure from precedent in *Brown* received a tremendous amount of publicity as people began to realize the political and social ramifications of this change in the law.

SOURCES OF AMERICAN LAW

In any governmental system, the primary function of the courts is to interpret and apply the law. In the United States, the courts interpret and apply numerous sources of law when deciding cases. We look here only at the **primary sources of law**—that is, sources that *establish* the law—and the relative priority of these sources when particular laws come into conflict.

Constitutional Law

The U.S. government and each of the fifty states have separate written constitutions that set forth the general organization, powers, and limits of their respective governments. **Constitutional law** consists of the rights and duties set forth in these constitutions.

The U.S. Constitution is the supreme law of the land. As such, it is the basis of all law in the United States. Any law that violates the Constitution is invalid and unenforceable. Because of its paramount importance in the American legal system, the complete text of the U.S. Constitution is found in Appendix A.

The Tenth Amendment to the U.S. Constitution reserves to the states and to the people all powers not granted to the federal government. Each state in the union has its own constitution. Unless they conflict with the U.S. Constitution or a federal law, state constitutions are supreme within the borders of their respective states.

Statutory Law

Statutes enacted by legislative bodies at any level of government make up another source of law, which is generally referred to as **statutory law.** Federal statutes—laws enacted by the U.S. Congress—apply to all of the states. State statutes—laws enacted by state legislatures—apply only within the state that enacted the law. Any state statute that conflicts with the U.S. Constitution, with federal laws enacted by Congress, or with the state's constitution will be deemed invalid and will not be enforced. Statutory law also includes the ordinances (such as local zoning or housing-construction

ADMINISTRATIVE LAW ● The body of law created by administrative agencies (in the form of rules, regulations, orders, and decisions) in order to carry out their duties and responsibilities.

ADMINISTRATIVE AGENCY ● A federal or state government agency established to perform a specific function. Administrative agencies are authorized by legislative acts to make and enforce rules to administer and enforce the acts.

ADMINISTRATIVE LAW JUDGE ● One who presides over an administrative agency hearing and who has the power to conduct legal hearings and make legal determinations.

CASE LAW ● The rules of law announced in court decisions. Case law includes the aggregate of reported cases that interpret judicial precedents, statutes, regulations, and constitutional provisions.

CIVIL LAW ● The branch of law that spells out the duties that individuals in society owe to other persons or to their governments, excluding the duty not to commit crimes.

CRIMINAL LAW ● The branch of law that defines and governs actions that constitute crimes. Generally, criminal law has to do with wrongful actions committed against society for which society demands redress.

laws) passed by cities and counties, none of which can violate the U.S. Constitution, the relevant state constitution, or any existing federal or state laws.

Administrative Law

Another important source of American law consists of **administrative law**—the rules, orders, and decisions of administrative agencies. At the federal level, Congress creates **administrative agencies,** such as the Food and Drug Administration or the Environmental Protection Agency, to perform specific functions. Typically, when Congress establishes an agency, it authorizes the agency to create rules that have the force of law and to enforce those rules by bringing legal actions against violators. Sometimes, these actions involve trial-like proceedings before an **administrative law judge,** who issues a decision in the matter.

As you will read in Chapter 18, the national government extensively regulates the economic life of this nation. Rules issued by various administrative agencies now affect virtually every aspect of our economy. For example, almost all of a business's operations, including the firm's capital structure and financing, its hiring and firing procedures, its relations with employees and unions, and the way it manufactures and markets its products, are subject to government regulation.

Administrative agencies exist at the state and local level as well. Commonly, state agencies are created that parallel federal agencies. Just as federal statutes take precedence over conflicting state statutes, federal agency regulations take precedence over conflicting state regulations.

Case Law

As is evident from the discussion of the common law tradition, another basic source of American law consists of the rules of law announced in court decisions, or **case law.** These rules of law include interpretations of constitutional provisions, of statutes enacted by legislatures, and of regulations issued by administrative agencies. Thus, even though a legislature passes a law to govern a certain area, how that law is interpreted and applied depends on the courts. The importance of case law, or judge-made law, is one of the distinguishing characteristics of the common law tradition. (See the feature on the following page entitled *Comparative Politics: Legal Systems of the World* for a discussion of another legal system that is used in many other countries.)

CIVIL LAW AND CRIMINAL LAW

All of the sources of law just discussed can be classified in other ways as well. One of the most significant classification systems divides all law into two categories: civil law and criminal law. **Civil law** spells out the duties that individuals in society owe to other persons or to their governments, excluding the duty not to commit crimes. Typically, in a civil case, a private party sues another private party (although the government can also sue a party for a civil law violation). The object of a civil lawsuit is to make the defendant—the person being sued—comply with a legal duty (such as a contractual promise) or pay money damages for failing to comply with that duty.

Criminal law, in contrast, has to do with wrongs committed against the public as a whole. Criminal acts are prohibited by local, state, or federal government statutes. Thus, criminal defendants are prosecuted by public officials, such as a district attorney (D.A.), on behalf of the government, not by their victims or other private parties. In a criminal case, the government seeks to impose a penalty (fines and/or imprisonment) on a person who has violated a criminal law. When someone robs a convenience store, that person has committed a crime and, if caught and proved guilty, will normally be in prison for some period of time.

comparative politics

Legal Systems of the World

Legal systems, of course, vary from country to country, because each country's law reflects the interests, customs, activities, and values that are unique to that nation's culture. Even though the laws and legal systems of various countries differ substantially, broad similarities do exist.

Basically, there are two legal systems in today's world. One of these systems is the common law system of England and the United States, which we have already discussed. The other system is based on Roman civil law, or "code law." The term *civil law,* as used here, refers not to civil as opposed to criminal law but to codified law—an ordered grouping of legal principles enacted into law by a legislature or governing body. In a *civil law system,* the primary source of law is a statutory code, and case precedents are not judicially binding, as they normally are in a common law system. Although judges in a civil law system commonly refer to previous decisions as sources of legal guidance, they are not bound by precedent; in other words, the doctrine of *stare decisis* does not apply.

Generally, those countries that were once colonies of Great Britain retained their English common law heritage after they achieved their independence. Similarly, the civil law system, which is followed in most of the continental European countries, was retained in the Latin American, African, and Asian countries that were once colonies of the continental European nations. Japan and South Africa also have civil law systems, and ingredients of the civil law system are found in the Islamic courts of predominantly Muslim countries. In the United States, the state of Louisiana, because of its historical ties to France, has in part a civil law system. The legal systems of Puerto Rico, Québec, and Scotland are similarly characterized as having elements of the civil law system.

For Critical Analysis

How might American laws and interpretations of them be different if the United States had a civil law system?

BASIC JUDICIAL REQUIREMENTS

A court cannot decide just any issue at any time. Before any court can hear and decide a case, specific requirements must be met. To a certain extent, these requirements act as restraints on the judiciary because they limit the types of cases that courts can hear and decide. Courts also have procedural requirements that frame the judicial process.

Jurisdiction

In Latin, *juris* means "law," and *diction* means "to speak." Thus, **jurisdiction** literally refers to the power "to speak the law." Jurisdiction applies either to the geographical area in which a court has the right and power to decide cases, or to the right and power of a court to decide matters concerning certain persons, property, or subject matter. Before any court can hear a case, it must have jurisdiction over the person against whom the suit is brought, the property involved in the suit, and the subject matter.

A state trial court (a **trial court** is, as the term implies, a court in which a trial is held and testimony taken), for example, usually has jurisdictional authority over the residents of a particular area of the state, such as a county or district. A state's highest court (often called the state supreme court)[11] has jurisdictional authority over all residents within the state. In some cases, if an individual has committed an offense such as

JURISDICTION ● The authority of a court to hear and decide a particular case.

TRIAL COURT ● A court in which trials are held and testimony taken.

Most cases start in some type of trial court, where testimony is taken and other evidence evaluated. Trial courts exist in all of the fifty state court systems. In the federal court system, trial courts are called district courts.

causing an automobile injury or selling defective goods within the state, the court can exercise jurisdiction even if the individual is a resident of another state. State courts can also exercise jurisdiction over people who do business within the state. A New York company that distributes its products in California, for example, can be sued by a California resident in a California state court.

Because the federal (national) government is a government of limited powers, the jurisdiction of the federal courts is limited. Article III, Section 2, of the Constitution states that the federal courts can exercise jurisdiction over all cases "arising under this Constitution, the Laws of the United States, and Treaties made, or which shall be made, under their Authority." Whenever a case involves a claim based, at least in part, on the U.S. Constitution, a treaty, or a federal law, a **federal question** arises. Any lawsuit involving a federal question can originate in a federal court.

Federal courts can also exercise jurisdiction over cases involving **diversity of citizenship.** Such cases may arise when the parties in a lawsuit live in different states or when one of the parties is a foreign government or a foreign citizen. Before a federal court can take jurisdiction in a diversity case, the amount in controversy must be more than $75,000.

Standing to Sue

To bring a lawsuit before a court, a person must have **standing to sue,** or a sufficient "stake" in the matter to justify bringing a suit. Thus, the party bringing the suit must have suffered a harm or been threatened with a harm by the action at issue, and the issue must be justiciable. A **justiciable[12] controversy** is one that is real and substantial, as opposed to hypothetical or academic.

The requirement of standing clearly limits the issues that can be decided by the courts. For example, suppose that an environmental interest group sues a company for polluting a local stream in violation of federal law. Even if the company is, in fact, violating federal law, the group cannot sue the firm unless it can produce evidence that its members have actually been harmed, or are about to be harmed, by the polluting activity.

Consider another example. After Congress passed the Line Item Veto Act of 1996 (see Chapter 14), six members of Congress brought a suit challenging the constitutionality of the act. They contended that the act gave the president powers that were intended for Congress, thus diluting their votes. When the case reached the Supreme Court, the Court did not even reach

FEDERAL QUESTION ● A question that pertains to the U.S. Constitution, acts of Congress, or treaties. A federal question provides a basis for federal court jurisdiction.

DIVERSITY OF CITIZENSHIP ● A basis for federal court jurisdiction over a lawsuit that arises when (1) the parties in the lawsuit live in different states or when one of the parties is a foreign government or a foreign citizen, and (2) the amount in controversy is more than $75,000.

STANDING TO SUE ● The requirement that an individual must have a sufficient stake in a controversy before he or she can bring a lawsuit. The party bringing the suit must demonstrate that he or she has either been harmed or been threatened with a harm.

JUSTICIABLE CONTROVERSY ● A controversy that is not hypothetical or academic but real and substantial; a requirement that must be satisfied before a court will hear a case.

the constitutionality issue. Why not? In the eyes of the Court, the challengers had not met the threshold requirement of standing. According to the Court, the injury they asserted was "wholly abstract" and would remain so until the president actually used the line-item veto.[13] (In a case brought *after* the president had used the line-item veto, the Supreme Court did address the constitutionality of the issue. As noted in Chapter 14, the Court invalidated the act because the procedures provided for in the act are not authorized by the Constitution.)

Court Procedures

Both the federal and the state courts have established procedural rules that apply in all cases. These procedures are designed to protect the rights and interests of the parties, ensure that the litigation proceeds in a fair and orderly manner, and identify the issues that must be decided by the court—thus saving court time and costs. Different procedural rules apply in criminal and civil cases. Generally, criminal procedural rules attempt to ensure that defendants are not deprived of their constitutional rights.

Parties involved in civil or criminal cases must comply with court procedural rules or risk being held in contempt of court. A party who is held in contempt of court can be fined, taken into custody, or both. A court must take care to ensure that the parties—and the court itself—comply with procedural requirements. Procedural errors often serve as grounds for a mistrial or for appealing the court's decision to a higher tribunal.

The Federal Court System

The federal court system is a three-tiered model consisting of U.S. district (trial) courts, U.S. courts of appeals, and the United States Supreme Court. Figure 16–1 shows the organization of the federal court system. (Not shown in the figure are certain "secret" courts—see the feature *A Question of Ethics: Do National Security Interests Justify Secret Courts?*)

Bear in mind that the federal courts constitute only one of the fifty-two court systems in the United States. Each of the fifty states has its own court system, as does the District of Columbia. No two state court systems are exactly the same, but generally each state has different levels, or tiers, of courts, just as the federal system does. Generally, state courts deal with questions of state law, and the decisions of a state's highest court on mat-

Figure 16–1
The Organization
of the Federal Court System

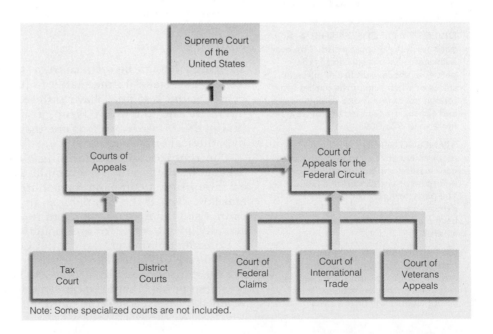

Note: Some specialized courts are not included.

a question of ethics

Do National Security Interests Justify Secret Courts?

In 1996, Congress passed the Anti-Terrorism Act, which was introduced into Congress shortly after the 1995 bombing of the Alfred P. Murrah Federal Building in Oklahoma City. In the debate over the act, the media often overlooked one provision: the establishment of an alien "removal court" to hear evidence against suspected "alien terrorists."

Secret Proceedings

Under the act, Justice Department officials need not abide by the criminal procedures that normally apply in criminal cases. Rather, they can argue deportation cases in a secret court. If the judges agree that the prosecution has established probable cause for deportation, then they issue an order that allows the government to seek a special public deportation proceeding in a U.S. district court.

At that point, the defendant learns of the action being taken against her or him and is given a summary of the evidence presented in the secret court. The defendant has no access to the actual documents or other evidence on which the government's charge is based. Even in the district court, part of the proceedings may not be public. A judge can conduct a secret review of whatever classified information the government prosecutor thinks that the judge can see. The deportee and her or his attorney do not have access to this information.

Why all this secrecy? The Justice Department claims that it is necessary to protect sensitive, classified information. The department argues that publicly disclosing key evidence, as normal courts require, could expose and endanger the sources of government intelligence.

The Secret FISA Court

The alien removal court is not the nation's first secret court. The Foreign Intelligence Surveillance Act (FISA) passed by Congress in 1978 established a court, known as the FISA court, to approve, in secret, warrants for the surveillance of suspected spies. If any evidence gathered as a result of the surveillance is used for prosecution, the government may prevent the defendant from having access to it. If the FISA court denies a request for a warrant, the government can appeal to a FISA court of review, but this higher FISA court has never once had to convene: the FISA court has approved all of the nearly 9,000 surveillance requests that the government has submitted.

Are Secret Courts Constitutional?

Civil liberties activists charge that these secret courts carve out a *de facto* national security exception to both the Fourth Amendment's prohibition of warrantless surveillance and the Fifth Amendment's guarantee of due process. Although the Supreme Court has never ruled on the constitutionality of FISA, the FISA court is probably consti-

tutional. There are numerous legal distinctions that separate aliens from citizens and national security investigations from law enforcement investigations.

What worries civil libertarians is that the secret courts may lead to abuses by intelligence agencies. Given the record of the FISA court, its judges do not seem to be able to turn down government requests. Because the public does not have access to the proceedings in the secret courts, there are few guarantees that they are applying a sufficiently rigorous standard of scrutiny to government applications. Only Justice Department prosecutors and the FISA judges are in a position to know what is truly happening behind the closed door of the FISA court.

The establishment of secret courts represents a policy decision, and ultimately any policy decision has ethical implications. The policy choice here trades off individual rights in the interests of national security and the welfare of all Americans. The Justice Department claims that this trade-off is necessary, because the alternative—allowing spies and terrorists to endanger national security and American lives—would be even worse.

For Critical Analysis

In your opinion, should Americans tolerate secret courts under any circumstances? Why or why not?

ters of state law are normally final. If a federal question is involved, however, a decision of a state supreme court may be appealed to the United States Supreme Court.

U.S. DISTRICT COURTS

On the lowest tier of the federal court system are the U.S. district courts, or federal trial courts. These are the courts in which cases involving federal laws begin, and the cases are decided by a judge or a jury (if it is a jury

APPELLATE COURT ● A court having appellate jurisdiction that normally does not hear evidence or testimony but reviews the transcript of the trial court's proceedings, other records relating to the case, and the attorneys' respective arguments as to why the trial court's decision should or should not stand.

trial). There is at least one federal district court in every state, and there is one in the District of Columbia. The number of judicial districts varies over time, primarily owing to population changes and corresponding caseloads. Currently, there are ninety-four judicial districts; Figure 16–2 shows their geographical boundaries. The federal system also includes other trial courts, such as the Court of International Trade and others shown in Figure 16–1. These courts have limited, or specialized, subject-matter jurisdiction; that is, they can exercise authority only over certain subjects.

U.S. COURTS OF APPEALS

On the middle tier of the federal court system are the U.S. courts of appeals. Courts of appeals, or **appellate courts,** do not hear evidence or testimony. Rather, an appellate court reviews the transcript of the trial court's proceedings, other records relating to the case, and the attorneys' respective arguments as to why the trial court's decision should or should not stand. In contrast to a trial court, where normally a single judge presides, an appellate court consists of a panel of three or more judges. The task of the appellate court is to determine whether the trial court erred in applying the law to the facts and issues involved in a particular case.

There are thirteen U.S. courts of appeals in the United States. The courts of appeals for twelve of the circuits, including the Court of Appeals for the D.C. Circuit, hear appeals from the U.S. district courts located within their respective judicial circuits (see Figure 16–2). Appeals from decisions made by federal administrative agencies, such as the Federal Trade Commission, may also be made to the U.S. courts of appeals. The Court of Appeals for

**Figure 16–2
U.S. Courts of Appeals
and U.S. District Courts**

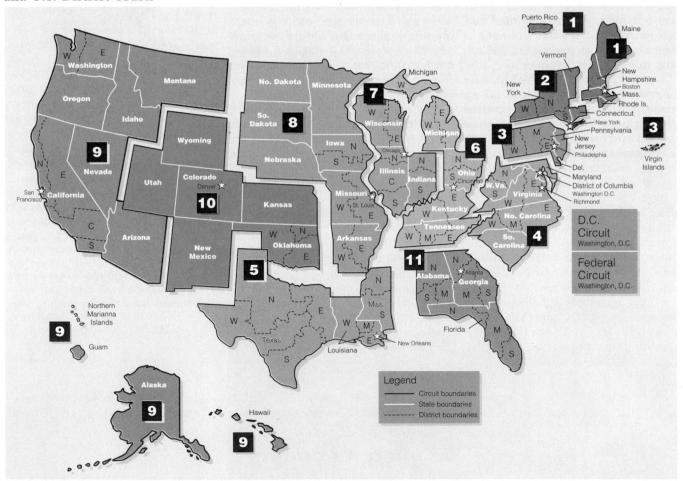

SOURCE: Administrative Office of The United States Courts, January 1983.

WRIT OF *CERTIORARI* ● An order from a higher court asking a lower court for the record of a case.

the Federal Circuit has national jurisdiction over certain types of cases, such as those concerning patent law and some claims against the national government.

The decisions of the federal appellate courts may be appealed to the United States Supreme Court. If a decision is not appealed, or if the high court declines to review the case, the appellate court's decision is final.

THE UNITED STATES SUPREME COURT

The highest level of the three-tiered model of the federal court system is the United States Supreme Court. According to Article III of the U.S. Constitution, there is only one national Supreme Court. Congress is empowered to create additional ("inferior") courts as it deems necessary. The inferior courts that Congress has created include the second tier in our model—the U.S. courts of appeals—as well as the district courts and any other courts of limited, or specialized, jurisdiction.

The United States Supreme Court consists of nine justices—a chief justice and eight associate justices—although that number is not mandated by the Constitution. The Supreme Court has original, or trial, jurisdiction only in rare instances (set forth in Article III, Section 2). In other words, only rarely does a case originate at the Supreme Court level. Most of the Court's work is as an appellate court. The Supreme Court has appellate authority over cases decided by the U.S. courts of appeals, as well as over some cases decided in the state courts when federal questions are at issue.

Which Cases Reach the Supreme Court?

There is no absolute right to appeal to the United States Supreme Court. Although thousands of cases are filed with the Supreme Court each year, on average the Court hears fewer than one hundred. As Figure 16–3 shows, the number of cases heard by the Court each year has declined significantly since the early 1980s. In large part, this is due to the Court's raising of its standards for accepting cases in recent years.

To bring a case before the Supreme Court, a party may request that the Court issue a **writ of *certiorari*,**[14] popularly called "cert.," which is an order that the Supreme Court issues to a lower court requesting the latter to send it the record of the case in question. Parties can petition the Supreme Court to issue a writ of *certiorari*, but whether the Court will do so is entirely within its discretion. The Court will not issue a writ unless at least four of the nine justices approve. In no instance is the Court required to issue a writ of *certiorari*.[15]

Most petitions for writs of *certiorari* are denied. A denial is not a decision on the merits of a case, nor does it indicate that the Court agrees with a lower court's opinion. Furthermore, the denial of a writ has no value as a precedent. A denial simply means that the decision of the lower court remains the law within that court's jurisdiction.

Figure 16–3
The Number of Supreme Court Opinions
During the 1952 term (the term beginning in October 1952 and ending in June 1953), the Supreme Court issued 65 decisions. The number of decisions peaked at 151 in the 1982 term and has been declining more or less steadily ever since.

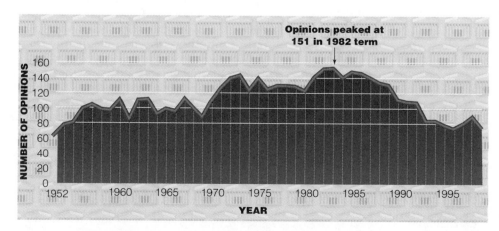

This is a photo of the Supreme Court chamber. In 1935, the Court moved from its quarters in the Capitol building to its own building, constructed with white Vermont marble. No television cameras have been allowed inside the Supreme Court chamber during the presentation of an actual case.

Typically, the petitions granted by the Court involve cases that raise important policy issues that need to be addressed. In recent years, for example, the Court has heard cases involving such pressing issues as whether the constitutional right to privacy included a right to commit assisted suicide and whether federal attempts to curb indecent expression on the Internet went too far in constraining the right to free speech. Also, if the lower courts have rendered conflicting opinions on an important issue, the Supreme Court may review a case involving that issue to define the law on the matter.

Supreme Court Opinions

Like all appellate courts, the United States Supreme Court normally does not hear any evidence. The Court's decision in a particular case is based on the written record of the case and the written arguments (legal briefs) that the attorneys submit. The attorneys can also present **oral arguments**—arguments presented in person rather than on paper—to the Court, after which the justices discuss the case in **conference.** The conference is strictly private—only the justices are allowed in the room.

When the Court has reached a decision, the chief justice, if in the majority, assigns the task of writing the Court's **opinion** to one of the justices. When the chief justice is not in the majority, the most senior justice voting with the majority assigns the writing of the Court's opinion. The opinion outlines the reasons for the Court's decision, the rules of law that apply, and the judgment.

Often, one or more justices who agree with the Court's decision may do so for different reasons than those outlined in the majority opinion. These justices may write **concurring opinions,** setting forth their own legal reasoning on the issue. Frequently, one or more justices disagree with the Court's conclusion. These justices may write **dissenting opinions,** outlining the reasons why they feel the majority erred in arriving at its decision. Although a dissenting opinion does not affect the outcome of the case before the Court, it may be important later. In a subsequent case concerning the same issue, a jurist or attorney may use the legal reasoning in the dissenting opinion as the basis for an argument to reverse the previous decision and establish a new precedent.

ORAL ARGUMENT ● An argument presented to a judge in person by an attorney on behalf of his or her client.

CONFERENCE ● In regard to the Supreme Court, a private meeting of the justices in which they present their arguments with respect to a case under consideration.

OPINION ● A written statement by a court expressing the reasons for its decision in a case.

CONCURRING OPINION ● A statement written by a judge or justice who agrees (concurs) with the court's decision, but for reasons different from those in the majority opinion.

DISSENTING OPINION ● A written opinion by a judge or justice who disagrees with the majority opinion.

Federal Judicial Appointments

Unlike state court judges, who are often elected, all federal judges are appointed. Article II, Section 2, of the Constitution authorizes the president to appoint the justices of the Supreme Court with the advice and consent of the Senate. Laws enacted by Congress provide that the same procedure be used for appointing judges to the lower federal courts as well. The process of nominating and confirming federal judges, especially Supreme Court justices, often involves political debate and controversy (see the discussion of ideology and judicial appointments later in the chapter).

Federal judges receive lifetime appointments (because under Article III of the Constitution they "hold their Offices during good Behaviour"). Federal judges may be removed from office through the impeachment process, but such proceedings are extremely rare and are usually undertaken only if a judge engages in blatantly illegal conduct, such as bribery. In the history of this nation, only thirteen federal judges have been impeached, seven of whom were removed from office. Normally, federal judges serve until they resign, retire, or die.

Although the Constitution sets no specific qualifications for those who serve on the Supreme Court, all who have done so share one characteristic: all have been attorneys. The backgrounds of the Supreme Court justices have been far from typical of the characteristics of the American public as a whole. Table 16–1 on the next page summarizes the backgrounds of all of the 108 Supreme Court justices to 1999.

THE NOMINATION PROCESS

The president receives suggestions and recommendations as to potential nominees for Supreme Court positions from various sources, including the Justice Department, senators, other judges, the candidates themselves, state political leaders, bar associations, and other interest groups. After selecting a nominee, the president submits his or her name to the Senate for approval. The Senate Judiciary Committee then holds hearings and makes its recommendation to the Senate, where it takes a majority vote to confirm the nomination.

When appointing judges to the district courts (and, to a lesser extent, the courts of appeals), the usual practice is to let the senator or senators of the president's political party from the state in which there is a vacancy recommend nominees to the presidential administration.

CONFIRMATION OR REJECTION BY THE SENATE

The president's nominations are not always confirmed. In fact, almost 20 percent of presidential nominations for the Supreme Court have been either rejected or not acted on by the Senate. Many bitter battles over Supreme Court appointments have ensued when the Senate and the president have disagreed on political issues.

From 1893 until 1968, the Senate rejected only three Court nominees. From 1968 through 1986, however, two presidential nominees to the highest court were rejected; both were appointed by President Richard Nixon and were rejected over questions about their conservative attitudes, among other things. In addition, one of President Lyndon Johnson's nominations was not acted on, and his nomination of Abe Fortas for chief justice in 1968 was withdrawn after a question arose involving Fortas's acceptance of $15,000 for teaching a summer college course. Another dispute about Fortas's finances led to his resignation in 1969.

Two of President Ronald Reagan's nominees to the Supreme Court failed. In 1987, the Senate rejected Robert Bork, who faced sometimes hostile questioning about his views of the Constitution during the confirmation hearings. Next, Reagan nominated Douglas Ginsburg, who ultimately

Table 16-1

Background of Supreme Court Justices to 1999

	NUMBER OF JUSTICES (108 = TOTAL)
Occupational Position before Appointment	
Private legal practice	25
State judgeship	21
Federal judgeship	28
U.S. attorney general	7
Deputy or assistant U.S. attorney general	2
U.S. solicitor general	2
U.S. senator	6
U.S. representative	2
State governor	3
Federal executive post	9
Other	3
Religious Background	
Protestant	83
Roman Catholic	11
Jewish	6
Unitarian	7
No religious affiliation	1
Age on Appointment	
Under 40	5
41–50	31
51–60	58
61–70	14
Political Party Affiliation	
Federalist (to 1835)	13
Democratic Republican (to 1828)	7
Whig (to 1861)	1
Democrat	44
Republican	42
Independent	1
Educational Background	
College graduate	92
Not a college graduate	16
Gender	
Male	106
Female	2
Race	
Caucasian	106
Other	2

SOURCES: Congressional Quarterly, *Congressional Quarterly's Guide to the U.S. Supreme Court* (Washington, D.C.: Congressional Quarterly Press, 1997); and authors' update.

withdrew his nomination when the press leaked information about his alleged use of marijuana during the 1970s. Finally, the Senate approved Reagan's third choice, Anthony Kennedy.

Both of President George Bush's nominees to the Supreme Court—David Souter and Clarence Thomas—were confirmed by the Senate. Thomas's confirmation hearings were extremely volatile and received widespread publicity on national television. The nation watched as Anita Hill, his former aide, leveled charges of sexual harassment at Thomas.

The Senate has the ultimate say over who becomes a justice of the United States Supreme Court. Here, Ruth Bader Ginsburg faces questioning by members of the Senate Judiciary Committee. On August 10, 1993, she became the 107th justice of the Supreme Court—and one of the only two women ever to be appointed to that tribunal.

In 1993, President Bill Clinton had little trouble gaining approval for his nominee to fill the seat left vacant by Justice Byron White. Ruth Bader Ginsburg became the second female Supreme Court justice, the first being Sandra Day O'Connor, who was appointed by President Reagan in 1981. When Justice Harry Blackmun retired in 1994, Clinton nominated Stephen Breyer to fill Blackmun's seat. Breyer was confirmed without significant opposition.

The Courts as Policymakers

INFOTRAC®

The Brennan legacy

In a common law system, such as that of the United States, judges and justices play a paramount role in government. In part, this is because of the doctrine of *stare decisis*, which theoretically obligates judges to follow precedents. Additionally, unlike judges in some other countries, U.S. judges have the power to decide on the constitutionality of laws or actions undertaken by the other branches of government.

Clearly, the function of the courts is to interpret and apply the law, not to make law—that is the function of the legislative branch of government. Yet judges can and do "make law"; indeed, they cannot avoid making law in some cases because the law does not always provide clear answers to questions that come before the courts. Constitutional and statutory provisions and other legal rules tend to be expressed in general terms, and the courts must decide how those general provisions and rules apply to specific cases.

Consider the Americans with Disabilities Act of 1990. The act requires employers to reasonably accommodate the needs of employees with disabilities. But the act does not say exactly what employers must do to "reasonably accommodate" such persons. Thus, the courts must decide, on a case-by-case basis, what this phrase means. Additionally, in some cases there is no relevant law or precedent to follow. In recent years, for example, courts have been struggling with new kinds of legal issues stemming from new communications technology, including the Internet. Until legislative bodies establish laws governing these issues, it is up to the courts to fashion the law that will apply—and thus make policy.

THE IMPACT OF COURT DECISIONS

As already mentioned, how the courts interpret particular laws can have a widespread impact on society. For example, in 1996, in *Hopwood v. State of*

Texas,[16] in the U.S. Court of Appeals for the Fifth Circuit held that an affirmative action program implemented by the University of Texas School of Law in Austin was unconstitutional. The program allowed admissions officials to take race and other factors into consideration when determining which students would be admitted. The court stated that the program violated the equal protection clause because it discriminated in favor of minority applicants. The court's decision in *Hopwood* set a precedent for all federal courts within the Fifth Circuit's jurisdiction (which covers Texas, Louisiana, and Mississippi). Thus, whenever similar affirmative action programs in those states are challenged, the federal courts hearing the cases must apply the law as interpreted by the Court of Appeals for the Fifth Circuit.

Decisions rendered by the United States Supreme Court, of course, have an even broader impact on American society, because all courts in the nation are obligated to follow precedents set by the high court. Thus, when the Supreme Court interprets laws, it establishes national policy. If the Court deems that a law passed by Congress or a state legislature violates the Constitution, for example, that law will be void and unenforceable in any court within the United States. The power of the courts to declare laws or actions of the other two branches unconstitutional is known as **judicial review,** a topic to which we now turn.

THE POWER OF JUDICIAL REVIEW

John Marshall (1755–1835) served as chief justice of the Supreme Court from 1801 to 1835.

The Constitution does not actually mention judicial review. Rather, the Supreme Court claimed the power for itself in *Marbury v. Madison.*[17] In that case, which was decided by the Court in 1803, Chief Justice John Marshall held that a provision of a 1789 law affecting the Supreme Court's jurisdiction violated the Constitution and was thus void. Marshall declared, "It is emphatically the province and duty of the judicial department [the courts] to say what the law is. . . . If two laws conflict with each other, the courts must decide on the operation of each. . . . So if a law be in opposition to the constitution . . . the court must determine which of these conflicting rules governs the case. This is the very essence of judicial duty."

Although the Constitution did not explicitly provide for judicial review, most constitutional scholars believe that the framers intended that the federal courts should have this power. In *Federalist Paper* No. 78, Alexander Hamilton clearly espoused the doctrine of judicial review. Hamilton stressed the importance of the "complete independence" of federal judges and their special duty to "invalidate all acts contrary to the manifest tenor of the Constitution." Without judicial review by impartial courts, there would be nothing to ensure that the other branches of government stayed within constitutional limits when exercising their powers, and "all the reservations of particular rights or privileges would amount to nothing." Chief Justice Marshall shared Hamilton's views and adopted Hamilton's reasoning in *Marbury v. Madison.*

Ideology and the Courts

The policymaking role of the courts gives rise to an important question: To what extent do ideology and personal policy preferences affect judicial decision making? Numerous scholars have attempted to answer this question, especially with respect to Supreme Court justices.

IDEOLOGY AND SUPREME COURT DECISIONS

In one study, judicial scholars Jeffrey Segal and Harold Spaeth concluded that "the Supreme Court decides disputes in light of the facts of the case vis-à-vis the ideological attitudes and values of the justices. Simply put, Rehnquist votes the way he does because he is extremely conservative."[18] The authors maintain that the Supreme Court justices base their decisions on policy pref-

politics on the far side

Our Changing Constitution

In the 1985 case of *Aguilar v. Felton*,[19] the Supreme Court ruled that New York City's program of remedial education violated the establishment clause of the First Amendment. The plan, which involved sending public school teachers into parochial schools to help needy children with math and English, constituted an excessive "entanglement" of church and state. New York City then set up an alternative program, which involved delivering remedial education to the parochial school students in leased vans parked next to the church schools but not on school property. It was a costly alternative: over a period of seven years, the city spent $93.2 million to continue its remedial education program in this way.

A provision in the Supreme Court's rules allows the Court to reopen a case if a party can show that there has been "a significant change either in factual conditions or in the law." When the Court reopened the case in 1997 on the basis of that rule, it reversed its 1985 decision: delivering federally funded remedial education services on parochial school premises no longer violated the establishment clause.[20] What change in factual conditions or in the law had occurred since 1985? According to Justice O'Connor, what had changed since *Aguilar* was "our understanding" of the establishment clause.

For Critical Analysis: What might result if the Supreme Court had no authority to overturn its previous decisions?

I N F O T R A C ®
The Court's Mr. Right

erences simply because they are free to do so—they are not accountable to the electorate, because they are not elected to their positions. The desire to attain higher office is also not a factor in the Court's decision making, because the justices are at the apex of the judicial career ladder.

Few doubt that ideology affects judicial decision making, although, of course, other factors play a role as well. Different courts (such as a trial court and an appellate court) can look at the same case and draw different conclusions as to what law is applicable and how it should be applied. Certainly, there are numerous examples of how ideology affects Supreme Court decisions. As new justices replace old ones and new ideological alignments are formed, the Court's decisions are affected (see, for example, the feature entitled *Politics on the Far Side: Our Changing Constitution*). Yet many scholars argue that there is no real evidence indicating that personal preferences influence Supreme Court decisions to an unacceptable extent.

IDEOLOGY AND JUDICIAL APPOINTMENTS

It should come as no surprise that ideology plays a significant role in the president's selection of nominees to the federal bench, particularly to the Supreme Court, the crown jewel of the federal judiciary. Traditionally, presidents have attempted to strengthen their legacies by appointing federal judges with similar political and philosophical views. In the history of the Supreme Court, fewer than 13 percent of the justices nominated by a president have been from an opposing political party.

During his first six years in office, President Bill Clinton appointed 296 district and appeals court judges. Thus, midway into his second term, Clinton appointees occupied about 36 percent of these judgeships. Most of his appointees have been political centrists. (See the feature on the next page entitled *Perception versus Reality: Clinton and Federal Judicial Appointments.*) Indeed, the moderation and compromise that have marked the Clinton administration's judicial-apppointment behavior have caused some in the president's Democratic constituency to view the Clinton years as a lost opportunity to pursue a liberal policy agenda.[21]

THE IDEOLOGICAL COMPLEXION OF THE REHNQUIST COURT

In contrast to the liberal Supreme Court under Earl Warren (1953–1969) and to a lesser extent under Warren Burger (1969–1986), today's Court is generally conservative. Three of the justices (William Rehnquist, Antonin Scalia, and Clarence Thomas) are notably rightist in their views. Four of the justices (John Paul Stevens, David Souter, Ruth Bader Ginsburg, and Stephen Breyer) hold liberal-to-moderate views. Sandra Day O'Connor and Anthony Kennedy tend to hold the middle ground, and when the Court is sharply divided on an issue, theirs are often the swing votes. The ideological alignments vary, however, depending on the nature of the case before the Court.

The Court began its rightward shift after President Ronald Reagan appointed conservative William Rehnquist as chief justice in 1986, and the Court moved further to the right as other conservative appointments to the bench were made during the Reagan and Bush administrations.

Clinton and Federal Judicial Appointments

Every year, there are numerous vacancies within the federal judiciary, and occasionally a vacancy occurs on the Supreme Court. In principle, a sitting president can make a mark on the future by appointing (always with the consent of the Senate) federal court judges who share the president's political philosophy.

The Perception

Before his first election to the presidency in 1992, Bill Clinton campaigned in favor of what generally are considered liberal causes—abortion rights, gay rights, and more aggressive environmental enforcement. Consequently, the public's initial perception of Clinton was that he was going to appoint liberal-leaning individuals to the federal judiciary.

The Reality

It is true that during Clinton's first six years in office, he appointed more women and minorities to the federal bench than his predecessors—fewer than 51 percent of his appointees were white males, compared with 72 percent for George Bush (1989–1993) and 86 percent for Ronald Reagan (1981–1989). For the most part, though, Clinton spurned activists and ideologues in his court appointments. Rather, he chose cautious moderates, such as respected state jurists and partners in large law firms. Prospective nominees have never been asked their views on abortion. Even some pro-lifers have been appointed by the Clinton administration. During his first term, his Supreme Court nominees—Ruth Bader Ginsburg and Stephen Breyer—were clear moderates who were easily confirmed.

You Be the Judge

Why might a "liberal" president appoint centrist federal judges?

Liberals worry that the Rehnquist Court's decisions are eroding too many rights through its conservative reading of the Constitution. In its 1997 decision on the right-to-die issue (see Chapter 4), for example, a unanimous Court declared that nothing in the Constitution granted people the right to commit physician-assisted suicide. Chief Justice Rehnquist wrote that it would be wrong to conclude that "any and all important, intimate, and personal decisions" are constitutionally protected. Thus, state laws banning assisted suicide did not violate the Constitution.[22]

This decision continued a long-standing debate, dating back to the Court's *Roe v. Wade* [23] decision of 1973 (which made abortion legal—see

The Rehnquist Court. Seated in the front row (from left to right) are Justices Antonin Scalia, John Paul Stevens, William Rehnquist, Sandra Day O'Connor, and Anthony Kennedy. Standing behind them (from left to right) are Justices Ruth Bader Ginsburg, David Souter, Clarence Thomas, and Stephen Breyer.

Chapter 4), over whether the judicial or political branches of government should decide controversial questions of social policy. By unanimously upholding state laws prohibiting assisted suicide, the Court tipped this debate in favor of the political branches and, according to one observer, "quietly exorcised the ghost of *Roe*."[24]

Other decisions also show that the Rehnquist Court is noticeably at odds with the Supreme Courts of yesteryear. In a landmark case decided in 1995, *United States v. Lopez*,[25] the Court held that Congress had exceeded its constitutional authority under the commerce clause when it passed the Gun-Free School Zones Act in 1990. This was the first time in sixty years that the Supreme Court had limited the national government's regulatory authority under the commerce clause. In several subsequent cases, the Court similarly placed limits on Congress's powers (see Chapter 3). Some contend that what we saw in the 1990s was an activist conservative Court. (For a discussion of judicial activism and judicial restraint, see the feature *The American Political Spectrum: Judicial Activism versus Judicial Restraint*.)

the american political spectrum

Judicial Activism versus Judicial Restraint

Judicial scholars like to characterize different Supreme Courts and different Supreme Court justices as being either activist or restraintist. Although the concepts of *judicial activism* and *judicial restraint* lack any precise definition, generally an activist justice believes that the Court should actively use its powers to check the activities of the legislative and executive branches to ensure that they do not exceed their authority. A restraintist justice, in contrast, generally assumes that the Court should defer to the decisions of the legislative and executive branches, because members of Congress and the president are elected by the people whereas justices of the Supreme Court are not. In other words, the Court should not thwart the implementation of legislative acts unless they are clearly unconstitutional.

One of the Court's most activist eras occurred during the period from 1953 to 1969 under the leadership of Chief Justice Earl Warren. The Warren Court propelled the civil rights movement forward by holding, among other things, that laws permitting racial segregation violated the equal protection clause.

Liberal Activism (or Restraint)

Because of the activism of the Warren Court, the term *judicial activism* has often been linked with liberalism. Indeed, many liberals are in favor of an activist federal judiciary because they believe that the judiciary can "right" the "wrongs" that result from "antiquated" legislation at the state and local levels.

Nonetheless, judicial activism and judicial restraint are not necessarily linked to a particular political ideology. Consider the liberals or "moderate liberals" on today's Supreme Court bench—Justices Stevens, Souter, Ginsburg, and Breyer. In the Court's 1997 decision on the right-to-die issue (discussed elsewhere in this chapter), these justices took a restraintist position; along with the other justices, they held that the Constitution did not provide for any such right and opted not to strike down state laws prohibiting assisted suicide. In the Court decisions limiting congressional powers (including the decision holding that parts of a federal gun-control act were unconstitutional),[26] some of the liberal justices seemed to be the ones exercising judicial restraint—they

were not convinced that the acts were unconstitutional.

Conservative Restraint (or Activism)

Judicial restraint is often associated with conservative justices and Courts. Certainly, the conservative justices on today's Supreme Court—Justices Rehnquist, Scalia, and Thomas, sometimes joined by Justices O'Connor and Kennedy—often exercise judicial restraint. They did so, for example, in 1997 when they voted (along with the liberal justices) to uphold the constitutionality of state laws prohibiting assisted suicide. Conservative justices may also be activist, however, as when they struck down as unconstitutional the act of Congress mentioned earlier relating to gun control.

For Critical Analysis

Should a court ever overturn a law passed by an elective body, such as Congress, which (at least in theory) represents the interests of the majority of American citizens?

Americans at Odds over the Judiciary

The federal judiciary in the United States plays a far more significant role than courts in most other countries do. Not surprisingly, the policymaking power of the courts generates controversy. After all, the power of the nine justices on the Supreme Court—none of whom has been elected by the people—to decide on national policy has serious implications in a democracy. A major question being debated today has to do with whether the courts, by making policy from the bench, have upset the balance of powers envisioned by the framers of the Constitution.

The Constitution and the Federal Judiciary

Several scholars have suggested, and many Americans believe, that the framers never intended the judiciary to have extensive policymaking powers, including the power of judicial review.

Alexander Hamilton, as already noted, clearly outlined the concept of judicial review in *Federalist Paper* No. 78. Adopting Hamilton's view, Chief Justice John Marshall claimed the power of judicial review for the Court in 1803 in *Marbury v. Madison*, thereby significantly enlarging the Court's authority. Hamilton also regarded the judiciary as the "least dangerous" branch of government. Indeed, in the early years of this nation, the Supreme Court had little prestige or power. In 1800, John Jay, having served from 1789 to 1795 as the first chief justice, had the following to say about the Court:

> I left the bench perfectly convinced that under a system so defective it [the Court] could not obtain the energy, weight, and dignity which are essential to its affording due support to the national government; nor acquire the public confidence and respect which, as the last resort of the justice of the nation, it should possess.[27]

Other framers, though, including James Madison and Thomas Jefferson, were aware of the potential danger of giving the judiciary too much power. Madison, in his *Federalist* essays, contended that to combine judicial power with executive and legislative authority was the "very definition of tyranny." Jefferson worried about the effects of allowing only the unelected judiciary to interpret the Constitution. Said Jefferson: "It is a very dangerous doctrine to consider the judges as the ultimate arbiters of all constitutional questions." According to Jefferson, such a doctrine "would place us under the despotism of an oligarchy."[28]

Those who would like to curb the Court's powers argue that even if the founders intended the Court to have the power of judicial review and be the final arbiter of the Constitution, they could not possibly have foreseen today's vast judicial enterprise and the extent to which judicial powers are currently exercised. This group argues that the Supreme Court and other federal courts have exceeded their constitutional limits. In doing so, they have also placed in jeopardy a basic principle of federalism—the division of powers between the national government and the states.

Reining in the Federal Courts

A movement to rein in the power of the federal courts, and particularly judicial activism, has been under way since 1995, when the Republicans took control of Congress. Several Republicans fear that judicial activism in the federal courts will result in a constitutional crisis in the near future unless steps are taken to limit the power of the federal courts. A number of

James Madison. Both Madison and Thomas Jefferson emphasized the need for an independent judiciary.

proposed bills and strategies for restraining the power of the federal judiciary are now being considered by Congress.

One bill introduced in the 105th Congress would have, among other things, allowed each party in a federal case to request that another judge be assigned to the case—without having to give any reason for the requested change. This would allow parties to avoid judges who are known to engage in improper courtroom behavior or who let their biases guide their decisions. Another bill would allow for the televising of federal criminal and civil trials and appeals, subject to the judges' approval. "[T]he American people deserve an opportunity to see how the federal courts operate," said the bill's co-sponsor, Representative Steve Chabot (R., Ohio). "We need to encourage deeper understanding and further discussion of the proper, and, properly limited, role of federal judges."[29]

Other proposals have included limiting the jurisdiction of the federal courts, blocking the appointment of activist federal judges by investigating the judicial philosophy of federal court nominees during the Senate confirmation process, and impeaching activist judges.

INFOTRAC

Impeaching abusive judges

Should Activist Judges Be Impeached?

As mentioned earlier in the chapter, federal judges hold office for life and have only rarely been impeached and removed from office. Representative Tom DeLay (R., Texas), however, has suggested that impeachment proceedings should be brought against activist judges who make decisions based on their political biases and policy preferences rather than on a plain reading of the law. According to DeLay, "The system of checks and balances so carefully crafted by our Founding Fathers is in serious disrepair" because activist judges are assuming the legislature's lawmaking power.[30]

DeLay's proposal, which found some support among conservative Republicans, raises a serious political question: Did the framers of the Constitution intend Congress to use the threat of sanction to influence judicial decision making? No, say several scholars, including Stanford history professor Jack Rakove. According to Rakove, "Neither the Federalists nor the Anti-Federalists envisioned sweeping use of the impeachment power to corral wayward judges. . . . The whole idea was to make judges independent of political pressures."[31] Others agree that the system of checks and balances would be in even greater disrepair if DeLay's proposal were implemented. Even some Republicans in Congress who are opposed to an activist judiciary are also opposed to such use of the impeachment power.

Some critics contend that from a practical point of view, the impeachment proposal is simply implausible. For one thing, judicial activism has no precise definition, and there is no objective standard for determining when a judicial decision is activist. Additionally, it would be difficult to garner the majority in the House of Representatives necessary to vote for impeachment and then get two-thirds of the Senate to vote to convict.

The Case for the Courts

Those who defend the federal courts against these attacks argue that giving Congress more power over the courts would limit the independence of the judicial branch of government and upset the separation of powers envisioned by the Constitution's framers. To be sure, Congress is the voice of the people but not *all* of the people. If a congressional majority decides to pass a law infringing on the rights of the minority, what is to stop Congress from doing so? Without the courts and their power of judicial review, the "tyranny of the majority" feared by the nation's founders could result. Besides, contends this group, there are already sufficient checks on the courts.

CHECKS ON THE COURTS

Defenders of the existing role of the courts point out that Supreme Court justices traditionally have exercised a great deal of self-restraint. Justices sometimes admit to making decisions that fly in the face of their personal values and policy preferences, simply because they feel obligated to do so in view of existing law. Self-restraint is also mandated by various judicially established traditions and doctrines, including the doctrine of *stare decisis*, which theoretically obligates the Supreme Court to follow its own precedents. Furthermore, the Supreme Court will not hear a meritless appeal just so it can rule on the issue. Finally, more often than not, the justices narrow their rulings to focus on just one aspect of an issue, even though there may be nothing to stop them from broadening their focus and thus widening the impact of their decisions.

The judiciary is subject to other checks as well. Courts may make rulings, but they cannot force legislatures at local, state, and federal levels to appropriate the funds necessary to carry out those rulings. For example, if the Supreme Court decides that prison conditions must be improved, a legislature has to find the funds to carry out the ruling. Additionally, legislatures can rewrite (amend) old laws or pass new ones to negate courts' rulings. This may happen when a court interprets a statute in a way that Congress had not intended. The Civil Rights Act of 1991 (see Chapter 5) is one example of a law passed by Congress to clarify legislative policy for the courts and to nullify Supreme Court rulings.

THE STATURE OF THE COURT

In the debate over whether the legislative or judicial branch should have the final say in interpreting the law, one factor is often overlooked: the American public's high regard for the Supreme Court and the federal courts generally.

The Court continues to be respected as a fair arbiter of conflicting interests and the protector of constitutional rights and liberties. Polls continue to show that Americans place more trust and confidence in the Supreme Court than they do in Congress. In the eyes of many Americans, the Supreme Court stands in sharp contrast to a White House nagged by scandals and a Congress that seems incapable of rising above partisan bickering and the quagmire of Washington politics.

This does not mean that the role of the Supreme Court is not controversial. Americans are at odds over the Court's decisions in many policy areas, including the area of criminal justice—as pointed out in this chapter's opening feature. Yet over time, the Court has been able to maintain its position as an important policymaker, remarkably protected from any serious attack on its authority.

key terms

administrative agency 393
administrative law 393
administrative law judge 393
appellate court 398
case law 393
civil law 393
common law 391
concurring opinion 400

conference 400
constitutional law 392
criminal law 393
dissenting opinion 400
diversity of citizenship 395
federal question 395
judicial review 404
judiciary 391

chapter summary

1. The American legal system is an offshoot of the legal system—the common law tradition—that developed in England over hundreds of years. The courts of the early English kings developed a uniform set of rules, based on decisions made by judges, that eventually became common to the English realm. These decisions are known as the common law, and thus the system is called a common law system. The cornerstone of the English and American legal systems is the doctrine of *stare decisis,* which theoretically obligates judges to follow precedents (previous court decisions in their jurisdiction) when interpreting the law.

2. Primary sources of American law include constitutional law (the U.S. Constitution and the constitutions of the various states), statutory law (laws passed by Congress and by state legislatures), administrative law (regulations issued by administrative agencies), and case law (the body of law developed by the courts when interpreting constitutional provisions, statutes, and other laws).

3. Law can also be classified in other ways. An important classification divides all law into civil law or criminal law. Civil law concerns the duties that individuals in society owe to other persons or to their governments, excluding the duty not to commit crimes. Criminal law has to do with wrongs committed against the public as a whole.

4. Certain judicial requirements limit the types of cases courts can hear and decide. Before a court can hear a case, it must have jurisdiction over the person against whom the case is brought, the property involved, and the subject matter. The party bringing the case must also have standing to sue—that is, the party must have a definable stake in the controversy at hand and the issue must be real and definite, not hypothetical or abstract. Additionally, both the federal and state courts have established procedural rules that apply in judicial proceedings.

5. The federal court system is a three-tiered model consisting of U.S. district (trial) courts, U.S. courts of appeals, and the United States Supreme Court. There is no absolute right of appeal to the Supreme Court. If the justices decide to hear a case, the parties present their arguments before the Court, and the justices then discuss the case and issue their decision in the form of a written opinion.

6. All federal judges are appointed by the president and confirmed by the Senate. Most nominees have the same political and ideological beliefs as the president who appoints them. For this reason, if the Senate and the president do not see eye to eye about political matters, a battle may ensue over a nominee's appointment.

7. Judges play an important policymaking role in the United States in part because of our common law system and the doctrine of *stare decisis.* Thus, court decisions, particularly those by the Supreme Court, can have a broad impact. How the Supreme Court interprets the Constitution or some other law establishes a precedent that all courts in the nation must follow. Additionally, courts in the United States have the power of judicial review. This means that judges can decide on the constitutionality of laws or actions undertaken by the other branches of government.

8. The extent to which ideology affects judicial decision making in the federal courts has led to substantial controversy because federal judges are appointed and are not accountable to the electorate. Some claim that the Supreme Court justices' ideologies influence their decisions in all cases. Others contend that although ideology influences how the Supreme Court decides issues, it does not do so to an unacceptable extent.

9. Presidents have attempted to strengthen their legacies by appointing federal judges with similar political, ideological, and philosophical views. During the Reagan and Bush administrations, several conservative justices were appointed, altering the ideological make-up of the Court considerably. The Rehnquist Court of today is far more conservative

than previous Supreme Courts (since the 1950s) have been. Although President Clinton has appointed two justices, they tend to be centrist, or moderate, in their views.

10. Americans are at odds over several issues relating to the federal judiciary. A major issue has to do with the ability of unelected judges to make policy.

Some members of Congress and other Americans claim that the framers of the Constitution never intended the courts to have such powers, particularly the power of judicial review. Several proposals to limit the powers of the federal courts are now being considered in Congress.

for critical analysis

1. Should the justices of the United States Supreme Court be elected, just as the president and members of Congress are? Why or why not?

2. "Diversity of citizenship should be abolished as a basis for federal jurisdiction so that the federal courts can focus their efforts on questions that truly involve federal issues." Do you agree with this statement? What might happen if diversity jurisdiction were abolished? Would anyone or any group be harmed as a result?

3. If the courts could not exercise the power of judicial review, what might result? Would Congress then be able to wield too much power? Is there anything wrong with having Congress, the representatives of the people, decide on the constitutionality of the laws it enacts?

4. Why do the president and the majority party in the Senate seem to place so much importance on the appointment of federal judges?

5. Is it possible to define "judicial activism" objectively?

6. Suppose that the United States Supreme Court did not have to abide by the doctrine of *stare decisis* but was free to decide cases simply as it chose without having to justify any departures from precedents. Would this be beneficial to our political system? Would it be harmful?

7. To what extent should judges consider public opinion in their decisions?

suggested readings

BAUM, Lawrence. *The Supreme Court*. 6th ed. Washington, D.C.: CQ Press, 1998. Written by a noted judicial scholar, this is a comprehensive treatment of the Supreme Court.

CLAYTON, Cornell W., and Howard Gillman. Eds. *Supreme Court Decision-Making*. Chicago: University of Chicago Press, 1999. In this collection of essays, a number of well-known Supreme Court scholars look closely at the institutional factors (the unique characteristics of the Supreme Court, the dynamics of coalition building, the effects of social movements, and so on) that influence decision making in the nation's highest court.

DWORKIN, Ronald. *Freedom's Law: The Moral Reading of the Constitution*. Cambridge, Mass.: Harvard University Press, 1997. The author takes a stand against those who would interpret the Constitution literally. He argues that the judicial function is not mechanical, as politicians and judges alike maintain, but creative. Only when we openly recognize this fact can there be democratic accountability: the public can understand what is being done on its behalf and have the opportunity to influence constitutional law by comment and criticism.

KAHN, Paul W. *The Reign of Law*: Marbury v. Madison *and the Construction of America*. New Haven, Conn.: Yale University Press, 1997. Kahn argues that the rule of law is a deep cultural myth, originating in divine right theories. He looks closely at the Supreme Court's *Marbury v. Madison* decision and its implications for American government.

SCALIA, Antonin. *A Matter of Interpretation: Federal Courts and the Law*. Ewing, N.J.: Princeton University Press, 1997. Supreme Court justice Antonin Scalia gives his views on several issues of importance today, including the question of how judges and justices can stay within their proper governmental sphere.

SUNSTEIN, Cass R. *One Case at a Time: Judicial Minimalism on the Supreme Court*. Cambridge, Mass.: Harvard University Press, 1999. The author argues that the Supreme Court, by avoiding broad rulings on controversial issues such as affirmative action, evidences a "minimalist" approach to judicial decision making. This, contends the author, helps to foster public debate on these issues and their ultimate resolution through the political system rather than the courts.

politics
on the web

An excellent Web site for information on the justices of the United States Supreme Court is

http://oyez.nwu.edu

This site offers biographies of the justices, links to opinions they have written, and, for justices who have served after 1920, video and audio materials. Oral arguments before the Supreme Court are also posted on this site. A planned addition to the site is a video tour of the Court.

Another helpful Web site is

http://supct.law.cornell.edu/supct

This is the index of the United States Supreme Court. It has recent Court decisions by year and name of party, and it also has selected historic decisions rendered by the Court.

FindLaw offers a free searchable database of Supreme Court decisions since 1907 at

http://www.findlaw.com

Increasingly, decisions of the state courts are also becoming available online. You can search through the texts of state cases that are on the Internet, as well as federal cases and state and federal laws, by accessing WashLaw at

http://www.washlaw.edu

To learn more about the federal court system, go to

http://www.uscourts.gov

This is the home page for the federal courts. Among other things, you can follow the "path" a case takes as it moves through the federal court system.

using
web resources

The United States Supreme Court plays a vital role in the American system of government. To inform the public of its origins, its significance, and its procedures, the Court published a pamphlet that is now online at

http://www.usscplus.com/info

Go to this site and click on the box titled "The Court and Constitutional Interpretation" in the left-hand margin of the screen. Read through this page, and then answer the following questions:

1. How does the Court describe its basic function in the American system of government?

2. What basic arguments did Alexander Hamilton and James Madison offer in support of the concept of judicial review?

3. When the Supreme Court rules on a constitutional issue, is that decision necessarily final? Can it ever be changed? Is so, how?

notes

1. *Duncan v. Louisiana*, 391 U.S. 145 (1968).

2. 372 U.S. 335 (1963).

3. 384 U.S. 436 (1966).

4. 367 U.S. 643 (1961).

5. 468 U.S. 897 (1984).

6. *New York v. Quarles*, 467 U.S. 649 (1984).

7. Note that the terms *justice* and *judge* are usually synonymous and simply represent two designations given to judges in various courts. All members of the United States Supreme Court, for example, are referred to as *justices*, whereas members of the lower federal courts are, for the most part, called *judges*.

8. Pronounced *ster*-ay dih-*si*-ses.

9. 347 U.S. 483 (1954).

10. See *Plessy v. Ferguson*, 163 U.S. 537 (1896).

11. Although a state's highest court is often referred to as the state supreme court, there are exceptions. In the New York court system, for example, the supreme court is a trial court, and the highest court is called the New York Court of Appeals.

12. Pronounced jus-*tish*-a-bul.

13. *Raines v. Byrd*, 521 U.S. 811 (1997).

14. Pronounced sur-shee-uh-*rah*-ree.

15. Between 1790 and 1891, Congress allowed the Supreme Court almost no discretion over which cases to decide. After 1925, in almost 95 percent of appealed cases the Court could choose whether to hear arguments and issue an opinion. Beginning with the term in October 1988, mandatory review was virtually eliminated.

16. 84 F.3d 720 (5th Cir. 1996).

17. 5 U.S. (1 Cranch) 137 (1803). The Supreme Court had considered the constitutionality of an act of Congress in *Hylton v. United States*, 3 U.S. 171 (1796), in which Congress's power to levy certain taxes was challenged. That particular act was ruled constitutional, rather than unconstitutional, however, so this first federal exercise of judicial review was not clearly recognized as such. Also, during the decade before the adoption of the federal Constitution, courts in at least eight states had exercised the power of judicial review.

18. Jeffrey A. Segal and Harold J. Spaeth, *The Supreme Court and the Attitudinal Model* (New York: Cambridge University Press, 1993), p. 65.

19. 473 U.S. 402 (1985).

20. *Agostini v. Felton*, 521 U.S. 203 (1997).

21. Sheldon Goldman and Elliot Slotnick, "Clinton's Second Term Judiciary: Picking Judges under Fire," *Judicature*, Vol. 82, No. 6 (May–June 1999), pp. 264–284.

22. See *Washington v. Glucksberg*, 521 U.S. 702 (1997).

23. 410 U.S. 113 (1973).

24. *The New York Times*, June 29, 1997, p. E15.

25. 514 U.S. 549 (1995).

26. *Printz v. United States*, 521 U.S. 898 (1997).

27. Jay wrote this in a letter to John Adams after Adams had appointed him to the Court for another term as chief justice. Jay refused the appointment.

28. Letter to William Jarvis, 1820.

29. As quoted in "Proposals Seek to Restrain Judges," *The National Law Journal*, April 21, 1997.

30. Statement to the House Judiciary Subcommittee on Courts and Intellectual Property during hearings held May 14–15, 1997.

31. As quoted in Harvey Berkman, "Some Republicans Declare a Judicial Open Season," *The National Law Journal*, June 30, 1997, p. A11.

DOMESTIC POLICY

Contents

Welfare Reform: Are We Abandoning Our Underclass?

When Bill Clinton campaigned for the presidency in 1992, he said he would change "welfare as we know it." Prior to his reelection in 1996, he signed into law the biggest welfare reform bill ever. In essence, the new welfare legislation allows the states to play a much greater role in establishing welfare rules, such as determining who is eligible to receive what types of benefits. The bill also shifted some of the financial burden of the welfare system to state governments. Perhaps more important, it imposed limits on the number of years people would be eligible for welfare assistance without going to work.

Go to CD-ROM

The results of the legislation have been striking. Indeed, by 1999 the number of former welfare recipients who had found work was estimated at about 50 percent for the nation as a whole. And many states had reduced their welfare caseloads by much higher percentages—85 percent in Idaho, for example, and 84 percent in Wyoming.

Yet the debate over welfare reform is not over. Some Americans maintain that there is another side to the story of welfare reform that is not being told.

Yes, We Are Abandoning Our Poor

According to the critics of the welfare reform legislation of 1996, we are indeed sacrificing the well-being of America's poor in the interest of promoting some puritanical notion of the work ethic. Getting off welfare is a process, not an event. It is unrealistic to think that welfare mothers and others ill equipped for the job market can simply "go off welfare" and get a job in two years.

Critics of welfare reform acknowledge that the number of people receiving welfare benefits has been dramatically reduced. Yet, say these critics, getting families off the welfare rolls is not in itself an adequate measurement of progress. What is not being factored into the welfare equation is the quality of life for the families who have been forced off the welfare rolls. Where do they go, and what do they do? Only a few studies have been conducted on this aspect of welfare reform, and their results are not encouraging. For example, a Tufts University survey concluded that in two-thirds of the states, welfare reform actually pushed the poor deeper into poverty, and in only fourteen states has welfare reform actually improved the lives of those most in need.[1]

These critics also point out that some surveys on which the national average is based have fairly loose definitions of employment. They include anyone earning at least $100 over a three-month period. Furthermore, claims this group, the samples are sometimes skewed. For example, a Manhattan Institute study managed to track only half of the original sample of former welfare recipients. And among those who could be located, about half were unemployed.[2]

Welfare Reform Is Just What We Need, Some Say

Those in favor of welfare reform—and many do not think it has gone far enough—argue that without giving the states the ability to run their own welfare programs, the system was destined to continuing failure. They point out that in the past fifty years, more than $5 trillion has been spent on helping the poor, yet the poverty rate has not dropped. Thus, they claim, letting the states impose work requirements on welfare recipients creates new incentives for getting these recipients off the dole.

Although some of the underclass may suffer in the

short run, in the long run society will be better off, because fewer individuals will become dependent on welfare payments. After all, long periods on welfare erode work skills and entrench the habit of depending on government handouts. Individual self-confidence and incentives to earn money are thereby destroyed.[3]

What about children? Proponents of welfare reform argue that children ultimately will be better off. Although welfare payments to their parents may make them better off in the short run, in the long run dependence on government payments corrupts a family's values. Children in families that are on welfare for long periods of time come to believe that it is normal to be supported by government. They therefore become emotionally incapable of becoming financially independent.

Where Do You Stand?

1. What additional arguments might you make to either support or counter the claim that the new welfare policy amounts to abandoning our underclass?

2. From the perspective of people living in poverty, will state management of the welfare system be more in their interests than federal management?

On the Web

You can find further information on welfare reform at the following Web site: http://www.welfareinfo.org.

DOMESTIC POLICY ● Public policy concerning issues within a national unit, such as national policy concerning welfare or crime.

POLICYMAKING PROCESS ● The procedures involved in getting an issue on the political agenda; formulating, adopting, and implementing a policy with regard to the issue; and then evaluating the results of the policy.

INFOTRAC®

The quiet success of welfare reform

Introduction

The Welfare Reform Act (the popular name for the Personal Responsibility and Work Opportunity Reconciliation Act) of 1996 marked a major change in this nation's welfare policy. Why was this change made? And who were the major participants in the decision-making process that led to this change?

To learn the answers to these and similar questions, you need to delve into the politics of policymaking. As stated in Chapter 1, policy, or public policy, can be defined as a government plan or course of action taken in response to a political issue or to enhance the social or political well-being of society. Public policy is the end result of the policymaking process, about which you will read shortly. **Domestic policy,** in contrast to foreign policy (discussed in Chapter 19), consists of public policy concerning issues *within* a national unit.

In this chapter, after discussing how policy is made through the policymaking process, we look at several aspects of domestic policy, including social welfare policy, crime policy, and economic policy. Bear in mind that although the focus here is on policy and policymaking at the national level, state and local governments also engage in policymaking and establish policies to achieve goals relating to activities within their boundaries.

The Policymaking Process

New laws, such as the Welfare Reform Act of 1996, do not appear out of nowhere. First, the problem addressed by the new law had to become part of the political agenda—that is, defined as a political issue to be resolved by government action. Furthermore, once the issue got on the political agenda, proposed solutions to the problem had to be formulated and then adopted. Agenda setting, policy formulation, and policy adoption are all parts of the **policymaking process.** The process does not end there, however. Once the law is passed, it has to be implemented and then evaluated.

Each phase of the policymaking process involves interactions between various individuals and groups. The president and members of Congress are

In August 1996, President Clinton signed the Welfare Reform Act into law. In so doing, he fulfilled a promise that he made during his 1992 campaign to "change welfare as we know it." The law ended individual entitlement benefits. Under new state programs, poor children may no longer be automatically entitled to cash benefits. The law gave states more program flexibility, but also imposed new federal requirements. (Some of the provisions of the 1996 law were later "softened" during the budget negotiations in 1997.)

A New Beginning
Welfare to Work

AGENDA SETTING ● The first stage of the policymaking process, which consists of getting an issue on the political agenda to be addressed by Congress.

obviously important participants in the process. Remember from Chapter 7 that interest groups play a key role in politics. Groups that may be affected adversely by a new policy will try to convince Congress not to adopt the policy. Groups that will benefit by a new policy will exert whatever influence they can on Congress to do the opposite. Congressional committees and subcommittees may investigate the problem to be addressed by the policy and, in so doing, solicit input from members of a certain group or industry.

Generally, the participants in policymaking and the nature of the debates involved depend on the particular policy being proposed, formed, or implemented. Whatever the policy, however, debate over its pros and cons usually occurs during each stage of the policymaking process.

AGENDA SETTING

The first stage of the policymaking process, often called **agenda setting** or *agenda building,* consists of getting an issue on the political agenda. A problem in society can become a political issue to be addressed by the government in a number of different ways. Sometimes, the social or economic effects of a national calamity, such as the Great Depression of the 1930s, create a need for government action. An event or series of events, such as an unusual number of airplane crashes, may lead to the perception that airline travel is unsafe and that the government should take action to rectify the problem. Dramatic increases in crime rates may make crime reduction a priority on the national political agenda.

The ideology of the dominant party in government may also affect agenda setting. In 1995, for example, the Republican-controlled Congress supported legislation endorsed predominantly by political conservatives. This legislation included welfare reform, budget reform, tougher crime laws, and tax cuts.

POLICY FORMULATION AND ADOPTION

The second stage in the policymaking process involves the formulation and adoption of specific plans for achieving a particular goal, such as welfare reform. The president, members of Congress, administrative agencies, and interest group leaders typically are the key participants in developing proposed legislation. Remember from Chapter 15 that iron triangles—subgovernments consisting of congressional committee members, interest group leaders, and bureaucrats in administrative agencies—work together in forming mutually beneficial policies. To a certain extent, the courts also establish policies when they interpret statutes passed by legislative bodies or make decisions concerning disputes not yet addressed by any law, such as disputes involving new technology (see Chapter 16).

Note that some issues may get on the political agenda but never proceed beyond that stage of the policymaking process. Usually, this happens when it is impossible to achieve a consensus over what policy should be adopted. Welfare reform had been on the political agenda for years, for example, but a new welfare policy was not developed and formally proposed until the Republican sweep of Congress in 1994. Even then, the president and Congress were unable to reach a consensus on the bill's specific provisions until 1996. To a significant extent, welfare reform is linked to the broad movement toward reducing federal government spending and turning more responsibilities over to state governments.

POLICY IMPLEMENTATION

Because of our federal system, the implementation of national policies necessarily requires the cooperation of the federal government and the various state and local governments. For example, the 1996 Welfare Reform Act required the states to develop plans for implementing the new welfare policy within their borders. The federal government, though, retained some authority over the welfare system by providing that state

politics on the far side

Implementing Public Policy—In Reverse

In 1967, Congress clearly enunciated a public policy against age discrimination with the passage of the Age Discrimination in Employment Act (ADEA). This act prohibits age-based employment discrimination against employees or job applicants who are forty years of age or older. Sometimes, however, policies get turned around in the process of implementing them, with unusual results.

Consider what happened to Professor Merwyn Bryan, a candidate for a professorship in geography at East Stroudsburg University of Pennsylvania (ESU). The search committee, when recommending Bryan to ESU's president, cited Bryan's age and experience as a reason to hire him. The president had misgivings: if age was a dominant factor in deciding to hire Bryan, then the decision might violate the ADEA. Based on this reasoning, the university decided not to hire Bryan. Instead, it hired an African American woman who had earlier been passed over because she was not qualified for the position. Even the woman agreed that she was not qualified to teach certain fields, such as meteorology.

For Critical Analysis: Can you think of other laws or regulations that, when implemented, have led to unintended consequences?

welfare plans had to be certified, or approved, by the federal government. Successful implementation also usually requires the support of groups outside the government. For example, the work requirements of the new welfare policy meant that the business sector would also play a key role in the policy's implementation.

Policy implementation also involves administrative agencies (see Chapter 15). Once Congress establishes a policy by enacting legislation, the executive branch, through its administrative agencies, enforces the new policy. The courts are also involved in policy implementation, because the legislation and administrative regulations enunciating the new policy must be interpreted and applied to specific situations by the courts. (Policy is also implemented by the public, although not always in the ways intended; see, for example, the feature entitled *Politics on the Far Side: Implementing Public Policy—In Reverse.*)

POLICY EVALUATION

The final stage of policymaking involves evaluating the success of a policy during and following its implementation. Once a policy has been implemented, groups both inside and outside the government evaluate the policy. Congress may hold hearings to obtain feedback from different groups on how a statute or regulation has affected those groups. Scholars and scientists may conduct studies to determine whether a particular law, such as an environmental law designed to reduce air pollution, has actually achieved the desired result—less air pollution. Sometimes, feedback obtained in these or other ways indicates that a policy has failed, and a new policymaking process may be undertaken to modify the policy or create a more effective one.

The Welfare Reform Act of 1996 was passed due to a perceived failure of the existing welfare policy to achieve its goal of improving the plight of the poor. Whether the new welfare policy will achieve its goal of reducing poverty in the long run is yet to be seen. Although the number of welfare recipients is declining, the poverty rate has not changed to any significant degree. Over time, as the states continue to implement their programs, data can be gathered and analyzed to accurately determine the policy's effectiveness in reducing poverty.

Social Welfare Policy

Social welfare policy consists of all government actions that are undertaken to give assistance to specific groups, such as the aged, the ill, and the poor. Social welfare policy is the government's response to the decision made by the American people, through their elected representatives, that everyone in the nation should be provided with a certain minimum level of income. Social welfare policy is often implemented through **income redistribution**—income is taken from some people through taxation and given to others. Government programs that redistribute income fall into two areas: social insurance programs (such as Social Security and Medicare) and public-assistance programs, often called welfare. (What, if anything, should be done about another pressing social issue—the homeless population in the United States—is the topic of this chapter's feature on the next page entitled *The American Political Spectrum: Homelessness.*)

SOCIAL WELFARE POLICY ● All government actions that are undertaken to give assistance to specific groups, such as the aged, the ill, and the poor.

INCOME REDISTRIBUTION ● The transfer of income from one group to another; income is taken from some people through taxation and given to others.

the american **political spectrum**

Homelessness

The existence of a homeless population in the United States, one of the most economically developed countries in the world, is—at least for many Americans, as well as other people around the globe—inexplicable. Although no one knows for sure how many Americans are homeless, it is estimated that there are as many as 600,000 people living in this country without homes. Some of them sleep in the streets. Others sleep in shelters provided by local governments. Still others find refuge with families and friends. Should the government be doing more to help this group of Americans? Generally speaking, liberals and conservatives have different views on this issue.

We Need to Provide Aid to the Homeless, Say Liberals

Liberals tend to believe that the government should take action to provide for the needs of the homeless population. Some liberals blame the 1996 welfare reform legislation for increasing the homeless population. They contend that since the implementation of that legislation, homeless shelters in major cities have been reporting that the demand for emergency

housing has increased by 60 percent. Their response is to call for more shelters and more services for the homeless population.

This group also claims that the cost of housing is so high that some Americans have no choice but to be "homeless." More federal and state funds should be allocated toward low-income housing to serve the needs of people who cannot afford the exorbitant housing costs in many of today's cities.

Additionally, something needs to be done about the fact that some cities are making homelessness a crime by enacting ordinances that prohibit sleeping on public property such as sidewalks, or in public parks. In effect, these ordinances only serve to swell the ranks of persons entering the criminal justice system—which leads to further problems, such as how to provide for prison cells for these people.

Aid to the Homeless Is No Solution, Say Conservatives

Conservatives take a different position on the issue. For one thing, they believe that the case for the homeless population is overstated. They claim that estimates of the homeless population

are too high—there are not really that many homeless people in the country. For another, more low-income housing and more homeless shelters will not cure the problem of homelessness. Such programs are simply a waste of time and money because they do not address the complexity of the causes that propel people into homelessness.

Conservatives point out that many (perhaps up to one-third) of the homeless population suffer from mental problems and that at least one-half of the homeless are addicted to alcohol or other drugs. Rather than spend money providing for more shelters and rehabilitation programs, society should focus its attention on the roots of these problems: broken homes and inadequate education. Public dollars would be better spent in efforts to restore family values and improve education.

For Critical Analysis

Some homeless people make it clear that they do not want any help from government. What can, or should, the government do to help homeless people who make such assertions?

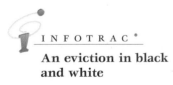

I N F O T R A C *

An eviction in black and white

SOCIAL SECURITY AND MEDICARE

A major aspect of income redistribution in the United States involves the Social Security system. Social Security includes what has been called old-age, survivors', and disability insurance (OASDI). This is essentially a program of compulsory saving financed from payroll taxes levied on both employers and employees. Workers pay for Social Security while working and receive the benefits later, usually after retirement. When the insured worker dies, benefits accrue to the survivors, including the spouse and children. Special benefits provide for disabled workers. Over 90 percent of all employed persons in the United States are covered by OASDI.

Medicare, launched in 1965, is a social insurance program under which the federal government pays for part of the cost of medical care for retired persons or persons with disabilities who are covered by Social Security. Like the Social Security program, Medicare is financed by payroll taxes on employers and employees.

The Problem with Social Security

Social Security was originally designed as a social insurance program that workers paid for themselves and that provided benefits that were determined by the size of a worker's past contributions. Today, Social Security is not really an insurance program because people are not guaranteed that the benefits they receive will be in line with the contributions they have made. The benefits are legislated by Congress, and there is no guarantee that Congress will continue to legislate the same amount of benefits in the future as it does today. Congress could (and probably will have to) legislate for lower real levels of benefits instead of higher ones. In essence, Social Security is an intergenerational income transfer that is only vaguely related to past earnings. It transfers income from Americans who work—the young through the middle-aged—to older, retired persons who do not work.

The real problem with the Social Security system is that the number of people who are working relative to the number of people who are retiring is declining. This means that workers will have to pay more of their income in Social Security taxes to pay for the retirement benefits of older, retired workers. Today, Social Security benefits cost about 15 percent of all taxable payroll income in the economy. By the year 2025, this figure is projected to be almost 23 percent. In today's dollars, that amounts to more than a trillion dollars of additional taxes annually. Clearly, increasing or even maintaining the current level of Social Security benefits will create a financial strain for the government. (For a discussion of the U.S. problem with Social Security compared with similar problems in other countries, see the feature on the next page entitled *Comparative Politics: If You Think We Have a Social Security Problem, Consider Europe.*)

Another Problem: Benefits Go to Wealthier Americans, Too

INFOTRAC®
Medicare scare

Benefit payments from OASDI redistribute income to some degree. Benefit payments, however, are not based on the recipients' needs. Participants' contributions give them the right to receive benefits even if they would be financially secure without the benefits. The same is true with Medicare. As a result, all classes in American society, regardless of income, benefit from these programs.

In fact, one study of Medicare recipients showed that wealthier Americans receive, on net, more Medicare benefits than poorer Americans. The authors of the study calculated that, among Americans born in 1925, the richest 10 percent will receive many times more in net Medicare benefits than the poorest 10 percent. Why? The reason is that wealthier Americans tend to live longer and use the Medicare system more intensively. Among persons over the age of eighty-five, the wealthiest 10 percent claim nearly 40 percent more in Medicare benefits than the poorest 10 percent.[4]

SUPPLEMENTAL SECURITY INCOME (SSI)

Many people who are poor but do not qualify for Social Security benefits are assisted through other programs. The federally financed and administered Supplemental Security Income (SSI) program was instituted in 1974. The purpose of SSI is to establish a nationwide minimum income for the aged, the blind, and the disabled. SSI has become one of the fastest-growing transfer programs in the United States: in 1974, less than $8 billion was spent; the estimate for 2000 is over $35 billion. Americans currently eligible for SSI include children and individuals claiming mental disabilities, including drug addicts and alcoholics.

TEMPORARY ASSISTANCE TO NEEDY FAMILIES

Traditionally, the basic welfare program in the United States was known as Aid to Families with Dependent Children (AFDC), a state-administered program financed in part by federal grants. The program was designed to

If You Think We Have a Social Security Problem, Consider Europe

Worries about Social Security and its future in the United States seem like child's play to those who are dealing with Europe's Social Security problem. Look at Table 17–1 to see what the state-funded pension liabilities are in selected countries.

The situation in the United States looks pretty good in comparison. Consider that in Europe, most pensions are 100 percent government paid. In contrast, in the United States we have relatively wide-ranging private pension plans funded either by companies or by individuals, or by both. In essence, for many—if not most—Americans, Social Security payments are supplementary retirement income, rather than the sole source of pension funds available on retirement. In Europe, the situation is different.

Consider France. In that country, over 99 percent of all pension payments are paid directly out of government (that is, taxpayer-financed) funds. The mandatory retirement age for the majority of workers in the country is sixty. For some workers, including train conductors, truck drivers, and subway and bus drivers working in Paris, the mandatory retirement age is fifty-five or lower. Individuals receiving government retirement funds are not allowed to work. Currently, 10 percent of annual national income goes to pension payments.

Moreover, France and the rest of Europe have even worse demographics than the United States with respect to the declining number of working individuals for every retired person. Consequently, over the next thirty years European countries must decide how to handle this challenge.

For Critical Analysis

Why do you think it is often illegal to work while receiving government-paid pensions in Europe?

Table 17–1

How the United States Stacks Up Relative to Other Countries with Respect to Pension (Social Security) Liabilities

COUNTRY	NET PENSION LIABILITIES AS A PERCENTAGE OF GROSS DOMESTIC PRODUCT (GDP)
United States	66
Germany	160
Belgium	165
United Kingdom	186
France	216
Japan	218
Italy	233
Canada	250

SOURCE: Organization of Economic Cooperation and Development.

provide aid to families in which dependent children did not have the financial support of the father because of desertion, disability, or death. Under the AFDC program, the federal government largely set the requirements that had to be met before a welfare applicant could receive welfare payments.

Medicare and Social Security have been considered "sacred cows," such that members of Congress rarely feel they can attack these programs if they want to be reelected. Not surprisingly, outlays for Medicare and Social Security continue to rise. In the 1990s, Medicare spending increased at a real rate of almost 10 percent per year. Social Security and Medicare combined account for one of every three dollars spent at the federal level. In spite of such real increases, senior citizens resist any threatened reduction in the rate of growth of their benefits.

The 1996 Welfare Reform Act replaced the AFDC program with a system that gives the states more discretion in establishing welfare rules and in managing the welfare program. Under the new welfare system, the federal government turns over to the states, in the form of "block" (lump-sum) grants, funds targeted for Temporary Assistance to Needy Families. Essentially, these block grants represent the funds that would otherwise have gone to the AFDC program. Unlike the AFDC program, in which the federal government paid for any increased welfare spending, the new system requires the states to pay any additional costs incurred in providing welfare assistance to the poor.

One of the goals of the 1996 act was to get individuals off welfare and into productive jobs. To this end, the act requires the states to limit welfare assistance to two years. After two years, welfare recipients may continue receiving benefits but only if they are are working, either in public-service jobs or in the private sector. The act limits lifetime welfare benefits to five years (but states may provide for a shorter period—or even a longer period, if they finance the additional costs).

Another key provision of the 1996 Welfare Reform Act allows states to deny welfare benefits to unmarried teenage mothers. Under the AFDC program, if an unwed mother had insufficient income to support a child, she could obtain welfare payments for that purpose. If the mother had another child, her welfare payments increased. Because the mother could be assured of welfare assistance, she had little incentive to get a job. After all, the income that the mother earned from a job (after taxes and paying for day-care, transportation, and other job-associated costs) often amounted to only a little more than she received from the government—without having to work. The 1996 act attempted to overcome this problem by discouraging illegitimate births. Not only does the act allow the states to deny welfare assistance to unwed teenage mothers, it also provides that "bonus payments" will be given to states that reduce illegitimate births among welfare mothers.

Much of domestic government spending is on some form of welfare payments. Here, a single parent applies for infant care and infant food assistance in California. When state welfare expenditures are added to federal welfare expenditures, we find that aggregate welfare expenses doubled from 1988 to 1998. In 1993, for the first time in American history, aggregate government welfare payments exceeded the total expenditures for national defense.

FOOD STAMPS

Food stamps are government-issued coupons that can be used to purchase food. The food stamp program was established in 1964, mainly to shore up the nation's agricultural sector by increasing demand for food through retail channels. In 1964, some 367,000 Americans were receiving food stamps. By 1999, that number had climbed to more than 28 million. The annual cost of the program jumped from $860,000 to more than $24 billion over the same period. Thus, the food stamp program has become a major part of the welfare system in the United States. The program has also become a method of promoting better nutrition among the poor.

THE EARNED INCOME TAX CREDIT (EITC) PROGRAM

In 1975, the Earned Income Tax Credit (EITC) program was created to provide rebates of Social Security taxes to low-income workers. Over one-fifth of all tax returns claim an earned-income tax credit. In some states, such as Mississippi, as well as the District of Columbia, nearly half of all families are eligible for the EITC.

The program works as follows: Households with reported incomes of less than $25,300 (exclusive of welfare payments) receive EITC benefits up to $2,528. Families with earnings between $8,425 and $11,000 receive a flat $2,528. Those earning between $11,000 and $25,300, however, get penalized 17.68 cents for every dollar they earn above $11,000. Thus, the EITC discourages work by low-income or moderate-income earners. In particular, it discourages low-income earners from taking on a second job. The General Accounting Office estimates that hours worked by employed wives in EITC-beneficiary households have consequently decreased by 10 percent. The average EITC recipient works 1,300 hours annually, compared to a normal work year of 2,000 hours.

Policies on Crime and Drugs

It is the subject we all love to hate—crime and illegal drugs. In the last several years, the American public has ranked crime as either the most seri-

This large drug seizure by Miami police officers reflects the part of the war on drugs that shows up in the media. When queried, many Americans express concern that illegal drugs are threatening the stability of our social structure.

ous problem or the second most serious problem facing the United States. Traditionally, crime was under the purview of state governments, but increasingly it has been placed on the national agenda. Crime committed by career criminals or related to drug trafficking is especially likely to be viewed as a problem for the national government to solve. (We have already examined the issue of whether the national government or the states should control drug legislation and enforcement—see the *America at Odds* feature that opens Chapter 3.)

Worries about crime are certainly not new in this nation. In fact, according to some criminologists, crime was probably as common in the mid-1700s as it is now. In the mid-1800s, citizens in some cities reported a notable increase in criminal activities.[5] In 1910, one author stated that crime was "increasing steadily" and "threatening to bankrupt the Nation."[6] In the 1920s, racial violence and labor union battles led to a sharp increase in social violence and crime. During the period from the 1930s to the 1960s, the United States experienced stable or slightly declining overall crime rates. As you can see in Figure 17–1, during the 1960s and subsequent decades, the crime rate rose dramatically. It climbed from fewer than 2,000 crimes per 100,000 inhabitants in 1960 to nearly 6,000 crimes per 100,000 inhabitants in 1991. Since then, we have seen a decline in the overall crime rate as well as the violent crime rate (which peaked in 1994).

THE RELATIONSHIP BETWEEN AGE AND CRIME

Perhaps the most startling development during the last decade has been the increase in the number of murders committed by younger Americans. It is true that throughout most of the twentieth century, young people have committed more violent crimes than have older Americans. Yet as Figure 17–2 on the next page shows, during the late 1980s and early 1990s homicide rates for Americans aged fourteen to seventeen rose significantly, as did the rates for those aged eighteen to twenty-four. Between 1985 and 1992, homicide rates for white males in this age group went up by 50 percent and tripled for African Americans in this age bracket. At the same time, homicide rates for those over the age of twenty-five have been notably declining, and persons over the age of fifty are responsible for only 4.3 percent of the violent crime arrests in this country.[7]

Criminologists and other observers have pointed out that serious crime is a young male's occupation. The proportion of young males in the population has been falling since 1980, as the baby-boom generation has aged.[8] Now, though, the percentage of young men in the population is beginning to rise again. Consequently, some criminologists and sociologists suggest that declining crime rates might be a temporary phenomenon.[9]

Figure 17–1
The Crime Index

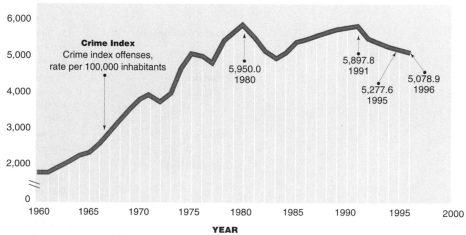

Source: Federal Bureau of Investigation.

Figure 17–2
Homicide Rates and Age,
1977–1997

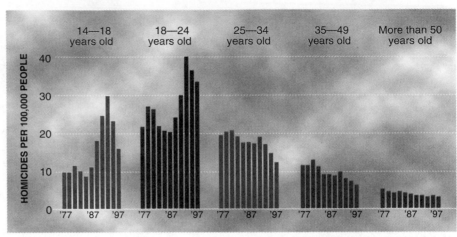

SOURCE: Bureau of Justice Statistics.

WHAT DOES CRIME COST US?

Look at Table 17–2. There you see that the cost of crime in the United States involves more than just the value of stolen goods. In fact, property loss is only about 10 percent of the total cost of crime. The other costs are (1) what we spend on the criminal justice system, including prison construction and maintenance; (2) private protection in the form of security systems, alarms, sensors, and so on; (3) urban decay; (4) destroyed lives; and (5) medical care.

One cost that is sure to rise is the cost of building and maintaining prisons. In 1999, the Department of Justice reported that the total U.S. prison population had risen to 1.8 million—more than twice what it was a decade earlier. As the number of incarcerations in the United States increases, so does the cost of building and operating prisons. Each week, an estimated 1,500 new prison beds are needed. When operational costs are included and construction costs are spread over the life of a facility, the cost of sentencing one person to one year in jail or prison now averages between $25,000 and $40,000. In all, the annual nationwide cost of building, maintaining, and operating prisons is about $35 billion today.

Table 17–2

The Total Yearly Cost of Crime in the United States

EXPENDITURE	EXPLANATION	TOTAL COST (PER YEAR)
Criminal justice	Spending on police, courts, and prisons at the federal, state, and local levels.	$95 billion
Private protection	Spending on private guards, security systems, alarms, and so on.	$70 billion
Urban decay	The cost of lost jobs and fleeing residents because of excessive crime in inner cities.	$50 billion
Property loss	The value of stolen goods and vandalized buildings.	$50 billion
Destroyed lives	The economic value of lost lives (death) and broken lives as a result of robberies, rapes, and other crimes.	$175 billion
Medical care	The cost of treating victims.	$10 billion
TOTAL		**$450 billion**

SOURCES: Federal Bureau of Investigation; *Business Week*, various issues.

Many American prisons are overcrowded. Here, four hundred inmates are crammed into a barracks-style prison in Alabama. Currently, over 1.8 million people are incarcerated in the United States.

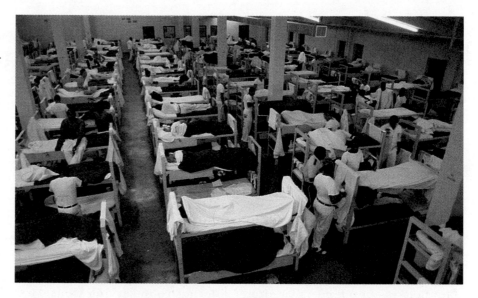

No matter how many prisons are built, they will continue to be overcrowded as long as we maintain the same legislation with respect to psychoactive drugs. The reason is that of the more than 1 million people arrested each year, the majority are arrested for drug offenses. Given that from 20 to 40 million Americans violate one or more drug laws each year, the potential "supply" of prisoners seems virtually without limit.

THE RELATIONSHIP BETWEEN CRIME RATES AND ILLEGAL DRUGS

There appear to be two relationships between crime rates and illegal drugs. The first one has to do with the number of individuals arrested each year for violations of drug laws. Contrary to popular belief, the majority of those arrested are drug users, not drug traffickers. Typically, these drug users are arrested for simple possession of small amounts of marijuana and other psychoactives.

The other relationship between crimes and illegal drugs has to do with murders and assaults that occur among drug traffickers, typically in gang battles over "turf." Gangs such as the Bloods and the Crips—two of the largest gangs—engage in shoot-outs across the country between themselves or with other rival gangs that are involved in the illegal drug trade.

Today, there is an ongoing debate over whether more funds should be used for education and rehabilitation or for the enforcement of existing drug laws (see the feature on page 428 entitled *A Question of Ethics: Has the War on Drugs Made Matters Worse?* for a discussion of this issue). Few politicians have ever suggested that the underlying drug legislation should be altered. Realistically, the "war on drugs" will be with us as long as we maintain our current legislation.[10]

Economic Policy

ECONOMIC POLICY ● All actions taken by the national government to smooth out the ups and downs in the nation's overall business activity.

MONETARY POLICY ● Actions taken by the Federal Reserve Board to change the amount of money in circulation so as to affect interest rates, credit markets, the rate of inflation, the rate of economic growth, and unemployment.

Economic policy consists of all actions taken by the government to smooth out the ups and downs in the nation's overall business activity. Economic policy is solely the responsibility of the national government.

One of the tools used in this process is **monetary policy,** which involves changing the amount of money in circulation so as to affect interest rates, credit markets, the rate of inflation, the rate of economic growth, and unemployment. Monetary policy is not specifically under the direct control of Congress and the president, because it is determined by the Federal Reserve System, an independent regulatory agency. As discussed in

a question of ethics

Has the War on Drugs Made Matters Worse?

Twenty years ago, in 1980, the "war on drugs" cost the federal government about $1 billion a year. Today, that figure exceeds $16 billion. Yet despite the billions of dollars spent on enforcing existing drug laws, drug abuse continues to be a serious problem. Consider that since 1980, the number of people incarcerated for violating drug laws has grown from 50,000 to over 400,000. In fact, as mentioned elsewhere, the majority of inmates in today's prisons are not violent offenders but drug users who violated one or another drug law.

A number of Americans believe that the war on drugs, by relying on incarceration as a "solution" to the drug problem, has made matters worse, not better, for American society.[11] Certainly, it has been responsible for prison overcrowding and the consequent need to spend more tax dollars on prison

construction and maintenance. It also does little, if anything, to mitigate the harms suffered by drug users and those around them.

What we need, claims this group, is a more pragmatic approach to the drug problem. Federal drug policy should focus less on trying to eradicate illegal drug use and more on drug rehabilation programs, ranging from prison rehabilitation programs to special drug courts that permit nonviolent drug abusers to undergo treatment as an alternative to serving time. The first drug court was established in Florida in 1989. Today, there are over three hundred such courts nationwide, a number that the Clinton administration would like to see tripled by the beginning of the new century.

A number of studies have indicated that rehabilitation programs monitored by drug courts are effective in reducing drug abuse. Accord-

ing to one such study, 60 percent of those who entered drug court programs were still in treatment after one year, and 50 percent eventually "graduated" from the programs.[12]

Another group of Americans, including many Republicans in Congress, argue that what we need is more spending on drug enforcement rather than treatment. In fact, according to recent public opinion surveys, the majority of Americans believe that tougher criminal penalties provide the best "solution" to the drug problem.

For Critical Analysis

The basic goal of the war on drugs is to create a "drug-free America." Is this goal realistic, or should the government acknowledge that drugs are here to stay and concentrate on harm-reduction innovations (ranging from rehabilitation programs to making sterile syringes available to drug abusers)?

Chapter 15, independent regulatory agencies are not directly controlled by either Congress or the president. Thus, monetary policy is not established through the policymaking process outlined earlier in this chapter.

The national government also controls **fiscal policy,** which is the use of changes in government expenditures and taxes to alter national economic variables. These variables include the rate of unemployment, the level of interest rates, the rate of inflation, and the rate of economic growth.

In this section we look briefly at the politics of monetary and fiscal policy, as well as the federal tax system and the issue of deficit spending.

MONETARY POLICY

As mentioned, monetary policymaking is under the authority of the Federal Reserve System (the Fed), which was established by Congress as the nation's central banking system in 1913. The Fed is governed by a board of seven governors, including the very powerful chairperson. The president appoints the members of the board of governors, and the Senate must approve the nominations. Members of the board serve for fourteen-year terms. Although the Fed's board of governors acts independently, the Fed has, on occasion, yielded to presidential pressure, and the Fed's chairperson must follow a congressional resolution requiring him to report monetary targets over each six-month period. Nevertheless, to date, the Fed has remained one of the truly independent sources of economic power in the government.

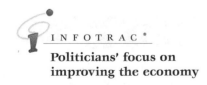

INFOTRAC®
Politicians' focus on improving the economy

FISCAL POLICY ● The use of changes in government expenditures and taxes to alter national economic variables, such as the employment rate and price stability.

FEDERAL OPEN MARKET COMMITTEE (FOMC) ● The most important body within the Federal Reserve System; the FOMC decides how monetary policy should be carried out by the Federal Reserve.

EASY-MONEY POLICY ● A monetary policy that involves stimulating the economy by expanding the rate of growth of the money supply. An easy-money policy supposedly will lead to lower interest rates and induce consumers to spend more and producers to invest more.

STAGFLATION ● A condition that occurs when both inflation and unemployment are rising.

KEYNESIAN ECONOMICS ● An economic theory proposed by British economist John Maynard Keynes that is typically associated with the use of fiscal policy to alter national economic variables. Keynesian economics gained prominence during the Great Depression of the 1930s.

Easy Money and Stagflation

The Fed and its **Federal Open Market Committee (FOMC)** make decisions about monetary policy several times each year. In theory, monetary policy is relatively straightforward. In periods of recession and high unemployment, we should pursue an **easy-money policy** to stimulate the economy by expanding the rate of growth of the money supply. An easy-money policy supposedly will lead to lower interest rates and induce consumers to spend more and producers to invest more. In periods of rising inflation, the Fed does the reverse: it reduces the rate of growth in the amount of money in circulation. This policy should cause interest rates to rise, thus inducing consumers to spend less and businesses to invest less. In theory, this sounds quite simple; the reality, however, is not simple at all. During periods of **stagflation**—rising inflation *and* rising unemployment—an expansionary monetary policy (increasing or expanding the rate of growth of the money supply) will lead to even more inflation.

Riding against the Wind

The economy goes through business cycles involving recessions (when unemployment is high) and boom times (when unemployment is low and the economy is in a period of growth). Monetary policy, in principle, should be countercyclical. The Fed should thus "ride against the wind" and create policies that go counter to business activity. Economic researchers have concluded, however, that, on average, the Fed's policy has been procyclical from the beginning. That is, by the time the Fed increased the money supply, it was time to decrease it; and by the time the Fed began to reduce the rate of growth in the amount of money in circulation, it was time to start increasing it.

These coordination difficulties are caused by the length of time it takes for a change in monetary policy to become effective. There is usually a lag of about fourteen months between the time the economy slows down (or speeds up) and the time the economy begins to feel the effects of a policy change.[13] Therefore, by the time a change in policy becomes effective, a different policy may be needed.

Perhaps the Fed's most devastating procyclical blunder occurred during the 1930s. Many economists believe that what would have been a severe recession became the Great Depression because the Fed's policy resulted in about a one-third decrease in the money supply.

FISCAL POLICY

The principle underlying fiscal policy, like that underlying monetary policy, is relatively simple: when unemployment is rising and the economy is going into a recession, fiscal policy should stimulate economic activity by increasing government spending, decreasing taxes, or both. When unemployment is decreasing and prices are rising (leading to inflation), fiscal policy should curb economic activity by reducing government spending, increasing taxes, or both. This particular view of fiscal policy is an outgrowth of the economic theories of the English economist John Maynard Keynes (1883–1943). Keynes's theories guided fiscal policymakers during the New Deal programs of Franklin D. Roosevelt in the 1930s.

Keynesian economics suggests that the forces of supply and demand operate too slowly in recessions, and therefore the government should undertake actions to stimulate the economy during such periods. Keynesian economists maintain that the Great Depression resulted from a serious imbalance in the economy. The public was saving more than usual, and businesses were investing less than usual. According to Keynesian theory, at the beginning of the depression, the government should have filled the gap that was created when businesses began limiting their investments. The government could have done so by increasing government spending or cutting taxes.

One of the problems with fiscal policy is that typically a lag exists between the government's decision to institute fiscal policy and the actual implementation of that policy. This is because the power to create fiscal policy does not rest with one individual or institution. Even if the president wants to institute a new fiscal policy, he is only one of many participants in the fiscal policymaking process. The president, with the aid of the director of the Office of Management and Budget, the secretary of the Treasury Department, and the Council of Economic Advisers, designs a desired mix of taxes and government expenditures. But they can only *recommend* this mix. It is up to Congress, with the help of many committees (such as the House Ways and Means Committee, the Senate Finance Committee, and the Senate Budget Committee), to enact the legislation necessary to implement fiscal policy.

THE FEDERAL TAX SYSTEM

The government raises money to pay its expenses in two ways: through taxes levied on business and personal income and through borrowing. In 1960, individuals paid 52 percent of total federal tax revenues. By 1999, this proportion had reached 74 percent (adding income taxes and Social Security payments together).

The Action-Reaction Syndrome

An examination of the Internal Revenue Code shows that it consists of thousands of pages, thousands of sections, and thousands of subsections. In other words, our tax system is not simple. Part of the reason for this is that tax policy has always been plagued by the **action-reaction syndrome,** a term describing the following phenomenon: *for every government action, there will be a reaction by the public.* Eventually, the government will react with another action, and the public will follow with further reaction. The ongoing action-reaction cycle is clearly operative in policymaking with respect to taxes.

ACTION-REACTION SYNDROME ●
For every government action, there will be a reaction by the public. The government then takes a further action to counter the public's reaction—and the cycle begins again.

PUBLIC DEBT ● The total amount of money that the national government owes as a result of borrowing; also called the national debt.

Tax Loopholes

Generally, the action-reaction syndrome means that the higher the tax rate—the action on the part of the government—the greater the public's reaction to that tax rate. Individuals and corporations facing high tax rates will react by making concerted attempts to get Congress to add various loopholes to the tax law that will allow them to reduce their taxable incomes.

When the Internal Revenue Code imposed very high tax rates on high incomes, it also provided for more loopholes. These loopholes enabled many wealthy individuals to decrease their tax bills significantly. For example, special tax provisions allowed investors in oil and gas wells to reduce their taxable income. Additional loopholes permitted individuals to shift income from one year to the next—which meant that they could postpone the payment of their taxes for one year. Still more loopholes let U.S. citizens form corporations outside the United States in order to avoid some taxes completely.

Will We Ever Have a Truly Simple Tax System?

The Tax Reform Act of 1986 was intended to lower taxes and simplify the tax code—and it did just that for most taxpayers. A few years later, however, large federal deficits forced Congress to choose between cutting spending and raising taxes, and Congress opted to do the latter. Tax increases occurred under both the Bush and the Clinton administrations. In fact, the tax rate for the highest income bracket rose from 28 percent in 1986 to 39.6 percent in 1993. Thus, the effective tax rate increased by over 40 percent.

In response to this sharp increase in taxes, those who were affected lobbied Congress to legislate special exceptions and loopholes so that the full impact of the rate increase would not be felt by the wealthiest and most powerful Americans. As a result, the tax code is now just as complicated as it was before the 1986 Tax Reform Act.

In 1997, lawmakers again talked about simplifying the tax rules. Nevertheless, the tax bill that was signed into law that year made the tax rules even more complicated. It added new forms to fill out, new instructions to decipher, and over eight hundred pages to the Internal Revenue Code.

DEFICIT SPENDING AND THE PUBLIC DEBT

When the government spends more than it receives, it has to finance this shortfall. Typically, it borrows. The U.S. Treasury sells IOUs on behalf of the U.S. government. They are called U.S. Treasury bills, or bonds. The sale of these bonds to corporations, private individuals, pension plans, foreign governments, foreign companies, and foreign individuals is big business. After all, until only very recently, federal government expenditures had exceeded federal government revenues virtually every year for many decades. The deficit reached its peak in recent years in 1982 when it amounted to almost 6 percent of total national income.

Every time there is a federal government deficit, there is an increase in the total accumulated **public debt** (also called national debt), which is defined as the total value of all outstanding federal government borrowing. If the existing public debt is $5 trillion and the government runs a deficit of $100 billion, then at the end of the year the public debt is $5.1 trillion. Table 17–3 shows what has happened to the public debt over time. We often hear about the burden of the public debt. Some analysts even maintain that the government will eventually go bankrupt. As long as the government can collect taxes to pay for interest on its public debt, however, that will never happen. What happens instead is that when Treasury bonds come due, they are simply "rolled over," or refinanced. That is, if a $1 million Treasury bond comes due today and is cashed in, the U.S. Treasury pays it off with the money it gets from selling another $1 million bond.

The interest on these bonds is paid by federal taxes. Even though most of the interest is being paid to American citizens, the more the federal

Table 17–3
The Public Debt

YEAR	NET PUBLIC DEBT (BILLIONS OF CURRENT DOLLARS)
1940	42.7
1945	235.2
1950	219.0
1955	226.6
1960	237.2
1965	261.6
1970	284.9
1975	396.9
1980	709.3
1985	1,499.4
1990	2,410.4
1995	3,603.3
1999	3,840.0

SOURCES: U.S. Department of the Treasury and Office of Management and Budget; 1999 data are estimated.

This photo shows the national debt counter that was placed in front of the Capitol building in Washington, D.C., by members of the Concord Coalition. The coalition is a nonpartisan organization founded in 1992 by the late senator Paul Tsongas (D., Mass.), former senator Warren Rudman (R., N.H.), and former U.S. secretary of commerce Peter Peterson. Former senator Sam Nunn (D., Ga.) was named co-chair of the coalition in April 1997. The Concord Coalition is dedicated to preventing federal budget deficits while ensuring the continuation of Social Security, Medicare, and Medicaid.

government borrows to meet these payments, the greater the percentage of its budget that is committed to making interest payments. This reduces the government's ability to supply money for needed community services, such as transportation, education, and housing programs.

Americans at Odds over Domestic Policy

Many groups in the United States are at odds today over this country's domestic and economic policies. As you learned in this chapter, the changes in welfare policy continue to fuel a controversy over how to deal with the problem of poverty. Americans are also at odds over how to reduce crime, including crimes related to drug trafficking and drug abuse. Here we look at two other issues over which Americans are at odds. One issue concerns the Social Security system. Another issue that seems to elicit ongoing debate has to do with whether the policymaking process as carried out at the national level is consistent with our democratic principles of government.

Should We Privatize Social Security?

Americans are at odds over whether we should privatize, partially or completely, the Social Security system. If Social Security were privatized, individuals would be given the choice of staying with the current government-financed system or placing the amount of money they would otherwise pay in Social Security taxes in private pension plans. When the Chilean government implemented such a system in 1981, more than 90 percent of the workers chose the private pension option. Under that option, workers invest 10 percent of their wages in private pension funds and choose investment firms that will manage the funds.

There is substantial support in the United States for the privatization of Social Security. Recent surveys indicate that the majority of adult respondents liked the idea of using part of their Social Security taxes to invest in a personal retirement account. Even some members of the Advisory Council on Social Security have advocated allowing workers to have the option of shifting all of their Social Security payroll taxes to private alternatives. The idea of privatizing Social Security has some Americans worried, though. The basic worry is that even partial privatization may eventually lead to the destruction of the benefits that are currently available to Social Security recipients.

One thing is certain: Social Security will continue to be an issue on the political agenda, and changing the current system may prove difficult. Remember from Chapter 7 that one of the most powerful interest groups in the United States is the AARP (the American Association of Retired Persons). Clearly, its members would not want to see a reduction in Social Security benefits. Neither would the current workers who have made substantial "contributions" to Social Security. Nevertheless, at some point, given the increasing number of retired persons relative to the number of workers who pay into the system, something will have to be done. The solution may very likely involve some form of partial privatization of the Social Security system.

Democracy and the Policymaking Process

Theoretically, at least, in a representative democracy such as the United States, those affected by a public policy should have a voice in the making of that policy. Some contend that American citizens do have a voice in policymaking—through their votes and through various interest groups interacting at the national level with Congress and the executive branch. Others contend that not all interests are represented by interest groups. For example, consider the Welfare Reform Act of 1996. Those affected by the change in welfare policy—the poor—had very little say in the policymaking process. Indeed, the poor are one of the most underrepresented groups in the nation.

A further issue over which Americans are at odds has to do with the amount of policymaking that is undertaken by unelected bodies, including regulatory agencies and the federal courts. Although Congress authorizes regulatory agencies to create new rules, which have the effect of law, the heads of these agencies are appointed, not elected. Therefore, an administrative agency, such as the Federal Reserve Board, can create economic policies that affect millions of Americans—yet those Americans have little voice in the agency's policymaking process.

Similarly, federal court judges are not elected but rather are appointed by the president and confirmed by the Senate. Yet these judges, by interpreting the law and applying it to particular situations, do, in fact, make policy, as you read in Chapter 16.

Public policies created at all levels of government frame the daily lives of Americans and touch on virtually every activity in our society. Americans will certainly continue to be at odds over how the voice of the electorate can be incorporated into the policymaking process.

key terms

action-reaction syndrome 430
agenda setting 418
domestic policy 417
easy-money policy 429
economic policy 427
Federal Open Market Committee (FOMC) 429
fiscal policy 428

income redistribution 419
Keynesian economics 429
monetary policy 427
policymaking process 417
public debt 431
social welfare policy 419
stagflation 429

chapter summary

1. Public policy can be defined as a government plan or course of action taken in response to a political issue or to enhance the social or political well-being of society. Domestic policy consists of public policy concerning issues within a national unit. Domestic policies are formed through a policymaking process involving several steps, or phases: agenda setting, policy formulation and adoption, policy implementation, and policy evaluation.

2. Social welfare policy consists of all government actions that are undertaken to give assistance to specific groups, such as the aged, the ill, and the poor. Social welfare policy is the government's response to the decision made by the American people, through their elected representatives, that everyone in the nation should be provided with a certain minimum level of income. Social welfare policy is implemented primarily through income redistribution—income is taken from some people through taxation and given to others. Government programs that redistribute income fall into two areas: social insurance programs (such as Social Security and Medicare) and public-assistance programs (often called welfare).

3. The Social Security program provides old-age, survivors', and disability insurance (OASDI) to retired workers who have made Social Security contributions while working. Today, Social Security is essentially an intergenerational income transfer in which the income paid by younger Americans who work is transferred to older, retired persons who do not work.

4. Major public-assistance programs designed to help the poor include Supplemental Security Income (SSI), Temporary Assistance to Needy Families (the basic welfare program), food stamps, and the Earned Income Tax Credit (EITC) program. The Welfare Reform Act of 1996 turned over significant welfare-management responsibilities to state governments. Under the new welfare policy, the federal government gives block grants to the states to help finance the state-run welfare programs.

5. Economic policy is established solely by the national government. Tools of economic policymaking include monetary policy and fiscal policy. Monetary policy is the use of changes in the amount of money in circulation to affect interest rates, credit markets, the rate of inflation, the rate of economic growth, and unemployment. Monetary policy is made by the Federal Reserve System (the Fed) and its Federal Open Market Committee (FOMC). Fiscal policy is the use of changes in government expenditures and taxes to alter national economic variables, including the rate of unemployment, the level of interest rates, the rate of inflation, and the rate of economic growth. No one person or government body makes fiscal policy; rather, fiscal policy is the outcome of a long and deliberative process involving both the executive branch and Congress.

6. The government raises revenues to pay its expenses by levying taxes on business and personal income or through borrowing. Individual income taxes constitute an increasing percentage of federal revenue. The action-reaction syndrome means that for every government action (such as an increase in the tax rate), there will be a reaction on the part of the public (such as efforts to get Congress to create exceptions and loopholes). We will probably never have a truly simple tax system because Congress often opts to increase taxes instead of cutting back on federal spending, thus setting in motion the action-reaction syndrome.

7. Until recently, federal government expenditures had exceeded federal government revenues virtually every year for decades, resulting in an increasing public (national) debt. To finance its deficit spending, the government sells Treasury bonds, on which it pays interest. Even though most of the interest is paid to American citizens, the more the federal government borrows to meet these interest payments, the less the government has to spend for needed community services.

8. Americans are at odds over a number of economic and domestic policies. One issue concerns what should be done about Social Security, given that the number of people who are working relative to the number of people who are retiring is declining. One alternative being debated is the full or partial privatization of the Social Security system. Some Americans are also concerned about the policymaking process itself and whether it is consistent with representative democracy.

for critical analysis

1. Some critics of the welfare reform legislation of 1996 claim that it was less "welfare reform" than "welfare repeal." Do you agree? Should the federal government have stepped back from the welfare system and turned so much authority over its implementation to the states?

2. How does public opinion affect the policymaking process?

3. Do you think you will ever collect Social Security? Would your future chances of collecting Social Security be greater if Social Security were privatized?

4. If you could choose between funding more schools or more prisons, which would you choose? Why?

5. In your opinion, what are the top three problems facing the nation today that Congress should address in the policymaking process?

6. Some people believe that the chair of the Federal Reserve Board is more powerful than the president of the country. Do you agree? Why or why not?

7. Suppose that the federal government decided to fully fund day-care centers for all children of working parents. What effect would this have on American society?

suggested readings

BROWN, Michael K. *Race, Money, and the American Welfare State.* Ithaca, N.Y.: Cornell University Press, 1999. The author examines America's "safety net" from its origins in the New Deal through much of its dismantling in the 1990s. He maintains that the forces of fiscal conservatism and racism combined to shape a welfare state in which blacks are disproportionately excluded from mainstream programs.

DIAMOND, Peter A. Ed. *Issues on Privatizing Social Security: Report of an Expert Panel of the National Academy of Social Service.* Cambridge, Mass.: MIT Press, 1999. This study addresses many important aspects of various proposals that have been made to change Social Security, including proposals that Social Security investments should be privately organized.

GUTMANN, Amy, and Dennis Thompson. *Democracy and Disagreement.* Cambridge, Mass.: Harvard University Press, 1996. These political theorists propose a solution to the challenge of making democracy more deliberative. The authors suggest that any argument about public policy, before being admitted to the public forum, should satisfy six basic principles, including reciprocity. Reciprocity means that any proposed policy should be "mutually acceptable" to all who will be bound by it.

JOHNSON, Haynes, and David S. Broder. *The System: The American Way of Politics at the Breaking Point.* Boston: Little, Brown, 1996. The authors, both Pulitzer Prize–winning journalists, offer a critical appraisal of the American political system. One of the strong points of the book is their examination of the agenda-building phase of the policymaking process.

MOYNIHAN, Daniel Patrick. *Miles to Go: A Personal History of Social Policy.* Cambridge, Mass.: Harvard University Press, 1997. Moynihan, a veteran Democratic senator from New York, gives his views on his thirty years in public service and the challenges that lie ahead. In writing about the issues of his time, he offers insights into contemporary problems facing Congress and the American people.

politics on the web

A wealth of data on everything that has to do with crime, including public attitudes, can be found on the interactive Web site offered by the Bureau of Justice Statistics called the Source Book of Criminal Justice Statistics. You can access this site at

http://www.albany.edu/sourcebook

The federal budget shows where federal funds go throughout the year. If you want to examine the budget to see how these funds are allocated, you might not want to go through the actual document (it's thicker than the Los Angeles phone book!). The following URL takes you to a site that is slightly shorter than the actual budget and a lot easier to navigate:

http://www.whitehouse.gov/WH/EOP/OMB/html/bud96gui.html

This site offers "A Citizen's Guide to the Federal Budget." If you can't get into this site, you can try going through the Welcome to the White House home page using the Virtual Library. You may have better luck, though, doing a search on a search engine (such as Excite or Yahoo) for the title of the document. The Welcome to the White House home page can be accessed at

http://www.whitehouse.gov

The national debt is a hot topic at the end of each federal fiscal year (October), as well as when national elections come around. The debt is the sum over time of each year's deficit. This URL will acquaint you with the size of the national debt:

http://www.census.gov/stat_abstract/brief.html

This site will give you "USA Statistics in Brief." If you can't get to it in this way, start with the U.S. Census Bureau's home page at

http://www.census.gov

Click on "Subjects A to Z." Then click on "S" in the alphabetic line-up and then on "Statistical Abstract."

If you are interested in reading an *Economic Report of the President,* go to

http://www.gpo.ucop.edu/catalog/erp.ct.html

Information on a variety of topics, including veterans' pensions, Medicare and Medicaid, disaster relief, and government departments (such as the Department of Agriculture and the Department of Health and Human Services) can be obtained at

http://www.whitehouse.gov/WH/Welcome.html

using web resources

Policymaking decisions go to the heart of the federal budgeting process. The Center for Community Economic Research at the University of California at Berkeley has created "The National Budget Simulation." This simple simulation is designed to illustrate the policy trade-offs needed to balance the budget. Access the center's Web site at

http://socrates.berkeley.edu:3333/budget/budget.html

1. Read the sections titled "How to play the game," "What categories of spending are used in the simulation?" and "Why tax expenditures are treated like general spending."

2. From the main page, select "The Long Version" and construct your budget. What categories did you cut? What categories did you increase?

3. How would you go about making your changes? Who might oppose your decisions? Why?

notes

1. Deborah L. Rhode, "Re-Reform Welfare Laws," *The National Law Journal,* May 10, 1999, p. A26.

2. *Ibid.*

3. Terry S. Becker, "What Makes the Welfare Bill a Winner," *Business Week,* September 23, 1996, p. 22.

4. Mark McClellan and Jonathan Skinner, "The Incidence of Medicare," National Bureau of Economic Research Working Paper, 1997, as reported in *The Economist,* August 2, 1997, p. 20.

5. President's Commission on Law Enforcement and Administration of Justice, *The Challenge of Crime in a Free Society* (Washington, D.C.: U.S. Government Printing Office, 1967), p. 19.

6. *Ibid.*

7. Federal Bureau of Investigation, *Crime in the United States, 1997* (Washington, D.C.: U.S. Government Printing Office, 1998), pp. 232–233.

8. U.S. Bureau of the Census, *Current Population Reports,* various issues.

9. William Bennett, Jr., *et al., Body Count: Moral Poverty . . . and How to Win America's War against Crime and Drugs* (New York: Simon & Schuster, 1996).

10. For an interesting proposal on how the drug problem might be solved, see Daniel K. Benjamin and Roger LeRoy Miller, *Undoing Drugs: Beyond Legalization* (New York: Basic Books, 1993), pp. 2–3.

11. For an argument in support of this view, see Ethan Nadelmann, "Rethinking the War on Drugs," *The Oregonian,* January 18, 1998, p. 1B.

12. Kalpana Srinivasen, "Forced Drug Rehabilitation Works, Bipartisan Health Experts Say," *The Fort Worth Star-Telegram,* November 11, 1998, p. 4.

13. Robert Gordon, *Macroeconomics,* 7th ed. (New York: HarperCollins, 1996), p. 431.

chapter

18

THE POLITICS OF REGULATION

Contents

Is the Payoff Worth the Cost of Stricter Air-Quality Rules?

Without question, clean air is good. The alternative, dirty air, is bad. No argument there, either. But how far should we go to ensure that the air is clean? The answer to this question is not so clear-cut, because stricter rules about air quality translate into additional costs to our society. When the Environmental Protection Agency (EPA) proposed stricter air standards in 1996, various groups of Americans were immediately at odds—as you would expect when a measure affects the health of our nation's citizens, including children, and imposes substantial costs on hundreds of thousands of businesses. Although the proposed standards became final in 1997, Americans continue to debate whether they are desirable or necessary.

Go to CD-ROM

The EPA and the Environmentalists Take a Stand

In a study funded by the EPA and published in 1995, researchers concluded that populations living in areas polluted by higher levels of particulates (very fine dust particles, measuring about 1/25th the diameter of a human hair) experience higher death rates. Subsequent to a 1993 lawsuit by the American Lung Association against the EPA, which was brought as part of an attempt to cause the EPA to reevaluate its standards, EPA chief Carol Browner announced tough new standards for particulates and ground-level ozone. She claimed that the new standards would save 15,000 lives a year, cut annual respiratory-related hospital admissions by 9,000, and reduce the number of chronic bronchitis cases by 60,000 a year. The EPA values a human life at $5 million a year, so the lives saved and medical expenses avoided would amount to $100 billion a year in benefits from the new standards. The EPA estimated that the cost to industry to comply with the new standards would be only $8.5 billion a year.

Supporters of the EPA's tougher air standards point out that particulates cause tens of thousands of Americans to die prematurely each year. Some proponents even suggest that the new regulations were too little, too late. The EPA's supporters include governors from the Northeast who have argued for years that polluted air from the Midwest contributes to air pollution in their region and who said that the tougher standards were a "bold response to this serious environmental threat."[1]

Not So Fast, Say the Critics

Small but vociferous groups of opponents claim that the tougher standards *will not* have a significant effect on public health, but that they certainly *will* be costly for businesses and communities to meet. Under the new standards, 250 communities around the nation will find themselves in violation of the standards for ozone and particulate pollution. Environmental researcher Lester Lave points out that Los Angeles cannot even meet the previous ozone standard, let alone the new one.

After the new EPA standards were proposed, a coalition of large industrial groups and a number of governors

and big-city mayors joined together in 1996 to fight the tougher standards. Governor George Voinovich of Ohio argued that the proposed rules would erode public support for environmental programs. Detroit's mayor, Dennis Archer, claimed that they would significantly hinder Detroit's economic recovery. Other critics contended that more research was needed—one study is not enough to justify the new regulations. Some critics even questioned the underlying studies that purported to show the dangers of particulates. These critics pointed out that no study has really demonstrated that particulates cause higher death rates. In other words, statistical correlation does not necessarily imply causation.

Where Do You Stand?

1. Ultimately, the public pays for tougher air standards in the form of higher-priced products and the reduced availability of certain services (such as local dry-cleaning establishments). Is there any way the public can affect the EPA's decisions regarding air standards?

2. Does calling oneself an "environmentalist" necessarily mean that one is in favor of tougher air-quality standards? Why or why not?

On the Web

For information about the EPA and its programs and regulations, go to http://www.epa.gov.

Introduction

REGULATION ● The exercise of government powers to influence the social and economic activities of a society.

INFOTRAC®

Air quality rules bear watching

The *Federal Register* is not light reading. This daily publication of the executive branch prints government orders, rules, and regulations and is filled with sentences such as "CFR part 1320 sets forth procedures for agencies to follow in obtaining OMB clearing for information collection requirements under the Paperwork Reduction Act of 1980, 44 U.S.C. 3501 *et seq.*"[2]

During the 1970s, a decade that witnessed an explosion of new regulations, the *Federal Register* grew to almost 100,000 pages each year. After President Ronald Reagan was elected in 1980 on a platform that promised to limit the size of the federal bureaucracy, the *Federal Register* became leaner for a time. In the late 1980s and early 1990s, the pendulum swung again toward increased government regulatory action, and today the *Register* is more than 130,000 pages thick.

Is a thick *Federal Register* "good" for the United States? Are greater amounts of government influence on daily life good for any country or community? These questions lie at the heart of the politics of regulation. The growth in the bureaucracy that you read about in Chapter 15 resulted from the increasing regulation of the nation's economic and social life during the twentieth century. It is the bureaucracy that implements the many rules and regulations issued by agencies of the U.S. government. Implicitly, those who criticize our extensive government bureaucracy also criticize the extensive government regulation that has necessitated that bureaucracy.

In this chapter, we focus on the regulatory system that has become such a dominant feature in today's political environment. We look at how that system evolved and at some of its pros and cons for American society. We begin the chapter by examining the constitutional basis for such regulation.

The Constitutional Basis for Regulation

Regulation can be broadly defined as the exercise of government powers to influence the social and economic activities of a society. The seeds for government regulation in the United States were planted by the framers of the Constitution, although it is doubtful that they envisioned the size of today's federal government. Article I, Section 8, of the Constitution expressly permits Congress "[t]o regulate Commerce with foreign Nations, and among the several States, and with the Indian Tribes." This clause, referred to as the *commerce clause,* has had a greater impact on business than has any other provision in the Constitution. The power it delegates to the federal government ensures the uniformity of rules governing the movement of goods through the states.

For some time, the commerce clause was interpreted as being limited to commerce *between* the states (*inter*state commerce) and not applicable to commerce *within* the states (*intra*state commerce). In 1824, however, the United States Supreme Court held that Congress has the power to regulate any activity—interstate or intrastate—that substantially "affects" interstate commerce.[3] Although Congress did not immediately exploit this broad grant of regulatory power, over time the commerce clause became the constitutional justification for extensive federal regulation. In 1942, for example, the Supreme Court held that even a farmer's wheat production intended wholly for consumption on his own farm was subject to federal regulation. The Court reasoned that the farmer's actions substantially affected interstate commerce because the home consumption of wheat reduces the demand for wheat in the marketplace.[4]

Virtually all commercial activities today can be regulated by the federal government. Although the Constitution only gives the federal government the power to regulate interstate commerce, the Supreme Court has interpreted that power expansively. Even if a farmer grows just enough food to consume at home, the activity can still be regulated by the federal government under its commerce power, according to the Supreme Court. Why? Because home consumption of home-grown food reduces the demand for that food in the marketplace and thus "substantially affects" interstate commerce.

A Brief History of Government Regulation

Federal regulation was almost nonexistent during the early years of the United States. U.S. citizens, still smarting from memories of King George III's colonial meddling, resisted (not entirely successfully) government interference in private affairs until after the Civil War (1861–1865). When the Industrial Revolution changed the economy and the "Robber Barons" (John D. Rockefeller, Andrew Carnegie, and Henry Ford, among others) began to assert more—and frequently unwelcome—influence over people's daily lives, those attitudes changed. The ensuing populist movement, driven by agrarian and labor groups, reflected mistrust by the "common people" of this new elite class of "big business" people.

"Robber Barons" Henry Ford (left), John D. Rockefeller, Sr. (middle), and Andrew Carnegie (right).

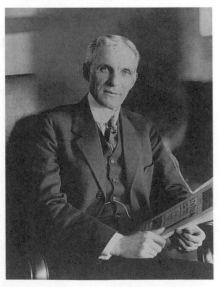

In the 1880s, the government began to react to the public's desire to rein in big business by passing legislation that marked the beginnings of the modern regulatory environment. (For an overview of regulation in the United States, see Figure 18–1.)

THE BEGINNINGS OF REGULATION

In 1887, the government attempted to regulate the railroad industry—then the nation's most powerful private sector—by passing the Interstate Commerce Act. The act prohibited railroads from charging discriminatory rates and different rates for short hauls and long hauls, except under certain circumstances. The act created the first regulatory agency, the Interstate Commerce Commission (ICC), to enforce these provisions.

Figure 18–1
A Time Line of Regulation in the United States

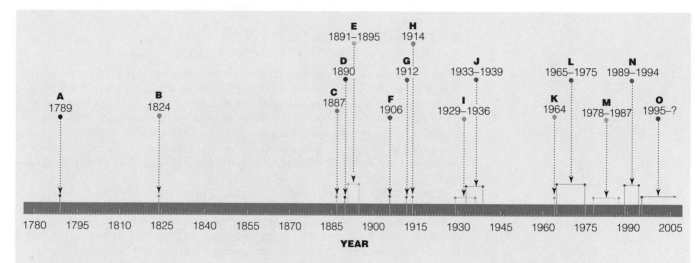

DESCRIPTION

A. The U.S. Constitution is ratified. Article 1, Section 8, of the Constitution—the commerce clause—provides the legal basis for regulation.

B. The U.S. Supreme Court rules that the commerce clause gives Congress the power to regulate any business activity that affects both interstate and intrastate trade. This broad interpretation paves the way for much of the federal legislation to follow.

C. Passage of the Interstate Commerce Act. This act establishes the control of the federal government over the railroad industry. Congress forms the nation's first federal regulatory agency, the Interstate Commerce Commission (ICC).

D. Passage of the Sherman Antitrust Act, the first major law to protect consumers from anticompetitive practices by business.

E. The populist movement reaches its peak. Farmer and labor groups voice mistrust of "big business" barons born of the Industrial Revolution. Populism makes early demands that government protect the people from business.

F. Passage of the Pure Food and Drug Act, the first major law to protect consumers from fraudulent or unsafe food and drugs.

G. Passage of the Sherley Amendment, which reinforces the Pure Food and Drug Act.

H. Passage of the Clayton Act and the Federal Trade Commission Act. Both laws strengthen the Sherman Antitrust Act.

I. The Great Depression. Economic hardships led many Americans to question business practices of the preceding decade.

J. The New Deal, a legislative program adopted by President Franklin D. Roosevelt to alleviate the effects of the Great Depression. The Securities Act of 1933 and the Securities Exchange Act of 1934 increase regulation of the stock market in order to restore investor confidence. The Banking Act of 1933 forms the Federal Deposit Insurance Corporation to protect depositors in the nation's banks. The Norris-LaGuardia Act of 1932 and the Wagner Act of 1935 strengthen the nation's labor unions.

K. Passage of the Civil Rights Act. This act attempts to protect Americans from being

discriminated against on the basis of race, color, national origin, religion, or gender.

L. A decade of increased social legislation along the line of the Civil Rights Act. Legislation passed during this period strengthens the rights of workers and consumers, provides financial assistance for poor Americans, and attempts to protect the environment.

M. Deregulation. In reaction to the regulation explosion of the late 1960s and early 1970s, this period of deregulation sees the removal of regulatory restraints on certain industries. Under Presidents Jimmy Carter (1977–1981) and Ronald Reagan (1981–1989), the airline, trucking, and communications industries are significantly deregulated.

N. Reregulation. Under Presidents George Bush and Bill Clinton, the trend of deregulation is reversed. A number of new regulations are placed on the banking and telecommunications industries, as well as many other sectors of the economy.

O. "Re"-deregulation? As Congress becomes more conservative, political pressure is rising to eliminate many regulations pertaining to the environment, workers' rights, and international trade.

ANTITRUST LAW ● The body of law that attempts to support free competition in the marketplace by curbing monopolistic and unfair trade practices.

Specifically, the ICC was charged with enforcing the act's mandate that all rates be "reasonable and just."

In 1890, Congress passed the Sherman Antitrust Act. The act was designed to destroy the large combinations of capital that were occurring in the American economy, particularly through the use of business organizations called "trusts," such as Standard Oil of New Jersey. That trust controlled over 80 percent of the nation's oil-refining capacity. The Sherman Act and subsequent legislation curbing monopolistic practices thus became known as **antitrust laws.** Section 1 of the Sherman Act declared that any "contract, combination in the form of trust or otherwise, or conspiracy, in restraint of trade or commerce among the several states, or with foreign nations" was illegal. Section 2 of the act stated that any person "who shall monopolize, or attempt to monopolize, or combine or conspire with any other person or persons to monopolize any part of the trade or commerce . . . shall be guilty of a misdemeanor."[5]

REGULATORY MOMENTUM IN THE TWENTIETH CENTURY

With the turn of the century came the Progressive Era in American politics. The public's hostility toward big business was at a high point, fueled by writers such as Upton Sinclair. Sinclair's *The Jungle,* which was published in 1906, was a harshly critical exposé of the nation's meat-packing industry. Fledgling grassroots organizations, such as the National Consumers' League, began questioning whether the prices being asked by business were fair and whether the products being sold were of the highest quality possible.

The national leaders of the time, Presidents Theodore Roosevelt (1901–1909), William Howard Taft (1909–1913), and Woodrow Wilson (1913–1921), echoed these concerns and oversaw a number of new regulatory developments. The Pure Food and Drug Act of 1906 and a 1912 amendment to that act attempted to protect consumers from unsafe food and drugs. In 1914, Congress passed the Clayton Act to sharpen the vague antitrust provisions of the Sherman Antitrust Act. The Clayton Act prohibited or limited a number of very specific business practices, such as charging different prices to different customers for the same goods, that were felt to be "unreasonable" attempts at restraining trade or commerce. The Federal Trade Commission Act was also passed in 1914. This act established the Federal Trade Commission to investigate unfair competitive practices, such as false or misleading advertising.

THE GREAT DEPRESSION AND THE NEW DEAL

President Franklin D. Roosevelt (1933–1945), in an attempt to spur the nation's recovery from the Great Depression that began in 1929, launched his New Deal—a series of programs that directly involved the federal government in big business. In the past, big business would have been resentful of such intrusions, but during the early 1930s it would take any help it was offered.

The Securities Act of 1933 and the Securities Exchange Act of 1934 increased federal regulation of the stock market and restored investor confidence. The Banking Act of 1933 created the Federal Deposit Insurance Corporation to protect most depositors by insuring their deposits. The Social Security Act of 1935 provided for income security in the form of old-age (retirement), survivors', and disability insurance. The Federal Unemployment Tax Act of the same year created a state system to provide unemployment compensation to eligible individuals. The decade also saw significant labor legislation: the Norris-LaGuardia Act of 1932 and the Wagner Act of 1935 permitted employees to organize unions and to engage in collective bargaining, respectively. Roosevelt's New Deal legislation dramatically extended the regulatory reach of the federal government into the economic and social life of the nation.

DEREGULATION ● The removal of regulatory restraints on business.

ECONOMIC REGULATION ● Government regulation of natural monopolies and inherently noncompetitive industries.

SOCIAL REGULATION ● Government regulation across all industries that is undertaken for the purpose of protecting the public welfare.

REGULATION AND DEREGULATION SINCE WORLD WAR II

After World War II (1939–1945), the U.S. economy was strengthened to the point where big business complained of being restricted by untoward government intrusion. The rise and fall of regulation since that time has been cyclical and has depended as much on public attitudes as on economic necessity. The *laissez-faire* attitude of the prosperous, postwar 1950s gave way to the idealistic policies of the 1960s and 1970s, during which much social legislation was passed—for example, the Civil Rights Act of 1964, the Water Quality Act of 1965, the Occupational Safety and Health Act of 1970, and the Consumer Product Safety Act of 1972.

A backlash against this regulatory atmosphere began in 1978, when President Jimmy Carter (1977–1981) instigated the deregulation of the airline and trucking industries. **Deregulation,** as the term implies, involves the removal of regulatory restraints on business. Ronald Reagan continued the deregulatory process during his two terms as president (1981–1989) by striking down regulatory controls of the telephone and bus industries. Reagan, in fact, pushed deregulation as one of the central tenets of his presidency. Rules and regulations increased again under the Bush and Clinton administrations, however.

Types of Regulation

It would be a mistake to try to gather all government regulation under one heading. Different regulations involve different methods and have different goals. Some forms of regulation are created with a specific industry in mind, whereas other forms cover the entire spectrum of the business world. Some regulation purports to control industry, and some claims to assist it.

In general, though, there are two types of government regulation. **Economic regulation** covers the regulation of natural monopolies and inherently noncompetitive industries. **Social regulation** tries to protect the public welfare and applies across all industries.[6] (See Table 18–1 for examples of both kinds of regulation.)

I N F O T R A C °

When competition results in fewer options

Table 18–1

Examples of Economic and Social Regulations and Corresponding Agencies

AGENCY	TYPE OF REGULATION
Product Markets	
Federal Communications Commission (FCC)	Economic
Federal Trade Commission (FTC)	Social and economic
Labor Markets	
Equal Employment Opportunity Commission (EEOC)	Social
Financial Markets	
Securities and Exchange Commission (SEC)	Social
Energy and Environment	
Environmental Protection Agency (EPA)	Social
Federal Energy Regulatory Commission	Economic
Health and Safety	
Occupational Safety and Health Administration (OSHA)	Social and economic

ECONOMIC REGULATION

Earlier in the chapter we saw examples of economic regulation with the creation of the Interstate Commerce Commission and the Federal Trade Commission. Other economic regulatory bodies control industries by setting maximum and minimum prices, restricting the entry of new companies, and controlling services that companies may offer.

For example, the Federal Communications Commission (FCC) was established in 1934 to regulate interstate communications and later was extended to cover the radio, telegraph, and telephone industries. After cable television companies were allowed to set their own rates in 1986, cable rates rose at three times the rate of inflation. Because cable operators hold nearly a 100 percent monopoly in cable-wired cities, consumer interest groups pressured the regulatory authorities to restrain costs. The result was the Cable TV Reregulation Act of 1992, which allowed the FCC to order a 10 to 15 percent cutback in cable rates. (The Telecommunications Act of 1996 deregulated cable rates again, however.)

SOCIAL REGULATION

Social regulation reflects concerns for how business activities affect the public welfare. In other words, social regulation focuses on the impact of production and services on the environment and society, on the working conditions under which goods and services are produced, and sometimes on the physical attributes of goods. The aim of social regulation is to improve the quality of life for everyone by creating a less polluted environment, better working conditions, and safer and better products.

For example, the Food and Drug Administration attempts to protect consumers from impure or unsafe foods, drugs, cosmetics, and other potentially hazardous products; the Consumer Product Safety Commission specifies minimum safety standards for consumer products in an attempt to reduce "unreasonable" risks of injury; the Environmental Protection Agency watches over the amount of pollutants released into the environment; the Occupational Safety and Health Administration attempts to protect workers against employment-related injuries and illnesses; and the Equal Employment Opportunity Commission seeks to provide fair access to jobs.

REGULATING NEGATIVE EXTERNALITIES

When a paper mill dumps its waste products into a nearby river, pollution obviously results. The paper company, though, does not pay the "cost" of the pollution, and therefore neither do its primary customers (through higher prices). Nevertheless, that pollution does represent a cost, and possibly a very high one, to the surrounding community. The quality of life for those who live on the banks of the river declines. Perhaps it is now unsafe for their children to swim in the river, or perhaps tainted groundwater has seeped into their underground wells. Additionally, the fauna and flora that live in the river suffer from the effects of the pollution.

The social costs paid by the community for decisions made by private decision makers are called *externalities* because some (or all) of the costs remain external to the private (business) decision-making process. **Negative externalities,** such as pollution, are often cited as reasons why government regulation is needed. After all, the full cost of using or harming a scarce resource, such as water, air, or the ozone layer, is borne one way or the other by all those who live in a society. When a firm that is producing a negative externality and the customers buying that firm's product do not take the external costs into consideration in their decision-making processes, society suffers. The problems of dealing with negative externalities become even more complicated when not just a single paper mill but an entire industry is involved.

Correcting for negative externalities is often expensive, and few firms are willing to shoulder the burden voluntarily and alone. For example, in

This paper mill in Port St. Joe, Florida, is emitting soot and smoke. Such emissions constitute negative externalities because they impose costs on third parties, such as homeowners and individuals, who have to breathe the polluted air. Government sometimes steps in to regulate such negative externalities.

1971, the federal government required new automobiles to have engines that run on unleaded gasoline instead of the more highly polluting leaded fuel. Subsequently, drivers in fifty of the country's most polluted cities were required to use a cleaner but more expensive blend of reformulated gasoline. Without government intervention, few automobile companies would have voluntarily changed their engine designs, and few consumers would have voluntarily spent 10 cents more per gallon for cleaner air. In these situations, as in many others involving air pollution, water pollution, or product safety, government regulation has been the primary way to control negative externalities.

Regulatory Agencies: Are They the Fourth Branch of Government?

In Chapter 2, we considered the system of checks and balances among the three branches of the U.S. government—executive, legislative, and judicial. Recent history, however, shows that it may be time to regard the regulatory agencies as a fourth branch of the government. Although the U.S. Constitution does not mention regulatory agencies, they can and do make **legislative rules,** or *substantive rules,* that are as legally binding as laws passed by Congress. With such powers, this administrative branch has an influence on the nation's businesses that rivals that of the president, Congress, and the courts.

Regulatory agencies have been on the American political scene since the last stages of the Industrial Revolution, but their golden age came during the regulatory explosion of the 1960s and 1970s. Congress itself could not have overseen the actual implementation of all of the laws that it was enacting at the time to control pollution and deal with other social problems. It therefore chose (and still chooses) to delegate to administrative agencies the tasks involved in implementing its laws. By delegating some of its authority to an administrative agency, Congress may indirectly monitor a particular area in which it has passed legislation without becoming bogged down in the details relating to the enforcement of that legislation—details that are often best left to specialists.

As we head into the new century, the government has been hiring increasing numbers of specialists to oversee its regulatory work. By the late 1990s, spending by federal regulatory agencies reached an all-time high: they spent more than $16 billion to administer their regulations, and they employed

LEGISLATIVE RULE ● An administrative agency rule that carries the same weight as a statute enacted by a legislature.

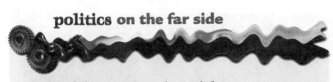

politics on the far side

Sparkling Apple Cider versus the U.S. Government

A few years ago, Benjamin Lacy III was running an apple cider establishment owned and operated by his family when twelve agents from the Federal Bureau of Investigation, the Environmental Protection Agency, the Virginia Department of Environmental Quality, and the state police stormed his place and seized all of his business documents. Why were these agents there? They believed that Lacy had not properly completed the complex paperwork required by the Clean Water Act.

Eighteen months later, following an investigation involving multiple government agencies, Lacy was found guilty by a jury of eight counts of violating the Clean Water Act. Lacy faced twenty-four years in jail and fines of $2 million for making eight errors in reviewing thousands of test results of the water discharged from his cider operation over a thirty-month period. (He was granted a new trial, but given no apologies for the raid on his place of business.)

The government never proved that he damaged the environment, and a local environmental group called Friends of the Shenandoah River testified that there was no pollution from apple juice run-off. The federal judge trying the case did not care. As former federal prosecutor David Geneson observed, there are so many rules on the books that there "is almost no point in time when a company won't be in violation of some regulation."[7]

For Critical Analysis

Has the government gone "too far" in protecting the environment?

over 130,000 federal workers to do so. Do these numbers represent the natural outgrowth of a capitalist country with over 272 million citizens and 15 million different businesses or a regulatory process gone mad? (See, for example, the feature entitled *Politics on the Far Side: Sparkling Apple Cider versus the U.S. Government.*) Before evaluating this issue, it is helpful to understand more about administrative agencies and how they operate.

AGENCY CREATION

To create an administrative agency, Congress passes **enabling legislation,** which specifies the name, purpose, composition, and powers of the agency being created. The Federal Trade Commission (FTC), for example, was created in 1914 by the Federal Trade Commission Act, as mentioned earlier. The act prohibits unfair and deceptive trade practices. The act also describes the procedures that the agency must follow to charge persons or organizations with violations of the act, and it provides for judicial review of agency orders.

Other portions of the act grant the agency powers to "make rules and regulations for the purpose of carrying out the Act," to conduct investigations of business practices, to obtain reports on business practices from interstate corporations, to investigate possible violations of federal antitrust statutes, to publish findings of its investigations, and to recommend new legislation. The act also empowers the FTC to hold trial-like hearings and to **adjudicate** (formally resolve) certain kinds of trade disputes that involve FTC regulations or federal antitrust laws.

Enabling legislation makes the regulatory agency a potent organization. For example, the Securities and Exchange Commission (SEC) imposes rules regarding the disclosures a company must make to those who purchase its stock. Under its enforcement authority, the SEC also prosecutes alleged violations of these regulations. Finally, the SEC sits as judge and jury in deciding whether its rules have been violated and, if so, what punishment should be imposed on the offender (although the judgment may be appealed to a federal court). These three operations—rulemaking, enforcement, and adjudication—are the basic functions of most regulatory agencies. Taken together, and supplemented by broad investigative powers, these three functions may be termed the **administrative process.**

RULEMAKING

A major function of a regulatory agency is **rulemaking**—the formulation of new regulations. The power that an agency has to make rules is conferred on it by Congress in the agency's enabling legislation. For example, the Occupational Safety and Health Administration (OSHA) was authorized by the Occupational Safety and Health Act of 1970 to develop and issue rules governing safety in the workplace. Under this authority, OSHA has issued various safety standards. For example, OSHA deemed it in the public interest to issue a rule regulating the health-care industry to prevent the spread of certain diseases, including acquired immune deficiency syndrome (AIDS). The rule specified various standards— on how contaminated instruments should be handled, for instance—with which employers in that industry must comply. Agencies cannot just make a rule at any time they wish, however. Rather, they must follow certain procedural requirements, particularly those set forth in the Administrative Procedure Act of 1946.

ENABLING LEGISLATION ● A law enacted by a legislature to establish an administrative agency; enabling legislation normally specifies the name, purpose, composition, and powers of the agency being created.

ADJUDICATE ● To render a judicial decision. In regard to administrative law, the process in which an administrative law judge hears and decides issues that arise when an agency charges a person or firm with violating a law or regulation enforced by the agency.

ADMINISTRATIVE PROCESS ● The functions—including rulemaking, enforcement, and adjudication— undertaken by administrative agencies in administering the law.

RULEMAKING ● The process undertaken by an administrative agency when formally proposing, evaluating, and adopting a new regulation.

NEGOTIATED RULEMAKING ● A type of administrative agency rulemaking in which the industries that will be affected by the new rule participate in the rule's formulation.

Agencies must also make sure that their rules are based on substantial evidence and are not "arbitrary and capricious." Therefore, prior to proposing a new rule, an agency may engage in extensive investigation (through research, on-site inspections of the affected industry, surveys, and so on) to obtain data on the problem to be addressed by the rule. Based on this information, the agency may undertake a cost-benefit analysis of a new rule to determine whether its benefits outweigh its costs. For example, when issuing new rules governing electrical equipment, OSHA predicted that they would cost business $21.7 billion annually but would save 60 lives and eliminate 1,600 worker injuries a year. The agency also estimated that its safety equipment regulations for manufacturing workers would cost $52.4 billion, save 4 lives, and prevent 712,000 lost workdays because of injuries each year.[8]

Don't get the idea that rulemaking is isolated from politics. Indeed, industries that will be affected by a new rule typically participate in its formulation through a process called **negotiated rulemaking.** The aim of negotiated rulemaking, which was approved by Congress in the Negotiated Rulemaking Act of 1990, is to avoid compliance problems. One way to conserve limited government resources and avoid protracted litigation is to negotiate the substance of a new rule with representatives of the industry or group to be regulated. An interest group can thus argue its case before the administrative agency. Recall from Chapter 15 that interest groups also participate in the iron triangles of the bureaucracy. In this way, an interest group can bring pressure to bear on both the president and certain members of Congress to help avoid new regulations that will affect it adversely.

ENFORCEMENT AND ADJUDICATION

Virtually every phase of the administrative process requires that regulatory agencies obtain information about the activities of the organizations or industry that they regulate. As already mentioned, the creation of new rules may require investigation into the problems faced by a particular industry.

An agency may also need to conduct investigations to make sure that businesses in the regulated industry are complying with the rules. After investigating a suspected rule violation, an agency may undertake an administrative action against an individual or organization. Most administrative actions are resolved in their initial stages through negotiated settlements. If a settlement cannot be reached, the agency may resort to an agency adjudication to resolve the dispute formally.

If the Environmental Protection Agency (EPA), for example, finds that a factory is polluting groundwater in violation of federal pollution laws, the EPA will issue a *complaint* against the violator in an effort to bring the plant into compliance with federal regulations. The factory charged in the complaint will respond by filing an *answer* to the EPA's allegations. If the factory and the EPA cannot agree on a settlement, the case is heard in a trial-like setting before an EPA administrative law judge (ALJ), who decides the matter and issues an order. The factory can petition a higher appeals board within the EPA to review the ALJ's order and, if still unsatisfied, can appeal the agency's decision to a federal court.

The rulemaking and enforcement powers of administrative agencies have led to complaints that administrative agency personnel—who are not accountable to the electorate—not only make laws but sit in judgment of those who allegedly violate agency regulations. Many people feel that there is potential for abuse because federal appellate courts (to which agency decisions can be appealed) generally defer to the expertise of agency adjudicators. (For another complaint about administrative agencies, see the feature *Politics on the Far Side: Say What?*)

politics on the far side

Say What?

The language of agency regulations can sometimes be a "tangled web" indeed. Suppose, for example, that you were on the board of directors of a charitable corporation and wanted to find out, for tax purposes, whether your organization qualified as a "private foundation." If you consulted Section 509(a) of the Internal Revenue Code, which deals with the definition of a private foundation, you would probably be mystified by the following statement: "For purposes of paragraph (3), an organization described in paragraph (2) shall be deemed to include an organization described in Section 501(c)(4), (5), or (6), which would be described in paragraph (2) if it were an organization described in section 501(c)(3)."

For Critical Analysis

Increasingly, government agencies are encouraging (and some agencies are requiring) rules to be written in "plain English." Should all government agencies be subject to plain-English requirements when formulating new rules?

Deregulation

As we noted previously, *deregulation* is the opposite of regulation and refers to the elimination or phasing out of regulations governing economic activity. Not surprisingly, the 1980s have been called the era of deregulation, and the deregulatory impulse has been intrinsically linked to the Reagan administration (1981–1989). The truth is, however, that although President Reagan enthusiastically carried out his 1980 campaign promise to reduce the regulation of American business (during his first term at least), the deregulation movement had already begun, as you can see in Table 18–2. (For a discussion of deregulation and political ideology, see the feature entitled *The American Political Spectrum: To Regulate or Not to Regulate.*)

In response to an economic downturn and rising federal budget deficit levels, the Carter administration (1977–1981) supported the deregulation of several industries. In 1978, President Carter signed the Airline Deregulation Act, which dismantled the Civil Aeronautics Board and gave airlines control over fares charged and routes flown.[9] His administration also favored the Motor Carriers Act of 1980, which deregulated the trucking industry. After the act was passed, trucking companies were gradually allowed to determine their own routes, as well as the prices they would charge companies and individuals who wanted to ship goods across state lines. In 1978, the Federal Communications Commission effectively completed the deregulation of the television broadcast industry, which freed up cable companies to compete directly with the three biggest networks—ABC, NBC, and CBS—and ultimately led to the multiple television channels that are available today.

THE REAGAN DEREGULATORY REVOLUTION

The Carter administration's efforts at deregulation evidently did not go far enough, as Reagan was elected in a landslide in 1980, partly for promising

Table 18–2

Some Milestones in Deregulation Legislation

LAW	YEAR	EFFECTS
Airline Deregulation Act	1978	Eliminated the Civil Aeronautics Board; gave airlines control over fares charged and routes flown.
Natural Gas Policy Act	1978	Decontrolled interstate natural gas prices but allowed states to control such prices within their boundaries.
Depository Institutions and Monetary Control Act	1980	Deregulated interest rates offered on deposits; also allowed savings and loans and banks to expand the services they offered.
Motor Carriers Act	1980	Reduced control of the Interstate Commerce Commission over interstate trucking rates and routes.
Staggers Rail Act	1980	Gave railroads more flexibility in setting rates and in dropping unprofitable routes.
Bus Regulatory Reform Act	1982	Allowed intercity bus lines to operate without applying for federal licenses in most circumstances.
Cable Communications Policy Act	1984	Deregulated 90 percent of cable TV rates by the end of 1986.
Telecommunications Act	1996	Allowed phone companies to enter the cable business as well as other communications markets.

To Regulate or Not to Regulate

Obviously, the public plays a large role in the regulatory relationship between government and business. The public casts its approval or disapproval of a politician's policies—including his or her stand on regulation—through its votes. The public also affects regulatory policy through special interest groups, which influence government regulation by lobbying Congress and seeking hearings before regulatory agencies.

What the Conservatives Believe

In general, conservatives are in favor of less rather than more regulation. They believe that the "invisible hand" within the free market allocates society's resources better than any government regulatory agency. Free market advocates, including economist Milton Friedman, argue against regulation in general. They contend that a well-informed public will punish companies that produce negative externalities, such as unsafe products. Consumers, insists Friedman, will take their dollars elsewhere, forcing the offending company to behave responsibly or go out of business. Conservatives point to the tremendous costs of government regulation and to the intransigence of government regulators toward those they regulate.

Conservative critics of regulation also maintain that regulators seem to lack common sense. As an example, they cite the record of the Occupational Safety and Health Administration (OSHA), which has been in existence since 1970. Although OSHA has issued over four thousand detailed regulations since its creation in 1970 and employs two thousand safety inspectors, safety in the American workplace has largely been unaffected by the agency's actions.

What the Liberals Say

Political liberals, who are also usually thought of as economic liberals, are in favor of regulation. Consumer advocacy groups, such as Ralph Nader's Public Citizen, push the government for regulatory curbs on businesses and for guidelines on the quality and safety of products. "Green" watchdog organizations, such as the Audubon Society and the Sierra Club, have been in the forefront of the movement to expand the regulations that protect the environment. The Civil Rights Act of 1964 and subsequent federal legislation prohibiting discrimination were a response by liberals in government to grassroots activity by minorities, women, older Americans, and persons with disabilities—groups that sought protection against discrimination by an underregulated American society.

According to economic liberals, the benefits of free markets are overstated, and their adverse effects are potentially catastrophic for the United States and the world economy. According to journalist Robert Kuttner, government regulation has helped, not hindered, American society, particularly in such areas as scientific research, electric power, and even city ambulance services.[10]

For Critical Analysis

What arguments could you present to demonstrate that the United States needs more regulation today than it may have needed one hundred years ago?

to "get the government off the people's backs." According to some estimates, during Reagan's eight years in office, the Department of Energy reduced its paperwork demands on the private sector by over 800,000 hours.[11] In the 1970s, the National Highway Traffic Safety Administration made about fifteen investigations each year into auto defects. During the first year of the Reagan administration, it undertook fewer than six. Activities at the EPA changed similarly: the EPA referred about two hundred cases a year to the Justice Department during the Carter administration, but referred fewer than thirty in the first year of the Reagan administration. At OSHA, the number of inspectors was reduced 16 percent while the number of workplaces grew and the number of workplace deaths increased.

Also, it was under the Reagan administration's Department of Justice that the Bell System, the huge government-sanctioned telephone monopoly, was ordered to be broken up. We are still witnessing the ramifications of this breakup today, including the Telecommunications Act of 1996 (which further decentralized the telecommunications industry) and its results. (For a discussion of communications deregulation in other countries, see the feature on page 452 entitled *Comparative Politics: Communications Deregulation Goes Worldwide.*)

Communications Deregulation Goes Worldwide

Since the breakup of AT&T and the Telecommunications Act of 1996, the United States has experienced more deregulation in communications than virtually any other country. On February 15, 1997, sixty-seven nations signed an international agreement that, in effect, applied the U.S. model for communications deregulation to the most important industrialized countries.

Given that the communications industry worldwide generates more than $600 billion per year, this is a major event for the world's communications consumers. One observer argues that the United States is now exporting something new: deregulation principles that have revolutionized the American long-distance telephone market since the 1980s. The biggest impact will be felt by consumers in Asia, Latin America, and Africa, where governments have done virtually nothing in the past to reform their state-controlled telephone monopolies.

One expected result of this international agreement will be foreign companies buying local telephone companies. AT&T, British Telecom, and NTT of Japan may eventually own all or parts of telephone companies throughout the world.

For Critical Analysis

Is there a "down side" to the deregulation of the communications industry?

THE LEGACY OF DEREGULATION

By the mid-1990s, the shine of deregulation as an instrument for regulatory reform had worn off for many. Deregulation, like any other regulatory action, appeared to have both costs and benefits. Consider the effects of deregulation on just one industry, the airline industry. Some argue that consumers of airline services were better off after deregulation. Deregulation of the airline industry, however, also had a number of costs, many of them social. For example, deregulation initially spurred the creation of numerous new airline companies, but a wave of mergers and acquisitions (as well as bankruptcies) then occurred and seemed to reduce competition. By 1993, 18 percent of the airline industry was in Chapter 11 bankruptcy, and one industry observer noted that the airlines had lost more than twice the accumulated profit they had earned since they began commercial service in the 1920s.[12] Major carriers such as Braniff, Pan Am, Eastern, Continental, and TWA have either been forced into bankruptcy or been liquidated.

The waging of seemingly constant price wars has helped consumers but has cut into the airlines' profits and hampered some technological, safety, and rehabilitative services. In the 1990s, U.S. commercial airlines had an older fleet of airplanes than did the airlines of Italy, France, Great Britain, Japan, Canada, or Germany.[13] Some consumers feel that airline safety in general has become compromised since deregulation. (For a discussion of whether air travel is safer or more hazardous as a result of airline deregulation, see the feature *Perception versus Reality: Airline Deregulation and Safety.*)

perception versus reality

Airline Deregulation and Safety

Airlines have been deregulated since 1978. Since that time, passenger revenue miles have skyrocketed in the United States. The question is, has airline deregulation led to less safe skies?

The Perception

The common perception is that indeed airline safety has deteriorated since deregulation. It is certainly true that some spectacular airplane crashes have occurred in the United States (and elsewhere, too). Some of these crashes involved large numbers of fatalities, as occurred when TWA Flight

800 went down in the Atlantic after takeoff from a New York airport in 1996.

The Reality

The reality is just the opposite of what people believe, at least with respect to airline safety. Although the *absolute* number of accidents and fatalities may have increased since deregulation (although for certain periods it did not), so many more passengers are flying that the probability of being in an accident has dropped. Contrary to most people's perception, fatal accidents per 100,000 departures

have decreased almost 75 percent. During the nine years before deregulation, total fatalities were 1,459. In the nine years after deregulation, total fatalities dropped to 1,036, despite an enormous increase in passenger miles traveled. This is a dramatic improvement. Fatal accidents per million miles traveled declined almost 60 percent during the nine years after deregulation.[14]

You Be the Judge

What factors, apart from deregulation, might explain the improved air-safety statistics?

The reconstruction of TWA Flight 800.

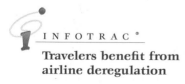

INFOTRAC®

Travelers benefit from airline deregulation

THE BACKLASH AGAINST DEREGULATION

After the 1988 presidential election, George Bush allowed a substantial increase in both regulatory rulemaking and expenditures. Under President Bush, Congress passed the Clean Air Act Amendments of 1990, the Americans with Disabilities Act of 1990, and the Civil Rights Act of 1991. These acts have increased the rulemaking and regulation that affect virtually every business in the United States. The Cable TV Reregulation Act of 1992 also was evidence of a regulatory revival during the Bush administration, though the president did not favor that particular legislation. (For further evidence that regulation is still alive and well, see the feature on the next page entitled *Politics on the Far Side: The Petty Regulations Still Keep Coming.*)

REREGULATION ● The act of regulating again. In the 1990s, certain groups began to call for the reregulation of industries that were deregulated in the 1970s and 1980s in order to avoid the unintended results of some of the earlier deregulatory policies.

By the early 1990s, public—and hence political—opinion was clearly turning against deregulation where individual safety was concerned, such as with prescription drugs, workplace safety, and airline travel. One survey of the Airline Pilots Association showed that 43 percent of its member pilots said deregulation had a "greatly adverse" effect on commercial aviation safety.[15] Along the same lines, a Gallup poll showed that nearly two-thirds of Americans had lost confidence in the safety and efficiency of airlines.[16] As we have seen, these feelings do not necessarily square with the facts, but the perceptions have opened a floodgate of questions about deregulation and, eventually, reregulation.

Reregulation

A sure sign of the backlash against deregulation has been the call, emanating from industry insiders and concerned consumer groups, for **reregulation.** Usually, the issue of reregulation is raised when deregulatory policies lead to unintended results. The most strident calls for reregulation typically come from heads of companies in formerly deregulated industries. For example, the head of USAir asked for reregulation of the airline industry as far back as 1987.

Why would the heads of firms in previously regulated industries ask for reregulation? Some argue that the lives of managers are much easier in a regulated industry than in a deregulated industry. Prior to deregulation in the airline industry in 1978, rates and schedules were controlled by the government. Consequently, there was virtually no competition for routes or fare wars. Before deregulation, most airlines were almost guaranteed profits, an enviable position for any industry.

Ironically, the one intended effect of deregulation—open competition—has not necessarily taken place. By the late 1990s, six airlines controlled 85 percent of U.S. air traffic. The reason lies in barriers to entry into the industry, which, if anything, are more stringent now than they were before deregulation. There are two basic reasons for these entry obstacles:

1. Gates and landing slots have been in short supply because deregulation spawned the hub-and-spoke system, which funnels most traffic through large, now overcrowded airports in such places as Atlanta, Chicago, and New York. Any potential newcomer airline can get gates only if an incumbent rival makes them available.
2. Frequent flyer bonus systems make it increasingly difficult for newcomer airlines to compete with established carriers. Business travelers, for example, would not necessarily switch to a lower-cost airline to save money for their companies, because doing so would eliminate the benefit of the frequent flyer miles they personally obtain.

These and other barriers to entry may be substantial enough to prevent the emergence of new airlines. Hence, Congress is giving more attention to reregulation. We will probably not see a return to the requirement of government approval for every airline schedule and rate, as was the case prior to 1978. Reregulation, however, would mean that the days of aggressive deregulation are over.

I N F O T R A C ®

Reregulation of the airline industry

politics on the far side

The Petty Regulations Still Keep Coming

In spite of attempts by the Clinton administration to streamline government, the petty regulations still keep coming. The Department of Housing and Urban Development recently issued a regulation concerning the ownership of pets by the elderly and disabled in public housing. It reads as follows:

Section 5.350;(2) In the case of cats and other pets using litter boxes, the pet rules may require the pet owner to change the litter (but not more than twice each week), may require pet owners to separate pet waste from litter (but not more than once each day), and may prescribe methods for the disposal of pet waste and used litter.

For Critical Analysis

How might you argue in support of this rule?

Americans at Odds over Regulation

Debates over more or less regulation, particularly at the federal level, continue and may be even more intense by the time you read this book. At issue in many debates over regulation is a fundamental question: Are the benefits of regulation worth the costs? We begin this section by exploring this issue.

Are the Benefits of Regulation Worth the Costs?

There is substantial disagreement over whether the costs of government regulation to business are greater than the benefits received by society. Would-be reformers of the regulatory process often argue that the projected costs of many individual regulations indeed outweigh their benefits.

CALCULATING THE BENEFITS

One of the potential benefits of regulation is, of course, the controlling of negative externalities. But what is the *value* of such benefits? The easiest way to answer this question is to examine some simple statistical evidence. For most of the 1970s and 1980s, for example, businesses spilled an average of 3.4 million gallons of oil each year. After a regulatory crackdown in the late 1980s, that number had dropped to 55,000 gallons in 1991.[17] By requiring new standards for workers in the manufacturing industry, the Occupational Safety and Health Administration estimated that it was preventing four deaths and over 60,000 injuries a year.[18] The Food and Drug Administration (FDA) points to the disastrous effects in Europe of certain drugs that the FDA has kept off the shelves in the United States: the pain reliever Indomethacin caused thirty-six deaths in Great Britain and Germany; the pain reliever Fenclofenac caused seven deaths in Great Britain; and a drug to prevent urinary problems, Terodilence, was responsible for numerous cases of heart trouble and fourteen deaths in Great Britain and Germany.[19]

While statistics indicate that there have been benefits, how do you place a dollar value on those benefits? Attempts to answer this question are rare, because that value is so difficult to calculate. "Try to put a dollar value on, say, drinking water in a community," said one proponent of environmental regulation.[20] This aspect of regulatory risk assessment troubles observers on both sides of the regulatory debate. The fact is, cost-benefit analysis requires that a monetary value be placed on items the humanist in each of us would rather not appraise—for example, health, safety, and, in some cases, human life.

WHAT IS A HUMAN LIFE WORTH?

According to an old saying, "You can't put a price on human life." Regulators, however, cannot simply say that the risk to society from automobile accidents, poisonous food products, flammable clothes, and so on must be zero. That is impossible. But how much are we willing to pay to save a human life? Implicitly, that cost will be the value we place on human life—and that value is not infinite. For example, if consumers were given the choice between reducing the probability of dying in an automobile accident by spending $5,000 more per car versus not spending that money, many would choose not to spend the additional money.

In the regulatory arena, the costs of saving a life have increased greatly in recent years. A study by the Center for Risk Analysis, a branch of the Harvard University School of Public Health, underscored this point by giving examples of what the median cost of saving one year of life through regulatory protection has been (see Table 18–3). Another study, by the World Bank, discovered that the value per cancer case avoided under the U.S. Clean Air Act rose from approximately $15 million in 1987 to $194 million in 1994.[21]

THE COST SIDE OF REGULATION

Basically, any regulation involves two types of costs—direct and indirect costs. The direct costs include all of the staffing, salaries, and so on that are required to implement and enforce the regulation. The indirect costs are not so easy to calculate. They usually show up in a higher price for goods and services. Consider an example. A building code requires you to install a certain amount of insulation in the attic of a new house, whether you want to or not. Your house will in fact cost more because of that regulation. The "hidden taxes" on new houses resulting from building regulations are estimated to run as high as one-third the price of the house.

Every business affected by government regulation faces indirect costs, and these are substantial. One of the most obvious indirect costs is the expense of the additional paperwork that American businesses must process because of increased regulation. Another indirect cost, particularly with respect to environmental regulations that restrict how natural resources can be used, is the limits such regulations impose on business opportunities. (See, for example, the feature entitled *A Question of Ethics: Was It a Love of the Environment, or Was It Politics?*)

The States versus the National Government

The state governments and Washington, D.C., are engaged in an ongoing battle over regulation, particularly as it concerns environmental rules.

Table 18–3
The Cost of Saving a Year of Life

PREVENTIVE MEASURE	NET COST PER ONE YEAR OF LIFE SAVED
Childhood immunizations	Less than zero
Drug and alcohol treatment	Less than zero
Helmet protection	$ 2,000
Water chlorination	4,000
Highway improvements	64,000
Asbestos controls	1,865,000
Pollution controls at paper mills	7,522,000
Radiation controls (at industrial sites and for radiologists)	27,386,000

REGULATORY AGENCY	NET COST PER ONE YEAR OF LIFE SAVED
Federal Aviation Administration	$ 23,000
Consumer Product Safety Commission	68,000
National Highway Traffic Safety Administration	78,000
Occupational Safety and Health Administration	88,000
Environmental Protection Agency	7,629,000

SOURCE: Harvard University School of Public Health, Center for Risk Analysis.

a question of ethics

Was It a Love of the Environment, or Was It Politics?

In the fall of 1996, less than two months before the presidential elections, President Bill Clinton visited the Grand Canyon. While there, he declared that 1.8 million acres in the Red Rock County of Utah would be established as the Escalante National Monument by presidential executive order (see Chapter 14). Under the Antiquities Act of 1906, "unique" American resources can be set aside by executive order.

With the stroke of a pen, one of the last big wilderness fights in the contiguous United States had been ended. The environmentalists seemed to have won. With the stroke of that pen, President Clinton removed forever the possibility of developing the nation's largest known reserves of clean-burning, low-sulfur coal. To be sure, the entire Utah congres-sional delegation opposed the new monument, but the monument was popular in the rest of the West and gave President Clinton a pro-environmental stance going into the elections.

The fight had basically been be-tween conservationists and min-ing interests. A Dutch-owned mining company, Andalex Resources, had planned to run a large coal-mining operation in what is now the heart of the new national monument. Andalex argued that it would employ almost one thousand people and develop the coal in an environ-mentally sound manner. Nonethe-less, such a mine would by necessity require new roads, power lines, and truck traffic.

Here's the catch, though. One of the few other places in the world where large deposits of clean-burning coal can be found just happens to be located in the South Kalimantan coal fields of Borneo, Indonesia. President Clinton received hundreds of thousands of dollars in contributions from for-eign sources, including Indonesia, during the 1996 presidential cam-paigns. Clinton has been accused of locking up U.S. coal reserves worth an estimated $1 trillion for the benefit of Indonesian coal-mining interests.[22]

For Critical Analysis

How can the public know whether a political leader's environmental policies are motivated by a concern over environmental health or by political ambitions?

The Clinton administration claims that violations of official EPA rules are underreported. The EPA has concluded, for example, that Pennsylvania and other big industrial states do not report the majority of major pollu-tion violations. Even Virginia, just across the river from the EPA's Potomac River headquarters, has been accused of resisting vigorous enforcement of federal environmental laws. Recently, the EPA brought a lawsuit against three companies accused of polluting the Pagan River in Virginia. The EPA said it had to sue because the state of Virginia, in the state's own law-suit against the companies, had sought penalties that were "too light." EPA administrator Carol Browner stated that "there is a disregard for the requirements of Federal laws, and I think there is a belief on the part of some in Virginia that ignoring the environment and public health stan-dards is what the business community wants."[23]

What is certain is that different cities and regions are never going to be completely in agreement with environmental regulations generated in Washington, D.C. (see, for example, the feature on the next page *A Question of Ethics: Is "Environmental Justice" Fair to Minority Communities?*). Even some major companies are starting to be at odds with government regula-tors. To cite one example: When the federal government requested Chrysler Corporation to recall some of its models on the basis of government crash-test results, Chrysler refused to do so. The government tests indicated that the seat belts were unsafe, but Chrysler argued that the cars were safe and that the government had tested the seat belts improperly. To force Chrysler to comply with its order, the government has sued the company.

a question of ethics

Is "Environmental Justice" Fair to Minority Communities?

In the first part of the 1990s, the Environmental Protection Agency (EPA) became concerned that too many factories, plants, and waste dumps were being situated in or near minority (primarily African American) communities. In effect, contended EPA director Carol Browner, this practice constituted a form of racial discrimination because African Americans suffered disproportionately (relative to white Americans) from the health effects of industrial pollutants. To counter this alleged "environmental racism," the EPA embarked on a policy of "environmental justice." The Office of Environmental Justice was created as a subagency within the EPA to monitor plant sitings and study the effects of pollutants emitted by new plants on the surrounding communities.

While environmental groups applauded the EPA's new policy, others were less enthusiastic. After all, if a plant is located in a minority or low-income community, that means more jobs and a higher standard of living for those living in that area. For example, when Shintech Corporation announced its plans to locate a $700 million polyvinyl plastics facility near the poor, largely African American community of Romeville, Louisiana, many of that community's residents looked

forward to the job opportunities that would result. In fact, polls showed that a majority of the area's residents supported the plant's construction there, as did six of the seven members of the local governing council. By 1997, the plant had passed both state and federal emissions requirements, and Shintech was ready to go forward with the plant's construction.

Nonetheless, the EPA ordered that plant construction be delayed. The agency concluded that the plant's proposed location would constitute environmental racism because cancer-causing emissions from the plant would disproportionately affect African Americans. Rather than tangle further with the EPA over the matter, Shintech eventually decided to build its facility in a largely white community some thirty miles from Romeville.

At issue in the Shintech case and in similar cases is whether the EPA should have the authority to unilaterally expand federal civil rights concepts through the concept of environmental justice. As mentioned, many Americans, particularly those actively involved in environmental causes, support the EPA's actions. Others, however, feel that it is not fair to let the EPA have the final say in what is, or is not, in a minority community's best interests. In the Shintech case,

for example, was the EPA really protecting that community by depriving it of economic benefits—even though it spared the community from Shintech's industrial emissions? What if the health risk posed by the emissions was not, in fact, as significant as the EPA contended (as the authors of one study concluded[24])? And if there was a significant health risk, why would it be more acceptable to impose this risk on whites rather than African Americans?

The EPA's Shintech decision has intensified the criticism of its environmental justice policy, which is currently under attack by some members of Congress. The EPA is also being challenged in court by the Washington Legal Foundation, a public-interest group, which claims that the EPA's policy, among other things, "stifles economic development in low-income and minority communities," thereby harming the very people the policy was designed to protect.[25]

For Critical Analysis

Assume that a proposed industrial plant's emissions would pose a significant health risk to a community. Should the decision about whether to accept that risk be left up to the community, or should the government have the final say in the matter?

The Red Tape Continues and May Lead to a Lack of Respect for the Law

In survey after survey, small and medium-sized businesses put government regulation and paperwork at the top of their list of problems. While purported overregulation creates costs to society, at least one observer believes that overregulation has more serious repercussions. Law professor Nicholas N. Kittri argues that the large increase in unnecessary and unreasonable laws, many of which are simply bureaucratic decrees, has generated an overall decline in the respect for the law.[26]

Even former Idaho senator Steve Symms agrees that there is too much government regulation. He recently co-authored a book entitled *A Citizen's*

Guide to Fighting Government. Meanwhile, the Institute for Policy Innovation in Texas has published a list of the ten most harmful federal regulations. Even abroad, articles have discussed the "overregulation" of America.[27]

The battle over regulation is certainly not over.

---

key terms

adjudicate 448	negative externality 446
administrative process 448	negotiated rulemaking 449
antitrust law 444	regulation 441
deregulation 445	reregulation 454
economic regulation 445	rulemaking 448
enabling legislation 448	social regulation 445
legislative rule 447	

---

chapter summary

1. The constitutional basis for regulation is found in the commerce clause, which, as interpreted by the United States Supreme Court, gives Congress the power to regulate interstate commerce as well as intrastate commerce that substantially affects interstate commerce.

2. The beginnings of regulation occurred in the late nineteenth century with the passage of the Interstate Commerce Act of 1887 (which created the first regulatory agency, the Interstate Commerce Commission) and the Sherman Antitrust Act of 1890. Regulatory momentum increased during the twentieth century, particularly with the New Deal legislation of Franklin D. Roosevelt and even more with the social legislation passed during the 1960s and 1970s. The deregulatory movement that began in the late 1970s represented a backlash against the extensive government regulation of the preceding decades.

3. Economic regulation involves statutes and rules covering monopolies and anticompetitive practices. Social regulation reflects concern for the effects of business activities on the social welfare. One of the reasons why government regulation is perceived to be necessary is to control negative externalities (such as pollution) that result from business decisions but impose costs on society.

4. Administrative agencies are sometimes regarded as the fourth branch of government because of the powers they wield. They can make legislative rules that are as legally binding as the laws passed by Congress. The three basic functions of agencies are rulemaking (forming new rules), enforcement (implementing rules), and adjudication (settling disputes). Agencies also exercise broad investigative powers in conjunction with their rulemaking and enforcement activities.

5. Deregulation has been linked to the Reagan administration of the 1980s but actually began during the late 1970s under the Carter administration. During the late 1970s and 1980s, a number of industries were deregulated, including the airline and trucking industries, the television broadcast industry (further deregulated by the Telecommunications Act of 1996), and the telephone industry.

6. Deregulation has involved both costs and benefits. Deregulation of the airline industry, for example, initially allowed for increased competition among numerous airline rivals. Eventually, however, as a result of mergers and bankruptcies, just a few airlines controlled the market for airline services. Barriers to entry prevent potential competitors from entering the industry. Some consumers have complained that the deregulation of the airline industry also compromised the safety of air travel, but statistics do not support this conclusion.

7. A backlash against deregulation occurred in the early 1990s, and during the Bush administration, significant regulatory legislation was passed, including the Americans with Disabilities Act of 1990.

8. Americans are at odds over whether there should be more or less regulation. The Clinton administration supports some deregulation, but at the same time is proposing increased regulation in some areas, such as environmental protection. State and local governments, as well as major companies, are beginning to be at odds with the government regulators in Washington, D.C. Some contend that the proliferation of unnecessary and unreasonable laws is generating an overall decline in the respect for the law.

for critical analysis

1. Regulatory agencies wield significant power in our government system. Do they have too much power? Are there sufficient checks on their actions?

2. Is there any alternative to allowing Congress to delegate some of its authority to administrative agencies? What if it could not delegate any lawmaking powers to agencies?

3. What are negative externalities, and how does their existence justify government regulation?

4. Why have the Democrats traditionally supported more government regulation and the Republicans less regulation? Can that be said of today's Democrats and Republicans?

5. Agency decisions made during adjudication may normally be appealed to a federal appellate court for review. Does the possibility of judicial review curb agency powers in any significant way? Why or why not?

6. Do you think that regulatory agencies should give economic costs more weight when creating new rules?

7. Can you think of any activities that could be better regulated by state governments than by the national government? In your opinion, what types of activities must be regulated at the national level?

suggested readings

DAVIS, Shelley L. *Unbridled Power: Inside the Secret Culture of the IRS.* New York: HarperBusiness, 1997. This is an insider's story of the Internal Revenue Service, written by a person who served as the agency's first and last historian—from 1989 to 1995. Davis argues that materials were uncovered that reveal an astonishing misuse of power. The book is an account of IRS misdeeds, from retaliating against whistleblowers to destroying incriminating documents.

FOREMAN, Christopher H., Jr. *The Promise and Peril of Environmental Justice.* Washington, D.C.: Brookings Institution Press, 1998. The author strongly criticizes the environmental justice movement and its approach to social justice.

GREIDER, William. *One World, Ready or Not.* New York: Simon & Schuster, 1997. The author reviews the trouble spots in the world economy. He points out where laborers have been shortchanged. He argues in favor of a tax on securities transactions worldwide to raise funds to help the poor. He views many of the "blowups" in the capitalist world as symptoms of deeper, systemic problems. He wants some-

one to be in charge of global capitalism because there is no one at the wheel.

KUTTNER, Robert. *Everything for Sale.* New York: Knopf, 1997. This liberal journalist has been writing for years about the benefits of bigger government. In this well-thought-out empirical broadside against free markets, he provides many examples of situations in which governments have outperfomed free markets. He argues in favor of a mixed economy, rather than a purely capitalistic one.

VOGEL, David. *Trading Up: Consumer and Environmental Regulation in a Global Community.* Cambridge, Mass.: Harvard University Press, 1997. The author, a professor of business and public policy at the University of California, Berkeley, looks at the increasingly controversial relationship between international trade and environmental regulatory policies. He concludes that, on balance, trade liberalization strongly reinforces regulations to improve the environment.

politics
on the web

In 1978, the Airline Deregulation Act was signed by President Carter. Most of the airline industry was deregulated, although some aspects of the industry are still regulated. For details, go to

http://www.air-transport.org

Under "General Info," select "The Airline Handbook." Then choose "Deregulation."

The Internet Law Library, sponsored by the U.S. House of Representatives, offers links to federal and state legislative and regulatory materials, including the *Code of Federal Regulations.* Go to

http://www.house.gov

If you are interested in learning more about the procedures that federal agencies follow in their rulemaking and other activities, you can access the Administrative Procedure Act of 1946 at

http://www.law.cornell.edu/uscode/5/ch5.html

For information on state administrative agencies and regulations, go to

http://www.law.vill.edu/State-Agency/statewebloc.html

The Web site of the U.S. Government Printing Office, called GPO Access, offers free online access to all of its databases, including the *Federal Register.* The URL for this site is

http://www.access.gpo.gov/su_docs

For information on the functions, organization, and administrators of federal departments and agencies, you can access the *United States Government Manual* online at

http://www.gpo.ucop.edu/catalog/govman.html

For news stories on environment-related topics from sources around the world, updated daily, you can go to the Web page of Australia-based Planet Ark Environmental Foundation at

http://www.planetark.org/new/worldnews.html

The site was launched on June 5, 1997, to commemorate World Environment Day.

using web resources

The Federal Trade Commission (FTC) is online at the following Web site:

http://www.ftc.gov

Access this site, browse through it, and then answer these questions:

1. What are the vision, mission, and goals of the FTC?

2. What legislation established the FTC? What areas of activity is the agency authorized to regulate?

3. In what circumstances might the FTC bring an action against an organization? When it does so, what procedures does it follow?

4. From the home page, select "Current News Releases." What topics do these releases address?

notes

1. As quoted in John H. Cushman, Jr., "E.P.A. May Extend Debate on Tougher Air Standards," *The New York Times,* February 2, 1997, p. A14.

2. "Rules and Regulations," *Federal Register,* December 6, 1991, p. 64004.

3. *Gibbons v. Ogden,* 22 U.S. (9 Wheat.) 1 (1824).

4. *Wickard v. Filburn,* 317 U.S. 111 (1942).

5. This is now a felony.

6. D. R. Wholey and S. M. Sanchez, "The Effects of Regulatory Tools on Organizational Population," *Academy of Management Review,* October 1991, p. 743.

7. As quoted in Max Boot, "A Rotten Fate," *The Wall Street Journal Europe,* December 6, 1995, p. 10.

8. R. B. Slater, "OSHA Goes on the Offensive," *Business and Society Review,* Spring 1994, p. 45.

9. M. B. Solomon, "Pro-Regulation Forces in U.S. See Chance to Alter Air Policy," *Journal of Commerce and Commercial Affairs,* September 16, 1992, p. 8A.

10. Robert Kuttner, *Everything for Sale* (New York: Knopf, 1997).

11. R. L. Miller and F. B. Cross, *The Legal and Regulatory Environment Today: Changing Perspectives for Business* (St. Paul: West Publishing Co., 1993), Chapter 8.

12. P. S. Dempsey, "The Bitter Fruits of Airline Deregulation," *The Wall Street Journal,* April 8, 1993, p. A15. (Note, though, that these numbers were not corrected for inflation and are therefore grossly exaggerated.)

13. *Ibid.*

14. A. Barnett, T. Curtis, J. Goranson, and A. Patrick, "Better Than Ever: Nonstop Jet Service in an Era of Hubs and Spokes," *Sloan Management Review,* Winter 1992, p. 49.

15. R. E. Dallos, "Sky-High Airline Debt Feeds Air Safety Debate," *The Los Angeles Times,* October 22, 1989, p. D1.

16. "The Nation," *The Los Angeles Times,* August 30, 1989, p. A2.

17. "Slants & Trends," *Air Water Pollution Report,* August 31, 1992, p. 2.

18. "52.4M Costs Seen by OSHA," *American Metal Market,* August 3, 1994, p. 10.

19. D. Levy, "FDA's Tough Drug Rules Save Lives," *USA Today,* February 3, 1995, p. A1.

20. "Weighing the Risks," *Nation's Business,* December 1994, p. 40.

21. "Is Saving a Life Too Costly?" *Haznews,* August 1, 1994, p. 2.

22. "Mining Money: A Monumental Loss of Clean Coal," *The Cincinnati Enquirer,* February 19, 1997, p. A10.

23. As quoted in John H. Cushman, Jr., "Virginia Seen as Undercutting U.S. Environmental Rules," *The New York Times,* January 19, 1997, p. 11.

24. Pranay Gupte and Bonner R. Cohen, "Carol Browner, Master of Mission Creep," *Forbes,* October 20, 1997, p. 175.

25. Henry Payne, "Red Zone," *Reason,* February 1999, p. 24.

26. Nicholas N. Kittri, *The War against Authority: From the Crisis of Legitimacy to a New Social Contract* (Baltimore: Johns Hopkins University Press, 1996).

27. See, for example, "Over-Regulating America," *The Economist,* July 27–August 2, 1996, pp. 19–21.

chapter

19

FOREIGN POLICY

Contents

Should the United States Be the World's Police Officer?

It used to be the United States against the "evil empire."[1] Today, at least for the time being, there is truly only one superpower, both militarily and economically, and it is the United States. Some contend that with this power come moral and ethical responsibilities. Others suggest that the United States should simply mind its own business and let the rest of the world solve its own problems in any way it wants.

Go to CD-ROM

The United States Has a Moral Obligation to Keep the Peace—Everywhere

Those in favor of U.S. intervention throughout the world when human rights are being violated have a strong argument: only the United States has the military might and the economic muscle to intervene successfully. If the United States does not intervene, no country will.

Perhaps U.S. politicians do not believe that we should put our hands into every cauldron of ethnic violence. Yet each time we have not, hundreds of thousands, and sometimes millions, have died. Look at what happened when the United States stood back and watched Hutu extremists slaughter hundreds of thousands of Tutsi in Rwanda in 1994. Consider what would have happened in Kosovo, Yugoslavia, without the intervention of NATO-led U.S. troops. The Serbian regime of Slobodan Milosevic would have continued the "cleansing" of ethnic Albanians in that province. More mass murders and other atrocities would have been committed against the Kosovars, and thousands more would have been forced to flee from their homes to other countries.

Many areas in the world, such as Afghanistan and parts of Africa, will never see stability unless the United States becomes the world's police officer. The United Nations and the Red Cross can provide humanitarian relief, but without concerted political pressure for solutions, relief alone can do very little.

In any event, the United States is the world's leading commercial power and therefore has a substantial interest in economic development, which can only occur if the world is at peace.

The United States Has Paid Enough—Yankee Stay Home

Those who favor a more isolationist foreign policy believe that the United States should keep its troops at home. So many ethnic battles are occurring at any one time throughout the world that it is impossible for the United States to act as the world's police officer. We pay good money to the United Nations—let its troops solve the world's minor ethnic flare-ups and other battles.

Every time we have intervened, we have made a mess of things. For example, we were in Somalia in the early 1990s, and that country is no better off now. In 1994, President Clinton sent the U.S. military to invade Haiti and reinstate the country's first freely elected president. The United States also spent $65 million to train thousands of civilian police officers, the first civilian police force in Haitian history, to serve as the cornerstone of the new democracy there. The result? According to recent reports, political factionalism in Haiti continues to provoke assassinations and bombings, just as it did in the past, and democracy remains just a word, not a reality, in that country.[2] And despite recent efforts by U.S. and other NATO-led forces to establish peace in Yugoslavia, Milosevic remains in power and ethnic hostilities continue.

Finally, the U.S. government has an obligation to defend the homeland. The best way to do this is to refrain from offending other nations or groups. To be sure, the United States should intervene in other nations' affairs to protect America's vital interests. But the interventions in Somalia, Haiti, and Kosovo had nothing to do with U.S. national security. According to Ivan Eland, the director of defense policy studies at the Cato Institute, "Such a casually interventionist foreign policy only provokes hostility from factions or groups within other countries." This hostility could lead to terrorist attacks against the United States—a very real threat in our times that the U.S. government should seek to prevent by all reasonable means.[3]

Where Do You Stand?

1. Should every nation have the right to intervene in other nations' affairs to protect human rights?

2. Does the fact that more countries will develop nuclear capabilities affect any of the arguments presented in this feature? If so, how?

On the Web

A good online source for information and views on U.S. foreign policy is the Chicago Council on Foreign Relations at http://www.ccfr.org.

Introduction

> **FOREIGN POLICY** ● A systematic and general plan that guides a country's attitudes and actions toward the rest of the world. Foreign policy includes all of the economic, military, commercial, and diplomatic positions and actions that a nation takes in its relationships with other countries.
>
> **ISOLATIONISM** ● A political policy of noninvolvement in world affairs.
>
> **MONROE DOCTRINE** ● A U.S. policy, announced in 1823 by President James Monroe, that the United States would not tolerate foreign intervention in the Western Hemisphere, and in return, the United States would stay out of European affairs.

INFOTRAC®
World's policeman

The idea that the United States has a moral responsibility toward the people of other nations is not new. Indeed, it has been one of the great shaping forces of this country's relations with other nations since at least the mid-1800s. The westward expansion of the United States—and the conquest of some 75,000 Spanish-speaking people and 150,000 Native Americans in the process—created a need for a rationale that could justify such expansion and conquest. In 1845, news reporter John O'Sullivan provided one. He stated that it was the "manifest destiny" of the United States "to overspread the continent allotted by Providence for the free development of our yearly multiplying millions."[4] O'Sullivan contended that Americans had a God-given right to extend—by force, if necessary—the benefits of American democracy to less civilized and more backward peoples (read: Mexicans and Native Americans).

The concept of manifest destiny provided an ideology for continued U.S. expansion in the Western Hemisphere. As the United States grew into a world superpower in the twentieth century, the concept of manifest destiny was left behind. The idea that the United States has a responsibility toward others in the world, however, continues to be reflected in U.S. foreign policy. **Foreign policy** is a systematic and general plan that guides a country's attitudes and actions toward the rest of the world. Foreign policy includes all of the economic, military, commercial, and diplomatic positions and actions that a nation takes in its relationships with other countries.

A Short History of American Foreign Policy

Although many U.S. foreign policy initiatives have been rooted in moral idealism, a primary consideration in U.S. foreign policy has always been national security—the protection of the independence and political integrity of the nation. Over the years, the United States has attempted to preserve its national security in many ways. These ways have changed over time and are not always internally consistent. This is because foreign policymaking, like domestic policymaking, reflects the influence of various political groups in the United States. These groups—including the voting public, interest groups, Congress, and the president and relevant agencies of the executive branch—are often at odds over what the U.S. position should be in regard to particular foreign policy issues. (See, for example, the feature entitled *The American Political Spectrum: Should We Keep Supporting the United Nations?*)

ISOLATIONISM

The nation's founders and the early presidents believed that avoiding political involvement with other nations—**isolationism**—was the best way to protect American interests. The colonies were certainly not yet strong enough to directly influence European developments. As president of the new nation, George Washington did little in terms of foreign policy. Indeed, in his farewell address in 1797, he urged Americans to "steer clear of permanent alliances with any portion of the foreign world." During the 1700s and 1800s, the United States generally stayed out of conflicts and political issues elsewhere.

In 1823, President James Monroe proclaimed what became known as the **Monroe Doctrine.** In his message to Congress in December 1823, Monroe made it clear that the United States would not tolerate foreign intervention in the Western Hemisphere. In return, promised Monroe, the

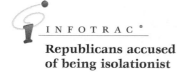

INFOTRAC®
Republicans accused of being isolationist

The General Assembly of the United Nations (UN) is composed of representatives of all of the member nations of that body. Each nation is entitled to one vote. On the most important questions, a two-thirds majority vote of those present and voting is required. For other questions, a simple majority vote is sufficient. The name *United Nations* was coined by President Franklin D. Roosevelt in 1941 to describe the countries fighting against the Axis nations in World War II. The term was first used officially on January 1, 1942, when twenty-six nations pledged, in a Declaration by the United Nations, to continue their joint war efforts and not to make peace separately. The UN Charter was drawn up at a conference held in San Francisco in 1945.

INTERVENTIONISM ● Direct involvement by one country in another country's affairs.

COLONIAL EMPIRE ● A group of colonized nations that are under the rule of a single imperial power.

NEUTRALITY ● A position of not being aligned with either side in a dispute or conflict, such as a war.

The second atomic bomb used in World War II, on August 9, 1945, devastated the Japanese city of Nagasaki.

United States would stay out of European affairs. The Monroe Doctrine buttressed the policy of isolationism toward Europe.

THE BEGINNING OF INTERVENTIONISM

Isolationism gradually became interventionism as the United States began to trade more with Japan, China, and other Asian countries and as it expanded westward across the North American continent. As a result of its westward expansion, the United States found itself in conflict with Mexico, France, Spain, and Great Britain. The first true step toward **interventionism** (direct involvement in foreign affairs) occurred with the Spanish-American War of 1898. The United States fought to free Cuba from Spanish rule. Spain lost and subsequently ceded control of several of its possessions, including Guam, Puerto Rico, and the Philippines, to the United States. The United States acquired a **colonial empire** and was acknowledged as a world power.

In 1899, Americans proclaimed the open-door policy, opening Chinese markets to the world's leading trading nations. In the early 1900s, President Theodore Roosevelt proposed that the United States could invade Latin America when it was necessary to guarantee U.S. political or economic stability.

THE WORLD WARS

When World War I broke out in 1914, President Woodrow Wilson initially proclaimed a policy of **neutrality**—the United States would not take sides in the conflict. The United States did not enter the war until 1917, after U.S. ships in international waters were attacked without cause by German submarines. After World War I ended in 1918, the United States returned to a policy of isolationism. We refused to join the League of Nations, an international body intended to resolve peacefully any future conflicts between nations.

Isolationism was relatively short-lived, lasting only until the Japanese attacked Pearl Harbor in 1941. The United States joined the Allies—Australia, Great Britain, Canada, China, France, and the Soviet Union—that fought the Axis nations of Germany, Italy, and Japan. One of the most significant foreign policy actions during World War II was the dropping of the atomic bombs on the Japanese cities of Hiroshima and Nagasaki.

Should We Keep Supporting the United Nations?

The United Nations (UN) is now more than fifty years old. When it was put together at the end of World War II, fifty-one nations signed its original charter. Today, it has 185 member states. Its six principal organs are (1) the General Assembly, (2) the Security Council, (3) the Economic and Social Council, (4) the Trusteeship Council, (5) the International Court of Justice (World Court), and (6) the Secretariat. The Secretariat is the administrative body of the organization and has more than 8,500 employees. Not counting the UN's 10,000 consultants and its peacekeeping forces, more than 64,500 people work for the UN.

When the UN turned fifty, numerous critics, both in the United States and elsewhere, argued that it had become riddled with wholesale corruption and inefficiency. As of 1999, the United States was still over $1 billion in arrears in its payments to the UN. Generally, political conservatives tend to attack the UN. Some have even suggested that the United States pull out of the UN and force the UN to move its headquarters out of New York City. Political liberals tend to support the UN, although even they agree that changes must be made.

The Extreme Right Is Truly Afraid of the UN's Power

During the presidential primary elections in 1996, Republican candidate Pat Buchanan campaigned on a platform that demonized the UN. He portrayed the UN as a central player in an international effort to deprive U.S. citizens of their national rights and liberties. The manager of Buchanan's campaign in Iowa said that the UN wants "the power to tax American citizens, to have its own central bank and treasury, to regulate trade between us and other countries. It's a blueprint for a socialist government spanning the world."[5] Since then, even conservatives who are not so "conspiracy minded" have argued that UN budgets are shrouded in secrecy and that there is a total lack of accountability. They point out that UN administrators are unwilling to undergo a thorough outside audit. Consequently, many political conservatives believe that the UN needs to be drastically downsized, and not just reformed. Some have suggested that many of the agencies could be privatized.[6]

Critics of the UN point out that the General Assembly has been dominated by non-Western nations whose political cultures are at odds with the democratic West. These non-Western states typically support antimarket economics. Most factions in the General Assembly have often voted against the United States. Given that the U.S. assessment is 25 percent of the UN's general budget, and 31 percent of the UN's peacekeeping budget, the United States should have more power in the General Assembly. Currently, ten countries pay about 80 percent of the UN's budget.[7]

But Some Political Liberals Think That the UN Is Worth Saving

Certainly, many who consider themselves political liberals agree that the UN should undergo reform. A significant group, though, believes that the UN is definitely worth saving. First of all, they point out that the UN is not developing a "covert one-world agency" to rule the world. Yes, it is true that the UN's thirty separate bureaucracies suffer from bloat and inefficiency. But since the end of the Cold War, the United States has been more successful than ever in using the UN as a tool for American diplomacy. The UN has helped contain the nations of Iraq and Libya, it has promoted free trade, and it has helped cultivate democracy in such places as Mozambique.

The $2 billion that the United States is supposed to pay the UN each year is equal to the annualized cost of a single aircraft carrier battle group. That is not very much for the benefits we receive, according to supporters of the UN today. When the United States intervenes along with the United Nations, we pay only 30 percent of the cost, and other nations provide most of the troops. Also, U.S. firms provide a significant portion of the goods and services the UN buys, so those purchases generate increases in income in the United States.

UN missions have achieved some great successes, including the World Health Organization's $30 million investment in eradicating smallpox worldwide, which was completed by 1977. Prior to that year, the United States alone spent $350 million a year on immunizations against that disease.

Finally, recent polls show that 60 percent of Americans think that the UN is "doing a good job" and 72 percent feel that it is "very important" that the United States continue to be an active member of the organization.[8]

For Critical Analysis

Should the wealthier and more powerful nations have a greater say in UN decision making than the less wealthy and less powerful nations? Why or why not?

COMMUNIST BLOC ● The group of Eastern European nations that fell under the control of the Soviet Union following World War II.

IRON CURTAIN ● A phrase coined by Winston Churchill to describe the political boundaries between the democratic countries in Europe and the Soviet-controlled communist countries in Eastern Europe.

MARSHALL PLAN ● A plan providing for U.S. economic assistance to European nations following World War II to help those nations recover from the war; the plan was named after George C. Marshall, secretary of state from 1947 to 1949.

CONTAINMENT ● A U.S. policy designed to contain the spread of communism by offering military and economic aid to threatened nations.

COLLECTIVE SECURITY ● A national defense and security policy that involved the formation of mutual defense alliances, such as the North Atlantic Treaty Organization, with other nations.

WESTERN BLOC ● The democratic nations that emerged victorious after World War II, led by the United States.

COLD WAR ● The war of words, warnings, and ideologies between the Soviet Union and the United States that lasted from the late 1940s through the early 1990s.

THE COLD WAR

Once World War II ended, the wartime alliance between the United States and the Soviet Union began to deteriorate quickly. The Soviet Union opposed American political and economic values. Many Americans thought that the Soviet Union and the spread of communism posed a major threat to democracy. After the war ended, one after another, the countries of Eastern Europe—Hungary, Poland, Bulgaria, Romania, and Czechoslovakia—fell under Soviet domination, forming what became known as the **communist bloc.**

The Iron Curtain

Britain's Prime Minister Winston Churchill established the tone for a new relationship between the Soviet Union and the Western allies in his famous "iron curtain" speech in Fulton, Missouri, on March 5, 1946:

> An iron curtain has descended across the Continent. Behind that line all are subject in one form or another, not only to Soviet influence but to a very high . . . measure of control from Moscow.

The reference to an **iron curtain** described the political boundaries between the democratic countries in Western Europe and the Soviet-controlled communist countries in Eastern Europe.

The Marshall Plan and the Policy of Containment

When it appeared that communists, backed by the Soviets, would take over Greece and Turkey in 1947 after Great Britain announced that it was withdrawing economic and military aid from those areas, President Harry Truman took action. He convinced Congress to appropriate $400 million in aid for those countries to prevent the spread of communism.[9] The policy of economic assistance to war-torn Europe was called the **Marshall Plan,** after George Marshall, who was then the U.S. secretary of state. During the next five years, Congress appropriated $17 billion for aid to sixteen European countries. By 1952, the nations of Western Europe, with U.S. help, had indeed recovered and were again prospering.

These actions marked the beginning of a policy of **containment**—a policy designed to contain the spread of communism by offering threatened nations U.S. military and economic aid.[10] To make the policy of containment effective, the United States initiated a policy of **collective security** involving the formation of mutual defense alliances with other nations. In 1949, by the North Atlantic Treaty, the United States, Canada, and ten European nations formed a military alliance—the North Atlantic Treaty Organization (NATO)—and declared that an attack on any member of the alliance would be considered an attack against all members. President Truman stationed four American army divisions in Europe as the nucleus of the NATO armed forces. President Truman also pledged military aid to any European nation threatened by communist expansion.

Thus, by 1949, almost all illusions of friendship between the Soviet Union and the Western allies had disappeared. The United States became the leader of the **Western bloc** of democratic nations that included France, Great Britain, Australia, Canada, Japan, the Philippines, and other countries in Western Europe and Latin America. The tensions between the Soviet Union and the United States became known as the **Cold War,** a war of words, warnings, and ideologies that lasted from the late 1940s through the early 1990s. The term *iron curtain,* from Winston Churchill's speech in 1946, became even more appropriate in 1961, when the Soviets insisted that Berlin be split by the Berlin Wall, which separated East Berlin from West Berlin.

Although the Cold War was mainly a war of words and belief systems, the wars in Korea (1950–1953) and Vietnam (1964–1975) are examples of confrontations that grew out of the efforts to contain communism.

DETERRENCE ● A policy of building up military strength for the purpose of discouraging (deterring) military attacks by other nations; the policy of "building weapons for peace" that supported the arms race between the United States and the Soviet Union during the Cold War.

MUTUAL-ASSURED DESTRUCTION (MAD) ● A phrase referring to the assumption, on which the policy of deterrence was based, that if the forces of two nations are equally capable of destroying each other, neither will take a chance on war.

THE ARMS RACE AND DETERRENCE

The tensions induced by the Cold War led both the Soviet Union and the United States to try to surpass each other militarily. They began competing for more and better weapons, with greater destructive power. This phenomenon, which was commonly known as the arms race, was supported by a policy of **deterrence**—of rendering ourselves and our allies so strong militarily that our very strength would deter (stop or discourage) any attack on us. Deterrence is essentially a policy of "building weapons for peace." Out of deterrence came the theory of **mutual-assured destruction (MAD)**, which held that if the forces of both nations were equally capable of destroying each other, neither would take a chance on war.

THE SECOND RUSSIAN REVOLUTION AND THE END OF THE COLD WAR

In August 1991, a number of disgruntled Communist Party leaders who wanted to curb the movement toward greater autonomy for the republics within the Soviet Union illegally seized control of the Soviet central government. Russian citizens rose up in revolt and defied those leaders. In particular, the democratically elected president of the Russian republic (the largest republic in the Soviet Union), Boris Yeltsin, openly defied the military troops in Moscow. This attempted coup was overthrown after three days in what has become known as the Second Russian Revolution (the first one having occurred seventy-four years earlier, in 1917, when the communists first established their power base in Russia). Over the next several weeks, the Communist Party in the Soviet Union lost virtually all of its power. Most of the fifteen republics constituting the Soviet Union declared their independence, and by the end of the year, the Union of Soviet Socialist Republics (U.S.S.R.) no longer existed.

Boris N. Yeltsin was elected president of the Russian Republic on June 13, 1991. On August 19 of that year, communist hard-liners attempted a coup. Yeltsin entered Moscow on August 23 and called for a general strike to resist the coup. Some of the tank commanders supported Yeltsin, and the coup leaders fled. Later that day, then Soviet President Mikhail Gorbachev, who had been under house arrest at his summer home in the Crimea, returned to Moscow. Gorbachev ordered the disbanding of the Communist Party and its apparatus, thus ending seventy-four years of communist rule.

The political destruction in 1991 of the Soviet Union, the only other superpower in the world besides the United States, led to an almost immediate response from George Bush, who was then the president of the United States. Bush ordered the American nuclear arsenal throughout the world to be dramatically, drastically, and permanently reduced. He did this without any promises from the leaders of the former Soviet republics that they would do the same. The reality was that the impoverished republics of the former Soviet Union could no longer bear the economic burden of maintaining (in working order) a huge nuclear arsenal.

Without question, the year 1991 will go down in history books as one of the most significant dates in modern times. It saw both the total collapse of communism in the former Soviet Union and the true end to the Cold War and the arms race. The demise of the Soviet Union also altered the framework and goals of U.S. foreign policy. During the Cold War, the moral underpinnings of American foreign policy were clear to all—the United States was the defender of the "free world" against the Soviet aggressor. When the Cold War ended, U.S. foreign policymakers were forced, for the first time in decades, to rethink the nation's foreign policy goals and adapt them to a world arena in which the United States was the only remaining superpower—at least, for a time.

Who Makes U.S. Foreign Policy?

The framers of the Constitution envisioned that the president and Congress would cooperate in developing American foreign policy. The Constitution did not spell out exactly how this was to be done, however. As commander in chief, the president has assumed much of the decision-making power in the area of foreign policy. Nonetheless, members of Congress, a number of officials, and a vast national security bureaucracy help to shape the president's decisions and to limit the president's powers.

THE PRESIDENT'S ROLE

Article II, Section 2, of the Constitution names the president commander in chief of the armed forces. As commander in chief, the president oversees the military and guides defense policies. Starting with Abraham Lincoln, presidents have interpreted this role broadly and have sent American troops, ships, and weapons to trouble spots at home and around the world. The Constitution also authorizes the president to make treaties, which must be approved by two-thirds of the Senate. In addition, the president is empowered to form executive agreements—pacts between the president and the heads of other nations. Executive agreements do not require Senate approval. Furthermore, the president's foreign policy responsibilities take on special significance because the president has ultimate control over the use of nuclear weapons.

As head of state, the president also influences foreign policymaking. As the symbolic head of our government, the president represents the United States to the rest of the world. When a serious foreign policy issue or international question arises, the nation expects the president to make a formal statement on the matter.

THE CABINET

All members of the president's cabinet concern themselves with international problems and recommend policies to deal with them. As U.S. power in the world has increased and as economic factors have become more important, the Departments of Commerce, Agriculture, Treasury, and Energy have become more involved in foreign policy decisions. The secretary of state and the secretary of defense, however, are the only cabinet members who concern themselves with foreign policy matters on a full-time basis.

The Department of State

The Department of State is, in principle, the government agency most directly involved in foreign policy. The department maintains diplomatic relations with nearly two hundred independent nations around the globe, as well as with the United Nations and other multilateral organizations, such as the Organization of American States. Most U.S. relations with other countries are maintained through embassies, consulates, and other U.S. offices around the world.

As the head of the State Department, the secretary of state has traditionally played a key role in foreign policymaking, and many presidents have relied heavily on the advice of their secretaries of state. Since the end of World War II, though, the preeminence of the State Department in foreign policy has declined dramatically.

The Department of Defense

The Department of Defense is the principal executive department that establishes and carries out defense policy and protects our national security. The secretary of defense advises the president on all aspects of U.S. military and defense policy, supervises all of the military activities of the U.S. government, and works to see that the decisions of the president as commander in chief are carried out. The secretary advises and informs the president on the nation's military forces, weapons, and bases and works closely with the U.S. military, especially the Joint Chiefs of Staff, in gathering and studying defense information.

The Joint Chiefs of Staff include the chief of staff of the Army, the chief of staff of the Air Force, the chief of naval operations, and the commandant of the Marine Corps. The chairperson is appointed by the president for a four-year term. The joint chiefs serve as the key military advisers to the president, the secretary of defense, and the National Security Council. They are responsible for handing down the president's orders to the nation's military units, preparing strategic plans, and recommending military actions. They also propose military budgets, new weapons systems, and military regulations.

The Pentagon houses the U.S. Department of Defense in Arlington, Virginia. The Pentagon was completed on January 15, 1943. At that time, it was the world's largest office building. It has 6.5 million square feet of floor space, 17 miles of corridors, and 7,748 windows.

OTHER AGENCIES

Several other government agencies are also involved in the foreign relations of the United States. The Arms Control Disarmament Agency was formed in 1961 to study and develop policies to deal with the nuclear arms race. The United States Information Agency works to strengthen communications and understanding between the United States and other nations. It is best known for running Voice of America, a round-the-clock radio program that is translated into approximately forty different languages. The Agency for International Development gives financial and technical help to other countries. The Peace Corps sends American volunteers to work on development and education projects in other countries. Two key agencies in the area of foreign policy are the National Security Council and the Central Intelligence Agency.

The National Security Council

The National Security Council (NSC) was established by the National Security Act of 1947. Its official function is "to advise the president with respect to the integration of domestic, foreign, and military policies relating to national security." The formal members of the NSC include the president, the vice president, the secretary of state, and the secretary of defense, but meetings are often attended by the chairperson of the Joint Chiefs of Staff, the director of the Central Intelligence Agency, and representatives from other departments. The assistant for national security affairs, who is a member of the president's White House staff, is the director of the NSC. The assistant informs the president, coordinates advice and information on foreign policy, and serves as a liaison with other officials.

The NSC and its members can be as important and powerful as the president wants them to be. Some presidents have made frequent use of the NSC, whereas others have convened it infrequently. Similarly, the importance of the role played by the assistant for national security affairs in shaping foreign policy can vary significantly, depending on the administration.

The Central Intelligence Agency

The Central Intelligence Agency (CIA) was created after World War II to coordinate American intelligence activities abroad. The CIA provides the president and his advisers with up-to-date information about the political, military, and economic activities of foreign governments. The CIA gathers much of its intelligence from overt sources, such as foreign radio broadcasts and newspapers, people who travel abroad, and satellite photographs. Other information is gathered from covert activities, such as its own secret investigations into the economic or political affairs of other nations. The CIA has tended to operate autonomously, and the nature of its work, methods, and operating funds are kept secret.

CONGRESS'S POWERS

Although the executive branch takes the lead in foreign policy matters, Congress also has some power over foreign policy. Remember that Congress alone has the power to declare war. It also has the power to appropriate funds to build new weapons systems, to equip U.S. armed forces, and for foreign aid. (For a comparison of foreign aid given by the United States with aid given by other countries, see the feature *Perception versus Reality: Foreign Aid.*) The Senate has the power to approve or reject treaties and the appointment of ambassadors.

In 1973, Congress passed the War Powers Resolution, which limits the president's use of troops in military action without congressional approval. Presidents since then, however, have not interpreted the resolution to mean that Congress must be consulted before military action is

perception **versus reality**

Foreign Aid

Every few years in Congress, a short but intense controversy arises over how much money should be given in foreign aid. These discussions center around an activity that appears to be an important part of U.S. foreign policy. Interestingly, the United States was the recipient of foreign aid in many of its earlier years while it was growing to become the world's number one economic powerhouse. During the Cold War, much of our foreign aid was given in an attempt to influence foreign governments to "side with" the United States and the Western democracies rather than with the Soviet Union and communism.

The Perception

In recent years, polls about foreign aid consistently have shown that the Americans polled believe that we are giving large amounts of money away to foreign nations. For example, a recent poll conducted jointly by the Center for the Study of Policy Attitudes and the Center for International Security Studies of the University of Maryland found that 75 percent of respondents thought that at least 15 percent of government spending was for foreign aid. When asked what portion of federal spending should go to foreign aid, those polled thought that 5 percent was about right.

The Reality

Expressed as a percentage of total federal government spending, foreign aid seems trivial. Currently, it accounts for only 0.1 percent of the federal budget. The United States gives less foreign aid as a percentage of its annual national income than most other developed countries. Indeed, Japan is now the leading giver of foreign aid (in proportionate terms) in the world.

You Be the Judge

What are the arguments for and against extending more foreign aid to other nations?

---

taken. On several occasions, presidents have ordered military action and then informed Congress after the fact.

Several congressional committees are directly concerned with foreign affairs. The most important are the Armed Services Committee and the International Relations Committee in the House and the Armed Services Committee and the Foreign Relations Committee in the Senate. Other congressional committees deal with matters such as oil, agriculture, and imports that indirectly influence foreign policy.

Nuclear Politics and Policy in an Unstable World

The Cold War may be over, but the threat of nuclear warfare—which formed the backdrop of foreign policy during the Cold War—has by no means disappeared. The existence of nuclear weapons in Russia and in other countries around the world continues to challenge U.S. foreign policymakers. Concerns about nuclear proliferation mounted in 1998 when India and Pakistan detonated nuclear devices within a few weeks of each other— events that took U.S. intelligence agencies by surprise. U.S. officials were also alarmed when they received information, in the summer of 1998, that North Korea was developing an underground nuclear arms site. Increasingly, American officials are becoming concerned about the threat of nuclear attack by a rogue nation that now possesses nuclear capabilities. (Many Americans are also concerned about accidental nuclear detonations—a topic discussed in the feature on the next page entitled *A Question of Ethics: Should the United States Part with Its Nuclear-Safety Secrets?*)

RUSSIA'S CURRENT NUCLEAR ARSENAL

Russia, the strongest of the fifteen republics that formerly constituted the Soviet Union, still has nearly seven thousand nuclear warheads, according to the Carnegie Endowment for International Peace. Such warheads could be

Should the United States Part with Its Nuclear-Safety Secrets?

Nuclear accidents do happen. During the Cold War, for example, a number of U.S. military aircraft carrying nuclear warheads crashed or accidentally dropped their bombs over U.S. soil and coastal waters. These accidents did not result in a crisis because the nuclear warheads did not detonate; they were equipped with safety devices. But what might happen today, when an increasing number of nations have the capacity to build nuclear weapons but do not have the capacity to protect those weapons against accidental detonations—or against unauthorized launches, sabotage, or theft by terrorist organizations?

The 1954 Atomic Energy Act expressly allows the United States to cooperate with other nations with respect to nuclear safety, but to date U.S. nuclear-safety assistance has been limited to Britain and France. With respect to other nations (such as Pakistan and India, which have recently demonstrated that they have nuclear capabilities), the United States has kept its nuclear-safety technologies cloaked in secrecy. One of the questions facing Americans and their political leaders today is whether the United States should declassify basic nuclear-safety technologies and share them with nations that are developing nuclear capabilities.

Critics of the idea of sharing nuclear-safety technology maintain that if the United States did declassify these technologies, it would essentially be condoning nuclear proliferation. Supporters of the idea, however, believe that such a step would be beneficial—it would help to protect against the use of nuclear warheads, accidental or otherwise.[11]

For Critical Analysis

Should Americans learn to "live with the bomb" by sharing safety technology?

delivered by land-based missiles, dropped from planes, or launched from submarines. Look at Figure 19–1. The array of intercontinental ballistic missiles (ICBMs), mobile ICBM launchers, submarine-launched ballistic missiles, and bombers throughout Russia is impressive. Under a bilateral agreement, no Russian missiles are targeted at the United States. Experts say, however, that Russia could reprogram its missiles within minutes.

Figure 19–1
Russia's Nuclear Arsenal

SOURCE: The Carnegie Endowment for International Peace.

Even today, proud displays of military power and nuclear capabilities are paraded before the Russian populace. Here, senior Russian military officers show Russia's military strength in a parade at Poklonnaya Gora in Moscow. Poklonnaya Gora (Russian for "a hill you bow to") is the site of a war memorial honoring Russian soldiers who died in World War II.

Russia, no matter how strapped for funds, wants to maintain its nuclear arsenal as a "badge" of first-class military status. Indeed, at one point in 1996 when member countries of the North Atlantic Treaty Organization (NATO) were negotiating to admit Eastern European countries (Poland, Hungary, and the Czech Republic), Russian Defense Minister Igor Rodionov threatened to aim missiles at the Eastern European countries if they should join NATO.

For some time, Western analysts and policymakers have debated the dangers posed by Russia's aging strategic missile forces. These concerns are now being voiced by some Russian military specialists as well. For example, General Vladimir Yakovlev, the head of Russia's land-based strategic missile forces, recently stated that 62 percent of Russia's combat-ready strategic rockets and 71 percent of the guidance systems were beyond their guaranteed service life. Another Russian specialist on strategic missiles has warned that Russia's older submarine-based nuclear-tipped rockets, which carry nuclear warheads, are wearing out and that Russia, by keeping the rockets in service, is risking "hundreds of Chernobyls."[12]

More worrisome perhaps is Russia's current economic and political instability. Many Russian troops remain unpaid and desperate. The chief of one Russian nuclear lab even committed suicide because its research was so curtailed by lack of funds. In the United States, the greatest fear among defense policymakers seems to be that some dissatisfied Russian officer could launch a strike or, alternatively, could sell a nuclear warhead or key substance to North Korea or Iraq. Small amounts of nuclear material have already turned up on the black market worldwide. Their source? Russia.

COULD A FALSE ALARM START A NUCLEAR WAR?

On January 25, 1995, President Boris Yeltsin of Russia saw a warning light on the nuclear briefcase that his aide was carrying. When the case was opened, it was tracking a ballistic missile coming over the Norwegian Sea. On the briefcase was an array of buttons that would authorize strike options for the 4,700 nuclear warheads that are on permanent alert in Russia. The choice was not easy. If it was a false alarm and Yeltsin gave the launch order, he could have started World War III. If it was not a false alarm and he did not retaliate, a nuclear warhead detonating over Russia would have crippled the nation. Yeltsin had four minutes to decide. Fortunately for all of us, he did not panic. A quick investigation showed that the blip on his computer screen was triggered by a meteorological rocket fired from Norway to obtain information about the aurora borealis.

The scenario just described was not an isolated event. In 1979, training data were slipped into the U.S. early warning system to mimic a large Soviet attack. The U.S. military decision makers fortunately figured out what had happened before any damage was done. In 1983, a solar storm caused an early warning system in the Soviet Union to indicate a massive U.S. attack.

The point is that in spite of the end of the Cold War, both the United States and Russia rely on extraordinarily rapid decision making. In the United States, from the time assessment occurs to the time of launch and preparation, only twenty-two minutes transpire; in Russia, this process takes thirteen minutes.

DISMANTLING RUSSIA'S NUCLEAR ARSENAL

In 1992, the United States signed the Strategic Arms Reduction Treaty (START I) with four former Soviet republics—Russia, Ukraine, Belarus, and Kazakhstan—to reduce the number of long-range nuclear weapons. The treaty obligates the United States and Russia to each reduce the number of their strategic nuclear weapons to about 6,500 by the year 2001. By the late 1990s, the U.S. and Russian arsenals of strategic warheads had been reduced to about 7,000 apiece—down from about 10,000 apiece in 1992. A second treaty (START II) signed in 1993 calls for these arsenals to be reduced even further—to approximately 3,500 apiece—by the year 2003. Russia, however, has not yet ratified START II.

Despite the apparent progress, a problem is inherent in the START process. Even though the United States has given the former Soviet Union hundreds of millions of dollars to dismantle parts of the former Soviet arsenal, Russia has resisted U.S. inspection. Therefore, the United States has not been able to monitor what Russian authorities have done with their nuclear warheads.

When President Clinton addressed the U.S. Air Force Academy graduating class of 1995, he stated, "For the first time since the dawn of the nuclear age, there are no Russian missiles pointed at the children of the United States." Unfortunately, at virtually the same time, the Russians unveiled a new mobile launcher for a high-powered missile—a first-strike weapon designed to attack the United States. Also at the same time, Russia successfully test-launched a new next-generation missile and indicated that it would replace all of its outdated missiles in the coming years.

The fact is, Russia has retained ten to fifteen thousand nonstrategic nuclear weapons, which is between seven and ten times as many as the United States has. Even if Russia ratifies START II, that treaty still does not cover nonstrategic nuclear weapons. Many critics of the START treaties argue that a new treaty should be negotiated that covers both strategic and nonstrategic nuclear weapons. If this were done, nonstrategic weapons would be included in arms control for the first time. The challenge, of course, would be how to verify the dismantling of such weapons.[13]

THE PROLIFERATION OF CRUISE AND BALLISTIC MISSILES—A NONNUCLEAR THREAT

In the last decade, nonnuclear ballistic and cruise missiles have been used to terrify, intimidate, and actually harm or kill civilians. During one six-month period, Iraq peppered Iran's capital, Tehran, with ballistic missiles, killing over two thousand Iranians and forcing half of the city to evacuate. During the Gulf War in 1991, Saddam Hussein's use of ballistic missiles against Israeli towns almost provoked retaliation. In 1996, China fired ballistic missiles into the sea near Taiwan to intimidate that country during its first democratic elections. In 1999, Pakistan test-fired a new missile that has a range of 1,200 miles, making it the longest-range missile in Pakistan's arsenal. India had conducted a similar missile test just three days earlier. In all, thirty-five non-NATO countries now have ballistic missiles. These missiles could be used for nuclear, chemical, or biological warheads.[14]

Some think that cruise and ballistic missiles pose little danger to the United States. Others think that these missiles do pose a threat, and a serious one. Consider the conclusion reached in 1998 by a bipartisan commission established to analyze the foreign ballistic missile threat to American territory. The commission, headed by former defense secretary Donald Rumsfeld, claimed that Iran, Iraq, and North Korea are aggressively seeking missile technology. Furthermore, these or other hostile nations would be able to "acquire the means to strike the U.S. within about five years of a decision" to build a ballistic missile. In early 1999, Defense Secretary William S. Cohen affirmed that "there is a threat, and the threat is growing, and it will pose a danger not only to our troops, but also to Americans here at home."[15] He proposed that a national missile shield be built to defend against possible missile attacks by rogue states.

Establishing a defense system against possible missile attacks is difficult because it would require a revision of the 1972 Anti-Ballistic Missile Treaty. Under that treaty, the Soviet Union and the United States agreed to limit their defenses against intercontinental ballistic missiles (ICBMs). The United States can have a maximum of one hundred interceptors aimed at ICBMs to give us early warning. The treaty permits only ground-based defense—no submarines are allowed—and specifically outlaws the use of orbiting lasers.

What Should Be Done about Biological and Chemical Weapons?

Biological warfare materials and chemical weapons are considered the poor person's nuclear bombs. While treaties to stop the spread of nuclear weapons have made the headlines, what to do about biological and chemical weapons has generated less concern.

In 1972, more than 130 nations ratified the Biological and Toxins Weapons Convention, which specifically prohibited the development and production of biological weapons. The treaty, however, contained no built-in checks. By the mid-1990s, at least twenty countries had undertaken military research programs that resulted in the development of biological weapons.[16] Just a few years ago, the United Nations charged Iraq with stockpiling biological warfare agents, including tens of thousands of liters of deadly botulinum and anthrax cultures.

All intelligence agencies generally agree that in addition to Iraq, other countries—including Iran, Syria, China, and North Korea—have developed and are holding vast quantities of biological weapons. Even white supremacists in the United States were able to purchase from commercial suppliers cultures of a bacteria that cause bubonic plague. In the future, we might see genetically engineered bacteria that are resistant to antibiotics.

WHAT THE UNITED STATES HAS DONE

According to some critics, the U.S. response to the threat of biological and chemical warfare has been too little, too late. While the threat of biological and chemical warfare has increased, the United States has spent very little for research on detection devices, antidotes to germ agents, and protective suits. During the Gulf War, U.S. troops in Iraq used chemical-agent detectors that were rudimentary at best. Troops that were at risk had to wear stifling suits and face masks. Given that to develop a vaccine takes from ten to twenty years, the United States is not in a position to protect its troops against biowarfare agents, particularly those that have been genetically engineered fairly recently.

The actual fighting during the Persian Gulf War lasted from January through February, 1991. Subsequently, many Gulf War veterans experienced what has become known as the "Gulf War Syndrome." The symptoms include nausea, cramps, rashes, fatigue, headaches, and joint and muscle pain. In 1997, the Department of Defense finally admitted that some Gulf War participants may have been exposed to biological and chemical warfare agents. Many U.S. soldiers at the time did don chemical suits, but their design was not appropriate for use in the high temperatures experienced in desert warfare.

INFOTRAC®
An unlikely threat

THE CHEMICAL WEAPONS TREATY

The Chemical Weapons Convention (CWC), a treaty ratified by the United States in 1997, was intended to abolish all chemical weapons worldwide. According to its critics, however, the CWC contains loopholes and weak enforcement mechanisms that might render it less effective than desirable. Specifically, these critics believe that Russia will continue to develop new chemical weapons. Many senators have expressed this concern, but the United States does not have the capability to verify other countries' compliance with the CWC. Moreover, according to a national intelligence estimate, the production of new classes of chemical weapons would be difficult to detect and confirm even through a CWC–sponsored investigation.

Perhaps more important, the clandestine production of chemical weapons, particularly in Russia, will probably continue despite the CWC. For example, a Pentagon report describes Foliante, the code name of a secret Soviet program to develop nerve agents lethal enough that a microscopic amount can kill. Under the CWC list of banned chemical weapons, many of the substances developed under the Foliante program technically would not be banned.

The destruction of chemical agents currently in existence also poses a problem. Even though the United States and other nations have offered to help Russia destroy its tens of thousands of tons of declared chemical agents, Russia has refused to accept any such help. In the meantime, the United States is already destroying its chemical-weapons stockpile. Although the CWC technically went into effect on April 29, 1997, because sixty-five nations had signed it, without Russian ratification, its effectiveness is probably limited.

How Should the United States Deal with China?

For years, the United States has attempted to encourage China to improve its human rights record. In spite of its impressive economic growth and the freeing up of its economy, China remains one of the world's least politically free nations. Indeed, it is the only remaining *major* power that still clings to communist ideas and concepts.

politics on the far side

Bargain Basement Prices for the Chinese Military

The Chinese government has developed a network of individuals in the United States to help buy defense-related equipment for China. The U.S. Defense Department estimates that up to eight hundred U.S.–based firms are involved. Because these firms concentrate on obtaining production equipment for making weapons, rather than the weapons themselves, they do not violate any laws against exporting military equipment to China. The Chinese network of brokers and buyers was put into place shortly after the Tiananmen Square massacre against pro-democracy demonstrators in 1989. During this same period, the Cold War was ending, and the decline in the demand for weapons forced the U.S. defense industry to downsize.

With this downsizing, huge amounts of surplus U.S. military equipment became available. Lockheed Martin Corporation, General Electric Company, and other companies unloaded production systems and sophisticated weapons for a small percentage of what taxpayers originally paid for those parts of our defense system. For example, Northrop Grumman Corporation auctioned off machines that were used to make fighters, bombers, and bombs at its Glen Arm facility in Maryland. One machine for stamping out aircraft wings that had cost $500,000 was sold for $2,500. Just prior to the auction, officials from a Chinese aircraft facility visited the plant and scrutinized that same machine.

For Critical Analysis: Why doesn't the U.S. government ban the export of equipment and other materials that could be used to make weapons?

MOST-FAVORED-NATION STATUS ● A status granted by a clause in an international treaty. Generally, most-favored-nation clauses are designed to establish equality of international treatment. For example, if the United States and the People's Republic of China have agreed in a treaty that each country will have most-favored-nation status with respect to international trade, then the United States must treat China at least as well as the country receiving the most favorable treatment from the United States and vice versa.

MOST-FAVORED-NATION STATUS VERSUS HUMAN RIGHTS

On several occasions, the United States has threatened to withdraw China's **most-favored-nation status** unless China improves its human rights record. (As long as China retains its most-favored-nation status, the United States must treat China at least as well as the country receiving the most favorable treatment from the United States with regard to imports or exports.) In the final analysis, though, the United States has always caved in and granted an additional year of such status, thereby benefiting the Chinese export sector. (For other favorable treatment of the Chinese, see the feature entitled *Politics on the Far Side: Bargain Basement Prices for the Chinese Military.*)

CHINA — THE NEXT SUPERPOWER?

China, even more than the former Soviet Union, has the potential to become a genuinely great power. After all, it is a country with a great culture, a great people, and, increasingly, a great economy. Given its impressive record of economic growth and its definite desire to become a superpower, China just may succeed in becoming the world's greatest superpower in the twenty-first century.

During the late 1990s, Jiang Zemin, the president of China, flew to India to mend fences with an old adversary, went to Pakistan to renew an old friendship, and saw European officials on a regular basis. More important, China undertook civilian and military cooperation in the nuclear arena with Pakistan. The United States has complained vociferously about such nuclear cooperation. China's answer has been, "Mind your own business." The Chinese have also been caught selling sophisticated weapons systems and nuclear technology to Iran and perhaps to other countries. Although China has stated on

several occasions that it has not done so and has promised not to do so in the future, the U.S. intelligence community believes that China is still supplying such weapons. In addition, a congressional committee report in 1999 alleged that Chinese spies had stolen a number of nuclear-weapons secrets from U.S. nuclear labs.

Critics of the Clinton administration argue that it has overlooked virtually everything negative that Beijing has done. Those who regularly visit China contend that its leaders have one goal—to overtake the United States as the preeminent global power. Foreign policy observers are worried that the United States will end up with a bipolar relationship similar to its relationship with the Soviet Union after World War II. Unlike the Soviet Union, however, China does not have dreams of territorial conquests. That means that relations between the United States and China will be much more multifaceted than relations between the United States and the Soviet Union were. China clearly needs the United States. A third of its exports go to the United States (with only 2 percent of American exports going to China).

Americans at Odds over Foreign Policy

Just because the United States no longer faces a single "enemy" does not mean that all is well and that foreign policy decision making is simpler. Indeed, some argue that foreign policy today is much more complicated than it was during the Cold War. After all, we knew who our "enemies" were then. Today, the United States continues to grapple with the problem of developing a foreign policy that will protect our short-run and long-run national interests and at the same time promote democracy and free markets, as well as human rights, throughout the world.

One foreign policy issue over which Americans are at odds today concerns international lending policies sponsored and paid for by the United States to help developing countries. Another issue involves cutbacks in the State Department's budget and their implications for the future of U.S. influence abroad. Finally, many Americans are at odds over the destruction of our nuclear arsenal and over how we can best combat terrorism.

The World Bank and Global Markets

In its heyday, the World Bank was the premier lending institution to developing countries. Its goal was to help those countries help themselves. Today, the World Bank and other multilateral lending institutions are under constant attack. Critics of such institutions—which are often financed disproportionately by American taxpayers—argue that loans provided by these lending institutions strengthen regimes that are opposed to American policy.[17]

Some critics question whether the World Bank is even needed anymore. In the past, the World Bank and other multilateral lending institutions controlled most of the money going to developing countries. Today, that is no longer true. It is estimated that in 1999, more than $220 billion in capital flowed to the developing world.[18] At most, $40 billion of this capital came from the World Bank and other official sources. Because of the great flow of private capital to developing countries, multilateral lending organizations such as the World Bank have to adapt themselves quickly and dramatically to global markets.

Nonetheless, multinational lenders can still play an important role in lending funds to the least developed countries. The poorest forty-eight countries in the world receive less than 1 percent of total private capital flows. One agency of the World Bank, the International Finance Corporation, is responding by expanding its reach into sixteen "high-risk" countries, such as Cambodia, Mongolia, Senegal, and Guyana. The World Bank is also putting more emphasis on helping poor countries strengthen their financial and legal systems.

This Wal-Mart in Mexico is a single example of the proliferation of U.S. companies doing business on a global scale.

Is U.S. Diplomacy Declining?

Since 1993, because of budget pressures and other reasons, the State Department has cut more than 2,000 employees and closed consulates in 26 foreign cities. The Agency for International Development has closed 23 overseas missions. That does not mean the State Department has died—it still has embassies in 162 countries and consulates in 81 foreign cities. Critics of the decline in the State Department's budget argue that over time, the cutbacks will have a negative impact on the ability of the United States to promote U.S. interests and influence events abroad.

DOES THE STATE DEPARTMENT STILL MATTER?

In 1997, soon after Madeleine Albright took over as secretary of state, policy analysts started evaluating the effectiveness of the State Department. Some asked whether the State Department still mattered. In 1997, only about 1 percent of the federal budget went toward foreign affairs. According to Madeleine Albright, however, "That 1 percent may well determine 50 percent of the history that is written about our era."[19]

Developments in communications technology have made much of what the State Department does abroad seem anachronistic. Every day outposts throughout the world send cables detailing the political situation, yet virtually anyone can obtain the same information on the Internet. Much of the work done in foreign countries could be done through encrypted e-mail and faxes from Washington, D.C., without embassies and consulates. One veteran foreign service officer agreed that communications technology has eliminated the traditional function of the ambassador.[20] Furthermore, many State Department employees are still guided by Cold War priorities, even though the Cold War is over. Many of the cables sent to Washington, D.C., from our foreign outposts are classified, even though they offer little more than what any citizen of the world can view on CNN.

THE STATE DEPARTMENT FIGHTS BACK

To fight the effects of budget cuts, the State Department is trying to get other agencies to pick up a greater share of the cost of operating abroad. For example, some ambassadors rely on CIA agents to obtain political information and analyses simply because the CIA can "afford" more agents.

Given the demise of one of the previous major missions of the State Department—keeping a lid on communist expansion—the department has turned to helping American companies. The U.S. acting ambassador for Germany, for example, kicked off a marketing promotion for McDonald's in Bonn. The typical U.S. ambassador now spends much more time going to economic conferences, opening shopping malls, and lobbying on trade issues than he or she spends dealing with possible threats to national security. Secretary of State Albright once stated that "one of the major goals of our administration is to make sure American economic interests can be pursued globally."[21] According to many observers of the State Department, business advocacy has allowed American diplomats to justify themselves to a Congress that wants to keep cutting their budgets.

How Far Should We Go in Destroying Nuclear Armaments?

A serious debate is under way over the merits of reducing our nuclear arsenal. On one side of the debate are those who would agree with the proposals of the Canberra Commission, an international body set up by the Australian government and run by a group of about forty American and Russian ex-military personnel. The commission argues that because the Cold War is over, the United States, Russia, Britain, France, and China should do the following:

■ Take all nuclear weapons off alert.
■ Store the warheads separately.
■ Decrease nuclear arsenals even more severely than the current treaties require.
■ Clamp down even more tightly on the transborder shipment of nuclear skills and materials.

The ultimate goal of the Canberra Commission is to abolish nuclear weapons completely. By destroying nuclear arsenals, we could create a nuclear-free world that, presumably, would be a safer place.

On the other side of the debate are those who argue that such thinking is pie in the sky. After all, nuclear technology is known worldwide—you can even get it off the Internet. Rogue states, such as Saddam Hussein's Iraq, will not abide by any nuclear treaty no matter what. Had Hussein had nuclear weapons when he attacked Kuwait in 1990, he might have used them. If the rest of the world did not have them, how could it have responded? The real question that we will undoubtedly have to face in the future is what to do with a nation or a group of terrorists that has a nuclear bomb and is willing to use it.

Terrorism

Perhaps one of the most troubling challenges to governments around the world is how to control terrorism. **Terrorism** is defined as the random use of staged violence at infrequent intervals to achieve political goals. International terrorism has occurred in virtually every region of the world, and the number of terrorist incidents is increasing.

Examples of terrorist acts include the attacks on Israeli Olympic athletes in Munich in 1972; various hijackings, such as the hijacking of TWA flight 847 in 1985; the seizure of the *Achille Lauro,* an Italian cruise ship, in 1986; the bombing of the World Trade Center in New York in 1993; the bombing of the Oklahoma City federal building in 1995; the bombing of an American military barracks in Saudi Arabia in 1996; the bombing of a fruit and vegetable market in Jerusalem in 1997 (as one of a long line of terrorist acts against Israel); the bombing of two U.S. embassies in Africa in 1998; and the recent terrorist acts in Russia (one bomb, on September 9, 1999, destroyed much of an apartment building in Moscow, killing forty-seven people and injuring dozens of others).

In 1996, in an effort to curb terrorism in the United States, Congress passed an antiterrorism bill that made it easier to conduct surveillance operations on suspected terrorists. Among other things, the act established special "deportation courts" (see Chapter 16), in which the government can argue deportation cases in secret. On an international level, the United States and six other nations, at a summit meeting in June 1996, decided to undertake a joint international effort to contain terrorism.

The U.S. government has also spent significant resources to find and bring to trial those who perpetrate terrorist acts that harm Americans. In 1998, immediately after the bombing of the American embassies in Kenya and Tanzania, hundreds of U.S. agents were sent to the bombing sites to conduct investigations. The magnitude of the suffering caused by the bombings—which killed more than 250 people (including 12 Americans) and injured more than 5,500 others—led to an unprecedented move on the part of the U.S. government. Less than three weeks later, President Clinton retaliated with air strikes against terrorist bases in Afghanistan and Sudan that apparently were instrumental in the bombings.

The problem with terrorism is that the enemy is so invisible and that terrorist acts, by their very nature, are random and unpredictable. Additionally, governments have found that the most effective way to contain terrorism and ward off terrorist attacks is to conduct extensive monitoring and surveillance activities.[22] The problem for Americans is whether it is in the nation's interests to sacrifice certain civil liberties (such as due process of law, protection against unreasonable searches and seizures, and privacy rights) to curb terrorism.

key terms

Cold War 468

collective security 468

colonial empire 466

communist bloc 468

containment 468

deterrence 469

foreign policy 465

interventionism 466

iron curtain 468

isolationism 466

Marshall Plan 468

Monroe Doctrine 466

most-favored-nation status 479

mutual-assured destruction (MAD) 469

neutrality 466

terrorism 482

Western bloc 468

chapter summary

1. A nation's foreign policy consists of a systematic and general plan that guides the country's attitudes and actions toward the rest of the world. Foreign policy includes all of the economic, military, commercial, and diplomatic positions and actions that a nation takes in its relationships with other countries. U.S. foreign policy has been guided by both moral idealism and the need to protect our national security.

2. Early U.S. political leaders felt that the best way to protect American interests was through isolationism—avoiding political involvement with other nations. The Monroe Doctrine of 1823 enunciated a policy of isolationism toward Europe but stressed that the United States, in turn, would not tolerate European intervention in the Western Hemisphere. Isolationism began to give way to interventionism as the United States expanded westward across the North American continent, coming into conflict with Mexico and other nations in the process, and as it began to trade more with Japan, China, and other Asian countries. The Spanish-American War of 1898 marked the first true step toward interventionism. By the end of the nineteenth century, the

United States had acquired a colonial empire and was acknowledged as a world power.

3. After World War I, the United States again returned to an isolationist foreign policy, which lasted until the Japanese attacked Pearl Harbor in 1941 and the United States entered World War II. The United States emerged from the war as a superpower, along with the Soviet Union. Soviet domination of the countries of Eastern Europe and the spread of communism led to a U.S. foreign policy of containment, a policy of containing communism by giving aid to countries threatened by a Soviet or Communist takeover. From the late 1940s until the early 1990s, the United States and the Soviet Union engaged in a Cold War—a war of words, threats and warnings, and ideologies. Political changes in the Soviet Union brought about its demise in late 1991—and the end of the Cold War.

4. As commander in chief, the president oversees the military and guides defense policy. The president's cabinet, particularly the secretary of state and the secretary of defense, assist the president in foreign policy, as do a number of agencies, including the National Security Council and the Central Intelligence Agency. Congress also plays a significant role in foreign policy. Only Congress can declare war, and through its control over budget appropriations, Congress wields significant influence over foreign policy. Additionally, although the president has the constitutional authority to form treaties with other nations, all treaties must be confirmed by two-thirds of the Senate.

5. After the end of the Cold War, the superpowers agreed to reduce the size of their nuclear arsenals dramatically. A major problem with nuclear disarmament is that the United States has not been able to monitor what Russian authorities have actually done with their nuclear warheads. The continued existence of nuclear weapons in the world poses the possibility that these weapons could be used in the future by disgruntled Russian generals, rogue states such as Iraq, or terrorists. The existence of nonnuclear ballistic and cruise missiles also poses a threat.

6. Less attention has been paid to the threat created by the existence of biological warfare agents and chemical weapons. Several countries, including Iraq, Iran, Syria, China, and North Korea, are believed to have vast quantities of biological weapons. Some criticize the United States for doing too little, too late, in response to the threat of biological and chemical warfare. It takes from ten to twenty years to develop vaccines against lethal biowarfare agents, so the United States would not be prepared for a biochemical war and could not protect its troops.

7. U.S. relations with China have been controversial, in part because of China's reluctance to ban nuclear weapons. According to the Pentagon, China even has nuclear missiles aimed at the United States. Although the United States has, on various occasions, threatened to withdraw China's most-favored-nation status, we have not done so. China, now under the leadership of an aggressive president, may well become the next superpower.

8. Americans are at odds over several foreign policy issues. One issue concerns the activities of the World Bank. Another issue focuses on the cutbacks in the U.S. Department of State's budget and how they will affect U.S. influence abroad in the future. A significant issue has to do with the implications of U.S. nuclear disarmament in the face of potential nuclear threats by hostile nations. A further issue has to do with the extent to which civil liberties may be sacrificed in the fight against terrorism.

for critical analysis

1. If Americans became involved in a violent civil war, would you want another nation or an international organization to step in and force the factions to the peace table? Why or why not?

2. Over the last decade or so, the United States has intervened in some conflicts around the globe but not in others. How do you explain this inconsistency in American foreign policy?

3. In your opinion, should the United States stay out of other nations' affairs, or should it assume the role of the world's peacekeeper?

4. Should the United States pursue a more selective trade policy? In other words, should the United States refuse to trade with nations whose governments oppress their citizens and violate human rights?

5. How has the end of the Cold War altered the international political arena? Generally, what are some of the major obstacles to peace in today's world?

6. Samuel Huntington argues that the dominant conflicts in the world following the end of the Cold War will be between major world cultures (Chinese,

Japanese, Islamic, Hindu, Western, Orthodox Christian, Latin American, and African) rather than between nations defined by geographic borders. Do you agree? Why or why not?

7. Why do so many conflicts in today's world involve struggles by different groups *within* nations instead of struggles *between* nations?

suggested readings

DENNIS, Anthony J. *The Rise of the Islamic Empire and the Threat to the West.* Bristol, Ind.: Wyndham Hall Press, 1996. According to this researcher, the violent fundamentalist strain of Islam constitutes a major threat to world peace. He argues that Islam is more than a religion; it is also a worldwide revolutionary movement that is no longer contained by worldwide communism.

FEIVESON, Harold A. Ed. *The Nuclear Turning Point: A Blueprint for Deep Cuts and De-Alerting of Nuclear Weapons.* Washington, D.C.: Brookings Institution Press, 1999. This book evaluates the policy of retaining and operating nuclear arsenals and the political challenges involved in reducing the size and readiness of nuclear forces.

JACKSON, Robert, and George Sorenson. *Introduction to International Relations.* New York: Oxford University Press, 1999. The authors provide readers with an excellent introduction to international relations and the principal theories in the field.

POLK, William R. *Neighbors and Strangers: The Fundamentals of Foreign Affairs.* Chicago: University of Chicago Press, 1997. The author sets forth an informed and comprehensive view of foreign relations, showing how a "fear of the foreigner" has been a pervasive force in shaping the foreign policies of nations throughout history.

STEEL, Ronald. *Temptations of a Superpower.* Cambridge, Mass.: Harvard University Press, 1996. The author, a leading foreign policy analyst, suggests that although the demise of the Soviet Union left the United States as the only remaining superpower, this means little in an age when foreign policy challenges often defy military solutions. He proposes that instead of continuing to abide by Cold War rules that no longer apply, the United States should be more realistic and pragmatic in its approach to foreign policy. Particularly, it should pursue a minimalist foreign policy and put domestic priorities first.

WEINBERGER, Casper, and Peter Schweizer. *The Next War.* Washington, D.C.: Regnery Publishing, 1997. This book on U.S. defense policy outlines the unconnected regional conflicts that might involve the United States over the next decade. It shows the impact of poor defense planning in such conflicts.

politics
on the web

You can find news about international events at an interesting Web site sponsored by the Institute for International Economics. You can also get access to the group's working papers at

http://www.iie.com

To learn more about national security policy and defense issues, you can go to the U.S. Department of Defense's DefenseLINK site at

http://www.defenselink.mil

For information on the U.S. Department of State and its activities, go to

http://www.state.gov/index.html

If you are interested in U.S. intelligence and terrorism, go to

http://www.spystuff.com/listsites.html

The Global Legal Information Network (GLIN) provides a database of national laws from countries around the world via the Web server of the U.S. Library of Congress. The site consists of more than 54,000 records of legislation enacted from 1976 to the present. To access this site, go to

http://lcweb2.loc.gov/glin/worldlaw.html

The World Bank's home page offers a wealth of information on international development, research studies containing economic data on various countries, and the like. Go to

http://www.worldbank.org

For worldwide news, an excellent site to visit is

http://www.start4all.com

Another site offering access to worldwide news is that created by the E&P Directory of Online Newspapers, which you can find at

http://www.mediainfo.com/emedia

The Washburn University Law School and Virtual Law Reference Desk offers, among other things, extensive information on international affairs, including United Nations materials. To access this site, go to

http://washlaw.edu/

Now that the Cold War is over, the Central Intelligence Agency has been declassifying a number of documents. Among them is a formerly classified report entitled "The CIA's Role in the Study of UFOs." If you are interested in learning what that role was, you can find the report at the following Web site:

www.ufomind.com/ufo/updates/1997/jun/m16-031.shtml

using web resources

Yale University professor John Lewis Gaddis has written several books and articles on U.S. foreign policy. One of his recent articles was published in the *Atlantic Monthly* and is included online at the magazine's Web site. Go to

http://www.theatlantic.com/issues/99apr/
9904candlestick.htm

Read through the article and then answer the following questions:

1. Why did Gaddis title the article "Living in Candlestick Park"?

2. What do earthquakes have to do with foreign policy, in Gaddis's opinion?

3. Why does he describe the Cold War as a "great game"?

4. How do the metaphors being used by scholars to describe international relations in the post–Cold War era differ from those used during the Cold War?

5. In Gaddis's opinion, what does this difference suggest in terms of future relations among nations?

notes

1. This was the way that President Ronald Reagan characterized the Soviet Union and its satellite countries during the 1980s.

2. Serge Kovaleski, "A Nation in Need: After Five-Year U.S. Intervention, Democracy in Haiti Looks Bleak," *The Washington Post*, September 21, 1999, p. A13.

3. Ivan Eland, "Protecting the Homeland: The Best Defense Is to Give No Offense," The Cato Institute, *Policy Analysis* No. 306, May 5, 1998.

4. As quoted in John Mack Faragher *et al., Out of Many: A History of the American People,* 2d ed. (Upper Saddle River, N.J.: Prentice Hall, 1997), p. 412.

5. *The International Herald Tribune,* September 24, 1996, p. 1.

6. See, for example, Stefan Halper, "A Miasma of Corruption: The United Nations at 50," The Cato Institute, *Policy Analysis* No. 253, April 30, 1996.

7. "Reforming the United Nations," *Economist,* August 8, 1998, p. 22. See also the Web site of the United Nations at **www.un.org.**

8. See, for example, the polls conducted by the Wirthlin Worldwide research organization in April 1996 and August 1998.

9. *Public Papers of the Presidents of the United States: Harry S Truman, 1947* (Washington, D.C.: U.S. Government Printing Office, 1963), pp. 176–180.

10. The containment policy was outlined by George F. Kennan, who was at that time the chief of the policy-planning staff for the Department of State, in an article that appeared in *Foreign Affairs,* July 1947, p. 575. The author's name was given as "X."

11. Todd Sechser, "How to Live with the Bomb," *The Wall Street Journal Europe,* September 2, 1998, p. 6.

12. David Hoffman, "Missile Expert Warns of '100s of Chernobyls,'" *The International Herald Tribune,* May 15, 1998, p. 7.

13. See, for example, A. B. Carter and J. M. Deutch, "No Nukes? Not Yet," *The Wall Street Journal,* March 4, 1997, p. A18.

14. Gerald Frost, "Wake Up America, before It's Too Late," *The Wall Street Journal Europe,* December 3, 1998, p. 10.

15. As cited in Paul Richter, "Pentagon Shifts on Missile Shield Warfare," *The Los Angeles Times,* January 21, 1999, p. A17.

16. "Ban the Bug Bomb: New Horrors Are Certain If the Convention on Biological Weapons Is Not Strengthened," *The Economist,* November 23, 1996, p. 19.

17. Caspar W. Weinberger, "Commentary on Events at Home and Abroad," *Forbes,* October 5, 1998, p. 39.

18. Institute of International Finance.

19. As quoted in *U.S. News & World Report,* January 27, 1997, p. 48.

20. *Ibid.*

21. As reported in *The Wall Street Journal,* January 21, 1997, p. A1.

22. For a discussion of the role of intelligence activities in combating terrorism, see Mortimer B. Zuckerman, "It's Time to Fight Back: America Must Take the Lead against Terrorism, with International Help," *U.S. News & World Report,* September 7, 1998, p. 92.

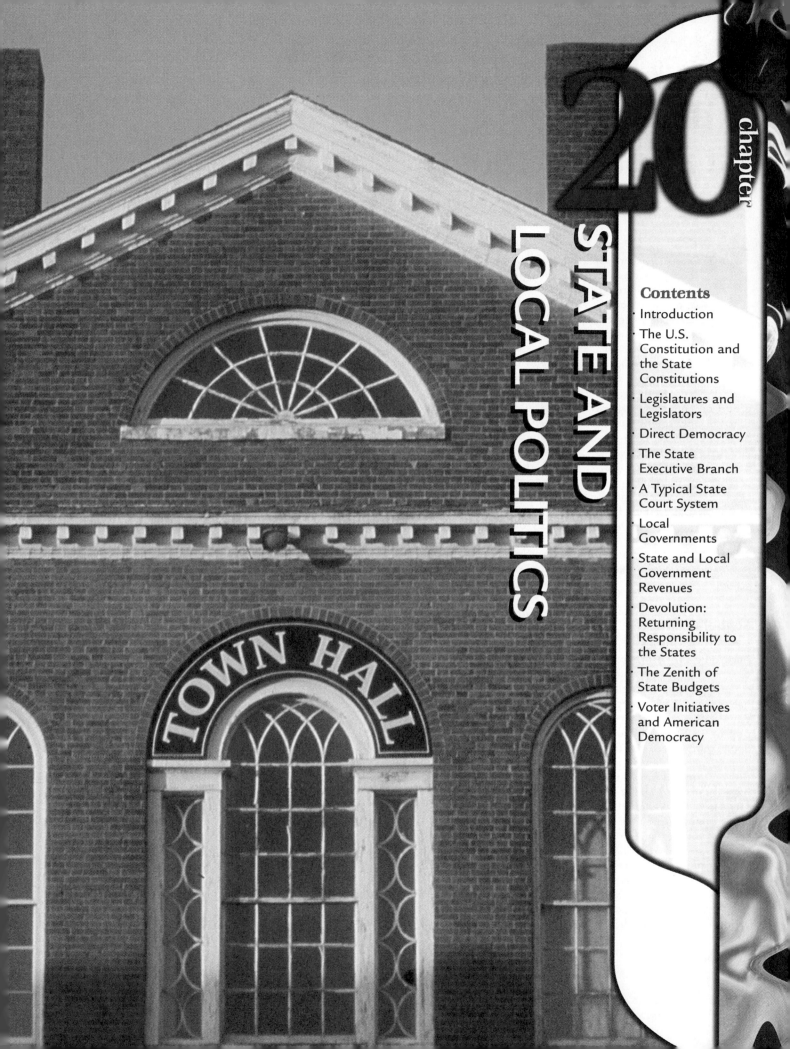

chapter

20

STATE AND LOCAL POLITICS

Contents

K through 12 Education: Should There Be a Choice?

Recent cross-nation comparisons of average scores on math and science tests put the achievement of U.S. schoolchildren below that of students in Japan, Korea, the Czech Republic, Bulgaria, Russia, and Germany. A significant and apparently growing group of Americans believes that the only solution to the "school problem" is to allow educational choice, which might include vouchers. Such vouchers, provided by the state and paid for with tax dollars, could be used by all families with children at any school.

Go to CD-ROM

School Choice Is the Only Choice

According to the proponents of school choice and vouchers, simply spending more money has accomplished nothing. The pupil-staff ratio was fifteen to one in 1890 and hovers at about thirty-five to one today. Annual per-student expenditures (corrected for inflation) have quintupled about every fifty years. Between 1970 and 1996, annual expenditures per student, on average, increased from $3,550 to $6,213,[1] and they continue to climb. In many districts, per-pupil annual expenditures exceed $11,000. Critics of public education often point to the per-

centage of education expenditures (often, nearly 50 percent) that goes to school administration, rather than to teachers or new educational resources (buildings, computers, and the like).

Critics of current public education also contend that many public schools fail because of poor curriculum, lack of personal safety, and few incentives to discipline disruptive students. With universal vouchers, parents could send their children to the public or private school of their choice. The private education sector would attract even more students by offering discipline, parental involvement, and more homework. Because the majority of public school teachers are dedicated to teaching, the ensuing competition will cause them to change their ways to attract better students with vouchers.

Proponents of this system point to the example of the U.S. Postal Service, which was forced to improve its service because of competition from FedEx and UPS. Some evidence also shows that even today the close proximity of Catholic private schools has caused nearby public schools to improve their academic performance.

Why Vouchers Won't Work

Opponents of school choice through vouchers argue that such a system would create

little incentive for public school reform. Parents who are dissatisfied with the performance of public schools would use the vouchers to send their children to private schools. The public schools would be emptied and their resources depleted.

Additionally, according to these critics, the very students who need school alternatives will not find any because new private schools will not be built in the inner cities. Moreover, existing private schools will not be obligated to take students with vouchers, just as private universities are not obligated to take applicants simply because they can pay.

Some critics of choice through educational vouchers also argue that allowing vouchers to be used at religious schools would violate the establishment clause of the First Amendment. After all, vouchers would represent public tax dollars. To allow families to use these dollars to send their children to religious schools would create an excessive entanglement with religion.

Finally, critics of school choice argue that there are

other ways to reform the public schools. They point to how Chicago's public schools are being turned around due to the influence of Mayor Richard Daley. Since taking direct control of the school system in 1995, the mayor has initiated reforms that have gotten results: reading test scores went up in fifty-two of Chicago's seventy-four high schools, and math scores improved in sixty-one schools.[2] Critics of school vouchers also contend that a curriculum established in Washington, D.C., and monitored in every town and city through achievement tests would help to solve our educational problems.

Where Do You Stand?

1. Do you agree or disagree with the argument that school vouchers are the solution to today's educational problems?

2. What might be some additional arguments both for and against the use of school vouchers?

3. What forces, if any, are currently preventing public schools from improving the educational process?

On the Web

For information on the types of reforms being implemented in various schools around the country, go to http://edreform.com/choice.htm.

Introduction

INFOTRAC®

**Voucher programs
stir new debates**

The resolution of independence passed on July 2, 1776, states that "These United Colonies are, and of right ought to be, free and independent States." In many ways, the states are independent: each has its own constitution and its own legislative, executive, and judicial branches. In 1787, when our federal system of government was created, the original thirteen colonies were included as "states" in that system. Also included in the American government system were the many local units of government that existed at that time. Since then, other states, cities, and local units of government have been created. The process has not yet ended: more local government units are still being created, while others are being eliminated.

State and local governments play a vital role in the American political system. Whether to implement school choice through a voucher system is just one example of the myriad policy choices that are made at the state and local levels. To understand how state and local governments function in the United States, the best place to start is at the constitutional level.

The U.S. Constitution and the State Constitutions

The U.S. Constitution never explicitly defines the powers of the states; rather, the Tenth Amendment to the Constitution states that the powers not delegated to the national government by the Constitution "are reserved to the States respectively, or to the people." The major reserved powers of the states include the power to regulate **intrastate commerce** (commerce *within* a state) and to exercise police powers. A state's police powers, as discussed in Chapter 3, refer to the state's right to pass and enforce laws in the areas of public safety, health, welfare, and morality.

STATE CONSTITUTIONS ARE LONG

The U.S. Constitution is a model of brevity: it consists of only seven thousand words. State constitutions, however, are typically models of excessive length and detail. Alabama's constitution, which contains 220,000 words, is the longest. Only one state constitution—that of Vermont, which has 6,880 words—is shorter than the U.S. Constitution.

Many Constitutional Changes

In contrast to the U.S. Constitution, which has only twenty-seven amendments, many state constitutions have hundreds of amendments. The Texas Constitution, for example, has been amended 364 times. The South Carolina Constitution has 465 amendments. The Alabama Constitution tops the list with 582 amendments. Additionally, whereas the U.S. Constitution has endured for over two hundred years, many states have rewritten their constitutions several times. Louisiana has had eleven constitutions; Georgia has had ten; South Carolina has had seven; Alabama, Florida, and Virginia have had six each; and Texas has had five.

Reasons for Lengthy State Constitutions

The length and mass of detail of many state constitutions reflect the loss of popular confidence in state legislatures between the end of the Civil War and the early 1900s. During that period, forty-two states adopted or revised their constitutions. Constitutions that were adopted before or after that period are shorter and contain fewer restrictions on the powers of state legislatures.

EXTRAORDINARY MAJORITY ●
More than a mere majority; typically, an extraordinary majority consists of two-thirds or three-fifths of the voting body (such as a legislature).

INITIATIVE ● A procedure by which voters can propose a change in state and local laws, including state constitutions, by means of gathering signatures on a petition and submitting it to the legislature (and/or the voters) for approval.

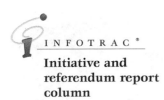

INFOTRAC ®

Initiative and referendum report column

An equally important reason for the length and detail of state constitutions is that the framers of state constitutions have had a difficult time distinguishing between constitutional law and statutory law. (Remember from Chapter 16 that statutory law is law made by legislatures, such as the U.S. Congress or the legislatures of the various states.) Many laws that are clearly statutory in nature have been put into state constitutions.

For example, South Dakota's state constitution has a provision authorizing the establishment of a cordage and twine plant at the state penitentiary. The Texas Constitution includes a pay schedule for state legislators. When Texas legislators want a raise, the constitution must be amended. The Alabama Constitution includes an amendment establishing the "Alabama Heritage Trust Fund." A provision of the California Constitution discusses the tax-exempt status of the Huntington Library and Art Gallery. In New York, the width of ski trails in state parks is a constitutional matter. Obviously, the U.S. Constitution contains no such details. It leaves to Congress the nuts-and-bolts activity of making specific statutory laws.

AMENDING STATE CONSTITUTIONS

Like the U.S. Constitution, most state constitutions can be amended through a process involving amendment proposal and ratification.

Proposing a Constitutional Amendment

Generally, a state constitutional amendment may be proposed in one of three ways: by legislative activity, by a constitutional convention, or by popular demand. Most commonly, amendments are proposed by the legislature. All states authorize their legislatures to propose constitutional amendments. Usually, an **extraordinary majority** of votes—typically two-thirds or three-fifths of the total number of legislators—is required to propose an amendment. In some states, a proposed amendment has to be passed in two successive sessions of the legislature.

A second method of proposing an amendment to a state constitution is by holding a state constitutional convention. On about 250 occasions, states have called constitutional conventions either to write new constitutions or to amend existing ones. This is not surprising, because four-fifths of all state constitutions expressly allow for such conventions. Some states, such as Illinois, New York, Ohio, and Michigan, require that constitutional conventions be called periodically to consider whether changes are needed and, if so, to propose them. Figure 20–1 shows how a constitutional convention must be called in each of the states.

Finally, some states provide that a constitutional amendment may be proposed by the citizens in what is known as an **initiative**—a procedure by which voters propose a new law or constitutional amendment. Eighteen states (Arizona, Arkansas, California, Colorado, Florida, Illinois, Massachusetts, Michigan, Mississippi, Missouri, Montana, Nebraska, Nevada, North Dakota, Ohio, Oklahoma, Oregon, and South Dakota) permit the use of the initiative to propose constitutional amendments. The constitutional initiative allows citizens to place a proposed amendment on the ballot without calling a constitutional convention. The number of signatures required to get a constitutional initiative on the ballot varies from state to state, but it is usually between 5 and 10 percent of the total number of votes cast in the last gubernatorial election. The use of the initiative is an example of direct democracy—a topic examined later in this chapter.

Ratification of a Constitutional Amendment

No matter which method of proposing an amendment is used, all of the states except Delaware require an amendment to be ratified by a majority of the voters in the general election. (To be ratified in Delaware, a constitutional amendment must receive a two-thirds vote by the state legislature in two consecutive sessions.) In the states in which voter approval is required,

Figure 20–1
Provisions for Calling State Constitutional Conventions

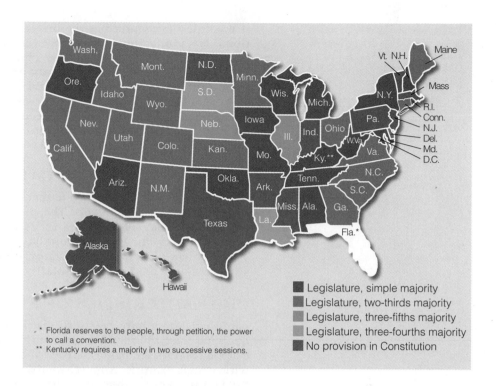

Legislature, simple majority
Legislature, two-thirds majority
Legislature, three-fifths majority
Legislature, three-fourths majority
No provision in Constitution

* Florida reserves to the people, through petition, the power to call a convention.
** Kentucky requires a majority in two successive sessions.

amendment proposals coming from the legislature are adopted far more often than those that originate by an initiative.

Legislatures and Legislators

During the early years of the American republic, the legislative branch of state government clearly was more important than the executive and judicial branches. Most state constitutions mention the legislative branch first.

This Connecticut state legislature, which is typical of the legislatures in many states, includes 36 Senate members and 151 House members. In contrast, New Hampshire's legislature has only 24 Senate members but 400 House members.

It was initially regarded as the primary method for putting state constitutional law into action. Today, however, state legislatures have lost much of their glow. Governors—the states' chief executives—have emerged as the leaders of the people in political affairs. Nonetheless, state legislatures are important forces in state politics and state governmental decision making. The task of these assemblies is to develop and pass laws on such matters as taxes, regulation of business and commerce, and funding for school systems and welfare payments. Allocation of state funds and program priorities are vital issues to residents and communities in every state.

ELEMENTS OF A TYPICAL STATE LEGISLATURE

All state legislatures, except for that of Nebraska, are bicameral—that is, they consist of two chambers. The size of state legislatures varies dramatically. Alaska has 40 members in its lower house, Delaware has 41, and Nevada has 42; but Pennsylvania has 203, and New Hampshire has 400.[3] There is less diversity in the states' upper houses. These range from 20 seats in Alaska to 67 in Minnesota.[4]

CHARACTERISTICS OF STATE LEGISLATORS

State legislators have been criticized as being less professional and less qualified than the members of the U.S. Congress. The reality is that most state legislators are paid relatively little and given relatively few resources with which to work. Almost twenty states pay their legislators less than $10,000 per year. Table 20–1 shows how well your state's legislators are paid relative to legislators in other states.

The low salaries for state legislators are partially explained by the fact that whereas members of the U.S. Congress have regular, year-round jobs as congressmen or congresswomen, most state legislators serve actively for erratic periods—full-time for a few months and at odd times for the remainder of their terms. Consequently, state legislators often have other jobs and look on their legislative duties as a sideline. In some states, including California and New York, the trend is toward making the job of legislator a full-time and adequately paid position and toward providing funds for professional staff and research assistants to assist the legislators.

About 40 percent of all state legislators are either lawyers or farmers; many others are business executives. The majority (about three-fourths) of state legislators have a college education. Most state legislators move on to other jobs in government and the private sector after serving their terms. In other words, state legislators have a higher rate of turnover than members of the U.S. Congress, who often have lengthy careers.

TERMS OF STATE LEGISLATORS AND TERM LIMITS

As you can see in Table 20–1, legislators serve either two-year or four-year terms. As with the U.S. Congress, state senators are often elected for longer terms than are state representatives. In all but four states—Alabama, Louisiana, Maryland, Mississippi, and North Dakota—representatives are chosen for two-year terms. In any given year, more than 25 percent of the 7,500 state legislators in the country are serving their first term in office.

Many citizens welcome a high turnover rate in their legislatures. Their reasoning is that newer members in a state legislature are more closely attuned to the wishes of their constituents than are legislators who have served for several terms and who tend to view politics as a career. This reasoning underlies the movement toward term limits. At least twenty-four states now limit the terms of their state legislators. Some of these states limit senators to two four-year terms, while representatives in the lower house may serve three two-year terms. Other states impose different limits, such as limiting the terms of all legislators to a total of eight years. The requirements vary from state to state.

Table 20-1

Characteristics of State Legislatures

	SEATS IN SENATE	LENGTH OF TERM	SEATS IN HOUSE	LENGTH OF TERM	YEARS SESSIONS ARE HELD	SALARY*
Alabama	35	4	105	4	Annual	$10(d)†
Alaska	20	4	40	2	Annual	24,012†
Arizona	30	2	60	2	Annual	15,000
Arkansas	35	4	100	2	Odd	12,500†
California	40	4	80	2	Even	75,600†
Colorado	35	4	65	2	Annual	17,500
Connecticut	36	2	151	2	Annual	16,760
Delaware	21	4	41	2	Annual	27,500†
Florida	40	4	120	2	Annual	24,012†
Georgia	56	2	180	2	Annual	11,348†
Hawaii	25	4	51	2	Annual	32,000†
Idaho	35	2	70	2	Annual	12,360†
Illinois	59	‡	118	2	Annual	47,039†
Indiana	50	4	100	2	Annual	11,600†
Iowa	50	4	100	2	Annual	20,120
Kansas	40	4	125	2	Annual	63(d)†
Kentucky	38	4	100	2	Even	103(d)†
Louisiana	39	4	105	4	Annual	16,800†
Maine	35	2	151	2	Even	10,500§
Maryland	47	4	141	4	Annual	29,700†
Massachusetts	40	2	160	2	Annual	46,410†
Michigan	38	4	110	2	Annual	51,895†
Minnesota	67	4	134	2	Odd	29,675†
Mississippi	52	4	122	4	Annual	10,000†
Missouri	34	4	163	2	Annual	26,803
Montana	50	4	100	2	Odd	58(d)†
Nebraska"	49	4	—	—	Annual	12,000†
Nevada	21	4	42	2	Odd	130(d)†
New Hampshire	24	2	400	2	Annual	200(b)
New Jersey	40	4	80	2	Annual	35,000
New Mexico	42	4	70	2	Annual	—†
New York	61	2	150	2	Annual	57,500†
North Carolina	50	2	120	2	Odd	13,951†
North Dakota	49	4	98	4	Odd	111(d)†
Ohio	33	4	99	2	Annual	42,427
Oklahoma	48	4	101	2	Annual	32,000†
Oregon	30	4	60	2	Odd	13,104†
Pennsylvania	50	4	203	2	Annual	57,367†
Rhode Island	50	2	100	2	Annual	10,250
South Carolina	46	4	124	2	Annual	10,400†
South Dakota	35	2	70	2	Annual	4,267#
Tennessee	33	4	99	2	Odd	16,500†
Texas	31	4	150	2	Odd	7,200†
Utah	29	4	75	2	Annual	100(d)†
Vermont	30	2	150	2	Odd	510(w)
Virginia	40	4	100	2	Annual	18,000†
Washington	49	4	98	2	Annual	28,800†
West Virginia	34	4	100	2	Annual	15,000
Wisconsin	33	4	99	2	Annual	39,211†
Wyoming	30	4	60	2	Annual	125(d)†

*Salaries annual unless otherwise noted as (d)–per day, or (b)–biennium, or (w)–per week.
†Plus *per diem* living expenses.
‡Terms vary from two to four years.
§For odd year; $7,500 for even year.
"Unicameral legislature.
#For odd year; $3,733 for even year.

SOURCE: Adapted from Council of State Governments, *The Book of the States, 1998–1999 Edition* (Lexington, Ky.: Council of State Governments, 1998).

Until 1995, these state laws also imposed term limits on members of the U.S. Congress. A Supreme Court decision in 1995, however, held that such limits were unconstitutional because the U.S. Constitution says nothing about limiting the terms of U.S. senators and representatives. The Court stated that the only way term limits can be imposed on national legislators is through an amendment to the U.S. Constitution.[5] Supporters of term limits continue to push for such an amendment. In fact, in the 1996 elections, the voters in nine states passed initiatives that require candidates for the U.S. Congress to declare their position on term limits before they can be elected. In this way, the voters will be able to elect representatives to Congress who will support term limits and try to influence Congress to propose a constitutional amendment requiring limits.

★ Direct Democracy

Lawmaking is somewhat different at the state level than it is at the national level. Many states exercise a type of direct democracy through the initiative, the referendum, and the recall—procedures that allow voters to control the government directly. Direct democracy at the state level was first instituted in Oregon before the 1920s. Remember from Chapter 1 that a form of direct democracy emerged in America at an early time in New England town meetings and continues to exist there. (But see the feature *Perception versus Reality: Direct Democracy in Early American New England Towns* for a candid look at how democratic these meetings really were.)

THE INITIATIVE

The *initiative* lets citizens themselves propose new laws for the voters' approval. As already mentioned, a majority of states now allow the use of the initiative. Eighteen states allow constitutional amendments to be proposed by initiative. Twenty-two states allow the initiative to be used for proposing new statutory laws. This type of initiative is called the *legislative initiative*. As with constitutional initiatives, most states require that a legislative initiative's backers circulate a petition to place the measure on the ballot. A certain percentage of the registered voters in the last gubernatorial election must sign the petition. If enough signatures are obtained, the issue is put on the ballot.

There are two types of initiatives—direct and indirect. A *direct initiative* goes directly on the ballot to be decided by popular vote. An *indirect*

INFOTRAC®
Organic planning a new approach

A citizen of Chatham, Massachusetts, voices his views at a town meeting. The tradition of the annual town meeting in New England is often cited as an example of direct democracy.

perception versus reality

Direct Democracy in Early American New England Towns

In the last decade or so, there have been a number of efforts—by historians, political scientists, and other scholars—to penetrate the screen of American mythology to discern "what really happened" in the past. Recently, in his book *The Good Citizen: A History of American Civic Life,*[6] historian Michael Schudson took a close look at New England town meetings and came up with a "reality" that is far different from the usual perception of what happened at those meetings.

The Perception

In the early days of this nation, settlers in the New England area organized local governing units called *towns*. As used here, the word *town* is not just another term for a small community, or city. Rather, it is a political unit similar to the county in other regions of America and typically comprises one or more urban communities and their outlying rural areas. Political decisions were made, just as they are today, in *town meetings*

attended by the town's residents. Town meetings have often been described as forums for direct democracy, in which all residents could come to the town hall and vote on what taxes would be levied, who should be elected to serve as the town's leaders, what laws should be enacted, and so on.

Although few residents turn out for town meetings today, the town meeting has been used by generations of historians and political scientists as an example of democracy in its purest form. In recent years, the labeling of Internet conferences as "electronic town-hall meetings" marks an attempt to call up the image of the intimate, deliberative democracy practiced in New England town meetings in the past.

The Reality

According to Schudson, the reality of the town meeting was far different from the myth that it inspired. For one thing, the meetings were open only to white male residents who owned property and, in some

cases, only to church members. And the idea that town meetings were forums for free expression or that they epitomized political freedom, contends Schudson, is "pure bunk." Rather, New England town halls were meant to showcase harmony and consensus. Far from being models of pure democracy, town meetings usually followed the agenda and preferences of the wealthiest residents in the town. The meetings were also not models of political participation, as has often been claimed. In eighteenth-century Massachusetts, for example, attendance at town meetings ranged from 20 to 60 percent of eligible voters. Apparently, then, as now, town meetings suffered from citizen apathy.

You Be the Judge

How do you explain the tendency—on the part of Americans as well as others around the globe—to idealize the past? Does such idealization serve any important function in a political culture?

REFERENDUM ● A form of direct democracy in which legislative or constitutional measures are proposed by a legislature and then presented to the voters for approval.

initiative goes first to the state legislature. If the legislature passes the initiative, the measure becomes law and does not go on the ballot. If the legislature does not pass the initiative, the measure is placed on the ballot, and the voters decide the issue.

THE REFERENDUM

The **referendum** is similar to the initiative, except that the issue (or constitutional change) is proposed first by the legislature and then directed to the voters for their approval. Whereas all of the states except Alabama currently provide for the use of the referendum for constitutional changes, only twenty-three states allow changes to statutory law through referenda.

The referendum is often used at the local level to approve local school bond issues and at the state level to amend state constitutions. In a number of states that provide for the referendum, a bill passed by the legislature may be "put on hold" by obtaining petitions with the required number of signatures from voters who oppose it. A statewide referendum election is then held, and if the majority of the voters disapprove of the bill, it is no longer valid.

Initially, the referendum was not intended for regular use. Indeed, it has been used infrequently in the past. Its opponents argue that it is an unnecessary check on representative government and that it weakens legislative responsibility. In recent years, the referendum has become increasingly popular as citizens have attempted to control their state and local governments. Interest groups have been active in sponsoring the petition drives necessary to force a referendum.

THE RECALL

The **recall**—a vote to dismiss an official—is directed at public officials who are deemed incompetent or grossly unethical in their conduct. Voters may circulate a petition calling for the removal of such an official, and if the petition obtains a sufficient number of signatures (which may be as high as 25 percent of the number of votes cast in the last gubernatorial election), then a recall election is held.

The recall is authorized in nearly half of the states. Being placed on a recall ballot does not necessarily mean that an elected person is guilty of anything, although charges of criminal activity are often a reason for recalling an official.

Although the recall is rarely used, it functions as a threat to public officials. Proponents of the recall in the states in which it exists argue that the possibility of recall prevents outrageously inappropriate official behavior. Opponents of the recall argue that it makes officeholders prey to well-financed special interest groups.

A California citizen signs a petition to support an initiative.

The State Executive Branch

The governor is the chief executive officer in each of the fifty states. In addition to her or his role as chief executive, the state governor is also the state's chief legislator and policymaker, chief political party leader, and chief spokesperson. Some of the most populous states have given their governors great control over the state executive branch. Even a few less populated states, such as Alaska and Hawaii, have made provisions for strong governors.

The formal qualifications for governor in most states are simple. A candidate for governor must be (1) a U.S. citizen, (2) of a certain age (normally, at least twenty-five or thirty years old), (3) a resident of the state for a minimum period of time (normally, five years), and (4) a qualified voter. A few states do not require even these qualifications. For example, Kansas has no formal qualifications for governor. In Ohio, the governor must be a U.S. citi-

RECALL ● A procedure that allows voters to dismiss an elected official from a state or local office before the official's term has expired.

These Texas state legislators hash out a proposed bill. State legislators work to carry out the business of state government in much the same way that legislators in Washington, D.C., work to carry out the business of governing the nation as a whole.

Governors from the various states convene at the National Governors' Association (NGA) annual conference. Typically, the sitting president addresses that conference. The NGA was founded in 1908 after state governors met with President Theodore Roosevelt to discuss conservation issues. The NGA's mission is to provide a forum for governors to exchange views and experiences among themselves. The group also seeks to implement policies on national issues.

zen and a qualified voter, but the state constitution does not specify any residency requirements. In some states, such as California, Massachusetts, Ohio, and Wisconsin, one can become governor at the age of eighteen.

Because millions of men and women can meet the formal requirements to become governor, the *informal* requirements are what truly determine who will be elected. No handbook is available to outline these qualifications, but they certainly include name familiarity, political experience, skill in relating to the media, and voter appeal in terms of personal demeanor and personality.

LENGTH OF SERVICE

Gone are the one-year terms of office that were so popular in the early days of this nation. Forty-seven states now have the governor serve for a minimum of four years.

Many states place limits on the number of terms that a governor may serve. Kentucky, New Mexico, and Virginia, for example, allow the governor to serve additional terms, but not consecutively. In twenty-seven states, governors may serve two consecutive terms. Nineteen states have a two-term limit.

Governors who choose to run for a second term almost always win. The power of incumbency is great at virtually all levels of government. The all-time record for gubernatorial service is held by Governor George Clinton of New York, who held office from 1777 to 1795 and from 1801 to 1804. He did this by winning seven three-year terms. The modern record goes to Orval Faubus, who was governor of Arkansas from 1955 to 1967—six consecutive two-year terms.

IMPEACHMENT AND RECALL

Removing a state governor by **impeachment** usually requires an indictment by the lower chamber of the legislature, a trial by the upper chamber (in which the senators are the jury members and the state supreme court justices are the judges), and conviction. State constitutions often provide that the chief justice of the state supreme court is to preside at the trial. Only Oregon does not allow the removal of the governor by impeachment.

Impeachment is not impossible, but it is infrequent. Governor Evan Mecham of Arizona was impeached and removed from office in 1988 when he was convicted of mishandling campaign finances and lending $80,000 of the state's money to his car dealership. (He was later acquitted of felony

IMPEACHMENT ● A formal criminal proceeding against a public official for misconduct or wrongdoing in office.

charges.) In the twentieth century, only four other governors have been removed in such a manner.[7]

About a third of the states provide for removal of the governor by recall. By signing petitions, voters in these states can call for a special election to determine whether or not the governor (or other state officials) will be removed before the term expires.

THE POWERS OF THE GOVERNOR

Whereas the U.S. Constitution defines the president as *the* "executive" of the federal government, most state constitutions describe their governors as *"chief* executive" in state government. The difference between *the* and *chief* may not seem significant, but it is. No one legally shares supreme executive power with the president of the United States. In many states, though, executive power may be shared by several executive officers, such as the lieutenant governor or the treasurer, who are often also popularly elected.

Appointment and Removal Powers

One of the most important executive powers of the governor is the power to appoint and remove state officials. A governor who can appoint her or his own department and agency heads is more likely to be able to coordinate policies and be more powerful than a governor without such powers. A governor who can reward supporters by appointing them to important department and agency positions will have a greater chance of success in carrying out his or her policies. One way to judge a governor's power is to see whether that governor can in fact select and appoint loyal and competent assistants.

A factor that can potentially reduce a governor's ability to appoint loyal followers is the requirement in most states that major appointees be confirmed by the state senate, which is part of the system of checks and balances. Some legislatures also set qualifications that appointees must meet in order to assume office. In states that have vigorous two-party competition, legislatures often require that a specified number of members of each commission or board be from each party. As a result, the governor must appoint members of the opposite party during her or his administration.

Power of the Purse

In the early years of this nation, governors had virtually no budgetary powers. In most states today, in contrast, planning and carrying out the budget is a significant responsibility for the governor. Just as the president of the United States prepares an annual budget, so too do many governors prepare annual or biennial budgets. After the governor finishes the budget, it is sent to the legislature for approval.

Once a budget is authorized by the legislature, most governors possess the power to control the pattern of expenditures through executive agencies and departments. Governors often have the power to decide which expenditures will be made in a particular year. A governor may withhold the funding for a particular project if he or she is not satisfied with the way the project is progressing.

Veto Power

Every state except North Carolina has given the governor the power to veto legislation. In some states, however, the governor has only a short time after the legislature passes a bill in which to veto it. The designated period is three days in Iowa, Minnesota, New Mexico, North Dakota, and Wyoming. In a number of other states, it is six or seven days. If the governor does not veto a measure during the designated period, the measure normally becomes law.

In forty-three states, the governor has some provision for a line-item veto. This allows the governor to veto a particular item in a bill with which he or she disagrees, while signing the rest of the bill into law.

A Typical State Court System

JUSTICE COURT ● A local court with limited jurisdiction; justice courts typically hear minor civil and criminal cases, perform marriages, and legalize documents.

JUSTICE OF THE PEACE ● A local judicial official who presides over the activities of a justice court; often popularly elected for a short term.

MAGISTRATE ● A local judicial official who presides over the activities of a magistrate's court; often popularly elected for a short term.

MAGISTRATE COURT ● A local court with limited jurisdiction, usually in a small town or city.

Figure 20–2
A Typical State Court System

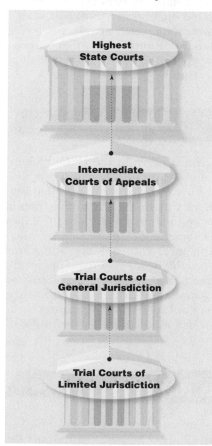

Highest
State Courts

Intermediate
Courts of Appeals

Trial Courts of
General Jurisdiction

Trial Courts of
Limited Jurisdiction

Every state has a different court system, but many systems are organized around three or four levels of courts. Any person who is involved in a lawsuit typically has the opportunity to plead the case before a *trial court,* which is on the lowest tier, or level, of state courts. If that person loses the case, he or she usually has the opportunity to appeal the decision to two other levels of courts, called *appellate courts* (review courts, or courts of appeals). About three-fourths of the states have intermediate appellate courts (courts on the level between the trial courts of general jurisdiction and the state's highest court). Every state has a highest court, which is usually called the state supreme court but may be called by some other name.[8]

In most states, a case proceeds first through a trial court with an automatic right to review by an appellate court. If the reviewing court is an intermediate court of appeals, the decision of that court may be appealed to the state's highest review court. Figure 20–2 shows the tiers of a typical state court system.

Each court has certain powers of jurisdiction. Recall from Chapter 16 that jurisdiction refers to a court's power to hear and decide cases. Courts with *limited* jurisdiction can only hear certain types of cases; courts with *general* jurisdiction can hear a broader range of cases.

LIMITED-JURISDICTION TRIAL COURTS

Most states have local trial courts that have limited jurisdiction, meaning that they can hear and decide only cases involving certain subject areas. These courts are often called special inferior trial courts or minor trial courts. Typical courts of limited jurisdiction are domestic relations courts, which handle only divorces and child custody cases; local municipal courts, which mainly handle traffic cases; probate courts, which handle the administration of wills and estate settlement problems; and small claims and justice courts. Usually, the minor trial courts do not keep complete written records of trial proceedings.

Justice Courts

One of the earliest courts of limited jurisdiction was the **justice court,** presided over by a **justice of the peace,** or JP. In the early days of this nation, JPs were found everywhere in the country. One of the most famous JPs was Judge Roy Bean, the "hanging judge" of Langtry, Texas, who presided over his court at the turn of the twentieth century.

Today, more than half the states have abolished justice courts. JPs still serve a useful function in some cities and in rural areas, however. JP courts still exist in Texas counties, for example. The jurisdiction of justice courts is limited to minor disputes between private individuals or companies and to crimes punishable by small fines or short jail terms. JPs are best known, however, for conducting marriage ceremonies. JPs are usually popularly elected.

Magistrate Courts

The equivalent of a county JP in the city is called a **magistrate.** **Magistrate courts** have the same limited jurisdiction as do justice courts in rural settings. Magistrates are often popularly elected for short terms.

GENERAL-JURISDICTION TRIAL COURTS

State trial courts that have general jurisdiction may be called county courts, district courts, superior courts, or circuit courts. In Ohio the name is Court of Common Pleas; in New York it is Supreme Court; and in Massachusetts, Trial Court. (The name sometimes does not correspond with the court's functions. For example, in New York the trial court is called the Supreme Court, whereas in most states the supreme court is the state's highest court.) General-jurisdiction trial courts have the authority to hear and decide cases involving many types of subject matter.

In trial courts, the parties to a controversy may dispute the particular facts, which law should be applied to those facts, and how that law should be applied. If a party is entitled to a trial by jury and requests one, the appropriate issues will be tried before a jury in a trial court. Generally, judges decide *questions of law* (what law applies to the facts of the case and how the law should be applied), and juries decide *questions of fact* (the outcome of the factual dispute before the court). If the trial is held without a jury, the judge decides both questions of law and questions of fact.

APPELLATE REVIEW

No jury and no witnesses are present during an appellate court's review of a trial court's decision. Rather, when a case is heard on appeal, normally a panel of judges reviews the records of the trial court to determine whether the trial court's judgment was correct. Appellate courts look at questions of law and procedure, but usually not at questions of fact. The decisions of each state's highest court on all questions of state law are final, unless the case can be appealed to the United States Supreme Court.

STATE COURT JUDGES

In the federal court system, as you read in Chapter 16, all judges are appointed by the president and confirmed by the Senate. It is difficult to make a general statement about how judges are selected in the state court systems, however, because procedures vary widely from state to state. In some states, such as Delaware, all judges are appointed by the governor and confirmed by a majority vote by the upper chamber of the legislature. In other states, such as Arkansas, all judges are elected on a partisan ballot. In still other states, such as Kentucky, all judges are elected on a nonpartisan ballot. In a number of states, judges in some of the lower state courts are elected, while judges of the appellate courts are appointed. Additionally, in some of those states in which judges are appointed for their initial terms, if they wish to retain their offices, they must run for reelection.[9]

Local Governments

Today, there are more than 83,000 local governments in the United States. Local government units include counties, municipalities, school districts, and other units. These governments undertake a variety of services, including public education, police and fire protection, city planning and zoning, public welfare, recreational and cultural activities, and many others. Table 20–2 lists and describes the characteristics of the basic types of local government.

The U.S. Constitution does not mention local governments, and states are not required by the Constitution to provide local governments at all. Every local government is therefore a creation of its parent state. Just as states can create local governments, so can they disband them. Since World War II, almost twenty thousand school districts have gone out of existence or been consolidated with other school districts—an example of how tenuous the existence of local government is.

State and Local Government Revenues

Relatively few limitations are placed on state and local taxing powers. The most obvious one was already discussed in Chapter 3—states cannot tax the

Table 20–2

Types of Local Government Units

TYPE OF UNIT	CHARACTERISTICS
Municipality	A political entity created by the people of a city or town to govern themselves locally. Almost all municipalities are fairly small cities. About three-fourths of municipal tax revenues come from property taxes. Municipalities rely heavily on financial assistance from both the federal government and the state.
County	The state sets up counties on its own initiative to administer state laws and state business at the local level. A county government's responsibilities include zoning, building regulations, health, hospitals, parks, recreation, highways, public safety, justice, and record keeping.
New England Town	The New England town is a unique feature of the New England states. In those states, the word *town* refers to a government unit that exercises the combined functions of a municipality and a county. The tradition of the annual town meeting is an example of direct democracy. Those who attend the meeting levy taxes, pass laws, elect town officers, and allocate funds for various activities.
Township	Townships are units of six square miles that were mapped out by federal land surveys that began in the 1780s. The township operates somewhat like a county and performs similar functions. Indiana, Iowa, Kansas, Michigan, Minnesota, New Jersey, New York, Ohio, Pennsylvania, and Wisconsin all have townships.
Special District	The special district is a one-function local government, such as a school district, that is usually created by the state legislature and governed by a board of directors. Most of the 83,000-plus local governments in the United States are special districts. In addition to school districts, there are special districts for mosquito control, fire protection, cemeteries, and numerous other concerns.

INFOTRAC®

State court judges

operations, land, buildings, or any other aspect of the federal government.[10] In addition, the U.S. Constitution prevents the states from taxing both imports into the United States and exports to other countries. The due process clause of the Fourteenth Amendment also places a restriction on methods of state and local government taxation. Taxes must be imposed and administered fairly and not be so great as to be the equivalent of seizing property. The equal protection clause of the same amendment also forbids unreasonable classifications for the purpose of collecting taxes. For example, a state can collect taxes on smokers by taxing cigarettes, but a state cannot make only blonde-haired citizens pay a state income tax.

In Figure 20–3 on the next page, you can see the various sources and relative importance of state and local revenues. By far the most important tax for most states is the general sales tax. The most important tax at the local level is the property tax. Other sources of state and local government revenues include federal grants, which were examined in Chapter 3; personal and corporate income taxes; and social insurance contributions. (For a comparison of U.S. state and local spending with that in other countries, see the feature on the following page entitled *Comparative Politics: The Importance of State and Local Government Spending*.)

Americans at Odds over State and Local Politics

With almost half of government spending taking place at the state and local levels, numerous issues arise over which different groups of Americans are at odds.

**Figure 20–3
Sources of State
and Local Revenues**

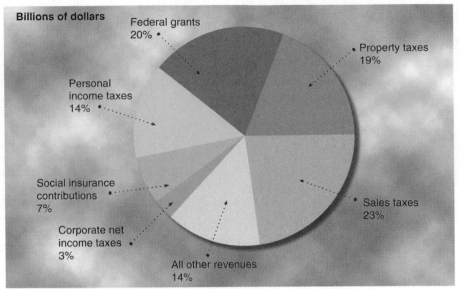

SOURCE: Bureau of Economic Analysis, U.S. Department of Commerce, 1998.

Devolution: Returning Responsibility to the States

A watchword of American politics in the 1990s was *devolution,* or the transfer of certain national government responsibilities back to state and local governments. The words *back to* are important. They indicate that the responsibilities in question were once the purview of state and local governments.

comparative politics

The Importance of State and Local Government Spending

As you can see in the accompanying table, only in Canada does state and local government spending account for more than 50 percent of total government spending. In the United States, the figure is about 45 percent, whereas in France it is less than 20 percent.

COUNTRY	PERCENTAGE OF TOTAL GOVERNMENT SPENDING ACCOUNTED FOR BY STATE AND LOCAL GOVERNMENT SPENDING
Canada	56
United States	45
Germany	39
Japan	32
United Kingdom	25
Italy	23
France	18

For Critical Analysis

What are the benefits of having a high percentage of total government spending be at the state and local levels?

Over time, as the nation grew, the national government did indeed assume regulatory responsibilities over areas traditionally governed by the states. In the 1930s, Franklin Roosevelt's New Deal legislation, including the Social Security Act, involved the national government in the nation's economic life to an unprecedented extent. Lyndon Johnson's Great Society programs of the 1960s, designed to improve the social and economic welfare of disadvantaged groups in society, vastly extended the regulatory role of the national government. Today, few activities are beyond the regulatory arm of the national government.

THE HIGH COST OF REGULATION

The problem is, government regulation is costly. By the 1990s, it was apparent that the federal government could no longer meet the costs of its regulatory burden without going further into debt. One result of the federal government's budgetary problems was the increasing use of unfunded federal mandates (requirements in federal legislation, such as an environmental law, with which state and local governments must comply—and for which they must pay). At the same time, there was a growing sentiment that many federal programs, such as welfare, were ineffective in combating the problems facing American society, such as poverty. The solution, according to many, was to give state and local governments more responsibility over areas that have been regulated by the national government since the 1930s. (See the feature on the next page entitled *The American Political Spectrum: Power to the States* for a discussion of how this solution is viewed across the political spectrum.)

IS DEVOLUTION THE ANSWER?

What does devolution mean for state and local governments? On the plus side, of course, is the ability to tailor programs to meet the needs of citizens in that particular state, which are often different from those of citizens in other areas of the country. On the minus side are the costs of administering programs, such as welfare, that have for decades been the responsibility of the national government. When state governments find it difficult to meet such costs, one option is to pass the costs on to local governments in the form of unfunded state mandates. Just as the federal and state governments have been at odds over unfunded federal mandates (see Chapter 3), now state and local governments are finding themselves at odds over the same issue. Devolution also raises the question as to which government—federal, state, or local—is the appropriate body to handle certain types of problems, such as welfare. Americans continue to be at odds over this issue.

THE THORNY ISSUE OF FEDERAL ENVIRONMENTAL MANDATES

The facts are clear: the federal government has been decreasing funding in the environmental area and reallocating those resources to fulfill other objectives. At the same time, the federal government has imposed additional (unfunded) mandates on state and local governments, all of which must be paid for somehow. Many of these mandates concern the environment. It is estimated that in the year 2000, local governments will have to pay 87 percent of the $55 billion total spending required to maintain environmental quality.[11]

The rising costs of complying with federal environmental mandates will probably force local governments to act. Local governments clearly are going to have to find less expensive ways of complying with federal mandates, and certainly, both local and state governments will be calling on Washington, D.C., to share part of the costs. (One of the problems with nationally created environmental mandates is that they apply nationwide and thus, by definition, cannot take specific state and local circumstances

Power to the States

Recall from Chapter 6 that a key distinction between conservatives and liberals is their perception of the role of government. Liberals tend to believe that the government has an obligation to solve the nation's economic and social problems; thus, liberals are likely to support programs to reduce poverty and to rely on government regulation to guide the activities of business and the economy. Conservatives, in contrast, tend to believe that the private sector should not be hampered by government regulations and controls. Conservatives also tend to believe that individuals should have the primary responsibility for their own well-being; thus, conservatives are less supportive of government initiatives to redistribute income or to craft programs that will change the status of individuals.

In view of this distinction, it is not surprising that conservatives and liberals disagree on the issue of devolution—returning power to the states.

How Conservatives View the Issue

Many conservatives strongly support the concept of devolution.

Generally, conservatives tend to believe that many social and economic programs are better handled by state and local governments because they can tailor the programs to fit the needs of their particular citizens—something that national programs, precisely because they are applied across the country, cannot do. Conservatives also tend to believe that certain programs, such as welfare, can be run more efficiently and cost-effectively at the state and local levels.

Furthermore, many conservatives argue that Democratic administrations (including those of Franklin Roosevelt and Lyndon Johnson), by expanding the regulatory role of the federal government, diminished the powers of state governments to control intrastate activities. Such powers, they contend, rightfully belong to the states as part of their reserved powers under the Tenth Amendment.

Liberals Have Their Doubts

Although many conservatives and some moderates support the idea of devolution, many liberals worry that society may suffer in the long run. What is to prevent state and local governments that are faced

with budget constraints from forgoing certain protections for disadvantaged groups? If more responsibility for environmental protection is turned over to state and local governments, will those governments be able to withstand the temptation of profiting financially from the development of areas now protected by federal environmental laws?

One of the reasons liberals have typically looked to the national government to solve certain problems is because national government officials are more impartial and less likely to be swayed by regional politics than government officials at the state and local levels. Thus, solutions to certain types of problems are best created and implemented by the national government.

For Critical Analysis

Explain how a liberal Democrat could be in favor of devolution.

---

into account. One bizarre result of this situation is discussed in the feature entitled *Politics on the Far Side: Dirty Water.*)

The Zenith of State Budgets

In the late 1990s, numerous states found themselves with budget surpluses. These states included Arizona, California, Indiana, Minnesota, North Carolina, South Carolina, Texas, and Washington. In all, projected budget surpluses for the 1999 fiscal year totaled $31 billion. (But see the feature *Perception versus Reality: Balancing State Budgets.*)

The Federation of Tax Administrators, however, points out that very soon many state coffers will be empty again. Why? The school-aged population is growing, and that means more public school expenditures will be required. Also, the fastest-growing age group consists of those over age

politics on the far side

Dirty Water

The Clean Water Act required that cities remove 30 percent of solid materials from sewage water. In Anchorage, Alaska, the water did not have that much solid material. The law did not allow for exceptions, however. So, to avoid penalties and the necessity of building an expensive new treatment facility, the city asked two local fish processors to dump five thousand pounds of fish waste into the sewer system. The waste was promptly removed—and Anchorage thus met the federal requirements.

For Critical Analysis: What might result if state and local governments were in charge of all environmental regulation?

sixty-five, and they will be putting pressure on state pension funds and especially on state payments to Medicaid.

At the same time, states are faced with the possibility of declining revenues from sales taxes. In part, this is because sales taxes apply only to goods, not services, but it is the service sector that is growing. Some state governors, including George W. Bush of Texas, have tried to expand sales taxes to services but without success. Additionally, the expansion in mail-order and Internet sales transactions, on which states are rarely able to collect taxes, will affect state revenues. Currently, the states are losing about $4 billion a year in taxes on these sales. It is estimated that by 2002, this loss may be as high as $20 billion a year.[12] State leaders have heavily lobbied Congress to allow states to tax Internet transactions, but as yet Congress has resisted such taxation, fearing that it might slow the growth of e-commerce.

Voter Initiatives and American Democracy

One of the issues over which Americans are at odds today concerns the use of voter initiatives to pass new laws. As mentioned earlier in this chapter, the initiative is often regarded as a form of direct democracy in that it allows the people themselves to both propose and vote for new laws. Early in

perception versus reality

Balancing State Budgets

Both the popular press and politicians give the distinct impression that the national government should be like the states. In other words, the federal government should be forced to balance its budget.

The Perception

The view that the states are required to balance their budgets has been around for a long time. Most state constitutions require that state budgets be balanced or run a surplus. Indeed, depending on how one interprets such laws, the number of states forced to balance their budgets ranges from a dozen to forty-nine.

The Reality

It is true that most states balance their *operating budgets* most of the time. Unlike the federal government, however, the states make a distinction between "operating" and "capital" budgets. Capital budgets include new airports, airport improvements, heavy machinery, highway construction, and so on. Almost all of the states permit debt financing (the sale of bonds to finance long-term improvements). Additionally, most states use special authorities to finance these outlays, which sometimes include operating costs. We really can't tell to what extent operating expenses are hidden in capital budgets. According to Richard

Briffault of Columbia University Law School, more than 50 percent of state expenditures are determined by authorities unconstrained by legal deficit spending limits.[13]

Sometimes, to fudge the numbers even further, states alter their fiscal year. Michigan did so to add three months of revenue during the summer when it did not have to make payments to school districts. Some states have fudged their pension accounting to not "run a deficit."

You Be the Judge

Does it matter whether in reality your state government is running a deficit?

this century, voter initiatives were viewed as a tool of the people against wealthy and powerful interests in a state. Nonetheless, the use of the initiative process was relatively rare. In recent years, however, their use has mushroomed, particularly in the western states. In the 1994 elections, 102 citizen-generated measures were placed on state ballots—the highest number ever. Although this number has declined since then, they continue to be widely used (there were 61 initiatives on state ballots in the 1998 elections).

Some Americans contend that the use of initiatives subverts the American system of government and thus results in bad laws. Furthermore, claim these critics, initiatives are no longer a tool of the people but of powerful national interest groups. Others disagree.

DO INITIATIVES MAKE BAD LAW?

Critics of voter initiatives claim that they subvert the American system of government because they bypass the checks and balances built into the traditional legislative process. That process allows the elected members of both chambers of a legislature to evaluate and debate the merits of a proposed law, including its costs and benefits and its potential impact on various groups within the state. It also allows the governor to veto proposed legislation. These critics assert that voter initiatives, because they bypass this process, often result in bad laws. Moreover, as with all laws, they are costly to implement. For example, the fourteen initiatives on the Oregon ballot in 1998, if they all had passed, would have cost $180 million annually to enforce—yet the state legislature had no say in what ultimately involves state budgeting decisions.[14]

Supporters of the initiative process point out that it does not result in bad laws.[15] Rather, it allows citizens to get laws passed when their elected representatives in the state legislature fail to act. It may take years, for example, for a legislature to take action on a divisive issue. Through the initiative process, the voters can have their say on controversial issues—and in recent years they have done just that. Consider just some of the initiatives passed in 1996 and 1998. Voters in California and Washington banned state-sponsored affirmative action. Oregon voters decided that the state should allow terminally ill people to commit physician-assisted suicide. In seven states, citizens approved the medical use of marijuana. Other issues addressed by voter initiatives in recent years include term limits for state legislators, abortion, animal rights, gambling, billboards, and union dues.

NATIONAL INTERESTS VERSUS STATE POLITICS

Critics of the initiative process also point out that it is not really all that democratic, nor is it strictly a state affair. They point out that many of the initiatives placed on state ballots during recent elections resulted from the efforts of well-funded national interest groups. These groups can afford to hire petitioners to gather enough signatures to place a measure on the state ballot and then pay millions of dollars to advertise the benefits of the measure and convince the voters to pass it. Rather than represent the wishes of the people, initiatives are simply another vehicle for interest groups to use when trying to get laws passed that are favorable to their causes. What was once a populist tool has turned into a multimillion-dollar industry dominated by professional firms and powerful national lobbyists.

Defenders of the initiative process claim that state governments should leave it alone. To be sure, interest groups do strongly influence the process, but such influence is pervasive in all government institutions, including state legislatures. For all its flaws, these defenders claim, the initiative process provides an important voice for the people, and its use should not be restrained.

STATE REGULATION AND THE FREE SPEECH ISSUE

In an attempt to curb the influence of national groups on state politics, several states are trying to devise ways to regulate the initiative process. Colorado launched an aggressive effort to do so by enacting statutes imposing various requirements on proponents of initiatives. These laws required that all persons who circulate initiative petitions in that state be registered Colorado voters and wear identification badges bearing the circulators' names. Additionally, proponents of any initiative had to report the names and addresses of all paid circulators and the amount paid to each of them.

The laws were soon challenged in court by a number of interest groups and individuals. These opponents claimed that the statutes violated the right of Americans, including members of national interest groups, to freely express their political opinions and preferences. Ultimately, the United States Supreme Court agreed, holding that the laws violated the First Amendment's guarantee of free speech.[16] Clearly, the decision will curb other state attempts to regulate the initiative process. Yet the controversy over this issue continues, and a future Supreme Court may view the matter differently.

key terms

extraordinary majority 492
impeachment 499
initiative 492
intrastate commerce 491
justice court 501

justice of the peace 501
magistrate 501
magistrate court 501
recall 498
referendum 496

chapter summary

1. Compared to the U.S. Constitution, state constitutions are lengthy and detailed. One of the reasons for this is the lack of confidence in state legislatures between the end of the Civil War and the early 1900s. Another reason is that constitution framers at the state level had a difficult time distinguishing between constitutional law and statutory law. State constitutional amendments may be proposed by the state legislature, by a constitutional convention, or by a constitutional initiative proposed by the citizens. All states but Delaware require an amendment to be ratified by a majority of the voters in a general election.

2. All state legislatures, except for that of Nebraska, are bicameral (have two chambers). The size of state legislatures varies significantly from state to state. In most states, state legislators are paid relatively little, compared to members of the U.S. Congress. One reason for this is that in most states the job of legislator is a part-time position. State legislators serve either two-year or four-year terms; usually, state senators serve longer terms than state representatives.

3. Many states exercise a type of direct democracy through the initiative, the referendum, and the recall. Twenty-two states allow their citizens to use

initiatives to place proposed laws on the ballots for popular vote; in eighteen states, the initiative can be used to propose constitutional amendments. The referendum is similar to the initiative, but the new law or constitutional change is proposed first by the legislature and then directed to the voters for their approval. The recall—a vote to dismiss an official—is aimed at public officials who are deemed incompetent or grossly unethical in their conduct. The recall is authorized in nearly half the states.

4. The governor is the chief executive officer in each state. Most states have few formal qualifications for governor. In most states, the governor serves for a minimum of four years. Only a few states have two-year terms. Many states limit the number of terms that a governor may serve. In all states but Oregon, governors may be removed through impeachment proceedings. About one-third of the states provide for removal of the governor by recall. The powers of the governor include the power to appoint and remove state officials, the power to plan and carry out the budget, and the power to veto legislation.

5. Every state's court system is different, but typically a state court system consists of three or four tiers, or levels. On the bottom tier are the trial courts of lim-

ited jurisdiction—courts that can handle only certain types of cases, such as probate courts and small claims courts. On the next tier are trial courts of general jurisdiction, which can hear and decide cases in many areas. About three-fourths of the states have intermediate appellate courts (courts of appeals, or reviewing courts). The highest appellate court is often called the state supreme court, but there are exceptions.

6. There are more than 83,000 local governments in the United States. Local governments, which are not mentioned in the U.S. Constitution, are created by the states. These governments perform a variety of services, including public education, police and fire protection, city planning and zoning, public welfare, recreational and cultural activities, and many others.

7. States have several sources of revenue, including general sales taxes (the most important source) and personal income taxes. The most important source of revenue at the local level is the property tax.

Federal grants to state and local governments are also important sources of state and local revenues.

8. Devolution—transferring powers back to the states—has led to controversy over whether state and local governments are really the appropriate governing bodies to handle certain problems, such as welfare. Federal and state mandates have imposed high costs on local government. Although state governments currently are experiencing budget surpluses, this may change in the future as an aging population puts pressure on state pension funds and state payments to fund Medicaid programs. Additionally, the federal government is starting to cut back on funds given to the states, and some states are passing tax-limitation measures.

9. Americans are at odds over a number of issues concerning state and local governments, including the costs imposed on state and local governments by federal mandates, declining revenues, and the widespread use of voter initiatives.

for critical analysis

1. Do you think that Republicans would be more likely to support school choice than Democrats, or vice versa? Why?

2. Does quality education have to do more with the quality of teaching or with other educational resources (school facilities, books, computers, and so on)?

3. How does school or classroom size affect the quality of teaching and learning? When it comes to education, are smaller classes necessarily better than larger ones?

4. Do you think that state initiatives are getting out of hand? Should states be able to make choices unilat-

erally, through an initiative, that contravene federal policy?

5. Does the state initiative process result in more radical policies than would result if policymaking were left solely in the hands of the state legislature?

6. In what ways are the functions of a state governor similar to the functions of the U.S. president? In what ways do these functions differ?

7. State court judges are often elected to their positions. Does this mean that state court judges need to heed the wishes of their electorates when making decisions? Should all state court judges be appointed, as federal judges are?

suggested readings

DONAHUE, John D. *Disunited States: What's at Stake as Washington Fades and the States Take the Lead.* Glenview, Ill.: Basic Books, 1997. The author candidly appraises the merits of devolution from a practical point of view. He argues that reality, not ideology, should shape policy. He sees no tremendous advantages associated with the devolution of government responsibilities from the national government to the states.

JOHNSON, William C. *Urban Planning and Politics.* Chicago: University of Chicago Press, 1997. The author offers insights into the planning process of local governments, including the major players and groups that influence the process.

LILLEY, William, III, Laurence J. DeFranco, and William M. Diefenderfer III. *The State Atlas of Political and Cultural Diversity.* Washington, D.C.: Congressional Quarterly Books, 1996. The authors have collected and analyzed data on the ethnic and ancestral make-up of the more than six thousand state legislative districts in the United States. The book, the first of its kind, is a comprehensive resource on racial and ethnic populations in state legislatures.

VAN HORN, Carl E. Ed. *The State of the States.* 3d ed. Washington, D.C.: Congressional Quarterly Books, 1996. This collection of essays describes state government institutions and political processes and looks at some of the challenges, such as welfare and educational reform, facing state governments today.

WASTE, Robert J. *Independent Cities: Rethinking U.S. Urban Policy.* Cambridge, Mass.: Harvard University Press, 1998.

The author evaluates the problems and challenges confronting America's local governments today and suggests some possible solutions.

politics
on the web

An excellent site, which gives you links to information about most of the fifty states, is

http://dir.yahoo.com/Government/U_S__Government

Another site that gives you information on state and local government can be found at

http://www.piperinfo.com

If you want to find the e-mail address or home page for your state's representative(s) in Congress, go to

http://www.house.gov

For e-mail addresses and home pages for your state's senators in the U.S. Senate, go to

http://www.senate.gov

To find newspapers that may be online in your state or local area, go to Newspapers Online at

http://www.newspapers.com

A good site for obtaining information on interest groups active in your state or local area is

http://www.yahoo.com/government/politics

The state of Washington has created a site to allow citizens to access legislative information on the current session of its state legislature and on how to contact Washington state officials. If you are interested in this information, go to

http://www.leg.wa.gov/wsladm/default.htm

using
web resources

The Center for Education Reform's Web site offers an abundance of articles on school reforms that are being undertaken in various areas of the country. Access its site at

http://www.edreform.com/choice.htm

1. Select the article entitled "Around the Reform World in 30 Days." What types of reforms are being considered or implemented in each of the four states discussed?

2. Go back to the main page and select the article titled "Florida Brings Accountability Home." Describe Florida's recent educational reform. Why does it stress "public school improvement and accountability"?

3. In your opinion, should similar legislation be passed in other states?

notes

1. *Forbes*, November 4, 1996, p. 149.

2. "The Difference a Mayor Makes," *The Economist*, July 26, 1997, pp. 24–25.

3. New Hampshire developed a strong dislike of government beyond its towns' borders when it was ruled directly from England as a royal colony. Its House of Representatives has at least one member for each town regardless of population. It is the third largest legislature in the English-speaking world, topped only by Congress and the British Parliament.

4. *The Book of the States, 1998–1999 Edition* (Lexington, Ky.: Council of State Governments, 1998), p. 68.

5. *U.S. Term Limits v. Thornton*, 514 U.S. 779 (1995).

6. Michael Schudson, *The Good Citizen: A History of American Civic Life* (New York: Free Press, 1998).

7. William Salzer of New York in 1913; James E. Ferguson of Texas in 1917; J. C. Walton of Oklahoma in 1923; and Henry S. Johnston of Oklahoma in 1929.

8. In New York, the state's highest court is called the Court of Appeals. In Texas and Oklahoma, there are two "highest" appellate courts. In Texas, for example, state district court decisions can be appealed to either the Texas Supreme Court or the Texas Court of Criminal Appeals, depending on the type of case.

9. *The Book of the States, 1998–1999 Edition*, pp. 135–137.

10. *McCulloch v. Maryland*, 4 Wheaton 316 (1819).

11. *The Preliminary Analysis of the Public Costs of Environmental Protection, 1981–2000* (Washington, D.C.: Environmental Protection Agency, May 1990).

12. David Broder, "Golden Years for Governors," *The Washington Post*, January 3, 1999, p. C7.

13. Richard Briffault, *Balancing Acts: The Reality behind State Balanced Budget Requirements* (Washington, D.C.: Twentieth Century Fund, 1996).

14. Lauren Dodge, "Ballot Initiatives Could Drain Oregon Budgets," *The Chicago Sun-Times*, October 4, 1998, p. 4.

15. "The People Get It Right, on the Whole," *The Economist*, November 7, 1998, p. 24.

16. *Buckley v. American Constitutional Law Foundation, Inc.*, 525 U.S. 182 (1999).

The Constitution of the United States

PREAMBLE

We the People of the United States, in Order to form a more perfect Union, establish Justice, insure domestic Tranquility, provide for the common defence, promote the general Welfare, and secure the Blessings of Liberty to ourselves and our Posterity, do ordain and establish this Constitution for the United States of America.

ARTICLE I

Section 1. All legislative Powers herein granted shall be vested in a Congress of the United States, which shall consist of a Senate and House of Representatives.

Section 2. The House of Representatives shall be composed of Members chosen every second Year by the People of the several States, and the Electors in each State shall have the Qualifications requisite for Electors of the most numerous Branch of the State Legislature.

No Person shall be a Representative who shall not have attained to the Age of twenty five Years, and been seven Years a Citizen of the United States, and who shall not, when elected, be an Inhabitant of that State in which he shall be chosen.

Representatives and direct Taxes shall be apportioned among the several States which may be included within this Union, according to their respective Numbers, which shall be determined by adding to the whole Number of free Persons, including those bound to Service for a Term of Years, and excluding Indians not taxed, three fifths of all other Persons. The actual Enumeration shall be made within three Years after the first Meeting of the Congress of the United States, and within every subsequent Term of ten Years, in such Manner as they shall by Law direct. The Number of Representatives shall not exceed one for every thirty Thousand, but each State shall have at Least one Representative; and until such enumeration shall be made, the State of New Hampshire shall be entitled to chuse three, Massachusetts eight, Rhode Island and Providence Plantations one, Connecticut five, New York six, New Jersey four, Pennsylvania eight, Delaware one, Maryland six, Virginia ten, North Carolina five, South Carolina five, and Georgia three.

When vacancies happen in the Representation from any State, the Executive Authority thereof shall issue Writs of Election to fill such Vacancies.

The House of Representatives shall chuse their Speaker and other Officers; and shall have the sole Power of Impeachment.

Section 3. The Senate of the United States shall be composed of two Senators from each State, chosen by the Legislature thereof, for six Years; and each Senator shall have one Vote.

Immediately after they shall be assembled in Consequence of the first Election, they shall be divided as equally as may be into three Classes. The Seats of the Senators of the first Class shall be vacated at the Expiration of the second Year, of the second Class at the Expiration of the fourth Year, and of the third Class at the Expiration of the sixth Year, so that one third may be chosen every second Year; and if Vacancies happen by Resignation, or otherwise, during the Recess of the Legislature of any State, the Executive thereof may make temporary Appointments until the next Meeting of the Legislature, which shall then fill such Vacancies.

No Person shall be a Senator who shall not have attained to the Age of thirty Years, and been nine Years a Citizen of the United States, and who shall not, when elected, be an Inhabitant of that State for which he shall be chosen.

The Vice President of the United States shall be President of the Senate, but shall have no Vote, unless they be equally divided.

The Senate shall chuse their other Officers, and also a President pro tempore, in the Absence of the Vice President, or when he shall exercise the Office of President of the United States.

The Senate shall have the sole Power to try all Impeachments. When sitting for that Purpose, they shall be on Oath or Affirmation. When the President of the United States is tried, the Chief Justice shall preside: And no Person shall be convicted without the Concurrence of two thirds of the Members present.

Judgment in Cases of Impeachment shall not extend further than to removal from Office, and disqualification to hold and enjoy any Office of honor, Trust, or Profit under the United States: but the Party convicted shall nevertheless be liable and subject to Indictment, Trial, Judgment, and Punishment, according to Law.

Section 4.   The Times, Places and Manner of holding Elections for Senators and Representatives, shall be prescribed in each State by the Legislature thereof; but the Congress may at any time by Law make or alter such Regulations, except as to the Places of chusing Senators.

The Congress shall assemble at least once in every Year, and such Meeting shall be on the first Monday in December, unless they shall by Law appoint a different Day.

Section 5.   Each House shall be the Judge of the Elections, Returns, and Qualifications of its own Members, and a Majority of each shall constitute a Quorum to do Business; but a smaller Number may adjourn from day to day, and may be authorized to compel the Attendance of absent Members, in such Manner, and under such Penalties as each House may provide.

Each House may determine the Rules of its Proceedings, punish its Members for disorderly Behavior, and, with the Concurrence of two thirds, expel a Member.

Each House shall keep a Journal of its Proceedings, and from time to time publish the same, excepting such Parts as may in their Judgment require Secrecy; and the Yeas and Nays of the Members of either House on any question shall, at the Desire of one fifth of those Present, be entered on the Journal.

Neither House, during the Session of Congress, shall, without the Consent of the other, adjourn for more than three days, nor to any other Place than that in which the two Houses shall be sitting.

Section 6.   The Senators and Representatives shall receive a Compensation for their Services, to be ascertained by Law, and paid out of the Treasury of the United States. They shall in all Cases, except Treason, Felony and Breach of the Peace, be privileged from Arrest during their Attendance at the Session of their respective Houses, and in going to and returning from the same; and for any Speech or Debate in either House, they shall not be questioned in any other Place.

No Senator or Representative shall, during the Time for which he was elected, be appointed to any civil Office under the Authority of the United States, which shall have been created, or the Emoluments whereof shall have been increased during such time; and no Person holding any Office under the United States, shall be a Member of either House during his Continuance in Office.

Section 7.   All Bills for raising Revenue shall originate in the House of Representatives; but the Senate may propose or concur with Amendments as on other Bills.

Every Bill which shall have passed the House of Representatives and the Senate, shall, before it become a Law, be presented to the President of the United States; If he approve he shall sign it, but if not he shall return it, with his Objections to the House in which it shall have originated, who shall enter the Objections at large on their Journal, and proceed to reconsider it. If after such Reconsideration two thirds of that House shall agree to pass the Bill, it shall be sent together with the Objections, to the other House, by which it shall likewise be reconsidered, and if approved by two thirds of that House, it shall become a Law. But in all such Cases the Votes of both Houses shall be determined by Yeas and Nays, and the Names of the Persons voting for and against the Bill shall be entered on the Journal of each House respectively. If any Bill shall not be returned by the President within ten Days (Sundays excepted) after it shall have been presented to him, the Same shall be a Law, in like Manner as if he had signed it, unless the Congress by their Adjournment prevent its Return in which Case it shall not be a Law.

Every Order, Resolution, or Vote, to which the Concurrence of the Senate and House of Representatives may be necessary (except on a question of Adjournment) shall be presented to the President of the United States; and before the Same shall take Effect, shall be approved by him, or being disapproved by him, shall be repassed by two thirds of the Senate and House of Representatives, according to the Rules and Limitations prescribed in the Case of a Bill.

Section 8.   The Congress shall have Power To lay and collect Taxes, Duties, Imposts and Excises, to pay the Debts and provide for the common Defence and general Welfare of the United States; but all Duties, Imposts and Excises shall be uniform throughout the United States;

To borrow Money on the credit of the United States;

To regulate Commerce with foreign Nations, and among the several States, and with the Indian Tribes;

To establish an uniform Rule of Naturalization, and uniform Laws on the subject of Bankruptcies throughout the United States;

To coin Money, regulate the Value thereof, and of foreign Coin, and fix the Standard of Weights and Measures;

To provide for the Punishment of counterfeiting the Securities and current Coin of the United States;

To establish Post Offices and post Roads;

To promote the Progress of Science and useful Arts, by securing for limited Times to Authors and Inventors the exclusive Right to their respective Writings and Discoveries;

To constitute Tribunals inferior to the supreme Court;

To define and punish Piracies and Felonies committed on the high Seas, and Offenses against the Law of Nations;

To declare War, grant Letters of Marque and Reprisal, and make Rules concerning Captures on Land and Water;

To raise and support Armies, but no Appropriation of Money to that Use shall be for a longer Term than two Years;

To provide and maintain a Navy;

To make Rules for the Government and Regulation of the land and naval Forces;

To provide for calling forth the Militia to execute the Laws of the Union, suppress Insurrections and repel Invasions;

To provide for organizing, arming, and disciplining, the Militia, and for governing such Part of them as may be employed in the Service of the United States, reserving to the States respectively, the Appointment of the Officers, and the Authority of training the Militia according to the discipline prescribed by Congress;

To exercise exclusive Legislation in all Cases whatsoever, over such District (not exceeding ten Miles square) as may, by Cession of particular States, and the Acceptance of Congress, become the Seat of the Government of the United States, and to exercise like Authority over all Places purchased by the Consent of the Legislature of the State in which the Same shall be, for the Erection of Forts, Magazines, Arsenals, dock-Yards, and other needful Buildings;—And

To make all Laws which shall be necessary and proper for carrying into Execution the foregoing Powers, and all other Powers vested by this Constitution in the Government of the United States, or in any Department or Officer thereof.

Section 9. The Migration or Importation of such Persons as any of the States now existing shall think proper to admit, shall not be prohibited by the Congress prior to the Year one thousand eight hundred and eight, but a Tax or duty may be imposed on such Importation, not exceeding ten dollars for each Person.

The privilege of the Writ of Habeas Corpus shall not be suspended, unless when in Cases of Rebellion or Invasion the public Safety may require it.

No Bill of Attainder or ex post facto Law shall be passed.

No Capitation, or other direct, Tax shall be laid, unless in Proportion to the Census or Enumeration herein before directed to be taken.

No Tax or Duty shall be laid on Articles exported from any State.

No Preference shall be given by any Regulation of Commerce or Revenue to the Ports of one State over those of another: nor shall Vessels bound to, or from, one State be obliged to enter, clear, or pay Duties in another.

No Money shall be drawn from the Treasury, but in Consequence of Appropriations made by Law; and a regular Statement and Account of the Receipts and Expenditures of all public Money shall be published from time to time.

No Title of Nobility shall be granted by the United States: And no Person holding any Office of Profit or Trust under them, shall, without the Consent of the Congress, accept of any present, Emolument, Office, or Title, of any kind whatever, from any King, Prince, or foreign State.

Section 10. No State shall enter into any Treaty, Alliance, or Confederation; grant Letters of Marque and Reprisal; coin Money; emit Bills of Credit; make any Thing but gold and silver Coin a Tender in Payment of Debts; pass any Bill of Attainder, ex post facto Law, or Law impairing the Obligation of Contracts, or grant any Title of Nobility.

No State shall, without the Consent of the Congress, lay any Imposts or Duties on Imports or Exports, except what may be absolutely necessary for executing its inspection Laws: and the net Produce of all Duties and Imposts, laid by any State on Imports or Exports, shall be for the Use of the Treasury of the United States; and all such Laws shall be subject to the Revision and Controul of the Congress.

No State shall, without the Consent of Congress, lay any Duty of Tonnage, keep Troops, or Ships of War in time of Peace, enter into any Agreement or Compact with another State, or with a foreign Power, or engage in War, unless actually invaded, or in such imminent Danger as will not admit of delay.

ARTICLE II

Section 1. The executive Power shall be vested in a President of the United States of America. He shall hold his Office during the Term of four Years, and, together with the Vice President, chosen for the same Term, be elected, as follows:

Each State shall appoint, in such Manner as the Legislature thereof may direct, a Number of Electors, equal to the whole Number of Senators and Representatives to which the State may be entitled in the Congress; but no Senator or Representative, or Person holding an Office of Trust or Profit under the United States, shall be appointed an Elector.

The Electors shall meet in their respective States, and vote by Ballot for two Persons, of whom one at least shall not be an Inhabitant of the same State with themselves. And they shall make a List of all the Persons voted for, and of the Number of Votes for each; which List they shall sign and certify, and transmit sealed to the Seat of the Government of the United States, directed to the President of the Senate. The President of the Senate shall, in the Presence of the Senate and House of Representatives, open all the Certificates, and the Votes shall then be counted. The Person having the greatest Number of Votes shall be the President, if such Number be a Majority of the whole Number of Electors appointed; and if there be more than one who have such Majority, and have an equal Number of Votes, then the House of Representatives shall immediately chuse by Ballot one of them for President; and if no Person have a Majority, then from the five highest on the List the said House shall in like Manner chuse the President. But in chusing the President, the Votes shall be taken by States, the Representation from each State having one Vote; A quorum for this Purpose shall consist of a Member or Members from two thirds of the States, and a Majority of all the States shall be necessary to a Choice. In every Case, after the Choice of the President, the Person having the greater Number of Votes of the Electors shall be the Vice President. But if there should remain two or more who have equal Votes, the Senate shall chuse from them by Ballot the Vice President.

The Congress may determine the Time of chusing the Electors, and the Day on which they shall give their Votes; which Day shall be the same throughout the United States.

No person except a natural born Citizen, or a Citizen of the United States, at the time of the Adoption of this Constitution, shall be eligible to the Office of President; neither shall any Person be eligible to that Office who shall not have attained to the Age of thirty five Years, and been fourteen Years a Resident within the United States.

In Case of the Removal of the President from Office, or of his Death, Resignation or Inability to discharge the Powers and Duties of the said Office, the same shall devolve on the Vice President, and the Congress may by Law provide for the Case of Removal, Death, Resignation or Inability, both of the President and Vice President, declaring what Officer shall then act as President, and such Officer shall act accordingly, until the Disability be removed, or a President shall be elected.

The President shall, at stated Times, receive for his Services, a Compensation, which shall neither be increased nor diminished during the Period for which he shall have been elected, and he shall not receive within that Period any other Emolument from the United States, or any of them.

Before he enter on the Execution of his Office, he shall take the following Oath or Affirmation: "I do solemnly swear (or affirm) that I will faithfully execute the Office of President of the United States, and will to the best of my Ability, preserve, protect and defend the Constitution of the United States."

Section 2. The President shall be Commander in Chief of the Army and Navy of the United States, and of the Militia of the several States, when called into the actual Service of the United States; he may require the Opinion, in writing, of the principal Officer in each of the executive Departments, upon any Subject relating to the Duties of their respective Offices, and he shall have Power to grant Reprieves and Pardons for Offenses against the United States, except in Cases of Impeachment.

He shall have Power, by and with the Advice and Consent of the Senate to make Treaties, provided two thirds of the Senators present concur; and he shall nominate, and by and with the Advice and Consent of the Senate, shall appoint Ambassadors, other public Ministers and Consuls, Judges of the supreme Court, and all other Officers of the United States, whose Appointments are not herein otherwise provided for, and which shall be established by Law; but the Congress may by Law vest the Appointment of such inferior Officers, as they think proper, in the President alone, in the Courts of Law, or in the Heads of Departments.

The President shall have Power to fill up all Vacancies that may happen during the Recess of the Senate, by granting Commissions which shall expire at the End of their next Session.

Section 3. He shall from time to time give to the Congress Information of the State of the Union, and recommend to their Consideration such Measures as he shall judge necessary and expedient; he may, on extraordinary Occasions, convene both Houses, or either of them, and in Case of Disagreement between them, with Respect to the Time of Adjournment, he may adjourn them to such Time as he shall think proper; he shall receive Ambassadors and other public Ministers; he shall take Care that the Laws be faithfully executed, and shall Commission all the Officers of the United States.

Section 4. The President, Vice President and all civil Officers of the United States, shall be removed from Office on Impeachment for, and Conviction of, Treason, Bribery, or other high Crimes and Misdemeanors.

ARTICLE III

Section 1. The judicial Power of the United States, shall be vested in one supreme Court, and in such inferior Courts as the Congress may from time to time ordain and establish. The Judges, both of the supreme and inferior Courts, shall hold their Offices during good Behaviour, and shall, at stated Times, receive for their Services a Compensation, which shall not be diminished during their Continuance in Office.

Section 2. The judicial Power shall extend to all Cases, in Law and Equity, arising under this Constitution, the Laws of the United States, and Treaties made, or which shall be made, under their Authority;—to all Cases affecting Ambassadors, other public Ministers and Consuls;—to all Cases of admiralty and maritime Jurisdiction;—to Controversies to which the United States shall be a Party;—to Controversies between two or more States;—between a State and Citizens of another State;—between Citizens of different States;—between Citizens of the same State claiming Lands under Grants of different States, and between a State, or the Citizens thereof, and foreign States, Citizens or Subjects.

In all Cases affecting Ambassadors, other public Ministers and Consuls, and those in which a State shall be a Party, the supreme Court shall have original Jurisdiction. In all the other Cases before mentioned, the supreme Court shall have appellate Jurisdiction, both as to Law and Fact, with such Exceptions, and under such Regulations as the Congress shall make.

The Trial of all Crimes, except in Cases of Impeachment, shall be by Jury; and such Trial shall be held in the State where the said Crimes shall have been committed; but when not committed within any State, the Trial shall be at such Place or Places as the Congress may by Law have directed.

Section 3. Treason against the United States, shall consist only in levying War against them, or, in adhering to their Enemies, giving them Aid and Comfort. No Person shall be convicted of Treason unless on the Testimony of two Witnesses to the same overt Act, or on Confession in open Court.

The Congress shall have Power to declare the Punishment of Treason, but no Attainder of Treason shall work Corruption of Blood, or Forfeiture except during the Life of the Person attainted.

ARTICLE IV

Section 1. Full Faith and Credit shall be given in each State to the public Acts, Records, and judicial Proceedings of every other State. And the Congress may by general Laws prescribe the Manner in which such Acts, Records and Proceedings shall be proved, and the Effect thereof.

Section 2. The Citizens of each State shall be entitled to all Privileges and Immunities of Citizens in the several States.

A Person charged in any State with Treason, Felony, or other Crime, who shall flee from Justice, and be found in another State, shall on Demand of the executive Authority of the State from which he fled, be delivered up, to be removed to the State having Jurisdiction of the Crime.

No Person held to Service or Labour in one State, under the Laws thereof, escaping into another, shall, in Consequence of any Law or Regulation therein, be discharged from such Service or Labour, but shall be delivered up on Claim of the Party to whom such Service or Labour may be due.

Section 3. New States may be admitted by the Congress into this Union; but no new State shall be formed or erected within the Jurisdiction of any other State; nor any State be formed by the Junction of two or more States, or Parts of States, without the Consent of the Legislatures of the States concerned as well as of the Congress.

The Congress shall have Power to dispose of and make all needful Rules and Regulations respecting the Territory or other Property belonging to the United States; and nothing in this Constitution shall be so construed as to Prejudice any Claims of the United States, or of any particular State.

Section 4. The United States shall guarantee to every State in this Union a Republican Form of Government, and shall protect each of them against Invasion; and on Application of the Legislature, or of the Executive (when the Legislature cannot be convened) against domestic Violence.

ARTICLE V

The Congress, whenever two thirds of both Houses shall deem it necessary, shall propose Amendments to this Constitution, or, on the Application of the Legislatures of two thirds of the several States, shall call a Convention for proposing Amendments, which, in either Case, shall be valid to all Intents and Purposes, as part of this Constitution, when ratified by the Legislatures of three fourths of the several States, or by Conventions in three fourths thereof, as the one or the other Mode of Ratification may be proposed by the Congress; Provided that no Amendment which may be made prior to the Year One thousand eight hundred and eight shall in any Manner affect the first and fourth Clauses in the Ninth Section of the first Article; and that no State, without its Consent, shall be deprived of its equal Suffrage in the Senate.

ARTICLE VI

All Debts contracted and Engagements entered into, before the Adoption of this Constitution shall be as valid against the United States under this Constitution, as under the Confederation.

This Constitution, and the Laws of the United States which shall be made in Pursuance thereof; and all Treaties made, or which shall be made, under the Authority of the United States, shall be the supreme Law of the Land; and the Judges in every State shall be bound thereby, any Thing in the Constitution or Laws of any State to the Contrary notwithstanding.

The Senators and Representatives before mentioned, and the Members of the several State Legislatures, and all executive and judicial Officers, both of the United States and of the several States, shall be bound by Oath or Affirmation, to support this Constitution; but no religious Test shall ever be required as a Qualification to any Office or public Trust under the United States.

ARTICLE VII

The Ratification of the Conventions of nine States shall be sufficient for the Establishment of this Constitution between the States so ratifying the Same.

AMENDMENT I [1791]

Congress shall make no law respecting an establishment of religion, or prohibiting the free exercise thereof; or abridging the freedom of speech, or of the press; or the right of the people peaceably to assemble, and to petition the Government for a redress of grievances.

AMENDMENT II [1791]

A well regulated Militia, being necessary to the security of a free State, the right of the people to keep and bear Arms, shall not be infringed.

AMENDMENT III [1791]

No Soldier shall, in time of peace be quartered in any house, without the consent of the Owner, nor in time of war, but in a manner to be prescribed by law.

AMENDMENT IV [1791]

The right of the people to be secure in their persons, houses, papers, and effects, against unreasonable searches and seizures, shall not be violated, and no Warrants shall issue, but upon probable cause, supported by Oath or affirmation, and particularly describing the place to be searched, and the persons or things to be seized.

AMENDMENT V [1791]

No person shall be held to answer for a capital, or otherwise infamous crime, unless on a presentment or indictment of a Grand Jury, except in cases arising in the land or naval forces, or in the Militia, when in actual service in time of War or public danger; nor shall any person be subject for the same offense to be twice put in jeopardy of life or limb; nor shall be compelled in any criminal case to be a witness against himself, nor be deprived of life, liberty, or property, without due process of law; nor shall private property be taken for public use, without just compensation.

AMENDMENT VI [1791]

In all criminal prosecutions, the accused shall enjoy the right to a speedy and public trial, by an impartial jury of the State and district wherein the crime shall have been committed, which district shall have been previously ascertained by law, and to be informed of the nature and cause of the accusation; to be confronted with the witnesses against him; to have compulsory process for obtaining witnesses in his favor, and to have the Assistance of Counsel for his defence.

AMENDMENT VII [1791]

In Suits at common law, where the value in controversy shall exceed twenty dollars, the right of trial by jury shall be preserved, and no fact tried by a jury, shall be otherwise re-examined in any Court of the United States, than according to the rules of the common law.

AMENDMENT VIII [1791]

Excessive bail shall not be required, nor excessive fines imposed, nor cruel and unusual punishments inflicted.

AMENDMENT IX [1791]

The enumeration in the Constitution, of certain rights, shall not be construed to deny or disparage others retained by the people.

AMENDMENT X [1791]

The powers not delegated to the United States by the Constitution, nor prohibited by it to the States, are reserved to the States respectively, or to the people.

AMENDMENT XI [1798]

The Judicial power of the United States shall not be construed to extend to any suit in law or equity, commenced or prosecuted against one of the United States by Citizens of another State, or by Citizens or Subjects of any Foreign State.

AMENDMENT XII [1804]

The Electors shall meet in their respective states, and vote by ballot for President and Vice-President, one of whom, at least, shall not be an inhabitant of the same state with themselves; they shall name in their ballots the person voted for as President, and in distinct ballots the person voted for as Vice-President, and they shall make distinct lists of all persons voted for as President, and of all persons voted for as Vice-President, and of the number of votes for each, which lists they shall sign and certify, and transmit sealed to the seat of the government of the United States, directed to the President of the Senate;—The President of the Senate shall, in the presence of the Senate and House of Representatives, open all the certificates and the votes shall then be counted;—The person having the greatest number of votes for President, shall be the President, if such number be a majority of the whole number of Electors appointed; and if no person have such majority, then from the persons having the highest numbers not exceeding three on the list of those voted for as President, the House of Representatives shall choose immediately, by ballot, the President. But in choosing the President, the votes shall be taken by states, the representation from each state having one vote; a quorum for this purpose shall consist of a member or members from two-thirds of the states, and a majority of all states shall be necessary to a choice. And if the House of Representatives shall not choose a President whenever the right of choice shall devolve upon them, before the fourth day of March next following, then the Vice-President shall act as President, as in the case of the death or other constitutional disability of the President.—The person having the greatest number of votes as Vice-President, shall be the Vice-President, if such number be a majority of the whole number of Electors appointed, and if no person have a majority, then from the two highest numbers on the list, the Senate shall choose the Vice-President; a quorum for the purpose shall consist of two-thirds of the whole number of Senators, and a majority of the whole number shall be necessary to a choice. But no person constitutionally ineligible to the office of President shall be eligible to that of Vice-President of the United States.

Amendment XIII [1865]

Section 1. Neither slavery nor involuntary servitude, except as a punishment for crime whereof the party shall have been duly convicted, shall exist within the United States, or any place subject to their jurisdiction.

Section 2. Congress shall have power to enforce this article by appropriate legislation.

Amendment XIV [1868]

Section 1. All persons born or naturalized in the United States, and subject to the jurisdiction thereof, are citizens of the United States and of the State wherein they reside. No State shall make or enforce any law which shall abridge the privileges or immunities of citizens of the United States; nor shall any State deprive any person of life, liberty, or property, without due process of law; nor deny to any person within its jurisdiction the equal protection of the laws.

Section 2. Representatives shall be apportioned among the several States according to their respective numbers, counting the whole number of persons in each State, excluding Indians not taxed. But when the right to vote at any election for the choice of electors for President and Vice President of the United States, Representatives in Congress, the Executive and Judicial officers of a State, or the members of the Legislature thereof, is denied to any of the male inhabitants of such State, being twenty-one years of age, and citizens of the United States, or in any way abridged, except for participation in rebellion, or other crime, the basis of representation therein shall

be reduced in the proportion which the number of such male citizens shall bear to the whole number of male citizens twenty-one years of age in such State.

Section 3. No person shall be a Senator or Representative in Congress, or elector of President and Vice President, or hold any office, civil or military, under the United States, or under any State, who having previously taken an oath, as a member of Congress, or as an officer of the United States, or as a member of any State legislature, or as an executive or judicial officer of any State, to support the Constitution of the United States, shall have engaged in insurrection or rebellion against the same, or given aid or comfort to the enemies thereof. But Congress may by a vote of two-thirds of each House, remove such disability.

Section 4. The validity of the public debt of the United States, authorized by law, including debts incurred for payment of pensions and bounties for services in suppressing insurrection or rebellion, shall not be questioned. But neither the United States nor any State shall assume or pay any debt or obligation incurred in aid of insurrection or rebellion against the United States, or any claim for the loss or emancipation of any slave; but all such debts, obligations and claims shall be held illegal and void.

Section 5. The Congress shall have power to enforce, by appropriate legislation, the provisions of this article.

Amendment XV [1870]

Section 1. The right of citizens of the United States to vote shall not be denied or abridged by the United States or by any State on account of race, color, or previous condition of servitude.

Section 2. The Congress shall have power to enforce this article by appropriate legislation.

Amendment XVI [1913]

The Congress shall have power to lay and collect taxes on incomes, from whatever source derived, without apportionment among the several States, and without regard to any census or enumeration.

Amendment XVII [1913]

Section 1. The Senate of the United States shall be composed of two Senators from each State, elected by the people thereof, for six years; and each Senator shall have one vote. The electors in each State shall have the qualifications requisite for electors of the most numerous branch of the State legislatures.

Section 2. When vacancies happen in the representation of any State in the Senate, the executive authority of such State shall issue writs of election to fill such vacancies: Provided, That the legislature of any State may empower the executive thereof to make temporary appointments until the people fill the vacancies by election as the legislature may direct.

Section 3. This amendment shall not be so construed as to affect the election or term of any Senator chosen before it becomes valid as part of the Constitution.

AMENDMENT XVIII [1919]

Section 1. After one year from the ratification of this article the manufacture, sale, or transportation of intoxicating liquors within, the importation thereof into, or the exportation thereof from the United States and all territory subject to the jurisdiction thereof for beverage purposes is hereby prohibited.

Section 2. The Congress and the several States shall have concurrent power to enforce this article by appropriate legislation.

Section 3. This article shall be inoperative unless it shall have been ratified as an amendment to the Constitution by the legislatures of the several States, as provided in the Constitution, within seven years from the date of the submission hereof to the States by the Congress.

AMENDMENT XIX [1920]

Section 1. The right of citizens of the United States to vote shall not be denied or abridged by the United States or by any State on account of sex.

Section 2. Congress shall have power to enforce this article by appropriate legislation.

AMENDMENT XX [1933]

Section 1. The terms of the President and Vice President shall end at noon on the 20th day of January, and the terms of Senators and Representatives at noon on the 3d day of January, of the years in which such terms would have ended if this article had not been ratified; and the terms of their successors shall then begin.

Section 2. The Congress shall assemble at least once in every year, and such meeting shall begin at noon on the 3d day of January, unless they shall by law appoint a different day.

Section 3. If, at the time fixed for the beginning of the term of the President, the President elect shall

have died, the Vice President elect shall become President. If the President shall not have been chosen before the time fixed for the beginning of his term, or if the President elect shall have failed to qualify, then the Vice President elect shall act as President until a President shall have qualified; and the Congress may by law provide for the case wherein neither a President elect nor a Vice President elect shall have qualified, declaring who shall then act as President, or the manner in which one who is to act shall be selected, and such person shall act accordingly until a President or Vice President shall have qualified.

Section 4. The Congress may by law provide for the case of the death of any of the persons from whom the House of Representatives may choose a President whenever the right of choice shall have devolved upon them, and for the case of the death of any of the persons from whom the Senate may choose a Vice President whenever the right of choice shall have devolved upon them.

Section 5. Sections 1 and 2 shall take effect on the 15th day of October following the ratification of this article.

Section 6. This article shall be inoperative unless it shall have been ratified as an amendment to the Constitution by the legislatures of three-fourths of the several States within seven years from the date of its submission.

AMENDMENT XXI [1933]

Section 1. The eighteenth article of amendment to the Constitution of the United States is hereby repealed.

Section 2. The transportation or importation into any State, Territory, or possession of the United States for delivery or use therein of intoxicating liquors, in violation of the laws thereof, is hereby prohibited.

Section 3. This article shall be inoperative unless it shall have been ratified as an amendment to the Constitution by conventions in the several States, as provided in the Constitution, within seven years from the date of the submission hereof to the States by the Congress.

AMENDMENT XXII [1951]

Section 1. No person shall be elected to the office of the President more than twice, and no person who has held the office of President, or acted as President, for more than two years of a term to which some other person was elected President shall be elected to the office of President more than once. But this Article shall not apply to any person holding the office of President when this Article was proposed by the Congress, and shall not prevent any person who may be holding the office of President, or acting as President, during the term within which this Article becomes operative from holding the office of President or acting as President during the remainder of such term.

Section 2. This article shall be inoperative unless it shall have been ratified as an amendment to the Constitution by the legislatures of three-fourths of the several States within seven years from the date of its submission to the States by the Congress.

AMENDMENT XXIII [1961]

Section 1. The District constituting the seat of Government of the United States shall appoint in such manner as the Congress may direct:

A number of electors of President and Vice President equal to the whole number of Senators and Representatives in Congress to which the District would be entitled if it were a State, but in no event more than the least populous state; they shall be in addition to those appointed by the states, but they shall be considered, for the purposes of the election of President and Vice President, to be electors appointed by a state; and they shall meet in the District and perform such duties as provided by the twelfth article of amendment.

Section 2. The Congress shall have power to enforce this article by appropriate legislation.

AMENDMENT XXIV [1964]

Section 1. The right of citizens of the United States to vote in any primary or other election for President or Vice President, for electors for President or Vice President, or for Senator or Representative in Congress, shall not be denied or abridged by the United States, or any State by reason of failure to pay any poll tax or other tax.

Section 2. The Congress shall have power to enforce this article by appropriate legislation.

AMENDMENT XXV [1967]

Section 1. In case of the removal of the President from office or of his death or resignation, the Vice President shall become President.

Section 2. Whenever there is a vacancy in the office of the Vice President, the President shall nominate a Vice President who shall take office upon confirmation by a majority vote of both Houses of Congress.

Section 3. Whenever the President transmits to the President pro tempore of the Senate and the Speaker of the House of Representatives his written declaration that he is unable to discharge the powers and duties of his office, and until he transmits to them a written declaration to the contrary, such powers and duties shall be discharged by the Vice President as Acting President.

Section 4. Whenever the Vice President and a majority of either the principal officers of the executive departments or of such other body as Congress may by law provide, transmit to the President pro tempore of the Senate and the Speaker of the House of Representatives their written declaration that the President is unable to discharge the powers and duties of his office, the Vice President shall immediately assume the powers and duties of the office as Acting President.

Thereafter, when the President transmits to the President pro tempore of the Senate and the Speaker of the House of Representatives his written declaration that no inability exists, he shall resume the powers and duties of his office unless the Vice President and a majority of either the principal officers of the executive department or of such other body as Congress may by law provide, transmit within four days to the President pro tempore of the Senate and the Speaker of the House of Representatives their written declaration that the President is unable to discharge the powers and duties of his office. Thereupon Congress shall decide the issue, assembling within forty-eight hours for that purpose if not in session. If the Congress, within twenty-one days after receipt of the latter written declaration, or, if Congress is not in session, within twenty-one days after Congress is required to assemble, determines by two-thirds vote of both Houses that the President is unable to discharge the powers and duties of his office, the Vice President shall continue to discharge the same as Acting President; otherwise, the President shall resume the powers and duties of his office.

AMENDMENT XXVI [1971]

Section 1. The right of citizens of the United States, who are eighteen years of age or older, to vote shall not be denied or abridged by the United States or by any State on account of age.

Section 2. The Congress shall have power to enforce this article by appropriate legislation.

AMENDMENT XXVII [1992]

No law, varying the compensation for the services of the Senators and Representatives, shall take effect, until an election of Representatives shall have intervened.

The Declaration of Independence

IN CONGRESS, JULY 4, 1776

A Declaration by the Representatives of the United States of America, in General Congress assembled. When in the Course of human Events, it becomes necessary for one People to dissolve the Political Bands which have connected them with another, and to assume among the Powers of the Earth, the separate and equal Station to which the Laws of Nature and of Nature's God entitle them, a decent Respect to the Opinions of Mankind requires that they should declare the causes which impel them to the Separation.

We hold these Truths to be self-evident, that all Men are created equal, that they are endowed by their Creator with certain unalienable Rights, that among these are Life, Liberty, and the Pursuit of Happiness— That to secure these Rights, Governments are instituted among Men, deriving their just Powers from the Consent of the Governed, that whenever any Form of Government becomes destructive of these Ends, it is the Right of the People to alter or to abolish it, and to institute new Government, laying its Foundation on such Principles, and organizing its Powers in such Forms, as to them shall seem most likely to effect their Safety and Happiness. Prudence, indeed, will dictate that Governments long established should not be changed for light and transient Causes; and accordingly all Experience hath shewn, that Mankind are more disposed to suffer, while Evils are sufferable, than to right themselves by abolishing the Forms to which they are accustomed. But when a long Train of Abuses and Usurpations, pursuing invariably the same Object, evinces a Design to reduce them under absolute Despotism, it is their Right, it is their Duty, to throw off such Government, and to provide new Guards for their future Security. Such has been the patient Sufferance of these Colonies; and such is now the Necessity which constrains them to alter their former Systems of Government. The History of the present King of Great-Britain is a History of repeated Injuries and Usurpations, all having in direct Object the Establishment of an absolute Tyranny over these States. To prove this, let Facts be submitted to a candid World.

He has refused his Assent to Laws, the most wholesome and necessary for the public Good.

He has forbidden his Governors to pass Laws of immediate and pressing Importance, unless suspended in their Operation till his Assent should be obtained; and when so suspended, he has utterly neglected to attend to them.

He has refused to pass other Laws for the Accommodation of large Districts of People, unless those People would relinquish the Right of Representation in the Legislature, a Right inestimable to them, and formidable to Tyrants only.

He has called together Legislative Bodies at Places unusual, uncomfortable, and distant from the Depository of their Public Records, for the sole Purpose of fatiguing them into Compliance with his Measures.

He has dissolved Representative Houses repeatedly, for opposing with manly Firmness his Invasions on the Rights of the People.

He has refused for a long Time, after such Dissolutions, to cause others to be elected; whereby the Legislative Powers, incapable of Annihilation, have returned to the People at large for their exercise; the State remaining in the mean time exposed to all the Dangers of Invasion from without, and Convulsions within.

He has endeavoured to prevent the Population of these States; for that Purpose obstructing the Laws for Naturalization of Foreigners; refusing to pass others to encourage their Migrations hither, and raising the Conditions of new Appropriations of Lands.

He has obstructed the Administration of Justice, by refusing his Assent to Laws for establishing Judiciary Powers.

He has made Judges dependent on his Will alone, for the Tenure of their offices, and the Amount and payment of their Salaries.

He has erected a Multitude of new Offices, and sent hither Swarms of Officers to harrass our People, and eat out their Substance.

He has kept among us, in Times of Peace, Standing Armies, without the consent of our Legislatures.

He has affected to render the Military independent of, and superior to the Civil Power.

He has combined with others to subject us to a Jurisdiction foreign to our Constitution, and unacknowledged by our Laws; giving his Assent to their Acts of pretended Legislation:

For quartering large Bodies of Armed Troops among us:

For protecting them, by a mock Trial, from Punishment for any Murders which they should commit on the Inhabitants of these States:

For cutting off our Trade with all Parts of the World:

For imposing Taxes on us without our Consent:

For depriving us, in many cases, of the Benefits of Trial by Jury:

For transporting us beyond Seas to be tried for pretended Offences:

For abolishing the free System of English Laws in a neighbouring Province, establishing therein an arbitrary Government, and enlarging its Boundaries, so as to render it at once an Example and fit Instrument for introducing the same absolute Rule into these Colonies:

For taking away our Charters, abolishing our most valuable Laws, and altering fundamentally the Forms of our Governments:

For suspending our own Legislatures, and declaring themselves invested with Power to legislate for us in all Cases whatsoever.

He has abdicated Government here, by declaring us out of his Protection and waging War against us.

He has plundered our Seas, ravaged our Coasts, burnt our towns, and destroyed the Lives of our People.

He is, at this Time, transporting large Armies of foreign Mercenaries to compleat the works of Death, Desolation, and Tyranny, already begun with circumstances of Cruelty and Perfidy, scarcely paralleled in the most barbarous Ages, and totally unworthy the Head of a civilized Nation.

He has constrained our fellow Citizens taken Captive on the high Seas to bear Arms against their Country, to become the Executioners of their Friends and Brethren, or to fall themselves by their Hands.

He has excited domestic Insurrections amongst us, and has endeavoured to bring on the Inhabitants of our Frontiers, the merciless Indian Savages, whose known Rule of Warfare, is an undistinguished Destruction, of all Ages, Sexes and Conditions.

In every state of these Oppressions we have Petitioned for Redress in the most humble Terms: Our repeated Petitions have been answered only by repeated Injury. A Prince, whose Character is thus marked by every act which may define a Tyrant, is unfit to be the Ruler of a free People.

Nor have we been wanting in Attentions to our British Brethren. We have warned them from Time to Time of Attempts by their Legislature to extend an unwarrantable Jurisdiction over us. We have reminded them of the Circumstances of our Emigration and Settlement here. We have appealed to their native Justice and Magnanimity, and we have conjured them by the Ties of our common Kindred to disavow these Usurpations, which, would inevitably interrupt our Connections and Correspondence. They too have been deaf to the Voice of Justice and of Consanguinity. We must, therefore, acquiesce in the Necessity, which denounces our Separation, and hold them, as we hold the rest of Mankind, Enemies in War, in Peace, Friends.

We, therefore, the Representatives of the UNITED STATES OF AMERICA, in General Congress Assembled, appealing to the Supreme Judge of the World for the Rectitude of our Intentions, do, in the Name, and by the Authority of the good People of these Colonies, solemnly Publish and Declare, That these United Colonies are, and of Right ought to be, Free and Independent States; that they are absolved from all Allegiance to the British Crown, and that all political Connection between them and the State of Great-Britain, is and ought to be totally dissolved; and that as Free and Independent States, they have full Power to levy War, conclude Peace, contract Alliances, establish Commerce, and to do all other Acts and Things which Independent States may of right do. And for the support of this declaration, with a firm Reliance on the Protection of divine Providence, we mutually pledge to each other our lives, our Fortunes, and our sacred Honor.

Twentieth-Century Supreme Court Justices

Chief Justices

NAME	YEARS OF SERVICE	STATE APP'T FROM	APPOINTING PRESIDENT	AGE APP'T	POLITICAL AFFILIATION	EDUCATIONAL BACKGROUND*
Fuller, Melville Weston	1888–1910	Illinois	Cleveland	55	Democrat	Bowdoin College; studied at Harvard Law School
White, Edward Douglass	1910–1921	Louisiana	Taft	65	Democrat	Mount St. Mary's College; Georgetown College (now University)
Taft, William Howard	1921–1930	Connecticut	Harding	64	Republican	Yale; Cincinnati Law School
Hughes, Charles Evans	1930–1941	New York	Hoover	68	Republican	Colgate University; Brown; Columbia Law School
Stone, Harlan Fiske	1941–1946	New York	Roosevelt, F.	69	Republican	Amherst College; Columbia
Vinson, Frederick Moore	1946–1953	Kentucky	Truman	56	Democrat	Centre College
Warren, Earl	1953–1969	California	Eisenhower	62	Republican	University of California, Berkeley
Burger, Warren Earl	1969–1986	Virginia	Nixon	62	Republican	University of Minnesota; St. Paul College of Law (Mitchell College)
Rehnquist, William Hubbs	1986–	Virginia	Reagan	62	Republican	Stanford; Harvard; Stanford University Law School

*SOURCE: Educational background information derived from Elder Witt, *Guide to the U.S. Supreme Court*, 2d ed. (Washington, D.C.: Congressional Quarterly Press, Inc., 1990). Reprinted with the permission of the publisher.

Associate Justices

NAME	YEARS OF SERVICE	STATE APP'T FROM	APPOINTING PRESIDENT	AGE APP'T	POLITICAL AFFILIATION	EDUCATIONAL BACKGROUND
Harlan, John Marshall	1877–1911	Kentucky	Hayes	61	Republican	Centre College; studied law at Transylvania University
Gray, Horace	1882–1902	Massachusetts	Arthur	54	Republican	Harvard College; Harvard Law School
Brewer, David Josiah	1890–1910	Kansas	Harrison	53	Republican	Wesleyan University; Yale; Albany Law School
Brown, Henry Billings	1891–1906	Michigan	Harrison	55	Republican	Yale; studied at Yale Law School and Harvard Law School
Shiras, George, Jr.	1892–1903	Pennsylvania	Harrison	61	Republican	Ohio University; Yale; studied law at Yale and privately
White, Edward Douglass	1894–1910	Louisiana	Cleveland	49	Democrat	Mount St. Mary's College; Georgetown College (now University)

Associate Justices (continued)

NAME	YEARS OF SERVICE	STATE APP'T FROM	APPOINTING PRESIDENT	AGE APP'T	POLITICAL AFFILIATION	EDUCATIONAL BACKGROUND
Peckham, Rufus Wheeler	1896–1909	New York	Cleveland	58	Democrat	Read law in father's firm
McKenna, Joseph	1898–1925	California	McKinley	55	Republican	Benicia Collegiate Institute, Law Dept.
Holmes, Oliver Wendell, Jr.	1902–1932	Massachusetts	Roosevelt, T.	61	Republican	Harvard College; studied law at Harvard Law School
Day, William Rufus	1903–1922	Ohio	Roosevelt, T.	54	Republican	University of Michigan; University of Michigan Law School
Moody, William Henry	1906–1910	Massachusetts	Roosevelt, T.	53	Republican	Harvard; Harvard Law School
Lurton, Horace Harmon	1910–1914	Tennessee	Taft	66	Democrat	University of Chicago; Cumberland Law School
Hughes, Charles Evans	1910–1916	New York	Taft	48	Republican	Colgate University; Brown University; Columbia Law School
Van Devanter, Willis	1911–1937	Wyoming	Taft	52	Republican	Indiana Asbury University; University of Cincinnati Law School
Lamar, Joseph Rucker	1911–1916	Georgia	Taft	54	Democrat	University of Georgia; Bethany College; Washington and Lee University
Pitney, Mahlon	1912–1922	New Jersey	Taft	54	Republican	College of New Jersey (Princeton); read law under father
McReynolds, James Clark	1914–1941	Tennessee	Wilson	52	Democrat	Vanderbilt University; University of Virginia
Brandeis, Louis Dembitz	1916–1939	Massachusetts	Wilson	60	Democrat	Harvard Law School
Clarke, John Hessin	1916–1922	Ohio	Wilson	59	Democrat	Western Reserve University; read law under father
Sutherland, George	1922–1938	Utah	Harding	60	Republican	Brigham Young Academy; one year at University of Michigan Law School
Butler, Pierce	1923–1939	Minnesota	Harding	57	Democrat	Carleton College
Sanford, Edward Terry	1923–1930	Tennessee	Harding	58	Republican	University of Tennessee; Harvard; Harvard Law School
Stone, Harlan Fiske	1925–1941	New York	Coolidge	53	Republican	Amherst College; Columbia University Law School
Roberts, Owen Josephus	1930–1945	Pennsylvania	Hoover	55	Republican	University of Pennsylvania; University of Pennsylvania Law School
Cardozo, Benjamin Nathan	1932–1938	New York	Hoover	62	Democrat	Columbia University; two years at Columbia Law School
Black, Hugo Lafayette	1937–1971	Alabama	Roosevelt, F.	51	Democrat	Birmingham Medical College; University of Alabama Law School
Reed, Stanley Forman	1938–1957	Kentucky	Roosevelt, F.	54	Democrat	Kentucky Wesleyan University; Foreman Yale; studied law at University of Virginia and Columbia University; University of Paris
Frankfurter, Felix	1939–1962	Massachusetts	Roosevelt, F.	57	Independent	College of the City of New York; Harvard Law School
Douglas, William Orville	1939–1975	Connecticut	Roosevelt, F.	41	Democrat	Whitman College; Columbia University Law School

Associate Justices (continued)

NAME	YEARS OF SERVICE	STATE APP'T FROM	APPOINTING PRESIDENT	AGE APP'T	POLITICAL AFFILIATION	EDUCATIONAL BACKGROUND
Murphy, Frank	1940–1949	Michigan	Roosevelt, F.	50	Democrat	University of Michigan; Lincoln's Inn, London; Trinity College
Byrnes, James Francis	1941–1942	South Carolina	Roosevelt, F.	62	Democrat	Read law privately
Jackson, Robert Houghwout	1941–1954	New York	Roosevelt, F.	49	Democrat	Albany Law School
Rutledge, Wiley Blount	1943–1949	Iowa	Roosevelt, F.	49	Democrat	University of Wisconsin; University of Colorado
Burton, Harold Hitz	1945–1958	Ohio	Truman	57	Republican	Bowdoin College; Harvard University Law School
Clark, Thomas Campbell	1949–1967	Texas	Truman	50	Democrat	University of Texas
Minton, Sherman	1949–1956	Indiana	Truman	59	Democrat	Indiana University College of Law; Yale Law School
Harlan, John Marshall	1955–1971	New York	Eisenhower	56	Republican	Princeton; Oxford University; New York Law School
Brennan, William J., Jr.	1956–1990	New Jersey	Eisenhower	50	Democrat	University of Pennsylvania; Harvard Law School
Whittaker, Charles Evans	1957–1962	Missouri	Eisenhower	56	Republican	University of Kansas City Law School
Stewart, Potter	1958–1981	Ohio	Eisenhower	43	Republican	Yale; Yale Law School
White, Byron Raymond	1962–1993	Colorado	Kennedy	45	Democrat	University of Colorado; Oxford University; Yale Law School
Goldberg, Arthur Joseph	1962–1965	Illinois	Kennedy	54	Democrat	Northwestern University
Fortas, Abe	1965–1969	Tennessee	Johnson, L.	55	Democrat	Southwestern College; Yale Law School
Marshall, Thurgood	1967–1991	New York	Johnson, L.	59	Democrat	Lincoln University; Howard University Law School
Blackmun, Harry A.	1970–1994	Minnesota	Nixon	62	Republican	Harvard; Harvard Law School
Powell, Lewis F., Jr.	1972–1987	Virginia	Nixon	65	Democrat	Washington and Lee University; Washington and Lee University Law School; Harvard Law School
Rehnquist, William H.	1972–1986	Arizona	Nixon	48	Republican	Stanford; Harvard; Stanford University Law School
Stevens, John Paul	1975–	Illinois	Ford	55	Republican	University of Colorado; Northwestern University Law School
O'Connor, Sandra Day	1981–	Arizona	Reagan	51	Republican	Stanford; Stanford University Law School
Scalia, Antonin	1986–	Virginia	Reagan	50	Republican	Georgetown University; Harvard Law School
Kennedy, Anthony M.	1988–	California	Reagan	52	Republican	Stanford; London School of Economics; Harvard Law School
Souter, David Hackett	1990–	New Hampshire	Bush	51	Republican	Harvard; Oxford University
Thomas, Clarence	1991–	District of Columbia	Bush	43	Republican	Holy Cross College; Yale Law School
Ginsburg, Ruth Bader	1993–	District of Columbia	Clinton	60	Democrat	Cornell University; Columbia Law School
Breyer, Stephen G.	1994–	Massachusetts	Clinton	55	Democrat	Stanford; Oxford University; Harvard Law School

A P P E N D I X   D

Twentieth-Century
Party Control of Congress

CONGRESS	YEARS	PRESIDENT	MAJORITY PARTY IN HOUSE	MAJORITY PARTY IN SENATE
57th	1901–1903	T. Roosevelt	Republican	Republican
58th	1903–1905	T. Roosevelt	Republican	Republican
59th	1905–1907	T. Roosevelt	Republican	Republican
60th	1907–1909	T. Roosevelt	Republican	Republican
61st	1909–1911	Taft	Republican	Republican
62d	1911–1913	Taft	Democratic	Republican
63d	1913–1915	Wilson	Democratic	Democratic
64th	1915–1917	Wilson	Democratic	Democratic
65th	1917–1919	Wilson	Democratic	Democratic
66th	1919–1921	Wilson	Republican	Republican
67th	1921–1923	Harding	Republican	Republican
68th	1923–1925	Coolidge	Republican	Republican
69th	1925–1927	Coolidge	Republican	Republican
70th	1927–1929	Coolidge	Republican	Republican
71st	1929–1931	Hoover	Republican	Republican
72d	1931–1933	Hoover	Democratic	Republican
73d	1933–1935	F. Roosevelt	Democratic	Democratic
74th	1935–1937	F. Roosevelt	Democratic	Democratic
75th	1937–1939	F. Roosevelt	Democratic	Democratic
76th	1939–1941	F. Roosevelt	Democratic	Democratic
77th	1941–1943	F. Roosevelt	Democratic	Democratic
78th	1943–1945	F. Roosevelt	Democratic	Democratic
79th	1945–1947	Truman	Democratic	Democratic
80th	1947–1949	Truman	Republican	Democratic
81st	1949–1951	Truman	Democratic	Democratic
82d	1951–1953	Truman	Democratic	Democratic
83d	1953–1955	Eisenhower	Republican	Republican
84th	1955–1957	Eisenhower	Democratic	Democratic
85th	1957–1959	Eisenhower	Democratic	Democratic
86th	1959–1961	Eisenhower	Democratic	Democratic
87th	1961–1963	Kennedy	Democratic	Democratic
88th	1963–1965	Kennedy/Johnson	Democratic	Democratic
89th	1965–1967	Johnson	Democratic	Democratic
90th	1967–1969	Johnson	Democratic	Democratic
91st	1969–1971	Nixon	Democratic	Democratic
92d	1971–1973	Nixon	Democratic	Democratic
93d	1973–1975	Nixon/Ford	Democratic	Democratic
94th	1975–1977	Ford	Democratic	Democratic
95th	1977–1979	Carter	Democratic	Democratic
96th	1979–1981	Carter	Democratic	Democratic
97th	1981–1983	Reagan	Democratic	Republican
98th	1983–1985	Reagan	Democratic	Republican
99th	1985–1987	Reagan	Democratic	Republican
100th	1987–1989	Reagan	Democratic	Democratic
101st	1989–1991	Bush	Democratic	Democratic
102d	1991–1993	Bush	Democratic	Democratic
103d	1993–1995	Clinton	Democratic	Democratic
104th	1995–1997	Clinton	Republican	Republican
105th	1997–1999	Clinton	Republican	Republican
106th	1999–2001	Clinton	Republican	Republican

Information on U.S. Presidents

	TERM OF SERVICE	AGE AT INAUGURATION	PARTY AFFILIATION	COLLEGE OR UNIVERSITY	OCCUPATION OR PROFESSION
1. George Washington	1789–1797	57	None		Planter
2. John Adams	1797–1801	61	Federalist	Harvard	Lawyer
3. Thomas Jefferson	1801–1809	57	Democratic-Republican	William and Mary	Planter, Lawyer
4. James Madison	1809–1817	57	Democratic-Republican	Princeton	Lawyer
5. James Monroe	1817–1825	58	Democratic-Republican	William and Mary	Lawyer
6. John Quincy Adams	1825–1829	57	Democratic-Republican	Harvard	Lawyer
7. Andrew Jackson	1829–1837	61	Democrat		Lawyer
8. Martin Van Buren	1837–1841	54	Democrat		Lawyer
9. William H. Harrison	1841	68	Whig	Hampden-Sydney	Soldier
10. John Tyler	1841–1845	51	Whig	William and Mary	Lawyer
11. James K. Polk	1845–1849	49	Democrat	U. of N. Carolina	Lawyer
12. Zachary Taylor	1849–1850	64	Whig		Soldier
13. Millard Fillmore	1850–1853	50	Whig		Lawyer
14. Franklin Pierce	1853–1857	48	Democrat	Bowdoin	Lawyer
15. James Buchanan	1857–1861	65	Democrat	Dickinson	Lawyer
16. Abraham Lincoln	1861–1865	52	Republican		Lawyer
17. Andrew Johnson	1865–1869	56	Nat/l. Union†		Tailor
18. Ulysses S. Grant	1869–1877	46	Republican	U.S. Mil. Academy	Soldier
19. Rutherford B. Hayes	1877–1881	54	Republican	Kenyon	Lawyer
20. James A. Garfield	1881	49	Republican	Williams	Lawyer
21. Chester A. Arthur	1881–1885	51	Republican	Union	Lawyer
22. Grover Cleveland	1885–1889	47	Democrat		Lawyer
23. Benjamin Harrison	1889–1893	55	Republican	Miami	Lawyer
24. Grover Cleveland	1893–1897	55	Democrat		Lawyer
25. William McKinley	1897–1901	54	Republican	Allegheny College	Lawyer
26. Theodore Roosevelt	1901–1909	42	Republican	Harvard	Author
27. William H. Taft	1909–1913	51	Republican	Yale	Lawyer
28. Woodrow Wilson	1913–1921	56	Democrat	Princeton	Educator
29. Warren G. Harding	1921–1923	55	Republican		Editor
30. Calvin Coolidge	1923–1929	51	Republican	Amherst	Lawyer
31. Herbert C. Hoover	1929–1933	54	Republican	Stanford	Engineer
32. Franklin D. Roosevelt	1933–1945	51	Democrat	Harvard	Lawyer
33. Harry S Truman	1945–1953	60	Democrat		Businessman
34. Dwight D. Eisenhower	1953–1961	62	Republican	U.S. Mil. Academy	Soldier
35. John F. Kennedy	1961–1963	43	Democrat	Harvard	Author
36. Lyndon B. Johnson	1963–1969	55	Democrat	Southwest Texas State	Teacher
37. Richard M. Nixon	1969–1974	56	Republican	Whittier	Lawyer
38. Gerald R. Ford‡	1974–1977	61	Republican	Michigan	Lawyer
39. James E. Carter, Jr.	1977–1981	52	Democrat	U.S. Naval Academy	Businessman
40. Ronald W. Reagan	1981–1989	69	Republican	Eureka College	Actor
41. George H. W. Bush	1989–1993	64	Republican	Yale	Businessman
42. William J. Clinton	1993–	46	Democrat	Georgetown	Lawyer

*Church preference; never joined any church.

†The National Union Party consisted of Republicans and War Democrats. Johnson was a Democrat.

**Inaugurated Dec. 6, 1973, to replace Agnew, who resigned Oct. 10, 1973.

‡Inaugurated Aug. 9, 1974, to replace Nixon, who resigned that same day.

§Inaugurated Dec. 19, 1974, to replace Ford, who became president Aug. 9, 1974.

APPENDIX E

Information on U.S. Presidents

RELIGION	BORN	DIED	AGE AT DEATH	VICE PRESIDENT	
1. Episcopalian	Feb. 22, 1732	Dec. 14, 1799	67	John Adams	(1789–1797)
2. Unitarian	Oct. 30, 1735	July 4, 1826	90	Thomas Jefferson	(1797–1801)
3. Unitarian*	Apr. 13, 1743	July 4, 1826	83	Aaron Burr	(1801–1805)
				George Clinton	(1805–1809)
4. Episcopalian	Mar. 16, 1751	June 28, 1836	85	George Clinton	(1809–1812)
				Elbridge Gerry	(1813–1814)
5. Episcopalian	Apr. 28, 1758	July 4, 1831	73	Daniel D. Tompkins	(1817–1825)
6. Unitarian	July 11, 1767	Feb. 23, 1848	80	John C. Calhoun	(1825–1829)
7. Presbyterian	Mar. 15, 1767	June 8, 1845	78	John C. Calhoun	(1829–1832)
				Martin Van Buren	(1833–1837)
8. Dutch Reformed	Dec. 5, 1782	July 24, 1862	79	Richard M. Johnson	(1837–1841)
9. Episcopalian	Feb. 9, 1773	Apr. 4, 1841	68	John Tyler	(1841)
10. Episcopalian	Mar. 29, 1790	Jan. 18, 1862	71		
11. Methodist	Nov. 2, 1795	June 15, 1849	53	George M. Dallas	(1845–1849)
12. Episcopalian	Nov. 24, 1784	July 9, 1850	65	Millard Fillmore	(1849–1850)
13. Unitarian	Jan. 7, 1800	Mar. 8, 1874	74		
14. Episcopalian	Nov. 23, 1804	Oct. 8, 1869	64	William R. King	(1853)
15. Presbyterian	Apr. 23, 1791	June 1, 1868	77	John C. Breckinridge	(1857–1861)
16. Presbyterian*	Feb. 12, 1809	Apr. 15, 1865	56	Hannibal Hamlin	(1861–1865)
				Andrew Johnson	(1865)
17. Methodist*	Dec. 29, 1808	July 31, 1875	66		
18. Methodist	Apr. 27, 1822	July 23, 1885	63	Schuyler Colfax	(1869–1873)
				Henry Wilson	(1873–1875)
19. Methodist*	Oct. 4, 1822	Jan. 17, 1893	70	William A. Wheeler	(1877–1881)
20. Disciples of Christ	Nov. 19, 1831	Sept. 19, 1881	49	Chester A. Arthur	(1881)
21. Episcopalian	Oct. 5, 1829	Nov. 18, 1886	57		
22. Presbyterian	Mar. 18, 1837	June 24, 1908	71	Thomas A. Hendricks	(1885)
23. Presbyterian	Aug. 20, 1833	Mar. 13, 1901	67	Levi P. Morton	(1889–1893)
24. Presbyterian	Mar. 18, 1837	June 24, 1908	71	Adlai E. Stevenson	(1893–1897)
25. Methodist	Jan. 29, 1843	Sept. 14, 1901	58	Garret A. Hobart	(1897–1899)
				Theodore Roosevelt	(1901)
26. Dutch Reformed	Oct. 27, 1858	Jan. 6, 1919	60	Charles W. Fairbanks	(1905–1909)
27. Unitarian	Sept. 15, 1857	Mar. 8, 1930	72	James S. Sherman	(1909–1912)
28. Presbyterian	Dec. 29, 1856	Feb. 3, 1924	67	Thomas R. Marshall	(1913–1921)
29. Baptist	Nov. 2, 1865	Aug. 2, 1923	57	Calvin Coolidge	(1921–1923)
30. Congregationalist	July 4, 1872	Jan. 5, 1933	60	Charles G. Dawes	(1925–1929)
31. Friend (Quaker)	Aug. 10, 1874	Oct. 20, 1964	90	Charles Curtis	(1929–1933)
32. Episcopalian	Jan. 30, 1882	Apr. 12, 1945	63	John N. Garner	(1933–1941)
				Henry A. Wallace	(1941–1945)
				Harry S Truman	(1945)
33. Baptist	May 8, 1884	Dec. 26, 1972	88	Alben W. Barkley	(1949–1953)
34. Presbyterian	Oct. 14, 1890	Mar. 28, 1969	78	Richard M. Nixon	(1953–1961)
35. Roman Catholic	May 29, 1917	Nov. 22, 1963	46	Lyndon B. Johnson	(1961–1963)
36. Disciples of Christ	Aug. 27, 1908	Jan. 22, 1973	64	Hubert H. Humphrey	(1965–1969)
37. Friend (Quaker)	Jan. 9, 1913	Apr. 22, 1994	81	Spiro T. Agnew	(1969–1973)
				Gerald R. Ford**	(1973–1974)
38. Episcopalian	July 14, 1913			Nelson A. Rockefeller§	(1974–1977)
39. Baptist	Oct. 1, 1924			Walter F. Mondale	(1977–1981)
40. Disciples of Christ	Feb. 6, 1911			George H. W. Bush	(1981–1989)
41. Episcopalian	June 12, 1924			J. Danforth Quayle	(1989–1993)
42. Baptist	Aug. 19, 1946			Albert A. Gore	(1993–)

Federalist Papers
No. 10 and No. 51

#10

Among the numerous advantages promised by a well-constructed Union, none deserves to be more accurately developed than its tendency to break and control the violence of faction. The friend of popular governments never finds himself so much alarmed for their character and fate as when he contemplates their propensity to this dangerous vice. He will not fail, therefore, to set a due value on any plan which, without violating the principles to which he is attached, provides a proper cure for it. The instability, injustice, and confusion introduced into the public councils have, in truth, been the mortal diseases under which popular governments have everywhere perished, as they continue to be the favorite and fruitful topics from which the adversaries to liberty derive their most specious declamations. The valuable improvements made by the American constitutions on the popular models, both ancient and modern, cannot certainly be too much admired; but it would be an unwarrantable partiality to contend that they have as effectually obviated the danger on this side, as was wished and expected. Complaints are everywhere heard from our most considerate and virtuous citizens, equally the friends of public and private faith and of public and personal liberty, that our governments are too unstable, that the public good is disregarded in the conflicts of rival parties, and that measures are too often decided, not according to the rules of justice and the rights of the minor party, but by the superior force of an interested and overbearing majority. However anxiously we may wish that these complaints had no foundation, the evidence of known facts will not permit us to deny that they are in some degree true. It will be found, indeed, on a candid review of our situation, that some of the distresses under which we labor have been erroneously charged on the operation of our governments; but it will be found, at the same time, that other causes will not alone account for many of our heaviest misfortunes; and, particularly, for that prevailing and increasing distrust of public engagements and alarm for private rights which are echoed from one end of the continent to the other. These must be chiefly, if not wholly, effects of the unsteadiness and injustice with which a factious spirit has tainted our public administration.

By a faction I understand a number of citizens, whether amounting to a majority or minority of the whole, who are united and actuated by some common impulse of passion, or of interest, adverse to the rights of other citizens, or the permanent and aggregate interests of the community.

There are two methods of curing the mischiefs of faction: the one, by removing its causes; the other, by controlling its effects.

There are again two methods of removing the causes of faction: the one, by destroying the liberty which is essential to its existence; the other, by giving to every citizen the same opinions, the same passions, and the same interests.

It could never be more truly said than of the first remedy that it was worse than the disease. Liberty is to faction what air is to fire, an aliment without which it instantly expires. But it could not be a less folly to abolish liberty, which is essential to political life, because it nourishes faction than it would be to wish the annihilation of air, which is essential to animal life, because it imparts to fire its destructive agency.

The second expedient is as impracticable as the first would be unwise. As long as the reason of man continues fallible, and his is at liberty to exercise it, different opinions will be formed. As long as the connection subsists between his reason and his self-love, his opinions and his passions will have a reciprocal influence on each other; and the former will be objects to which the latter will attach themselves. The diversity in the faculties of men, from which the rights of property originate, is not less an insuperable obstacle to a uniformity of interests. The protection of these faculties is the first object of government. From the protection of different and unequal faculties of acquiring property, the possession of different degrees and kinds of property immediately results; and from the influence of these on the sentiments and views of the respective proprietors ensues a division of the society into different interests and parties.

The latent causes of faction are thus sown in the nature of man; and we see them everywhere brought into different degrees of activity, according to the different circumstances of civil society. A zeal for different opinions concerning religion, concerning government, and many other points, as well of speculation as of practice; an attachment to different leaders ambitiously contending for pre-eminence and power; or to persons of other descriptions whose fortunes have been interesting to the human passions, have, in turn, divided mankind into parties, inflamed them with mutual animosity, and rendered them much more disposed to vex and oppress each other than to co-operate for their common good. So strong is this propensity of mankind to fall into mutual animosities that where no substantial occasion presents itself the most frivolous and fanciful distinctions have been sufficient to kindle their unfriendly passions and excite their most violent conflicts. But the most common and durable source of factions has been the various and unequal distribution of property. Those who hold and those who are without property have ever formed distinct interests in society. Those who are creditors, and those who are debtors, fall under a like discrimination. A landed interest, a manufacturing interest, a mercantile interest, a moneyed interest, with many lesser interests, grow up of necessity in civilized nations, and divide them into different classes, actuated by different sentiments and views. The regulation of these various and interfering interests forms the principal task of modern legislation and involves the spirit of party and faction in the necessary and ordinary operations of government.

No man is allowed to be a judge in his own cause, because his interest would certainly bias his judgment, and, not improbably, corrupt his integrity. With equal, nay with greater reason, a body of men are unfit to be both judges and parties at the same time; yet what are many of the most important acts of legislation but so many judicial determinations, not indeed concerning the rights of single persons, but concerning the rights of large bodies of citizens? And what are the different classes of legislators but advocates and parties to the causes which they determine? Is a law proposed concerning private debts? It is a question to which the creditors are parties on one side and the debtors on the other. Justice ought to hold the balance between them. Yet the parties are, and must be, themselves the judges; and the most numerous party, or in other words, the most powerful faction must be expected to prevail. Shall domestic manufacturers be encouraged, and in what degree, by restrictions on foreign manufacturers? Are questions which would be differently decided by the landed and the manufacturing classes, and probably by neither with a sole regard to justice and the public good. The apportionment of taxes on the various descriptions of property is an act which seems to require the most exact impartiality; yet there is, perhaps, no legislative act in which greater opportunity and temptation are given to a predominant party to trample on the rules of justice. Every shilling with which they overburden the inferior number is a shilling saved to their own pockets.

It is in vain to say that enlightened statesmen will be able to adjust these clashing interests and render them all subservient to the public good. Enlightened statesmen will not always be at the helm. Nor, in many cases, can such an adjustment be made at all without taking into view indirect and remote considerations, which will rarely prevail over the immediate interest which one party may find in disregarding the rights of another or the good of the whole.

The inference to which we are brought is that the causes of faction cannot be removed and that relief is only to be sought in the means of controlling its effects.

If a faction consists of less than a majority, relief is supplied by the republican principle, which enables the majority to defeat its sinister views by regular vote. It may clog the administration, it may convulse the society; but it will be unable to execute and mask its violence under the forms of the Constitution. When a majority is included in a faction, the form of popular government, on the other hand, enables it to sacrifice to its ruling passion or interest both the public good and the rights of other citizens. To secure the public good and private rights against the danger of such a faction, and at the same time to preserve the spirit and the form of popular government, is then the great object to which our inquiries are directed. Let me add that it is the great desideratum by which alone this form of government can be rescued from the opprobrium under which it has so long labored and be recommended to the esteem and adoption of mankind.

By what means is this object attainable? Evidently by one of two only. Either the existence of the same passion or interest in a majority at the same time must be prevented, or the majority, having such coexistent passion or interest, must be rendered, by their number and local situation, unable to concert and carry into effect schemes of oppression. If the impulse and the opportunity be suffered to coincide, we well know that neither moral nor religious motives can be relied on as an adequate control. They are not found to be such on the injustice and violence of individuals, and lose their efficacy in proportion to the number combined together, that is, in proportion as their efficacy becomes needful.

From this view of the subject it may be concluded that a pure democracy, by which I mean a society consisting of a small number of citizens, who assemble and administer the government in person, can admit of no cure for the mischiefs of faction. A common passion or interest will, in almost every case, be felt by a majority of the whole; a communication and concert results from the form of government itself; and there is nothing to check the inducements to sacrifice the weaker party or an obnoxious individual. Hence it is that such democracies have ever been spectacles of turbulence and contention; have ever been found incompatible with personal security or the rights of property; and have in general been as short in their lives as they have been violent in their deaths. Theoretic politicians, who have patronized this species of government, have erroneously supposed that by reducing mankind to a perfect equality in their political rights, they would at the same time be perfectly equalized and assimilated in their possessions, their opinions, and their passions.

A republic, by which I mean a government in which the scheme of representation takes place, opens a different prospect and promises the cure for which we are seeking. Let us examine the points in which it varies from pure democracy, and we shall comprehend both the nature of the cure and the efficacy which it must derive from the Union.

The two great points of difference between a democracy and a republic are: first, the delegation of the government, in the latter, to a small number of citizens elected by the rest; secondly, the greater number of citizens and greater sphere of country over which the latter may be extended.

The effect of the first difference is, on the one hand, to refine and enlarge the public views by passing them through the medium of a chosen body of citizens, whose wisdom may best discern the true interest of their country and whose patriotism and love of justice will be least likely to sacrifice it to temporary or partial considerations. Under such a regulation it may well happen that the public voice, pronounced by the representatives of the people, will be more consonant to the public good than if pronounced by the people themselves, convened for the purpose. On the other hand, the effect may be inverted. Men of factious tempers, of local prejudices, or of sinister designs, may, by intrigue, by corruption, or by other means, first obtain the suffrages, and then betray the interests of the people. The question resulting is, whether small or extensive republics are most favorable to the election of proper guardians of the public weal; and it is clearly decided in favor of the latter by two obvious considerations.

In the first place it is to be remarked that however small the republic may be the representatives must be raised to a certain number in order to guard against the cabals of a few; and that however large it may be they must be limited to a certain number in order to guard against the confusion of a multitude. Hence, the number of representatives in the two cases not being in proportion to that of the constituents, and being proportionally greatest in the small republic, it follows that if the proportion of fit characters be not less in the large than in the small republic, the former will present a greater option, and consequently a greater probability of a fit choice.

In the next place, as each representative will be chosen by a greater number of citizens in the large than in the small republic, it will be more difficult for unworthy candidates to practice with success the vicious arts by which elections are too often carried; and the suffrages of the people being more free, will be more likely to center on men who possess the most attractive merit and the most diffusive and established characters.

It must be confessed that in this, as in most other cases, there is a mean, on both sides of which inconveniencies will be found to lie. By enlarging too much the number of electors, you render the representative too little acquainted with all their local circumstances and lesser interests; as by reducing it too much, you render him unduly attached to these, and too little fit to comprehend and pursue great and national objects. The federal Constitution forms a happy combination in this respect; the great and aggregate interests being referred to the national, the local and particular to the State legislatures.

The other point of difference is the greater number of citizens and extent of territory which may be brought within the compass of republican than of democratic government; and it is this circumstance principally which renders factious combinations less to be dreaded in the former than in the latter. The smaller the society, the fewer probably will be the distinct parties and interests composing it; the fewer the distinct parties and interests, the more frequently will a majority be found of the same party; and the smaller the number of individuals composing a majority, and the smaller the compass within which they are placed, the more easily will they concert and execute their plans of oppression. Extend the sphere and you take in a greater variety of parties and interests; you make it less probable that a majority of the whole will have a common motive to invade the rights of other citizens; or if such a common motive exists, it will be more difficult for all who feel it to discover their own strength and to act in unison with each other. Besides other impediments, it may be remarked that, where there is a consciousness of unjust or dishonorable purposes, communication is always checked by distrust in proportion to the number whose concurrence is necessary.

Hence, it clearly appears that the same advantage which a republic has over a democracy in controlling the effects of faction is enjoyed by a large over a small republic—is enjoyed by the Union over the States composing it. Does this advantage consist in the substitution of representatives whose enlightened views and virtuous sentiments render them superior to local prejudices and to schemes of injustice? It will not be denied that the representation of the Union will be most likely to possess these requisite endowments. Does it consist in the greater security afforded by a greater variety of parties, against the event of any one party being able to outnumber and oppress the rest? In an equal degree does the increased variety of parties comprised within the Union increase this security. Does it, in fine, consist in the greater obstacles opposed to the concert and accomplishment of the secret wishes of an unjust and interested majority? Here again the extent of the Union gives it the most palpable advantage.

The influence of factious leaders may kindle a flame within their particular States but will be unable to spread a general conflagration through the other States. A religious sect may degenerate into a political faction in a part of the Confederacy; but the variety of sects dispersed over the entire face of it must secure the national councils against any danger from that source. A rage for paper money, for an abolition of debts, for an equal division of property, or for any other improper or wicked project, will be less apt to pervade the whole body of the Union than a particular member of it, in the same proportion as such a malady is more likely to taint a particular county or district than an entire State.

In the extent and proper structure of the Union, therefore, we behold a republican remedy for the diseases most incident to republican government. And according to the degree of pleasure and pride we feel in being republicans ought to be our zeal in cherishing the spirit and supporting the character of federalists.

Publius
(James Madison)

#51

To what expedient, then, shall we finally resort, for maintaining in practice the necessary partition of power among the several departments as laid down in the Constitution? The only answer that can be given is that as all these exterior provisions are found to be inadequate the defect must be supplied, by so contriving the interior structure of the government as that its several constituent parts may, by their mutual relations, be the means of keeping each other in their proper places. Without presuming to undertake a full development of this important idea I will hazard a few general observations which may perhaps place it in a clearer light, and enable us to form a more correct judgment of the principles and structure of the government planned by the convention.

In order to lay a due foundation for that separate and distinct exercise of the different powers of government, which to a certain extent is admitted on all hands to be essential to the preservation of liberty, it is evident that each department should have a will of its own; and consequently should be so constituted that the members of each should have as little agency as possible in the appointment of the members of the others. Were this principle rigorously adhered to, it would require that all the appointments for the supreme executive, legislative, and judiciary magistracies should be drawn from the same fountain of authority, the people, through channels having no communication whatever with one another. Perhaps such a plan of constructing the several departments would be less difficult in practice than it may in contemplation appear. Some difficulties, however, and some additional expense would attend the execution of it. Some deviations, therefore, from the principle must be admitted. In the constitution of the judiciary department in particular, it might be inexpedient to insist rigorously on the principle: first, because peculiar qualifications being essential in the members, the primary consideration ought to be to select that mode of choice which best secures these qualifications; second, because the permanent tenure by which the appointments are held in that department must soon destroy all sense of dependence on the authority conferring them.

It is equally evident that the members of each department should be as little dependent as possible on those of the others for the emoluments annexed to their offices. Were the executive magistrate, or the judges, not independent of the legislature in this particular, their independence in every other would be merely nominal.

But the great security against a gradual concentration of the several powers in the same department consists in giving to those who administer each department the necessary constitutional means and personal motives to resist encroachments of the others. The provision for defense must in this, as in all other cases, be made commensurate to the danger of attack. Ambition must be made to counteract ambition. The interest of the man must be connected with the constitutional rights of the place. It may be a reflection on human nature that such devices should be necessary to control the abuses of government. But what is government itself but the greatest of all reflections on human nature? If men were angels, no government would be necessary. If angels were to govern men, neither external nor internal controls on government would be necessary. In framing a government which is to be administered by men over men, the great difficulty lies in this: you must first enable the government to control the governed; and in the next place oblige it to control itself. A dependence on the people is, no doubt, the primary control on the government; but experience has taught mankind the necessity of auxiliary precautions.

This policy of supplying, by opposite and rival interests, the defect of better motives, might be traced through the whole system of human affairs, private as well as public. We see it particularly displayed in all the subordinate distributions of power, where the constant aim is to divide and arrange the several offices in such a manner as that each may be a check on the other—that the private interest of every individual may be a sentinel over the public rights. These inventions of prudence cannot be less requisite in the distribution of the supreme powers of the State.

But it is not possible to give to each department an equal power of self-defense. In republican government, the legislative authority necessarily predominates. The remedy for this inconveniency is to divide the legislature into different branches; and to render them, by different modes of election and different principles of action, as little connected with each other as the nature of their common functions and their common dependence on the society will admit. It may even be necessary to guard against dangerous encroachments by still further precautions. As the weight of the legislative authority requires that it should be thus divided, the weakness of the executive may require, on the other hand, that it should be fortified. An absolute negative on the legislature appears, at first view, to be the natural defense with which the executive magistrate should be armed. But perhaps it would be neither altogether safe nor alone sufficient. On ordinary occasions it might not be exerted with the requisite firmness, and on extraordinary occasions it might be perfidiously abused. May not this defect of an absolute negative be supplied by some qualified connection between this weaker department and the weaker branch of the stronger department, by which the latter may be led to support the constitutional rights of the former, without being too much detached from the rights of its own department?

If the principles on which these observations are founded be just, as I persuade myself they are, and they be applied as a criterion to the several State constitutions, and to the federal Constitution, it will be found that if the latter does not perfectly correspond with them, the former are infinitely less able to bear such a test.

There are, moreover, two considerations particularly applicable to the federal system of America, which place that system in a very interesting point of view.

First. In a single republic, all the power surrendered by the people is submitted to the administration of a single government; and the usurpations are guarded against by a division of the government into distinct and separate departments. In the compound republic of America, the power surrendered by the people is first divided between two distinct governments, and then the portion allotted to each subdivided among distinct and separate departments. Hence a double security arises to the rights of the people. The different governments will control each other, at the same time that each will be controlled by itself.

Second. It is of great importance in a republic not only to guard the society against the oppression of its rulers, but to guard one part of the society against the injustice of the other part. Different interests necessarily exist in different classes of citizens. If a majority be united by a common interest, the rights of the minority will be insecure. There are but two methods of providing against this evil: the one by creating a will in the community independent of the majority—that is, of the society itself; the other, by comprehending in the society so many separate descriptions of citizens as will render an unjust combination of a majority of the whole very improbable, if not impracticable. The first method prevails in all governments possessing an hereditary or self-appointed authority. This, at best, is but a precarious security; because a power independent of the society may as well espouse the unjust views of the major as the rightful interests of the minor party, and may possibly be turned against both parties. The second method will be exemplified in the federal republic of the United States. Whilst all authority in it will be derived from and dependent on the society, the society itself will be broken into so many parts, interests and classes of citizens, that the rights of individuals, or of the minority, will be in little danger from interested combinations of the majority. In a free government the security for civil rights must be the same as that for religious rights. It consists in the one case in the multiplicity of interests, and in the other in the multiplicity of sects. The degree of security in both cases will depend on the number of interests and sects; and this may be presumed to depend on the extent of country and number of people comprehended under the same government. This view of the subject must particularly recommend a proper federal system to all the sincere and considerate friends of republican government, since it shows that in exact proportion as the territory of the Union may be formed into more circumscribed Confederacies, or States, oppressive combinations of a majority will be facilitated; the best security, under the republican forms, for the rights of every class of citizen, will be diminished; and consequently the stability and independence of some member of the government, the only other security, must be proportionally increased. Justice is the end of government. It is the end of civil society. It ever has been and ever will be pursued until it be obtained, or until liberty be lost in the pursuit. In a society under the forms of which the stronger faction can readily unite and oppress the weaker, anarchy may as truly be said to reign as in a state of nature, where the weaker individual is not secured against the violence of the stronger; and as, in the latter state, even the stronger individuals are prompted, by the uncertainty of their condition, to submit to a government which may protect the weak as well as themselves; so, in the former state, will the more powerful factions or parties be gradually induced, by a like motive, to wish for a government which will protect all parties, the weaker as well as the more powerful. It can be little doubted that if the State of Rhode Island was separated from the Confederacy and left to itself, the insecurity of rights under the popular form of government within such narrow limits would be displayed by such reiterated oppressions of factious majorities that some power altogether independent of the people would soon be called for by the voice of the very factions whose misrule had proved the necessity of it. In the extended republic of the United States, and among the great variety of interests, parties, and sects which it embraces, a coalition of a majority of the whole society could seldom take place on any other principles than those of justice and the general good; whilst there being thus less danger to a minor from the will of a major party, there must be less pretext, also, to provide for the security of the former, by introducing into the government a will not dependent on the latter, or, in other words, a will independent of the society itself. It is no less certain than it is important, notwithstanding the contrary opinions which have been entertained, that the larger the society, provided it lie within a practicable sphere, the more duly capable it will be of self-government. And happily for the *republican cause,* the practicable sphere may be carried to a very great extent by a judicious modification and mixture of the *federal principle.*

Publius
(James Madison)

Spanish Equivalents for Important Political Terms

Acid Rain: Lluvia Acida

Acquisitive Model: Modelo Adquisitivo

Actionable: Procesable, Enjuiciable

Action-reaction Syndrome: Sídrome de Acción y Reacción

Actual Malice: Malicia Expresa

Administrative Agency: Agencia Administrativa

Advice and Consent: Consejo y Consentimiento

Affirm: Afirmar

Affirmative Action: Acción Afirmativa

Agenda Setting: Agenda Establecida

Aid to Families with Dependent Children (AFDC): Ayuda para Familias con Niños Dependientes

Amicus Curiae Brief: Tercer persona o grupo no involucrado en el caso, admitido en un juicio para hacer valer el intéres público o el de un grupo social importante.

Anarchy: Anarquía

Anti-Federalists: Anti-Federalistas

Appellate Court: Corte de Apelación

Appointment Power: Poder de Apuntamiento

Appropriation: Apropiación

Aristocracy: Aristocracia

Attentive Public: Público Atento

Australian Ballot: Voto Australiano

Authority: Autoridad

Authorization: Autorización

Bad-Tendency Rule: Regla de Tendencia-mala

"Beauty Contest": Concurso de Belleza

Bicameralism: Bicameralismo

Bicameral Legislature: Legislatura Bicameral

Bill of Rights: Declaración de Derechos

Blanket Primary: Primaria Comprensiva

Block Grants: Concesiones de Bloque

Bureaucracy: Burocracia

Busing: Transporte Público

Cabinet: Gabinete, Consejo de Ministros

Cabinet Department: Departamento del Gabinete

Cadre: El núcleo de activistas de partidos políticos encargados de cumplir las funciones importantes de los partidos políticos americanos.

Canvassing Board: Consejo encargado con la encuesta de una violación.

Capture: Captura, Toma

Casework: Trabajo de Caso

Categorical Grants-in-Aid: Concesiones Categóricas de Ayuda

Caucus: Reunión de Dirigentes

Challenge: Reto

Checks and Balances: Chequeos y Equilibrio

Chief Diplomat: Jefe Diplomático

Chief Executive: Jefe Ejecutivo

Chief Legislator: Jefe Legislador

Chief of Staff: Jefe de Personal

Chief of State: Jefe de Estado

Civil Law: Derecho Civil

Civil Liberties: Libertades Civiles

Civil Rights: Derechos Civiles

Civil Service: Servicio Civil

Civil Service Commission: Comisión de Servicio Civil

Class-action Suit: Demanda en representación de un grupo o clase.

Class Politics: Política de Clase

Clear and Present Danger Test: Prueba de Peligro Claro y Presente

Climate Control: Control de Clima

Closed Primary: Primaria Cerrada

Cloture: Cierre al voto

Coattail Effect: Effecto de Cola de Chaqueta

Cold War: Guerra Fría

Commander in Chief: Comandante en Jefe

Commerce Clause: Clausula de Comercio

Commercial Speech: Discurso Comercial

Common Law: Ley Común, Derecho Consuetudinario

Comparable Worth: Valor Comparable

Compliance: De acuerdo

Concurrent Majority: Mayoría Concurrente

Concurring Opinion: Opinión Concurrente

Confederal System: Sistema Confederal

Confederation: Confederación

Conference Committee: Comité de Conferencia

Consensus: Concenso

Consent of the People: Consentimiento de la Gente

Conservatism: Calidad de Conservador

Conservative Coalition: Coalición Conservadora

Consolidation: Consolidación

Constant Dollars: Dólares Constantes

Constitutional Initiative: Iniciativa Constitucional

Constitutional Power: Poder Constitucional

Containment: Contenimiento

Continuing Resolution: Resolució Contínua

Cooley's Rule: Régla de Cooley

Cooperative Federalism: Federalismo Cooperativo

Corrupt Practices Acts: Leyes Contra Acciones Corruptas

Council of Economic Advisers (CEA): Consejo de Asesores Económicos

Council of Government (COG): Consejo de Gobierno

County: Condado

Credentials Committee: Comité de Credenciales

Criminal Law: Ley Criminal

De Facto Segregation: Segregación de Hecho

De Jure Segregation: Segregación Cotidiana

Defamation of Character: Defamación de Carácter

Democracy: Democracia

Democratic Party: Partido Democratico

Détente: No Spanish equivalent.

Dillon's Rule: Régla de Dillon

Diplomacy: Diplomácia

Direct Democracy: Democracia Directa

Direct Primary: Primaria Directa

Direct Technique: Técnica Directa

Discharge Petition: Petición de Descargo

Dissenting Opinion: Opinión Disidente

Divisive Opinion: Opinión Divisiva

Domestic Policy: Principio Político Doméstico

Dual Citizenship: Ciudadanía Dual

Dual Federalism: Federalismo Dual

Economic Aid: Ayuda Económica

Economic Regulation: Regulación Económica

Elastic Clause, or Necessary and Proper Clause: Cláusula Flexible o Cláusula Propia Necesaria

Elector: Elector

Electoral College: Colegio Electoral

Electronic Media: Media Electronica

Elite: Elite (el selecto)

Elite Theory: Teoría Elitista (de lo selecto)

Emergency Power: Poder de Emergencia

Enumerated Power: Poder Enumerado

Environmental Impact Statement (EIS): Afirmación de Impacto Ambiental

Equal Employment Opportunity Commission (EEOC): Comisión de Igualdad de Oportunidad en el Empleo

Equality: Igualdad

Equalization: Igualación

Era of Good Feeling: Era de Buen Sentimiento

Era of Personal Politics: Era de Política Personal

Establishment Clause: Cláusula de Establecimiento

Euthanasia: Eutanasia

Exclusionary Rule: Régla de Exclusión

Executive Agreement: Acuerdo Ejecutivo

Executive Budget: Presupuesto Ejecutivo

Executive Office of the President (EOP): Oficina Ejecutiva del Presidente

Executive Order: Orden Ejecutivo

Executive Privilege: Privilegio Ejecutivo

Expressed Power: Poder Expresado

Extradite: Entregar por Extradición

Faction: Facción

Fairness Doctrine: Doctrina de Justicia

Fall Review: Revision de Otoño

Federalist: Federalista

Federal Mandate: Mandato Federal

Federal Open Market Committee (FOMC): Comité Federal de Libre Mercado

Federal Register: Registro Federal

Federal System: Sistema Federal

Federalists: Federalistas

Fighting Words: Palabras de Provocación

Filibuster: Obstrucción de iniciativas de ley

Fireside Chat: Charla de Hogar

First Budget Resolution: Resolució Primera Presupuesta

First Continental Congress: Primér Congreso Continental

Fiscal Policy: Político Fiscal

Fiscal Year (FY): Año Fiscal

Fluidity: Fluidez

Food Stamps: Estampillas para Comida

Foreign Policy: Política Extranjera

Foreign Policy Process: Proceso de Política Extranjera

Franking: Franqueando

Fraternity: Fraternidad

Free Exercise Clause: Cláusula de Ejercicio Libre

Full Faith and Credit Clause: Cláusula de Completa Fé y Crédito

Functional Consolidation: Consolidación Funcional

Gag Order: Orden de Silencio

Garbage Can Model: Modelo Bote de Basura

Gender Gap: Brecha de Género

General Law City: Régla General Urbana

General Sales Tax: Impuesto General de Ventas

Generational Effect: Efecto Generacional

Gerrymandering: División arbitraria de los distritos electorales con fines políticos.

Government: Gobierno

Government Corporation: Corporación Gubernamental

Government in the Sunshine Act: Gobierno en la acta: Luz del Sol

Grandfather Clause: Cláusula del Abuelo

Grand Jury: Gran Jurado

Great Compromise: Grán Acuerdo de Negociación

Hatch Act (Political Activities Act): Acta Hatch (acta de actividades políticas)

Hecklers' Veto: Veto de Abuchamiento

Home Rule City: Régla Urbana

Horizontal Federalism: Federalismo Horizontal

Hyperpluralism: Hiperpluralismo

Ideologue: Ideólogo

Ideology: Ideología

Image Building: Construcción de Imágen

Impeachment: Acción Penal Contra un Funcionario Público

Inalienable Rights: Derechos Inalienables

Income Transfer: Transferencia de Ingresos

Incorporation Theory: Teoría de Incorporación

Independent: Independiente

Independent Candidate: Candidato Independiente

Independent Executive Agency: Agencia Ejecutiva Independiente

Independent Regulatory Agency: Agencia Regulatoria Independiente

Indirect Technique: Técnica Indirecta

Inherent Power: Poder Inherente

Initiative: Iniciativa

Injunction: Injunción, Prohibición Judicial

In-kind Subsidy: Subsidio de Clase

Institution: Institución

Instructed Delegate: Delegado con Instrucciones

Intelligence Community: Comunidad de Inteligencia

Intensity: Intensidad

Interest Group: Grupo de Interés

Interposition: Interposición

Interstate Compact: Compacto Interestatal

Iron Curtain: Cortina de Acero

Iron Triangle: Triágulo de Acero

Isolationist Foreign Policy: Política Extranjera de Aislamiento

Issue Voting: Voto Temático

Item Veto: Artículo de Veto

Jim Crow Laws: No Spanish equivalent.

Joint Committee: Comité Mancomunado

Judicial Activism: Activismo Judicial

Judicial Implementation: Implementación Judicial

Judicial Restraint: Restricción Judicial

Judicial Review: Revisión Judicial

Jurisdiction: Jurisdicción

Justiciable Dispute: Disputa Judiciaria

Justiciable Question: Pregunta Justiciable

Keynesian Economics: Economía Keynesiana

Kitchen Cabinet: Gabinete de Cocina

Labor Movement: Movimiento Laboral

Latent Public Opinion: Opinión Pública Latente

Lawmaking: Hacedores de Ley

Legislative History: Historia Legislativa

Legislative Initiative: Iniciativa de legislación

Legislative Veto: Veto Legislativo

Legislature: Legislatura

Legitimacy: Legitimidad

Libel: Libelo, Difamación Escrita

Liberalism: Liberalismo

Liberty: Libertad

Limited Government: Gobierno Limitado

Line Organization: Organización de Linea

Literacy Test: Exámen de alfabetización

Litigate: Litigar

Lobbying: Cabildeo

Logrolling: Práctica legislativa que consiste en incluir en un mismo proyecto de ley temas de diversa ídole.

Loophole: Hueco Legal, Escapatoria

Madisonian Model: Modelo Madisónico

Majority: Mayoría

Majority Floor Leader: Líder Mayoritario de Piso

Majority Leader of the House: Líder Mayoritario de la Casa

Majority Opinion: Opinión Mayoritaria

Majority Rule: Régla de Mayoría

Managed News: Noticias Manipuladas

Mandatory Retirement: Retiro Mandatorio

Matching Funds: Fondos Combinados

Material Incentive: Incentivo Material

Media: Media

Media Access: Acceso de Media

Merit System: Sistema de Mérito

Military-Industrial Complex: Complejo Industriomilitar

Minority Floor Leader: Líder Minoritario de Piso

Minority Leader of the House: Líder Minorial del Cuerpo Legislativo

Monetary Policy: Política Monetaria

Monopolistic Model: Modelo Monopólico

Monroe Doctrine: Doctrina Monroe

Moral Idealism: Idealismo Moral

Municipal Home Rule: Régla Municipal

Narrow Casting: Mensaje Dirigído

National Committee: Comité Nacional

National Convention: Convención Nacional

National Politics: Politica Nacional

National Security Council (NSC): Concilio de Seguridad Nacional

National Security Policy: Política de Seguridad Nacional

Natural Aristocracy: Aristocracia Natural

Natural Rights: Derechos Naturales

Necessaries: Necesidades

Negative Constituents: Constituyentes Negativos

New England Town: Pueblo de Nueva Inglaterra

New Federalism: Federalismo Nuevo

Nullification: Nulidad, Anulación

Office-Block, or Massachusetts, Ballot: Cuadro-Oficina, o Massachusetts, Voto

Office of Management and Budget (OMB): Oficina de Administració y Presupuesto

Oligarchy: Oligarquía

Ombudsman: Funcionario que representa al ciudadano ante el gobierno.

Open Primary: Primaria Abierta

Opinion: Opinión

Opinion Leader: Líder de Opinión

Opinion Poll: Encuesta, Conjunto de Opinión

Oral Arguments: Argumentos Orales

Oversight: Inadvertencia, Omisión

Paid-for-Political Announcement: Anuncios Políticos Pagados

Pardon: Perdón

Party-Column, or Indiana, Ballot: Partido-Columna, o Indiana, Voto

Party Identification: Identificación de Partido

Party Identifier: Identificador de Partido

Party-in-Electorate: Partido Electoral

Party-in-Government: Partido en Gobierno

Party Organization: Organización de Partido

Party Platform: Plataforma de Partido

Patronage: Patrocinio

Peer Group: Grupo de Contemporáneos

Pendleton Act (Civil Service Reform Act): Acta Pendleton (Acta de Reforma al Servicio Civil)

Personal Attack Rule: Regla de Ataque Personal

Petit Jury: Jurado Ordinario

Pluralism: Pluralismo

Plurality: Pluralidad

Pocket Veto: Veto de Bolsillo

Police Power: Poder Policiaco

Policy Trade-offs: Intercambio de Políticas

Political Action Committee (PAC): Comité de Acción Política

Political Consultant: Consultante Político

Political Culture: Cultura Política

Political Party: Partido Político

Political Question: Pregunta Política

Political Realism: Realismo Político

Political Socialization: Socialización Política

Political Tolerance: Tolerancia Política

Political Trust: Confianza Política

Politico: Político

Politics: Política

Poll Tax: Impuesto Sobre el Sufragio

Poll Watcher: Observador de Encuesta

Popular Sovereignty: Soberanía Popular

Power: Poder

Precedent: Precedente

Preferred-Position Test: Prueba de Posición Preferida

Presidential Primary: Primaria Presidencial

President Pro Tempore: Presidente Provisoriamente

Press Secretary: Secretaría de Prensa

Prior Restraint: Restricción Anterior

Privileges and Immunities: Privilégios e Imunidades

Privatization, or Contracting Out: Privatización

Property: Propiedad

Property Tax: Impuesto de Propiedad

Public Agenda: Agenda Pública

Public Debt Financing: Financiamiento de Deuda Pública

Public Debt, or National Debt: Deuda Pública o Nacional

Public Interest: Interes Público

Public Opinion: Opinión Pública

Purposive Incentive: Incentivo de Propósito

Ratification: Ratificación

Rational Ignorance Effect: Effecto de Ignorancia Racional

Reapportionment: Redistribución

Recall: Suspender

Recognition Power: Poder de Reconocimiento

Recycling: Reciclaje

Redistricting: Redistrictificación

Referendum: Referédum

Registration: Registración

Regressive Tax: Impuestos Regresivos

Relevance: Pertinencia

Remand: Reenviar

Representation: Representación

Representative Assembly: Asamblea Representativa

Representative Democracy: Democracia Representativa

Reprieve: Trequa, Suspensión

Republic: República

Republican Party: Partido Republicano

Resulting Powers: Poderes Resultados

Reverse: Cambiarse a lo Contrario

Reverse Discrimination: Discriminación Reversiva

Rule of Four: Régla de Cuatro

Rules Committee: Comité Regulador

Run-off Primary: Primaria Residual

Safe Seat: Asiento Seguro

Sampling Error: Error de Encuesta

Secession: Secesión

Second Budget Resolution: Resolución Segunda Presupuestal

Second Continental Congress: Segundo Congreso Continental

Sectional Politics: Política Seccional

Segregation: Segregación

Select Committee: Comité Selecto

Selectperson: Persona Selecta

Senatorial Courtesy: Cortesia Senatorial

Seniority System: Sistema Señiorial

Separate-but-Equal Doctrine: Separados pero Iguales

Separation of Powers: Separación de Poderes

Service Sector: Sector de Servicio

Sex Discrimination: Discriminación Sexual

Sexual Harassment: Acosamiento Sexual

Slander: Difamación Oral, Calumnia

Sliding-Scale Test: Prueba Escalonada

Social Movement: Movimiento Social

Social Security: Seguridad Social

Socioeconomic Status: Estado Socioeconómico

Solidary Incentive: Incentivo de Solideridad

Solid South: Súr Sólido

Sound Bite: Mordida de Sonido

Soviet Bloc: Bloque Soviético

Speaker of the House: Vocero de la Casa

Spin: Girar/Giro

Spin Doctor: Doctor en Giro

Spin-off Party: Partido Estático

Spoils System: Sistema de Despojos

Spring Review: Revisión de Primavera

Stability: Estabilidad

Standing Committee: Comité de Sostenimiento

Stare Decisis: El principio característico del ley comú por el cual los precedentes jurisprudenciales tienen fuerza obligatoria, no sólo entre las partes, sino tambien para casos sucesivos análogos.

State: Estado

State Central Committee: Comité Central del Estado

State of the Union Message: Mensaje Sobre el Estado de la Unión

Statutory Power: Poder Estatorial

Strategic Arms Limitation Treaty (SALT I): Tratado de Limitación de Armas Estratégicas

Subpoena: Orden de Testificación

Subsidy: Subsidio

Suffrage: Sufrágio

Sunset Legislation: Legislación Sunset

Superdelegate: Líder de partido o oficial elegido quien tiene el derecho de votar.

Supplemental Security Income (SSI): Ingresos de Seguridad Suplementaria

Supremacy Clause: Cláusula de Supremacia

Supremacy Doctrine: Doctrina de Supremacia

Symbolic Speech: Discurso Simbólico

Technical Assistance: Asistencia Técnica

Third Party: Tercer Partido

Third-Party Candidate: Candidato de Tercer Partido

Ticket Splitting: División de Boletos

Totalitarian Regime: Régimen Totalitario

Town Manager System: Sistema de Administrador Municipal

Town Meeting: Junta Municipal

Township: Municipio

Tracking Poll: Seguimiento de Encuesta

Trial Court: Tribunal de Primera

Truman Doctrine: Doctrina Truman

Trustee: Depositario

Twelfth Amendment: Doceava Enmienda

Twenty-fifth Amendment: Veinticincoava Enmienda

Two-Party System: Sistema de Dos Partidos

Unanimous Opinion: Opinión Unánime

Underground Economy: Economía Subterráea

Unicameral Legislature: Legislatura Unicameral

Unincorporated Area: Area no Incorporada

Unitary System: Sistema Unitario

Unit Rule: Régla de Unidad

Universal Suffrage: Sufragio Universal

U.S. Treasury Bond: Bono de la Tesoreria de E.U.A.

Veto Message: Comunicado de Veto

Voter Turnout: Renaimiento de Votantes

War Powers Act: Acta de Poderes de Guerra

Washington Community: Comunidad de Washington

Weberian Model: Modelo Weberiano

Whip: Látigo

Whistleblower: Privatización o Contratista

White House Office: Oficina de la Casa Blanca

White House Press Corps: Cuerpo de Prensa de la Casa Blanca

White Primary: Sufragio en Elección Primaria/Blancos Solamente

Writ of Certiorari: Prueba de certeza; orden emitida por el tribunal de apelaciones para que el tribunal inferior dé lugar a la apelación.

Writ of Habeas Corpus: Prueba de Evidencia Concreta

Writ of Mandamus: Un mandato por la corte para que un acto se lleve a cabo.

Yellow Journalism: Amarillismo Periodístico

Glossary

A

ABSOLUTE MONARCHY ● A form of monarchy in which the monarch has complete and unlimited power as a matter of divine right.

ACTION-REACTION SYNDROME ● For every government action, there will be a reaction by the public. The government then takes a further action to counter the public's reaction—and the cycle begins again.

ADJUDICATE ● To render a judicial decision. In regard to administrative law, the process in which an administrative law judge hears and decides issues that arise when an agency charges a person or firm with violating a law or regulation enforced by the agency.

ADMINISTRATIVE AGENCY ● A federal or state government agency established to perform a specific function. Administrative agencies are authorized by legislative acts to make and enforce rules to administer and enforce the acts.

ADMINISTRATIVE LAW JUDGE ● One who presides over an administrative agency hearing and who has the power to conduct legal hearings and make legal determinations.

ADMINISTRATIVE LAW ● The body of law created by administrative agencies (in the form of rules, regulations, orders, and decisions) in order to carry out their duties and responsibilities.

ADMINISTRATIVE PROCESS ● The functions—including rulemaking, enforcement, and adjudication—undertaken by administrative agencies in administering the law.

AFFIRMATIVE ACTION ● A policy calling for the establishment of programs that involve giving preference, in jobs and college admissions, to members of groups that have been discriminated against in the past.

AGENDA SETTING ● The first stage of the policymaking process, which consists of getting an issue on the political agenda to be addressed by Congress.

AGENTS OF POLITICAL SOCIALIZATION ● People and institutions that influence the political views of others.

AMERICAN CREED ● The principles set forth in a document written by William Tyler Page in 1917 and based on the Declaration of Independence.

ANTI-FEDERALISTS ● A political group that opposed the adoption of the Constitution because of the document's centralist tendencies and because it did not include a bill of rights.

ANTITRUST LAW ● The body of law that attempts to support free competition in the marketplace by curbing monopolistic and unfair trade practices.

APPELLATE COURT ● A court having appellate jurisdiction that normally does not hear evidence or testimony but reviews the transcript of the trial court's proceedings, other records relating to the case, and the attorneys' respective arguments as to why the trial court's decision should or should not stand.

APPORTIONMENT ● The distribution of House seats among the states on the basis of their respective populations.

APPROPRIATION ● A part of the congressional budgeting process that involves determining how many dollars will be spent in a given year on a particular set of government activities.

ARTICLES OF CONFEDERATION ● The nation's first national constitution, which established a national form of government following the American Revolution. The articles provided for a confederal form of government in which the central government had few powers.

ATTACK AD ● A negative political advertisement that attacks the character of an opposing candidate.

AUSTRALIAN BALLOT ● A secret ballot that is prepared, distributed, and counted by government officials at public expense; used by all states in the United States since 1888.

AUTHORITY ● The ability to exercise power, such as the power to make and enforce laws, legitimately.

AUTHORIZATION ● A part of the congressional budgeting process that involves the creation of the legal basis for government programs.

AUTOCRACY ● A form of government in which the power and authority of the government are in the hands of a single person.

B

BIASED SAMPLE ● A poll sample that does not accurately represent the population.

BICAMERAL LEGISLATURE ● A legislature made up of two chambers, or parts. The United States has a bicameral legislature, composed of the House of Representatives and the Senate.

BILL OF ATTAINDER ● A legislative act that inflicts punishment on particular persons or groups without granting them the right to a trial.

BILL OF RIGHTS ● The first ten amendments to the U.S. Constitution. They list the freedoms—such as the freedoms of speech, press, and religion—that a person enjoys and that cannot be infringed on by the government.

BLANKET PRIMARY ● A "wide open" primary in which each voter receives a single ballot listing each party's candidates for each nomination.

BLOCK GRANT ● A federal grant given to a state for a broad area, such as criminal justice or mental health programs.

BUREAUCRACY ● A large, complex, hierarchically structured administrative organization that carries out specific functions.

BUREAUCRAT ● An individual who works in a bureaucracy; as generally used, the term refers to a government employee.

BUSING ● The transportation of public school students by bus to schools physically outside their neighborhoods to eliminate school segregation based on residential patterns.

C

CABINET ● An advisory group selected by the president to assist with decision making. Traditionally, the cabinet has consisted of the heads of the executive departments and other officers whom the president may choose to appoint.

CAMPAIGN MANAGER ● The person who coordinates and plans a political candidate's campaign and the strategy that will be used for it.

CASE LAW ● The rules of law announced in court decisions. Case law includes the aggregate of reported cases that interpret judicial precedents, statutes, regulations, and constitutional provisions.

CATEGORICAL GRANT ● A federal grant targeted for a specific purpose as defined by federal law.

CAUCUS ● A meeting held by party leaders to choose political candidates. The caucus system of nominating candidates was eventually replaced by nominating conventions and, later, by direct primaries.

CHECKS AND BALANCES ● A major principle of American government in which each of the three branches is given the means to check (to restrain or balance) the actions of the others.

CHIEF DIPLOMAT ● The role of the president in recognizing and interacting with foreign governments.

CHIEF EXECUTIVE ● The head of the executive branch of government. In the United States, the president is the head of the executive branch of the federal government.

CHIEF OF STAFF ● The person who directs the operations of the White House Office and who advises the president on important matters.

CHIEF OF STATE ● The person who serves as the ceremonial head of a country's government and represents that country to the rest of the world.

CIVIL DISOBEDIENCE ● The deliberate and public act of refusing to obey laws thought to be unjust.

CIVIL LAW ● The branch of law that spells out the duties that individuals in society owe to other persons or to their governments, excluding the duty not to commit crimes.

CIVIL LIBERTIES ● Individual rights protected by the Constitution against the powers of the government.

CIVIL RIGHTS ● The rights of all Americans to equal treatment under the law, as provided for by the Fourteenth Amendment to the Constitution.

CIVIL RIGHTS MOVEMENT ● The movement in the 1950s and 1960s, by minorities and concerned whites, to end racial segregation.

CIVIL SERVICE ● Employees of the civil government, or civil servants.

CLASSICAL LIBERALISM ● Liberalism in its traditional form. Like modern liberalism, classical liberalism stressed political democracy, constitutionally guaranteed civil liberties, political equality, free political competition, and separation of church and state. Unlike modern liberalism, classical liberalism opposed government intervention in the economy and stressed free enterprise, individual initiative, and free trade.

CLOSED PRIMARY ● A primary in which only party members can vote to choose that party's candidates.

CLOTURE ● A method of ending debate in the Senate and bringing the matter under consideration to a vote by the entire chamber.

COALITION ● An alliance of individuals or groups with a variety of interests and opinions who join together to support all or part of a political party's platform.

COLD WAR ● The war of words, warnings, and ideologies between the Soviet Union and the United States that lasted from the late 1940s through the early 1990s.

COLLECTIVE SECURITY ● A national defense and security policy that involved the formation of mutual defense alliances, such as the North Atlantic Treaty Organization, with other nations.

COLONIAL EMPIRE ● A group of colonized nations that are under the rule of a single imperial power.

COMMANDER IN CHIEF • The supreme commander of the military forces of the United States.

COMMERCE CLAUSE • The clause in Article I, Section 8, of the Constitution that gives Congress the power to regulate interstate commerce (commerce involving more than one state).

COMMERCIAL SPEECH • Advertising statements that describe products. Commercial speech receives less protection under the First Amendment than ordinary speech.

COMMON LAW • The body of law developed from judicial decisions in English and U.S. courts, not attributable to a legislature.

COMMUNIST BLOC • The group of Eastern European nations that fell under the control of the Soviet Union following World War II.

COMPETITIVE FEDERALISM • A model of federalism devised by Thomas R. Dye in which state and local governments compete for businesses and citizens, who in effect "vote with their feet" by moving to jurisdictions that offer a competitive advantage.

CONCURRENT MAJORITY • A principle advanced by John C. Calhoun that states that democratic decisions should be made only with the agreement of all segments of society affected by the decisions. Without their agreement, a decision should not be binding on those whose interests it violates.

CONCURRENT POWERS • Powers held by both the federal and state governments in a federal system.

CONCURRING OPINION • A statement written by a judge or justice who agrees (concurs) with the court's decision, but for reasons different from those in the majority opinion.

CONFEDERAL SYSTEM • A league of independent sovereign states, joined together by a central government that has only limited powers over them.

CONFEDERATION • A league of independent states that are united only for the purpose of achieving common goals.

CONFERENCE COMMITTEE • A temporary committee that is formed when the two chambers of Congress pass separate versions of the same bill. The conference committee, which consists of members from both the House and the Senate, works out a compromise form of the bill.

CONFERENCE REPORT • A report submitted by a congressional conference committee after it has drafted a single version of a bill.

CONFERENCE • In regard to the Supreme Court, a private meeting of the justices in which they present their arguments with respect to a case under consideration.

CONGRESSIONAL DISTRICT • The geographical area that is served by one representative in Congress.

CONSENSUS • A general agreement among the citizenry (often defined as an agreement among 75 percent or more of the people) on matters of public policy.

CONSERVATISM • A set of beliefs that includes a limited role for the national government in helping individuals, support for traditional values and lifestyles, and a cautious response to change.

CONSERVATIVE • One who subscribes to a set of political beliefs that includes a limited role for government, support for traditional values, and a preference for the status quo.

CONSTITUTIONAL CONVENTION • The convention (meeting) of delegates from the states that was held in Philadelphia in 1787 for the purpose of amending the Articles of Confederation. In fact, the delegates wrote a new constitution (the U.S. Constitution) that established a federal form of government to replace the governmental system that had been created by the Articles of Confederation.

CONSTITUTIONAL LAW • Law based on the U.S. Constitution and the constitutions of the various states.

CONSTITUTIONAL MONARCHY • A form of monarchy in which the monarch shares governmental power with elected lawmakers; the monarch's power is limited, or checked, by other government leaders and perhaps by a constitution or a bill of rights.

CONTAINMENT • A U.S. policy designed to contain the spread of communism by offering military and economic aid to threatened nations.

CONTINUING RESOLUTION • A resolution, which Congress passes when it is unable to pass a complete budget by October 1, that enables the executive agencies to keep on doing whatever they were doing the previous year with the same amount of funding.

COOPERATIVE FEDERALISM • The theory that the states and the federal government should cooperate in solving problems.

COUNCIL OF ECONOMIC ADVISERS (CEA) • A three-member council created in 1946 to advise the president on economic matters.

CREDENTIALS COMMITTEE • A committee of each national political party that evaluates the claims of national party convention delegates to be the legitimate representatives of their states.

CRIMINAL LAW • The branch of law that defines and governs actions that constitute crimes. Generally, criminal law has to do with wrongful actions committed against society for which society demands redress.

CYBER DEMONSTRATION • A labor protest, or demonstration, organized and executed by the use of e-mail communications among labor union members.

D

DE FACTO SEGREGATION • Racial segregation that occurs not as a result of deliberate intentions but because of past social and economic conditions and residential patterns.

DE JURE SEGREGATION • Racial segregation that is legally sanctioned—that is, segregation that occurs because of laws or decisions by government agencies.

DELEGATE • A person selected to represent the people of one geographical area at a party convention.

DEMOCRACY • A system of government in which the people have ultimate political authority. The word is derived from the Greek demos (people) and kratia (rule).

DEREGULATION • The removal of regulatory restraints on business.

DETERRENCE • A policy of building up military strength for the purpose of discouraging (deterring) military attacks by other nations; the policy of "building weapons for peace" that supported the arms race between the United States and the Soviet Union during the Cold War.

DEVOLUTION • In the context of American politics, the transfer to the states of some of the responsibilities assumed by the national government since the 1930s.

DICTATORSHIP • A form of government in which absolute power is exercised by a single person who has usually obtained his or her power by the use of force.

DIPLOMAT • In regard to international relations, a person who represents one country in dealing with representatives of another country.

DIRECT DEMOCRACY • A system of government in which political decisions are made by the people themselves rather than by elected representatives. This form of government was widely practiced in ancient Greece.

DIRECT PRIMARY • An election held within each of the two major parties—Democratic and Republican—to choose the party's candidates for the general election.

DISSENTING OPINION • A written opinion by a judge or justice who disagrees with the majority opinion.

DIVERSITY OF CITIZENSHIP • A basis for federal court jurisdiction over a lawsuit that arises when (1) the parties in the lawsuit live in different states or when one of the parties is a foreign government or a foreign citizen, and (2) the amount in controversy is more than $75,000.

DIVINE RIGHT THEORY • A theory that the right to rule by a king or queen was derived directly from God rather than from the consent of the people.

DIVISION OF POWERS • A basic principle of federalism established by the U.S. Constitution. In a federal system, powers are divided between units of government (such as the federal and state governments).

DOMESTIC POLICY • Public policy concerning issues within a national unit, such as national policy concerning welfare or crime.

DOUBLE JEOPARDY • To prosecute a person twice for the same criminal offense; prohibited by the Fifth Amendment in all but a few circumstances.

DUAL FEDERALISM • A system of government in which both the federal and state governments maintain diverse but sovereign powers.

DUE PROCESS CLAUSE • The constitutional guarantee, set out in the Fifth and Fourteenth Amendments, that the government will not illegally or arbitrarily deprive a person of life, liberty, or property.

DUE PROCESS OF LAW • The requirement that the government use fair, reasonable, and standard procedures whenever it takes any legal action against an individual; required by the Fifth and Fourteenth Amendments.

E

EASY-MONEY POLICY • A monetary policy that involves stimulating the economy by expanding the rate of growth of the money supply. An easy-money policy supposedly will lead to lower interest rates and induce consumers to spend more and producers to invest more.

ECONOMIC POLICY • All actions taken by the national government to smooth out the ups and downs in the nation's overall business activity.

ECONOMIC REGULATION • Government regulation of natural monopolies and inherently noncompetitive industries.

ELECTOR • A member of the electoral college.

ELECTORAL COLLEGE • The group of electors who are selected by the voters in each state to officially elect the president and vice president. The number of electors in each state is equal to the number of that state's representatives in both chambers of Congress.

ELECTORATE • All of the citizens eligible to vote in a given election.

ELECTRONIC MEDIA • Communication channels that involve electronic transmissions, such as radio, television, and, to an extent, the Internet.

ENABLING LEGISLATION • A law enacted by a legislature to establish an administrative agency; enabling legislation normally specifies the name, purpose, composition, and powers of the agency being created.

ENCRYPTION SOFTWARE • Computer programs that enable the user to encode ("encrypt") data to prevent access to the data by unauthorized persons.

ENTITLEMENT PROGRAM • A government program (such as Social Security) that allows, or entitles, a certain class of people (such as the elderly) to receive special benefits. Entitlement programs operate under open-ended budget authorizations that, in effect, place no limits on how much can be spent.

EQUAL EMPLOYMENT OPPORTUNITY • A goal of the 1964 Civil Rights Act to end employment discrimination based on race, color, religion, gender, or national origin and to promote equal job opportunities for all individuals.

EQUAL PROTECTION CLAUSE • Section 1 of the Fourteenth Amendment, which states that no state shall "deny to any person within its jurisdiction the equal protection of the laws."

EQUALITY • A concept that holds, at a minimum, that all people are entitled to equal protection under the law.

ESPIONAGE • The practice of spying, on behalf of a foreign power, to obtain information about government plans and activities.

ESTABLISHMENT CLAUSE • The section of the First Amendment that prohibits Congress from passing laws "respecting an establishment of religion." Issues concerning the establishment clause often center on prayer in public schools, the teaching of fundamentalist theories of creation, and government aid to parochial schools.

EVOLUTIONARY THEORY • A theory that holds that government evolved gradually over time as families first joined together into clans, then into tribes, and then into a larger, more formal unit.

EX POST FACTO **LAW** • A criminal law that punishes individuals for committing an act that was legal when the act was committed but that has since become a crime.

EXCLUSIONARY RULE • A criminal procedural rule requiring that any illegally obtained evidence will not be admissible in court. The rule is based on Supreme Court interpretations of the Fourth and Fourteenth Amendments.

EXECUTIVE AGREEMENT • A binding international agreement, or pact, that is made between the president and another head of state and that does not require Senate approval.

EXECUTIVE OFFICE OF THE PRESIDENT (EOP) • A group of staff agencies that assist the president in carrying out major duties. Franklin D. Roosevelt established the EOP in 1939 to cope with the increased responsibilities brought on by the Great Depression.

EXECUTIVE ORDER • A presidential order to carry out a policy or policies described in a law passed by Congress.

EXPRESSED POWERS • Constitutional or statutory powers that are expressly provided for by the Constitution or by congressional laws.

EXTRAORDINARY MAJORITY • More than a mere majority; typically, an extraordinary majority consists of two-thirds or three-fifths of the voting body (such as a legislature).

F

FACTION • A group or clique within a larger group.

FEDERAL MANDATE • A requirement in federal legislation that forces states and municipalities to comply with certain rules.

FEDERAL OPEN MARKET COMMITTEE (FOMC) • The most important body within the Federal Reserve System; the FOMC decides how monetary policy should be carried out by the Federal Reserve.

FEDERAL QUESTION • A question that pertains to the U.S. Constitution, acts of Congress, or treaties. A federal question provides a basis for federal court jurisdiction.

FEDERAL SYSTEM • A form of government in which a written constitution provides for a division of powers between a central government and several regional governments. In the United States, the division of powers between the national government and the fifty states is established by the Constitution.

FEDERALISTS • A political group, led by Alexander Hamilton and John Adams, that supported the adoption of the Constitution and the creation of a federal form of government.

"FIGHTING WORDS" • Words that, when uttered by a public speaker, are so inflammatory that they could provoke the average listener to violence.

FILIBUSTERING • The Senate tradition of unlimited debate, undertaken for the purpose of preventing action on a bill.

FIRST BUDGET RESOLUTION • A budget resolution, which is supposed to be passed in May, that sets overall revenue goals and spending targets for the next fiscal year, which begins on October 1.

FIRST CONTINENTAL CONGRESS • The first gathering of delegates from twelve of the thirteen colonies, held in 1774.

FISCAL FEDERALISM • The power of the national government to influence state policies through grants.

FISCAL POLICY • The use of changes in government expenditures and taxes to alter national economic variables, such as the employment rate and price stability.

FISCAL YEAR • A twelve-month period that is established for bookkeeping or accounting purposes. The government's fiscal year runs from October 1 through September 30.

FORCE THEORY ● A theory that holds that government originated when strong persons or groups conquered territories and forced everyone living in those territories to submit to their will.

FOREIGN POLICY ● A systematic and general plan that guides a country's attitudes and actions toward the rest of the world. Foreign policy includes all of the economic, military, commercial, and diplomatic positions and actions that a nation takes in its relationships with other countries.

FREE EXERCISE CLAUSE ● The provision of the First Amendment stating that the government cannot pass laws "prohibiting the free exercise" of religion. Free exercise issues often concern religious practices that conflict with established laws.

FUNDAMENTAL ORDERS OF CONNECTICUT ● America's first written constitution, developed by some of the Pilgrims who left the Massachusetts Bay Colony and settled in what is now Connecticut. The document provided for an assembly of elected representatives from each town and for the popular election of a governor and judges.

FUNDAMENTAL RIGHT ● A basic right of all Americans, such as all First Amendment rights. Any law or action that prevents some group of persons from exercising a fundamental right will be subject to the "strict scrutiny" standard, under which the law or action must be necessary to promote a compelling state interest and must be narrowly tailored to meet that interest.

G

GENERAL ELECTION ● A regularly scheduled election to elect the U.S. president, vice president, and senators and representatives in Congress; general elections are held in even-numbered years on the first Tuesday after the first Monday in November.

GERRYMANDERING ● The drawing of a legislative district's boundaries in such a way as to maximize the influence of a certain group or political party.

GLASS CEILING ● The often subtle obstacles to advancement faced by professional women in the workplace.

GOVERNMENT ● The individuals and institutions that make society's rules and that also possess the power and authority to enforce those rules.

GOVERNMENT CORPORATION ● An agency of the government that is run as a business enterprise. Such agencies engage in primarily commercial activities, produce revenues, and require greater flexibility than that permitted in most government agencies.

GREAT COMPROMISE ● A plan for a bicameral legislature in which one chamber would be based on population and the other chamber would represent each state equally.

The plan, also known as the Connecticut Compromise, resolved the small-state/large-state controversy.

I

IDEOLOGUE ● An individual who holds very strong political opinions.

IMPEACHMENT ● A formal criminal proceeding against a public official for misconduct or wrongdoing in office.

IMPLIED POWERS ● The powers of the federal government that are implied by the expressed powers in the Constitution, particularly in Article I, Section 8.

INCOME REDISTRIBUTION ● The transfer of income from one group to another; income is taken from some people through taxation and given to others.

INDEPENDENT EXECUTIVE AGENCY ● A federal bureaucratic agency that is not located within a cabinet department.

INDEPENDENT EXPENDITURE ● An expenditure for activities that are independent from (not coordinated with) those of a political candidate or a political party.

INDEPENDENT REGULATORY AGENCY ● A federal bureaucratic organization that is responsible for creating and implementing rules that regulate private activity and protect the public interest in a particular sector of the economy.

INHERENT POWERS ● The powers of the national government that, although not expressly granted by the Constitution, are necessary to ensure the nation's integrity and survival as a political unit. Inherent powers include the power to make treaties and the power to wage war or make peace.

INITIATIVE ● A procedure by which voters can propose a change in state and local laws, including state constitutions, by means of gathering signatures on a petition and submitting it to the legislature (and/or the voters) for approval.

INSTITUTIONS ● Organizations and establishments in a society that are devoted to the promotion of a particular cause. Some of the institutions in our government are the legal system, Congress, and the social welfare system.

INSTRUCTED DELEGATE ● A representative (such as a member of Congress) who is expected to mirror the views of those whom he or she represents (such as a congressional member's constituents).

INTEREST GROUP ● An organized group of individuals sharing common objectives who actively attempt to influence policymakers in all three branches of the government and at all levels.

INTERGOVERNMENTAL LOBBY ● A special interest lobby formed by governors, mayors, highway commissioners, and others for the purpose of obtaining federal funds for state and local governments.

INTERSTATE COMMERCE ● Trade that involves more than one state.

INTERVENTIONISM ● Direct involvement by one country in another country's affairs.

INTRASTATE COMMERCE ● Commerce that takes place within state borders. State governments have the power to regulate intrastate commerce.

IRON CURTAIN ● A phrase coined by Winston Churchill to describe the political boundaries between the democratic countries in Europe and the Soviet-controlled communist countries in Eastern Europe.

IRON TRIANGLE ● A three-way alliance among legislators, bureaucrats, and interest groups to make or preserve policies that benefit their respective interests.

ISOLATIONISM ● A political policy of noninvolvement in world affairs.

ISSUE AD ● A negative political advertisement that focuses on flaws in an opposing candidate's position on a particular issue.

J

JUDICIAL REVIEW ● The power of the courts to decide on the constitutionality of legislative enactments and of actions taken by the executive branch.

JUDICIARY ● The courts; one of the three branches of the federal government in the United States.

JURISDICTION ● The authority of a court to hear and decide a particular case.

JUSTICE COURT ● A local court with limited jurisdiction; justice courts typically hear minor civil and criminal cases, perform marriages, and legalize documents.

JUSTICE OF THE PEACE ● A local judicial official who presides over the activities of a justice court; often popularly elected for a short term.

JUSTICIABLE CONTROVERSY ● A controversy that is not hypothetical or academic but real and substantial; a requirement that must be satisfied before a court will hear a case.

K

KEYNESIAN ECONOMICS ● An economic theory proposed by British economist John Maynard Keynes that is typically associated with the use of fiscal policy to alter national economic variables. Keynesian economics gained prominence during the Great Depression of the 1930s.

KITCHEN CABINET ● The name given to a president's unofficial advisers. The term was coined during Andrew Jackson's presidency.

L

LABOR FORCE ● All of the people over the age of sixteen who are working or actively looking for jobs.

LEGISLATIVE RULE ● An administrative agency rule that carries the same weight as a statute enacted by a legislature.

LEMON TEST ● A three-part test enunciated by the Supreme Court in the 1971 case of *Lemon v. Kurtzman* to determine whether government aid to parochial schools is constitutional. To be constitutional, the aid must (1) be for a clearly secular purpose; (2) in its primary effect, neither advance nor inhibit religion; and (3) avoid an "excessive government entanglement with religion." The Lemon test has also been used in other types of cases involving the establishment clause.

LIBEL ● A published report of a falsehood that tends to injure a person's reputation or character.

LIBERAL ● One who subscribes to a set of political beliefs that includes the advocacy of active government, government intervention to improve the welfare of individuals, support for civil rights, and political change.

LIBERTY ● The freedom of individuals to believe, act, and express themselves freely so long as doing so does not infringe on the rights of other individuals in the society.

LIMITED GOVERNMENT ● A form of government based on the principle that the powers of government should be clearly limited either through a written document or through wide public understanding; characterized by institutional checks to ensure that government serves public rather than private interests.

LITERACY TEST ● A test given to voters to ensure that they could read and write and thus evaluate political information; a technique used in many southern states to restrict African American participation in elections.

LOBBYING ● All of the attempts by organizations or by individuals to influence the passage, defeat, or contents of legislation or to influence the administrative decisions of government.

LOBBYIST ● An individual who handles a particular interest group's lobbying efforts.

LOOPHOLE ● A legal way of evading a certain legal requirement.

M

MADISONIAN MODEL ● The model of government devised by James Madison in which the powers of the government are separated into three branches: executive, legislative, and judicial.

MAGISTRATE COURT ● A local court with limited jurisdiction, usually in a small town or city.

MAGISTRATE ● A local judicial official who presides over the activities of a magistrate's court; often popularly elected for a short term.

MAGNA CARTA ● The great charter that King John of England was forced to sign in 1215 as protection against the absolute powers of the monarchy. It included such fundamental rights as trial by jury and due process of law.

MAJORITY LEADER ● The party leader elected by the majority party in the House or in the Senate.

MAJORITY PARTY ● The political party that has more members in the legislature than does the opposing party.

MALAPPORTIONMENT ● A condition that results when, based on population and representation, the voting power of citizens in one district becomes more influential than the voting power of citizens in another district.

MANAGED NEWS COVERAGE ● News coverage that is manipulated (managed) by a campaign manager or political consultant to gain media exposure for a political candidate.

MANDATORY PREFERENCE POLL ● A form of the preference poll in which delegates to the national party convention are selected at a state convention, and the delegates must vote for the candidate chosen by the voters.

MARKUP SESSION ● A meeting held by a congressional committee or subcommittee to approve, amend, or redraft a bill.

MARSHALL PLAN ● A plan providing for U.S. economic assistance to European nations following World War II to help those nations recover from the war; the plan was named after George C. Marshall, secretary of state from 1947 to 1949.

MASS MEDIA ● Communication channels, such as newspapers and radio and television broadcasts, through which people can communicate to mass audiences.

MAYFLOWER COMPACT ● A document drawn up by Pilgrim leaders in 1620 on the ship Mayflower. The document stated that laws were to be made for the general good of the people.

MEDIA ● Newspapers, magazines, television, radio, the Internet, and any other printed or electronic means of communication.

MEDIATING INSTITUTIONS ● Institutions that assume a mediating role between Americans and their government. Mediating institutions include political party conventions (which decide who will be candidates for political office) and network news organizations (which determine what political events should be reported to the public).

MINORITY LEADER ● The party leader elected by the minority party in the House or in the Senate.

MINORITY PARTY ● The political party that has fewer members in the legislature than does the opposing party.

MINORITY-MAJORITY DISTRICT ● A congressional district whose boundaries are drawn in such a way as to maximize the voting power of a minority group.

MIRANDA WARNINGS ● A series of statements informing criminal suspects, on their arrest, of their constitutional rights, such as the right to remain silent and the right to counsel; required by the Supreme Court's 1966 decision in *Miranda v. Arizona*.

MODERATE ● With regard to the political spectrum, a person whose views fall in the middle of the spectrum.

MODERN LIBERALISM ● A political ideology that stresses political democracy, constitutionally guaranteed civil liberties, political equality, free political competition, and separation of church and state. Unlike classical liberalism, modern liberalism supports the notion that the national government should take an active role in solving the nation's domestic problems and in protecting the interests of poor and disadvantaged groups in society.

MONARCHY ● A form of autocracy in which a king, queen, emperor, empress, tsar, or tsarina is the highest authority in the government; monarchs usually obtain their power through inheritance.

MONETARY POLICY ● Actions taken by the Federal Reserve Board to change the amount of money in circulation so as to affect interest rates, credit markets, the rate of inflation, the rate of economic growth, and unemployment.

MONROE DOCTRINE ● A U.S. policy, announced in 1823 by President James Monroe, that the United States would not tolerate foreign intervention in the Western Hemisphere, and in return, the United States would stay out of European affairs.

MOST-FAVORED-NATION STATUS ● A status granted by a clause in an international treaty. Generally, most-favored-nation clauses are designed to establish equality of international treatment. For example, if the United States and the People's Republic of China have agreed in a treaty that each country will have most-favored-nation status with respect to international trade, then the United States must treat China at least as well as the country receiving the most favorable treatment from the United States and vice versa.

MULTICULTURALISM ● The belief that the many cultures that make up American society should remain distinct and be protected and even encouraged by our laws.

MUTUAL-ASSURED DESTRUCTION (MAD) ● A phrase referring to the assumption, on which the policy of deterrence was based, that if the forces of two nations are equally capable of destroying each other, neither will take a chance on war.

N

NARROWCASTING ● Catering media programming to the specialized tastes and preferences of targeted audiences.

NATIONAL CONVENTION ● The meeting held by each major party every four years to select presidential and vice presidential candidates, to write a party platform, and to conduct other party business.

NATIONAL PARTY CHAIRPERSON ● An individual who serves as a political party's administrative head at the national level and directs the work of the party's national committee.

NATIONAL PARTY COMMITTEE ● The political party leaders who direct party business during the four years between the national party conventions, organize the next national convention, and plan how to obtain a party victory in the next presidential election.

NATIONAL SECURITY COUNCIL (NSC) ● A council that advises the president on domestic and foreign matters concerning the safety and defense of the nation; established in 1947.

NATURAL RIGHTS ● Rights that are not bestowed by governments but are inherent within every single man, woman, and child by virtue of the fact that he or she is a human being.

NECESSARY AND PROPER CLAUSE ● Article I, Section 8, Clause 18, of the Constitution, which gives Congress the power to make all laws "necessary and proper" for the federal government to carry out its responsibilities; also called the elastic clause.

NEGATIVE EXTERNALITY ● An effect of private decision making, such as pollution, that imposes social costs on the community. Negative externalities resulting from business decisions are often cited as reasons for government regulation.

NEGATIVE POLITICAL ADVERTISING ● Political advertising undertaken for the purpose of discrediting an opposing candidate in the eyes of the voters; attack ads and issue ads are forms of negative political advertising.

NEGOTIATED RULEMAKING ● A type of administrative agency rulemaking in which the industries that will be affected by the new rule participate in the rule's formulation.

NEUTRAL COMPETENCY ● The application of technical skills to jobs without regard to political issues.

NEUTRALITY ● A position of not being aligned with either side in a dispute or conflict, such as a war.

NEW DEAL ● A program ushered in by the Roosevelt administration in 1933 to bring the United States out of the Great Depression. The New Deal included many government spending and public-assistance programs, in addition to thousands of regulations governing economic activity.

NEW FEDERALISM ● A plan to limit the federal government's role in regulating state governments and to give the states increased power to decide how they should spend government revenues.

NOMINATING CONVENTION ● An official meeting of a political party to choose its candidates. Nominating conventions at the state and local levels also select delegates to represent the people of their geographical areas at a higher-level party convention.

NORTHWEST ORDINANCE ● A 1787 congressional act that established a basic pattern for how states should govern new territories north of the Ohio River.

O

OBSCENITY ● Indecency or offensiveness in speech or expression, behavior, or appearance; what specific expressions or acts constitute obscenity normally are determined by community standards.

OFFICE OF MANAGEMENT AND BUDGET (OMB) ● An agency in the Executive Office of the President that assists the president in preparing and supervising the administration of the federal budget.

OFFICE-BLOCK BALLOT ● A ballot that lists together all of the candidates for each office.

"ONE PERSON, ONE VOTE" RULE ● A rule, or principle, requiring that congressional districts must have equal population so that one person's vote counts as much as another's vote.

OPEN PRIMARY ● A primary in which voters can vote for a party's candidates regardless of whether they belong to the party.

OPINION ● A written statement by a court expressing the reasons for its decision in a case.

ORAL ARGUMENT ● An argument presented to a judge in person by an attorney on behalf of his or her client.

P

PARLIAMENT ● The name of the national legislative body in countries governed by a parliamentary system, as in England and France.

PARLIAMENTARY DEMOCRACY ● A form of democracy in which the lawmaking and law-enforcing branches of government overlap. In Great Britain, for example, the prime minister and the cabinet are members of the legislature, meaning that they both enact and enforce the laws.

PARTISAN POLITICS ● Political actions or decisions that are influenced by a particular political party's ideology.

PARTY ELITE ● A loose-knit group of party activists who organize and oversee party functions and planning during and between campaigns.

PARTY IDENTIFIER ● A person who identifies himself or herself as being a member of a particular political party.

PARTY PLATFORM ● The document drawn up by each party at its national convention that outlines the policies and positions of the party.

PARTY TICKET ● A list of a political party's candidates for various offices.

PARTY-COLUMN BALLOT ● A ballot (also called the Indiana ballot) that lists all of a party's candidates under the party label; voters can vote for all of a party's candidates for local, state, and national offices by making a single "X" or pulling a single lever.

PATRONAGE ● A system of rewarding the party faithful and workers with government jobs or contracts.

PEER GROUP ● Associates, often those close in age to oneself; may include friends, classmates, co-workers, club members, or church group members. Peer group influence is a significant factor in the political socialization process.

PLURALIST THEORY ● A theory that views politics as a contest among various interest groups—at all levels of government—to gain benefits for their members.

PLURALITY ● A situation in which a candidate wins an election by receiving more votes than the others but does not necessarily win a majority (over 50 percent of the votes). Most federal, state, and local laws allow for elections to be won by a plurality vote.

POCKET VETO ● A special type of veto power used by the chief executive after the legislature has adjourned. Bills that are not signed by the president die after a specified period of time and must be reintroduced if Congress wishes to reconsider them.

POLICE POWERS ● The powers of a government body that enable it to create laws for the protection of the health, morals, safety, and welfare of the people. In the United States, most police powers are reserved to the states.

POLICYMAKING PROCESS ● The procedures involved in getting an issue on the political agenda; formulating, adopting, and implementing a policy with regard to the issue; and then evaluating the results of the policy.

POLITICAL ACTION COMMITTEE (PAC) ● A committee that is established by a corporation, labor union, or special interest group to raise funds and make contributions on the establishing organization's behalf.

POLITICAL ADVERTISING ● Advertising undertaken by or on behalf of a political candidate to familiarize voters with the candidate and his or her views on campaign issues.

POLITICAL AGENDA ● The issues that politicians will address; often determined by the media.

POLITICAL CONSULTANT ● A person who, for a large fee, devises a political candidate's campaign strategies, monitors the campaign's progress, plans all media appearances, and coaches the candidate for debates.

POLITICAL CULTURE ● The set of ideas, values, and attitudes about government and the political process held by a community or nation.

POLITICAL PARTY ● A group of individuals outside the government who organize to win elections, operate the government, and determine policy.

POLITICAL SOCIALIZATION ● A learning process through which most people acquire their political attitudes, opinions, beliefs, and knowledge.

POLITICS ● The process of resolving conflicts over how society should use its scarce resources and who should receive various benefits, such as wealth, status, health care, and higher education. According to Harold Lasswell, politics is the process of determining "who gets what, when, and how" in a society. According to David Easton, politics is "the authoritative allocation of values" in a society.

POLL TAX ● A fee of several dollars that had to be paid in order to vote; a device used in some southern states to prevent African Americans from voting.

POLL WATCHER ● A representative from one of the two major political parties who is allowed to monitor a polling place to make sure that the election is run fairly and to avoid fraud.

POWER ● The ability to influence the behavior of others, usually through the use of force, persuasion, or rewards.

PRECEDENT ● A court decision that furnishes an example or authority for deciding subsequent cases involving identical or similar facts and legal issues.

PRECINCT ● A political district within a city (such as a block or a neighborhood) or a portion of a rural county; the smallest voting district at the local level.

PREEMPTION ● A doctrine rooted in the supremacy clause of the Constitution that provides that national laws or regulations governing a certain area take precedence over conflicting state laws or regulations governing that same area.

PREFERENCE POLL ● A method of voting in a primary election in which the names of the candidates for the nomination and the delegates appear separately, and voters cast separate votes for candidates and for delegates.

PRESIDENTIAL DEMOCRACY ● A form of democracy in which the lawmaking and law-enforcing branches of government are separate but equal, as in the United States.

PRESS CONFERENCE ● A scheduled interview with the media.

PRESS SECRETARY ● A member of the White House staff who holds press conferences for reporters and makes public statements for the president.

PRIMARY ● A preliminary election held for the purpose of choosing a party's final candidate.

PRIMARY SOURCE OF LAW ● A source of law that establishes the law. Primary sources of law include constitutions, statutes, administrative agency rules and regulations, and decisions rendered by the courts.

PRINT MEDIA ● Communication channels that consist of printed materials, such as newspapers and magazines.

PRIVATIZATION ● The replacement of government agencies that provide products or services to the public by private firms that provide the same products or services.

PROBABLE CAUSE ● Cause for believing that there is a substantial likelihood that a person has committed or is about to commit a crime.

PUBLIC DEBT ● The total amount of money that the national government owes as a result of borrowing; also called the national debt.

PUBLIC OPINION ● The individual attitudes or beliefs about politics, public issues, and public policies that are shared by a significant portion of adults; a complex collection of opinions held by many people on issues in the public arena.

PUBLIC OPINION POLL ● A numerical survey of the public's opinion on a particular topic at a particular moment.

PUBLIC POLICIES ● Plans of action to support or achieve government goals that are designed to improve the lives of citizens.

PUBLIC SERVICES ● Essential services that individuals cannot provide for themselves, such as building and maintaining roads, providing welfare programs, operating public schools, and preserving national parks.

PUBLIC-INTEREST GROUP ● An interest group formed for the purpose of working for the "public good"; examples of public-interest groups are the American Civil Liberties Union and Common Cause.

PUSH TECHNOLOGY ● Software that enables Internet users to customize the type of information they receive from Web sources. The information is "pushed" to the user automatically as it is put on the Web.

Q

QUOTA SYSTEM ● A policy under which a specific number of jobs, promotions, or other types of selections, such as university admissions, must be given to members of selected groups.

R

RADICAL LEFT ● Persons on the extreme left side of the political spectrum who would like to significantly change the political order, usually to promote egalitarianism. The radical left includes socialists, communists, and, often, populists.

RADICAL RIGHT ● Persons on the extreme right side of the political spectrum. The radical right includes reactionaries (who would like to return to the values and social systems of some previous era), fascists (who pursue strongly nationalistic policies), and libertarians (who believe in no regulation of the economy and individual behavior, except for defense).

RANDOM SAMPLE ● In the context of opinion polling, a sample in which each person within the entire population being polled has an equal chance of being chosen.

RATING SYSTEM ● A system by which a particular interest group evaluates (rates) the performance of legislators based on how often the legislators have voted consistently with the group's position on particular issues.

RATIONAL BASIS TEST ● A test (also known as the "ordinary scrutiny" standard) used by the Supreme Court to decide whether a discriminatory law violates the equal protection clause of the Constitution. Few laws evaluated under this test are found invalid.

REALIGNING ELECTION ● An election in which the popular support for and relative strength of the parties shift so that either (1) the minority (opposition) party emerges as the majority party or (2) the majority party is reestablished with a different coalition of supporters.

RECALL ● A procedure that allows voters to dismiss an elected official from a state or local office before the official's term has expired.

REFERENDUM ● A form of direct democracy in which legislative or constitutional measures are proposed by a legislature and then presented to the voters for approval.

REGULATION ● The exercise of government powers to influence the social and economic activities of a society.

REPRESENTATIVE DEMOCRACY ● A form of democracy in which the will of the majority is expressed through smaller groups of individuals elected by the people to act as their representatives.

REPRESENTATIVE GOVERNMENT ● A form of government in which representatives elected by the people make and enforce laws and policies.

REPUBLIC ● Essentially, a term referring to a representative democracy—in which the will of the majority is expressed through smaller groups of individuals elected by the people to act as their representatives.

REREGULATION ● The act of regulating again. In the 1990s, certain groups began to call for the reregulation of industries that were deregulated in the 1970s and 1980s in order to avoid the unintended results of some of the earlier deregulatory policies.

REVERSE DISCRIMINATION ● The assertion that affirmative action programs that require preferential treatment for minorities discriminate against those who have no minority status.

RULE OF LAW ● A basic principle of government that requires both those who govern and those who are governed to act in accordance with established law.

RULEMAKING ● The process undertaken by an administrative agency when formally proposing, evaluating, and adopting a new regulation.

RULES COMMITTEE ● A standing committee in the House of Representatives that provides special rules governing how particular bills will be considered and debated by the House. The Rules Committee normally proposes time limitations on debate for any bill, which are accepted or modified by the House.

S

SABOTAGE ● A destructive act intended to hinder a nation's defense efforts.

SAMPLE ● In the context of opinion polling, a group of people selected to represent the population being studied.

SAMPLING ERROR ● In the context of opinion polling, the difference between what the sample results show and what the true results would have been had everybody in the relevant population been interviewed.

SEARCH ENGINE ● A special computer program that allows users to perform "key word" searches of documents on the Internet. Popular search engines include Yahoo, WebCrawler, Excite, Infoseek, HotBot, and Lycos.

SECESSION ● The act of formally withdrawing from membership in an alliance; the withdrawal of a state from the federal Union.

SECOND BUDGET RESOLUTION ● A budget resolution, which is supposed to be passed in September, that sets "binding" limits on taxes and spending for the next fiscal year, which begins on October 1.

SECOND CONTINENTAL CONGRESS ● The congress of the colonies that met in 1775 to assume the powers of a central government and establish an army.

SEDITIOUS SPEECH ● Speech that urges resistance to lawful authority or that advocates the overthrowing of a government.

SELF-INCRIMINATION ● Providing damaging information or testimony against oneself in court.

SEPARATE BUT EQUAL DOCTRINE ● A Supreme Court doctrine holding that the equal protection clause of the Fourteenth Amendment did not forbid racial segregation as long as the facilities for blacks were equal to those provided for whites. The doctrine was overturned in the *Brown v. Board of Education of Topeka* decision of 1954.

SEPARATION OF POWERS ● The principle of dividing governmental powers among the executive, the legislative, and the judicial branches of government.

SEXUAL HARASSMENT ● Unwanted physical contact, verbal conduct, or abuse of a sexual nature that interferes with a recipient's job performance, creates a hostile environment, or carries with it an implicit or explicit threat of adverse employment consequences.

SHAYS' REBELLION ● A rebellion of angry farmers in western Massachusetts in 1786, led by former Revolutionary War captain Daniel Shays. This rebellion and other similar uprisings in the New England states emphasized the need for a true national government.

SINGLE-MEMBER DISTRICT SYSTEM ● A method of election in which only one candidate can win election to each office.

SLANDER ● The public utterance (speaking) of a statement that holds a person up for contempt, ridicule, or hatred.

SOCIAL CONFLICT ● Disagreements among people in a society over what the society's priorities should be with respect to the use of scarce resources.

SOCIAL CONTRACT ● A voluntary agreement among individuals to create a government and to give that government adequate power to secure the mutual protection and welfare of all individuals.

SOCIAL REGULATION ● Government regulation across all industries that is undertaken for the purpose of protecting the public welfare.

SOCIAL WELFARE POLICY ● All government actions that are undertaken to give assistance to specific groups, such as the aged, the ill, and the poor.

SOFT MONEY ● Campaign contributions that are made to political parties, instead of to particular candidates.

SOLIDARITY ● Mutual agreement with others in a particular group.

SOUND BITE ● In televised news reporting, a brief comment, lasting for only a few seconds, that captures a thought or a perspective and has an immediate impact on the viewers.

SPEAKER OF THE HOUSE ● The presiding officer in the House of Representatives. The speaker has traditionally been a long-time member of the majority party and is often the most powerful and influential member of the House.

SPECIAL ELECTION ● An election that is held at the state or local level when the voters must decide an issue before the next general election or when vacancies occur by reason of death or resignation.

SPIN ● A reporter's slant on, or interpretation of, a particular event or action.

SPIN DOCTOR ● A political candidate's press adviser who tries to convince reporters to give a story or event concerning the candidate a particular "spin" (interpretation, or slant).

STAGFLATION ● A condition that occurs when both inflation and unemployment are rising.

STANDING COMMITTEE ● A permanent committee in Congress that deals with legislation concerning a particular area, such as agriculture or foreign relations.

STANDING TO SUE ● The requirement that an individual must have a sufficient stake in a controversy before he or she can bring a lawsuit. The party bringing the suit must demonstrate that he or she has either been harmed or been threatened with a harm.

STARE DECISIS ● A common law doctrine under which judges normally are obligated to follow the precedents established by prior court decisions.

STATUTORY LAW ● The body of law enacted by legislatures (as opposed to constitutional law, administrative law, or case law).

STORE AND FORWARD PROCEDURE ● A process by which information is divided into separate packets, transmitted over the Internet, and then reassembled at the destination. The procedure was devised to ensure that information, once transmitted, could be rerouted and retrieved in the event of a nuclear attack.

STRAW POLL ● A nonscientific poll; a poll in which there is no way to ensure that the opinions expressed are representative of the larger population.

SUBCOMMITTEE ● A division of a larger committee that deals with a particular part of the committee's policy area. Each of the standing committees in Congress has several subcommittees.

SUFFRAGE ● The right to vote; the franchise.

SUPREMACY CLAUSE ● Article VI, Clause 2, of the Constitution, which makes the Constitution and federal laws superior to all conflicting state and local laws.

SUSPECT CLASSIFICATION ● A classification based on race, for example, that provides the basis for a discriminatory law. Any law based on a suspect classification is subject to strict scrutiny by the courts—meaning that the law must be justified by a compelling state interest.

SYMBIOTIC RELATIONSHIP ● The complex relationship that exists between political consultants and the media during political campaigns; derived from the biological term *symbiosis*.

SYMBOLIC SPEECH ● The expression of beliefs, opinions, or ideas through forms other than speech or print; speech involving actions and other nonverbal expressions.

T

TERRORISM ● The random use of staged violence at infrequent intervals to achieve political goals.

THIRD PARTY ● In the United States, any party other than one of the two major parties (Republican and Democratic) is considered a minor party, or third party.

THREE-FIFTHS COMPROMISE ● A compromise reached during the Constitutional Convention by which it was agreed that three-fifths of all slaves were to be counted both for tax purposes and for representation in the House of Representatives.

TOTALITARIAN ● A term describing a dictatorship in which a political leader (or group of leaders) seeks to control almost all aspects of social and economic life. Totalitarian dictatorships are rooted in the assumption that the needs of the nation come before the needs of individuals.

TRACKING POLL ● Polls that are taken almost every day toward the end of a political campaign to find out how well the candidates are competing for votes.

TRADE ORGANIZATION ● An association formed by members of a particular industry, such as the oil industry or the trucking industry, to develop common standards and goals for the industry. Trade organizations, as interest groups, lobby government for legislation or regulations that specifically benefit their groups.

TREASON ● As enunciated in Article III, Section 3, of the Constitution, the act of levying war against the United States or adhering (remaining loyal) to its enemies.

TREATY ● A formal agreement between the governments of two or more countries.

TRIAL COURT ● A court in which trials are held and testimony taken.

TRUSTEE ● In regard to a legislator, one who acts according to his or her conscience and the broad interests of the entire society.

TWO-PARTY SYSTEM ● A political system in which two strong and established parties compete for political offices.

TYRANNY ● The arbitrary or unrestrained exercise of power by an oppressive individual or government.

U

UNICAMERAL LEGISLATURE ● A legislature with only one chamber.

UNITARY SYSTEM ● A centralized governmental system in which local or subdivisional governments exercise only those powers given to them by the central government.

V

VETO • A Latin word meaning "I forbid"; the refusal by an official, such as the president of the United States or a state governor, to sign a bill into law.

VETO POWER • A constitutional power that enables the chief executive (president or governor) to reject legislation and return it to the legislature with reasons for the rejection. This prevents or delays the bill from becoming law.

VITAL CENTER • The center of the political spectrum, or those who hold moderate political views. The center is vital because, without it, it may be difficult, if not impossible, to reach the compromises that are necessary to a political system's continuity.

W

WARD • A local unit of a political party's organization, consisting of a division or district within a city.

WEB BROWSER • The name given to software that allows Internet users to navigate through the World Wide Web. Web browsers enable users to browse, or "surf," across many Web sites through a system of hypertext links. Two of the most popular Web browsers today are Netscape Communications Corporation's *Netscape Navigator* and Microsoft Corporation's *Internet Explorer*.

WESTERN BLOC • The democratic nations that emerged victorious after World War II, led by the United States.

WHIP • A member of Congress who assists the majority or minority leader in the House or in the Senate in managing the party's legislative preferences.

WHISTLEBLOWER • In the context of government employment, someone who "blows the whistle" on (reports to authorities) gross governmental inefficiency, illegal action, or other wrongdoing.

WHITE HOUSE OFFICE • The personal office of the president. White House Office personnel handle the president's political needs and manage the media.

WINNER-TAKE-ALL SYSTEM • A term used to describe the electoral college system, in which the candidate who receives the largest popular vote in a state is credited with all that state's electoral votes—one vote per elector.

WRIT OF *CERTIORARI* • An order from a higher court asking a lower court for the record of a case.

WRIT OF HABEAS CORPUS • An order that requires an official to bring a specified prisoner into court and explain to the judge why the person is being held in prison.

WRITE-IN CANDIDATE • A candidate whose name is written on the ballot by the voter on election day.

Index